Finance for Professionals

Finance for Professionals is a collection of carefully curated books designed to provide advanced, practical knowledge to finance practitioners. The series includes a wide range of books, covering topics such as financial management, banking operations, investment strategies, risk management, corporate finance, and fintech innovations. Each title is structured to meet the needs of professionals like financial analysts, bankers, portfolio managers, and corporate executives, offering insights and methodologies essential for success in the industry. Aimed at both experienced professionals and those aspiring to advance their careers, "Finance for Professionals" delivers authoritative resources tailored to support professional growth and address the evolving demands of the finance sector.

Antonio Scalia
Editor

Corporate Credit Analysis and AI

Advancing the Rating System at a Central Bank

Springer

Editor
Antonio Scalia
Directorate Financial Risk Management
Bank of Italy
Rome, Italy

ISSN 3059-3654 ISSN 3059-3530 (electronic)
Finance for Professionals
ISBN 978-3-032-13421-9 ISBN 978-3-032-13422-6 (eBook)
https://doi.org/10.1007/978-3-032-13422-6

This Springer imprint is published by the registered company Springer Nature Switzerland AG
The registered company address is: Gewerbestrasse 11, 6330 Cham, Switzerland

For Lucilla, Giuseppe, Carlo, Riccardo, and Francesco

Foreword

Why are central banks concerned with corporate risk analysis? The answer becomes evident when looking at key figures. At the height of the Covid-19 crisis, in 2021, counterparties' use of Eurosystem liquidity peaked at €2.2 trillion, with an increase of about 1.6 trillion relative to the pre-Covid period. The refinancing operations were backed by €2.8 trillion in collateral. Nearly one third of these assets consisted of credit claims, mainly to non-financial corporations. At peak, the increase in this type of collateral was 0.5 trillion. In the same period several other central banks that also accept corporate loans in their refinancing framework introduced a range of measures to support the flow of credit to the economy.

These facts show that, especially in situations of market tension, the central banks' ability to reliably and quickly assess the creditworthiness of non-financial companies is key for the conduct of monetary policy.

To evaluate the credit quality of collateral, the Eurosystem relies on three sources: external credit assessment institutions, banks' internal ratings-based systems, and the so-called in-house credit assessment systems (ICASes), developed by several National Central Banks. Such systems were introduced in the aftermath of the great financial crisis, in response to the Financial Stability Board's call to reduce reliance on external ratings. They have been enabling banks without internal models to pledge loans to non-rated firms as collateral. The Bank of Italy launched its own system in 2013.

The Eurosystem has recently expanded the role of in-house systems in monetary policy, by giving them priority over other rating sources and integrating the so-called statistical ICAS ratings (obtained by purely statistical modelling, without recourse to expert judgement) into the general collateral framework. These changes, which entail full risk-sharing across the Eurosystem, are underpinned by harmonized principles, transparent methodologies, and rigorous oversight.

This volume describes the existing ICAS process at the Bank of Italy and includes several new empirical studies that pave the way for further developments of the approach. It is published at a time of profound transformation. One major driver of change is the progress in artificial intelligence, which enables the exploration and interpretation of new types of information and big data with unprecedented efficiency and depth—and introduces methodological challenges and snags, which must be carefully managed. Another emerging challenge stems from new sources of corporate risk—particularly those linked to cyber threats and operational risk, climate change, and broader sustainability concerns.

Against this backdrop, at the Bank of Italy we are eager to engage with other central banks and experts in the field. By illustrating our ICAS techniques and exposing them to external challenge we aim to stimulate debate and criticism, to ensure they remain fit for purpose in a rapidly changing environment.

Rome, Italy Paolo Angelini

Preface

Corporate credit analysis (CCA) involves assessing the likelihood that a company may fail to meet its financial obligations. In 2013, the Bank of Italy opted to develop and manage its own in-house credit assessment system (ICAS) to support monetary policy implementation. Since its inception, ICAS has been playing a key role in evaluating large volumes of bank loans pledged as collateral in refinancing operations.

This book offers a comprehensive illustration of the Bank's approach to CCA, reflecting years of development and refinement. It serves both as a guide to the relevant literature and as a presentation of the analytical framework and methodologies that underpin ICAS. The volume includes practical examples, summary statistics, regression analyses, performance indicators, and back-testing results. It also features case studies on emerging applications of AI, showcasing how innovations are being integrated into ICAS to improve the assessment of risk factors such as climate physical risk, sustainability-related risks, adverse market sentiment, and cyber risk. More technical material is presented in appendices to the relevant chapters.

The book is designed for a dual audience: practitioners and researchers. Practitioners include professionals involved in credit risk assessment for banks, rating agencies, and corporate finance teams. Researchers will find material to support the advancement of statistical techniques and AI applications, along with extensive empirical evidence. The volume may also be a useful resource for graduate-level courses in financial risk management.

The structure of the book is organized into four parts:

- "Overview" introduces the fundamentals of CCA, the role of AI, and related risk management considerations.
- "The Current System" describes the methodology of the current ICAS version, including its outputs and performance.
- "The Models at Commercial Banks" reviews best practices in commercial bank rating systems, comparing their performance with ICAS.
- "AI and New Risk Sources" explores recent research on AI and emerging sources of corporate credit risk.

With the exception of Chapter A SAFE Model for AI Risk Management—authored by a leading academic expert—the content has been developed within the Financial Risk Management Directorate of the Bank of Italy, with contributions from credit analysts across its branch network.

I am grateful to Paolo Angelini and Paolo Del Giovane for their support throughout the project. I also thank the participants to the workshop *Corporate credit analysis: Advances in methodologies and the use of AI*, held in Palermo on 6 June 2025, for their valuable feedback. Special thanks go to Tommaso Perez and Francesco Columba for their encouragement and insightful comments, and to Federica Orsini and Federica Vassalli for their invaluable help in coordinating the editorial process.

The usual disclaimer applies: the views expressed in this book are those of the authors and do not necessarily reflect those of the Bank of Italy.

Rome, Italy Antonio Scalia

Glossary and Abbreviations

ABS	Asset-Backed Security	A type of financial investment backed by a pool of underlying assets that generate cash flow—such as loans, leases, credit card debt, or receivables. Typically issued as bonds or notes, ABS pay income at a fixed rate for a defined period until maturity. For investors focused on income, ABS can serve as an alternative to other debt investments like corporate bonds or bond funds
ACC	Additional Credit Claims	A temporary extension of the types of assets eligible as collateral to ensure that banks have full access to central bank liquidity, even in adverse economic condition. ACCs are credit claims that do not fulfil all the eligibility criteria applicable under the general collateral framework
Altman z-score		A financial metric developed by Edward Altman in 1968 to assess the likelihood of a company going bankrupt. It combines five key financial ratios—covering profitability, leverage, liquidity, solvency, and activity—into a single score. A lower score indicates higher risk of financial distress, while a higher score suggests better financial health
AnaCredit		A database containing detailed information on individual bank loans within the euro area. Its name stands for "analytical credit datasets"
AUROC	Area under the Receiver Operating Characteristic curve	A measure of the ability of the model to assign higher PDs to firms that will default compared with financially sound firms
Basel Accord		A set of international banking regulations developed by the Basel Committee on Banking Supervision to strengthen the stability of the global banking system. The Basel Accord consists of three major versions—Basel I, Basel II, and Basel III—each introducing more rigorous standards for capital adequacy, risk management, and supervisory review of banks
BoD	Board of Directors	
CBAM	Carbon Border Adjustment Mechanism	A fiscal measure established by Regulation (EU) 2023/956 to prevent carbon leakage by applying a carbon price on imported goods from non-EU countries. The CBAM aligns the cost of embedded emissions in imports with the price paid by EU producers under the EU ETS. It supports the European Green Deal and "Fit for 55" goals of reducing emissions by 55% by 2030 and achieving climate neutrality by 2050

(continued)

(continued)

CCA	Corporate Credit Analysis	The process of evaluating the risk that a company may default on its financial obligations
CCR	Climate Change Risk	The potential adverse effects of climate change on assets, investments, and economic systems. These risks can be physical (such as damage from extreme weather events or sea level rise), transition (related to policy, technology, and market changes aimed at mitigating climate change)
CONSOB	*Commissione Nazionale per le Società e la Borsa*	The public authority responsible for regulating the Italian financial markets
CQS	Credit Quality Step	A bucket of the ECAF harmonised rating scale
Credit claims		Banks can pledge credit claims to central banks in exchange for funding. Credit claims include loans, credit lines, or other receivables that meet the eligibility criteria set by the central bank
CRR	Capital Requirements Regulation	The regulatory framework that sets out the rules and standards for the minimum capital banks and financial institutions must hold in the European Union. These requirements ensure that firms have enough capital to cover their risks and absorb potential losses, promoting stability in the financial system. CRR is part of the broader Basel regulatory framework and is particularly important in the EU context, forming part of the Capital Requirements Directive and Regulation package
CSRD	Corporate Sustainability Reporting Directive	EU directive that enhances and expands the sustainability reporting requirements for companies. The CSRD requires large companies and listed SMEs to disclose detailed information on environmental, social, and governance (ESG) factors, promoting transparency and accountability in sustainability practices. It updates and replaces the previous Non-Financial Reporting Directive (NFRD)
CV	Coefficient of Variation	A statistical measure defined as the ratio of the standard deviation over the mean of a data set, expressed as a percentage. The CV is useful for comparing the relative variability or risk of different data sets, regardless of their units or magnitudes. A higher CV indicates greater relative variability
CVAH	Collateral Value After Haircuts	The adjusted value of collateral after applying a "haircut," which is a percentage reduction that accounts for the potential decline in the asset's value or its liquidity risk. This value determines the amount of credit a lender can rely upon when securing a loan or other credit exposure. The haircut protects the lender from the risk of market fluctuations in the value of the collateral
CVaR	Conditional Value at Risk	The risk assessment metric that measures the expected loss of an investment or portfolio in the worst-case scenarios beyond a certain confidence level. Unlike Value at Risk (VaR), which only provides a threshold value, CVaR is the average of losses that exceed the VaR, giving a fuller picture of tail risk. It's also known as Expected Shortfall (ES)
D-FRM	Directorate Financial Risk Management	The Bank of Italy's Directorate, within the Directorate General Markets and Monetary Policy Operations, in charge of managing risks
Discriminatory power		The ability of a credit risk model to differentiate between levels of corporate risk, such as distinguishing between borrowers who are likely to default and those who are not. Higher discriminatory power indicates that the model is more effective at identifying and ranking risks accurately. The discriminatory power is usually measured by the AuROC

(continued)

(continued)

DL	Deep Learning	A subset of machine learning techniques that uses artificial neural networks with multiple layers (deep networks) to model complex patterns and relationships in the data. Deep learning excels at handling large amounts of structured or unstructured data, such as images, audio files, and text
EAD	Exposure At Default	An estimate of the total value a lender is exposed to if a borrower defaults on a loan
ECAF	Eurosystem Credit Assessment Framework	ECAF defines the minimum credit quality requirements as well as the rules and procedures which ensure that the Eurosystem only accepts adequate collateral, as required by article 18.1 of the Protocol on the Statute of the European System of Central Banks and of the European Central Bank
ECAI	External Credit Assessment Institution	Credit rating agencies accepted as external credit assessment institutions by the ECAF
ES	Expected Shortfall	See CVaR
ESG	Environmental, Social, and Governance	Acronym for the *environmental, social, and governance* dimensions of corporate practices not closely related to economic and financial practices
EU ETS	European Union Emissions Trading System	It is the European Union's regulated market for trading greenhouse gas emission allowances, based on a cap-and-trade mechanism, setting a limit on greenhouse gas emissions from key sectors and allowing trading of emission allowances to incentivize cost-effective reductions
EUA	European Union Allowances	As defined in Article 3(a) of the EU ETS Directive, an EU Allowance represents the right to emit one tonne of carbon dioxide equivalent during a specific time period and can be transferred according to the directive's rules
Expert assessment		The second stage of the ICAS process, involving two analysts and possibly the rating committee to obtain the final rating of the firm
FSB	Financial Stability Board	The FSB is an international organisation that promotes international financial stability; it does so by coordinating national financial authorities and international standard-setting bodies as they work toward developing strong regulatory, supervisory and other financial sector policies. It fosters a level playing field by encouraging coherent implementation of these policies across sectors and jurisdictions
Full ICAS		The 'full' ICAS rating, including the expert assessment, is regularly produced for 4,000 Italian firms that are debtors of a large share of the loans posted as collateral in refinancing operations
GARCH	Generalized Autoregressive Conditional Heteroskedasticity	A statistical model used to estimate and forecast the volatility of time series data, particularly in financial markets. GARCH models capture the tendency of volatility to cluster over time—periods of high volatility are followed by high volatility, and low volatility by low volatility—by modelling current variance as a function of past squared residuals and past variances
GB	Gradient Boosting	A machine learning technique for building predictive models by sequentially combining multiple weak models (often decision trees) to form a stronger model. Each new model is trained to correct the errors of the previous one, with the overall process guided by minimizing a loss function. Gradient boosting is popular for tasks like regression and classification due to its high accuracy and flexibility

(continued)

(continued)

GHGs	Green House Gases	Acronym of greenhouse gases, i.e. gases considered in the Kyoto Protocol: carbon dioxide (CO_2), methane (CH_4), nitrous oxide (N_2O) and the so-called F-gases (hydrofluorocarbons and perfluorocarbons) and sulphur hexafluoride (SF_6). These gases retain the heat produced by solar radiation on the earth's surface and prevent it from being dispersed into the atmosphere, resulting in an increase of the temperature on the earth's surface
Gini Index		A statistical measure of concentration, commonly used to assess inequality in income distributions or other data sets. In a machine learning context, it is also used in decision trees to evaluate the quality of splits. A Gini index of zero means perfect equality (or uniformity) in the distribution, while higher values indicate greater concentration or inequality
Haircut		A reduction applied to the market value of an asset used as collateral to reflect its risk or potential volatility. The haircut ensures that lenders or counterparties have a safety margin in case the collateral value declines
ICAS	In-House Credit Assessment System	One of the sources in the ECAF for assessing the credit quality of eligible assets as collateral in monetary policy operations. The Bank of Italy's ICAS rating process is based on a two-stage procedure which combines a statistical model with an expert assessment, performed by two analysts and possibly the rating committee, to obtain the final rating of the firm
INVIND	*Indagine sulle imprese industriali e dei servizi* (Survey of Industrial and Services Firms)	The survey that collects information on investments, gross sales, workforce and other economic variables relating to Italian industrial and services firms with 20 or more employees
IRB	Internal Rating Based (model or system)	Systems managed by banks to assess the counterparties' creditworthiness
ISPRA	*Istituto Superiore per la Protezione e la Ricerca Ambientale*	The Italian public research institute for environmental protection, established in 2008 and operational since 2010, under the supervision of the Ministry of Environment and Energy Security. ISPRA coordinates regional environmental protection agencies (ARPA) and provides technical and scientific support to the Ministry. It also manages national environmental monitoring and emergency response, produces environmental data and indicators, and collaborates with European and international networks
IVASS	*Istituto per la Vigilanza sulle Assicurazioni*	The public authority responsible for supervising and regulating the insurance and reinsurance markets in Italy
LDA	Linear Discriminant Analysis	A statistical and machine learning technique used for classification and dimensionality reduction. LDA seeks to find a linear combination of features that best separates two or more classes by maximizing the ratio of between-class variance to within-class variance. This makes it effective for distinguishing categories in datasets with multiple variables
LGD	Loss Given Default	The amount of money that a lender loses when a borrower defaults on a loan, after considering any recovery, represented as a percentage of total exposure at the time of loss

(continued)

(continued)

LIME	Local Interpretable Model-agnostic Explanations	A method for explaining the predictions of complex machine learning models by approximating them locally with simpler, interpretable models (like linear regressions). LIME creates an interpretable explanation for individual predictions, helping users understand how specific features contribute to the model's output. Is model-agnostic, i.e. it can be applied to any predictive model regardless of its complexity
ML	Machine Learning	A field of artificial intelligence that develops systems that can learn from data and improve their performance over time without being explicitly programmed. Machine learning involves training models using algorithms and statistical techniques to identify patterns and make predictions or decisions based on new data. It is widely used in applications like image recognition, natural language processing, and predictive analytics
MoF	Ministry of Finance	
NCB	National Central Bank	
NCR	National Credit Register	The data repository managed by the Bank of Italy that collects information on the debts of households and businesses to the banking and financial system. The CR is fed with data submitted by participating intermediaries (banks, financial companies, and other intermediaries), including information on loans and guarantees granted to their customers, guarantees received from their clients, and loans or guarantees acquired from other intermediaries
NFC	Non-Financial Corporations	Businesses and entities that produce goods or provide non-financial services
NFD	Non-Financial Declaration	A report that companies must publish to disclose information on ESG issues relevant to their business activities. This declaration provides transparency on sustainability practices and impacts, and is often required under regulations such as the EU's Non-Financial Reporting Directive (NFRD)
NGFS	Network for Greening the Financial System	The NGFS is a group of central banks and regulatory authorities established in 2017 following the Paris Agreement to enhance international cooperation towards reaching the target of a maximum temperature rise below 2°C with respect to the pre-industrial levels
NGFS Scenarios		The NGFS Climate Scenarios explore the impacts of climate change and climate policy to provide a common reference framework. The Orderly and Disorderly scenarios explore a transition consistent with limiting global warming to below 2°C. The Hothouse world scenario leads to severe physical risks
Paris Agreement		A landmark international treaty adopted in 2015 under the United Nations Framework Convention on Climate Change (UNFCCC). Its main goal is to limit global warming to well below 2°C above pre-industrial levels, while pursuing efforts to limit it to 1.5°C. The agreement commits countries to submit climate action plans and to regularly strengthen them to meet long-term climate goals
PD	Probability of Default	A credit risk measure for the likelihood that a borrower will default on a debt obligation within a specified time horizon, typically one year
PEFA	Physical Energy Flow Accounts	They are are part of environmental economic accounts that record the flows of energy products—in physical units—from the environment into the economy, within the economy, and from the economy back to the environment

(continued)

(continued)

PIT	Point-in-time	A method of estimating risk or creditworthiness that reflects the current economic environment and borrower conditions. Point-in-Time models are highly responsive to real-time changes, capturing fluctuations in market conditions, borrower health, and macroeconomic factors at a specific moment in time. This contrasts with Through-the-Cycle (TTC) models, which smooth out short-term volatility to provide a long-term view of risk
PR	Physical Risk	A type of climate-related risk arising from the direct physical impacts of climate change, such as extreme weather events (e.g., floods, storms, heatwaves - acute risk) or long-term changes in climate patterns (e.g., rising sea levels, desertification - chronic risk). Physical risks can lead to damage or loss of assets, disruptions to supply chains, and increased costs for businesses and communities
Predictive power		A measure of how accurately a credit risk model can identify and rank borrowers' likelihood of default or credit deterioration
Refinancing operations		Monetary policy tools used by the European Central Bank (ECB) to provide liquidity to banks within the euro area. These operations allow banks to borrow money from the ECB, usually in the form of loans secured by eligible collateral
Repo transactions		Short-term borrowing and lending arrangements where one party sells securities to another and simultaneously agrees to repurchase them at a later date for a higher price. Repos are widely used in money markets to manage liquidity, secure short-term funding, and facilitate market stability
RF	Random Forests	A machine learning algorithm that builds multiple decision trees and combines their predictions to improve accuracy and stability. Each tree in the forest is trained on a random subset of the data and features (a technique called bagging). By averaging or taking the majority vote of all the trees, the random forest reduces overfitting and increases predictive performance compared to a single decision tree
SAFE	Survey on the Access to Finance of Enterprises	The survey provides information on the latest developments in the financial situation of enterprises, documents trends in the need for and availability of external financing, and measures firms' expectations about their selling prices, costs, and employment, as well as about euro area inflation. The survey results are broken down by firm size, sector, country, firm age, financial autonomy and ownership
SNPA	*Sistema Nazionale per la Protezione dell'Ambiente*	It is the network of ISPRA and the regional and provincial environmental protection agencies (ARPA/APPA) in Italy, responsible for providing uniform and integrated environmental monitoring, control, and technical support across the country
SSM	Single Supervisory Mechanism	The system of banking supervision in the EU, comprising the ECB and national supervisory authorities of participating countries
SVM	Support Vector Machine	A supervised machine learning algorithm used for classification and regression tasks. SVMs work by finding the optimal hyperplane (or decision boundary) that best separates data points into different classes. In cases where data is not linearly separable, SVMs use kernel functions to project data into higher dimensions, enabling better separation and more flexible decision boundaries

(continued)

(continued)

TR	Transition Risk	A type of climate-related risk associated with the shift to a low-carbon economy. It arises from changes in policies, technologies, market preferences, and regulations aimed at mitigating climate change. Transition risk can affect asset values, business models, and financial stability by making certain sectors or investments less viable in a carbon-constrained future
Transition plan		A climate transition plan is a detailed action plan that outlines how a firm will modify its business model to achieve net zero carbon emissions by 2050. Transition plans are essential for showing stakeholders that the firm is committed to reducing emissions and ensuring the business remains profitable in a net-zero carbon economy
TTC	Through-the-cycle	A risk assessment approach that smooths out short-term fluctuations in economic and borrower-specific factors to provide a stable, long-term estimate of credit risk or other financial metrics. TTC models are less sensitive to current economic conditions and instead capture the average risk profile over a full economic cycle, providing a more structural view of risk
UK CCRA	Climate Change Risk Assessment	The UK Government is required under the 2008 Climate Change Act to publish a UK-wide Climate Change Risk Assessment every five years. The Act stipulates that the Government must assess "the risks for the United Kingdom from the current and predicted impacts of climate change"
Winsorization		A statistical technique used to limit extreme values in a dataset, effectively reducing the influence of outliers. It works by replacing the extreme values in the dataset with less extreme values from the same dataset, usually at specific percentiles
XAI	Explainable Artificial Intelligence	A set of methods and techniques that make the decision-making processes of complex machine learning models more transparent and understandable to humans
XGB or XGBoost	Extreme Gradient Boosting	An advanced implementation of gradient boosting algorithms designed for speed and performance. XGBoost builds an ensemble of decision trees sequentially, where each new tree corrects the errors of the previous ones, and uses regularization to prevent overfitting

Contents

Editor and Contributors

About the Editor

Antonio Scalia is the Head of the Financial Risk Management Directorate at the Bank of Italy and a member of the ECB's Risk Management Committee. After graduating summa cum laude in Economics at LUISS University in Rome, he obtained the M.Sc. in Economics from the LSE and the Ph.D. from the London Business School. He joined the Bank of Italy's Research Department as an Adviser in the Financial Markets Division. His research concerns prudential regulation and banks' behaviour, information asymmetries in financial markets, and the government bond market. In 2023, he published the book on *Financial Risk Management and Climate Change Risk. The Experience in a Central Bank*, with Springer. In 2025, the Bank of Italy won the *Risk Manager of the Year* award from CentralBanking.com.

Contributors

Francesca Colletti Bank of Italy, Turin Branch, Turin, Italy

Francesco Columba Bank of Italy, Financial Risk Management Directorate, Rome, Italy

Manuel Cugliari Bank of Italy, Financial Risk Management Directorate, Rome, Italy

Stefano Di Virgilio Bank of Italy, Financial Risk Management Directorate, Rome, Italy

Lorenzo Esposito Bank of Italy, Milan Branch, Milan, Italy

Enrico Foscolo Bank of Italy, Financial Risk Management Directorate, Rome, Italy

Marisa Franzoni Bank of Italy, Bologna Branch, Bologna, Italy

Giulio Gariano Bank of Italy, Financial Risk Management Directorate, Rome, Italy

Paolo Giudici Department of Economics and Management, University of Pavia, Pavia, Italy

Massimo Guglielmi Bank of Italy, Financial Risk Management Directorate, Rome, Italy

Alessandra Iannamorelli Bank of Italy, Financial Risk Management Directorate, Rome, Italy

Francesco Monterisi Bank of Italy, Financial Risk Management Directorate, Rome, Italy

Simone Narizzano Bank of Italy, Financial Risk Management Directorate, Rome, Italy

Marco Orlandi Bank of Italy, Financial Risk Management Directorate, Rome, Italy

Federica Orsini Bank of Italy, Financial Risk Management Directorate, Rome, Italy

Paolo Parlamento Bank of Italy, Financial Risk Management Directorate, Rome, Italy

Anna Maria Rossi Bank of Italy, Financial Risk Management Directorate, Rome, Italy

Antonio Scalia Directorate Financial Risk Management, Bank of Italy, Rome, Italy

Raffaella Sorgente Bank of Italy, Venice Branch, Venice, Italy

Laura Tozzi Bank of Italy, Florence Branch, Florence, Italy

Stefano Tranquillo Bank of Italy, Financial Risk Management Directorate, Rome, Italy

Federica Vassalli Bank of Italy, Financial Risk Management Directorate, Rome, Italy

Part I
Overview

Corporate Credit Analysis and AI Applications: An Overview

Antonio Scalia

> *"Vita brevis, ars longa, occasio praeceps, experimentum periculosum, iudicium difficile."*
>
> (Life is short, art is long, opportunity is fleeting, experiment is dangerous, judgment is difficult)
>
> Lucius Annaeus Seneca

1 Introduction

Corporate credit analysis (CCA) entails evaluating the risk that a company may default on its financial obligations, whether in terms of interest payments or principal repayment. A robust CCA framework is essential for the effective risk management of institutions that extend credit to firms—such as commercial banks—or that accept corporate loans as collateral in refinancing operations—such as central banks. Investors rely on credit assessments provided by rating agencies regarding bond issuers to guide their portfolio allocation decisions.

CCA seeks to reduce the information asymmetry that typically characterizes investment decisions and lending relationships, thereby lowering the agency costs of the corporate sector, as envisaged by Jensen and Meckling (1976). It thus plays a pivotal role in facilitating credit provision to the economy (see, e.g., Bernanke, 1992) and in safeguarding financial system stability, as acknowledged in banking capital regulations (BCBS, 2010). CCA is equally relevant for the implementation

A. Scalia (✉)
Directorate Financial Risk Management, Bank of Italy, Rome, Italy
e-mail: antonio.scalia@bancaditalia.it

A. Scalia (ed.), *Corporate Credit Analysis and AI*, Finance for Professionals,
https://doi.org/10.1007/978-3-032-13422-6_1

of monetary policy via the bank lending channel (Mishkin, 1996). From a macroeconomic perspective, CCA and the evaluation of balance sheet positions constitute a fundamental mechanism for the efficient allocation of financial resources across the economy and for fostering sustainable economic growth (Bernanke & Gertler, 1989).

To provide context, since the great financial crisis the Eurosystem has adopted full allotment in its refinancing operations as a standard for liquidity provision. Counterparties are entitled to obtain the full amount of liquidity they request, provided they supply sufficient high-quality collateral in the form of marketable assets and credit claims. As a side effect, the use of the marginal lending facility—the equivalent of the discount window in the U.S. Federal Reserve framework—is rare. Importantly, euro area counterparties face no stigma in prepositioning collateral with their respective National Central Bank (NCB).[1] Besides, the opportunity cost of encumbering bank loans at the NCB is low. Against this background, banks in the euro area may preposition loans as a form of inexpensive insurance against liquidity shocks.

CCA is a highly interdisciplinary field, drawing on expertise in corporate finance, financial statement analysis, risk management, statistics, and econometrics. Although grounded in theoretical models of the firm, CCA is fundamentally empirical in nature. The seminal work by Altman (1968) introduced multiple discriminant analysis applied to corporate financial ratios, laying the foundation for subsequent research. Building on Professor Altman's Z-score notion, the discipline has progressively incorporated a broad array of statistical techniques. In recent years, significant progress has been driven by the proliferation of big data and the advancement of artificial intelligence (AI) methods. Under certain conditions, empirical models based on AI have demonstrated superior performance compared to traditional approaches in estimating corporate credit risk (Shi et al., 2022).

This volume presents the state-of-the-art in CCA as developed by the Bank of Italy over the years. In 2013, the Bank opted to design and operate its own in-house credit assessment system (ICAS). Comparable systems are also maintained by other NCBs within the euro area (Auria et al., 2021). ICAS ratings, which are not publicly disclosed, are primarily used for central bank risk management purposes.[2] As such, ICASes contribute to the effective transmission of monetary policy throughout the economy. Moreover, they may prove particularly valuable during episodes of financial market stress, when emergency liquidity assistance to individual banks may become necessary. The importance of banks' ability—or lack thereof—to mobilize collateral at the central bank was underscored during the crises involving four mid-sized U.S. banks and a major Swiss institution in March–April 2023, which revealed certain vulnerabilities in this area (Angelini, 2023; BCBS, 2023).

---

[1] This framework differs from that in place in the US (see, e.g., Gorton et al., 2025).

[2] ICAS is also employed for banking supervision and research purposes. An example of the latter is Iannamorelli et al. (2024), which investigates the role of asymmetric information in corporate bond issuance.

The volume serves both as a guide to the existing literature and as a detailed exposition of the analytical framework and methodologies underpinning the Bank of Italy's ICAS.

The publication is motivated by two primary objectives. First, it aims to promote transparency and accountability in the functioning of ICAS, particularly in view of the increasing relevance of such systems within the ECB's credit assessment framework. Notably, in November 2024, the ECB's Governing Council resolved that ICAS ratings would have priority over other credit assessment sources—namely, agency ratings and commercial banks' internal ratings—for collateral valuation purposes. In the private sector, rating agencies typically disclose general documentation, research outputs, and detailed methodological reports to support their assessments.

Second, the volume fosters knowledge exchange among practitioners regarding recent advancements in CCA. It may also prove valuable to corporate entities wishing to gain deeper insight into the factors that shape financial soundness.

A few definitions are warranted. The principal output of CCA is the estimated probability that a given company will default on any of its financial obligations within a given time horizon—expressed as a percentage between 0 and 100. This probability of default (PD) can be mapped to a credit rating, an ordinal variable indicating the sub-range within the admissible PD spectrum to which the company belongs. For companies issuing bonds in the market, the standard metric for credit risk is the agency rating assigned to the bonds, which is typically solicited by the issuer and made publicly available for investor evaluation. The PD concept is more general, as it applies to all companies regardless of their financing channels. Throughout this volume, both terms will be employed, with the understanding that PD represents the fundamental output of any CCA system, while the rating is a derived variable, often used for ease of communication. For firms that issue bonds, we will refer to the issuer's PD or rating, not to the rating of specific bonds, which may differ according to their structure. Besides, our reference time horizon will be twelve months, unless otherwise specified.

The concept of default—often associated with insolvency—differs fundamentally from that of bankruptcy. While bankruptcy represents a legal and terminal resolution for a corporation, default is a potentially reversible condition. A firm may, at a given point, fail to meet its financial obligations; however, under favourable financial circumstances, it may subsequently restore its solvency and resume normal operations.

The best practices in CCA involve combining a statistical model with expert judgment provided by credit analysts. A rating committee composed of senior managers typically oversees the entire process. ICAS, in line with this framework, is structured as a two-stage system supervised by a rating committee.

ICAS has some general features that may be of interest for CCA practice.

First, it employs a broad and diverse set of data sources, including macroeconomic projections, financial ratios, credit performance indicators, sector studies, climate risk indicators, news articles, sustainability scores, cyber threat metrics, and more. Some of these data are publicly available or accessible to rating agencies and banks; others are proprietary to the Bank of Italy, developed internally using advanced techniques.

Second, as we aim to demonstrate throughout the book, ICAS stands at the forefront of applied research on emerging risk sources and methodologies for CCA.

For clarity, this volume is not a textbook on CCA methodologies, but rather a coherent collection of essays focused on the application and results of various approaches. This has two implications for the reader. First, those wishing to explore advanced topics—such as the principles of machine learning (ML) in credit risk management—will find concise literature reviews and bibliographic references in each chapter. Second, while we have aimed to minimize redundancy, each chapter is largely self-contained. In some cases, more technical material is included in appendices.

One of the key factors behind the successful launch and sustained performance of the ICAS project is the availability, within the Bank of Italy, of two electronic data repositories that provide fully automated access to the project's core input data. The first archive contains the financial statements of Italian corporations. The second, more restricted and managed directly by the Bank, is the National Credit Register (NCR), which offers detailed monthly data on the credit performance of individual Italian firms.

This seamless access to high-quality data, combined with the development of a robust statistical model, enabled ICAS to be implemented within a relatively short time frame and have been a pillar for the functioning of the system over the years. For this reason, all professionals involved in the management of ICAS are grateful to colleagues in the Bank's statistical and IT departments, whose work makes these data infrastructures available and operational.

The volume is structured into four parts. Part I provides an overview of CCA, the use of AI, and related risk management issues. Part II presents the methodology behind the current version of ICAS, along with its outputs and performance. Part III reviews best practices in the rating systems of commercial banks, comparing their performance with that of ICAS. Part IV explores recent research on AI and emerging sources of corporate credit risk. After a suitable period of calibration and testing, this research may guide future developments of ICAS. In the remainder of this chapter, I will provide an overview of the key themes of the book.

2 AI Risk Management

AI offers significant opportunities for enhancing financial services, particularly by improving the quality and efficiency of processes such as credit risk assessment. To fully harness these benefits, it is essential that both private sector actors and public authorities carefully manage the risks associated with AI, as is the case with any emerging technology (Signorini, 2025). This is particularly relevant in the field of cybersecurity (FSB, 2025).

AI systems are advanced machine-based frameworks capable of learning from data and generating outputs—such as predictions, recommendations, or decisions—that influence both physical and virtual environments. Unlike traditional software, AI systems can actively shape the contexts in which they operate. This transformative potential has prompted regulatory attention, most notably through the European Union AI Act, which sets out general principles for all AI systems as well as specific provisions for those that are prohibited or classified as high-risk.

In the United States, no comprehensive federal legislation has been enacted to regulate the development or use of AI, nor to prohibit its application (Congressional Research Services, 2025). Stakeholders continue to debate how best to foster AI innovation and regulation—seeking to leverage its benefits, while mitigating risks like bias and inaccuracies in AI-generated outputs. The Department of Commerce has issued general guidelines recognizing that AI presents unique challenges for both organizational deployment and societal integration (NIST, 2023).

AI risk management is thus a key component of responsible development and use of AI systems. Responsible AI practices can help align the decisions about AI system design, development, and use with intended aims and values.

While the practical application of AI techniques to CCA is addressed in Part IV of this volume, Chapter 2 introduces a general risk management framework aligned with the AI Act. This framework, which may specifically apply to credit risk assessment systems, aims to balance innovation with safeguards for individuals, organizations, and society. It identifies four guiding principles: security, accuracy, fairness, and explainability.

The AI Act classifies systems into prohibited, high-risk, and limited-risk categories, each subject to different levels of scrutiny. Building on this, the framework offers a structured approach to assess and monitor AI risks. Measuring compliance with the above principles enables organizations to ensure that AI systems remain responsible and human centred.

By integrating regulatory compliance with robust risk metrics, the proposed framework supports the development of trustworthy AI systems that deliver benefits while minimizing potential harms. Notably, the chapter presents a rigorous risk measurement process and illustrates it with practical examples.

3 The Current System

The current ICAS process stems from a comprehensive review of its two core components—the statistical model and the expert assessment—carried out in 2023. Before this update, the operational versions had been working rather well for years (Giovannelli et al., 2023), as confirmed in the monitoring exercise performed regularly by the ECB. Still, they showed some room for improvement.

The statistical model (S-ICAS), based on logistic regressions, faced structural limitations in handling key variables that exhibit non-linear or non-monotonic relationships with default events. For instance, firm-level sales growth displays empirically a U-shaped relationship with default rates: both very high and very low growth levels are linked to higher default probabilities, while moderate growth tends to correlate with lower risk.

Credit scoring models generally fall into two categories: statistical models and ML models. While ML models lack transparency—making them hard for credit analysts to interpret—a growing body of research highlights the potential of hybrid approaches. These combine ML techniques with traditional statistical methods, aiming to enhance predictive accuracy without sacrificing interpretability.

In developing the current version of S-ICAS, we adopted this hybrid strategy to balance predictive power and transparency. The ICAS statistical framework retains simplicity and clarity by using logistic regressions, while integrating ML components for variables that exhibit a non-monotonic relationship with the event of default, such as sales growth. These variables are transformed using decision trees, and the resulting discretized versions are then incorporated into the logistic regression model, yielding improved discriminatory power, predictive power, and model stability.

As discussed in Chapter 3, the statistical model demonstrates robust and reliable properties, allowing for strong discrimination between healthy and risky firms, with stable results over time. Its discriminatory power increases with firm size, ensuring an accurate assessment of the largest exposures involved in monetary policy operations.

The model's architecture is also quite flexible, providing a solid foundation for future enhancements that may further improve its ability to distinguish between different credit risk profiles.

Chapter 4 presents two further enhancements to S-ICAS for improving the accuracy and stability of its predictions, with a focus on systemic risk and idiosyncratic risk, respectively.

The first enhancement integrates the effects of the business cycle into the statistical model (Pesaran et al., 2006). S-ICAS relies on microeconomic variables—specifically, financial ratios and indicators obtained from the NCR, which are inherently backward-looking. To incorporate broader economic conditions, we have developed a satellite macroeconomic model that captures business cycle dynamics and embeds them into the system's PD estimates.

Prior to this development, the α coefficient in the logistic regressions—that reflects the one-year ahead expected average default rate under the overall business conditions—was adjusted mainly based on expert judgment.

The second enhancement fully exploits the cross-sectional heterogeneity of firms by applying panel estimation techniques.

Our main finding is that the macroeconomic model estimates average default rates with four times greater accuracy than the original S-ICAS. As a result, the enhanced system better reflects macroeconomic conditions across economic sectors, especially during recessions, thereby improving its discriminatory power.

Estimation results for the two most representative sub-models of S-ICAS indicate that panel methods can lead to gains in discriminatory power, although with limited improvements in the Area Under the Receiver Operating Characteristic (AUROC) curve.

The macroeconomic model has already been implemented in the operational system. In contrast, the potential adoption of panel econometric techniques for operational use requires further investigation. We aim to extend coverage to all economic sectors and conduct additional robustness checks. This will allow us to better assess the empirical benefits of applying panel econometric techniques to S-ICAS, weighing them against their increased operational and technical complexity.

In the assessment of a firm's credit risk, the two designated analysts adopt a forward-looking perspective and draw on a wide range of information sources. As illustrated in Chapter 5, each analyst independently evaluates predefined assessment modules that capture firm-specific characteristics—such as financial flexibility, business sector, and governance. Based on their evaluation, analysts assign a score to each module. These scores are then weighed and aggregated to produce the final rating.

Following the internal review conducted in 2023, several improvements have been introduced to enhance the quality and consistency of expert assessments. Structured checklists now guide analysts through the evaluation of each risk profile, ensuring a comprehensive and more consistent analysis of all relevant risk factors and reducing the likelihood of omissions or subjective bias. A Bayesian aggregation methodology has been adopted to combine the partial scores assigned to each risk area.

In the years prior to the 2023 review, expert assessment provided significant added value in terms of discriminatory power, predictive power, and rating stability compared with statistical ratings. We believe that, thanks to the improvements introduced as of 2024 in both the statistical model and expert assessment, this added value may have further increased. We will test this hypothesis as soon as a sufficiently large data sample will be available.

Climate transition and physical risks affect creditworthiness through their impact on growth, financial performance, and business models. Integrating these risks into credit assessment poses two main challenges: methodological issues—such as scenario design, risk endogeneity, and non-linear effects—and the limited availability of firm-level data (Angelini, 2022). To address these issues, the Eurosystem has established minimum common standards for incorporating climate risks into ICASes managed by NCBs (Körding & Resch, 2022).

As part of this effort, in 2024 the Bank of Italy conducted an experimental survey to collect firm-level data on greenhouse gas emissions, energy use, financial impacts of climate events, and qualitative aspects of governance and organizational structure. The goal was to improve the assessment of climate change risk (CCR) and enhance ICAS rating accuracy, overcoming the limitations of sectoral averages.[3]

Chapter 6 presents the 2024 survey results and illustrates their contribution to CCR evaluation. Key findings include gaps in firms' climate risk management, such as limited transition planning and insufficient mitigation of physical risks. The

[3] The survey was repeated in 2025; its results are not yet available at the time of going to press.

survey also highlights a disconnect between firms' perceived exposure to physical risks and the potential impact of extreme climate events. While most firms report low exposure, many acknowledge possible disruptions to production—especially in agriculture and manufacturing. This suggests that progress is still needed in governance and data reporting to effectively integrate climate risks into credit assessments.

Survey responses demonstrate the value of firm-level data for ICAS. For transition risk, PDs based on individual data differ significantly from those estimated using sectoral averages. These findings support the use of climate survey data within ICAS, particularly for firms that do not publish non-financial statements—at least until more systematic firm-level CCR data become available.

Chapter 7 presents the evolution of Italian firms' creditworthiness as measured by S-ICAS over the period 2013–2024. The data show a gradual improvement during the sample period. Following the sovereign debt crisis and up to the COVID-19 pandemic, PDs declined significantly, reflecting the economic recovery and the strengthening of firms' financial structures, supported by accommodative monetary policy. The impact of the pandemic was uneven across sectors.

The strong post-pandemic recovery led to a further decline in PDs by the end of 2022. Estimates for end-2023 show a slight deterioration, entirely attributable to changes in the macroeconomic environment. At the end of 2024, firms' creditworthiness remained broadly stable. Our projections suggest a default rate of around 3 per cent in 2025, driven by persistently high financing costs, weak economic growth, and rising geopolitical risks.

4 The Models at Commercial Banks

CCA systems similar to ICAS are developed internally by major commercial banks for risk management and capital requirement calculations; in addition, they may be used for collateral valuation in Eurosystem refinancing. Chapter 8 examines the role of banks' internal ratings-based (IRB) systems in assessing credit claims for the latter purpose.

The chapter presents three key insights. First, in a bank-based financial system, IRB systems enhance banks' ability to mobilize credit claims and diversify credit risk assessments, complementing rating agencies and ICAS ratings.

Second, the regulatory framework for IRB systems is evolving. Their role is being reduced for supervisory purposes—following the implementation of the Capital Requirements Regulation 3 (or CRR3) in the European Union—and for monetary policy, as the Eurosystem has decided to prioritize ICAS ratings within its collateral framework.

Third, despite these changes, IRB systems remain essential for assessing small and medium-sized enterprises (SMEs), especially in jurisdictions and sectors not covered by ICASes. They help ensure collateral availability and support the transmission of monetary policy. According to the latest data for Italy, even after ICAS prioritization, IRB systems remain the credit assessment source for over one third of the total volume of credit claims pledged as collateral.

From 2026, the statistical component of ICASes across the euro area may be used to assess SMEs, many of which are not covered by other sources (Duarte et al., 2025). In line with this ECB decision, full ratings continue to apply to large firms. To support the specialization of expert assessment by firm size, in Chapter 9 we review the methodologies used by various rating entities to evaluate large non-financial firms, identifying best practices and recent developments.

The review covers the credit assessment sources accepted for Eurosystem collateral purposes: external credit assessment institutions (ECAIs) such as Moody's, S&P, and Fitch; selected ICASes with established use and public documentation, such as those managed by Banco de España, Banque de France, and Bundesbank; commercial banks' IRB systems; and the two main Italian rating agencies, Cerved and CRIF.[4]

The analysis shows that rating entities rely on a broad set of financial and non-financial information. Qualitative judgment—based on interviews with top management and assessments of governance and market positioning—plays a key role in evaluating complex firms. Common features include sector-specific methodologies, group-level assessments, early warning tools, and structured procedures for overriding model outputs when appropriate.

Chapter 10 examines the benchmarking of banks' IRB ratings against the central bank's ICAS ratings for monetary policy purposes. The research question concerns the potential underreporting of risk by banks (Behn et al., 2022), which could lead to unwarranted exposure for the central bank.

We present a detailed empirical analysis showing that both the rating systems of Italian banks and the central bank exhibit satisfactory discriminatory power and predictive accuracy, supporting the view that credit risk is adequately assessed. On average, banks' internal models are slightly less conservative than the central bank's model for borrowers whose loans are eligible as collateral.

There is only mild evidence—of small economic significance—that banks may strategically manage credit risk assessments for pledged loans. Moreover, there is no indication that banks with higher central bank liquidity usage assign more lenient PDs to their debtors.

5 AI and New Risk Sources

Chapter 11 presents a comparative study of widely used ML methods versus S-ICAS, and proposes a practical tool based on eXplainable Artificial Intelligence (XAI) to support analysts in the second stage of the ICAS evaluation process.

[4] Other credit assessment sources are available, including those that specialize on SMEs and employ AI techniques. A notable example of the latter is Wiserfunding, Ltd., co-founded by Prof. Altman.

ML methods make minimal assumptions about the data-generating process, as they aim to optimize predictive accuracy by capturing complex, non-linear relationships. However, their complexity limits explainability, which is essential in regulatory contexts. In contrast, traditional models like S-ICAS offer simpler, interpretable outputs. To bridge this gap, XAI techniques have been developed to enhance the transparency of ML models (Apley & Zhu, 2020; Bussmann et al., 2021). The chapter explores how XAI can support ICAS analysis.

We replicate the S-ICAS structure using three ML models—random forests, extreme gradient boosting, and deep learning—and combine them in a meta-model. XAI techniques are then used to build an interpretation tool that highlights the most relevant factors behind discrepancies between ML-estimated PDs and those from S-ICAS.

Our findings show that ML models offer valuable insights that complement—but do not replace—S-ICAS. This aligns with concerns about overreliance on automated decisions, and with regulatory emphasis on transparency and accountability (Angelini, 2025; European Banking Authority, 2023).

Overall, ML methods can enhance the ICAS process by refining outputs and integrating additional data sources, including unstructured information. Indeed, while the empirical study in Chapter 11 uses the same input dataset as S-ICAS, future developments might extend ML applications to much broader information sets. This represents a promising direction for further research.

Climate change is intensifying natural disasters, with significant economic repercussions that may undermine firms' financial soundness. Events such as floods and landslides can destroy physical assets and cause prolonged operational disruptions, potentially leading to insolvency (Grimwade, 2022).

However, assessing physical risks remains challenging. The most severe events are typically localized, and detailed data on the geographic distribution of firms' assets are often lacking. Chapter 12 evaluates the impact of hydro-geological (HG) risks on the one-year PD of a large sample of Italian non-financial firms, seeking to overcome the data limitations that have hindered research in this area.

The analysis shows that over one third of Italian firms are exposed to HG risks, particularly floods. Accounting for the location of all business units—not just headquarters—is crucial: relying solely on headquarters data leads to misestimation of risk for many firms.

The results indicate that, when accounting for HG risks, a large share of firms experiences a mild increase in PDs—with sectoral and regional heterogeneity—and the effect on collateral pledged for monetary policy operations is negligible. However, both the frequency and intensity of extreme events are expected to increase relative to our sample period, potentially amplifying their impact on firms' creditworthiness.

Chapter 13 leverages the dataset on verified emissions from the European Union Emissions Trading System (EU-ETS) to estimate the impact of carbon-price related transition risk on the one-year PD of Italian firms. Emissions represent a key component of production, and their associated costs are a critical factor in assessing PD. The EU-ETS market offers direct insights into firm-level emissions, enabling a more accurate bottom-up evaluation of transition risk.

The analysis combines market-based stochastic simulations of carbon price trajectories with fundamentals-based stress testing of PDs to quantify firm-specific transition risk linked to emission costs. To identify a risk-sensitive extreme scenario, the study applies the Conditional Value at Risk (CVaR) across simulated paths. The resulting carbon price shocks are then used to reassess each firm's financial position and update its PD accordingly.

The framework also accounts for the potential revenue generation from EU-ETS allowances. Firms emitting less than their allocated quota can sell surplus allowances on the market, thereby generating additional income. The main finding is that PDs derived from EU-ETS-based scenario analysis exhibit greater sensitivity to transition risk compared to those obtained using the scenarios developed by the Network for Greening the Financial System (NGFS). This allows for a more realistic estimation of rating migrations, capturing both downgrades and upgrades.

The integration of broader ESG considerations is becoming increasingly relevant for constructing a comprehensive risk assessment framework. Altman et al. (2023) highlight the benefits of incorporating social and governance (S and G) indicators—such as board gender composition, managers' age, management experience, and hiring/firing ratios—into the estimation of PDs for SMEs. Similarly, sound governance practices, including independent boards and audit functions, robust control systems, and transparent communication, can enhance corporate performance, reduce the risk of fraud and conflicts of interest, and improve creditworthiness (Moody's Ratings, 2021; S&P Global Ratings, 2021).

Chapter 14 explores the role of the S and G pillars in predicting corporate default among Italian firms, as assessed within the S-ICAS framework. Default risk is evaluated using two independent scores—one based on social metrics and the other on governance metrics—and combining statistical and ML methods.

Social indicators such as layoff rate, employee turnover, and average wages enhance both the discriminatory power and predictive power of default risk models, corroborating earlier evidence. These metrics reflect the link between employment stability, workforce engagement, and financial resilience, reinforcing the notion that investment in human capital and long-term financial sustainability support each other (Houston et al., 2024). Governance factors influence the S-ICAS PD differently depending on firm size.

The enhanced S-ICAS model—incorporating both social and governance scores—displays improved discriminatory power compared to the baseline specification.

Natural language processing has significantly broadened the scope for integrating unstructured textual data into quantitative analysis, as shown e.g., by prior research on the effect of sentiment scores on the prediction of credit default swap spreads (Lu et al., 2016). More recently, the advent of large language models (LLMs) has introduced powerful new capabilities for interpreting complex linguistic content.

Chapter 15 applies cutting-edge LLMs—including Bidirectional Encoder Representations from Transformers (BERT), LLaMA 3 by Meta, Microsoft's Phi 3, and Google's Gemma 2—to extract sentiment indicators from a corpus of company-related news sourced from the Dow Jones Factiva database. These models serve as a bridge between qualitative insights and quantitative evaluation, enabling a holistic assessment of corporate creditworthiness.

To maintain computational efficiency, while ensuring analytical precision, the study employs compression techniques that reduce the resource demands of these models without significantly compromising performance. The results show that sentiment indicators derived from LLMs enhance the discriminatory power of the S-ICAS framework and provide a robust methodology for integrating unstructured data into predictive credit risk models.

Chapter 16, the final study of this volume, focuses on the cyber risk exposure of firms. It presents a comprehensive framework for measuring corporate vulnerability to cyber threats in Italy. We introduce a novel taxonomy for assessing cyber risk, around six dimensions. Data are sourced from financial statements, web scraping of corporate cybersecurity disclosures, and media reports on cyberattacks.

The study then applies LLMs and ML techniques to the resulting dataset. Specifically, it evaluates: (i) firm-reported signals of cyber risk and defensive measures, classified using a supervised learning algorithm trained on the bespoke taxonomy; and (ii) cyber incidents and mitigation strategies. The resulting cyber risk indicator enables an assessment of vulnerability distribution across firms.

Key findings reveal a consistent rise in both the frequency and variety of cyberattacks affecting firms since 2019. The cyber risk index has remained high since 2020, pointing to structural weaknesses in firms' cybersecurity profiles. Sector-specific threats vary according to operational models, digital exposure, and the nature of data. For instance, data breaches are the prevalent type of attack across all sectors, while ransomware is common in manufacturing, professional services, and retail.

These patterns underscore the need for systematic monitoring and robust evaluation of corporate cyber risk. The impact of cyber risk on corporate creditworthiness will be explored in future research.

More broadly, as emphasized throughout this overview, the findings presented in the book are expected to guide future research and potential enhancements to ICAS in the years ahead.

AI applications in this area will continue to be inspired by some guiding principles: (i) compliance with the Eurosystem standards for collateral valuation; (ii) assessment of performance benefits against development and running costs; (iii) compliance with the general principles of the AI Act, in particular the notion that AI processes should be supervised by human intelligence and adhere to sound risk management rules.

To conclude my overview, I would like to offer a reflection inspired by Seneca's words. I sincerely hope that the insights gathered in this volume may contribute to making the art of corporate credit analysis long-lasting and judgment less difficult.

References

Altman, E. I. (1968). Financial ratios, discriminant analysis and the prediction of corporate bankruptcy. *Journal of Finance, 23*, 589–609.

Altman, E. I., Balzano, M., Giannozzi, A., & Srhoj, S. (2023). Revisiting SME default predictors: The omega score. *Journal of Small Business Management, 61*(6), 2383–2417.

Angelini, P. (2022). The financial risks posed by climate change: information gaps and transition plans, Speech at the Meeting of *Associazione nazionale per lo studio dei problemi del credito*, Milan, 15 November.

Angelini, P. (2023). The banking crises of 2023: some initial reflections, Remarks at the event "*Promoting Accountability in Times of Crisis*", Tenth Annual Meeting of the Working group on financial and economic stability of the International Organization of Supreme Audit Institutions (INTOSAI). Rome, 8 November 2023.

Angelini, P. (2025). Data Science in Central Banking, Closing remarks at the 4th Irving Fisher Committee and Bank of Italy Workshop, Rome, 20 February.

Apley, D. W., & Zhu, J. (2020). Visualizing the effects of predictor variables in black box supervised learning models. *Journal of the Royal Statistical Society Series b: Statistical Methodology, 82*(4), 1059–1086.

Auria, L., Bingmer, M., Caicedo Graciano, C. M., Charavel, C., Gavilá, S., Iannamorelli, A., Levy, A., Maldonado, A., Resch, F., Rossi, A. M., Sauer, S. (2021). Overview of central banks' in-house credit assessment systems in the euro area, ECB Occasional Paper, No. 284.

Basel Committee on Banking Supervision—BCBS. (2010, August). *An assessment of the long-term economic impact of stronger capital and liquidity requirements.* BIS.

Basel Committee on Banking Supervision—BCBS. (2023). *Report on the 2023 banking turmoil.* BIS.

Behn, M., Haselmann, R., & Vig, V. (2022). The limits of model-based regulation. *Journal of Finance, 77*, 1635–1684.

Bernanke, B. S. (1992). Credit in the macroeconomy. *Federal Reserve Bank of New York Quarterly Bulletin*, Spring 1992–1993, 50–70.

Bernanke, B. S., & Gertler, M. (1989). Agency costs, net worth, and business fluctuations. *American Economic Review, 79*, 14–31.

Bussmann, N., Giudici, P., Marinelli, D., & Papenbrock, J. (2021). Explainable machine learning in credit risk management. *Computational Economics, 57*, 203–216.

Congressional Research Service. (2025, June). *Regulating Artificial Intelligence: U.S. and International approaches and considerations for congress.*

Duarte, C., Engel, J., Reichmann, O., & Džaja, T. (2025). Introducing statistical in-house credit assessment systems (S-ICASs) as an additional source of credit assessments under the general collateral framework. *ECB Economic Bulletin*, 3/2025, Frankfurt.

European Banking Authority. (2023). Machine learning for IRB models: Follow-up report from the consultation on the discussion paper on machine learning for IRB models (EBA/REP/2023/28).

Financial Stability Board—FSB. (2025, September). *G7 cyber expert group statement on Artificial Intelligence and cybersecurity.*

Giovannelli, F., Iannamorelli, A., Levy, A., & Orlandi, M. (2023). The Bank of Italy's in-house credit assessment system for non-financial firms. In A. Scalia (Ed.), *Financial risk management and climate change risk. The experience in a central bank.* Springer.

Gorton, G. B., Ross, C. P., & Ross, S. Y. (2025). *Where collateral sleeps* (NBER Working Paper, No. 34266).

Grimwade, M. (2022). How climate change may impact operational risk. *Journal of Operational Risk, 17*, 41–81.

Houston, L., Shah, D., Wang, X. (2024). *Social risks and opportunities for corporates: Long-term performance in global equity markets.* MSCI Research.

Iannamorelli, A., Nobili, S., Scalia, A., & Zaccaria, L. (2024). Asymmetric information and corporate lending: Evidence from SME bond markets. *Review of Finance, 28*, 163–201.

Jensen, M., & Meckling, W. (1976). Theory of the firm: Managerial behavior, agency costs and ownership structure. *Journal of Financial Economics, 3*, 305–360.

Körding, J., & Resch, F. (2022). Common minimum standards for incorporating climate change risks into in-house credit assessment systems in the Eurosystem. *ECB Economic Bulletin, 6/* 2022, Frankfurt.

Lu, H. M., Hung, M. W., & Tsai, F. T. (2016). The impact of news articles and corporate disclosure on credit risk valuation. *Journal of Banking and Finance, 68*, 100–116.

Mishkin, F. S. (1996). *The channels of monetary transmission: Lessons for monetary policy* (NBER Working Paper, No. 5464).

Moody's Ratings. (2021). *General principles for assessing environmental, social and governance risks*. Cross-Sector Rating Methodology.

National Institute of Standards and Technology—NIST. (2023). *Artificial Intelligence risk management framework*.

Pesaran, M. H., Schuermann, T., Treutler, B.-J., & Weiner, S. M. (2006). Macroeconomic dynamics and credit risk: A global perspective. *Journal of Money, Credit and Banking, 38*, 1211–1261.

Shi, S., Tse, R., Luo, W., D'Addona, S., & Pau, G. (2022). Machine learning-driven credit risk: A systemic review. *Neural Computing and Applications, 34*, 14327–14339.

Signorini, L. F. (2025). Artificial intelligence in finance, speech at the fourth G20 finance ministers and central bank governors' meeting, South Africa's Financial Sector Conduct Authority (FSCA) and the OECD, Durban, South Africa.

Standard and Poor's Global Ratings. (2021). *The evolution of ESG factors in credit risk assessment: Corporate governance*.

A SAFE Model for AI Risk Management

Paolo Giudici

1 Introduction

An AI system is a sophisticated machine-based framework designed to perform tasks that involve learning from data and making informed predictions or decisions based on those data. These systems operate with either explicit objectives—clear, predefined goals that guide their processes—or implicit objectives, which may be less evident but nonetheless drive the system's behaviour. The hallmark of an AI system is its capability to analyse the input it receives and utilise that analysis to generate a range of outputs. These outputs may result in predictions, content creations, recommendations, or strategic decisions tailored to specific contexts.

One of the defining features of AI systems is their ability to influence both physical and virtual environments. This means that the outcomes produced by AI can have tangible effects on the real world, be they in the realm of digital interactions or in the physical domain where human activities take place. This distinguishes AI from traditional software or standard machine-based systems. While conventional systems may process information and return outputs, AI systems possess a deeper level of sophistication that allows their outputs to actively shape and alter the settings in which they operate.

These considerations are now being included in governmental regulations and recommendations. The first law to be issued is the European AI Act, from which we report the legal definition of an AI system:

> An AI system is a machine-based system that, for explicit or implicit objectives, infers, from the input it receives, how to generate outputs such as predictions, content, recommendations, or decisions, that can influence physical or virtual environments.

P. Giudici (✉)
Department of Economics and Management, University of Pavia, Pavia, Italy
e-mail: paolo.giudici@unipv.it

A. Scalia (ed.), *Corporate Credit Analysis and AI*, Finance for Professionals,
https://doi.org/10.1007/978-3-032-13422-6_2

The definition indirectly implies that, because of their potential influence on the contextual environment, the applications of AI systems must be 'controlled' and 'managed', for the benefit of all.

The objective of this chapter is to present an AI risk management framework which, while addressing the compliance with the European AI Act, provides a consistent and rigorous set of assessment metrics that can be used to measure and monitor the risk that AI may cause on individuals, organisations, or the planet at large, thereby balancing opportunities with risks.

2 AI Risk Management

The most important risks of AI are the following.

- **Security Risks**: The integration of AI into IT systems can introduce vulnerabilities that might be exploited by malicious actors. AI can be used to launch sophisticated cyberattacks, necessitating robust cybersecurity measures to safeguard sensitive information (see e.g. Aldasoro et al., 2022).
- **Accuracy Risks**: The accuracy and reliability of AI models depend on the quality of the data and on the model used for training. Poor quality data and models can lead to erroneous predictions, which can have serious implications in critical sectors such as finance, healthcare, and law enforcement (see e.g. Babaei & Giudici, 2024).
- **Explainability Risks**: The rapid advancement of AI technologies outpaces the capacity to fully understand their functioning. This discrepancy can lead to challenges in governance, particularly concerning accountability, control, and human oversight on the actions of AI systems (see e.g. Bracke et al., 2019).
- **Fairness Risks**: AI systems can inadvertently perpetuate or exacerbate existing biases, particularly if they are trained on datasets that are not representative. This concern is more relevant in areas like recruitment, lending, and law enforcement, where discriminatory outcomes can have far-reaching consequences for the affected individuals and communities (see e.g. Agarwal et al., 2023).

To address these risks and ensure responsible AI deployment, various organisations, public and private, are working collaboratively to develop codes of practice and international standards for AI providers and deployers. These guidelines aim at the establishment of frameworks that promote ethical practices, accountability and transparency in AI development and usage. By creating standardised protocols, organisations can better manage the risks associated with AI, ensuring that its benefits are realised while minimising potential harms.

An important regulatory effort in the AI field is the European Union's AI Act. It categorises AI systems according to their level of risk and distinguishes between three types of AI practices, subject to varying degrees of regulatory scrutiny.

- **Prohibited AI Practices**: Certain AI applications deemed too risky or fundamentally harmful are banned outright. An example of this includes social scoring systems that rank individuals based on their behaviours and interactions, raising serious ethical concerns regarding privacy and discrimination.
- **High-Risk AI Practices**: This category of AI systems, such as credit scoring and life insurance pricing, are permitted but must adhere to stringent risk management protocols. Providers must implement measures to mitigate potential risks, ensuring compliance with established standards and practices.
- **Limited Risk Practices**: AI applications classified as limited risk, such as chatbots and virtual assistants, are allowed but must conform to specific transparency requirements. This may include disclosures about the system's AI nature and limitations, allowing users to make informed decisions during their interactions.

Following a similar risk-based perspective, we can map the principles contained in the European AI Act, the compliance with which can be measured in a quantitative fashion, in four classes, as first suggested in Giudici and Raffinetti (2023). This approach allows for a consistent and effective measurement of the degree of compliance with the principles, which could be made difficult in the presence of many different risk classes.

The four identified principles, and the corresponding risk classes, are the following:

- **Security**: AI systems should achieve an appropriate level of robustness and cybersecurity. The risk of not achieving an adequate level of security is akin to the notions of operational risk and cyber risk, well known in the risk management community.
- **Accuracy**: AI systems should achieve an adequate level of accuracy. The risk of a model not being accurate is similar to the notion of model risk, well known in the risk management community.
- **Fairness**: Input data for AI systems should be relevant, representative, and complete, as regards the persons and groups on which the AI system is used. The risk of generating discrimination is a new risk type, mainly because it does not impact directly an organisation, as the previous risks, but its customers and, thus, it requires an external independent assessment. Organisational risks are usually defined as the probability/severity that an organisation incurs into a loss. Discrimination risk refers instead to the probability/severity that a customer of an organisation, rather than the organisation itself, suffers a loss, due to discrimination and unfair treatment.
- **Explainability**: AI systems should be designed so that they can be effectively overseen and controlled by natural persons. This risk type is related to governance risk, already known in the risk management community.

Putting together the four stated principles we get the acronym SAFE, which stands for Secure, Accurate, Fair and Explainable AI.

We postulate that a valid risk management framework should measure the risks that an AI system is not SAFE or, in other words, that there is a lack of compliance with the SAFE principles. If a risk management framework can measure, monitor, and mitigate such risks, the corresponding AI system can become responsible and human centred.

3 AI Risk Measurement

A risk management framework is different from a pure compliance framework. In a compliance framework, the aim is assessing whether a set of principles, including the SAFE principles, are fulfilled by an AI system of a provider or a deployer. This type of assessment is mostly qualitative and has the advantage that it can cover different types of principles, including those that are difficult to measure. At the same time, compliance assessment is by nature more subjective, as it needs to be conducted by groups of experts or auditors. For this reason, it has the disadvantage of being more expensive, in cost and time.

Conversely, a risk management framework is mostly quantitative, as it aims at measuring in continuous time that the stated principles are fulfilled by the AI system of a provider or deployer. This has the advantage of allowing an automated or semi-automated quality control on AI applications. The disadvantage is that it can be applied only to criteria that can be measured in a quantitative manner, so that they can be monitored, managed, and mitigated.

The distinction between compliance and risk management is reflected in the organisation of the control functions of financial organisations worldwide. Many of them have two separate sub-functions: a compliance function, with strong regulatory and legal skills; and a risk management function, with strong quantitative and data science skills.

It is likely that the same subdivision will be implemented in organisations whose core activity involves developing and running AI applications, in line with the emerging regulations and recommendations that mirror those of the financial sector. This implies that risk measurement will be required for managing the most important risks of AI, those that need to be monitored and, possibly, managed and mitigated in continuous time. This may be the case for the SAFE risks described above.

Less important risks, or less frequent ones, can be subject to qualitative compliance checks. This may be the case, for example, for accountability, book-keeping, transparency, and the respect of human rights, the fulfilment of which is difficult to assess quantitatively.

In the remainder of this Chapter, we focus on risk measurement. To this aim, next we present a review of the state-of-the-art methods to measure the fulfilment of the SAFE principles.

The best-known SAFE AI principle is Accuracy. It is usually measured in terms of the distance between the predicted and the 'true' values of the output variable, where 'true' means actually observed or expected (see e.g. Gneiting, 2011; Hand &

Till, 2001). If the response is numeric, the main metrics are the Mean Squared Error (MSE) and the Root Mean Squared Error (RMSE). If the response is binary or categorical, the main accuracy metrics are the True Positive Rate (TPR) and the False Positive Rate (FPR), summarised into the Receiver Operating Characteristics (ROC) curve, which shows how TPR and FPR change as the rank threshold changes. Giudici and Raffinetti (2024) have shown that the AUC can be generalised into a Rank Graduation Accuracy measure (RGA) which, while equal to AUC for binary variables, can be calculated in the same way also for ordinal and continuous response target variables.

Explainability has a positive impact on all the stakeholders of an AI system. If the system is interpretable, a data scientist can effectively manage it (see e.g. Bracke et al., 2019), while auditors and regulators can better validate it. Customers and users can understand the reasons of the predictions that involve themselves and can thus learn how to improve their situation. While some techniques are explainable by design, in terms of their parameters (e.g. regression models), AI methods usually are black boxes (like neural networks and random forests) and need post-processing tools to be made explainable to the extent possible. For black-box models, the most employed and effective tools are Shapley values (see e.g. Lundberg & Lee, 2017; Ribeiro et al., 2016; Bussman et al., 2021; Giudici & Gramegna, 2021). Shapley values, introduced in the context of game theory (Shapley, 1953), are based on the idea that there is a game for the prediction of each observation. For each game, the players are the model predictors which, during the game, compete for a share of the total reward, equal to the value of the prediction. At the end of the game, the predicted value is shared in unequal parts, one for each predictor.

Security can be assessed by evaluating the impact of a model perturbation, such as a cyberattack on the input data, on the model's output. This gives rise to a metric similar to RGA, defined as Rank Graduation Robustness (RGR) in Babaei et al. (2025). In light of the development of AI, it is important to consider how secure an AI model is for its surrounding environment, that is, to evaluate its sustainability and, in particular, its environmental sustainability. Energy and $CO2$ consumption increase with model complexity, which in turn increases with the number of input variables. In this respect, dimensional reduction methods such as principal components and whitening, as well as regularisation methods such as LASSO and RIDGE, can reduce the number of input variables, without compromising on predictive accuracy. Doing so, we can obtain a more parsimonious model which, while retaining predictive accuracy, will be simpler and less time- and energy-consuming, as well as more stable against extreme variations and perturbations in the data.

Finally, since human decisions may be unfair, it is obvious that, when automatic decisions, based on machine learning, are taken, algorithmic injustice may arise, in terms of some 'protected' variables, such as gender, race, nationality, and/or religion (Kozodoi et al., 2022). The most popular measures of fairness are based on the notion of statistical parity, which is simple and intuitive: all individuals should receive the same outcome from a model (prediction, recommendation, or content), regardless of their belonging to one or another group of the protected variable. To exemplify, suppose that a credit scoring model is applied separately by gender. The difference between the accuracy of the model chosen for the men and the accuracy of that chosen for the women is an example of parity metrics. Other types of fairness measures relate to the provision of counterfactuals, or to the notion of individual fairness. All fairness measures are strictly related to the measurement of explainability of the protected variables.

4 AI Risk Metrics

Accuracy. A recent paper (Giudici & Raffinetti, 2024) proposes a new accuracy metric, the Rank Graduation Accuracy (RGA), which unifies the case of a categorical response with that of a continuous response, and that can be utilised as a general criterion to measure SAFE AI risks. RGA is expressed as a percentage and it coincides with the AUC when the response is binary. The higher is the value of RGA, the better is the predictive accuracy of a model. In particular, RGA $= 1$ means that the predicted ranks are all equal to the observed ranks, and RGA $=$ 0.5 means that the predicted ranks are equal to that of a random model.

Explainability. The Shapley value of a variable, SHAP (X_k), expresses the average contribution of variable X_k to the predictions of the machine learning models that contain it (Lundberg & Lee, 2017; Shapley, 1953). A small Shapley value means that the average added value of the variable is small, i.e. it does not change the prediction of the *i-th* observation. A large Shapley value means that the average added value of the variable is large, i.e. it significantly changes the prediction of the *i*-th observation. The disadvantage of Shapley values is that they are not normalised and, therefore, are difficult to interpret. To solve this issue, Giudici and Raffinetti (2021) introduced Shapley Lorenz values, which measure the contribution of a variable X_k not to the predictions of the machine learning models, but to their accuracy, thereby generating a percentage: the higher is the Shapley Lorenz Values, (SLV), the more important is that variable. We can then calculate the overall explainability of a model as the sum of the explainability of its variables.

Note that, applying Shapley Lorenz Values, we add to the AI model an extra modelling layer that helps to make it explainable. In our language, this is equivalent to making it safer.

Security. The security of a model can be defined in terms of its resilience, or robustness, against adversarial attacks and extreme events. We refer the reader to the paper of Babaei et al. (2025), in which a Rank Graduation Robustness measure (RGR), similar to RGA, is proposed, to improve the safety of a machine learning model against cyberattacks. Doing so, we add to the AI model an extra modelling layer that helps to make it safer.

The robustness of a model can also improve via feature selection, that is, eliminating variables which do not make a significant contribution to predictive accuracy, either in terms of Diebold and Mariano's test when the response variable is continuous (Diebold & Mariano, 1995) or in terms of DeLong's test when the response variable is binary (De Long et al., 1988). For a detailed explanation, see for example the paper of Babaei et al. (2022).

Fairness. Mathematically, we can measure fairness by comparing the accuracy of a model, when applied separately to different population groups (Mitchell et al., 2021; Passach & Shmueli, 2022) defined by a protected variable. For example, comparing the RGA of a binary classification model applied separately to males and females (where the protected variable is gender) or to white people and non-white people (where the protected variable is race). A better approach is to measure fairness conditionally on the available variables, as in a recent paper by Chen et al. (2024). In this case we can compare explainability metrics, such as the Shapley Lorenz Values, for different population groups. We note that, applying a (conditional) fairness parity metrics, we add to the AI model an extra modelling layer that helps to make it fairer. In our language, this is equivalent to making it safer. We remark that fairness is measurable only in the presence of a protected variable of interest.

Lorenz curve metrics. From the state-of-the-art-metrics described in the previous Section, we next build a general risk measurement framework for a SAFE and responsible AI. As it occurs in financial risk management, we seek to integrate the four risk types into a single measure, to provide a comprehensive risk assessment score, similarly to what is done when integrating market, credit, and operational risk into a unified measure of capital requirement.

To this aim, each SAFE metric can be interpreted as a probability of compliance with the related principle, and the complement of such probability can be interpreted as a risk measure: of security, accuracy, fairness, and explainability. To integrate the four risk types, we need four metrics with similar scales and interpretation. This can be done by normalising all metrics in terms of the underlying concordance curve, related to the Lorenz Curve (Lorenz, 1905).

In this way, we obtain four different measures, RGA, RGR, RGE, and RGF, which can be compounded into a unified risk measure, equal to the product of the four risks. This is made possible because the four measures share the same mathematical background, and they are all expressed as a percentage.

To illustrate the application of the metrics, we consider a use case, taken from the paper of Giudici et al. (2024). The authors consider five deep learning models to predict the returns of a financial asset: Multi-Layer Perceptron (MLP), Radial Basis Function (RBF), Neural Network Autoregressive (NNAR), Long-Short Term Memory (LSTM), and Gated Recurrent Unit (GRU). A classic approach based on the minimisation of the RMSE of the predictions would lead to choose GRU (with RMSE $= 0.04$), against NNAR (0.13), MLP (0.10) RBF (0.09), LSTM (0.05). In the application of the SAFE AI framework, instead, we consider not only accuracy, but also robustness and explainability. For each model we can calculate the risk of security, accuracy and explainability, as previously defined (fairness is not applicable), and take their product. Then, the probability that at least one SAFE principle is violated is the complement to one of the products. Choosing the model with the lowest such probability leads to choosing the RBF (Probability = 0.75), against NNAR (0.93), MLP (0.77) GRU (0.91), LSTM (0.85).

This occurs because GRU, while highly accurate (RGA = 0.88 vs 0.45 for RBF), is less secure (RGR = 0.92 vs 0.95 for RBF) and, more importantly, much less explainable (RGE = 0.17, vs 0.54 of RBF).

This use case illustrates a clear difference between using a SAFE AI approach as opposed to an alternative approach. If a provider or deployer of AI only looks at the performance capability of the AI model, RMSE may indicate that a rather complex one should be employed, such as GRU. On the other hand, if SAFE and human centred AI principles are taken into account, the same provider or deployer may chose a model that is easier to interpret and, therefore, to be explained, controlled, and managed.

References

Agarwal, S., Muckley, C., & Neelakantan, P. (2023). Countering racial discrimination in algorithmic lending: A case for model agnostic interpretation methods. *Economics Letters, 226*.

Aldasoro, I., Gambacorta, L., Giudici, P., & Leach, T. (2022). The drivers of cyber risk. *Journal of Financial Stability, 60*, Article 100989.

Babaei, G., Giudici, P., & Raffinetti, E. (2022). Explainable fintech lending. *Journal of Economics and Business, 125*, 106126.

Babaei, G., & Giudici, P. (2024). GPT lending classifications. *Machine Learning with Applications, 16*, 100534.

Babaei, G., Giudici, P., & Raffinetti, E. (2025). A rank graduation box for safe artificial intelligence. *Expert Systems with Applications, 259*, 125239.

Bracke, P., Datta, A., Jung, C., & Sen, S. (2019) *Machine learning explainability in finance: An application to default risk analysis* (Bank of England Working Paper, 816).

Bussman, N., Giudici, P., Marinelli, D., & Papenbrock, J. (2021). Explainable machine learning in credit risk management. *Computational Economics, 57*(1), 203–216.

Chen, Y., Giudici, P., Kailang, L., & Raffinetti, E. (2024). Measuring fairness in credit ratings. *Expert Systems with Applications, 258*, Article 125184.

DeLong, E. R., DeLong, D. M., & Clarke-Pearson, D. L. (1988). Comparing the areas under two or more correlated receiver operating characteristic curves: A nonparametric approach. *Biometrics, 44*(3), 837–845.

Diebold, F., & Mariano, R. (1995). Comparing predictive accuracy. *Journal of Business and Economic Statistics, 13*(3), 253–263.

Giudici, P., & Gramegna, A. (2021). SHAP and LIME: An evaluation of discriminative power in credit risk. *Frontiers in Artificial Intelligence, 4*, 752558.

Giudici, P., Piergallini, A., & Recchioni, M. C. (2024). Explainable AI methods for financial time series. *Physica A: Statistical Mechanics with Applications, 2024*(655), Article 130176.

Giudici, P., & Raffinetti, E. (2021). Shapley-Lorenz eXplainable Artificial Intelligence. *Expert Systems with Applications, 167*, Article 114104.

Giudici, P., & Raffinetti, E. (2023). SAFE Artificial Intelligence in Finance. *Finance Research Letters, 56*, Article 104088.

Giudici, P., & Raffinetti, E. (2024). RGA: A unified measure of predictive accuracy. *Advances in Data Analysis and Classification, 19*(1), 67–93.

Gneiting, T. (2011). Making and evaluating point forecasts. *Journal of the American Statistical Association, 106*, 746–762.

Hand, D., & Till, R. J. (2001). A simple generalisation of the area under the ROC Curve for multiple classification problems. *Machine Learning, 45*, 171–186.

Kozodoi, N., Jacob, J., & Lessmann, S. (2022). Fairness in credit scoring: Assessment, implementation and profit implications. *European Journal of Operational Research, 297*, 1083–1094.
Lorenz, M. O. (1905). Methods of measuring the concentration of wealth. *Publications of the American Statistical Association, 9*, 209–219.
Lundberg, S. M., & Lee, S. (2017). A unified approach to interpreting model predictions. In *Advances in Neural Information Processing Systems*, (NIPS 2017) (Vol. 30, pp. 4768–4777).
Passach, D., & Shmueli, E. (2022). A review on fairness in machine learning. *ACM Computing Surveys, 55*(3), 1–44.
Mitchell, S., Potash, E., Barocas, S., D'Amour, A., & Lum, K. (2021). Algorithmic fairness: Choices, assumptions and definitions. *Annual Review of Statistics and Its Applications, 8*, 141–163.
Ribeiro, M. T., Singh, S., & Guestrin, C. (2016). Why should I trust you? Explaining the predictions of any classifiers. In *Proceedings of the 22nd ACM SIGKDD International Conference on Knowledge Discovery and Data Mining* (pp. 1135–1144).
Shapley, L. S. (1953). A value for n-person games. In *Contributions to the Theory of Games II* (pp. 307–317). Princeton University Press.

Part II

The Current System

The Statistical Model

Simone Narizzano, Marco Orlandi, and Antonio Scalia

1 Introduction

Since 2013 the Bank of Italy has been managing the in-house credit assessment system (ICAS) for Italian non-financial firms, for use in the Eurosystem's collateral framework. Similar systems are also employed in other National Central Banks (NCBs) of the Eurosystem. The Bank of Italy's ICAS rating process is based on a two-stage procedure which combines a statistical model with an expert assessment, performed by two analysts and possibly the rating committee, to obtain the final rating of the firm. The 'full' ICAS (F-ICAS) rating, including the expert assessment, is regularly produced for 4,000 Italian firms that are debtors of a large share of the loans posted as collateral in refinancing operations. The statistical model (S-ICAS), that is the first stage of the rating process, covers a much larger sample by means of a fully automated procedure. Every month the model produces estimates of the probability of default (PD) over a one-year horizon for about 370,000 non-financial firms, namely all those that: (i) are incorporated as a limited-liability company in Italy; (ii) publish a financial statement; and (iii) have an exposure towards the banking system, as reported in the National Credit Register (NCR).

While the credit assessment of firms is a well-established practice among banks and rating agencies, and the Bank of Italy's ICAS obviously shares many features with the models of private entities, it has one information advantage, because it

S. Narizzano (✉) · M. Orlandi · A. Scalia
Bank of Italy, Rome, Italy
e-mail: simone.narizzano@bancaditalia.it

M. Orlandi
e-mail: m.orlandi@bancaditalia.it

A. Scalia
e-mail: antonio.scalia@bancaditalia.it

A. Scalia (ed.), *Corporate Credit Analysis and AI*, Finance for Professionals,
https://doi.org/10.1007/978-3-032-13422-6_3

exploits full access to the detailed credit performance of each firm as recorded in the NCR. ICAS ratings, like those of commercial banks, are not public. The ICASes of the NCBs play a crucial role in monetary policy implementation in the euro area as they allow all counterparties to pledge credit claims to non-financial firms. The ICAS contribution to the transmission of monetary policy is even more important during episodes of market tension, as ICASes support the overall availability of collateral. This chapter illustrates the methodology underlying the Bank of Italy's ICAS statistical model and its validation process.

Default forecasting is of key importance for financial institutions and investors. Banks use PDs to evaluate the risks stemming from their lending activity, while investors exploit PDs for bond pricing and portfolio management. The related literature, developed since the 1960s, is substantial (Altman, 1968; Blum, 1974; Deakin, 1972; Edmister, 1972). Although credit models vary widely, they can be divided into two main categories: statistical models and machine learning (ML) models. Several studies compare the performance of statistical models and ML models in corporate default prediction. The majority of these studies concludes that ML models on average slightly outperform statistical models thanks to the ability to capture variables with a non-linear or non-monotonic relationship with default. However, ML models are opaque for the credit analyst and this 'black box' feature makes their use and interpretation rather difficult. A recent strand of the literature has shown that hybrid credit scoring models, which integrate ML techniques with statistical methods, offer a promising approach to default prediction (Dumitrescu et al., 2022; Van Gestel et al., 2005). In the development of the statistical model, we have followed the latter approach, which tries to solve the trade-off between predictability and transparency by combining features of traditional models and ML models. The ICAS statistical approach preserves simplicity and 'readability' by relying on a logit regression, while it tries to improve predictive performance with ML components for some variables that display a non-monotonic behaviour towards default prediction. For these variables we develop a discretized transformation obtained with a decision tree and employ the transformed variables in the logit regression.

Every month the model produces an estimate of the PD over a one-year horizon for virtually all Italian non-financial firms with a fully automated procedure. The model shows robust and satisfactory properties that enable a high discrimination between healthy and risky firms with a fair stability of the results. The discriminatory power improves as the size of the company increases, thus ensuring a proper evaluation of the largest exposures in monetary policy operations. The architecture of the model is rather flexible, enabling us to work on possible developments to further improve the model's discriminatory power.

The remainder of the chapter is organized as follows. Section 2 outlines the Eurosystem framework within which the ICAS operates. Section 3 describes the architecture of the ICAS model. Section 4 reviews the main approaches used in the literature to estimate the probability of default of a firm. Section 5 provides details on the ICAS statistical model. Section 6 describes the validation process and Sect. 7 presents the main results on performance and a comparison with the previous version of the model (Giovannelli et al., 2023). Section 8 concludes.

2 The Eurosystem Credit Quality Standards for Collateral

The collateral framework is one of the key pillars that support the implementation of monetary policy. All Eurosystem liquidity providing operations require counterparties to provide adequate collateral. The concept of collateral adequacy has two dimensions. First, collateral has to protect the Eurosystem against losses in its credit operations, that might affect its financial independence and credibility. Second, there should be enough collateral potentially available, to enable the transmission of monetary policy and provide a level playing field for counterparties in each country in the area.

The eligibility requirements set by the Eurosystem are mainly aimed at mitigating financial, legal, and operational risks incurred in the conduct of monetary policy. The Eurosystem Credit Assessment Framework (ECAF)[1] defines the minimum credit quality requirements as well as the rules and procedures which ensure that the Eurosystem only accepts adequate collateral, as required by article 18.1 of the Protocol on the Statute of the European System of Central Banks and of the European Central Bank.

With a view to accepting a very broad range of marketable and non-marketable assets as collateral, the Eurosystem relies on three sources of credit assessment:

- credit rating agencies accepted as external credit assessment institutions (ECAIs): five of them are currently in the list (DBRS, Fitch, Moody's, Scope Ratings, and Standard & Poor's)[2];
- in-house credit assessment systems (ICASes) managed by NCBs: such systems are currently operated in Austria, France, Germany, Greece, Italy, Portugal, and Spain;
- internal rating-based (IRB) systems managed by banks: around 40 systems are currently authorized in the whole euro area.

ECAIs are mainly used for the assessment of marketable collateral, whereas ICASes and IRB systems are largely used for non-marketable assets. The ECAF maps each rating grade into a single harmonised rating scale to make the credit ratings comparable across systems and sources.

ECAF foresees that all accepted credit assessment systems are subject to due diligence and a yearly performance monitoring process. The monitoring process has two components: (1) quantitative statistical methods are employed to check

[1] For more information, see https://www.ecb.europa.eu/paym/coll/risk/ecaf/html/index.en.html.

[2] On 2 November 2023, the Governing Council decided to accept the credit rating agency Scope Ratings as a new ECAI for the purposes of the ECAF.

whether each system has accurately predicted default rates and the mapping of the ratings is appropriate; (2) a qualitative assessment is performed on credit assessment processes and methodologies.

The ICASes of the NCBs play a key role in ECAF as they allow any counterparty to pledge credit claims to non-financial firms as collateral. In particular, ICASes can be used by small and medium-sized banks that do not have an IRB system and are not in a position to easily fund themselves through structured finance operations, such as asset-backed securities or covered bonds. The development of ICASes has thus contributed to increasing collateral availability for a wide range of counterparties with different business models, thus paving the way for a smooth implementation of monetary policy. The use of credit claims as collateral in monetary policy operations enables counterparties to use liquid assets to guarantee market financing operations and comply with regulatory liquidity requirements (Grandia et al., 2019). Credit claims have a low opportunity cost as collateral, whereas marketable assets, such as sovereign bonds, are largely used as collateral in private repo transactions. ICASes provide an even greater contribution to the correct transmission of monetary policy in times of market tension, as they support the overall availability of collateral. This crucial role is confirmed by the measures adopted by the Eurosystem in April 2020, during the financial and economic crisis brought about by the pandemic, when the Governing Council decided to enlarge the scope of the so-called additional credit claim (ACC) framework, that allows NCBs to expand the eligibility rules for credit claims in their own jurisdiction. The effectiveness of these measures is shown by the significant increase in the use of ICAS assessment in several countries since 2020.

ICASes also offer other related benefits for the Eurosystem. First, they foster the direct transmission of monetary policy measures to the real economy, especially to small and medium-sized enterprises (SMEs) that do not issue marketable instruments. Second, supporting the pledge of credit claims contributes to diversifying risk in the Eurosystem balance sheet and reduces the reliance on external credit rating agencies. Besides, NCBs may use ICAS ratings for other purposes along with monetary policy operations, such as emergency liquidity assistance (ELA) operations, financial stability analysis, economic research, and supervisory tasks. Finally, the development of ICASes contributes to increasing the Eurosystem internal credit risk assessment capabilities as a complement to external ratings, thus reducing the reliance on ECAIs, as recommended by the Financial Stability Board (FSB, 2010).

3 The Architecture of the In-House Credit Assessment System

3.1 Aims and Governance

Since 2013 the Bank of Italy has developed its own internal model for assessing the creditworthiness of Italian non-financial firms (Giovannelli et al., 2023), for use in the context of the Eurosystem's collateral framework. The credit ratings and other information on non-financial firms managed by ICAS are also employed for other purposes, such as financial stability analysis, economic research, and occasionally for banking supervision purposes.

ICAS is managed by the Directorate Financial Risk Management (D-FRM). Within D-FRM, the Credit Risk Assessment Division (CRA) is in charge of model development, production of ratings and coordination tasks, while the Financial Risk Control Division (FRC) is responsible for the validation of the model, thus ensuring separation of tasks.[3] Nine ICAS Divisions in the Bank of Italy's network of local branches cooperate with D-FRM in the rating production process.

3.2 Rating Process

The rating process is based on a two-stage procedure, which combines the statistical model with the expert assessment by rating analysts to produce the final rating (Fig. 1).

The rating of a non-financial firm hinges on its estimated probability of default (PD) over a one-year horizon. In the first stage of the rating process the estimated PD is obtained from the statistical model; in the second stage the expert assessment is performed on the firm's credit worthiness. This process is similar to that in place for public ratings at the ECAIs.

The PD estimates are categorized into risk classes on the internal rating scale and the ratings are then mapped to the corresponding credit quality step (CQS) of the Eurosystem harmonized rating scale (Table 1).

Fig. 1 Rating process

[3] Antonio Scalia is the head of D-FRM, responsible for the whole ICAS process. Simone Narizzano and Marco Orlandi are members of the CRA Division and of the FRC Division, respectively.

Table 1 Rating scale (percentage values)

Risk class of ICAS	Minimum PD	Maximum PD	Eurosystem credit quality step
1	0	0.001	CQS 1 and 2
2 +	0.001	0.01	
2	0.01	0.03	
2-	0.03	0.05	
3 +	0.05	0.07	
3	0.07	0.09	
3-	0.09	0.1	
4 +	0.1	0.17	CQS 3
4	0.17	0.3	
4-	0.3	0.4	
5 +	0.4	0.8	CQS 4
5	0.8	1	
5-	1	1.5	CQS 5
6 +	1.5	2	CQS 6
6	2	3	
6-	3	5	CQS 7
7	5	25	CQS8
8	25	100	
9	100	100	Default

Every month the statistical model yields the PD over a one-year horizon for about 370,000 Italian firms. The statistical model procedure is fully automated.

The expert assessment is performed by two credit analysts. The first analyst can either confirm the rating obtained from the statistical model or revise the risk class up or down. The second analyst reviews all the previous steps and produces an independent assessment. The final assessment is upper-bounded: analysts can downgrade the rating without limitations, while they can raise the statistical rating by one notch only. If they intend to upgrade the statistical rating by more than one level, or if they disagree on the level, they are required to submit the proposal(s) to the ICAS rating committee for the final decision, which can involve a rating upgrade by up to three notches (Fig. 2). A detailed description of the expert assessment procedure is provided in Chap. 5.

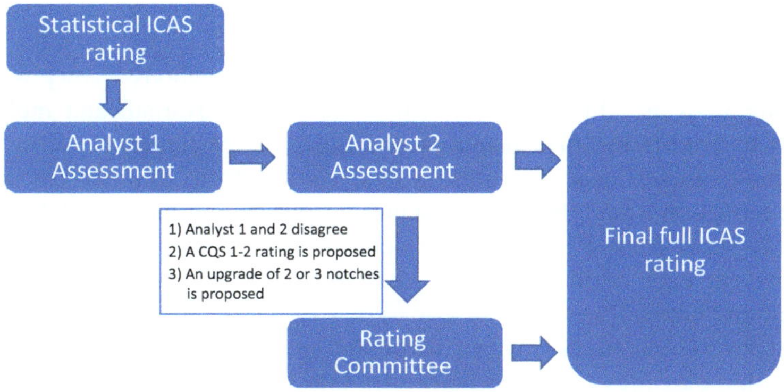

Fig. 2 Rating decision process

4 Credit Scoring: Statistical Models vs Machine Learning Models

Default forecasting is of key importance for financial institutions and investors. Banks use PDs to screen potential borrowers, evaluate the terms of new loans, and manage the risks stemming from lending activities. Investors also make extensive use of PDs and probabilities of migration across different credit rating classes for bond pricing and portfolio management. Macroprudential authorities have an interest in the surveillance of default risk as it is a major source of risk for lenders.

Since the Basel II Accord, credit scoring methods have become popular in the banking industry. They apply multivariate models to the firm characteristics, such as economic and financial ratios, to predict its credit quality. The output of these methods is a credit score, namely a continuous numerical indicator of creditworthiness, which can be translated into a probability of default. Credit scoring models can be divided into two categories: statistical models and machine learning (ML) models.

Statistical models are particularly fit for the purpose of inference, since they rely on assumptions regarding the structural relationship between variables, the number of parameters that can be robustly estimated, and the distribution properties of the data generating process. ML models are mostly aimed at prediction accuracy, and make very weak assumptions on the structure of the data generating process. This allows for the detection of data-driven interactions and non-linear or non-monotonic relationships between predictors and the outcome variable. A recent strand of the literature has shown that hybrid credit scoring models, which integrate ML techniques with traditional statistical methods, offer a promising approach to default prediction, balancing interpretability and discriminatory power. In the remainder of this Section we briefly describe these categories in turn.

4.1 Statistical Models

The literature about default prediction with statistical methods is very wide. The pioneering work is Altman (1968), which develops univariate and multivariate methods to predict the firm bankruptcy using a set of financial ratios. Altman uses a multivariate linear discriminant analysis (LDA) to estimate the so-called Z-score model on a sample of manufacturing firms during the period 1946–1965. The study starts from a list of 22 financial ratios and ends up selecting five of them, one for each of the following categories: liquidity, profitability, leverage, solvency, and activity.[4]

LDA provides an assessment of corporate credit quality using a discriminant function that classifies corporate borrowers into groups (default and non-default) based on their characteristics. Using sample observations, the set of parameters (β_i) is estimated for each independent variable (X_i): the discriminant score Z_i, obtained as the product of X_i and the β_i parameters, allows the mapping of firms into (non-continuous) default probability classes. This leads to the following equation:

$$Z_i = \sum_{i=1}^{n} \beta_i \times X_i \tag{1}$$

LDA has been extensively use by practitioners, with a fairly good performance in predicting bankruptcy and other types of distress of non-financial firms worldwide (Altman, 1968, 1983; Altman et al., 2017; Deakin, 1972; Micha, 1984). Over time LDA has also attracted criticism on some of its underlying assumptions, mainly based on the following arguments: failing firms and non-failing firms belong to two different populations; the choice of the normal distribution for the independent variables may not be appropriate; the covariance matrices for the two populations may differ. Besides, in LDA the standardized coefficients cannot be interpreted like the slopes of a regression equation and, consequently, the coefficients do not represent the relative weight of the variables. With these caveats in mind, researchers and practitioners have employed new methodologies to estimate the probability of default; in particular, Ohlson (1980) uses a conditional logit model to predict corporate default.

The logistic regression model (logit) provides estimates of the continuous probability of default from firms' observable characteristics using the two extreme values for the probability of default as the dependent variable: 0 for financially sound firms and 1 for defaulted firms. The model assumes that firms belong to the same population and that a known structural relationship (additive and linear) exists between the observable characteristics of the firm and the probability of

[4] The original Z-score model uses the following ratios: working capital/total assets, retained earnings/total assets, EBIT/total assets, market value equity/book value of total debt, and total debt and sales/total assets.

default, as in the following equation:

$$\ln\left(\frac{PD}{1-PD}\right) = \alpha + \sum_{i=1}^{n} \beta_i \times X_i + \varepsilon \quad (2)$$

where PD is the probability that a default event occurs e.g. within the next 12 months, and $\ln(PD/(1 - PD))$ is the log-odds ratio (or logit). The above expression can be solved for PD as follows:

$$PD = \frac{1}{1 + e^{\ (\alpha + \sum_{i=1}^{n} \beta_i \times X_i)}} \quad (3)$$

The parameters β_i of the model are usually estimated with the maximum likelihood procedure to find the smallest possible deviation between the observed variable and the predicted variable.[5]

The logit has two practical advantages: first, it relaxes the restrictive assumptions of LDA, such as multivariate normality and equal covariance matrices; second, it can work with unbalanced samples. From a statistical point of view, the logit regression fits well the characteristics of the default prediction problem, where the dependent variable is binary (failure/non-failure) and it has the important advantage of ease of calibration of its results, by delivering a score between zero and one, which corresponds to the probability of default of the borrower. Another advantage is the interpretation of the outcomes: the estimated coefficients show the economic significance of each of the independent variables in the explanation of the PD.

These features have attracted a strong interest for the logit model from the academic literature (Giannozzi et al., 2013; Gentry et al., 1985; Mossman et al., 1998) and have prompted its adoption among practitioners. Logit is particularly fit for use in banks' IRB models. They should be intuitive (CRR, art. 179),[6] and the logistic regression guarantees an interpretable and quantifiable link between risk drivers and the default indicator. The logit model is also employed by several National Central Banks in their ICAS models (Auria et al., 2021).

In spite of its large diffusion, the logit model still has some limitations. They include: (a) the lack of non-linear or complex interactions between observables and defaults; (b) the sensitivity to outliers or missing data; and (c) the difficulty to fully exploit large datasets owing to the intrinsic parsimony of the model.

---

[5] $\beta_{LOG} = \arg\min\left[\frac{1}{n} \times \sum_{i=1}^{n}\left(y_i\beta^T x_i + \ln\left(1 + e^{\beta^T x_i}\right)\right)\right]$.

[6] For more information, see https://www.eba.europa.eu/regulation-and-policy/single-rulebook/interactive-single-rulebook/100971.

4.2 Machine Learning Models

Machine learning involves teaching a computer routine to parse data, learn from them, and then make a prediction. The methodology 'learns' using large amounts of data and algorithms. The ML field has a long tradition, and recent improvements in data storage and computing power have made ML ubiquitous across many different fields and applications. Regarding credit scoring models, in recent years a growing strand of research indicates that the use of models based on ML algorithms for default prediction may provide a suitable alternative to statistical modelling. The ML approach to default prediction differs from the standard approach: (1) ML models are free from assumptions regarding their functional form, that is, they are non-parametric and allow for non-linear and non-monotonic modelling of the relationship between explanatory variables and outcomes; (2) ML algorithms are more computationally intensive, since they estimate multiple models and then select the best performing one using cross-validated accuracy measures. The discriminatory power of a model is typically assessed with the Area under the receiver operating characteristic (AUROC). AUROC is a measure of the ability of the model to assign higher PDs to firms that will default compared with financially sound firms. By construction, the AUROC statistic ranges from 0 ('the model is completely wrong') to 1 ('the model discriminates perfectly'), whereas 0.5 indicates a purely random model. In practice, a rating system with AUROC ≥ 0.7 is usually considered as adequate.[7]

ML algorithms can be grouped into two classes: supervised learning and unsupervised learning. In the first class, the algorithm learns from the associations between the category attributed to each outcome observation (for example default or non-default) and the observable characteristics for these observations. In turn the algorithm can predict the category an observation belongs to, given its characteristics (that is the algorithm performs a classification task). In the second class of algorithms, the observations are not grouped in different categories (i.e. an outcome variable is not provided) and the model puts forward a classification of the observations.

Several studies compare the performance of ML models and statistical models in corporate default prediction. Using a large dataset covering the North American corporate sector, Barboza et al. (2017) show that ML provides a significant improvement over the statistical model. Bachman and Zhao (2017) compare the performance of ML models with Moody's proprietary regression model in the US corporate sector; ML models achieve an AUROC statistic which turns out to be 2–3 percentage points larger than that of the regression approach. Fantazzini and Figini (2009) compare the performance of a specific ML model (the random forest model, or RDF) with that of the logit model for the probability of survival using SME data in Germany. The study finds a weak association between in-sample and

[7] For illustrative purposes, suppose that the sample of firms displays an ex post frequency of default equal to 2%. A model that assigns ex ante the largest (smallest) 2% PDs to the same firms that eventually defaulted has an AUROC equal to 1 (0). See Fawcett (2004) and Chawla (2009).

out-of-sample forecasting performance, revealing an overfitting problem that can be associated to ML. The logit model outperforms the RDF model in the out-of-sample forecast of default probability. Using a large dataset of Italian non-financial firms, Moscatelli et al. (2020) show that the use of ML techniques (RDF and gradient boosted trees, or GBT), can improve the performance of credit scoring models if the latter only rely on financial statement information. The value added of ML models declines when the scoring models also rely on credit behaviour indicators based on the NCR. This suggests that ML models, which are relatively opaque, may be used as a benchmark for the probability of default obtained using more transparent statistical models.

Most researchers conclude that ML models, on average, outperform traditional statistical models thanks to their ability to capture more precisely indicators with a non-linear or non-monotonic relationship with default. This feature of ML models is very important for credit risk applications, but it comes at the cost of lower transparency relative to statistical models. ML models do not provide estimates of the parameters that relate predictors to the outcome variable, that is the models are non-parametric. Such 'black box' feature can make their rationale and forecasts difficult to grasp. For this reason, European banks have been hesitant to apply ML techniques to their IRB models for credit risk (EBA, 2021).

4.3 Hybrid Models

A strand of the literature has explored hybrid credit scoring models that combine ML techniques with traditional statistical methods. Van Gestel et al. (2005) propose a model that combines the interpretability of the linear logistic regression with the flexibility and the ability to capture complex non-linearities of a support vector machine (SVM) model. Their results show that the hybrid model outperforms a simple statistical model. Dumitrescu et al. (2022) put forward a penalised logistic tree regression (PLTR) which tries to improve the predictive performance of the logistic regression through data pre-processing and short-depth decision trees. The hybrid model performs better than traditional statistical models while being comparable to machine learning methods.

5 The Statistical Model

5.1 Overview

In the development of the statistical model, we have tried to solve the trade-off between predictive power and transparency by combining features of traditional models and ML models. In particular, we preserve the simplicity and transparency of the logit model, and, at the same time, we try to improve its predictive performance using ML techniques that allow for the inclusion of non-linear or non-monotonic relationships of the model variables with the default event.

A common type of non-linearity may arise from the existence of one or more univariate threshold effects on a single predictive variable (Dumitrescu et al., 2022). ML decision tree methods (such as random forest) are powerful at detecting univariate threshold effects by exploiting the non-linear relationship with default, but these methods lack interpretation. This opaqueness hinders credit scoring, especially when the final credit rating involves also expert analysis. Consequently, there is a trade-off between predictive performance and transparency. To solve this issue, one could seek an explanation for the decision-making process of machine learning techniques (Cascarino et al., 2022). Alternatively, one could preserve the simplicity of traditional models while improving their performance with the introduction in the model of variables with non-linear effects or univariate threshold effects (Dumitrescu et al., 2022; Van Gestel et al., 2005). Moscatelli et al. (2020) show that the value added of ML models declines when scoring models also rely on credit behaviour indicators, as in our case. To enhance the comprehension of the statistical model by credit analysts, we decided to follow the second approach, leaving the first one for future research. Therefore, we try to improve the discriminatory power of the logit model by employing, for certain variables, a discretized transformation obtained with the use of several decision trees (Sect. 2).

The model draws from a pre-existing model, in operation from 2013 to 2022 (see Giovannelli et al., 2023). For the estimation of the new model, we started by checking whether each variable in the previous model still significantly contributes to default prediction. We also tried completely new variables. The development of the new version of the statistical model pursues the following objectives:

- improving the discriminatory power compared to the previous model;
- increasing the stability and consistency across different phases of the economic cycle;
- enhancing the transparency and including financial ratios that are widely recognized as explanatory of company creditworthiness based on experience and the recent empirical literature.

The model tries to achieve the above objectives with the introduction of some new features compared to the previous model. First, to increase stability and consistency, the observation period for the development of the model has been extended. The estimation sample considers six years of default history (from 2014 to 2019): four years are used as the training sample (from 2015 to 2018) and two years form the test sample (2014 and 2019).[8] By doing so, we use for both estimation and testing a suitable mix of 'good' and 'bad' years, which are representative of the likely range of variability of one-year default rates. The default data for 2020 are excluded from the estimation analysis owing to the extraordinary nature of

[8] The previous version of the statistical model was developed using a two-years' time period (Giovannelli et al., 2023).

that year, with the spreading of the Covid-19 pandemic and the ensuing government support measures. Nevertheless, we assess the model performance in terms of discriminatory power and back testing also for 2020 (see Sect. 7).

Second, separate models for different sectors usually improve predictive performance, as they allow for the selection of the most appropriate sector-specific financial ratios (Hajek, 2012; Lee & Choi, 2013). We find supporting evidence for this hypothesis and apply it to the following macro-sectors that were also employed in the pre-existing model: manufacturing, trade, construction, services, real estate, and holdings. To further improve predictive performance, we apply a new distinction for the type of financial statement (ordinary financial statement or simplified financial statement).[9] Usually, simplified financial statements do not provide the breakdown of debt between financial and other liabilities and, consequently, the use of financial ratios including financial debt is precluded without making arbitrary assumptions. The distinction enables us to exploit some ratios that are widely employed in the literature and in expert analysis (such as the ratio between equity and net financial debt). As a result, the number of financial statement sub-models increases from six to eleven (for the holdings we developed only one model due to the small number of firms in this sector).

Third, the firm-bank relationship and credit availability differ significantly across firm size (Angori et al., 2020; Kosekova et al., 2023). Our analysis confirms the important role of size in the credit behaviour of non-financial firms. We thus estimate separate credit behaviour models according to company size.[10]

Fourth, we use a discretized transformation for certain variables in order to catch non-linear relationships with default (Sect. 4) and we introduce new risk areas, such as business development in the financial statement sub-models and quality of credit receivables in the credit behaviour sub-models.

Finally, the updated statistical model consists of a system of logit models with two independent components providing separate credit scores:

- a financial component, employing a logit regression on yearly financial statement data, such as the debt sustainability ratio, financial structure, and liquidity ratios. This component consists of eleven sub-models, that account for different sectors and types of financial statement;
- a credit behaviour component, employing a logit regression on data from the NCR, which hinges on the credit record of each company. Three sub-models

[9] The simplified accounts may only be employed by joint stock companies that, for two consecutive financial years, have not exceeded any two of the following limits (micro and small enterprises): (1) total assets = EUR 4.4 million; (2) total revenues = EUR 8.8 million; (3) average number of employees during the year = 50 persons.

[10] In the previous model, the size of a firm was approximated by the financial exposure towards the banking system. In a limited number of cases this classification could generate a distortion. In particular, if a large firm had a low financial exposure reported in the NCR it was classified as a small company.

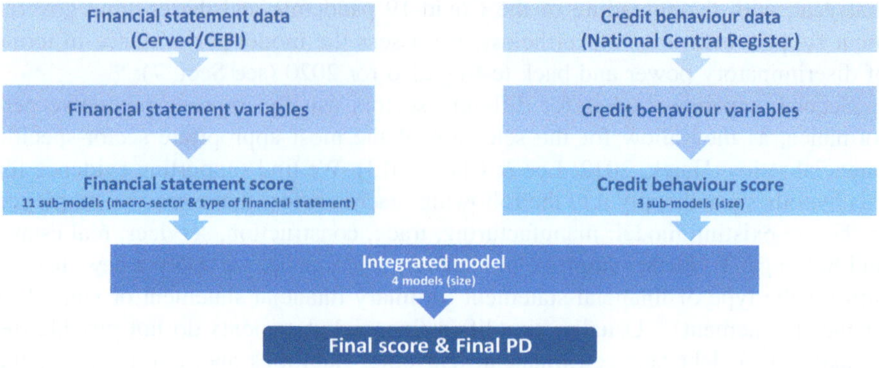

Fig. 3 Statistical model architecture

are set up for different firms considering their size (micro, small, and medium-large) based on the European Commission definition (Recommendation 2003/361/EC).[11]

In line with banking industry practice, the two components are estimated separately and then merged into the final model through a further logistic regression that yields the final score. This is transformed into a PD via the inverse logit function:

$$PD = \frac{1}{1 + e^{-(\text{final score})}} \tag{4}$$

This approach is used to aggregate different information in the rating system. Under a hypothetical single model, the potentially high correlation between accounting variables and credit relationship variables could generate biased results, with a cost in terms of predictive power. Besides, the different timing of data (monthly data for NCR and annual data for the financial statement) and time lag of the data sources (up to 12 months for financial statements, 2 months for NCR) could generate distortion in the PD estimates (Giannozzi et al., 2013).

The final stage of the model, namely the integration of the two components, is carried out with four models by size (micro, small, medium, and large firms). This distinction allows the relative importance of financial information and credit behaviour information to change with firm size (Fig. 3).

The estimation of separate sub-models, a common practice in the banking industry, enables us to select the most appropriate variables considering the characteristics of different firms (Fig. 4). Sector-specific financial statement sub-models improve the discriminatory power (Hajek, 2012; Lee & Choi, 2013), while the breakdown according to the type of financial statement improves the usability of

[11] For more information, see https://ec.europa.eu/growth/smes/sme-definition_en.

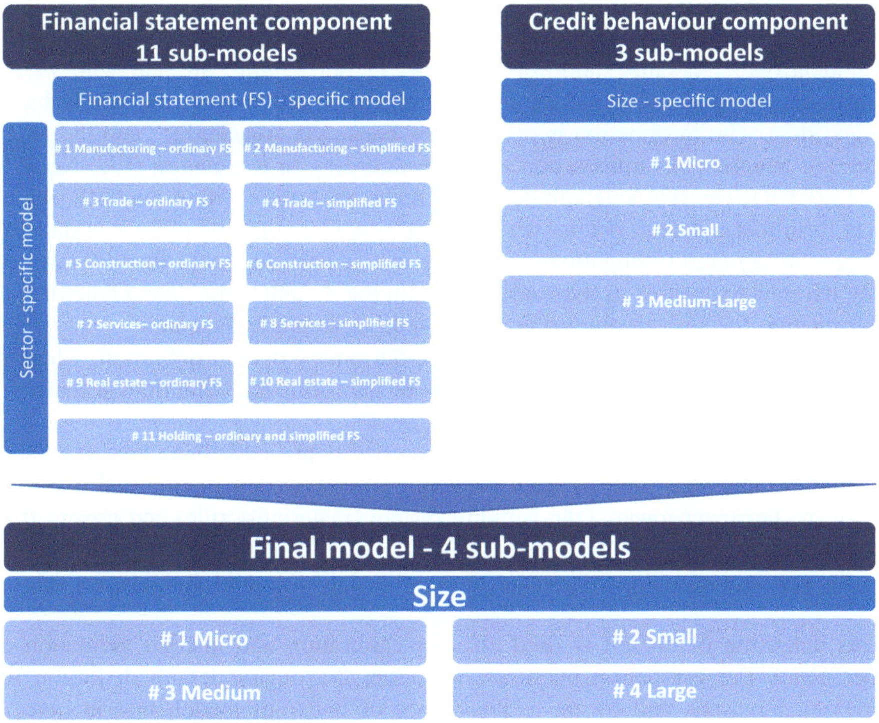

Fig. 4 Statistical model overview

the model by the credit analysts.[12] For the credit behaviour component, the estimation of size specific models reflects the importance of company size in the credit relationship with the banking system.[13] For each sub-model we perform a variable selection process (described in Appendix A).

[12] The expert assessment starts with an analysis of the consistency and validity of the data for the statistical model. Next, the assessment involves possible adjustments to the data (e.g. finance leasing is not included in financial debt according to Italian GAAP financial statements).

[13] In the credit behaviour component, we consider medium and large firms together to increase the statistical significance of some ratios, owing to the low number of defaults among large firms. In the final stage of the model, though, we separate large and medium firms because the relative importance of financial information and credit behaviour information changes widely according to firm size (see Sect. 3).

5.2 Default Definition

To identify the default status of the firms in our sample, in line with ECAF standards, we perform a merger of reporting information from the whole banking system. The information is provided by banks via AnaCredit[14] and the NCR, through which banks must report defaults according to Regulation (EU) No 575/2013 (CRR). The ICAS default definition relies on Article 178 of the CRR, which sets forth that a default occurs when a bank considers that the obligor is unlikely to pay (UTP) credit obligations, or the obligor is past due more than 90 days on any material exposures to the bank. To obtain the default status, the whole default information for a given obligor is aggregated into a single indicator.

For the estimation of the model we use the binary default definition, whereby a borrower is considered in default if both of the following conditions are met:

- the total amount of exposure reported as bad debt, unlikely to pay, and more than 90 days past due by each bank is greater than 5% of the total exposure of the borrower towards the banking system (materiality rule) and greater than 500€;
- the previous condition is met for three consecutive months (persistency rule).

This definition of default is used also for calibration and internal validation of the model. For estimation purposes, we adopt the binary default definition for prudential reasons and owing to the choice of the logit model, that involves a binary independent variable.

As of January 2020, the new harmonised definition of 'fractional default' has been introduced for evaluating the performance of ICAS models in the yearly ECAF monitoring process. The new default definition aggregates the whole default information into a single default indicator. Two thresholds are applied:

- a materiality threshold of 2.5% of the defaulted amount over the total exposure of the debtor;
- persistence for three consecutive months.

Over a given monitoring period, fractional default is equal to the maximum proportion in default which fulfils the two above conditions. In the case of bankruptcy, insolvency, judicial administration, or similar measures (legal default) the materiality is considered equal to 100% and no persistency is required. This definition is used for internal and external validation.

[14] Analytical Credit (AnaCredit) is a dataset containing detailed information on individual bank loans in the euro area, harmonized across all Member States. The AnaCredit dataset project was launched in 2011 and data collection started in September 2018. On 18 May 2016 the ECB adopted Regulation (EU) 2016/867 on the collection of granular credit and credit risk data (known as 'AnaCredit Regulation'), following the principles approved by the Governing Council in 2015.

5.3 Data

The model relies on two types of information: (1) financial statement data, and (2) credit behaviour data.

For financial statement data, we employ the Bank of Italy's financial statement archive which stores data collected by Cerved Group. Such data are available in two datasets: *Centrale dei Bilanci* (Cebi) and Cerved. The Cebi dataset contains around 80,000 financial statements per year covering nearly all the medium-sized and large firms and about half of the small ones. These data are collected partly through banks participating in the Cebi program and for the rest through the National Official Business Register (NOBR). Cerved manages a more comprehensive dataset of the Italian corporate sector that includes nearly all the small and micro limited-liability firms. Data are provided by NOBR. Financial statement data are available according to the Cebi reclassification accounting scheme, which can be applied to both the national GAAP and IFRS financial statements.

The NCR is a database with granular information on households' and firms' debt towards the banking and financial system. On a monthly basis, banks and other financial intermediaries are legally required to send to the central register a wide set of information about the financial liabilities and payment behaviour of individual firms and households. In return, banks have access to information on the debt exposure of their borrowers towards the whole banking system. The NCR collects information about all credit relationships with a minimum size of 30,000€. We use the NCR data for the default definition and the estimation of the credit behaviour model.

For data collection we use a cross-sectional approach: default data and independent variables refer to different time periods (Fig. 5). For each year T, we start by selecting limited-liability firms reported to the NCR at the end of the year and that are not in default. Then, we collect data according to the respective reference date, that is the most recent date prior to the reference date. The credit behaviour data have a two-months lag (31 October of year T), and the financial statement data are those for year T−1. The default monitoring period spans the following 12 months (from 1 January to 31 December of year T + 1).

For the development of the model, we used an extensive dataset of financial and credit behaviour indicators for Italian non-financial firms for the years 2014–19.

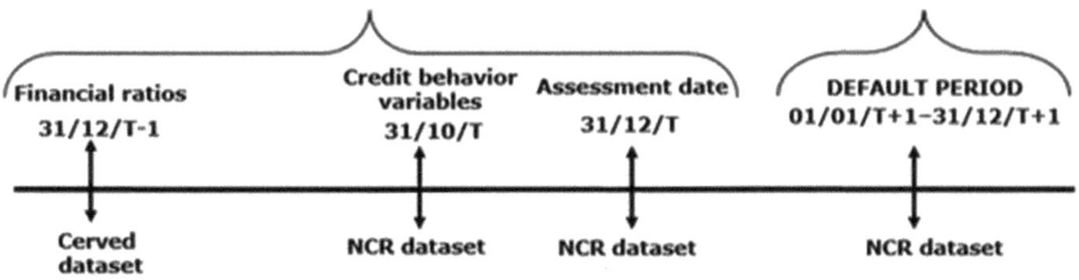

Fig. 5 Data timeline

Table 2 Historical default rate

Period	Year	Firms (#)	Binary default rate (%)	Fractional default rate (%)
Out-of-sample	2014	255,189	7.01	5.35
In-sample	2015	232,937	6.23	4.65
In-sample	2016	257,590	4.64	3.61
In-sample	2017	257,328	3.61	2.81
In-sample	2018	257,461	3.34	2.6
Out-of-sample	2019	267,341	2.96	2.36

Note Own calculation on NCR data

Our dependent variable, binary default (Sect. 2), reflects a system-wide definition of the non-performing status of a borrower. The historical default rate gives an aggregate measure of credit risk, which we model at firm level (Table 2). Credit risk peaked in 2014, in the aftermath of the European sovereign debt crisis and of the ensuing slowdown of the Italian economy. Following the monetary measures undertaken by the European Central Bank, the gradual improvement in the business cycle, and the exit of vulnerable firms from the market, aggregate default risk constantly declined, to below 3% in 2019.

As stated earlier, the use of the binary default definition introduces a suitable degree of conservatism in the model estimation compared to the use of the fractional default definition (Table 2). In the remainder of this Section, we will only refer to the binary default definition.

The estimation sample covers the years 2015–2018, while the test sample consists of the years 2014 and 2019. The latter are chosen to evaluate the performance of the model in a year with a higher default rate (2014) compared to the estimation sample and a year with a lower default rate (2019). The choice of four years as estimation sample and the large number of firms ensure a robust estimation, using a suitable mix of 'good' and 'bad' years.

Structural differences in default risk levels are usually associated with firm size and sector; consistently, credit risk models in the first place relate the firm PD to these factors (Altman et al., 2017; Dwyer and Wang, 2011). Medium and large firms record lower default rates compared with micro and small firms and these differences become wider in periods of economic distress (Fig. 6). In 2014 and 2015 the differences in default risk by size class are at their peak, and then gradually decline with the improvement of the economic cycle.

The lower riskiness of larger firms can be explained by their larger market shares and better profitability (measured e.g. by return on assets), leverage (measured by the ratio between equity and total debt), and debt sustainability (measured by interest expenses over EBITDA or sales; Table 3).

The economic sector is another important dimension of firm credit risk, with more cyclical sectors (usually investment goods and construction) leading to more volatile revenues and greater fragility. Indeed, construction presents a significantly higher default rate than other sectors, such as manufacturing and services (Fig. 7).

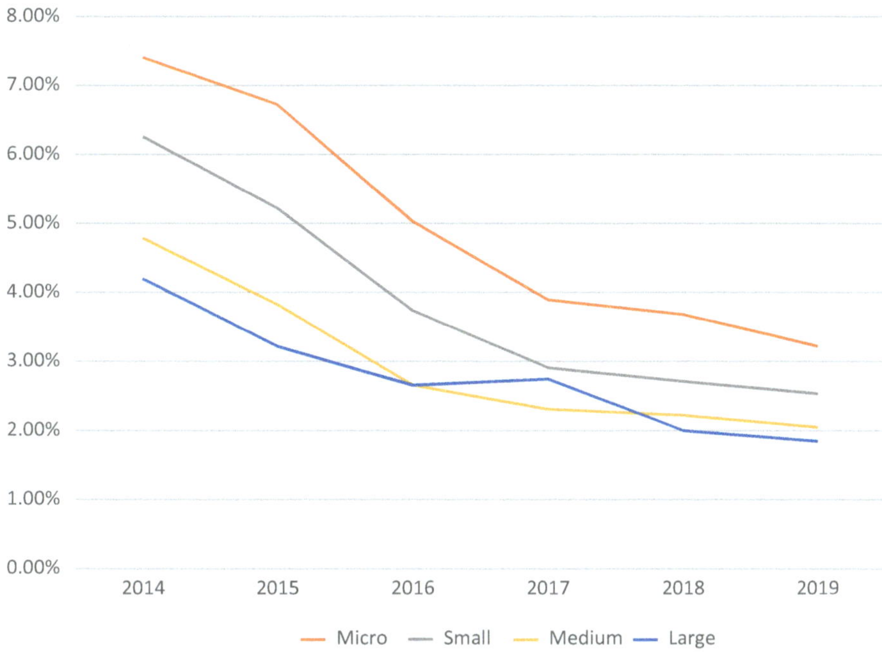

Fig. 6 Default rate by size. *Source* Own calculation on NCR and Cerved data. Binary default definition. Firm size classes are defined according to the European Commission definition

Table 3 Key firm indicators by size (2014–2019, median value)

Size	Firms (#)	Total Assets (EUR mln)	Net Sales (EUR mln)	ROA (%)	Equity / Total debt (%)	Interest Expenses / EBITDA (%)	Interest Expenses / Sales (%)
Micro	1,100,481	0.8	0.5	3.2	18.8	19.3	2.3
Small	317,288	3.6	3.8	3.6	26.9	15	1
Medium	88,164	15.9	17	3.6	39.1	11.2	0.7
Large	21,913	87.8	89.5	3.5	44.4	9.4	0.7

Note Own calculation on Cerved data. Firm size classes are defined according to the European Commission definition

The latter sectors usually present more diversified businesses with greater exposure to foreign markets.

Construction firms show on average a lower profitability and capitalization, and a worse debt servicing capacity (Table 4).

Within the same macro-sector, firms subject to different accounting standards (ordinary financial statement or simplified financial statement) show significant differences in terms of total assets and net sales (Table 5).

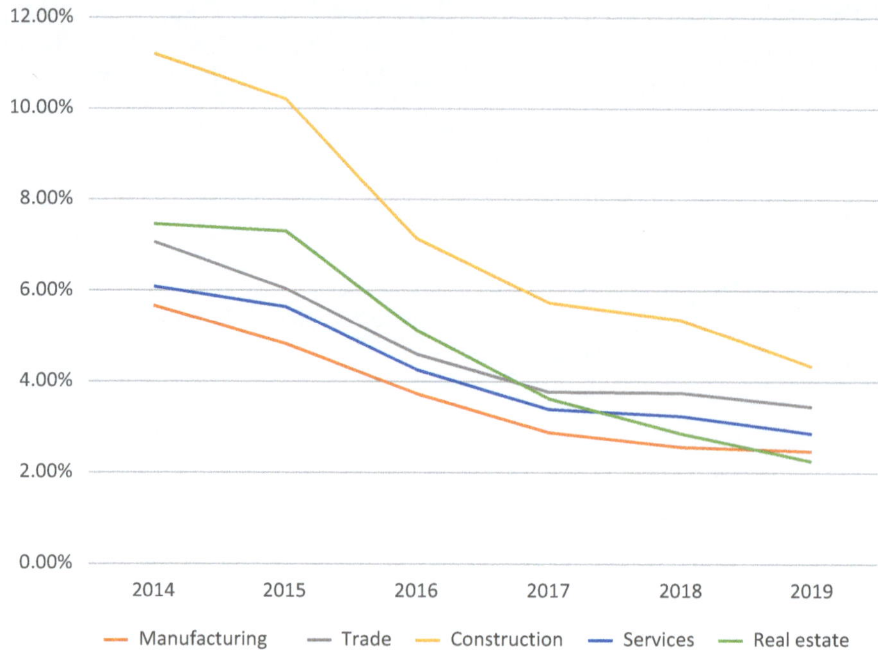

Fig. 7 Default rate by macro-sectors. *Source* Own calculation on NCR and Cerved data. Binary default definition. Firm economic sector affiliation is based on Cerved data

Table 4 Key firm indicators by macro-sectors (2014–2019, median value)

Sector	Firms (#)	Total assets (EUR mln)	Net sales (EUR mln)	ROA (%)	Equity / Total debt (%)	Interest expenses / EBITDA (%)	Interest expenses / Sales (%)
Manufacturing	437,728	1.7	1.4	3.9	26.4	15.7	1.4
Trade	326,731	1.2	1.5	3.5	18.8	20.8	1.1
Construction	169,683	1.5	0.8	3.1	17.6	24	2.4
Services	397,260	0.8	0.7	3.7	19.7	14.7	1.6
Real Estate	183,765	1.6	0.1	1.7	30.7	20	11.2

Note Own calculation on Cerved data. Firm economic sector affiliation is based on Cerved data

5.4 Variables

As shown in Sect. 1, the statistical model has a financial statement component and a credit behaviour component, each with a suitable sub-model distinction. The distinction in the first component allows for the selection of financial ratios based on the sectoral specific characteristics and the information on financial liabilities, available only in the ordinary financial statement. The model distinction implicitly

Table 5 Firm distribution by macro-sectors and financial statement type (2014–2019, median value)

Sector	Financial statement type	Firms (#)	Total assets (EUR mln)	Net sales (EUR mln)	ROA (%)	Equity / Total debt (%)	Interest expenses / EBITDA (%)	Interest expenses / Sales (%)
Manufacturing	ordinary	231,636	3	3	3.9	31.7	13.9	1.2
	simplified	206,092	1	0.9	3.8	21.2	17.9	1.8
Trade	ordinary	177,208	1.9	2.9	3.6	20.6	19.7	0.9
	simplified	149,523	0.8	0.9	3.4	16.7	22.4	1.4
Construction	ordinary	77,929	2.1	1.2	3.2	20.7	22.1	2
	simplified	91,754	1.1	0.6	3	15.3	25.9	2.9
Services	ordinary	153,300	1.4	1.4	3.7	21.9	13.2	1.2
	simplified	243,960	0.6	0.5	3.7	18.3	15.7	1.9
Real Estate	ordinary	41,971	2.6	0.2	1.4	31.4	19.3	11.7
	simplified	141,794	1.4	0.1	1.7	30.5	20.4	9.8

Note Our calculation on Cerved data. Firm economic sector affiliation is based on Cerved data

considers the firm size, as firms with an ordinary financial statement are larger than those with simplified reporting (Table 5).

The credit behaviour model distinction captures the structural differences in the use of credit lines and the relationship with the financial sector by firms of different size. For each sub-model, the best discriminatory function is selected by means of the methodology described in Appendix A. The two components are merged via a logistic regression according to firm size. The remainder of this subsection reviews the rationale for the selection of variables for each component and provides summary statistics.

Financial Statement Variables

The empirical literature employs a large variety of accounting ratios to predict firm default. Chen and Shimerda (1981) note that nearly 50 different financial ratios are significant in at least one empirical study. They group the ratios in several risk areas and note that the inclusion of correlated variables as regressors distorts the relationship between variables and default.

Consistently with previous research, and in line with financial industry practice, we start by defining a long list of over 90 variables (considering all the 11 sub-models) grouped in the following risk areas:

profitability—profitability has a negative relationship with the PD (Altman, 1968; Altman et al., 1977; Campbell et al., 2008; Ohlson, 1980). We test over 20 variables including net profit and loss, EBITDA, EBIT, net sales, and cash flow at the numerator and total assets, tangible assets, and net sales at the denominator;

capitalization and financial structure—high leverage increases the riskiness of a company. (e.g. Bonaccorsi et al., 2015). We try several variables including the ratios between equity or tangible equity, and total debt, net debt, total financial debt, or net financial debt (the latter variables apply only to the sub-models for firms with ordinary financial statements);

debt sustainability—poor debt sustainability reduces the credit worthiness of a company. In this risk category we try over 30 indicators including the ratios that measure the firm's ability to generate net sales, EBITDA, EBIT, or cash flow to cover interest payments or some other measure at the denominator, such as total debt or financial debt. De Socio and Michelangeli (2017) measure firm vulnerability using the ratio between interest expenses and EBITDA. Other studies (Beaver, 1966; Blum, 1974) investigate the discriminant power of the ratio between EBITDA or cash flow and financial debt, showing a positive relationship with credit soundness. In addition, for ordinary financial statements, we include also interest rate risk exposure such as return on debt (ROD), measured as the ratio between interest expenses and average financial debt. Based on Modigliani and Miller (1958), we expect a direct relationship between ROD and PD;

liquidity—high liquidity reduces the PD. Altman and Sabato (2007) find that the PD in the US economy is negatively related to the ratio of cash over total assets. This risk area measures the extent to which a company has liquid assets relative to the size of its current or total liabilities. We consider over 10 variables including cash and marketable assets over total debt or financial debt, and traditional variables such as the current ratio (Altman et al., 1977; Beaver, 1966), quick ratio (Giannozzi et al., 2013), and other ratios between assets and liabilities such as financial mismatch;

activity and efficiency—the firm's operating efficiency has an impact on the PD. Following several studies (Alberici, 1975; Luerti, 1992; Piatti et al., 2015), we test the discriminatory power of several cash conversion cycle variables, such as days receivables outstanding, days inventory outstanding and days payables outstanding;

business development—the variables in this group capture the stability and trend of firm performance. We consider sales growth, total asset growth, change in value added, and equity;

size and age—large firms default less often (Fig. 6). Charalambakis and Garret (2019) find that size is negatively correlated with the probability of default of Greek private firms. Other authors find that the logarithm of age is negatively correlated with the PD (Altman et al., 2010; Antunes et al., 2016). We measure size using the natural logarithm of total assets or net sales; we measure age by its natural logarithm.

Following the procedure described in Appendix A, for each financial statement sub-model we define the final combination of variables and the relative weights

(Table 8 and 9). Table 6 provides summary statistics for default and non-default firms for the variables selected for at least one of the eleven financial statement sub-models.

Table 6 Financial statement variables (2014–2019)

Risk area	Variable	Mean (non-default)	Mean (default)	Median (non-default)	Median (default)
Profitability	Cash flow / Net sales (%)	8.1	1.3	5.1	2.5
	Cash flow / Total assets (%)	5.2	1.8	4.3	1.6
	Value Added / Total assets (%)	25.9	17.5	20.3	12.1
Capitalization and financial structure	Equity / Financial net debt (%)	245.7	98.6	79.3	29.4
	Equity / Total net debt (%)	61.9	27.4	24.6	9.9
Debt sustainability	Interest expenses / EBITDA (%)	36.5	63.4	20.3	56.6
	Interest expenses / Cash flow (%)	84.4	166.6	31.3	136.4
	Interest expenses / Net sales (%)	5.5	10.1	1.6	3.7
	ROD (%)	5.8	7.1	4.0	5.4
	Net sales / Total net debt	1.9	1.1	1.4	0.8
Liquidity	Current ratio = (current assets / current liabilities) (%)	1.6	1.5	1.2	1.1
	Financial mismatch = [(current liabilities—current assets) / total assets] (%)	−0.1	−0.1	−0.1	−0.0
	Cash / Total short-term debt (%)	17.2	6.9	4.9	1.7
Activity and efficiency	Days receivables and inventory outstanding	339	612	82	153
	Days receivables outstanding	84	112	54	63
	Days payables outstanding	520	654	140	194
Business development	Sales growth (%)	5.5	1.9	0.0	0.0
Age	Log(age)	2. 6	2.4	2.6	2.4

Note our calculation on Cerved data. The mean and median are computed after winsorization and transformation (see Appendix A)

As expected, profitability measures, such as cash flow over sales, cash flow over total assets, and value added over total assets, are associated with credit worthiness; low or negative values for these ratios can be a signal of future financial problems. Firm capitalization has a negative relationship with default rate and probability of default. For firms with ordinary financial statements, we employ the ratio between equity and net financial debt (financial debt—cash), commonly used by analysts to assess the level of capitalization of a company; for firms with the simplified financial statement, we employ the ratio between equity and net total debt (total debt—cash).

As concerns debt sustainability, interest expenses over EBITDA (or cash flow), and interest expenses over net sales show a positive relationship with default and a high discriminatory power. The numerator of these variables captures the effect of credit conditions, as it includes the impact of the level of debt and its cost, while the denominator reflects operating profitability and business activity, respectively. Within the same risk area, we also consider: the debt coverage ratio, measured by net sales over net debt, which shows a negative relationship with default; and ROD, which measures the cost of debt, and is available only for firms with an ordinary financial statement.

The ratio of cash over total short-term debt and that of current assets over current liabilities increase the possibility to meet the firm's financial obligations on time; empirically, both variables show a negative relationship with default.

The age of firms displays a negative impact on PD, indicating a greater soundness of firms which stand in the market for longer.

The variables generally display a linear relationship with the default rate (Table 6). The linear relationship of the variables with default allows for their direct use as input to logit (Fig. 8).

Nonlinearity

Some variables of interest from the financial statement exhibit a non-linear relationship with default risk in our sample. This is the case e.g. of sales growth (Fig. 9a). Other variables belonging to the 'activity and efficiency' risk area show a relationship with default rate that is non-monotonic for a large portion of the distribution. Nevertheless, we note that riskiness increases with a linear trend after reaching a certain threshold (Fig. 9b, 9c and 9d).

These non-linear variables cannot be accommodated in the standard logistic regression of default. Nevertheless, to fully exploit the financial statement information, we apply decision tree techniques to these variables and create new discretized variables as candidate indicators for the logit. Decision trees are partition algorithms that recursively split the dataset into smaller subgroups (or branches) that best separate defaulters from non-defaulters. At each iteration, the decision tree algorithm chooses a value for the classification variable, so as to minimize a measure of heterogeneity (impurity index) in the resulting branches with

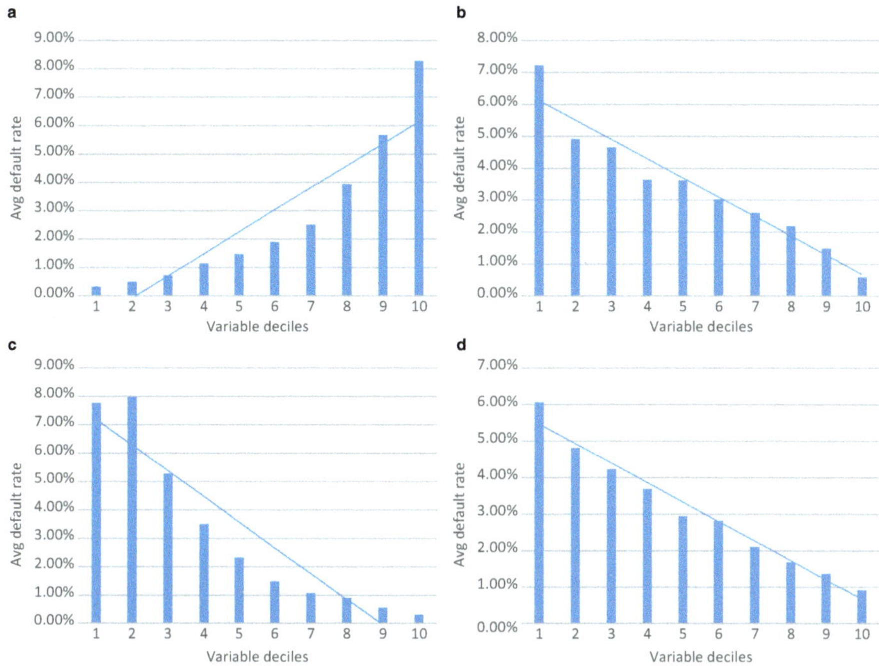

Fig. 8 Default rate by deciles—linear relationship variables. **(a)** Interest expenses / EBITDA; **(b)** Equity / net financial debt; **(c)** Net sales / total net debt; **(d)** Current ratio. 2014–2019, manufacturing, ordinary financial statement

respect to the classification variable.[15] The process continues within each branch until a stopping condition is reached, such as a small number of observations in the branch or no significant reduction in impurity (Fig. 10).

As concerns sales growth, empirically both a large growth and a large decline lead to an increase in default rate. From a judgemental point of view, it is easier for a credit analyst to understand a negative effect on PD of a decline in sales rather than of their growth; hence we apply the decision tree to identify thresholds related only to negative sales growth.[16] As shown in Fig. 10, we apply a simple classification tree containing only the sales growth variable as the splitting parameter (X_1). The first level of the tree splits the whole sample into two middle branches depending on the value of sales growth. Firms with sales growth higher than −0.1

[15] We use the Gini coefficient as a measure of impurity. Given a set of observations O with a binary value for each observation $y_i \in \{0, 1\}$, the Gini impurity coefficient is defined as $GI(O) = 2 \cdot \sum_i p_i(1 - p_i)$, where p_i is the percentage of observations in O such that $y_i = 1$. The Gini impurity ranges between 0 ($p_i = 0$ or $p_i = 1$) and 0.5 ($p_i = 0.5$).

[16] All firms with positive net sales growth were considered as firms with a constant level of turnover (the variable sales growth was set equal to zero).

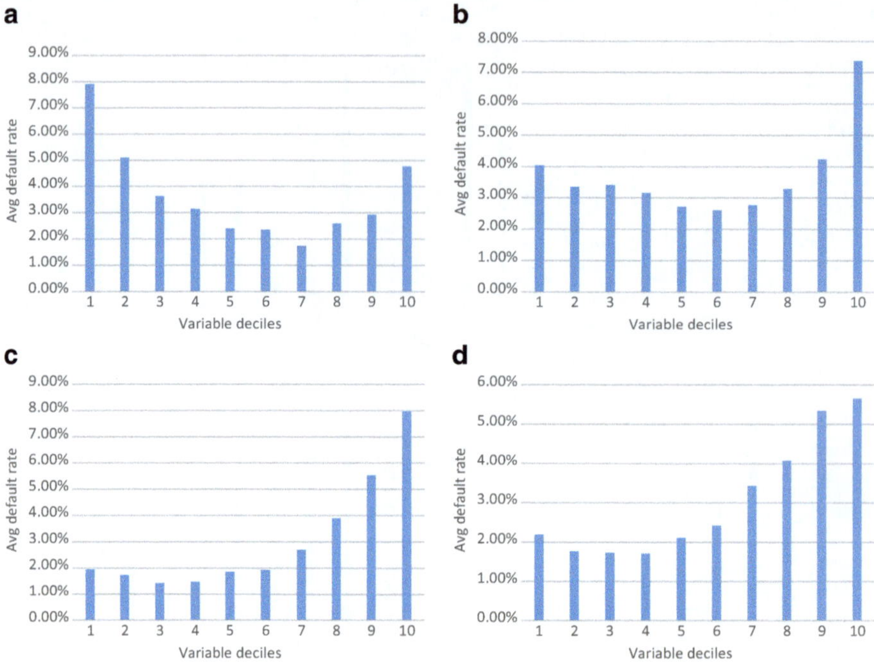

Fig. 9 Default rate by deciles—non-linear relationship. **(a)** Sales growth; **(b)** Days receivables outstanding. 2014–2019, services, ordinary financial statement. **(c)** Days receivables and inventory outstanding; **(d)** Day payables outstanding. 2014–2019, manufacturing, ordinary financial statement

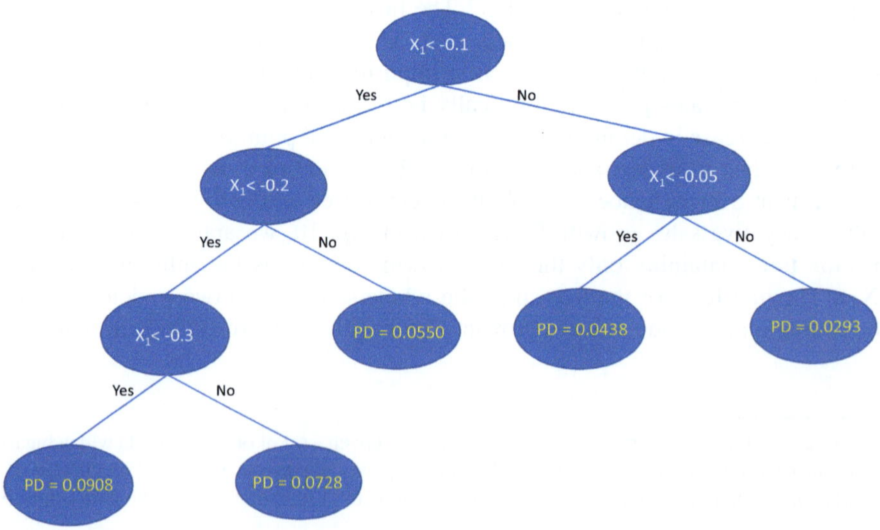

Fig. 10 Sales growth, decision tree techniques

are further divided according to their sales growth value. Firms with negative sales growth up to −0.05 end up in a leaf with a PD equal to 0.0293, while firms with negative sales growth between −0.05 and −0.1 have a PD equal to 0.0438. On the other branch, firms with sales growth worse than −0.1 are divided between firms with negative growth up to −0.2 that end up in a leaf with a PD equal to 0.055, while firms with sales growth lower than −0.2 undergo a further split distinguishing those with sales growth lower than −0.3 (PD equal to 0.0903) and those with sales growth between −0.2 and −0.3, that end up in a leaf with a PD equal to 0.0728.

At the end of the procedure, the new discretized variable has a linear relationship with default, thus fitting the logistic regression model (Fig. 11).

On the liability side, days payables outstanding (DPO) measure how long it takes on average for a company to pay its suppliers. A large DPO may be preferable for working capital management, as it may suggest favourable credit terms with suppliers. Nevertheless, after breaching a certain threshold, a large value of DPO is an indication of the company struggling to meet its obligations on time, thus revealing an increase in default risk. Consequently, the decision tree suggests considering only the extreme part of the distribution. The resulting four discretized classes show a linear and positive relationship with default rate (Fig. 12).

On the asset side, days receivables outstanding (DRO) is a measure of the average number of days for a company to collect payment from customers. A large number of days indicates an inadequate operating efficiency and/or customers who are not financially creditworthy. Late payment or the default of customers can have negative effects, such as cash flow shortages and economic losses. Days inventory outstanding (DIO) is the average number of days for the inventory to be sold. A high level of inventories could signal difficulties for a company in selling its products, with the risk of writing off a portion of the inventories. We use two discretized variables created from DRO and the sum between DRO and DIO, respectively. For

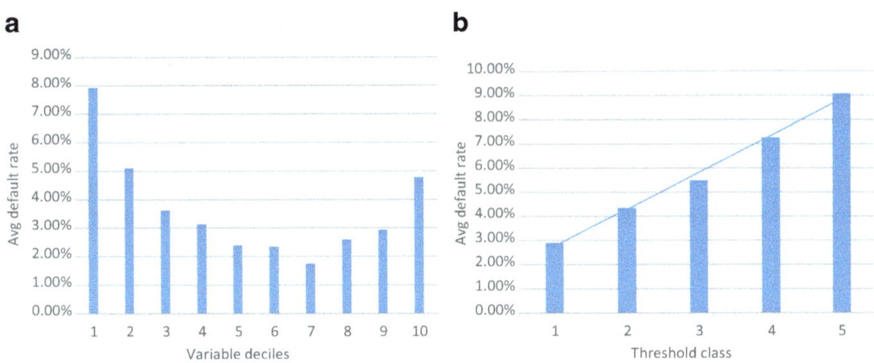

Fig. 11 Sales growth. 2014–2019, services, ordinary financial statement. **(a)** Default rate by decile; **(b)** Default rate by discretized class

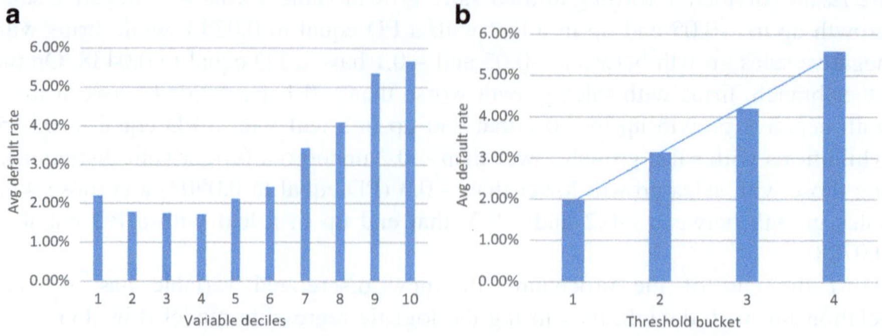

Fig. 12 Days payable outstanding. 2014–2019, manufacturing, ordinary financial statement. **(a)** Default rate by decile; **(b)** Default rate by discretized class

the first ratio, the procedure identifies three classes with a positive relationship with default. For the second ratio, the discretized risk classes are four (Fig. 13).

Credit Behaviour Variables

The NCR dataset is extremely granular, as it contains information about different credit lines held by each firm, distinguishing three classes of loans: term loans, current account revolving credit lines, and account receivables revolving credit lines. For each credit line, the dataset records drawn and undrawn amount, excess and unauthorized overdrafts, and default classification.

Several studies examine the role of credit behaviour in predicting default. Firms that draw more on their credit lines have a higher default rate (Jimenez et al., 2009). Such firms may have liquidity issues, and high leverage or bad financial performance may make it difficult for them to acquire additional funding other than drawing down their credit lines (Zhao et al., 2014). Credit line usage and excess overdraft are significant explanatory variables of default, especially for small business firms (Norden & Weber, 2010). More specifically, the utilization rate for current account revolving credit lines and excess overdrafts are good predictors of default for Italian SMEs and, more generally, the inclusion of credit behaviour variables improves the accuracy of credit scoring models (Giannozzi et al., 2013).

Based on the existing empirical studies and the industry best practices, we define a list of over 70 variables for all the 3 sub-models, that cover the following risk areas:

utilization rate—this variable is defined as the ratio between drawn amount and granted amount, for each type of credit line and at various frequencies (last quarter, last six-months, etc.);

financial distress—this is defined alternatively as the number of months, or absolute and relative amounts of overdrafts, for each type of credit line at

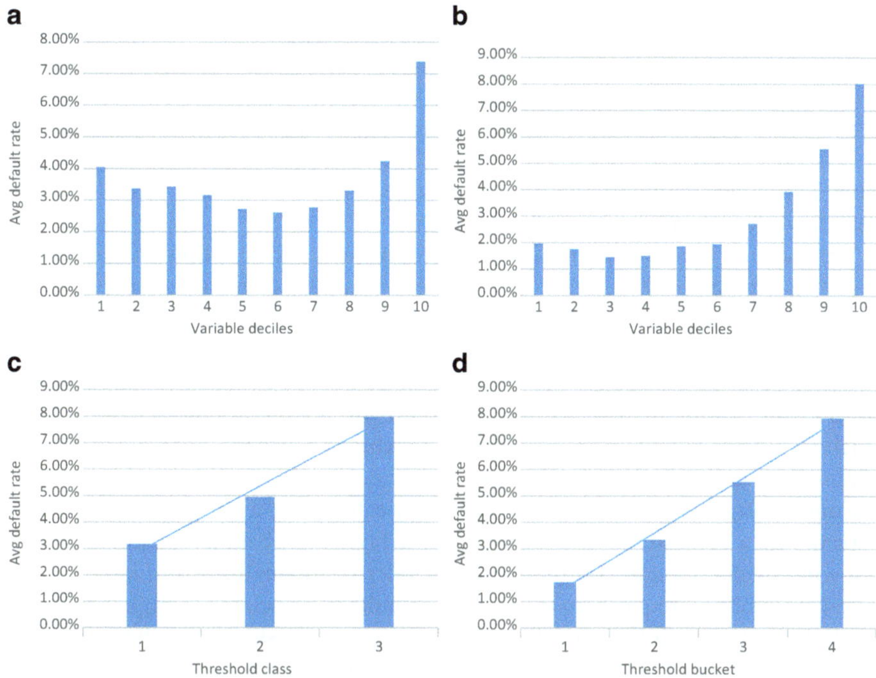

Fig. 13 Days receivables outstanding. **(a)** Default rate by decile; **(c)** Default rate by discretized class. 2014–2019, services, ordinary financial statement. Days receivables and inventories outstanding. **(b)** Default rate by decile; **(d)** Default rate by discretized class. 2014–2019, manufacturing, ordinary financial statement

various frequencies, or as past delinquencies and past default status. Previous studies show that excess overdrafts or past delinquencies are positively correlated with default (Gallucci et al., 2022; Norden & Weber, 2010);

debt composition—this is measured by variables that describe the debt characteristics of a given company, including a dummy for the presence of medium-long term loans and the breakdown of total debt by different types of loans. Earlier research shows that longer maturities are associated with better financial conditions and lower informational opacity of the borrower, and that creditors use shorter maturities to enforce monitoring of riskier borrowers (Ortiz-Molina & Penas, 2008);

quality of credit receivables—the indicators in this area capture the quality of the credit portfolio used in account receivables revolving credit lines, like the ratio of unpaid credit receivables over the total amount of credit expires or over net sales. We expect that a large amount of unpaid credit receivables is associated with a large PD;

trend ratio—it is measured alternatively as the change of utilization rate, evolution of credit lines, change in the number of reporting banks, and number of first information requests, all of them at different frequencies. Previous evidence is that the overall effect of more concentrated banking relationships involves a higher probability of incurring into financial distress, due to an increase in liquidity risk (Carmignani & Omiccioli, 2007). In the last year before default, the number of reporting banks decreases (Salvadè et al., 2024).

Table 7 provides summary statistics on a selection of the above variables with a breakdown for default and non-default firms.

We find that the utilization rate variables, under various definitions, are significantly associated with default. As expected, financial distress variables are also clearly associated with future default.

The ratio of overdraft percentage on term loans has been discretized due to the skewness of its distribution, with only a small number of firms having an overdraft. The number of months with an overdraft on revolving credit lines and term loans, which is discrete and bounded by definition, exhibits a strong linear and monotonic relationship with default risk (Fig. 14).

Consistently with Salvadè et al. (2024), we find that a decline in the number of banks in a semester is associated with a higher probability of default in the following twelve months. Furthermore, for micro and small firms, a large number of first information requests in the last six-months is associated to higher riskiness. Similarly to Ortiz-Molina and Penas (2008), our data show that the absence of medium-long term loans for micro and small firms is associated with an increase in PD.

As expected, we find that a bad quality of credit receivables has a positive relationship with default. Unrecoverable receivables have a direct impact on profit and liquidity. Within this area, we try measures of the general level of customer credit worthiness. We consider both a relative indicator, measured by the ratio between unpaid and expired amount on account receivables credit lines in the last six months, and an absolute indicator, namely the ratio between the average amount over the last six months of unpaid amount on account receivables credit lines over net sales. For both variables, we find a non-linear and non-monotonic relationship with default. Nevertheless, both variables exhibit an increase in default rate (with a linear trend) in the final part of the distribution, when a significant portion of the customer credit portfolios is not financially sound or when the amount of trade credit in default is above a certain amount compared to the size of the company, measured by net sales (Fig. 15a and 15b). Hence, with the decision tree technique we obtain two discretized variables with, respectively, five and three risk classes associated linearly with default (Fig. 15c and 15d).

Table 7 Credit behaviour variables (2014–2019)

Risk area	Variable	Mean (non-default)	Mean (default)	Median (non-default)	Median (default)
Utilization rate	Drawn amount/granted amount—current account revolving credit lines—average last three-months (%)	40.8	78.6	33.0	95.9
	Drawn amount/granted amount—short-term credit lines—average last six-months (%)	27.7	49.7	1.24	60.1
	Drawn amount/granted amount—account receivables revolving credit lines—average last six-months (%)	48.1	66.9	49.1	75.1
Financial Distress	No. of months (last six-months) with overdraft on current account revolving credit lines	0.4	2.1	0.0	2.0
	No. of months (last six-months) with overdraft on term loans	0.2	1.6	0.0	0.0
	Overdraft % on term loans, 6-month average (%)	0.2	1.8	0.0	0.0
	Dummy default status (last 6 months)	0.0	0.1	0.0	0.0
Debt composition	Dummy no medium-long term credit lines	0.0	0.1	0.0	0.0
Quality of credit receivables	Unpaid/Expired amount on account receivables credit lines—average last six-months (%)	12.3	31.0	1.2	14.4
	Unpaid amount on account receivables credit lines—average last six-months / net sales (%)	2.3	10.2	0.0	0.4
Trend	Dummy reduction in the number of reporting banks—last six-months	0.1	0.1	0.0	0.0
	No. of first information requests—last six-months	0.4	0.5	0.0	0.0

Note Own calculation on NCR data

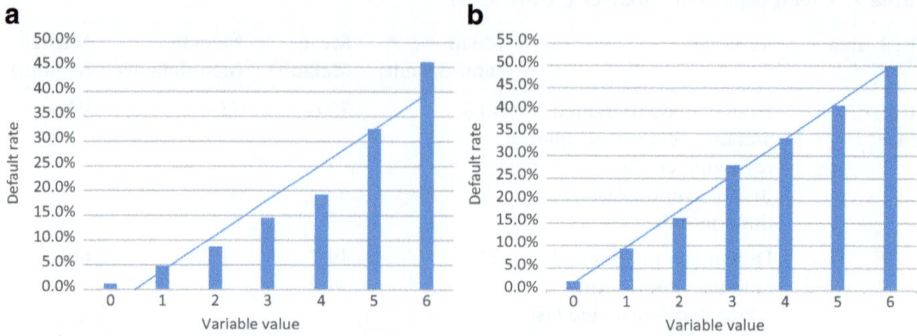

Fig. 14 Overdraft analysis. 2014–2019, small firms. **(a)** No. of months w/overdrafts, account revolving credit lines; **(b)** No. of months w/overdrafts, term loans

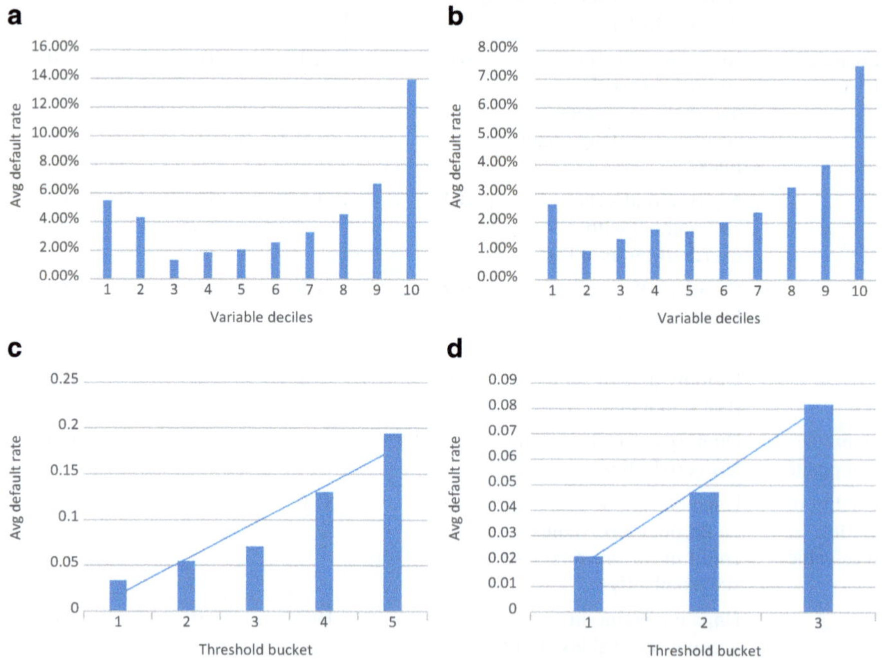

Fig. 15 Quality of credit receivables. **(a)** Unpaid/Expired amount on account receivables credit lines avg six-months; **(c)** Discretized Unpaid/Expired amount on account receivables credit lines avg six-months 2014–2019, micro firms. **(b)** Unpaid amount on account receivables credit lines avg six-months / net sales; **(d)** Discretize unpaid amount on account receivables credit lines avg six-months / net sales 2014–2019, medium-large firms

5.5 Model Development

Financial Statement Model

As shown in Sect. 1, the financial statement model consists of eleven sub-models based on the company macro-sector and type of financial statement. The breakdown according to the sector enables us to take into account the characteristics of different kinds of firms, while the type of financial statement enables us to fully exploit financial information (see Sect. 1). For each sub-model we perform an independent variable selection process (see Appendix A). We provide below a parsimonious representation of the main economic relationships estimated with each of the sub-models. These are summarised in Table 8 for firms with the ordinary financial statement and in Table 9 for those with the simplified financial statement. A ' + ' ('-') indicates a positive (negative) relationship of the variable with the default rate, i.e. whether an increase in the variable is associated with a higher (lower) PD. Variables with no sign are not considered in the specific sub-model.

To estimate the relative weight of the variables, we use the standardized coefficient for each variable within a specific sub-model. We find that, on average, debt sustainability is the most important risk dimension, with the ratio interest expenses over EBITDA among the most significant variables for manufacturing, trade, and services, for both ordinary and simplified financial statement sub-models. Besides, our results indicate that interest expenses over net sales is highly significant for trade firms, while net sales over total net debt is more important for services.

Leverage and liquidity are also significant risk dimensions. Within the liquidity area we find that the ratio between cash and total short-term debt is a good predictor for each economic sector, and it is more important than other ratios that compare current assets with short-term liabilities. In the leverage risk area, capitalization ratios are good predictors for capital intensive sectors, such as real estate and construction. We use the ratio between equity and net financial debt for the ordinary financial statement sub-models and the ratio between equity and total net debt for the simplified financial statement sub-models.

Overall, the distinction for the type of financial statement and the introduction of efficiency and business development variables with decision tree techniques significantly improve the discriminatory power of the sub-models in comparison with their previous version.

Credit Behaviour Model

The credit behaviour model consists of three sub-models (micro, small, and medium-large firms). The main relationships for the credit behaviour sub-models are summarised in Table 10. A ' + ' ('-') indicates a positive (negative) relationship of the variable with the default rate, i.e. whether an increase in the variable is associated with a higher (lower) PD.

Consistently with an earlier study (Giannozzi et al., 2013), according to the standardized coefficient methodology, the most important risk area for all the sub-models is the utilization rate and, in particular, the rate on the current account revolving credit lines. Unfortunately, these ratios are not always available due to

Table 8 Ordinary annual financial statement models

Risk area	Variable	Industrial sector				
		Manufacturing	Trade	Construction	Services	Real Estate
Profitability	Cash flow / Net sales	–	–		–	
	Cash flow / Total assets			–		
	Value added / Total assets					-
Leverage and financial structure	Equity / Net financial debt	–	–	–	–	–
	Fixed assets / Total assets					–
Debt sustainability	Interest expenses / EBITDA	+	+	+	+	
	Interest expenses / Cash flow					+
	Interest expenses / Net sales	+	+		+	
	Net sales / Total net debt	–	–		–	
	ROD (return on debt) = Interest expenses / Average financial debt	+	+	+	+	+
Liquidity	Current ratio = current assets / current liabilities	-		–		
	Financial mismatch = (current liabilities—current assets) / total assets		+		+	
	Cash / Total short-term debt	–	–	–	–	–
Activity	Days receivables outstanding + Days inventory outstanding (discretize)	+				
	Days receivables outstanding (discretize)			+	+	+

(continued)

Table 8 (continued)

Risk area	Variable	Industrial sector				
		Manufacturing	Trade	Construction	Services	Real Estate
	Days payables outstanding (discretize)	+	+	+		
Business development	Net sales negative variation (discretize)	+	+		+	
Age	Log(age)	−	−	−	−	

some missing values, arising from the absence of short-term loans or of other loan types. When this happens, we set the ratio equal to 0 (best possible value) and introduce a specific dummy variable which adjusts the credit score for the average riskiness of the sub-set of firms within the estimation sample for which this type of loans is not reported in the NCR.

The second most important risk dimension is financial distress, in particular the ratio constructed with the amount of overdraft on (discretized) term loans and the ratio that employs the number of months with excess overdraft on account revolving credit lines and term loans. The breakdown of the type of loan for overdraft indicators is one of the main improvements in comparison with the previous version of the credit behaviour model.

Other risk areas, such as the quality of credit receivables and the trend variables, are statistically significant but, as expected, their relative weights are less important compared to those of the average utilization rate and overdraft indicators. Nevertheless, the introduction of the former is the second most significant change compared with the previous model.

Within the medium-large firms' sub-model, we hypothesize that larger firms have a greater bargaining power towards their bank counterparties. The firm's bargaining power may enable it to perform more loosely on credit lines without jeopardising its credit standing. We thus adjust the credit score for large firms with a discretized variable based on net sales (starting from 0 for firms with net sales below 100 million euro and up to 5 for firms with net sales above 5 billion euro), with an inverse effect on the probability of default. Our conjecture is supported by the model.

Table 9 Simplified financial statement models

Risk area	Variable	Industrial sector					
		Manufacturing	Trade	Construction	Services	Real estate	Holdings
Profitability	Cash flow / Net sales	–	–		–		
	Cash flow / Total assets			–			
	Value added / Total assets					–	
	Ebit / Total assets						–
	Delta returns						–
Leverage and Financial structure	Equity / Total net debt	–	–	–		–	
	Equity / Total assets						–
	Fixed assets / Total assets					–	
	Financial assets / Total assets						–
Debt sustainability	Interest expenses / EBITDA	+	+	+	+		
	Interest expenses / Cash flow					+	
	Interest expenses / Net sales		+		+	+	
	Net sales / Total net debt	–	–		–		
Liquidity	Financial mismatch = (current liabilities—current assets) / total assets	+	+	+	+		
	Cash / Total short-term debt	–	–	–	–	–	
	Cash / Total debt						–
Activity	Days receivables outstanding + Days inventory outstanding (discretized)	+	+		+		
Business development	Net sales negative change (discretized)	+	+		+		
Age	Log(age)	–	–	–	–		

Table 10 Credit behaviour models

Risk area	Variable	Credit size		
		Micro	Small	Medium-Large
Average utilization rate	Drawn amount/granted amount—current account revolving credit lines—average last three-months	+	+	+
	Dummy no-current account revolving credit lines—last three-months	+	+	+
	Drawn amount/granted amount—short-term credit lines—average last six-months			+
	Dummy no-short-term credit lines—last six-months			+
	Drawn amount/granted amount—account receivables revolving credit lines—average last six-months	+	+	
	Dummy no-account receivables revolving credit lines—last six-months	+	+	
Debt composition	Dummy no medium/long term credit—last six-months	+	+	
Financial distress	No. of months (out of last six) with overdraft on current account revolving credit lines	+	+	+
	No. of months (out of last six) with overdraft on term loans	+	+	+
	Overdraft % on term loans, 6-month average (discretized)	+	+	+
	Dummy default status—last six-months	+	+	+
Quality of credit receivables	Unpaid/Expired amount on account receivables credit lines—average last six-months (discretized)	+	+	
	Unpaid amount on account receivables credit lines—average last six-months / net sales (discretized)			+
Trend	Dummy reduction in the number of reporting banks—last six-months	+	+	+
	No. of first information requests—last six-months	+	+	
Size	Net sales (discretized)			–

Integrated Model

Following a standard approach in rating systems for the integration of information from different sources (e.g. Balduini et al., 2017; Figini & Giudici, 2011; Giannozzi et al., 2013), the partial scores obtained from the financial model and the credit behaviour model are integrated by means of a logistic regression that yields the final score; in turn, this is transformed into a PD via the inverse logit function (Eq. 3.3).

The integration approach produces four distinct models by size (micro, small, medium, and large firms) according to the EC definition. This procedure reflects some underlying facts. We find that credit behaviour information has a large explanatory power for micro and small firms with a larger weight than that of the financial statement model. For medium and large firms, when an ordinary financial statement is available, the accounting module has a larger relative weight than that of the credit behaviour model. The ratio between the standardized beta of the credit behaviour component and that of the financial statement component ranges between 0.80 for large firms to 2.06 for micro firms (Fig. 16).

As described in Sect. 1, the model has been developed with the observations from 2015 to 2018 as the training sample and those for 2014 and 2019 as the test sample. Within the logit modelling framework, this implies that the (in-sample) average firm-level PD equals the average default rate recorded in the training sample. Considering that more recent data about the economic cycle in Italy are somewhat different from those of the years 2015–2018, in the statistical model we

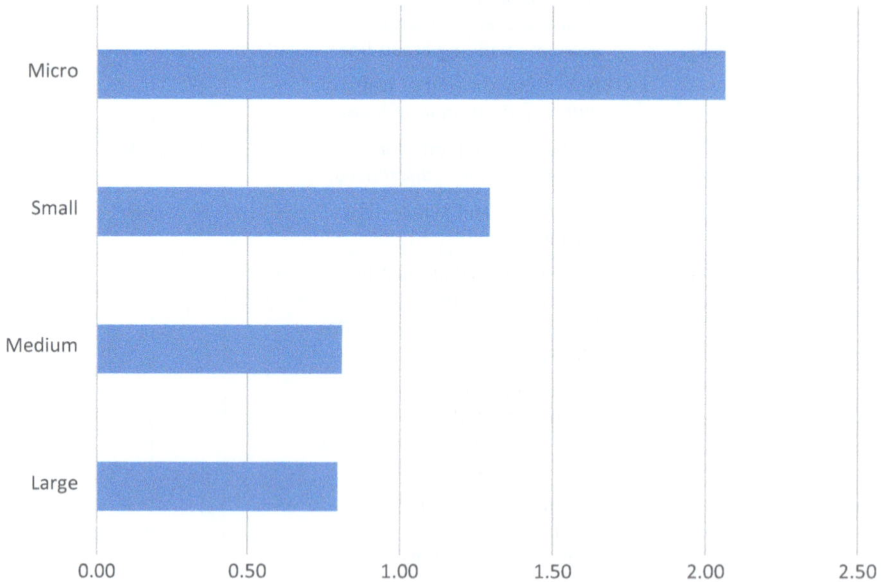

Fig. 16 Ratio of standardized betas between credit behaviour model and financial statement model

Table 11 Alpha-adjustment by size

Size	Default rate (2014–21)	Default rate (2015–18)	Difference	Alpha-adjustment
	(%)	(%)	(%)	
Micro	4.36	4.84	−0.48	−0.11
Small	3.39	3.64	−0.25	−0.07
Medium	2.63	2.76	−0.13	−0.05
Large	2.39	2.66	−0.27	−0.11

apply the so-called alpha-adjustment. We adjust the intercept α to match the default rate recorded over the longer period 2014–2021, with the following formula.

$$\alpha_{adjusted} = \ln\left(\frac{1 - DefRate_{15-18}}{DefRate_{15-18}} \cdot \frac{DefRate_{14-21}}{1 - DefRate_{14-21}}\right) \tag{5}$$

We apply the alpha-adjustment procedure for each sub-model by size. The default rate in the longer period 2014–2021 is lower than that in-sample. Hence the average PD of each statistical model is adjusted on the downside (Table 11).

6 Validation

The best practices in the field of credit risk assessment envisage the separation of validation from model development and rating production. Separation guarantees the independence and impartiality of validators. At the Bank of Italy, the responsibility for rating production and model validation is assigned to two separate units.[17] The validation activity involves a one-off internal validation step as well as an ongoing monitoring process.

Internal validation aims at checking that the rating process is carried out consistently with the best methodological practices, thus providing adequately robust and efficient PD estimates. This activity is performed each time a new version of the model is developed, or a significant innovation is introduced. The checks are applied to the whole model, both in the statistical component and in the expert system component.

The goal of performance monitoring is assessing the stability of the rating system over time and verifying the predictive ability of the model on a yearly basis.

Since ICAS is mainly aimed at PD estimation, internal validation does not include the assessment of the Loss Given Default (LGD) nor of the Exposure at

[17] This is in line with a specific ECB Governing Council recommendation. While approving the Bank of Italy's ICAS on 4 July and 7 November 2013, the Governing Council issued several recommendations, in particular that internal validation and monitoring of the model performance should be separated from methodology development and rating production.

Default (EAD).[18] The validation and monitoring of the PDs are mainly performed with benchmarking and back testing.

Benchmarking techniques compare the PDs estimated with the model with those estimated with other models on the same sample of firms. These techniques typically involve the calculation of the statistical distance between the models. The main limitation of this approach is the small number of ratings usually obtained with other models, since ICAS assesses small and medium-sized enterprises that are seldom assessed with other systems. Besides, benchmarking requires strong confidence in the rating system used for the comparison.

Back testing procedures are employed to compare the ratings estimated ex-ante with the number of defaults observed ex-post. The literature provides several statistical tests which help assess the model accuracy. Within the validation framework, three aspects are typically considered: discriminatory power, predictive power (or calibration quality), and performance stability.

Discriminatory power tests assess the ability of the model to distinguish firms on the basis of their future status (default or non-default) over a predefined time horizon. Predictive power tests compare the number of defaults that actually occurred in a given rating class with the number of defaults predicted by the model. Stability tests concern the ability of the rating system to distinguish between real causes/effects and purely random relationships; unstable rating systems have a disappointing performance (i.e. they lose discriminatory power or predictive power) if applied to databases other than that for which they were developed.

Discrimination, prediction, and stability of a model are not necessarily correlated. For instance, a rating system may show a high discriminatory power but a poor predictive performance; this can occur e.g. in the presence of small samples, as is often the case in practice. Alternatively, a rating system could have a good predictive power but a weak discriminatory power. This could occur if, for instance, in a population of obligors with an actual default rate equal to x per cent, the rating system assigns ratings randomly, attributing a probability of default of x per cent to each rating class; hence the probability of default is correctly assigned to each rating class, but the discriminatory power is nil.

Discriminatory power and predictive power are linked by an asymmetric relationship. Obtaining a good calibration (i.e. predictive power) is sometimes difficult; we note that it is easier to calibrate a model with a good discriminatory power than to improve the discriminatory power of the model, even if it is well calibrated. Furthermore, the discriminatory power of a rating system limits the quality of its calibration: it is the discriminatory power of a rating system that a priori makes it possible to obtain probabilities close to 0 or 1.

The next three subsections present the tools for discriminatory power analysis, predictive power analysis, and stability analysis, respectively. Section 7 shows the test results for our model.

[18] The approach that tackles also the analysis of the LGD and the EAD is typically followed in the IRB model validation (see also BIS, 2005).

6.1 Discriminatory Power

The main purpose of a rating system is to distinguish between 'sick' and 'healthy' units (firms), depending on whether the occurrence of the default event is considered likely for each of them within a given time horizon. In most cases, the model is expected to draw a line between the two types of units; the most common procedure involves setting a cut-off probability. The units that have an estimated default probability below (above) the cut-off level are considered healthy (sick). The model must have discriminatory power, that is it should show precision in assigning a default probability below (above) the cut-off level to the healthy (sick) firms.

The discriminatory power should reflect the following properties:

- specificity, that is the ability to correctly classify the units for which the event does not occur;
- sensitivity, that is the ability to correctly classify the units for which the event occurs.

There is a clear trade-off between specificity and sensitivity. For instance, as the cut-off level for the probability of default increases, the model will be less specific but more sensitive.

The standard measure for the discriminatory power of a model is the Receiver operating characteristic (ROC) curve, which in turn yields the AUROC statistic (see Sect. 4.2). We note that the evidence about the units gone into default and those that survived in the time period under consideration is only one of the possible realizations from the probability distributions of the defaulters and the non-defaulters. In other words, the default phenomenon has a stochastic nature. If the same experiment were repeated, different realizations of these distributions would be obtained, with every realization showing a different value of the AUROC.

The stochastic nature of the default phenomenon can be investigated with the statistic known as U of Mann–Whitney, which is strictly linked to AUROC (Cortes and Mohri, 2005); the statistical properties of the Mann–Whitney U are thus applicable to the study of the stochastic behaviour of the AUROC.

The Mann–Whitney U statistic can help measure how far the value achieved by the AUROC is from its expected value, by calculating appropriate confidence intervals; this allows for hypothesis testing, for example to check whether the discriminatory power of the rating system is significantly different from the value under total randomness.

6.2 Predictive Power

The predictive power (or calibration quality) refers to the model's ability to identify the 'real' probability of default for an individual debtor or a class of homogeneous debtors. Since the real PD is unknown, it is not possible to accurately estimate it. Therefore, to test the quality of the PD calibration the observed (ex-post) default frequency is compared with the estimated (ex-ante) probability of default and hypothesis testing is performed. Typically, a rating system includes various classes of risk, and the validator must assess each risk class separately.

Conditional and unconditional tests can be used. The notions of conditional and unconditional testing can be best understood if related to the notions of 'point-in-time' (PIT) and ''through-the-cycle' (TTC) probability of default. The probability of default can be based (or 'conditioned') on the current state of the economy, for example by including macroeconomic variables in the regression equation. Typical macro variables are the GDP growth rate and the unemployment rate. In this case the estimated probabilities of default are PIT PDs. Credit events can then be treated as independent, because most of the dependence among them is captured by incorporating the macroeconomic variables into the PD forecasts. In contrast, the unconditional estimates of the PD are not based on the current state of the economy. Such estimates, based on data referring to a complete economic cycle, are denominated TTC PDs. When using unconditional PDs, no independence assumption between the credit events can be accepted, given that the change in the observed default rates cannot any longer be explained by the change in the conditional PDs, which are themselves random variables (Tasche, 2006).

The estimated PDs provided by ICAS are generally of the PIT type (Auria et al., 2021) because they capture the perspective creditworthiness of firms as closely as possible, to better control the credit risk of collateral in monetary policy refinancing operations. Thus, the validation of the predictive power of ICAS is performed mainly with conditional tests on the state of the economy. These tests are illustrated below.

The first approach for testing multiple risk classes at the same time involves multiple comparisons. As an alternative, a single statistical test is used to compare risk classes simultaneously (joint testing). When multiple testing is applied, each risk class is assessed individually in the first stage. Under the usual assumption of independence among the defaults, the number of defaults by risk class follows a binomial distribution. In the second stage the results of the individual tests are considered, to check if the rating system adopts appropriate PD estimates for all classes.

It is important to clarify a definition issue. The ICAS 'statistical model' produces probabilities; based on them, each sample company is assigned to a specific risk class. To assess the eligibility of the company and obtain the prudential haircut for monetary policy purposes, the ICAS 'rating system' gives each company a probability equal to that of the upper limit of the risk class.

For the validation of ICAS, we perform multiple testing to check: (1) for the absence of underestimation of the ICAS *system* PDs in each rating class (adopting a risk aversion profile towards default typical of a 'supervisor'); (2) whether the ICAS *system* is too conservative or too loose, i.e. whether its PDs are in line with actual defaults (adopting a risk aversion profile of a 'production unit' with business objectives); (3) whether the ICAS *model* PDs are in line with the actual defaults. Under the null hypothesis that 'the expected defaults are higher than those observed' (the supervisor view), a one-tailed binomial test is conducted for each rating class.

The test distribution has an average value equal to the PD value of the upper bound in each rating class. The test is evaluated at the 99% confidence level. When the number of actual defaults is significantly lower than that of the expected defaults for all rating classes, the ICAS system is prudential, i.e. it does not lead to underestimating default risk.

Employing as the null hypothesis the statement 'the expected defaults are equal to those observed, for each rating class's' (the production unit view)—which is equivalent to 'the ICAS system is precise'—a two-tailed binomial test is conducted for each rating class. As in the previous case, the distribution of each test has the average value equal to the upper end of the probability range of each rating class. The test is evaluated at the 99% confidence level. If the number of actual defaults is significantly higher or lower than that of the expected defaults for a given rating class, the null hypothesis is rejected.

Lastly, under the null hypothesis 'the expected defaults of the statistical model underlying the ICAS rating system are equal to those observed, for each rating class's'—which is equivalent to 'the ICAS model is precise'—a two-tailed binomial test is conducted for each rating class. The distribution of each test has the average value equal to the average of the probabilities of default assigned by the statistical model to the borrowers that belong to each rating class. The test is evaluated at the 99% confidence level. If the number of actual defaults is significantly higher or lower than that of the expected defaults for some rating class, the hypothesis 'the ICAS model is precise' is rejected.

However, when multiple testing analysis is conducted, the so-called alpha-inflation problem should be accounted for. This is related to the fact that, as the number of hypotheses to be simultaneously tested increases, the probability of type 1 error on the global hypothesis rises.

Some methods can be employed to keep this error under control. The most common in the literature consists in increasing the *p*-values on the single class tests. Some of these methods are applied also in the ICAS validation process, either under the supervisor approach or under the production unit approach.

Within the family of joint tests, those put forward by Spiegelhalter and Hosmer and Lemeshow are the most used. The Spiegelhalter test, based on the Brier Score,[19] combines the information on the calibration quality available at the individual level. Under the null hypothesis of perfect calibration (the expected value of

[19] The Brier Score is a score function that measures the accuracy of probabilistic predictions. For unidimensional predictions, it is strictly equivalent to the mean squared error as applied to predicted probabilities. The Brier score is applicable to tasks in which predictions must assign

the default distribution is equal to the PD estimate for each unit), the test statistic is distributed as a standardized normal. The test assumes of independence among the defaults. The Spiegelhalter test results should be interpreted carefully, since the test statistic is based on a weighted average PD that is estimated on the entire sample of debtors. Only an average overestimation/underestimation of the probabilities of default causes the rejection of the null hypothesis of perfect calibration at the individual level. The test therefore fails to identify as unacceptable those situations in which the overestimation of PDs for some units is offset by the underestimation of PDs for other units in the sample. To overcome this issue, the Hosmer–Lemeshow test compares expected defaults and realized defaults within each rating class. The test, like the Spiegelhalter test, uses a normal approximation of the binomial distribution that leads to a chi-square distribution of the statistic.[20]

6.3 Stability

The stability of a rating system is usually validated by applying the rating system to a data sample different from the one which is used to develop the system. The latter is referred to as the 'training sample', while the sample employed for stability evaluation is called the 'validation sample'. There are three ways to construct the validation sample:

- out-of-sample: the training sample is obtained by randomly selecting a part of a larger sample. The complement of the training sample within the larger sample is used for validation;
- out-of-universe: the training sample is formed by deterministically selecting a part of a larger sample (e.g. considering only data from specific regions or sectors). The complement of the training sample within the larger sample is used for validation;
- out-of-time: the training sample is made up of data covering a given time period. Data from outside this period is used for validation.

In practice, the availability of data may be an issue. The full starting sample, to be split into a training sample and a validation sample, is often small. If, on the one hand, the training sample is too small, there will be uncertainty in the estimation and an excessive adaptation to the available data (overfitting); then the validation

probabilities to a set of mutually exclusive discrete outcomes or classes. The set of possible outcomes can either be binary or categorical in nature, and the probabilities assigned to this set of outcomes sum to one (where each individual probability is in the range of 0 to 1). The Brier score can be thought of as a cost function. More precisely, across all items $i \in 1 \ldots N$ in a set of N predictions, the Brier score measures the mean squared difference between the predicted probability assigned to the possible outcomes for item i and the actual outcome o_i. Therefore, the lower the Brier score is for a set of predictions, the better the predictions are calibrated.

[20] This approximation could be questionable with a small number of borrowers.

will end up confirming what is obvious. If, on the other hand, the validation sample is too small, validation will be of little use.

An approach that is often applied in practice is the 'walk-forward testing'. The rating system to be validated is set up using data from a certain period of time only. Data from the following periods are added gradually and the exercise is repeated, leading to a time series of results that can be used to assess performance. This approach is very useful because it replicates the process which the rating system will undergo over time. In the light of new data, there will be an ongoing review and re-fitting of the system.

7 Model Performance: Back Testing and Comparison with the Previous Model

In this Section we illustrate the performance of the model in terms of discriminatory power, predictive power, and stability by means of a back testing exercise. Besides, we benchmark the model performance against that of the previous version of the model (Giovannelli et al, 2023). Back testing is based on the following criteria:

- discriminatory power—the model's AUROC should be as large as possible (above 70%);
- predictive power—in the first place, the model's default forecast should be conservative; besides, a model that provides precision, by forecasting default rates as close as possible to actual default rates, should be preferred;
- stability—the measures of discriminatory power and predictive power should change as little as possible over time; validation should favour the model with a stationary behaviour.

We recall that:

- the previous model was estimated on the defaults of the years 2015–2016, with an alpha correction based on 2016;
- the new model is estimated on the defaults of the years 2015–2018, with an alpha correction based on 2014–2021.

A fully informative validation would in principle involve an out-of-sample analysis. We employ the actual defaults for the years 2019–2021, available at the time of the analysis. This procedure is partially in-sample because the alpha-adjustment also employs the defaults of the years 2019–2021. However, we also note that the overlap between the estimation sample and the test sample is limited, and alpha is calibrated over a suitably large number of years.

The performance of the two models is examined at the following reference dates: December 2018 (default period from January to December 2019), June 2019 (default period July 2019-June 2020), December 2019 (default period January-December 2020), June 2020 (default period July 2020- June 2021), December 2020 (default period January-December 2021). For completeness, the probabilities of default have been compared with the subsequent defaults of fractional type and binary type.

In Sect. 5 we describe the time period used for the model development carried out by the CRA Division. In this Section we report the independent validation of the model carried out by the FRC Division. The validation function also looks at different default periods compared to those used in the estimation process. The validation analysis refers to the one-year default period (all PDs have a one-year horizon). For completeness, the PDs are validated using both the binary and the fractional default definition (Sect. 2).

In terms of discriminatory power, the new model achieves fairly large AUROC values, at 84% or better. These are always larger that the corresponding figures for the previous model at each date (Table 12). For large firms the AUROC is as large as 90% (see Appendix A).

In terms of predictive power, the two models pass the test on the absence of underestimation of the PD in each rating class. As concerns accuracy, the new model generally performs better than the previous one. In fact, using the third test presented in the previous Section and considering the number of rating classes for which the relevant model presents a significant deviation between the number of actual defaults and the number of estimated defaults, the new model features the absence of 'slack' classes, that is in no case is the number of forecast defaults smaller than that of the actual ones.

The standard deviation of the results presented in the above tables turns out to be smaller for the new model in almost all cases. Thus, the new model exhibits a lower volatility of the results.

We can conclude that, compared to the previous version of the statistical model, the new model features a larger discriminatory power, a larger predictive power, and greater stability. In addition, as argued above, the new model is more transparent for analysts. All these properties are highly desirable and represent a substantial improvement over the previous model.

Table 12 AUROC (percentage values)

Default period	December 2018	June 2019	December 2019	June 2019	December 2020
Binary defaults					
Previous model	87.6	87	87.6	87.4	83.3
New model	88.5	88.1	88.9	88.6	84.5
Fractional defaults					
Previous model	83.3	84.4	84.3	83.8	81.6
New model	84	84.8	84.9	84.3	82.8

Table 13 Number of rating classes: estimated and actual defaults

Default period	December 2018	June 2019	December 2019	June 2020	December 2020
Binary defaults					
Previous model	2	1	1	1+4	1
New model	2	3	5	4	1
Fractional defaults					
Previous model	1	0	2	4	0
New model	2	4	5	5	2

Note the total number of rating classes (CQS) is eight. The numbers: (i) in blue show for how many classes: forecasted defaults > effective defaults (the model is conservative); (ii) in red show for how many classes: forecasted defaults < effective defaults (the model is slack); (iii) in black indicate a situation in which for every class: forecasted defaults = effective defaults (the model is precise)

Next, we examine the behaviour of the in-sample calibration version of the model (or base model), to find out if and to what extent it provides robust PD estimates with respect to the actual defaults, without considering the alpha-adjustment.

First, we note that the discriminatory power of the base model is the same as in Table 12. A shift of the PDs such as that implied by the alpha-adjustment does not affect the ordering of the PDs among themselves.

The predictive power worsens, since in this case there is a larger number of 'not precise' classes, even if the base model is never slack, as it happens for the previous model (Table 13). That is, the base model is rather conservative; based on the data, the alpha-adjustment partially contains the degree of prudence of the model (Table 14).

As concerns the stability of the results, the base part of the statistical model exhibits a less volatile behaviour than that of the previous model, as well as that of the recalibrated model. The standard deviation of the results presented in the previous tables is almost always smaller than in the base model.

Table 14 Number of rating classes: comparison between estimated and actual default. Base model

Default period	December 2018	June 2019	December 2019	June 2020	December 2020
Binary defaults					
Previous model	2	1	1	1+4	1
New model	5	4	5	5	2
Fractional defaults					
Previous model	1	0	2	4	0
New model	4	5	5	5	5

Note the total number of rating classes (CQS) is eight. The numbers: (i) in blue show for how many classes: forecasted defaults > effective defaults (the model is conservative); (ii) in red show for how many classes: forecasted defaults < effective defaults (the model is slack); (iii) in black indicate a situation in which for every class: forecasted defaults = effective defaults (the model is precise)

To conclude, the statistical model described in this chapter has a robust structure, as it yields PD estimates that enable the system to discriminate between healthy and sick firms and that never predict a number of defaults below that of actual defaults. Likewise, it appears that the base model is highly prudent. This property can be managed by means of the alpha-adjustment (see Sect. 3).

The validation analysis was also conducted for each size class of the firms for which a PD is provided by the model. This approach has confirmed the evidence regarding similarities and differences between the new model and the previous one. We also find that the discriminatory power of the statistical model improves as the size of the company increases. This is a favourable property, as the largest exposures are usually held towards the largest firms.

As far as predictive power is concerned, although the new model is more prudent than the previous version towards smaller firms, the two models tend to converge and become more precise as the size of the company increases (see Appendix B). This result will guide possible future methodological developments of the model.

8 Conclusions

This chapter describes the methodology underlying the Bank of Italy's statistical credit assessment model and its validation process. Each month the model produces with an automated procedure an estimate of the one-year PD for 370,000 Italian non-financial firms. The model preserves the transparency of the traditional logistic model, while trying to improve the performance with ML techniques that capture complex relationships of some variables with the default event.

Empirically, the model shows satisfactory features that enable it to properly discriminate between healthy and risky firms, with an AUROC statistic between 84 and 90%. The stability of the results is high. Furthermore, the discriminatory power of the model improves as the size of the company increases, thus ensuring a proper evaluation of the largest exposures in monetary policy operations.

The architecture of the model will enable us to work on possible future enhancements, such as the integration of the analysis of climate risk and press news, to further improve the performance of the model.

Appendix A

Model Development

The first step in model development consists in (i) the choice of the dependent variable with the specification of the default definition, and (ii) the collection of all the data with an initial analysis on quality and consistency.

The second step consists in splitting the data sample for the purpose of estimation and testing (see Sect. 1).

The third step, for each component of the model (11 financial statement sub-models and 3 credit behaviour sub-models), is a univariate analysis on a list of variables of interest that are potentially predictive of default. The variables are chosen after consulting credit analysts and reviewing the literature and other credit scoring models. For both the financial statement sub-models and the credit behaviour sub-models, we divide the list of variables into classes that reflect different hypotheses regarding a firm's creditworthiness (like profitability, debt sustainability, liquidity). Within the univariate analysis, we analyse and treat the outliers that could cause distortions in the development of the models. For continuous variables, we examine the frequency distribution and the key statistics and apply winsorization methods to the outliers, by replacing each outlier with a given percentile of the frequency distribution (Barnett & Lewis, 1994). Besides, we examine missing or inconsistent values for each variable. When a missing or inconsistent value is related to a situation that could be 'extremely positive' or 'extremely negative', we replace that value with the extreme value used in the winsorization process. When a missing value is not related to a positive or negative condition, it can be replaced with the median or average value of the distribution or with a dummy variable. For example, the ratio drawn amount to granted amount for a certain type of credit line reported in the NCR could be missing. In this case we assign a value of 0 (positive value) and introduce a dummy variable to set the credit score equal to the average default rate of the firms that do not have this type of credit line.

The aim of the univariate analysis is to shorten the list of variables and to identify, for each group of candidate regressors, the most significant ones for the multivariate analysis. The variable selection uses the following criteria:

- variables with a lot of missing values and outliers are dropped;
- variables not having a linear and monotonic relationship with default are usually dropped. Nevertheless, for some variables of interest (such as sales growth and days of receivables turnover) we consider as potential predictors also the discretized transformation obtained with the application of decision tree techniques;
- using a *t*-test, the variables with insignificant differences in the mean value between the default and non-default groups are dropped;
- using univariate logit regression for the probability of default, the variables with an accuracy ratio below 55% are dropped;
- for each risk group, we retain the variables with a high accuracy ratio and some other variables based on a qualitative assessment.

The fourth step involves the analysis of collinearity. To assess the possible informative redundancies and reduce the collinearity between variables, we verify their independence. To this aim, we construct a correlation matrix between the variables selected in the previous step. If two or more variables have a correlation above 0.7 or below −0.7 we keep the one with the highest discriminatory power.

For each sub-model, the final step is the selection process that involves the choice of the final combination of variables and the definition of their relative weights. We use a multivariate logistic regression with a statistical selection of indicators performed via a stepwise algorithm with a 1% minimum significance level for a variable to enter the model. We review the results of the statistical process to make sure that (a) all the relevant risk areas are represented, and (b) the estimated sign of the coefficient of each indicator is consistent with the underlying economic assumptions.

Appendix B

Firm Size

The behaviour of the statistical model against the previous model can be further investigated by splitting the sample according to firm size.

The new model displays a higher discriminatory power. This is even more true in the case of large firms, both under the definition of binary default and of fractional default. Larger firms generally have larger credit exposures, hence the ability to discriminate correctly in this context can be very important. These results are shown in the following Tables 15 and 16.

The new version of the model is more prudent than the previous one, in particular for the micro enterprises, which are approximately 70% of all sample firms. As the size increases, the two models become more precise. The previous model shows a slack in several periods, under both binary and fractional defaults, while the new model never presents this problem. This result is reported in the following table.

Table 15 AUROC by firm size (percentage values)

Default period	December 2018	June 2019	December 2019	June 2019	December 2020
Binary defaults					
Micro firms					
Previous model	87.1	86.6	87	87.3	82.9
New model	87.6	87.3	88	88.1	83.5
Small firms					
Previous model	88.3	87.7	88.7	87.6	84.1
New model	90.2	89.5	90.4	89.5	86.3
Medium firms					
Previous model	88.2	87	88.3	86.1	84.3
New model	90.7	89.2	90.6	89.1	86.4
Large firms					
Previous model	89.3	85	85.7	84.5	84.1
New model	90.9	86.8	88.4	89	90
Fractional defaults					
Micro firms					
Previous model	82.5	83.9	83.5	83.2	80.6
New model	82.7	83.8	83.8	83.3	81.2
Small firms					
Previous model	84.2	84.8	82.9	83.9	82.9
New model	86.2	86.4	86.6	85.6	85.5
Medium firms					
Previous model	84.5	83.8	85.8	83.6	82.6
New model	86.7	85.5	87.1	86.3	85.3
Large firms					
Previous model	86.7	82.9	83.5	79.7	78.5
New model	87.3	85.5	86.2	82.7	84.9

Table 16 Number of classes with issues on estimated PDs, by firm size

Default period	December 2018	June 2019	December 2019	June 2020	December 2020
Binary defaults					
Micro firms					
Previous model	1	0	1	4	0
New model	2	3	4	4	1
Small firms					
Previous model	2	0	0	3	1
New model	0	0	1	3	0
Medium firms					
Previous model	0	1	0	0	0
New model	1	0	2	2	0
Large firms					
Previous model	0	0	1	0	0
New model	0	0	0	0	0
Fractional defaults					
Micro firms					
Previous model	1	0	3	4	2
New model	2	3	5	5	1
Small firms					
Previous model	0	0	0	4	2
New model	0	0	4	4	1
Medium firms					
Previous model	0	0	0	2	1
New model	1	0	2	2	2
Large firms					
Previous model	0	1	0	0	0
New model	0	0	0	0	0

Note the total number of rating classes (CQS) is eight. The numbers: (i) in blue show for how many classes: forecasted defaults > effective defaults (the model is conservative); (ii) in red show for how many classes: forecasted defaults < effective defaults (the model is slack); (iii) in black indicate a situation in which for every class: forecasted defaults = effective defaults (the model is precise)

References

Alberici, A. (1975). *Analisi dei bilanci e previsione delle insolvenze*. Isedi, Milano

Altman, E. I. (1968). Financial ratios, discriminant analysis and the prediction of corporate bankruptcy. *J Finance, 23*, 589–609.

Altman, E. I. (1983). *Corporate financial distress: A complete guide to predicting, avoiding, and dealing with bankruptcy*. John Wiley and Sons.

Altman, E. I., Halderman, R. G., & Narayanan, P. (1977). Zeta-analysis: A new model to identify bankruptcy risk of corporations. *Journal of Banking & Finance, 1*, 29–54.

Altman, E. I., Iwanicz-Drozdowska, M., Laitinen, E. K., & Suvas, A. (2017). Financial distress prediction in an international context: A review and empirical analysis of Altman's Z-score model. *J Int Financ Manag Account, 28*, 131–171.

Altman, E. I., & Sabato, G. (2007). Modelling credit risk for SMEs: Evidence from the U.S. market. *Abacus 43*(3).

Altman, E. I., Sabato, G., & Wilson, L. (2010). The value of non-financial information in SME risk management. *J Credit Risk, 6*(2), 1–33.

Angori, G., Aristei, D., & Gallo, M. (2020). Banking relationship, firm-size heterogeneity and access to credit: Evidence from European firms. *Finance Res Lett 33.*

Antunes, A., Gonçalves, H., & Prego, P. (2016, April). Firm default probabilities revisited. *Econ Stud*, Banco de Portugal.

Auria, L., Bingmer, M., Mateo, C., Graciano, C., Charavel, C., Gavilá, S., Iannamorelli, A., Levy, A., Maldonado, A., Resch, F., Rossi, A. M., & Sauer. S. (2021). Overview of central banks' in-house credit assessment systems in the euro area. *ECB Occas Pap Ser 284.*

Bacham, D., & Zhao, J. (2017, July). Machine learning: Challenges, lessons, and opportunities in credit risk modeling. *Moody's Analytics Risk Perspect, 9.*

Balduini, A., Dwyer, D., Gianfreda, S., Hemminki, R., Yang, L., & Zhao, J. Y. (2017). Combining financial and behavioral information to predict default for small and medium-sized enterprises—A dynamic weighting approach. *Moody's Analytics and Credit Data Research.*

Barboza, F., Kimura, H., & Altman, E. (2017). Machine learning models and bankruptcy prediction. *Expert Systems with Applications, 83*, 405–417.

Barnett, V., & Lewis T. (1994). *Outliers in statistical data.* J. Wiley & Sons, XVII.

Beaver, W. H. (1966). Financial ratios as predictors of failure. *Journal of Accounting Research, 4*, 71–111.

BIS. (2005). *Studies on the validation of internal rating systems*. Work Pap 14. https://www.bis.org/publ/bcbs_wp14.pdf

Blum, M. (1974). Failing company discriminant analysis. *Journal of Accounting Research, 12*(1), 1–25.

Bonaccorsi di Patti, E., D'Ignazio, A., Gallo, M., & Micucci, G. (2015). The role of leverage in firm solvency: Evidence from bank loans. *Ital Econ J, 1*(2), 253–286.

Brier, G. W. (1950). Verification of forecasts expressed in terms of probability. *Monthly Weather Review, 78*(1), 1–3.

Campbell, J. Y., Hilscher, J., & Szilagyi, J. (2008). In search of distress risk. *J Finance, 63*(6), 2899–2939.

Carmignani, A., & Omiccioli, M. (2007). *Costs and benefits of creditor concentration: An empirical approach.* Work Pap 645, Bank of Italy.

Cascarino, G., Moscatelli, M., & Parlapiano, F. (2022). *Explainable artificial intelligence: Interpreting default forecasting models based on machine learning*. Occas Pap 674, Bank of Italy.

Charalambakis, C., & Garrett, I. (2019). On corporate financial distress prediction: What can we learn from private firms in a developing economy? Evidence from Greece. *Rev Quant Financ Account, 52*, 467–491.

Chawla, N. V. (2009). Data mining for imbalanced datasets: An overview. In O. Maimon & L. Rokach (Eds.), *Data mining and knowledge discovery handbook* (pp. 875–886). Springer.

Chen, K. H., & Shimerda, T. A. (1981). An empirical analysis of useful financial ratios. *Financ Manag, 10*(1), 51–60.

Cortes, C., & Mohri, M. (2005). Confidence intervals for the area under the ROC curve. *Adv Neural Inf Process Syst*, 305–312.

De Socio, A., & Michelangeli, V. (2017). Modelling Italian firms' financial vulnerability. *Journal of Policy Modelling, 39*, 147–168.

Deakin, E. (1972). A discriminant analysis of predictors of business failure. *Journal of Accounting Research, 10*(1), 167–179.

Dumitrescu, E., Hué, S., Hurlin, C., & Tokpavi, S. (2022). Machine learning for credit scoring: Improving logistic regression with non-linear decision-tree effects. *European Journal of Operational Research, 297*(3), 1178–1192.
EBA. (2021). EBA discussion paper on machine learning for IRB models. EBA/DP/2021/04, Nov 2021.
Edmister, R. (1972). An empirical test of financial ratio analysis for small business failure prediction. *J Financ Quant Anal, 7*(2), 1477–1493.
FSB. (2010). Principles for reducing reliance on CRA ratings.
Fantazzini, D., & Figini, S. (2009). Random survival forests models for SME credit risk measurement. *Methodology and Computing in Applied Probability, 11*, 29–45.
Fawcett, T. (2004). ROC graphs: Notes and practical considerations for researchers. *Machine Learning, 31*(1), 1–38.
Figini, S., & Giudici, P. (2011). Statistical merging of rating models. *The Journal of the Operational Research Society, 62*(6), 1067–1074.
Gallucci, C., Santulli, R., Modina, M., & Formisano, F. (2022). Financial ratios, corporate governance and bank-firm information: A Bayesian approach to predict SMEs' default. *Journal of Management and Governance*. https://doi.org/10.1007/s10997-021-09614-5
Gentry, J. A., Newbold, P., & Whitford, D. T. (1985). Classifying bankrupt firms with funds flow components. *Journal of Accounting Research, 23*(1), 146–160.
Giannozzi, A., Altman, E. I., Roggi, O., & Sabato, G. (2013). Building SME rating: Is it necessary for lenders to monitor financial statements of the borrowers? *Bancaria Editrice, 10*, 54–71.
Giovannelli, F., Iannamorelli, A., Levy, A., & Orlandi, M. (2023). The Bank of Italy's in-house credit assessment system for non-financial firms. In A. Scalia (Ed.), *Financial risk management and climate change risk* (pp. 107–137). Springer.
Grandia, R., Hänling, P., Lo Russo, M., & Âberg, P. (2019). *Availability of high-quality liquid assets and monetary policy operations: An analysis for the euro area.* ECB Occas Pap Ser 218.
Hajek, P. (2012). Credit rating analysis using adaptive fuzzy rule-based systems: An industry-specific approach. *Cent Eur J Oper Res, 20*(3), 421–434.
Jiménez, G., Lopez, J., & Saurina, J. (2009). Empirical analysis of corporate credit lines. *Rev Financ Stud, 22*, 5069–5098.
Kosekova, K., Maddaloni, A., Papoutsi, M., & Schivardi, F. (2023). *Firm-bank relationship: A cross-country comparison.* ECB Work Pap Ser 2826.
Lee, S., & Choi, W. S. (2013). A multi-industry bankruptcy prediction model using back-propagation neural network and multivariate discriminant analysis. *Expert Systems with Applications, 40*(8), 2941–2946.
Luerti, A. (1992). La previsione dello stato di insolvenza delle imprese. Il modello AL/93. Etaslibri, Milano.
Micha, B. (1984). Analysis of business failure in France. *Journal of Banking & Finance, 8*, 281–291.
Modigliani, F., & Miller, M. (1958). The cost of capital, corporation finance and the theory of investment. *The American Economic Review, 48*(3), 261–297.
Moscatelli, M., Narizzano, S., Parlapiano, F., & Viggiano, G. (2020). Corporate default forecasting with machine learning. *Expert Systems with Applications, 161*, Article 113567.
Mossman, C. E., Bell, G. G., Swartz, L. H., & Turtle, H. (1998). An empirical comparison of bankruptcy models. *The American Economic Review, 48*(2), 35–54.
Norden, L., & Weber, M. (2010). Credit line usage, checking account activity, and default risk of bank borrowers. *Rev Financ Stud, 23*, 3665–3699.
Ohlson, J. (1980). Financial ratios and the probabilistic prediction of bankruptcy. *Journal of Accounting Research, 18*(1), 109–131.
Ortiz-Molina, H., & Penas, M. F. (2008). Lending to small business: The role of loan maturity in addressing information problems. *Small Business Economics, 30*(4), 361–383.
Salvadè, F., Troege, M., & Taillet, N. (2024). Passing the parcel? *Banking Relationships at the Onset of Financial Distress.* SSRN. https://ssrn.com/abstract=3936411 or https://doi.org/10.2139/ssrn.3936411

Tasche, D. (2006). Validation of internal rating systems and PD estimates. In *The analytics of risk model validation*, pp. 169–196.
Van Gestel, T., Baesens, B., Van Dijcke, P., Suykens, J. A. K., Crispiniano Garcia, J. B., & Alderweireld, T. (2005). Linear and non-linear credit scoring by combining logistic regression and support vector machines. *Journal of Credit Risk, 1*(4).
Zhao, Y. J., Dwyer, D. W., & Zhang, J. (2014). Usage and exposures at default of corporate credit lines: An empirical study. *Journal of Credit Risk, 10*(1).

Macroeconomic Variables and Panel Estimation

Francesco Columba, Stefano Di Virgilio, Giulio Gariano, Alessandra Iannamorelli, Simone Narizzano, Marco Orlandi, and Federica Vassalli

1 Introduction

This Chapter presents two enhancements of S-ICAS to refine the accuracy and stability of its predictions addressing both systemic and idiosyncratic risks.

The first enhancement incorporates the effects of the business cycle into S-ICAS. So far, the system has shown a very high discriminatory power in ranking firms according to their credit risk; still, S-ICAS is only based on microeconomic variables, namely firm balance-sheet data and reports from the NCR. To account for changes in the general economic conditions, while preserving the discriminatory power of S-ICAS, we develop a satellite macroeconomic model that captures the effects of the business cycle allowing for their inclusion in S-ICAS PDs.

F. Columba (✉) · S. Di Virgilio · G. Gariano · A. Iannamorelli · S. Narizzano · M. Orlandi · F. Vassalli
Bank of Italy, Financial Risk Management Directorate, Rome, Italy
e-mail: francesco.columba@bancaditalia.it

S. Di Virgilio
e-mail: stefano.divirgilio@bancaditalia.it

G. Gariano
e-mail: giulio.gariano@bancaditalia.it

A. Iannamorelli
e-mail: alessandra.iannamorelli@bancaditalia.it

S. Narizzano
e-mail: simone.narizzano@bancaditalia.it

M. Orlandi
e-mail: m.orlandi@bancaditalia.it

F. Vassalli
e-mail: federica.vassalli@bancaditalia.it

A. Scalia (ed.), *Corporate Credit Analysis and AI*, Finance for Professionals,
https://doi.org/10.1007/978-3-032-13422-6_4

The second enhancement exploits to a full extent the cross-section heterogeneity of firms using panel estimation methods. We try to overcome the limitations that hinder the use of panel econometrics in standard credit risk models owing to the scarcity of the events of default.

Our main finding is that the macroeconomic model estimates the aggregate default rate for the economic system four times more accurately than S-ICAS.[1] Thus, the enhanced S-ICAS better reflects the macroeconomic conditions in the economic sectors, especially during recessions, improving the discriminatory power of the model.

The results for the panel estimation on two sub-models of S-ICAS show that panel models may yield an improvement in discriminatory power, measured by an increase in the AUROC[2] between 0.3 and 0.1 percentage points.

The macroeconomic model has already been implemented in the running system. The possible adoption of the panel techniques for operational purposes requires further investigation, to cover all economic sectors and perform additional robustness tests.

The remainder of the Chapter is organized as follows: Section 4.2 describes the current S-ICAS model and discusses the methodologies for the inclusion of macroeconomic factors in the S-ICAS PD. Section 4.3 presents the validation of the models which incorporate macroeconomic factors. Section 4.4 discusses the panel analysis for estimating S-ICAS PDs. Section 4.5 concludes.

2 S-ICAS and Business Cycle

The model involves the estimation of the intercept α and of the vector of coefficients β for the explanatory variables.

The $X\beta$ component of the model is the part of the firm's PD explained by its microeconomic variables, while α reflects systematic latent factors, in particular the business cycle. Every year the S-ICAS intercept is calibrated with the so-called alpha-adjustment, which aims to capture the factors that affect the default of firms, but that are not included in the model, primarily the macroeconomic outlook. The calibration, so far largely reliant on judgmental assessment, is based on expectations about the prevailing average default rate across firms.

We set out to enhance the S-ICAS by accounting for the impact of the business cycle on the borrowers' creditworthiness via the estimation of the intercept α with a satellite macroeconomic model.

[1] Considering year 2022 as out-of-sample, the Root Mean Square Error (RMSE) of the macroeconomic model is 0.0012 per cent while that of S-ICAS is 0.0049 per cent.

[2] AUROC is a measure of the ability of the model to assign higher PDs to firms that will default compared with financially sound firms.

2.1 A Macroeconomic Model for the Average Default Rate

The models for estimating the PD are usually based on micro and macroeconomic data (financial statement information, credit behaviour data, macroeconomic variables) and are generally used to assess loans granted to small and medium-sized firms, for which market information is unavailable.[3] These models may be classified into three categories (Chaun-Lau, 2006). The first category consists of macroeconomic models that assess how the state of the economy affects the average probability of insolvency. The second category includes models, employing financial statement data, that estimate the PD for individual firms using financial information. The third category includes models that use credit behaviour data, available from credit registers, to estimate PDs. Models that estimate PDs with a combination of macroeconomic variables, financial statement data, and credit behaviour information have been put forward since the increase in firms' and households' default rates observed during the major recessions in the last fifteen years (Jarrow, 2009; Simons and Rolwes, 2018).

S-ICAS uses financial statement information and credit behaviour data (that is microeconomic data) and adjusts PDs based on expectations about the average default rate consistent with those about the economic outlook. In this Section we illustrate the macroeconomic model to estimate the average default rate.[4] This estimate is then used to adjust the intercept of S-ICAS and yield the PDs. For parsimony, a multivariate linear regression model with exogenous lagged variables is chosen, as in the following equation:

$$y_t = \alpha + \sum_{l=0}^{L} \boldsymbol{x}_{t-l}^{T} \boldsymbol{\beta}_l + \varepsilon_t \tag{4.1}$$

where y_t is the average default rate at time t for the sample of non-financial firms assessed with S-ICAS, α is the intercept, $\boldsymbol{x}_{t-l}$ is the vector of macroeconomic variables at lag l, and ε_t is the error term. The choice of the specification affects the correction of the intercept and modifies the predictive and discriminatory power of the PDs estimated by S-ICAS.[5]

To estimate the average default rate y_t, we adopt the Fully Modified Least Squares (FM-OLS) estimation method, due to its valid asymptotic properties in small samples and its consistency in case of cointegration.[6] Starting with a broad

[3] PD estimation models fall into two broad categories: market-based models, which employ asset prices, and fundamental-based models, which employ financial statement data, economic indicators, and credit behaviour data.

[4] The model allows to incorporate information on the business cycle not yet included in the firms' balance sheets, which are released with a lag of several quarters.

[5] The statistical tests are defined according to the ECAF, the collection of rules and procedures for the credit risk management of the collateral pledged for monetary policy operations. See Appendix C for details on the tests.

[6] Phillips (1995). For robustness, we also run OLS regressions which yield similar results.

set of variables and after evaluating a range of possible specifications previously used to forecast the Italian non-financial firm default rate,[7] we select the following regression equation and run it on quarterly data:

$$y_t = c + \beta_1 STAT\ PD_t + \beta_2 CREDIT\ DEM_{t-2} + \beta_3 \Delta TCR_{W\,t-2} + \beta_4 \Delta RGDP_{W\,t-4} + \varepsilon_t \tag{4.2}$$

Where $STAT\ PD_t$ is the S-ICAS average PD with a 12-month horizon, $CREDIT\ DEM_{t-2}$ represents Italian banks' expectations for changes in credit demand over the next three months with a two-quarter lag, $\Delta TCR_{W\,t-2}$ is the average interest rate applied to new loans with a two-quarter lag and $\Delta RGDP_{W\,t-4}$ is the change of real GDP with a four-quarter lag. The S-ICAS average PD provides a benchmark for the default rate, incorporating microeconomic information from financial statements and the NCR. $CREDIT\ DEM_{t-2}$ and $\Delta RGDP_{W\,t-4}$ capture financial and real demand-side factors. While NCR data already cover credit usage by firms, $CREDIT\ DEM_{t-2}$ reflects banks' expectation for loan demand over the next quarter.[8] Lastly, $\Delta TCR_{W\,t-2}$ represents the supply side of credit, where higher interest rates on new loans signal banks' perception of increased firm risk.

We estimate the model from the third quarter of 2012 to the third quarter of 2019, to avoid possible structural breaks during the COVID-19 period. The estimated coefficients align with economic theory and findings in the literature (Table 4.1).[9] The average PD estimated with S-ICAS is the most significant regressor. We find that a 1 per cent increase in the interest rate on credit results in a 0.44 per cent increase in the default rate. Italian firms heavily rely on bank loans as a primary source of financing (with the ratio of bank loans to total financial debt at approximately 60 per cent in 2019).[10] Thus, an increase in loan interest rates tightens financial conditions for these firms. Additionally, a 1 per cent increase in real GDP reduces the default rate by 0.1 per cent, as GDP growth typically signals rising demand for goods and services, positively impacting all sectors.

When comparing the actual default rate with the average PD estimated by S-ICAS, we observe that, after the COVID-19 period, the PD estimated by S-ICAS tends to underestimate the actual default rate (Fig. 4.1). This discrepancy may be due to a decrease in the accuracy of the creditworthiness information conveyed by the firms' financial variables during the COVID-19 pandemic, because of the debt moratoria and public guarantee programs introduced. Conversely, the default rate estimated with the FM-OLS model captures the upward trend of the actual default

---

[7] We considered alternative variables and specifications stemming from the models used to develop S-ICAS, and also related models by Bofondi and Ropele (2011), Bonaccorsi di Patti and Cascarino (2020), Moscatelli et al. (2020), Simons and Rolwes (2018). See Appendix A for more details.

[8] The Governing Council of the ECB carries out the euro area bank lending survey (BLS). BLS provides information on bank lending conditions in the euro area. It supplements existing statistics with information on the supply of, and demand for, loans to enterprises and households. The Change in Credit Demand Index for Italian Firms is part of the BLS.

[9] Abaidoo (2018), Simons and Rolwes (2018), Carvalho et al. (2022) and Bocchio et al. (2023) among others.

[10] Visco (2019).

Table 4.1 Default rate - FM-OLS Model

Variable	Coefficient	Std. Error	Prob.
PD $STAT_t$	0.9343	0.0419	0
CREDIT DEM_{t-2}	−0.0001	0	0.007
$\Delta TCRw_{,t-2}$	0.4384	0.0961	0
$\Delta RDGPw_{,t-4}$	−0.104	0.048	0.041
C	0.0053	0.0023	0.033
R-squared	0.9876	Mean dependent var	0.0553
Adjusted R-squared	0.9856	S.D. dependent var	0.0203
Long-run variance	4.10E-06	Sum squared resid	0.0001

rate from the end of 2020. Also, the model captures the rise in the actual default rate after the third quarter of 2022, which follows the sharp rise in interest rates started in July 2022. In fact, considering the observations for 2022, the macroeconomic model Mean Square Error (MSE) is four times smaller than the S-ICAS MSE (0.0012 per cent against 0.0049 per cent). Our forecasts are consistent with the profile of the ABI-Cerved forecast of non-performing loans rate for the years 2019–2024 (ABI-Cerved, 2023).

2.2 The Sector Models

In line with the S-ICAS financial sub-models, we estimate the macroeconomic model for each primary NACE sector (see Chap. 3). In terms of number of firms, the most significant sectors within the ICAS sample are manufacturing, trade, construction, and real estate. Developing specific models for each sector allows us to capture more accurately the deterioration of firms' conditions in the run-up to default, given the heterogeneity in their financial vulnerability and default rates across sectors.[11]

The specifications for the manufacturing and construction sectors mirror the macroeconomic model (Eq. 4.2), as their credit risk is particularly reactive to credit and GDP. Both manufacturing and construction are capital-intensive industries, requiring substantial investment for machinery, raw materials, infrastructure, and labour, making access to credit essential. GDP growth generally implies a rising demand for goods and services, which positively affects these sectors through the demand for manufactured goods and, in turn, housing, commercial spaces, and infrastructure projects.

For the trade sector, the specification incorporates the euro-dollar exchange rate rather than GDP, as this sector depends particularly on import and export markets,

[11] See Chap. 3; Bank of Italy (2023).

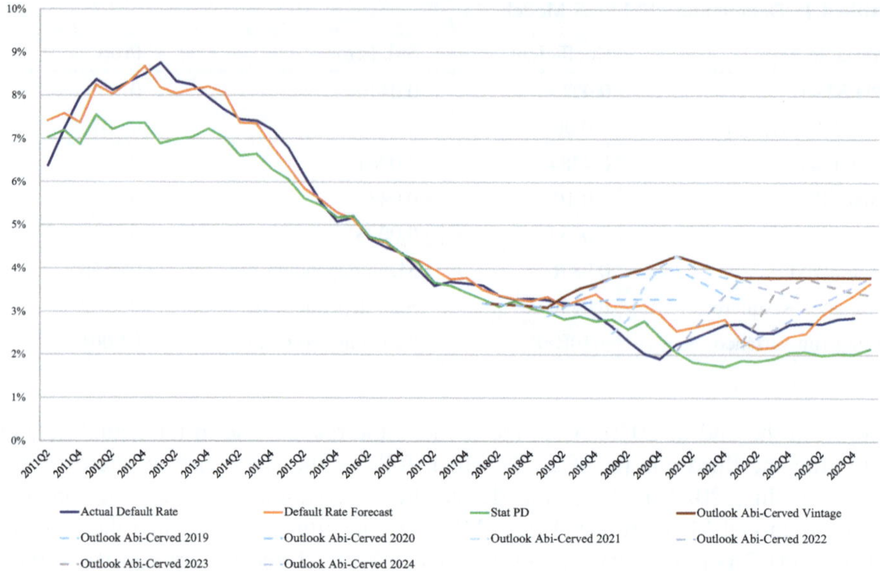

Fig. 4.1 Comparison between default rates. The graph shows the actual default rate, the default rate predicted by the macroeconomic model, the average PD estimated by S-ICAS, the non-performing loans rate forecast by ABI-Cerved over the last five years. The Outlook Abi-Cerved line shows the one-year forecast of the non-performing loans rate and it consists of the upper envelope of the yearly Outlook Abi-Cerved forecast lines from 2019 to 2024 (Source: ABI-Cerved, Bank of Italy)

making exchange rates a critical factor for firm activity. The real estate specification is different, including house price inflation ($INFL\_HPI_{t-8}$) and changes in unemployment (ΔUMP_{t-4}), which influence both demand and supply within the real estate market.[12] We use a general specification for the other sectors by replacing credit demand variation with the four-quarter lagged annual inflation rate (Carvalho et al., 2022). The estimated coefficients align with economic theory and findings in the literature (Table 4.2).[13] The statistical PD remains the most significant explanatory variable across all sectors, followed by the interest rate on new loans and the unemployment rate. A one per cent increase in the interest rate raises the default rate by 0.45 percentage points on average, while a one per cent rise in the unemployment rate results in an average 0.18 percentage points increase in the default rate. Conversely, a one per cent increase in GDP growth is associated with an average 0.1 per cent decline in the default rate.

[12] Klamargias et al. (2018), Carvalho et al. (2022) and Bocchio et al. (2023).

[13] Abaidoo (2018), Simons and Rolwes (2018), Carvalho et al. (2022) and Bocchio et al. (2023) among others. The results for other sectors are also aligned with the literature and are not reported in Table 4.2 and Fig. 4.2 for simplicity.

Table 4.2 Sector default rate - FM-OLS model

Manufacturing				**Construction**			
Variable	Coef.	Std. Error	Prob.	Variable	Coef.	Std. Error	Prob.
PD $STAT_t$	0.81	0.05	0.00	PD $STAT_t$	1.12	0.05	0.00
CREDIT DEM_{t-2}	0.00	0.00	0.09	CREDIT DEM_{t-2}	0.00	0.00	0.00
$\Delta TCRw_{,t-2}$	0.39	0.12	0.00	$\Delta TCRw_{,t-2}$	0.67	0.14	0.00
$\Delta RDGPw_{,t-4}$	−0.07	0.05	0.21	$\Delta RDGPw_{,t-4}$	−0.14	0.07	0.06
C	0.01	0.00	0.00	C	0.00	0.00	0.78
R-squared	0.98	Mean dep var	0.04	R-squared	0.99	Mean dep var	0.08
Adj R-squared	0.98	S.D. dep var	0.02	Adj R-squared	0.99	S.D. dep var	0.03
Long-run var	0.00	Sum sq. resid	0.00	Long-run var	0.00	Sum sq. resid	0.00
Retail and wholesale trade				**Real estate activities**			
Variable	Coef.	Std. error	Prob.	Variable	Coef.	Std. error	Prob.
PD $STAT_t$	0.76	0.04	0.00	PD $STAT_t$	1.12	0.05	0.00
$\Delta TCRw_{,t-2}$	0.39	0.10	0.00	INFL HPI $_{t-8}$	−0.06	0.02	0.03
$EXUSEUR_{t-2}$	0.02	0.01	0.00	$\Delta TCRw_{,t-2}$	0.65	0.17	0.00
CREDIT DEM_{t-2}	0.00	0.00	0.00	ΔUMP_{t-4}	0.18	0.09	0.05
C	−0.01	0.01	0.06	C	−0.02	0.00	0.00
R-squared	0.99	Mean dep var	0.05	R-squared	0.99	Mean dep var	0.05
Adj R-squared	0.98	S.D. dep var	0.02	Adj R-squared	0.99	S.D. dep var	0.02
Long-run var	0.00	Sum sq. resid	0.00	Long-run var	0.00	Sum sq. resid	0.00
		Aggregate					
		Variable	Coef.	Std. error	Prob.		
		PD $STAT_t$	0.95	0.05	0.00		
		$\Delta TCRw_{,t-2}$	0.12	0.15	0.45		
		$\Delta RDGPw_{,t-4}$	−0.06	0.04	0.17		
		INFL $DEFw_{,t-4}$	0.22	0.09	0.02		
		C	0.00	0.00	0.91		
		R-squared	0.99	Mean dep var	0.05		
		Adj R-squared	0.98	S.D. dep var	0.02		
		Long-run var	0.00	Sum sq. resid	0.00		

The estimated default rate for manufacturing, construction, and trade forecasts well the actual default rate, which tends to be higher than the S-ICAS PD after the COVID-19 pandemic (Fig. 4.2). Only for the real estate activities sector, the S-ICAS PD tends to overestimate the default rate. This may depend on the circumstance that the average decline in the actual default rate over the sample period is about 50 per cent, against 70 per cent for the real estate activity. Financial statements may not promptly reflect such a sharp variation, as real estate firms usually have a special financial statement format (De Socio et al., 2020) and the share of simplified financial statements is larger than in other sectors (see Chap. 3). These peculiarities may alter the predictive power of the statistical PD estimation and warrant an integration within S-ICAS of macroeconomic factors.

We conclude that the output of the satellite macroeconomic model applied to the economic sectors produces accurate estimates of the average default rate of each sector. These estimates can be used to adjust the alpha parameter in S-ICAS, enabling the model to account for the heterogeneity of the business cycle effect on economic sectors.

3 Macroeconomic Model Validation

The validation of a model is a requirement in regulatory and commercial practice (Stein, 2007), as well as for S-ICAS models within the ECAF. Validation analysis involves three features of the behaviour of the model. The first feature is the ability to sort firms from the riskiest to the safest (discriminatory power); the second feature is the ability to forecast the true default frequency of a certain group of firms (predictive power); the third feature is the ability to produce results in line with the true defaults over time (performance stability).[14]

We validate the general macroeconomic model and the sector models using S-ICAS as a benchmark. As for the first feature of these models, the discriminatory power does not change compared to S-ICAS, since the macroeconomic model operates an upward translation of all the PDs.[15] The AUROC is above 80 per cent, which seems fairly good if compared to similar exercises. For the sector models we find an increase in discriminatory power (Table 4.3).

To verify the second feature of a model, namely predictive power, on an annual basis the Eurosystem performs a battery of tests on the ICAS operated by the national central banks, under the so-called Traffic Light Approach (TLA).[16] We

[14] Appendix C discusses in more detail the methodology employed.

[15] The discriminatory power depends on the order that a model assigns to the analysed firms, distinguishing between riskier and safer companies. If all the PDs change equally, the order and discriminatory power do not change.

[16] The approach applies a binomial test with regard to every risk class of the analysed rating system. TLA involves a single-tail test based on an upper bound PD. The total number of rating classes (CQS, Credit Quality Step) examined is seven, in line with ECAF practices. ECAF mitigates the credit risk of collateral pledged in monetary policy operations, together with appropriate valuation

Fig. 4.2 Default rates by sector. **a** Manufacturing; **b** Construction; **c** Retail and Wholesale Trade; **d** Real Estate Activities. (Source: Bank of Italy)

Table 4.3 AUROC (percentage values)

Reference date	S-ICAS / FM_OLS	FM_OLS_SECTORS
31.03.2011	86.18	86.18
30.06.2011	85.82	85.85
30.09.2011	85.84	85.84
31.12.2011	86.61	86.62
30.09.2021	80.87	80.27
31.12.2021	81.72	82.01
31.03.2022	82.5	83.02
30.06.2022	82.72	83.08

Table 4.4 Rating classes with issues

Reference date	S-ICAS	FM_OLS	FM_OLS_SECTORS
31.03.2011	0	0	0
30.06.2011	0	0	0
30.09.2011	0	1	0
31.12.2011	0	0	0
30.09.2021	3	0	0
31.12.2021	1	0	0
31.03.2022	0	0	0
30.06.2022	0	0	0

Note: The numbers in red show how many classes report predicted defaults below actual defaults; the model is rated as not prudent if actual defaults are above an alarm threshold, or "red" alarm. Numbers in yellow show how many classes report predicted defaults below actual defaults; in this case the model is rated as not prudent according to a pre-alarm threshold or "yellow" alarm that is lower than the red one. The zeros in green show that all classes report predicted defaults above or equal to actual defaults (the model is prudent)

run the same predictive tests on the general macroeconomic model and the sector models; they pass the tests and are preferable to S-ICAS (Table 4.4).

Since the general macroeconomic model and the sector models show performance stability and better results than S-ICAS,[17] they are validated.

and risk control measures. See Appendix C for more details on the tests implemented in the traffic light approach.

[17] The stability is assessed with the standard deviation calculated on the columns in tables 3 and 4.

4 Panel Econometric Methods and S-ICAS

The granularity of the ICAS data set and the heterogeneity of non-financial firms suggest the adoption of a panel approach for the estimation of the PD, to fully exploit the available information.[18]

A panel approach for the estimation of S-ICAS PDs has not been employed so far due to implementation difficulties, at the Bank of Italy and in similar rating systems developed by other National central banks of the Eurosystem and by commercial banks.

Since default is a binary variable, the models traditionally used to estimate PDs are logit and probit models. Three main types of panel estimators may be used for such models: the random effects estimator, the fixed effects estimator, and the correlated random effects estimator. The first two types present issues incompatible with the current S-ICAS, while the third category of model fits with the ICAS setting, though it requires a considerable investment in its estimation.[19]

The random effects estimator cannot bring appreciable benefits to S-ICAS, since one of the underlying assumptions of the estimator is the absence of correlation between the unobserved fixed effects and the independent variables.[20] Such hypothesis is not plausible in the S-ICAS data set, therefore the estimation of the coefficients would be biased. As for the fixed effects estimator, it does not allow the calculation of PDs, since the estimator is obtained by maximizing a conditional likelihood function that does not depend on the fixed effects.[21]

The correlated random effects (CRE) estimator, instead, allows for the estimation of unobserved effects for firms.[22] We conduct a preliminary analysis of the performance of the CRE estimator on one of the eleven S-ICAS financial sub-models and on one of the three S-ICAS credit behaviour sub-models. We select the sub-model for firms in the services sector for the financial component and the sub-model for medium-large firms for the credit behaviour component.[23]

---

[18] 95 percent of firms appears more than once in the estimation sample, at different moments in time.

[19] Appendix B illustrates the details of the econometric and operational issues to be overcome.

[20] For binary models the stronger assumption of independence is required.

[21] It would be possible to maximize the unconditional likelihood function, in which the fixed effects appear, but the estimators would be inconsistent. Moreover, when maximizing the conditional likelihood function, only firms in the sample that are detected as both in default and not in default through time are considered, and, since the number of defaults accounts for less than five percent of the sample, the estimator would be imprecise.

[22] From an operational perspective, calculating fixed effects for new firms that have not previously been evaluated (around 2000 monthly in the ICAS case) is not feasible. Fixed effects values derived from other firms must be used to estimate a PD for these new firms. For each of the fourteen S-ICAS sub-models, a function is needed to map each new firm into a group of similar firms, allowing us to estimate the new firm's fixed effect by averaging the fixed effects of firms in the same group. Constructing these groups of similar firms is crucial, as it significantly impacts the performance of these models.

[23] We select these two sub-models because their sample size is small enough to ensure robust estimation and acceptable computational time, making the analysis more tractable.

Table 4.5 Comparison between out-of-sample AUROC of pooled and CRE logit estimators

Model	Pooled Logit	Correlated RE Logit
NCR	86.05	86.33
Financial	75.38	75.49

We compare the AUROC values between the current baseline model (pooled logit) and the panel model in the CRE specification (Table 4.5). Both models are estimated over the period 2013–2019, while 2012 and 2022 are used as out-of-sample to evaluate discriminatory power.[24] The AUROC improvement ranges between about 0.3 percentage points for the NCR model and 0.1 for the financial sub-model.[25]

We also present the differences between the estimated coefficients of the pooled logit and the CRE logit models for the NCR sub-model (Table 4.6) and for the financial statement sub-model (Table 4.7).[26] We find that the signs of the coefficients are consistent across models and align with economic theory. However, the coefficients differ in magnitude, and some variables lose significance in the CRE model.

The CRE generally yields smaller coefficients than those of the pooled logit model. Including fixed effects[27] (group average values) mitigates the time-invariant omitted variable bias, which appears to be negative. The time-fixed effects also capture a macroeconomic shock impacting all firms equally relative to the baseline year, 2013. Notably, the average default rate declines from 2014 to 2019, reflecting easing monetary policy conditions, improved access to credit, and recovery from the 2008 great financial crisis and the 2012 sovereign debt crisis.

In conclusion, the preliminary findings based on two of the fourteen S-ICAS sub-models indicate that panel models yield an improvement in the discriminatory power, albeit small at this stage of the analysis. Further analyses on the other sub-models are required to evaluate the overall gain for the accuracy of S-ICAS stemming from the implementation of panel methods.[28]

[24] The COVID-19 period, years 2020 and 2021, has been excluded from the dataset given its peculiarity.

[25] We estimate confidence bands for AUROC differences with bootstrapping.

[26] The coefficients of these two models are not directly comparable with those of the current S-ICAS model (Narizzano et al., 2024), due to differences in the training periods. We selected the time frame to align with the macroeconomic model, allowing for a consistent comparison of AUROC improvements.

[27] The averages of some variables could not be introduced into the correlated random effects model, due to the high correlation with the corresponding variable.

[28] Such analyses include: i) the study of 14, potentially new, models; ii) the construction of comparable firm groups, utilizing machine learning techniques, particularly decision trees and random forests; iii) the analysis of the models' discriminatory power, predictive power and stability; iv) the development of the IT infrastructure to implement the models, including the exploration of the required data tables.

Table 4.6 NCR sub-model—Medium-Large firms

Risk area	Variable	NCR - Medium-Large	
		Pooled Logit	CRE Logit
Average utilization rate	Drawn amount/granted amount - current account revolving credit lines - average last three months	1.628*** (−0.066)	1.546*** (−0.066)
	Dummy no-current account revolving credit lines - last three months	1.130*** (−0.078)	1.091*** (−0.078)
	Drawn amount/granted amount—Short term credit lines - average last six months	1.278*** (−0.078)	0.607*** (−0.106)
	Dummy no-short term credit lines - last six months	0.891*** (−0.094)	0.901*** (−0–094)
Financial distress	No. of months (out of last six) with overdraft on current account revolving credit lines	0.265*** (−0.010)	0.213*** (−0.016)
	No. of months (out of last six) with overdraft on term loans	0.257*** (−0.020)	0.257*** (−0.024)
	Overdraft % on term loans, six month average (discretized)	0.764*** (−0.067)	0.746*** (−0.068)
	Dummy default status—Last six months	0.730*** (−0.064)	0.572*** (−0.072)
Quality of credit receivables	Unpaid amount on account receivables credit lines - average last six months / net sales (discretized)	0.236*** (−0.024)	0.216*** (−0.024)
Trend	Dummy reduction in the number of reporting banks—Last six months	0.114** (−0.047)	0.048 (−0.051)
Size	Net sales (discretized)	−0.197*** (−0.041)	0.232* (−0.122)
Year	Year = 2014	−0.336*** (−0.051)	−0.347*** (−0.051)
	Year = 2015	−0.250*** (−0.051)	−0.262*** (−0.052)
	Year = 2016	−0.424*** (−0.054)	−0.427*** (−0.054)
	Year = 2017	−0.555*** (−0.055)	−0.565*** (−0.056)

(continued)

Table 4.6 (continued)

Risk area	Variable	NCR - Medium-Large	
		Pooled Logit	CRE Logit
	Year = 2018	−0.518*** (−0.057)	−0.536*** (−0.057)
	Year = 2019	−0.634*** (−0.058)	−0.638*** (−0.058)
Group mean	Drawn amount/granted amount—Short term credit lines - average last six months		0.948*** (−0.099)
	No. of months (out of last six) with overdraft on current account revolving credit lines		0.074*** (−0.024)
	No. of months (out of last six) with overdraft on term loans		0.139*** (−0.032)
	Dummy default status—Last six months		0.621*** (−0.136)
	Dummy reduction in the number of reporting banks—Last six months		0.328*** (−0.095)
	Net sales (discretized)		−0.482*** (−0.119)
	Constant	−5.161*** (−0.063)	−5.245*** (−0.064)
	Observations	156,066	156,066

Standard errors in parentheses; *** p < 0.01, ** p < 0.05, * p < 0.1

Table 4.7 Financial sub-model—Services sector

Risk area	Variable	Financial statement - Services	
		Pooled Logit	CRE Logit
Profitability	Cash flow / net sales	−0.878*** (−0.144)	0.158 (−0.271)
Leverage & financial structure	Equity / net financial debt	−0.053*** (−0.006)	−0.050*** (−0.006)
Debt sustainability	Interest expenses / EBITDA	0.641*** (−0.052)	0.253*** (−0.079)
	Interest expenses / net sales	1.172*** (−0–275)	1.010*** (−0.285)
	Net sales / Total net debt	−0.231*** (−0.014)	−0.229*** (−0.017)

(continued)

Table 4.7 (continued)

Risk area	Variable	Financial statement - Services	
		Pooled Logit	CRE Logit
	ROD (return on debt) = interest expenses / average financial debt	4.452*** (−0.227)	4.380*** (−0.27)
Liquidity	Financial mismatch = (current liabilities—Current assets) / total assets	0.194*** (−0.059)	0.194*** (−0.062)
	Cash / Total short-term debt	−0.873*** (−0.091)	−0.863*** (−0.100)
Activity	Days receivables outstanding (discretized)	0.147*** (−0.022)	0.145*** (−0.022)
Business development	Net sales negative variation (discretized)	0.132*** (−0.010)	0.136*** (−0.010)
Age	Log(age)	−0.280*** (−0.014)	−0.275*** (−0.014)
Year	Year = 2014	−0.316*** (−0.062)	−0.296*** (−0.061)
	Year = 2015	−0.389*** (−0.064)	−0.365*** (−0.063)
	Year = 2016	−0.689*** (−0.054)	−0.675*** (−0.054)
	Year = 2017	−0.768*** (−0.054)	−0.765*** (−0.054)
	Year = 2018	−0.745*** (−0.052)	−0.740*** (−0.052)
	Year = 2019	−0.770*** (−0.050)	−0.771*** (−0.051)
Group mean	Cash flow / net sales		−1.157*** (−0.326)
	Interest expenses / EBITDA		0.543*** (−0.101)
	Constant	−1.917*** (−0.068)	−1.982*** (−0.075)
	Observations	160,171	160,171

Standard errors in parentheses; *** $p < 0.01$, ** $p < 0.05$, * $p < 0.1$

5 Conclusions

In this Chapter we explored two types of improvement of the S-ICAS model. The first one consists in incorporating the effects of macroeconomic conditions into the model to improve its accuracy through the business cycle. We find that the mean square error of the macroeconomic model is four times smaller than that of S-ICAS. This allows for the inclusion of the effects of the business cycle in S-ICAS PDs with greater accuracy. We also find that developing sectoral macroeconomic models may further improve the PDs' sensitivity to cyclical conditions.

The second experiment consists in applying a panel econometric approach for S-ICAS to fully exploit the heterogeneity of firms' behaviour and discuss the options to address the constraints that have so far prevented its application. We experiment a panel regression on two out of the fourteen S-ICAS sub-models and the preliminary results show a small improvement in discriminatory power. Further investigation of the robustness and economic significance of these results for all the sub-models of S-ICAS is warranted.

Appendix A

Analysis of the Variables

The macroeconomic dataset consists of the variables identified as key drivers of the average default rate in the literature (Table 4.8),[29] observed from 2011Q1 to 2023Q3 and forecasted until 2025Q4.

Table 4.8 Macroeconomic variables. Identification and sources

Variables	Id	Source
Harmonized index of consumer prices	IPCA	*Bank of Italy*
GDP deflator	DEF	*Bank of Italy*
Real GDP	RGDP	*Bank of Italy*
Unemployment rate	UMP	*Bank of Italy*
Per capita productivity	PROD	*Bank of Italy*
Current account balance	SALDO_CC	*Bank of Italy*
Average interest rate on non-financial corporate loans	TCR	*Bank of Italy*
House Price index	HPI	*Bank of Italy*
Brent crude oil Price in USD	BRENTEU	*FRED St. Louis*
Euro-Dollar exchange rate	EXUSEU	*ECB SDW*
Credit conditions tightening index for Italian firms	CREDIT_ST	*ECB SDW*
Change in credit demand index for Italian firms	CREDIT_DEM	*ECB SDW*
Economic policy uncertainty index	EPU	*EPU*

Note: all data from Bank of Italy come from the Bank of Italy Economic Bulletin 4/2023. EPU is derived from Baker et al. (2016). ECB-SDW stands for Statistical Data Warehouse, the data repository of the ECB as FRED St. Louis is the one of the Federal Reserve Bank

The univariate analysis involves tests for the stationarity of the time series, searching for seasonality and structural breaks and identifying the data generating process (DGP). Based on the univariate analysis, we find that some variables are

[29] See e.g. Bofondi and Ropele (2011), Simons and Rolwes (2018), Moscatelli et al. (2019), Bonaccorsi di Patti and Cascarino (2020).

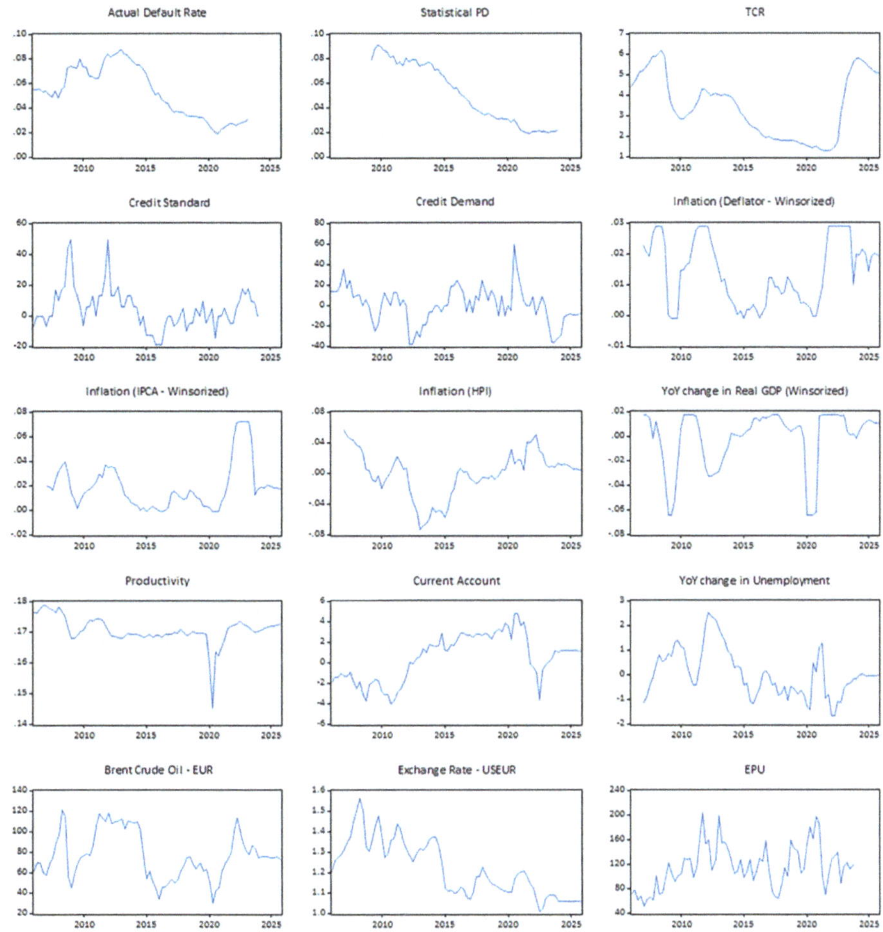

Fig. 4.3 Macroeconomic variables. (Source: Bank of Italy)

stationary while others are integrated.[30] Fig. 4.3 shows the trends of the variables, reported in first differences for non-stationary variables.

The graphical inspection of the real variables, such as the inflation rate (calculated with the deflator and with the IPCA) and the GDP growth rate, shows significant peaks and troughs. These values have to be treated as outliers to avoid distorted estimates. Therefore, we winsorize the three variables with a subscript W

[30] The non-stationary variables are real GDP, the three inflation rates computed by three indicators (i.e. IPCA, GDP deflator and House Price Index). The variables with a structural break are the unemployment rate, interest rate on loans to non-financial firms.

in Fig. 4.3.[31] For the inflation rate, the primary correction occurs in the most recent period following the price increases triggered by the post-COVID-19 recovery, but especially by supply shocks resulting from the Russian aggression to Ukraine. For the GDP growth rate, the main corrections occur after the disruption of the production due to the COVID-19 lockdown and the subsequent rebound. Besides, we winsorize the change in credit interest rate, using twice the standard deviation as the threshold value.

We employ multivariate analysis to spot the presence of correlation and covariance between variables. In analysing correlation, we observe positive and significant correlation between the dependent variable (DEF_RATE) and the ICAS Statistical PD, credit interest rate (also significantly correlated with ICAS Statistical PD), BRENT price (positively and statistically correlated with both ICAS Statistical PD and credit rate), credit access conditions (significantly correlated with credit interest rate and with low significance to ICAS Statistical PD), unemployment rate, per capita productivity, and inflation calculated with the deflator. Instead, there is a negative correlation for demand variables, such as house price inflation (significantly correlated with ICAS Statistical PD and credit rate) and current account balance and credit demand variations.

We tend to exclude variables that, although correlated with the default rate, present a correlation exceeding 70 per cent.[32] Second, we observe a positive monotonic relationship between the default rate with ICAS Statistical PD (Fig. 4.4) the credit access index change, the unemployment rate, and the euro-dollar exchange rate. Conversely, variables with a negative trend are the change in the index of credit demand and house price inflation. In this case, the trend also reflects expectations regarding the relationship between supply and demand variables with the default rate.

Following the univariate and multivariate analysis, we select the following regressors: the change in the index of credit demand with a two-quarter lag; the interest rate on credit with a two-quarter lag; the real GDP change with a four-quarter lag. We estimate the model on the central 75 per cent of the sample, from 2012Q3 to 2019Q3, to avoid possible structural breaks during the COVID-19 period.

The in-sample goodness of fit of the FM-OLS model is more than satisfactory, excluding serial correlation and cointegration among the residuals.[33] Fig. 4.5 illustrates the predictive capacity out-of-sample, the 2011Q2-2012Q2 and 2022Q1-2022Q4 periods.[34]

Figure 4.6 illustrates the results of the in-sample and out-of-sample estimation (2011Q2 - 2012Q2 and from 2022 Q1 to 2022 Q4 in this case), as well as the

[31] Winsorization is a statistical procedure that consist of substituting a variable extreme values with those of a specific percentile. It is common to use as threshold values the 5° and 95° percentile.

[32] Threshold already adopted in the S-ICAS model.

[33] The Engle-Granger test rejects the hypothesis of cointegration.

[34] We exclude the Covid period to not bias the results.

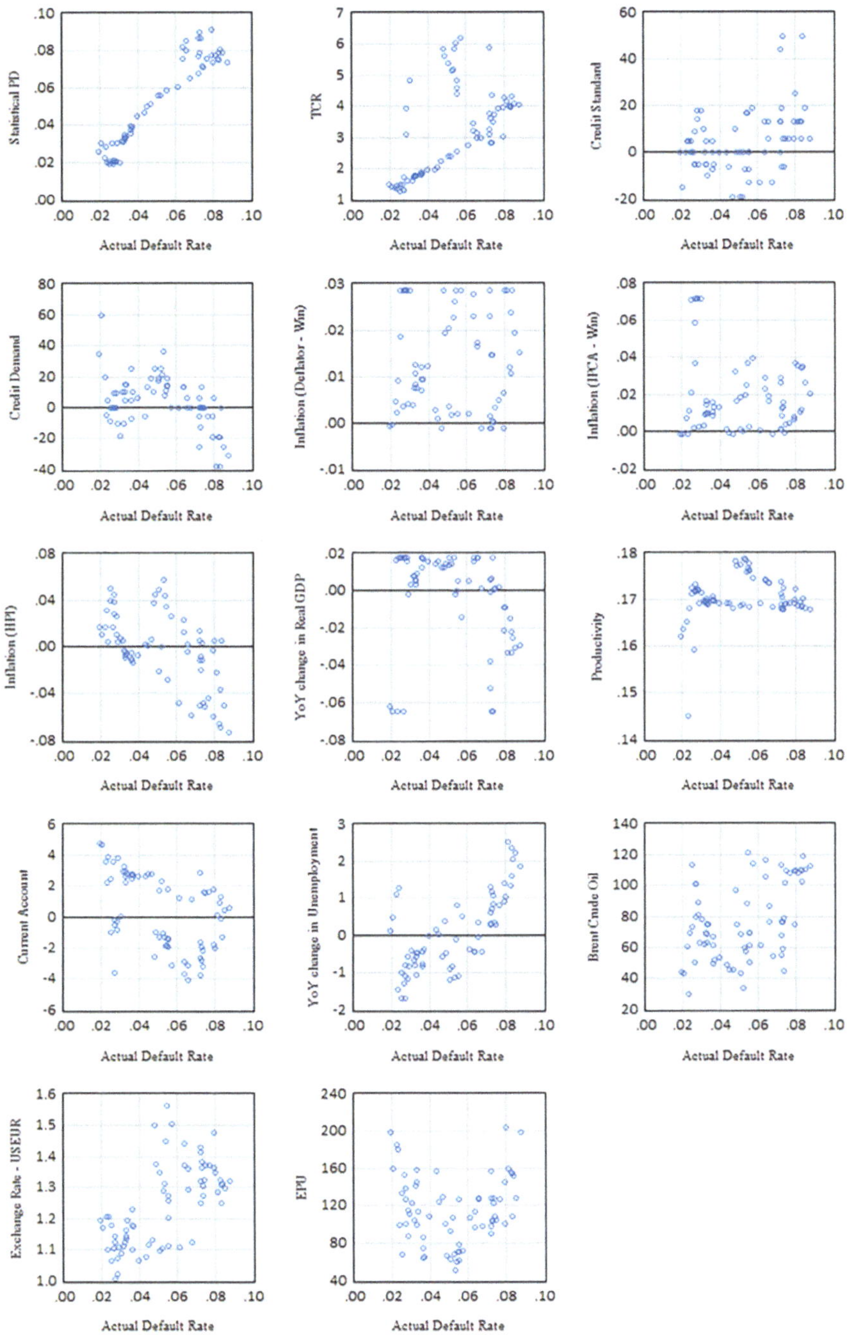

Fig. 4.4 Scatterplot XY, ICAS default rate versus exogenous variables. Each graph plots the candidate regressor against the dependent variable. The goal is to observe whether there is a monotonic relationship. If this is the case, the candidate regressor is considered. (Source: Bank of Italy)

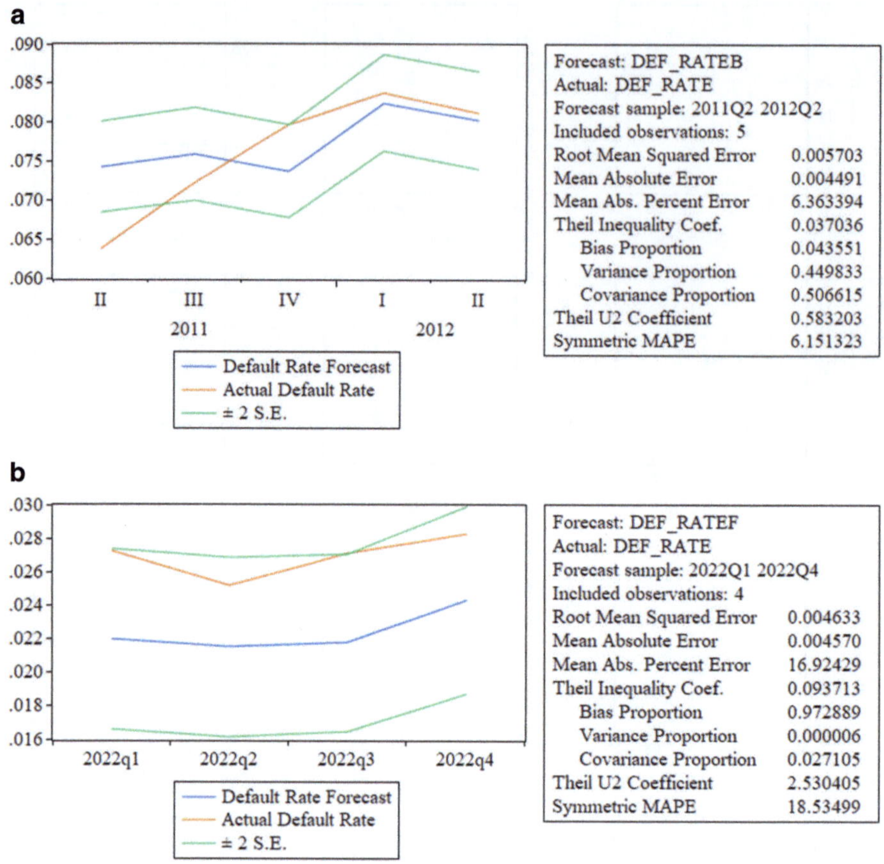

Fig. 4.5 Out-of-sample estimates. **a** Out-of-sample estimates for the period 2011Q2-2012Q2 **b** Out-of-sample estimates for the period 2022Q1-2022Q4. The blue line is the forecasted default rate (DEF_RATE_B), the brown line the actual default (Actuals), the green lines are the confidence bands at 95 per cent. (Source: Bank of Italy)

forecast up to 2023Q4. Except for the COVID-19 period, the estimated value of the ICAS default rate is close to the actual default rate, and the prediction metrics are satisfactory.

Appendix B

The Constraints on the Use of Panel Techniques in S-ICAS

Logistic regressions within S-ICAS are pooled logit models that consider repeated observations of the same firm over time as independent. The estimation does not consider the longitudinal nature of the data. When dealing with longitudinal data,

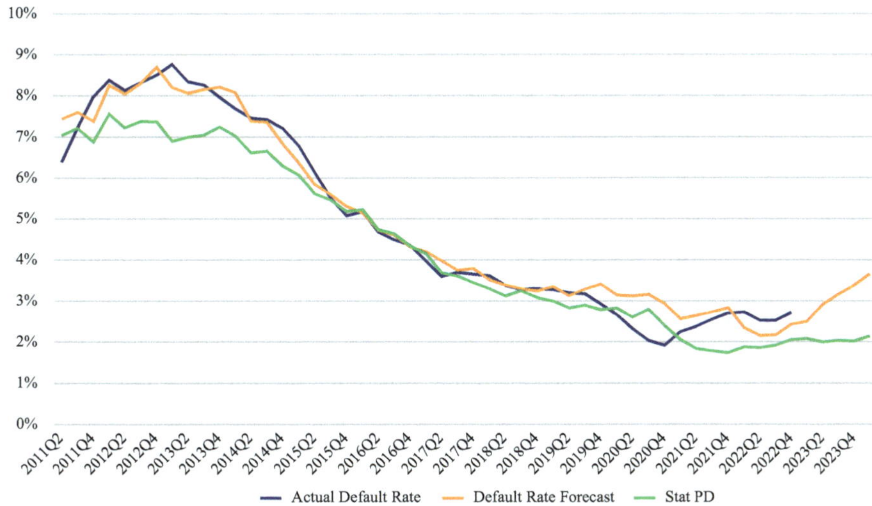

Fig. 4.6 Results of the estimation of the FM-OLS model in-sample, out-of-sample, and forecast

panel techniques can capture possible correlations between independent variables and unobserved time-invariant variables, enabling consistent estimates of model coefficients. However, panel techniques for PD estimation within S-ICAS face two types of problems: one related to the model structure and another related to its purposes.

Regarding the model structure, the existence of the two components described in Chap. 3 would not yield consistent estimators of the coefficients within each component, not even using panel estimators. In each model, there are omitted variables not fixed in time and correlated with independent variables, causing an omitted variable bias. In the financial component, the error term includes the NCR variables that are correlated with some of the financial statement variables. For example, a greater incidence of the ratio between credit drawn and granted (an NCR variable) is generally accompanied by a greater importance of debt in the financial statement, with effects in terms of capitalization and sustainability indicators (net equity on net financial position, revenues on financial debt, cash on short-term debt, financial charges on EBITDA). This causes a bias in the estimation of the coefficients of the financial component. The NCR component of S-ICAS faces the same problem.

S-ICAS estimates one-year ahead PDs. Since default is a binary variable, traditionally models used for PD estimation are logit or probit. The main estimators used in the panel literature for binary logit or probit models are of three types: panel models with random effects; panel models with fixed effects; and panel models with correlated random effects.

A binary panel model with random effects, unlike pooled logit, correctly identifies observations of the same firm over time as belonging to the same entity.

However, it assumes that the fixed unobserved effect of the firm and the independent variables of the model are independent. With this assumption, unobserved effects are generally modelled as random variables which, conditional on the independent variables of the model, are distributed according to a normal distribution with zero mean. This implies that, if we were to use this estimator, we could not take into account the likely correlation between a firm's fixed effect and the independent variables of S-ICAS.

A binary panel model with fixed effects is applicable only to a logit model[35] and in the estimation it considers only firms that appear both in default and in non-default status. Indeed, this estimator takes into account the variability in the response (a binary default variable) within the observations of each firm. If there is no variability, i.e. if the firm in the sample is always in default or it is never in default, the observations related to this firm have no weight in the estimation phase.[36] Since the number of defaults is very low (less than five percent in the estimation sample), such an estimator would only consider few observations and would thus be imprecise. There is also a second issue with the fixed effects logit estimator. In fact, unlike the linear fixed effects estimator, for a logit estimator it is not possible to estimate the value of the unobserved fixed effect even for firms in the estimation sample.[37] Since the PD of a firm also depends on the value of the corresponding fixed effect, such an estimator may not be used by ICAS, which seeks to calculate default probabilities.

A binary panel model with correlated random effects models the unobserved effects of a firm as a linear function of the average of the independent variables associated with the firm over time. Thus, it estimates the corresponding fixed effect for each firm in the sample. Moreover, during the estimation, the observations related to firms that are never in default or always in default are also considered (unlike in the fixed effects logit estimator). However, this estimator has also a drawback. S-ICAS calculates new default probabilities every month on a sample of

[35] The probit model suffers from the incidental parameter problem. By treating the fixed effects as parameters to be estimated, the obtained estimators of the coefficients are not consistent, i.e. they do not converge in probability.

[36] To obtain consistent estimators, it is necessary to eliminate the fixed effects from the likelihood function of each firm, since otherwise we would fall into the incidental parameter problem. This is possible in logit models thanks to the particular functional form of the logistic function, which determines for each firm a conditional likelihood function, both with respect to the fixed effects and with respect to the number of defaults the firm has in the sample, that does not depend on the value of fixed effects. However, if the firm in the sample is always in default or if it is never in default, the state of the firm is not random, but is completely determined. Therefore, observations relating to those firms do not contribute to the maximization of the overall likelihood and to the estimation of the coefficients.

[37] As explained in the previous note, the estimation of the coefficients is obtained by maximizing a conditional likelihood function, which does not depend on fixed effects. Therefore, with this methodology it is not possible to obtain estimators of firms' unobserved effects. If we tried to maximize an unconditional likelihood function, in which fixed effects appear, we would fall into the incidental parameter problem.

firms partially different from that of the previous months. On average, over 2,000 firms that have never been evaluated before enter the sample each month. This turnover is due to both the establishment of new firms and the fact that existing firms may exceed the NCR reporting threshold for the first time, a requirement for inclusion in the S-ICAS sample. For these firms there is no time series of NCR variables to calculate the average over time of the variables and estimate the fixed effects. Since the estimation of fixed effects is necessary for calculating default probabilities under correlated random effects, it would not be possible to calculate a PD for firms that have never been evaluated before. To overcome this problem, the fixed effect of a new firm could be estimated by determining a group of similar firms and using the average over time of the variables of firms that belong to this group. This methodology has been tested as part of a preliminary analysis and we obtained a small improvement in the discriminatory power (see Sect. 4.4).

In the credit scoring literature, the use of panel logistic regression is not very common, but, when used, fixed effects estimates are rarely encountered, except in studies that employ static and balanced samples. In some cases, a theoretical framework is proposed for the dynamic assessment of creditworthiness in credit scoring, using models with random effects for static and balanced samples.[38] In other cases, a panel logit regression with fixed effects is applied, but the estimation occurs only once, the sample is not dynamic, and it is balanced.[39] In other cases, random effects logistic regressions are used to estimate the models, but the study is theoretical and may not be replicated over time, unlike the case of S-ICAS.[40]

Based on our investigation, the estimators present the following issues regarding their application to S-ICAS. The random effects estimator would not bring appreciable benefits to S-ICAS due to the assumption of independence between unobserved effects and independent variables. The fixed effects estimator would not allow the calculation of default probabilities. The correlated random effects estimator, for firms never evaluated so far, could produce default probabilities only using estimated fixed effects of similar firms. This would imply a monthly dependence of the evaluations of more than 2,000 firms on data related to other firms.

The correlated random effects estimator could be implemented within S-ICAS. However, since preliminary tests showed a small improvement in the discriminatory power with respect to the pooled logit model, further analyses are required.

[38] Bijak et al. (2013), Erdogan (2016).

[39] Berg et al. (2019); Bandyopadhyay (2006).

[40] Carvalho et al. (2022).

Appendix C

Validation

In this study we are interested in validating the proposed models. We seek to verify whether they bring improvements and, if so, whether the improvements are robust. Furthermore, in choosing the validation tests, we use the same procedures as those approved in the ECAF. We validate the models with regard to discriminatory power, predictive power, and performance stability.

For the assessment of the discriminatory power, see the validation procedure described in Chap. 3.

For predictive power, the validation procedure should investigate if the new models are closer to reality, concerning default frequencies in each risk class. Therefore, in line with the ECAF, we adopt the TLA first, to obtain granular information.

The purpose of the TLA test is to verify the ability of a rating system to provide predicted defaults that are larger than realized defaults. This approach applies a multiple one-tail binomial test. For every risk class, a binomial distribution has an average value equal to the predicted defaults. It is possible to define two different thresholds on the binomial distribution, one (yellow) smaller than the other (red). If realized defaults are larger than the yellow threshold, but smaller than the red threshold, then a monitoring procedure is run. If realized defaults are larger than the red threshold, then an alarm procedure is run, to fix the issues. These procedures are performed even with only one critical rating class. Otherwise, if realized defaults are smaller than the yellow threshold, the rating system is in a "green area", and no monitoring/correction procedures are performed.

The TLA aims to verify the conservatism of a rating system, compared to the accuracy of the underlying model. For the sake of clarity, "rating system" refers to the combined i) statistical model, which assigns a firm to a risk class based on statistical PD, and ii) the rule whereby the firm is then assigned the upper extreme PD of that risk class; "model" refers to the underlying model, which assigns the "statistical" PD. Therefore, the rating system assigns each firm a "base" PD and adds a prudential buffer. In general, in terms of predictive power, a desirable rating system is one that i) is based on an accurate model, where predicted defaults statistically match actual defaults; and ii) adjusts the model's PDs in a simple and conservative manner, but not too drastically.

The TLA could approve a rating system based on a model that is already conservative and that, due to the adjustment of PDs to the upper extreme, could in the future prove to be excessively prudent (assigning firms to a higher risk class than the correct one). Similarly, the TLA could approve a rating system that starts from a model that is inherently lenient and that, despite the adjustment of PDs to the upper extreme, could in the future prove to be not sufficiently prudent (assigning firms to a lower risk class than the correct one).

In addition to the TLA, validation can also apply multiple binomial tests based on average PDs and double tails. We also carry out this type of analysis, which confirms the results reported in the main text. For the sake of brevity, we do not report the related evidence.

References

Abaidoo, R. (2018). Loan delinquency and macroeconomic conditions: An ARDL and error correction approach. *Am J Bus, 33*(3), 82–95.

ABI-Cerved (2023) Aumentano npl, in 2023 livelli oltre pre-Covid. https://www.abi.it/abi-cerved-aumentano-npl-in-2023-livelli-oltre-pre-covid/

Baker, S. R., Bloom, N., & Davis, S. J. (2016). Measuring economic policy uncertainty. *Quarterly Journal of Economics, 131*(4), 1593–1636.

Bandyopadhyay, A. (2006). Predicting probability of default of Indian corporate bonds: Logistic and Z-score model approaches. *J Risk Finance, 7*(3), 255–272.

Bank of Italy (2023) Financial Stability Report, No. 2, November.

Berg, T., Burg, V., Gombovic, A., & Puri, M. (2019). On the rise of fintechs: Credit scoring using digital footprints. *Review of Financial Studies, 33*(7), 2845–2897.

Bijak K, Thomas L, Mues C (2013) Assessing affordability using random effects models of income and consumption growth. Credit scoring and credit control XIII conference, Edinburgh, United Kingdom, 27–29 Aug 2013.

Bocchio, C., Crook, J., & Andreeva, G. (2023). The impact of macroeconomic scenarios on recurrent delinquency: A stress testing framework of multi-state models for mortgages. *International Journal of Forecasting, 39*(4), 1655–1677.

Bofondi, M., & Ropele, T. (2011). Macroeconomic determinants of bad loans: Evidence from Italian banks. *Bank of Italy Occasional Pap, 89.*

Bonaccorsi di Patti, E., & Cascarino, G. (2020). Modelling the dynamics of nonperforming loans in Italy. *Bank of Italy Notes on Financial Stability and Supervision, 19.*

Carvalho, P., Curto, J. D., & Primor, R. (2022). Macroeconomic determinants of credit risk: Evidence from the eurozone. *Int J Finance Econ, 27*(2), 2054–2072.

Chan-Lau, J. A. (2006). Fundamentals-based estimation of default probabilities: A survey. *IMF Work Pap, 149.*

De Socio A, Narizzano S, Orlando T, Parlapiano F, Rodano G, Sette E, Viggiano G (2020) The effects of the Covid-19 shock on corporates' liquidity needs, balance sheets and riskiness. Bank of Italy Covid-19 notes 13.

Erdogan, B. E. (2016). Long-term examination of bank crashes using panel logistic regression: Turkish banks failure case. *Int J Stat Probab, 5*(3), 42–48.

Jarrow, R. A. (2009). Credit risk models. *Annual Review of Financial Economics, 1*(1), 37–68.

Klamargias, A., Petropoulos, A., Siakoulis, V., & Mylonas, D. (2018). A combined statistical framework for forecasting default rates of Greek financial institutions' credit portfolios. *Bank of Greece Work Pap, 243.*

Moscatelli, M., Parlapiano, F., Narizzano, S., & Viggiano, G. (2020). Corporate default forecasting with machine learning. *Expert Systems with Applications, 161*, 11356.

Phillips, P. C. B. (1995). Fully modified least squares and vector autoregression. *Econometrica, 63*(5), 1023–1078.

Simons, D., & Rolwes, F. (2018). Macroeconomic default modeling and stress testing. *International Journal of Central Banking, 5*(3), 177–204.

Stein, R. (2007). Benchmarking default prediction models: Pitfalls and remedies in model validation. *J Risk Model Valid, 1*(1), 77–113.

Visco I (2019) Corporate finance in Italy: Recent developments and future prospects. Speech of the Bank of Italy governor at the conference on the Italian corporate bond market: What's happening to the capital structure of Italian non-financial companies?, Milan.

The Expert Assessment

Lorenzo Esposito, Massimo Guglielmi, Francesco Monterisi, Simone Narizzano, and Marco Orlandi

1 Introduction

As discussed in chapter "The Statistical Model", the Bank of Italy's ICAS consists of two components: (i) the statistical model, covering a broad sample of Italian firms, and (ii) the expert assessment, applied to the subsample of the most significant firms for collateral purposes. The structure of ICAS reflects a common approach in the banking and finance industry. Statistical models, valued for their objectivity, scalability, and reliance on historical data, offer speed and consistency in credit assessment. However, they may fall short of capturing forward-looking variables or incorporating qualitative factors. The expert assessment, described in detail in this chapter, introduces a forward-looking perspective and qualitative judgement, helping to address the limitations of purely statistical approaches, albeit at the cost of increased subjectivity.

At the Bank of Italy, the expert assessment is carried out by two credit analysts who may either confirm the rating obtained from the statistical model (the

L. Esposito
Bank of Italy, Milan Branch, Milan, Italy
e-mail: lorenzo.esposito@bancaditalia.it

M. Guglielmi · F. Monterisi (✉) · S. Narizzano · M. Orlandi
Bank of Italy, Financial Risk Management Directorate, Rome, Italy
e-mail: francesco.monterisi@bancaditalia.it

M. Guglielmi
e-mail: massimo.guglielmi@bancaditalia.it

S. Narizzano
e-mail: simone.narizzano@bancaditalia.it

M. Orlandi
e-mail: m.orlandi@bancaditalia.it

A. Scalia (ed.), *Corporate Credit Analysis and AI*, Finance for Professionals,
https://doi.org/10.1007/978-3-032-13422-6_5

'statistical rating') or revise it upward or downward. Starting from the statistical rating, the analysts independently review the main characteristics of the firm (size, business sector, geographical location, etc.) along with the variables underlying the statistical assessment; they then assess a set of predefined risk profiles (also dubbed as 'assessment modules') and determine a score for each of them. Each score reflects whether the analyst believes that an individual module improves, confirms, or worsens the risk assessment of the statistical model. The module scores are subsequently weighted and aggregated to determine the final rating, also dubbed as the 'full rating'. If the two analysts broadly agree and their assessment does not lead to a major improvement vis-à-vis the statistical rating, the process stops. Otherwise, the rating proposal is submitted for further review to the Rating committee, composed of senior staff members, that takes the final decision.

This chapter has two aims. First, it illustrates the expert assessment framework and its recent methodological developments, including the integration of climate-related risks and major changes in sector analysis. Second, it provides evidence on the value added by the expert assessment to the whole credit evaluation process. The current methodology benefits from improvements carried out over time to increase the homogeneity, reliability, and transparency of the qualitative credit assessment conducted by the analysts. In particular, a comprehensive review was carried out in 2023.

An internal validation exercise performed before the review of the methodology showed that the expert assessment had significantly enhanced the discriminatory power, the predictive power and the stability of the statistical model. Specifically, over the review period the AUROC had improved by nearly 2 percentage points, from 85.3 to 87%. Furthermore, the expert assessment had introduced some degree of conservatism, thus strengthening the robustness of the system during periods of heightened uncertainty, such as financial crises or abrupt macroeconomic shifts.

Our validation results, as well as the substantial enhancement under the current version, suggest that the gains of the expert assessment have significantly increased compared with the estimates presented in this chapter. We will compute an empirical estimation of the value added by the current methodology once an adequate statistical sample will be available.

The remainder of the Chapter is organized as follows: Sect. 2 reviews the best practices in the credit risk industry; Sect. 3 describes the ICAS expert assessment model in its current version; Sect. 4 describes the main findings from the internal validation exercise as applied to the previous version of the expert assessment, which was employed until 2023; Sect. 5 discusses how analysts can deal with emerging risk categories, like ESG risks and geopolitical risks; Sect. 6 concludes.

2 The Expert Assessment of Credit Risk

Counterparty credit risk is the primary source of risk in banking operations, as noted e.g. by the Basel Committee and national banking regulators (BCBS, 2024). The development of a robust credit rating system is thus of paramount importance for each financial institution as well as for the financial system. To this end, credit risk service providers and lenders managing credit risk systems have established comprehensive databases, tools, and procedures that collectively define credit risk management activities. Corporate credit analysis is centred around the company's structural ability to generate income and service its debt.

The practice of corporate credit analysis generally relies on common components as concerns input data and models. Ratings are usually updated annually, in accordance with the fiscal year, as a market and regulatory standard (BCBS, 2015). Major credit risk agencies (CRAs) manage a range of models, because ratings cannot be applied uniformly to borrowers of different size or from different sectors (Garcia Alcubilla & Ruiz del Pozo, 2012). Pro-cyclicality and reputational risks may affect ratings (Amato & Furfine, 2003). Markets and financial players have long valued the comparability and the general clarity of CRA ratings. The use of these ratings for regulatory purposes increased in the 1990s, in the run-up to the great financial crisis (EU, 2009).

The CRAs' rating methodology is based on two components: a quantitative model and a qualitative assessment. The output of the quantitative model results from the integration of a few predictive variables of the default event and serves as the starting point for the rating process. The qualitative assessment incorporates expert and market views, based on general guidelines. The qualitative assessment is even more important for large corporates and in the current international economic and financial context marked by exceptional uncertainty (Ballis et al., 2024). CRAs prioritize sector risk as it helps understand the outlook for the corporation and its competitive environment. Governance and group structure are also examined, owing to their effect on corporate strategy, business model, transparency, and integrity. Rating agencies carry out due diligence and meetings with the firm's top management as part of the qualitative assessment of the company. The rating is accompanied by an 'outlook', that shows the likely direction of the rating over the medium term, i.e. in twelve months time.[1]

IRB models managed by banks are subject to certain requirements to be eligible for regulatory purposes, at the outset and on an ongoing basis.[2] Like CRAs' models, IRB methodologies: (i) vary significantly with firm size[3]; (ii) include a quantitative component and a qualitative assessment; (iii) share the same input data. However, IRB models have a comparative advantage over CRAs because banks own a richer information set concerning payment flows, which is particularly important in the case of SMEs.

[1] As for banks, our second source of ratings, in the 1990s, several major financial institutions developed advanced credit risk models such as CreditMetrics (J.P. Morgan) and CreditRisk+ (Crédit Suisse), that have since become market standards, and, with Basel II, also regulatory standards (Gallo, 2021).

[2] See BCBS (2001) and EBA (2017).

[3] For instance, transactional behaviour detected from current account flows is less important for large corporates than SMEs.

CRAs faced significant criticism after the Enron and WorldCom scandals, and even more so following the 2008 financial crisis, with accusations of lax rating standards and potential conflicts of interest (Alp, 2013). The credibility of CRAs rating models was questioned (deHaan, 2017) due also to increased competition (Becker & Milbourn, 2011). Standard setters observed that supervisors should be cautious against over-reliance on internal models for credit risk management (BIS, 2015). More recently, geopolitical factors may have contributed to cyclicality in credit ratings, with data indicating optimistic ratings during risky periods, linked to conflict-of-interest issues (Singhal et al., 2024).

3 Methodology

3.1 General Principles and New Features

The ICAS rating methodology follows a two-stage approach that combines a statistical model with the expert assessment. The statistical model is described in detail in chapter "The Statistical Model".

The expert assessment involves the financial analysts' assessment of credit risk with a forward-looking perspective, employing a wide range of information sources. The analysis can either confirm the rating obtained from the statistical model or revise it upward or downward.

In particular, two credit analysts review the statistical rating employing quantitative data and qualitative information. Each analyst independently evaluates predefined assessment modules that capture firm-specific features (financial statement, financial flexibility, business sector, governance, etc.). They assign a score to each module based on their evaluation of the firm's creditworthiness, in comparison with the statistical rating. These scores are then weighted and aggregated to obtain the full rating.

The Bank of Italy has identified several principles and desirable properties for the expert assessment methodology:

- objectivity and credibility: credit ratings must be perceived as reliable and trustworthy by all users;
- quality, completeness, and integrity: the methodology should encompass all key factors affecting default risk. The data used in developing credit ratings must be of high quality and sourced from reliable providers;
- transparency and disclosure: the methodology should guide analysts through a clear and traceable decision-making process[4];

[4] Each phase of the credit assessment should be consistently and transparently reflected in the full rating. Any deviation from the general methodology should be explained and justified using a 'comply or explain' approach.

- homogeneity: the rating process should ensure a uniform treatment of information to maintain consistency across analysts and over time[5];
- robustness: the weighting of the qualitative and quantitative stages should be based on robust analysis, ideally grounded in observed data and/or aligned with industry best practices;
- flexibility: the rating process should allow analysts to address all potential business idiosyncrasies without being constrained by overly rigid rules.[6]

Following the internal review conducted in 2023, several improvements have been introduced in 2024 to improve the quality and consistency of expert assessments. Structured questionnaires (or checklists) have been developed to guide analysts through the evaluation of each risk profile. This ensures a more comprehensive and consistent assessment of all relevant risk factors, reducing the possibility of omissions or subjective biases. A Bayesian aggregation methodology now combines the partial scores attributed to each risk area. This provides analysts with a coherent statistical framework that supports final decisions (to confirm, upgrade, or downgrade the initial model-based rating) based on the overall assessment derived from the single profiles modules.

Analysts may preliminarily adjust the statistical PD by changing some predictive variables or adding new ones, where justified by firm-specific accounting practices or data peculiarities (e.g. finance leasing not included in financial debt according to Italian GAAP financial statements). Sector and group analyses have been strengthened to better capture a firm's competitive position within its economic sector and its financial interlinkages within the group.[7] The coverage of risk profiles has been expanded, with the inclusion of climate-related risks in line with evolving standards for integrating sustainability considerations into credit assessments.

3.2 Procedure

The expert assessment procedure is organized into the following steps, which analysts are required to perform sequentially through the dedicated modules that capture firm-specific characteristics (Fig. 1):

---

[5] Similar business cases should be evaluated in a homogeneous manner to support comparability and methodological coherence.

[6] The value added of qualitative assessment often lies in the ability to integrate subjective or 'soft' information that is typically not included in statistical models. However, the exercise of such flexibility should be properly documented and consistently monitored throughout the rating process.

[7] If the company is affiliated to a group, we estimate the intensity of the interlinkages within the group and establish the impact of the creditworthiness of the parent company at a consolidated level.

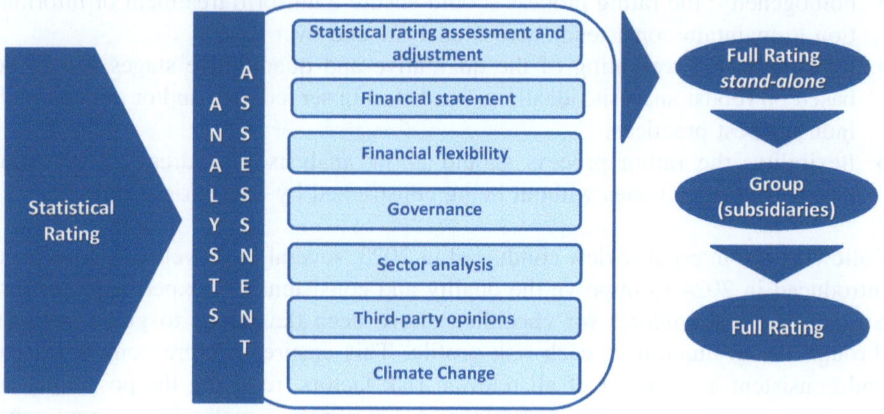

Fig. 1 The expert assessment procedure

- initial statistical rating adjustment;
- financial statement (module1);
- financial flexibility (module 2);
- governance (module 3);
- sector analysis (module 4);
- third-party opinions (module 5);
- climate change (module 6);
- overall assessment and stand-alone full rating;
- for subsidiaries only: group analysis (module 7) and full rating.

For each module the analysts assign a score (the 'module score') on a five-point scale: very positive, positive, neutral, negative, and very negative, corresponding to the cardinal values +2, +1, 0, −1, and −2, respectively. These scores result from the aggregation of the answers given by the analysts to the checklist for each module. The answers are standardized on the same five-point scale as above.

The stand-alone rating is obtained by means of the Bayesian integration of the scores assigned to modules 1–6 (see section "Overall Assessment and Stand-Alone Full Rating"). In the case of subsidiaries, in module 7, an adjustment to the stand-alone rating may be made based on the strength of the interlinkages with the group and the creditworthiness of the parent company.

Automated aggregation criteria ensure consistency across different analyses. However, analysts may override both the scores and the stand-alone rating, provided that such deviations are properly explained.

The expert assessment is carried out in sequential steps by two different analysts; in specific cases, the rating committee reviews the assessment and makes the final decision on the full rating. The first analyst assesses the modules. Every score is accompanied by an explanation; this should be sufficiently detailed to allow the second analyst and, possibly, the rating committee[8] to check the motivation. The second analyst reviews and double-checks the coherence of the analysis performed by the first analyst, under a four-eyes approach.

Initial Statistical Rating Adjustment

The expert assessment starts by reviewing the quality and consistency of the input data for the statistical rating. This step serves also to integrate any additional information obtained by the analysts through their own research on the firm (financial reports, NCR and Analytical Credit data, non-financial reports—NFR) that may lead to a revision of the statistical rating. The assessment of the financial statement component concerns: financial leases, cash and cash equivalents, non-recurring items in the income statement, dividends, interest expenses, hybrid shareholders' loans. The assessment of the credit behaviour component involves average utilization rates and financial distress variables (see Appendix A for details). The statistical rating resulting from the initial adjustment made by the analysts is the starting point for the expert assessment.

Financial Statement

Financial statement analysis involves the examination of a broader set of indicators than those considered by the statistical model. This module includes peer group analysis and any other new information (e.g., infra-annual reporting) with a forward-looking perspective. The empirical literature confirms the role of financial ratios towards the prediction of firm default.[9]

Financial statement analysis covers four aspects: (i) profitability; (ii) capital adequacy and financial structure; (iii) debt sustainability; (iv) liquidity and cash generation.[10]

The corresponding sections include a broad set of indicators available over the last four financial years, accompanied by a quintile-based classification in the peer group of companies (Fig. 2).

The first analyst notes the elements obtained from financial reporting and any other useful information. The first and second analyst fill out independently a checklist. Each answer is weighted, contributing to the module score. This can be reviewed by both analysts. Once the assessment is completed, the procedure weights equally to the profile scores to yield an overall score of the financial

---

[8] The rating committee is composed of senior managers within the Financial Risk Management Directorate. The analysts involved in the assessment are also required to attend the committee meeting. The Committee is responsible for the review of the ratings that involve significant financial and/or reputational risks. It also acts as the decision-making body in case of discrepancies between the ratings put forward by the two analysts. The Committee takes the final decision, which can involve a rating upgrade of more than 1 notch.

[9] Modigliani and Miller (1958) and Altman (1968).

[10] The web-based platform automatically provides analysts with detailed information on financial reporting data (balance sheet, income, cash-flow statement, etc.) to facilitate their assessment.

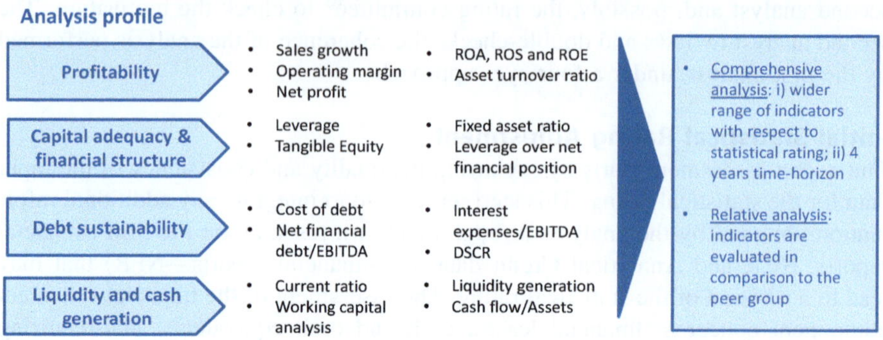

Fig. 2 Financial statement

statement module. The final score can be reviewed by both analysts, enabling them to reach independent conclusions.

Financial Flexibility

As part of the financial flexibility module, the analysts evaluate the company's ability to mitigate the negative impact on financial resources of external shocks relating to the economic cycle or of internal shocks linked to its own activity. The assessment involves an in-depth analysis of the NCR dataset and of additional information (Fig. 3).

The NCR dataset provides extensive information on different credit lines held by each firm. The dataset distinguishes three classes of loans: term loans, current account revolving credit lines, and accounts receivable revolving credit lines for both short term and medium to long-term credit lines. For each credit line, the

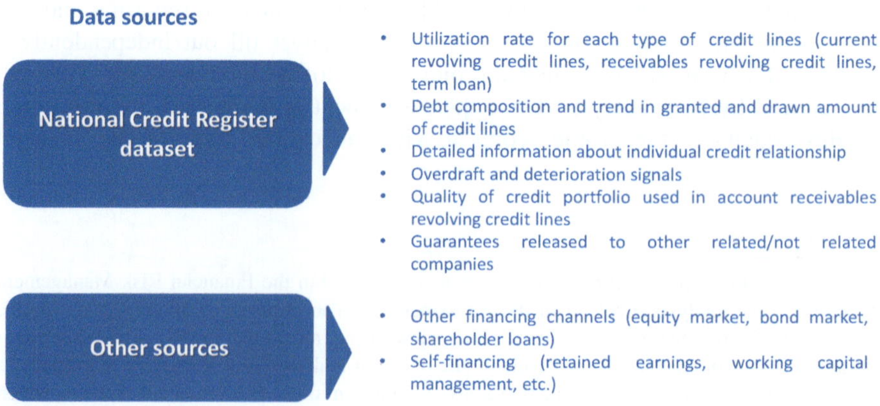

Fig. 3 Financial flexibility

dataset records drawn and undrawn amounts, excess and unauthorized overdrafts, and default classifications.

Several studies confirm the role of credit behaviour in discriminating between good and bad firms.[11] Credit line usage and excess overdraft are significant explanatory variables of default, especially for small business firms (Giannozzi et al., 2013; Norden & Weber, 2010). Additionally, past delinquencies are positively correlated with default (Gallucci et al., 2022). Firms with significant credit line usage may face liquidity issues, and high leverage or poor financial performance may hinder their ability to acquire additional funding (Zhao et al., 2014). The utilization rate for current account revolving credit lines and excess overdrafts are good in discriminating between non-defaulted and defaulted firms among Italian SMEs.

Analysts have access to the credit-related flows primarily from the NCR. This module automatically provides data covering the last 13 months. This information helps assess the relationship between the firm and the banking system, which is particularly important in Italy where firms, especially small ones, heavily rely on bank financing. Changes in the usage patterns of granted credit lines or the frequency of overdrafts are critical for identifying potential tensions in financial resources.

The analysis is structured along three sections, leading to the score on financial flexibility.

The first section contains NCR data on: (i) the amount drawn and granted for short-term credit lines according to different technical forms, such as current account revolving credit lines and accounts receivable revolving credit lines; (ii) the distribution of credit lines by maturity; (iii) detailed data on term loans and lease financing. The analysts assess the amount of undrawn short-term financing lines to check for sufficient financial flexibility in the event of a liquidity shortage. While the statistical model incorporates the used-to-granted-credit ratios, it does not account for the absolute amount of undrawn credit lines. Analysts therefore complement the statistical model's output by evaluating whether the residual availability on short-term credit lines is sufficient to absorb any temporary liquidity shortfall. They verify if the statistical model has correctly assessed the firm, considering that used-to-granted-credit ratios are already included in the statistical model. They also assess the adequacy of the firm's debt structure in relation to its net working capital and the evolution of financial leverage.

In the second section the analysts examine the quality of credit receivables and check for potential risks related to off-balance sheet guarantees issued by the firm and negative fair value on derivatives. Besides, the analysts assess whether the firm has actual or potential access to additional financing sources, such as private equity capital, debt and capital markets, the international banking system. The number of active banking relationships, the nature of the intermediaries (local vs big banks,

[11] Agarwal et al. (2006), Jiménez et al. (2009), and Sufi (2009).

factoring and leasing intermediaries, etc.), and their changes over time can provide additional insight.

The last section contains information on overdrafts and non-performing loans over the past 13 months. The analysts check whether a fractional default[12] has occurred using both NCR and AnaCredit sources.

Governance

The academic literature has long highlighted the importance of corporate governance in the context of corporate stability and efficiency.[13] Firms with better management practices tend to perform better: they are larger in scale, more profitable, have higher labour productivity, and are more likely to export (Bloom & Van Reenen, 2007). Strong corporate governance can also mitigate conflicts of interest between shareholders and company management, thus reducing risks for creditors. It also contributes to greater transparency and better disclosure of information, which are crucial elements for assessing credit risk (Diamond, 1984). Finally, the composition of the board of directors, particularly the presence of independent directors, strong internal control mechanisms and well-structured risk management correlate with a robust corporate governance (Anderson et al., 2004).

The analysis of this risk factor is conducted through a questionnaire (or checklist), to evaluate the key aspects of corporate governance, that are known to influence a firm's risk profile and creditworthiness. Factors such as stock exchange listing and adherence to governance codes of conduct signal transparency and external accountability. The structure and functioning of the board—especially the presence of independent directors, managerial competence, and internal committees—are viewed as indicators of effective oversight. Robust internal controls, including rules on conflicts of interest and related-party transactions, help reduce operational and reputational risks. The quality and transparency of financial reporting, along with the auditor's findings, are also considered as essential for the evaluation of the reliability of disclosed information. Adverse legal rulings, public controversies, and exposure to social risks are monitored as potential red flags. Overall, strong governance practices are viewed as a positive signal, enhancing the credibility of the firm's rating in addition to the results of quantitative models.

Based on the analysts' responses, the procedure computes the module risk score. The analysts may override the score, explaining the reason for the change in a specific comment line.

Sector Analysis

This module has three sections: (i) strategic positioning, (ii) country risk, and (iii) environmental risk. Based on the analysts' responses, a score is produced for each section.[14]

[12] For further details on the ICAS default definition see chapter "The Statistical Model".

[13] Jensen and Meckling (1976) and Shleifer and Vishny (1997).

[14] Environmental risks and opportunities are included in this area of the expert assessment because the exposure to environmental factors (i.e. Energy and Fuel Management, Air and water pollution,

With reference to strategic positioning, the analysts consider the conditions and potential evolution of the economic sector in which the company primarily operates, in view of the macroeconomic outlook. To support the analysis of the economic environment and industrial sectors, industry forecasts and other data are obtained from an external provider. The sector outlook is evaluated from both a structural and a forward-looking perspective. The analysts examine the company's positioning within the sector, considering factors such as market size/share, product differentiation, brand recognizability, innovation, and diversification of offerings. Additionally, the analysis encompasses broader sectoral dynamics, including the sensitivity of sector demand to macroeconomic trends, the sector's stage in its lifecycle, the intensity of competition, capital requirements, and the economies of scale.

The country risk section is applicable if net revenues produced abroad exceed 30% of total revenues. In this case, the score attribution is guided by a checklist and quantitative indicators obtained from external providers. These indicators measure the country's attractiveness in terms of export and investment opportunities, political and legal risks, and social situation.

The section relating to environmental risk assesses the possibility that the company business may cause (or be negatively affected by) environmental issues. The exposure to environmental factors is strictly related to the sector in which the firm operates. Examples include air, water, and soil pollution, loss of biodiversity, soil deterioration and habitat loss, and exposure to hazardous chemicals. The environmental risk questions address the company's exposure to environmental risks, its reliance on natural resources, the impact of its production processes, and its ability to operate sustainably. The analysts also consider reputational and legal risks arising from lack of corporate attention to environmental sustainability and their negative externalities. The analysts rely on sector-level opinions and scores produced by an external provider.

Finally, the overall risk score for this module is reviewed by the analysts. Similarly to the other modules, the analysts may override the overall score, providing the reason for the adjustment in a dedicated comment.

Third-Party Opinions

This module requires that analysts consider three data sources, if available:

- the firm analysis carried out by other financial institutions;
- the ratings assigned to the company by rating agencies;
- the company score produced by an independent credit assessment source.

When assessing third-party opinions, analysts are required to map each third-party rating or score into the equivalent ICAS rating. To reconcile possible differences across external ratings, the analysts are guided through a list of questions for each

Waste of row materials, Water usage, Biodiversity and ecological impact) is related to the sector in which the firm operates.

external rating source. Based on the answers, a risk score is computed.[15] The analysts can override the automatic score, explaining the reason for the deviation in a dedicated comment.

Climate Change Risks

The ECB is committed to addressing climate change risk (CCR) within its mandate. With the decision No. 541 of 22 June 2022, the Governing Council outlined its action plan to include the integration of CCR into the expert assessment of the ICASes by the end of 2024.

The assessment of CCR covers transition risk and physical risk. The analysts assess both categories and integrate them into a single score. Given the unique nature of these risks, which are not captured by the statistical model, in this module analysts assign a score that reflects the firm's exposure to CCR using a best-in-class/best-in-universe approach. The ECB encourages ICASes to use as the primary data source on CCR the self-disclosed information by firms. However, the current approach predominantly relies on data obtained from external or sectoral sources; individual data provided by firms in non-financial disclosures (NFD), if available, are used to supplement the analysis. To address the scarcity of granular firm-level data on CCR, initiatives are underway.[16]

The analysis of transition risk has two stages, in line with the ECB's minimum requirements.[17] First, we estimate the impact of a carbon tax on the firm's creditworthiness (see Di Virgilio et al., 2024). The 12-months' PD of the firm is computed under different NGFS scenarios. The resulting transition risk score is compared with those of external data providers. The qualitative approach for transition risk involves a checklist including items such as best-in-class/universe firm behaviour, governance sensitivity, transition plans. The analysts answer qualitative questions (e.g., on internal governance, commitment of corporate bodies, insurance coverage, investments, and damages already suffered from physical risks) using information collected from NFR and financial statements.

The quantitative methodology for the evaluation of physical risk employs a benchmark physical risk score provided by an external provider. Hazards such as landslides and floods are captured through a synthetic indicator on a five-point

[15] This choice is related to the fact that IRBs and ECAIs are eligible rating sources for the ECAF.

[16] In Italy the Coordination Table on Sustainable Finance (chaired by the Ministry of Economy and Finance, with participation from the Bank of Italy, Consob, Ivass, the Ministry of Environment and Energy Security, and Covip) facilitates the accessibility and integration of currently available databases on the environmental risks of firms and households. It also seeks to encourage SMEs not subject to CSRD obligations to provide sustainability information voluntarily, harmonized and proportionate to their size, to meet the informational needs of banks, non-financial firms, and investors with whom SMEs have financial or commercial relationships.

[17] See *Common minimum standards for incorporating climate change risks into in-house credit assessment systems in the Eurosystem*, European Central Bank, Economic Bulletin Issue 6, 2022, box 6.

scale. The resulting physical risk score considers the location of the company headquarters and operating units, but it does not account for mitigating actions (such as insurance or physical devices) undertaken by the company to reduce potential risks. In the subsequent qualitative assessment, the analysts incorporate possible mitigation measures if the information is available, for instance, from the non-financial statement. The assessment is supported by a questionnaire about recent disaster events and insurance coverage.[18]

An internal model is later used to integrate the transition and the physical risk scores. The final score contributes to the stand-alone rating.

Overall Assessment and Stand-Alone Full Rating

The integration of the expert assessment into the statistical rating is performed using Bayesian statistical techniques. We update the statistical rating with new information, given by the scores provided by the various modules. The reformulation of the PD estimate can be seen as an extended version of the standard logistic model. Formally, the logistic model for the PD is defined by the following sigmoidal function:

$$\mathrm{PD} = \frac{1}{1 + e^{-(\beta_0 + \beta_1 x_1 + \beta_2 x_2 + \ldots)}} \tag{1}$$

The extended model incorporates the original logistic model and the module scores which capture the judgement of the analysts. The extended model implements a Bayesian approach using numerical techniques such as Markov Chain Monte Carlo (MCMC), which is standard practice for this type of application. In our extended model, we use the formula:

$$\mathrm{PD} = \frac{1}{1 + e^{-(Score + \alpha_1 z_1 + \alpha_2 z_2 + \ldots)}} \tag{2}$$

where *Score* is the result of the original logistic model, and z_1, z_2, ... are the module scores.

We note that the above is a simplified representation of the methodology, for illustrative purposes. While the traditional logistic model follows a frequentist approach, the extended model adopts a Bayesian approach, whereby the PD is not a point estimate, but it is obtained as the median of a probability distribution. Unlike the statistical PD, the Bayesian model strictly requires numerical methods such as MCMC.

In frequentist statistics, probability is interpreted as the long-term frequency of an event in repeated samples. In contrast, the Bayesian view sees probability as a measure of belief or credibility which can be updated as new information becomes available using Bayes' theorem. This approach allows for greater flexibility and the

---

[18] Additionally, analysts can leverage individual information from a survey involving a sample of Italian non-financial firms (see chapter "The Climate Risk Survey").

inclusion of a priori knowledge in the model. The Bayesian approach is particularly suitable when working with small samples and it allows for the integration of analysts' assessments in a flexible and yet rigorous manner. This enhances both the accuracy and the value of expert assessment. While the model requires somewhat complex computational techniques, its output is rather intuitive and easy to interpret. It also provides an objective benchmark for full ratings, against which analysts can compare their own assessment. The internal rules foresee that the analysts retain the option to override the resulting rating under certain conditions. They may lower the rating without restrictions, but they can raise it by one notch only. If they intend to raise it by more than one notch, they must submit the proposal for review to the Rating committee.

In the following example, we illustrate how module scores affect the posterior distribution of PD estimates to yield the full rating. The process begins with the statistical rating. Let's assume that our representative firm has a statistical rating equal to 5+ on the Bank of Italy's scale. A neutral expert assessment would confirm this estimate, while the integration of positive or negative module scores could produce a different full rating (Fig. 4).

Group Analysis

For subsidiaries, group analysis is conducted once the stand-alone full rating is assigned. The methodology foresees that the higher is the degree of integration between the company and its group, the greater is the weight assigned to the parent company in the full rating of the subsidiary. To support this assessment, analysts are provided with a set of indicators and information on group entities. They are expected to identify the appropriate parent company, assess the strength of the interlinkages, and evaluate the parent's creditworthiness, drawing on the ratings available within ICAS or from external sources. Group analysis is divided into three steps. In the first one, companies are sorted. The first analyst is required to identify the parent company.[19] If the company under assessment does not belong to a group or is a parent company at the highest level of consolidation, the final assessment coincides with the stand-alone assessment of the company and the process stops.

In the second step, the first and second analyst independently fill out a checklist on the interlinkages between the subsidiary and its parent company. Responses are classified into three levels of strength: weak, medium, and strong. The questions pertain to three dimensions: (i) governance and corporate integration; (ii) economic and operational integration; and (iii) financial integration. Each dimension is equally weighted to obtain the overall intensity of the interlinkages. The analysts may apply a motivated override to the resulting level of intensity; for instance, if the subsidiary is expected to be divested in the near term, a lower degree of integration is typically assumed. The subsequent step consists in the credit risk assessment of the parent company. The first analyst verifies whether a full rating

[19] The second analyst must explicitly validate the choice made by the first analyst.

a All module scores are neutral

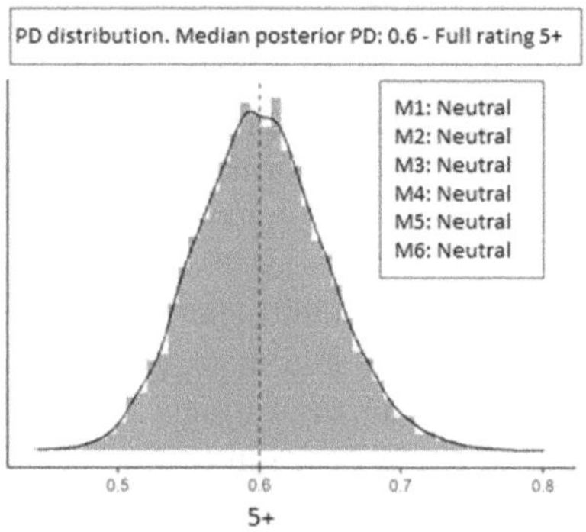

The median of the posterior PD distribution coincides with the statistical PD statistical rating; besides posterior PDs are concentrated in the interval [0.5–0.7] corresponding to the full rating 5+

The model yields the full rating 5+

b Prevalence of negative scores

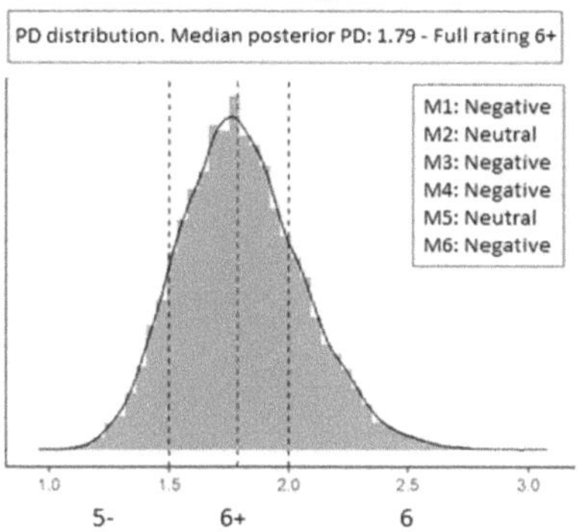

The median of the posterior PD distribution falls in the interval of PDs corresponding to the full rating 6+, worse than the statistical rating. Most posterior PDs fall in the interval corresponding to 6+ [1.5–2.0] but a non-negligible percentage of posterior PDs falls in the interval corresponding to the full rating 6 [2.0-3.0]

The model yields the full rating 6+, but also 6 is plausible

c Prevalence of positive scores

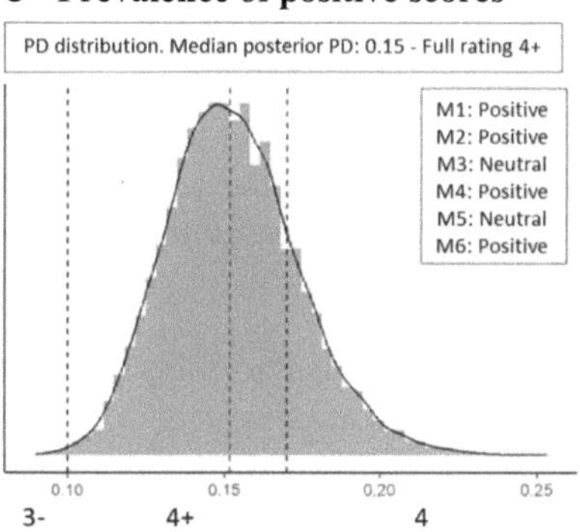

The median of the posterior PD distribution falls in the interval of PDs corresponding to the full rating 4+, better than the statistical rating (+3 notches). Most posterior PDs fall in the interval corresponding to 4+ [0.1–0.17], but a non-negligible percentage of posterior PDs falls in the interval corresponding to the full rating 4 [0.17-0.3]

The model yields the full rating 4+, but also 4 is plausible

Fig. 4 Posterior PD distribution according to module scores—Examples (statistical PD: 0.6%; statistical rating: 5+)

for the parent company is available, based on financial data from the same year as that of the individual entity. If the parent company is a foreign entity, the analyst checks for an ICAS rating issued by other National Central Banks. In the absence of such ratings, the analysts provide a qualitative assessment of the parent's financial position relative to the individual entity, on a five-point scale (from 'very positive' to 'very negative'), drawing on all available information, including third-party assessments (e.g., external ratings, IRB PDs) and the statistical ICAS rating, if available.

In the third step, based on previous information, the system generates a rating proposal. If a full rating for the parent company is available, a weighted average is computed between the individual and parent company ratings, where the weights reflect the interlinkage intensity. In the absence of a rating for the parent company, the system applies an adjustment (notching upward or downward) using a transition matrix that incorporates both the parent's creditworthiness and the interlinkage factor. In all cases, the proposed rating can be overridden by either analyst. Generally, when a strong link is identified between an entity and its group, the subsidiary's rating cannot exceed that of the parent company. If the subsidiary's rating exceeds that of the parent company, the former rating must be submitted to the Rating committee for approval.

4 Validation

4.1 General Principles

The validation of the expert assessment is based on the dataset covering the period from 2016 to 2022, with over 25,000 records.[20] The validation exercise draws on interviews with staff from the Bank of Italy's division responsible for managing the ICAS. The dataset comprises the expert assessment output grouped by analyst, firm, and date. For each observation, the statistical rating, the full rating, the module scores assigned by the analysts and any default event in the 12 months following the rating assignment are recorded. The exercise addresses the following questions:

- does the expert assessment provide incremental value relative to the statistical model? If so, is this value statistically significant?
- what is the relationship between each module of the analysis and the full rating? Specifically, how does each module contribute to the explanatory power and performance of the full rating?

[20] The default state for each assessment is binomial; we chose this type of default to have a larger dataset (evidence of fractional defaults is only available from January 1, 2019).

- are there significant differences across analysts in deriving the full rating? If that is the case, do these differences produce a different performance of the full rating?

We perform backtesting on both the statistical rating and the full rating, evaluating their discriminatory power, predictive power, and performance stability. We adopt the following guiding principles:

discriminatory power: we favour rating systems that exhibit higher values of the AUROC;
predictive power: we prefer conservative default forecasts; hence we favour rating systems whose forecasted default rate closely aligns with the observed default frequency;
stability: we value time consistency in both discriminatory and predictive power; we therefore prefer rating systems that exhibit stationary behaviour over time.

Besides, the validation process seeks to ensure broad accessibility and interpretability of its results. Therefore, we follow the testing procedures recommended by the ECAF.

We evaluate whether any changes in discriminatory power, predictive power and stability arising from the transition from the statistical rating to the full rating are statistically significant. Concerning the predictive power, we apply a rule of the ECAF framework: two rating systems are considered as significantly different if the difference is due to one or more rating classes.

4.2 Performance

We present the results concerning the overall performance of the expert assessment, without disaggregating the specific contributions of individual components to the full rating (see the following sections for a detailed analysis). We examine the alignment between full ratings and observed defaults, evaluating the discriminatory power and the predictive power of ratings and the stability of their performance. We estimate the incremental value added by the expert assessment over the statistical ratings and assess its significance.

The results indicate that the expert assessment improves the discriminatory power of ICAS. The AUROC increases from 85.3% for the statistical rating to 87% for the full rating (Fig. 5).

The ROC curve for the full rating lies strictly above that for the statistical rating across the entire range of thresholds. This implies that, in terms of discriminatory power, the full rating strictly dominates the statistical rating. To evaluate the significance of this improvement, we apply a bootstrapping procedure to estimate the distribution of AUROC differences simulated between the two types of rating for each firm. The observed difference falls in the tail of the empirical distribution,

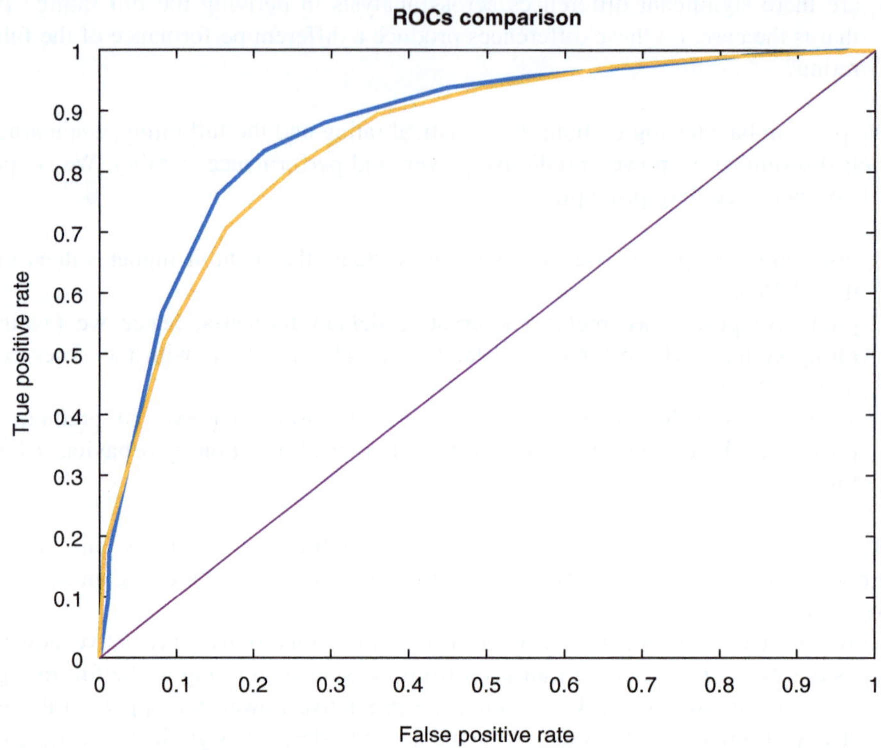

Fig. 5 ROC curves for statistical and full rating (2016–2022). The yellow line refers to the statistical rating, the blue line to the full rating

Table 1 AUROC, by firm size (2016–2022, percentage values)

	Statistical rating	Full rating
Micro	71.7	79
Small	77.1	84.3
Average	86.4	87
Large	87.3	89.3

outside of the 95% confidence interval, indicating statistical significance. These results are robust to dataset stratification, since ssimilar conclusions hold when the analysis is repeated by firm size and year (Tables 1 and 2).

A bootstrapping exercise reveals that some of the differences between the statistical rating and the full rating reported in the above tables are statistically significant, while others are not.[21] We conclude that the full rating consistently

[21] The subsample analysis by firm size and year is based on relatively small samples; as such the corresponding results should be interpreted with caution due to limited statistical robustness.

Table 2 AUROC, by year (percentage values)

	Statistical rating	Full rating
2016	82.1	86.9
2017	82.4	83
2018	89.7	89
2019	85.6	87.9
2020	87.2	91.2
2021	86.6	91.2
2022	84.2	85.9

achieves higher AUROC values than the statistical rating across all firm size categories in nearly all years in the sample. These findings suggest that the expert assessment improves the discriminatory power and is stable over time.

Secondly, the expert assessment enhances the predictive power of ICAS. The full rating tends to be more conservative than the statistical rating, often resulting in lower ratings (Table 3). While this may reduce precision in matching actual defaults, it increases prudence. In practice, the analysts frequently assign lower ratings than those implied by the statistical model, reflecting a cautious stance. This behaviour is corroborated by additional statistical tests, including the Redelmeier test.[22]

Although the full rating is less precise in a narrow predictive sense, it shows greater robustness to year-to-year fluctuations in default rates. The statistical rating does not always forecast deteriorating credit conditions, whereas the full rating tends to overestimate defaults. This conservative bias enables the expert assessment to act as a safeguard against unexpected defaults, thereby contributing to a more stable and resilient predictive performance over time.

4.3 Behaviour of the Analysts[23]

In this section we examine how the community of analysts derives the full rating from the module scores and how this rating performs in relation to observed defaults. We thus view the performance of the analysts without distinction across the individuals. We proceed as follows:

- we estimate a regression model to identify how the analysts combine the module scores, taking note of systematic deviations from the general guidelines;
- we assess the effectiveness of the score aggregation in predicting defaults, in terms of discriminatory power and predictive power.

[22] For technical details, see Appendix B.

[23] In this section we examine the first analyst's behaviour.

Table 3 Multiple tests for statistical rating and full rating (2016–2022)

CQS	Members number	Lower bound	Expected defaults	Upper bound	Defaults
Statistical rating					
CQS1&2	1489	0	1	5	1
CQS3	6933	7	19	34	8
CQS4	7673	34	56	81	29
CQS5	2734	18	34	54	32
CQS6	4325	63	91	122	105
CQS7	2090	57	84	113	127
CQS8	221	24	41	59	64
Full rating					
CQS1&2	937	0	1	5	0
CQS3	6145	5	16	30	9
CQS4	6809	29	49	72	13
CQS5	3904	28	49	72	22
CQS6	3561	49	74	102	47
CQS7	1868	50	75	103	71
CQS8	2241	454	516	580	204

Note The table above refers to the assignment to individual debtors of the full ratings produced by ICAS, according to which the debtors are allocated to the different CQS. For each CQS we apply a binomial test with 2 tails centred on the average rating. The aim of the test is to verify if the expected defaults are different from the observed defaults. The test confidence level is 0.95. The numbers in red signal that the number of the observed defaults is greater than the number of the expected ones[24]

On average we find that:

- the analysts combine the module scores in a rather discretionary fashion;
- certain modules significantly contribute to the performance of ICAS, others do not.

Deviations from the Guidelines

We run the following regression, for each firm and year (the suffixes are suppressed for simplicity):

$$ln\left(\frac{\mathrm{PD}_{\mathrm{full}}}{\mathrm{PD}_{\mathrm{statistical}}}\right) = \beta_0 + \beta_{FS} * \mathrm{AST}_{FS} + \beta_{FF} * \mathrm{AST}_{FF} + \beta_{GV} * \mathrm{AST}_{GV} + \beta_{SA} * \mathrm{AST}_{SA} + \beta_{GR} * \mathrm{AST}_{GR} + \beta_{3P} * \mathrm{AST}_{3P} + \eta \quad (3)$$

where:

- the dependent variable is the natural logarithm of the ratio between the full rating, assigned by the analysts for each firm and year, and the statistical rating;
- the independent variables are the module scores assigned by the analyst.

[24] For further details, see chapter "The Statistical Model".

Financial statement	Financial flexibility	Governance	Group	Sector analysis	Third-party opinions	Residual component
1.97%	0.61%	0.13%	0.13%	-0.08%	0.26%	-1.35%

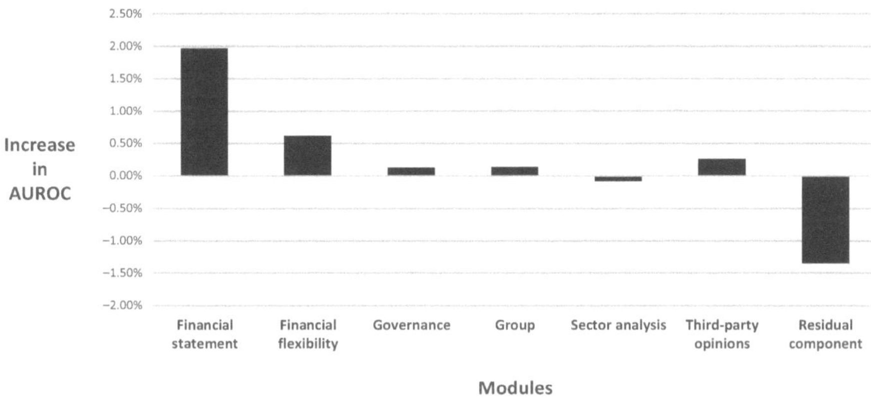

Fig. 6 Contribution to discriminatory power. The x-axis reports the names of the modules, the y-axis shows the increase in discriminatory power

The regression results[25] reveal that the analysts' weighting of the modules partially diverges from the guidelines. Specifically:

- the financial statement score receives the highest weight in the transition to the full rating;
- the financial flexibility score and the third-party opinions scores are roughly equivalent;
- the remaining modules appear to have a limited impact on the full rating.

Performance of the Analysts

Starting from the regression results, we reconstruct the full ratings by sequentially adding the contributions of the constant term and each module score to the baseline statistical rating.

At each step, we obtain a distinct set of marginal contributions of each module to the full rating. We then compare the contributions against observed defaults, which enables us to measure the corresponding discriminatory power and predictive power (Fig. 6).

We test whether each module provides a statistically significant increase in discriminatory power, and whether the module contributions are significantly different from each other.[26]

Regarding the discriminatory power, we find that:

[25] For technical details, see Appendix C.

[26] These significance analyses were conducted using appropriate bootstrap procedures, identifying the threshold quantiles at a 95% confidence level.

- the financial statement module provides the largest marginal contribution, followed by the financial flexibility and the third-party opinions modules;
- these three modules are the only ones that make a positive and significant contribution;
- the sector analysis module, while not statistically significant, exhibits a negative marginal contribution;
- a residual component, attributable to other independent variables[27] or to individual choices made by the analysts, shows a negative contribution that turns out to be statistically significant.

Building on these findings, we decompose the overall predictive power of the full ratings, isolating the marginal contribution of each module to the system's forecasting accuracy.[28] The main results are as follows:

- the transition from the statistical rating to the full rating results in a more conservative assessment of credit risk;
- none of the six modules, considered in isolation, significantly enhances the predictive power of the rating system;
- the inclusion of the constant term (β_0) in the regression introduces a shift in the rating level, changing the assessment from a relatively lenient to a conservative stance. In other words, even in the absence of specific signals from the modules, the analysts tend to worsen the statistical rating, showing a precautionary bias.

4.4 Heterogeneity in the Analysts' Behaviour

We extend[29] the previous analysis to investigate the following questions:

- whether the individual analyst behaviour significantly deviates from that of the group;
- whether any such deviations result in a statistically significant improvement in rating performance.

We analyse some partitions of the original dataset, each corresponding to a different analyst. For each sub-dataset we estimate a regression model similar to the one described in the previous section. These results reveal substantial heterogeneity across analysts. Specifically, we find that:

---

[27] This is the case for instance of the climate change risk considerations, formerly not considered, and recently introduced in the expert assessment.

[28] For each contribution we run the multiple binomial test (Dohler, 2011; Dudoit et al., 2003) as reported in Table 3. The predictive power of two contributions is compared by examining the results of their respective tests.

[29] For methodological details and results, see Appendix D.

- the analysts often differ in the selection of modules and their weights;
- some analysts do not employ all the modules in their assessment.

These findings reveal that the analysts employ in practice a broad range of rating strategies. Each strategy features a distinct combination of modules and weighting schemes. We then set out to assess the performance of these strategies in terms of their discriminatory power and predictive power. Concerning the discriminatory power, we find that some strategies yield performance improvements relative to the average analyst, while others lead to performance deterioration. In terms of predictive power, no individual strategy appears to produce significant differences compared to the average. None of the strategies significantly outperforms the analysts as a group in either discriminatory power or predictive power. We conclude that the heterogeneity in analysts' behaviour does not translate into performance gains.

5 Developments: Geopolitics and ESG

As shown above,[30] the validation highlights, among other things, that on average, analysts used other elements beyond the variables included in the modules. This phenomenon suggests to extend the expert assessment to additional factors with a view to improving its contribution to the performance of the rating system.

Geopolitical considerations are playing an increasing role in credit ratings, as country risk may be affected by rising global tensions. The pandemic and the war in Ukraine have accelerated the reconfiguration of global supply chains, a trend that began in the aftermath of the 2008 financial crisis. The future of a liberalized, rule-based global trade system is uncertain, with the US exemplifying this shift (Mercurio, 2024). International trade with geopolitically aligned partners and trade tariffs are increasing for economic and political reasons. Global supply chains have shown their fragility during the pandemic and afterwards (Shih, 2022). From a political standpoint, the number of new global trade restrictions has increased from approximately 650 in 2017 to over 3,000 in 2023 (MGI, 2024), while 'friendshoring', the alignment of supply chains with the political orientation of the country, is spreading (Yellen, 2022). These developments have led to a closer alignment between states and firms, influencing credit ratings, and triggering rapid demand shifts across sectors, with a move away from export-led strategies (Cherif & Hasanov, 2024). The approaches of CRAs and IRBs must adapt to this volatile environment by identifying which industries are likely to benefit or be adversely affected by the global changes.

The importance of environmental, social and governance (ESG) concerns has grown among the public, governments, and in corporate strategies. The number of companies acknowledging climate change risks in their financial reporting has

[30] See, in particular, paragraph 4.3.

significantly increased (KPMG, 2020). ESG-related investments have surged in recent years, prompting CRAs to explicitly integrate ESG factors into their rating methodologies (EC, 2022). However, ESG scores are heterogeneous across rating providers.[31] This heterogeneity has fueled the investors' skepticism about the reliability of ESG ratings (Del Giudice et al., 2024). Nonetheless, the importance of integrating ESG factors into corporate credit assessment is increasing, as shown by studies linking carbon neutrality to credit risk (Umar et al., 2021) and green innovation to default risk (Meles et al., 2023). ESG issues may affect corporate risk both directly, through the business model, and indirectly, via reputational channels. Numerous studies have shown that sustainable companies tend to exhibit a stronger financial performance.[32] Financial market data corroborate these findings, with ESG funds outperforming their peers (Morgan Stanley, 2024). The rationale is that sustainability becomes profitable when it is embedded in the firm's core business model (Kim & Yoon, 2023).[33]

Due to market demand and the growing body of research linking ESG factors to investment outcomes and financial performance, CRAs nowadays incorporate ESG considerations into their ratings, albeit in different ways. ESG factors can affect credit risk either directly, by influencing a specific rating component such as the governance quality, or indirectly, by reducing profitability or liquidity through additional costs. It is also essential to establish whether the impact stems from one-off events, such as a controversy, or it reflects a structural, sector-wide shift that may alter long-term risk.

CRAs assess whether climate-related physical and transition risks are significant for the firm. The most frequent approach is to integrate ESG factors into the standard rating procedure, treating them as a component of the overall assessment, despite the often-limited quality of ESG data. Given the heterogeneity of the indicators, CRAs typically develop E, S and G scores separately. The IRB approach to ESG is similar to CRAs'. Since IRB models are used for regulatory purposes related to capital requirements, it seems likely that, should ESG-related requirements materialize, banks would align their own ESG ratings more closely (EBA, 2022).

In line with this trend, ICAS has recently been tasked with the integration of ESG factors into its credit assessment process.

---

[31] This variability in rating criteria has been empirically shown to result in divergent opinions on the same firms (Billio et al., 2021), with differences in weighting and social and governance indicators being the primary drivers of these divergences (Capizzi et al., 2021).

[32] Notably, a comprehensive study by Whelan et al. (2021) reviewed over 1,000 research papers from 2015 to 2020, finding a positive relationship between ESG and financial performance in 58% of the corporate studies, with only 8% showing a negative relationship.

[33] Companies that merely declare sustainable intentions, such as signing the Principles for Responsible Investment, do not show distinguishable performance improvements, despite widely advertising their affiliation (Kim & Yoon, 2023).

6 Conclusions

This chapter shows the contribution of the expert assessment in the Bank of Italy's ICAS system towards the predictive power and discriminatory power of credit ratings. By integrating qualitative considerations within a robust statistical framework, the expert assessment improves the PD estimates and serves as a safeguard against the inherent limitations of statistical models, particularly during periods of rising economic uncertainty.

The validation results confirm that the expert assessment enhances the accuracy and the conservatism of credit ratings. Notably, the AUROC improves significantly. Furthermore, the adjustments introduced by the analysts ensure that the ICAS framework responds to evolving economic conditions.

Our findings underscore the importance of an adequate structure for the expert assessment process. The recent introduction of detailed checklists and Bayesian aggregation techniques has significantly enhanced transparency, homogeneity, and accountability. These advancements mitigate any subjective bias and allow the ICAS system to address complex, forward-looking factors such as climate risks and sector dynamics.

Our work suggests several avenues for future development. The expert assessment framework lends itself to further enhancements, notably in the areas of ESG integration and geopolitical risk, and to the use of new data sources, to ensure that the system remains at the forefront of the credit risk assessment practice.

In conclusion, our study reaffirms the importance of the interplay between statistical rigour and expert insight in corporate credit analysis. By bridging these dimensions, the ICAS system exemplifies a comprehensive and resilient approach, providing valuable insights for risk management, financial institutions, and researchers. It is important to keep the rigorous standards of the system as well as its ability to incorporate new developments in credit risk analysis, to integrate emerging risk factors, such as climate risks and geopolitical risk, and new estimation techniques, in particular artificial intelligence tools.

Appendix A: Initial Adjustment of the Statistical Rating

The analysts may adjust the statistical rating obtained from the financial component for the following considerations.

- Finance Leases: According to Italian GAAP, finance leases are usually recognized among off-balance sheet items. Italian accounting standards emphasize form, leading to the recognition of lease payments as operating costs over the term of the lease agreement. Italian GAAP stipulates that in a finance lease, involving the transfer to the lessee of most risks and rewards of asset ownership, the company should report in the financial statement notes a table detailing the implicit debt of the lease contract, the total amount of assets leased, yearly amortization, and interest expenses. Analysts must extract information from these notes and adjust for leasing according to IFRS methodology (known as the 'financial method'). Under this method, companies recognize finance leases as assets and liabilities on the balance sheet, valued at their fair value and implicit financial debt, respectively. Annual lease payments are divided between interest expense and asset amortization on the income statement.

- Cash and Cash Equivalents: For conservatism, the statistical model for calculating net financial debt considers only cash, cheques, and bank and postal deposits as liquidity. Other financial instruments are classified as 'current financial assets'. Analysts must review the notes to the financial statement to include highly liquid instruments that are readily convertible to cash and subject to low risk of value change (e.g., sovereign bonds or time deposits) within liquidity. Conversely, companies may have cash or equivalents unavailable for general purposes (e.g., restricted cash). To ensure the statistical model accounts for the reduced amount of available cash to repay debt, analysts must exclude restricted cash from 'cash and cash equivalents'.
- Non-recurring Items in the Income Statement: The income statement information used by the statistical model sometimes includes positive or negative transactions that could be considered as 'non-recurring'. These non-recurring items should be reclassified among extraordinary items and excluded from operating income, as they are neither part of ongoing core operations nor an accurate reflection of future performance.
- Dividends: Dividends are proposed by the company's Board of Directors and approved at the general shareholders' meeting. The statistical PD typically reflects information as of the reporting date and does not incorporate declared dividends. Analysts are required to adjust for declared dividends by reducing equity and increasing short-term liabilities accordingly.
- Interest Expenses: Interest expenses are crucial variables for the statistical model, as they are used in predictive variables (e.g., interest expenses to EBITDA or return on debt). Sometimes, companies include items not related to financial debt within interest expenses (e.g., unwinding of the discount of certain assets or liabilities, foreign exchange gains and losses). This reporting distorts the statistical ratios based on the relationship between interest expenses and financial debt. To address this issue, analysts must reclassify the portion of interest expenses not coherent with financial debt as operating expenses, preserving interest coverage ratios and interest rate risk ratios.
- Hybrid Shareholders' Loans: Some instruments possess characteristics of both equity and debt. For subordinated interest-free shareholders' loans without a specified maturity date, analysts must follow different reclassifications based on the type of company. For predominantly mutual cooperative corporations,[34]

[34] According to Article 2511 of the Italian Civil Code, 'cooperatives' are companies with variable capital with a mutual purpose registered in the register of cooperative companies. Cooperative societies differ from other corporations because they are aimed at providing goods or services directly to the members, on more profitable terms than those offered by the market. They may be predominantly or not predominantly mutual, depending on whether there are conditions in the company's

these loans must be reclassified as equity if they are considered financial debt by the statistical model. For other companies, these instruments should not be considered financial debt for calculating the ratios used by the statistical model (e.g., equity to net financial debt ratio or return on debt).

The analysts may adjust the statistical rating obtained from the credit behaviour component for the following considerations.

- Average Utilization Rates: These variables are defined as the ratio between the drawn amount and granted amount for each type of credit line (e.g., current account revolving credit lines, accounts receivable revolving credit lines, total short-term credit lines). When these ratios are not available due to the absence of short-term loans in the NCR, the model sets the ratio to 0 (best possible value) and introduces a specific dummy variable that adjusts the credit score for the average riskiness of the subset of firms within the estimation sample without this type of loan reported in the NCR. In specific cases, when analysts observe that one or more ratios are computed incorrectly due to a specific form of credit line (e.g. credit card), they must rectify the ratios used by the statistical model.
- Financial Distress: The statistical model employs variables such as the number of months, or absolute and relative amounts of overdrafts, for each type of credit line at various frequencies, as well as past delinquencies and default status. In this context, analysts must check for erroneous reporting or technical overdrafts and rectify them in the statistical model.

Appendix B: Redelmeier Test

The Redelmeier test (Redelmeier et al., 1991) verifies which one, between two rating systems, has the best predictive power. The test involves a comparison of the mean squared errors (MSE) computed by the two rating systems using the same data sample. The test checks whether the deviation of the realized MSE from its expected value, computed for the first rating system, is significantly different from the deviation of the realized MSE from its expected value, computed for the second rating system. The rating system with the lowest MSE is the best.

The test statistic is:

$$Z_R = \frac{\left[\sum_{i=1}^{N}\left(\hat{\pi}_{i,m1}^2 - \hat{\pi}_{i,m2}^2\right) - 2\left(\hat{\pi}_{i,m1}^2 - \hat{\pi}_{i,m2}^2\right) * y_i\right]}{\left[\sum_{i=1}^{N}[\left(\hat{\pi}_{i,m1}^2 - \hat{\pi}_{i,m2}^2\right)^2 * (\hat{\pi}_{i,m1} + \hat{\pi}_{i,m2}) * (2 - \hat{\pi}_{i,m1} - \hat{\pi}_{i,m2})]\right]^{0,5}} \tag{4}$$

where:

statute limiting the distribution of profits to members, and the activity is carried out primarily for the benefit of the latter.

$\hat{\pi}_{i,mn}$ = expected default frequency from the model/rating system of rating *mn* ($n = 1, 2$) for the firm *i*;

y_i = true *default* state for the firm I ($y = 0$ – healthy firm –, 1 – defaulted firm –).

The test statistics follows a standard normal distribution under these hypotheses:

$$H_0 : E[(E(\text{MSE}_{m1}) - \text{MSE}_{m1}) - (E(\text{MSE}_{m2}) - \text{MSE}_{m2})] = 0,$$

$$H_1 : E[(E(\text{MSE}_{m1}) - \text{MSE}_{m1}) - (E(\text{MSE}_{m2}) - \text{MSE}_{m2})] \neq 0$$

Appendix C: Contribution of the Modules

We run the following regression:

$$ln\left(\frac{\text{PD}_{\text{full}}}{\text{PD}_{\text{statistical}}}\right) = \beta_0 + \beta_{FS} * \text{AST}_{FS} + \beta_{FF} * \text{AST}_{FF} + \beta_{GV} * \text{AST}_{GV} + \beta_{SA} * \text{AST}_{SA} + \beta_{GR} * \text{AST}_{GR} + \beta_{3P} * \text{AST}_{3P} + \eta \quad (5)$$

where:

- the dependent variable is the natural logarithm of the ratio between the full rating and the statistical rating;
- the independent variables are the scores assigned for each company by the analysts (denoted by AST for assessment) to the modules, identified by the acronyms:
  - FS: financial statement
  - FF: financial flexibility
  - GV: governance
  - SA: sector analysis
  - GR: group
  - 3P: third-party opinions
- β_i is the coefficient of the *i*th module in the regression, including the intercept
- η denotes the error term.

By construction, the dependent variable is defined on the set of real numbers; the independent variables are defined on the set of integers and are rescaled to allow a comparison between the modules. We can apply the OLS method.

The expert assessment practice requires the analysts to issue scores for each module. This provides a significant incentive for the analysts to incorporate any prior considerations on the modules into their evaluation. Therefore, it is assumed that a dynamic specification for the modules in the regression is unnecessary.

Running this regression, the Breusch-Pagan test and the Breusch-Godfrey test, with p-values below 1%, confirm the presence of heteroscedasticity and

Table 4 Significance of the coefficients

Regressor	Coefficient		
Intercept	0.2115	***	(0.0050)
FS	–0.3790	***	(0.0061)
FF	–0.1436	***	(0.0052)
GV	–0.1224	***	(0.0060)
SA	–0.1248	***	(0.0047)
GR	–0.1076	***	(0.0054)
3P	–0.1557	***	(0.0051)

Note In the 'coefficient' column the coefficients of the OLS regression described above are reported, the Newey-West standard errors are reported in parentheses. The asterisks (***,**,*) indicate a statistical significance of 1 per thousand, 1%, 5% respectively

autocorrelation of the residuals. This suggests that the regression omits some variables.

Nevertheless, the primary interest here is to obtain the best indication regarding the behaviour of the analysts with respect to the modules. To this end, we continue using the coefficient estimates obtained in the first run of the regression, without including other explanatory variables and employing the standard errors provided by the Newey-West procedure (Verbeek, 2010) in the tests. The coefficients of all modules are significant in explaining the full rating (Table 4).

Additionally, these coefficients can be ranked (following a specific F-test) as shown in Table 5.

From the previous table, we note that in absolute terms:

- the largest coefficient pertains to the financial statement module;
- the coefficients for financial flexibility and for third-party opinions follow in magnitude;
- the coefficients for the remaining modules, though not significantly different from each other, exhibit the smallest magnitude.

Appendix D: Differences Between the Analysts

We study portions of the original dataset, each one referring to an analyst. To derive the behavioural characteristics of each analyst, we consider only those who performed at least 100 assessments over sufficiently differentiated firms. This approach results in the selection of over 50 analysts, with individual datasets containing between 100 and 700 assessments.

While the size of datasets can lead to a credible estimate of the analysts' patterns, the main feature of default events is their rarity. Consequently, the results

Table 5 Significance of the differences between the coefficients

Test hypotesis	F	Pr(F)	Significance
FS - FF = 0	688.53	<2.2e-16	***
FS - GV = 0	911.51	<2.2e-16	***
FS - SA = 0	899.73	<2.2e-16	***
FS - GR = 0	1,006.1	<2.2e-16	***
FS - 3P = 0	723.76	<2.2e-16	***
FF - GV = 0	6.52	0.01	*
FF - SA = 0	6.79	0.01	**
FF - GR = 0	21.60	3.37e-06	***
FF - 3P = 0	2.70	0.10	
GV - SA = 0	0.10	0.76	
GV - GR = 0	3.22		
GV - 3P = 0	20.38	6.375e-06	***
SA - GR = 0	5.52	0.02	*
SA - 3P = 0	21.47	3.616e-06	***
GR - 3P = 0	43.26	4.896e-11	***

Note In the previous table, the 'F' column shows the values assumed by the F statistic used to test the hypotheses in the 'Hypothesis under test' column. The value of the p-value relating to column F is reported in the 'Pr(F)' Column. The related outcomes in terms of statistical significance are reported in the 'Significance' Column. The asterisks (***,**,*) indicate a statistical significance of 1 per thousand, 1%, 5% respectively. The dot (.) indicates a statistical significance of 10%. The absence of an asterisk or dot indicates a significance greater than 10%

regarding the performance of the analysts' patterns generally have only a heuristic value.

We conduct a regression analysis like the one shown in the previous section, for each analyst. The results are summarized in the following table, which, for simplicity, is only an excerpt from a larger table relating to all the selected analysts.

The regression results show a fairly good explanatory power. Specifically:

- the null hypothesis of the F-test is rejected in all cases;
- the R-squared value is medium-high;
- the sign of the constant term is positive and aligns with expectations;
- the sign of the module coefficients is negative and aligns with expectations.

These regressions also indicate that the assessment methods may differ among analysts.

Approximately 80% of the analysts differ from the average analyst as concerns the adoption of modules for the full rating. A significant part of this is attributable to the omission of one or two modules.

The analysts also differ in their choice of the modules that are not employed and of the weights that are attributed to the modules. These differences are often statistically significant. This enables the identification of a set of assessment strategies.

The dendrogram below provides a detailed view of the set of the assessments; we construct the dendrogram by computing proximity in terms of Ward's distance between individual analysts or groups of analysts. We compute the distance between the coefficients of the different regressions reported in Table 6. The dendrogram helps in studying the strategies adopted by the analysts. For instance, we study strategies that appear as distant as possible in the dendrogram to see if they differ significantly in terms of discriminatory power and predictive power (and if they differ from that of the average analyst) (Fig. 7).

We conclude that the heterogeneity in the analysts' behaviour is not rewarding in terms of performance, neither is it in terms of discriminatory power or predictive power.

Table 6 Regressions by analyst (excerpt)

analyst	const	FS	FF	GV	SA	GR	3P	F-test	Adjusted R square
1	0.2802	−0.3792	0.0000	0.0000	−0.1789	−0.2133	0.0000	0.0000	0.5281
2	0.0963	−0.2406	−0.1448	−0.1222	−0.0768	−0.0877	−0.1050	0.0000	0.5317
3	0.1148	−0.2502	−0.0739	−0.0816	−0.0691	−0.1254	−0.1311	0.0000	0.5561
4	0.1704	−0.4793	0.0000	0.0000	−0.0972	−0.1110	−0.1627	0.0000	0.5995
5	0.0000	−0.1599	−0.2079	−0.1986	0.0000	0.0000	−0.1418	0.0000	0.5222
6	…	…	…	…	…	…	…	…	…

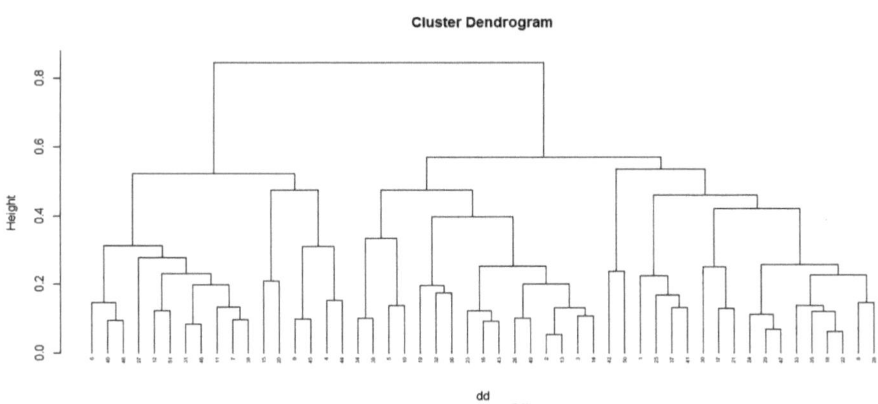

Fig. 7 Proximity between analysts. On the abscissa, we report the identification number for each analyst; on the ordinate, we report the Ward distance between analysts or groups of analysts

References

Agarwal, S., Ambrose, B. W., & Liu, C. (2006). Credit lines and credit utilization. *Journal of Money, Credit, and Banking, 38*, 1–22.
Alp, A. (2013). Structural shifts in credit rating standards. *Journal of Finance, 68*(6), 2435–2470.
Altman, E. I. (1968). Financial ratios, discriminant analysis and the prediction of corporate bankruptcy. *Journal of Finance, 23*, 589–609.
Amato, J. D., & Furfine, C. H. (2003). *Are credit ratings procyclical* (BIS Working Papers No. 129).
Anderson, R. C., Mansi, S. A., & Reeb, D. M. (2004). Board characteristics, accounting report integrity, and the cost of debt. *Journal of Accounting and Economics, 37*, 315–342.
Ballis, A., Ioannidis, C., & Sifodaskalikis, E. (2024). Structural shifts in bank credit ratings. *Journal of Financial Stability, 73*, 101272.
BCBS. (2001). *The internal ratings-based approach.* BIS, Basel.
BCBS. (2015). *Developments in credit risk management across sectors: Current practices and recommendations.* BIS, Basel.
BCBS. (2024). *Guidelines for counterparty credit risk management.* BIS, Basel.
Becker, B., & Milbourn, T. (2011). How did increase competition affect credit ratings? *Journal of Financial Economics, 108*, 493–514.
Billio, M., et al. (2021). Inside the ESG ratings: (Dis)agreement and performance. *Corporate Social Responsibility and Environmental Management, 28*, 1426–1445. https://doi.org/10.1002/csr.2177
BIS. (2015). *Developments in credit risk management across sectors: Current practices and recommendations.*
Bloom, N., & Van Reenen, J. (2007). Measuring and explaining management practices across firms and countries. *The Quarterly Journal of Economics, 122*, 1351–1408.
Capizzi, V., et al. (2021). The divergence of ESG ratings: An analysis of Italian listed companies. *Journal of Financial Management Markets and Institutions, 9*, 2150006. https://doi.org/10.1142/S2282717X21500067
Cherif, R., & Hasanov, F. (2024). *The pitfalls of protectionism: Import substitution vs. export-oriented industrial policy* (IMF Working Paper 24/86). Washington.
deHaan, D. (2017). The financial crisis and corporate credit ratings. *The Accounting Review, 4*, 161–189.
Del Giudice, A., et al. (2024). *I rating ESG: un confronto internazionale.* Università Cattolica del Sacro Cuore.
Diamond, D. W. (1984). Financial intermediation and delegated monitoring. *Review of Economic Studies, 51*(3), 393–414.
Di Virgilio, S., et al. (2024). Assessing credit risk sensitivity to climate and energy shocks: Towards a common minimum standards in line with the ECB climate agenda. *Journal of Policy Modelling, 46*(3), 552–568.
Dohler, S. (2011). Validation of credit default probabilities using multiple-testing procedures. *Journal of Risk Model Validation, 4*(4), 59–92.
Dudoit, S., et al. (2003). Resampling-based multiple testing for microarray data analysis. *TEST, 12*(1), 1–77.
EBA. (2017). *Guidelines on PD estimation, LGD estimation and defaulted exposures.* European Banking Authority, Paris.
EBA. (2022). *The role of environmental risks in the prudential framework* (EBA Discussion Paper 2022/02). Paris.
EC. (2022). *Targeted consultation on the functioning of the ESG ratings market in the European Union and on the consideration of ESG factors in credit ratings.* European Commission, Brussels.
EU. (2009). Regulation (EC) No 1060/2009 of the European Parliament and Council on credit rating agencies. https://eur-lex.europa.eu/legal-content/EN/TXT/PDF/?uri=CELEX:32009R1060

Gallo, R. (2021). *The IRB approach and bank lending to firms* (Temi di discussione 1347), Bank of Italy, Rome.
Gallucci, C., et al. (2022). Financial ratios, corporate governance and bank-firm information: A Bayesian approach to predict SMEs' default. *Journal of Management and Governance*. https://doi.org/10.1007/s10997-021-09614-5
Garcia Alcubilla, R., & Ruiz del Pozo, J. (2012). *Credit rating agencies on the watch list: Analysis of European regulation*. Oxford University Press.
Giannozzi, A., et al. (2013). Building SME rating: Is it necessary for lenders to monitor financial statements of the borrowers? *Bancaria Editrice, 10*, 54–71.
Jensen, M. C., & Meckling, W. H. (1976). Theory of the firm: Managerial behaviour, agency costs and ownership structure. *Journal of Financial Economics, 3*, 305–360.
Jiménez, G., Lopez, J., & Saurina, J. (2009). Empirical analysis of corporate credit lines. *The Review of Financial Studies, 22*, 5069–5098.
Kim, S., & Yoon, A. S. (2023). Analyzing active fund managers' commitment to ESG: Evidence from the United Nations principles for responsible investment. *Management Science, 69*, 741–758.
KPMG. (2020). *The time has come: The KPMG survey of sustainability reporting*. Amsterdam.
Meles, A., et al. (2023). The influence of green innovation on default risk: Evidence from Europe. *The International Review of Economics & Finance, 84*, 692–710. https://doi.org/10.1016/j.iref.2022.11.036
Mercurio, B. (2024). The demise of globalization and rise of industrial policy: Caveat emptor. *World Trade Review, 23*, 242–250.
MGI. (2024). *Geopolitics and the geometry of global trade*. McKinsey Global Institute.
Modigliani, F., & Miller, M. (1958). The cost of capital, corporation finance and the theory of investment. *The American Economic Review, 48*, 261–297.
Morgan Stanley. (2024). *Sustainable funds outperformed peers in 2023*. Institute for Sustainable Investing.
Norden, L., & Weber, M. (2010). Credit line usage, checking account activity, and default risk of bank borrowers. *The Review of Financial Studies, 23*, 3665–3699.
Redelmeier, D. A., et al. (1991). Assessing predictive accuracy: How to compare brier score. *Journal of Clinical Epidemiology, 44*, 1141–1146.
Shih, W. C. (2022, March 21). *Are the risks of global supply chains starting to outweigh the rewards?* Harvard Business Review.
Shleifer, A., & Vishny, R. W. (1997). A survey of corporate governance. *Journal of Finance, 52*, 737–783.
Singhal, H., et al. (2024). The quality of credit ratings amid geopolitical risk. *Economics Letters, 234*.
Sufi, A. (2009). Bank lines of credit in corporate finance: An empirical analysis. *The Review of Financial Studies, 22*, 1057–1088.
Umar, M., et al. (2021). Carbon neutrality, bank lending, and credit risk: Evidence from the Eurozone. *Journal of Environmental Management, 296*.
Verbeek, M. (2010). *Econometria*. Zanichelli.
Whelan, T., et al. (2021). *ESG and financial performance: Uncovering the relationship by aggregating evidence from 1,000 plus studies published between 2015–2020*. NYU STERN Rockfeller Asset Management.
Yellen, J. (2022, April 13). *Remarks by secretary of the treasury Janet L. Yellen on way forward for the global economy*. Atlantic Council.
Zhao, Y. J., et al. (2014). Usage and exposures at default of corporate credit lines: An empirical study. *The Journal of Credit Risk, 10*(1), 65.

The Climate Risk Survey

Francesca Colletti, Francesco Columba, Manuel Cugliari, Alessandra Iannamorelli, Paolo Parlamento, and Laura Tozzi

1 Introduction

This Chapter presents the results of a survey devoted to climate change risk management practices by Italian non-financial corporations (NFCs). The survey was conducted in 2024 as part of the ongoing efforts of ICAS to integrate climate change risks into its evaluation process, using high-quality data.

F. Colletti
Bank of Italy, Turin Branch, Turin, Italy
e-mail: francesca.colletti@bancaditalia.it

F. Columba · M. Cugliari · A. Iannamorelli · P. Parlamento (✉)
Bank of Italy, Financial Risk Management Directorate, Rome, Italy
e-mail: paolo.parlamento@bancaditalia.it

F. Columba
e-mail: francesco.columba@bancaditalia.it

M. Cugliari
e-mail: manuel.cugliari@bancaditalia.it

A. Iannamorelli
e-mail: alessandra.iannamorelli@bancaditalia.it

L. Tozzi
Bank of Italy, Florence Branch, Florence, Italy
e-mail: laura.tozzi@bancaditalia.it

A. Scalia (ed.), *Corporate Credit Analysis and AI*, Finance for Professionals,
https://doi.org/10.1007/978-3-032-13422-6_6

So far, in the second step, the Bank of Italy's ICAS has applied a top-down approach for climate risk assessment, using sector-level data on climate change risks (CCR), with limited use of firm-level data.[1]

Climate transition and physical risks affect firms' creditworthiness, via the impact on economic and financial performance, and business model. The integration of climate-related risks into credit risk assessment presents two main challenges. The first one pertains to methodological issues, such as those related to the design of scenarios for climate change risks, the endogeneity of such risks, and the non-linearity of climate effects.[2] The second challenge is the scarcity of firm-level data on climate change risks (Angelini, 2022b, 2023; Lavecchia et al., 2022).[3] To address these challenges, the Eurosystem has set minimum common standards for integrating climate change risks into the ICASes managed by NCBs.[4]

In 2024 the Bank of Italy carried out an experimental survey to collect information on firms' greenhouse gas emissions, energy consumption, financial impact of extreme climate events and qualitative information on corporate governance and organization. The objective of the survey was to enhance the evaluation of the impact of CCR on credit risk and improve the accuracy of ICAS ratings by means of granular firm-level data to be used in assessments for 2025.[5] This approach overcomes the limitations of the use of sectoral averages.

This Chapter presents the results of the survey and shows how they contribute to the evaluation of climate-related risks. The survey identifies some shortfalls in Italian firms' climate risk management, such as in emission reporting and insufficient physical risk mitigation, highlighting significant differences with the results estimated on the basis of sectoral data.

According to the survey, in the manufacturing sector two thirds of the firms have governance bodies that deal with CCR; in the services and agriculture sectors only

[1] Top-down approaches incorporate climate risk into credit assessment using sector-level or macroeconomic data, applying broad adjustments across portfolios to capture systemic risk but with limited firm-specific detail. In contrast, bottom-up approaches integrate firm-specific data, such as emissions and adaptation plans, into credit assessment for tailored analysis of climate risks, though they require high-quality, granular data (Auria et al., 2021). A bottom-up approach for ICAS climate risk methodology has been developed. However, it is currently applied only to firms participating in the EU Emissions Trading System (EU-ETS), due to the availability of firm-specific emissions data (see chapter "Transition-Risk Adjusted Credit Analysis").

[2] The design of climate scenarios involves methodologies whose development is not settled yet, endogeneity refers to the mutual influence between climate policies and economic behaviors, and non-linearity describes how climate effects can rapidly escalate beyond certain thresholds (Monasterolo, 2020).

[3] The sustainable data gap for analysing climate change and sustainable finance includes deficiencies in availability, usability, access, and reliability of information (Network for Greening the Financial System—NGFS, 2021), also in Italy.

[4] See ECB (2022).

[5] The sample of surveyed firms was targeted to maximize the amount of potential collateral to be assessed; as such, the findings cannot be used for statistical inference on Italian NFCs as the sample is not random nor stratified.

half of the firms do. Less than half of the firms track their emissions and almost all of them belong to sectors with high emissions; firms that do not track emissions often deem them as being irrelevant or cite resource constraints. Stronger governance practices and investments in emission reduction are more common in firms of higher credit worthiness; only a minority of firms have formalized transition plans to achieve their climate goals.

The survey also reveals a disconnect between firms' perceived exposure to physical risks and the potential impact of extreme climate events. Most firms report low risks, despite one-third of them being associated with medium or high physical risk,[6] yet they acknowledge potentially large disruptions to production capacity, especially in the agriculture and manufacturing sectors. This evidence indicates that substantial progress is still required in firm governance and data reporting in order for self-assessed climate risk evaluations to be integrated into credit risk assessment.

The survey responses illustrate the advantages of incorporating firm-level data into ICAS in the place of currently available proxies. Regarding transition risk, PDs based on individual survey data significantly differ from those estimated with sectoral averages. Sectoral data lead to an overestimation of PD compared to the granularly estimated PD for 48% of the firms in the survey and an underestimation for 52% of them. The mean and standard deviation of granular PDs are higher than for sectoral PDs.[7] We believe individual survey data also allow for a more accurate assessment of firm exposure to physical risks than that based on sectoral data. Incorporating precise survey information on weather-related damage and mitigation measures leads to an override of third-party scores for around 25% of physical risk assessments.

These results support the use of climate change survey data, for participating firms that responded to the survey, for the purposes of ICAS, especially for firms that do not publish the non-financial statement, at least until more systematic firm-level information on CCR becomes available. In the coming years some initiatives might increase the availability and quality of this type of information, including the Corporate Sustainability Reporting Directive (CSRD)[8] and, in Italy, the 'MoF Platform on Sustainable Finance' (MoF Platform on Sustainable Finance, 2024).[9]

[6] The firms' exposure to physical risk considers its headquarters and local units' locations, with their relevance estimated based on the number of employees.

[7] The two figures are, respectively, 0.19 and 0.65 for granular PDs and, respectively, 0.03 and 0.07 for sectoral PDs.

[8] CSRD has updated and expanded the scope of the Non-Financial Reporting Directive (Directive 2014/95/EU, NFRD) by requiring reporting for large, listed, companies from 2025, for large, unlisted, companies from 2026, for small and medium-sized companies listed from 2027. Approximately 2,000 firms evaluated by ICAS should report such data by 2027. However, in February 2025 the EU Commission proposed to simplify sustainability reporting requirements removing around 80% of companies from the scope of CSRD. These changes are subject to approval by the European Parliament and EU Member States.

[9] The initiative is chaired by the Ministry of Economy and Finance (MoF) and involves the Ministry of Environment and Energy Security, the Ministry of Enterprises and Made in Italy, the

The remainder of the chapter is organized as follows. Section 2 outlines the structure of the survey. Section 3 describes the sample. Section 4 provides details on the respondents. Section 5 presents the main results. Section 6 analyses the impact of granular data on climate risk-adjusted PDs. Section 7 concludes.

2 Structure

The survey launched by the Bank of Italy intends to collect granular information from firms on CCR and other qualitative data not otherwise available. Given the experimental nature of the survey, a limited number of firms among those assessed by ICAS was contacted, selecting the most relevant ones in terms of collateral. Participation in the survey was voluntary, but it was fostered by supplying the respondents with a feedback report comparing individual responses to those of a reference group.

The survey has two sections: (i) a first one on CCR; (ii) a second section on corporate governance and other qualitative information. The climate section consists of 13 questions which span seven areas: (i) the existence of dedicated internal climate committees; (ii) the monitoring of greenhouse gas (GHG) emissions[10]; (iii) energy consumption data[11]; (iv) the assessment of physical risks and the firm's ability to manage them; (v) the investments in energy transition to assess the firm's commitment to reducing its carbon emissions; (vi) the emission targets; (vii) the participation in the Emissions Trading Scheme (ETS).

The second section investigates corporate governance and organizational aspects that are important for credit risk assessment of the firm. This section includes 12 questions that explore three areas: (i) the firm's strategic positioning and competitive advantage; (ii) the communication with stakeholders; (iii) the economic and financial outlook.

Bank of Italy, the Italian Companies and Stock Exchange Commission (CONSOB), the Institute for the Supervision of Insurance (IVASS), and the Italian Pension Fund Supervisory Authority (COVIP). Recently, the Sustainability Dialogue between SMEs and Banks (https://www.dt.mef.gov.it/it/attivita_istituzionali/sistema_bancario_finanziario/finanza_sostenibile/dialogo_sostenibilita/index.html) was published by the MoF Platform on Sustainable Finance. The document aims to support SMEs in gathering and producing information on environmental, social, and governance (ESG) impacts, facilitating dialogue with banks on sustainability issues and improving access to financing.

[10] Including both direct and indirect emissions (Scope 1 and 2).

[11] Renewable sources are distinguished from non-renewable sources to assess the carbon footprint.

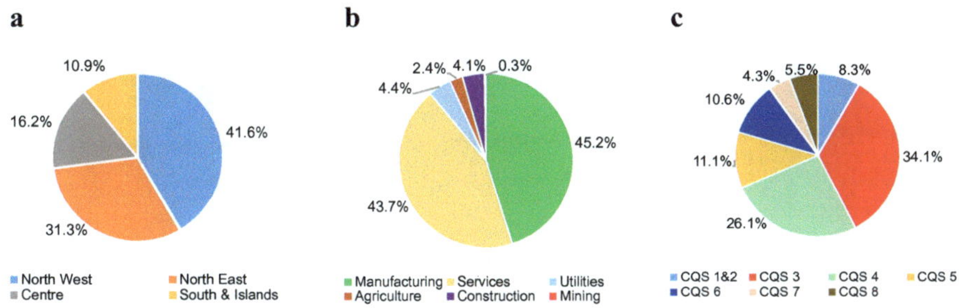

Fig. 1 Distribution of NFCs eligible for the Full ICAS rating by **a** geographical area; **b** economic activity sector; **c** CQS. *Note* CQS are the credit risk categories defined by the Eurosystem to classify assets eligible as collateral in monetary policy operations (see also chapter "The Statistical Model"). The scale ensures the comparability of credit assessments across all accepted systems, such as ECAIs, IRB systems, and ICASes. CQS 1&2 and CQS 3 correspond approximately to ECAI ratings from AAA to AA– and from A+ to A–, respectively

3 Sample

To define the survey sample, we considered the 5,040 NFCs eligible for the Full ICAS rating in 2024 (Fig. 1).[12]

The survey sample is designed to address specific information gaps for the ICAS expert assessment. Hence the sample is not stratified and it should therefore not be used for statistical inference about the population of all Italian NFCs.

We selected a candidate group of 1,102 firms from the ICAS sub-sample that we had initially identified,[13] aiming to obtain responses from 680 firms, balancing the need for a sufficient number of valid responses with the goal of containing the survey costs (Fig. 2).[14] The firms were selected with the following criteria:

[12] Chosen according to criteria based on characteristics of the firms and of the associated loans eligible for use as collateral from the 370,000 firms assessed with the statistical model.

[13] Initially, 1,912 firms stood out as the most interesting for ICAS and selected according to purposive sampling, 871 were assessed relevant for climate change risks and 1,041 for governance and organizational aspects. The relevant companies for climate change risks were identified as being ex ante exposed to transition or physical climate risks based on Di Virgilio et al. (2024), external ratings, or third-party climate risk assessment services. Following the ineligibility criteria of the American Association for Public Opinion Research (AAPOR, 2023), for example, in cases where the company could not be reached or was no longer operational, only 1,102 firms were included in the candidate group (95 companies were also included in the Bank of Italy—Survey of Industrial and Service Firms in 2023, the so called INVIND Survey).

[14] The target included 540 significant firms in terms of climate change risk (with particular reference to exposure to transition risk and participation in the EU ETS) and the remaining 140 chosen for qualitative significance (including those with the highest statistical ratings or with a possible role as a parent company).

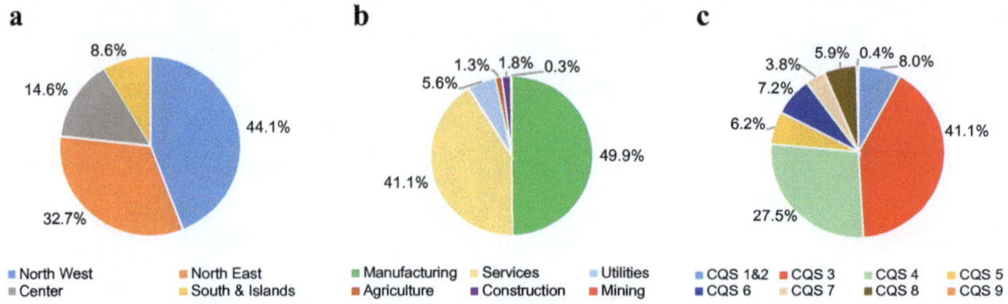

Fig. 2 Distribution of candidate NFCs by **a** geographical area, **b** economic activity sector and **c** CQS. *Note* **c** includes CQS 9 as some firms have gone into default since the start of the survey

(a) non-default status[15]; (b) medium or large size[16]; (c) relevance for monetary policy, based on the collateral exposure of the lending banks.[17] The survey was conducted by ICAS analysts in the regional branches between February and June 2024.[18]

4 Respondents

The NFCs that responded to the survey are 577, more than half of the contacted firms, and not far from the target of 680.[19]

The number of responses declined slightly as the questionnaire progressed beyond the first question, it dropped after reaching 80% of questions answered

[15] The ICAS default definition relies on Article 178 of the Capital Requirements Regulation (CRR), which sets forth that a default occurs when a bank considers that the obligor is unlikely to pay its credit obligations or the obligor is past due more than 90 days on any material credit obligation to the bank (Auria et al., 2021). A new harmonized definition of 'fractional default' has been introduced for evaluating the performance of ICAS models in the yearly Eurosystem ECAF monitoring process (see chapter "The Statistical Model").

[16] According to Commission Recommendation 2003/361/EC, large companies are those with over 250 employees and revenues above €50 million or assets over €43 million, while medium-sized firms have 50–250 employees and revenues or assets between €10 million and €50 million.

[17] Additional details on the characteristics of the candidate group are provided in Table 7 in the Appendix.

[18] Analysts reached out to companies by sending out questionnaires, followed by phone contact.

[19] In the absence of statistical objectives and due to the non-priority nature of certain questions, even a single response is considered valuable, as it provides otherwise unavailable information that ICAS analysts can use in creditworthiness assessments (AAPOR, 2023). The survey was submitted to 1,102 NFCs. The response rate can be considered satisfactory as it is not far from that obtained in other Bank of Italy surveys, in which there is often a significant share of collaborative firms for several years (e.g. the participation rate was 64.2, 62.2 and 69.6%, respectively, for industrial, service and construction firms in the Bank of Italy's 2023 INVIND).

Table 1 Responses (number of respondents)

% of completed answers	Climate section	Corporate governance section	Both sections	Only one section
At least 1 answer	569	546	538	577
30	536	536	525	547
50	525	536	522	539
60	523	536	520	539
70	515	536	512	539
80	479	533	475	537
90	288	527	285	530
100	55	509	55	509

Note The column "only one section" reports the cases in which firms responded either to the climate section or to the corporate governance section
Source ICAS Survey

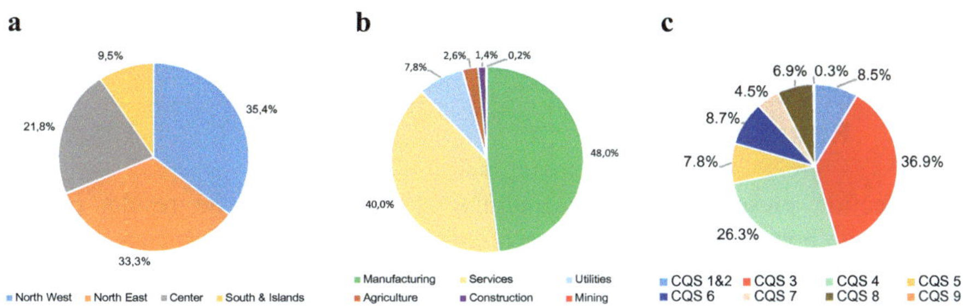

Fig. 3 Distribution of the respondents' sample by **a** geographical area, **b** economic activity sector and **c** CQS. *Note* **c** includes CQS 9 as some firms have gone into default since the start of the survey

(Table 1). The most significant reduction occurred in the climate section, where some questions required detailed responses.[20]

Regarding the geographical distribution, 69% of respondents are from the northern regions, a slightly lower share compared to the ICAS population distribution (73%). As for the distribution across sectors, nearly half of the responses are from the manufacturing sector (48%), followed by services (40%), in line with the distribution within the ICAS population. From a credit quality perspective, 63% of respondents are in the intermediate risk classes (Fig. 3),[21] as in the ICAS sub-sample.

[20] Questions on energy consumption and emissions required detailed internal data that some firms, particularly those without established environmental reporting, found difficult to provide.
[21] CQS 3 and 4.

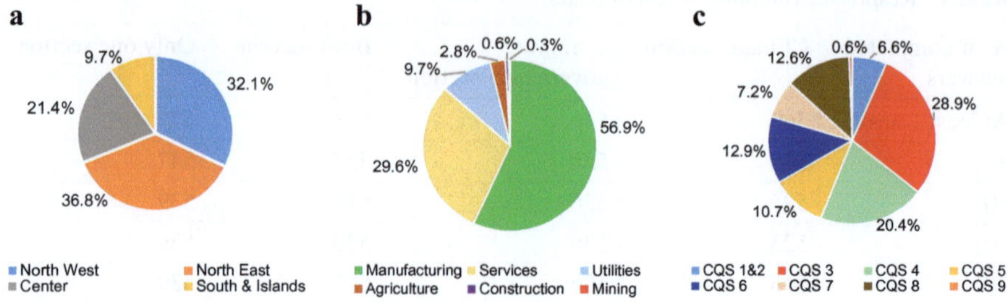

Fig. 4 Distribution of climate respondents' sample by **a** geographical area, **b** economic activity sector and **c** CQS. *Note* **c** includes CQS 9 as some firms have gone into default since the start of the survey

The share of respondents to the climate section that operate in the manufacturing sector is 57% of the section and the share in the higher credit quality steps is 35% (CQS 1–3, Fig. 4).

Conversely, the firms that responded to the corporate governance section are more concentrated in the services sector and more creditworthy.[22]

5 Results

This Section presents the main findings of the survey. The results provide insights into how Italian firms approach climate-related risk governance, emission monitoring, and qualitative aspects important to the ICAS framework.

5.1 Climate Change Risk Governance

The first section of the survey investigates how firms manage climate risk. 565 firms (98% of the respondents) provided an answer regarding the presence of a governing body responsible for climate-related risk management.

The results indicate in many cases the absence of designated structures: 46% of the NFCs report no governance structure specifically tasked with climate risk management (Fig. 5).

This gap is prominent in the services and agricultural sectors, where 58 and 60% of firms, respectively, lack a designated governance body; the share drops to 35% in manufacturing. A minority of firms (25%) indicate that they have structures exclusively devoted to climate risk management (sustainability committee or dedicated figures external to the Board of Directors, BoD), more frequently in the manufacturing sector. Additionally, in nearly one-third of the firms, climate-related

[22] For additional details on the ICAS sub-sample and the respondents' sample, see Tables 7, 8, 9, and 10.

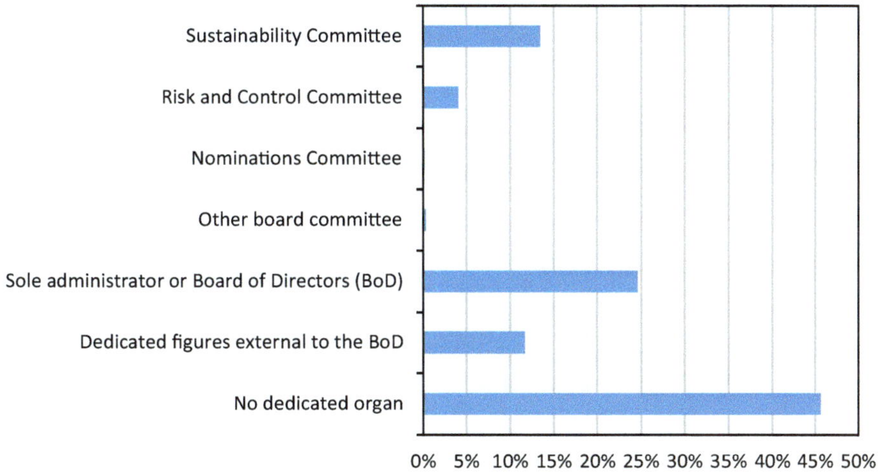

Fig. 5 Climate risk management. *Source* ICAS Survey

responsibilities are integrated into existing governance bodies (risk and control committee, nominations committee, other board committee, sole administrator, or BoD).

The absence of designated bodies is less frequent among firms with higher credit quality scores: only 37% of the NFCs in CQS 1&2 and 39% in CQS 3 report no specific climate governance roles. In contrast, the share rises to 73% in CQS 6 and 62% in CQS 7 and 8. This pattern should not be interpreted as an indicator of a causal relation: lower attention to climate risks does not necessarily lead to lower credit scores. Causality, if any, may also be running in the opposite direction (reverse causality): NFCs with better credit profiles may naturally adopt stronger governance practices, including those related to climate risks, due to a broader attention to organizational resilience.

5.2 Emission Accounting

Another section of the survey examines the tracking of direct and indirect greenhouse gas emissions (Scope 1 and Scope 2 emissions, respectively). Of the 554 respondents to this section of the questionnaire, only 44% state that they track emissions and only one tenth of the remaining firms plan to begin the tracking; awareness and prioritization of climate risks thus show ample room for improvement. Emission accounting is more widespread in the manufacturing sector, where the majority of firms (54%) monitor their emissions.

Of the firms that do not track emissions, 40% cite "lack of relevance or significance" as the primary reason and 14% the lack of skills or resources (Fig. 6).

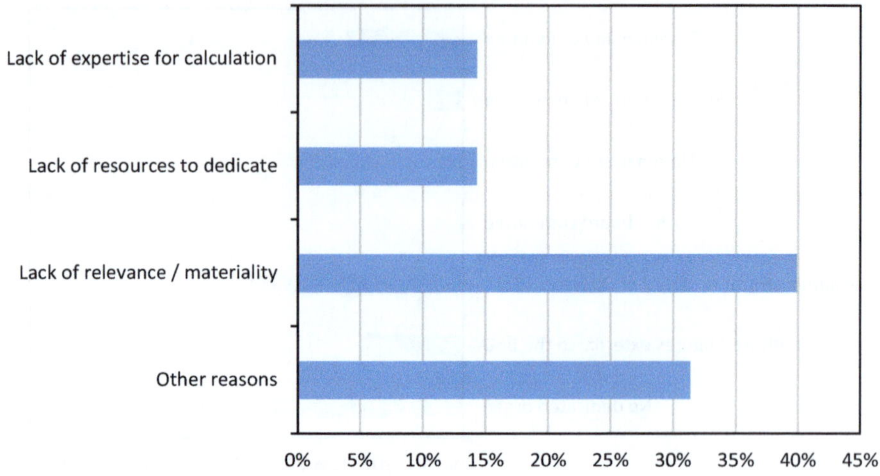

Fig. 6 Reasons for not reporting emissions. *Source* ICAS Survey

Among the firms that do not track emissions only three per cent belong to low-emission sectors,[23] 81% belong to medium-emission sectors and 16% belong to high-emission sectors.[24] The firms in sectors with high emissions report that the lack of tracking is due in 22% of the cases to their own emissions being not significant[25] and in 24% of cases to the lack of skills or resources.

5.3 Investments in Emission Reduction

The survey also examines firms' investments towards reducing their greenhouse gas emissions ('eco-sustainable investments'). Among the 524 respondents to this question, 40% report having made such investments in 2023. Investments in emission reduction are more common among firms with higher credit quality scores: 55% of the respondent NFCs with CQS 1&2 and 46% of those with CQS 3 invest in such initiatives. This finding may suggest a relation between credit quality and the (willingness and) capacity to allocate resources to emission reduction, though it is unclear whether stronger credit profiles act as an enabling factor for such investments or whether the underlying organizational strength supports both creditworthiness and sustainability.

[23] The classification of the sectors with low, medium and high emissions is described in Di Virgilio et al. (2024).

[24] Of these firms in high emission sectors, 34% belong to the land transportation sector, 26% to the metal sector, 16% to the chemical sector.

[25] This may be the case, for example, for firms operating in paper production or in the metallurgical industry, generally considered as high-emissions entities.

Table 2 Distribution of financing instruments for eco-sustainable investments (percentage values)

Type of financing	Firms	Average share of investment
Self-financing	75.4	73.5
Interfirm financing	5.8	70.6
Banks and other financial intermediaries	45.4	70.9
Issuance of bonds and similar instruments	1.9	38.6
Equity	0.5	66
Public funding	11.1	37.1
Other	4.3	72.6

Note The column "Firms" indicates the percentage of firms using the specific financing instrument. The average share of investments financed by this financing instrument is calculated only for firms using it
Source ICAS Survey

In addition, the survey revealed that large firms are more financially committed in reducing their environmental impact; about 80% of the companies that made investments towards reducing their greenhouse gas emissions in 2023 were large. This finding aligns with the ECB's Survey on the Access to Finance of Enterprises (SAFE; Ferrando et al., 2023).

On average, firms indicate 1.4 financing instruments. Self-financing is the most common funding source for investments towards reducing own emissions, reported by 75% of firms, followed by bank loans, indicated by 45% of respondents. Public funding is used by only 11% of the firms; this share rises in Southern Italy and the Islands to 27% of the respondents. Firms with better CQS scores favour self-financing (91%); those with CQS 3 to 5 rely more on bank loans. Financing instruments such as bonds and equity are less common yet finance substantial portions of investments when used. Specifically, bonds fund on average 39% of investment, equity 66% and inter-firm financing over 70% (Table 2). Only 11% of firms resorts to public funding, which on average covers only 37% of eco-sustainable investments. These results confirm the findings for the euro area from SAFE, which identifies public subsidies to climate-related investment as insufficient.

For firms that do not invest in the reduction of emissions, 56% cite "other reasons", including ongoing planning due to regulatory uncertainty. This is consistent with the idea that a clear regulatory framework could stimulate investment. Additionally, 16% of the respondents report that further investments are not economically viable due to the nature of their production processes, highlighting sector-specific challenges (Fig. 7).

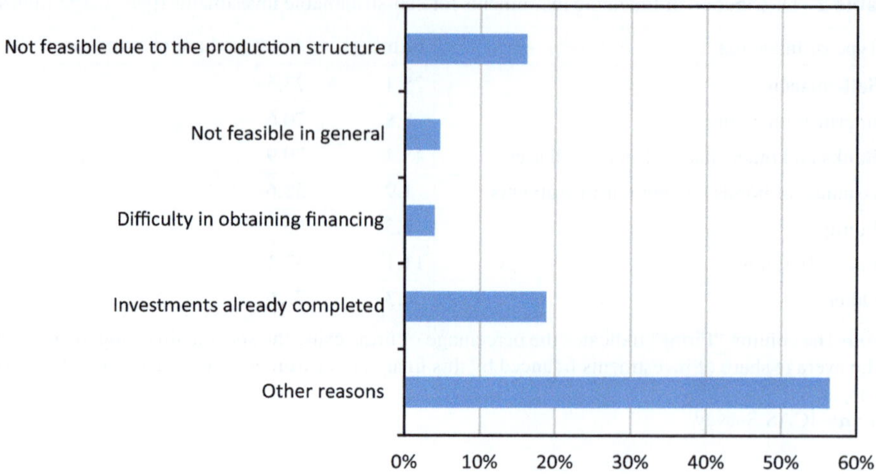

Fig. 7 Reasons for no eco-sustainable investments. *Source* ICAS Survey

5.4 Investment Forecasts for the Energy Transition

In terms of economic outlook, 76% of responding firms provide forecasts for own investments in the energy transition. Among these, 43% plan no new investments, 25% plan to increase their investment flows, and 24% expect to maintain current flows. Only a small portion foresees reducing their annual investments, while 19% of the companies that reported no investments in the previous year foresee them in the future.

5.5 Long-Term Goals

Among the 519 respondents to this question, 43% have set emission reduction targets for the next five years. These targets are more widespread in the construction and manufacturing sectors (63 and 51%, respectively) and less frequent in the services sector (33%). Over two-thirds of firms in CQS 1&2 have set targets; while this share declines significantly for firms in lower CQS. For the firms with established targets, the majority (over 80%, Fig. 8) expect reducing Scope 1 emissions relative to 2023. Nearly three-fifths of respondents report having no emission reduction targets; a similar share has not made any related investments.

Just over 60% of the respondents expect a reduction in Scope 2 emissions or in the use of non-renewable energy sources.

Among firms that have set emission reduction targets for the next five years, however, only a limited number of firms have formalized a plan to achieve these goals, more often in the manufacturing sector. No clear relation emerges between having defined a transition plan and the firm CQS score. Many firms appear

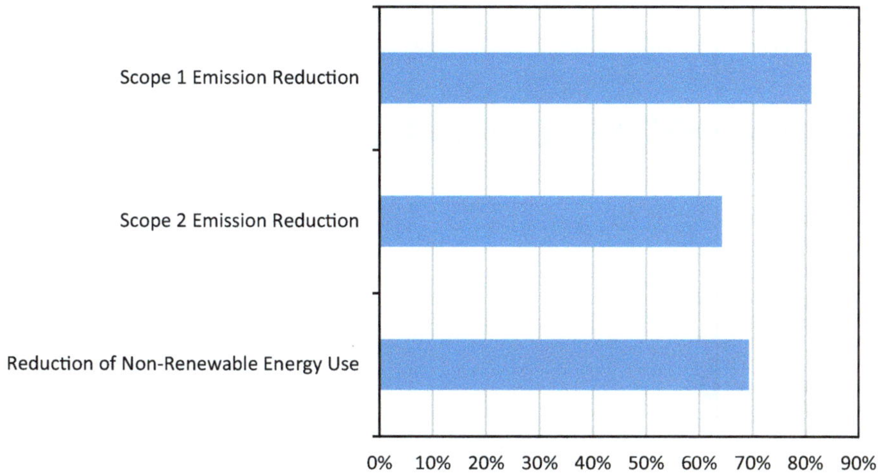

Fig. 8 Emissions and non-renewable energy reduction targets. *Source* ICAS Survey

to lack the governance and resources necessary to translate the objectives into actions, regardless of the credit standing; more than half of the firms that have not defined a plan in fact have not identified a body responsible for following up on sustainability issues.

5.6 Physical Risk

Among the 541 respondents to this question, 25% of firms report to have suffered direct damages from extreme weather events over the past five years, with a higher incidence in the North East and North West areas. However, the impact on productive capacity is low, with more significant effects in the agriculture and utilities sectors.

In terms of perceived exposure to physical climate risk, 70% of the firms indicate a low or zero risk level; of these 68%, according to data based on ISPRA maps, appear to be in areas with low physical risk, 19% in medium risk areas and 13% in high risk areas.[26] Only one per cent of firms, all in northern Italy, assess their exposure as very high (Fig. 9).

To evaluate the accuracy of this risk perception, self-assessed risk scores (on a 1-to-5 scale) are compared with those from an external provider. Across the 432 respondents to this question, 29% show alignment between internal and external scores; 35% of firms underestimate the risk compared with the external provider, while 36% overestimate risk. This symmetric distribution reveals no

[26] The firms answer for the group, if existing, to which they belong. We compare the survey responses with data based on ISPRA risk maps.

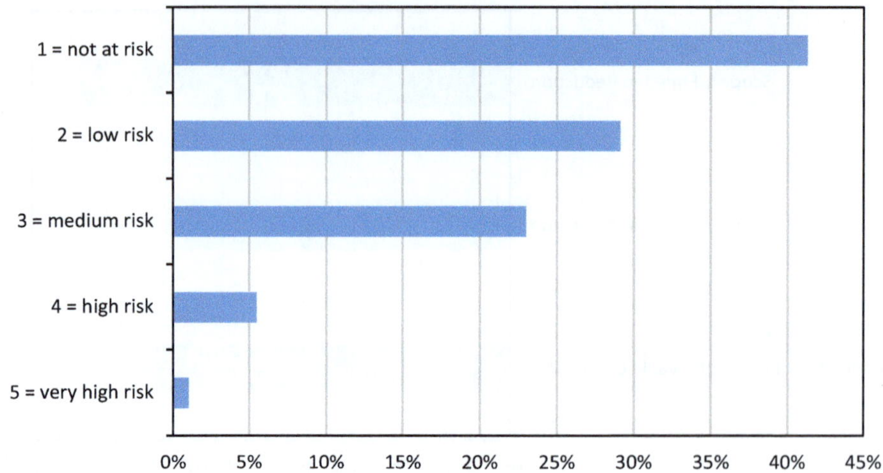

Fig. 9 Perceived exposure to climate risk. *Source* ICAS Survey

systematic bias, but rather a prevailing misalignment between perceived and externally assessed exposure. The divergence is particularly clear among firms operating in areas with a high physical risk: although nearly one-fifth of the respondents operate in such areas, more than two-thirds of them perceive their exposure as minimal, and the majority of those acknowledging some exposure report only limited expected impacts on production capacity.[27] These findings suggest that firms' perception of climate-related physical risk may be disconnected from objective indicators of exposure and vulnerability, although we are not in a position to verify this possibility.

Despite the moderate risk perception reported by firms, the potential impact of extreme climate events on productive capacity is assessed as more substantial: based on the 279 responses received to the dedicated question, the average estimated impact is 19%. This apparent contradiction may stem from the distinction between perceived probability ("exposure") and perceived severity ("vulnerability"): firms may consider the occurrence of extreme events unlikely, yet still recognize their potentially significant consequences on operations if such events were to materialize. These estimates of the potential impact of extreme climate events are significantly higher than the damages reported over the past five years, likely reflecting either an underestimation of past losses or expectations of worsening climatic phenomena.

[27] The external provider assigns a five-tier score based on the geographical location of the company's headquarters and any secondary sites (for the latter, information on the number of assigned employees, where available, is used to estimate their relative importance). For the purposes of our elaboration, firms with a score in the two lowest tiers are classified as high physical risk.

The discrepancy between the low perceived risk and the high expected impact may reflect the coexistence of limited recent experience and growing awareness of the potential consequences of extreme events. This could be due to heightened salience of recent climate disasters without excluding a dynamic adjustment of expectations over time. Although the recent impacts on productive capacity have been limited, firms may be factoring in the growing intensity of climate-related risks. This apparent contradiction may reflect cognitive and structural aspects of risk perception. Firms may perceive low risk based on the limited frequency of past events, influenced by short institutional memory and a lack of recent direct experience. At the same time, recent high-impact disasters—widely reported in the news and socially salient—may amplify their perception of potential severity (Kunreuther et al., 2014). From a modelling perspective, this aligns with the standard separation between the probability of occurrence and the conditional severity distribution: climate-related physical risks are often characterised by low expected frequency, but potentially extreme consequences, consistent with fat-tailed loss distributions (Batteson et al., 2014).[28]

5.7 Insurance Coverage and Mitigation Strategies

The survey indicates that 73% of firms are insured against physical risks, with higher coverage among manufacturing and services (81 and 67%, respectively); most of these firms are large ones (76%). These results are in line with the findings of Gallo et al., (2022), based on Bank of Italy's 2021 INVIND data, which showed that 68% of firms had bought insurance coverage at the time.[29] However, the reasons for the lack of insurance coverage differ across the two surveys. In the ICAS survey, about one-third of respondents cite non-economic factors, such as the perceived insignificance of risk, while INVIND participants primarily flag high insurance costs and insufficient information. These differences may reflect the characteristics of the respective samples: the higher share of smaller firms in the INVIND sample may explain their greater focus on cost-related barriers.

Participation in the insurance market is lower for smaller firms and for those located in the South and Islands consistently with previous analyses (Angelini, 2022a; Frigo & Venturini, 2024; Gallo et al., 2022). Insurance coverage is instead more widespread among firms with higher CQS ratings (coverage rates between 73 and 81%), compared to firms with lower CQS scores, which display coverage rates between 41% (CQS 7) and 63% (CQS 6).

Among the firms without insurance coverage, 58% indicate that they consider climate risk irrelevant for their operations (Fig. 10). Common strategies include

[28] The Third UK Climate Change Risk Assessment Technical Report (CCRA, 2021) and Rising et al. (2022) report that risk perception often trails empirical risk indicators for firms with limited resources devoted to resilience.

[29] The same survey also found that damages from climate events more than doubled between 2016 and 2021, while insurance adoption remained largely unchanged (Gallo et al., cit.).

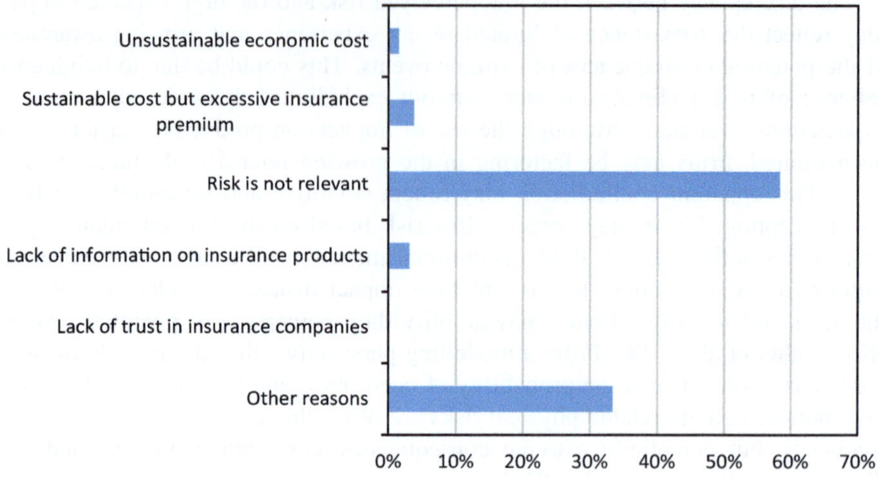

Fig. 10 Reasons for no insurance coverage. *Source* ICAS Survey

investment in safety measures, the diversification of production and storage sites, general insurance, disaster recovery plans, and relocating operations to areas with lower exposure to climate risk. Italian firms will nevertheless have to gradually adapt to the national regulations concerning compulsory insurance against damages resulting from catastrophic events.[30]

5.8 Corporate Governance Survey

This Section presents the findings from the survey's second section, which does not investigate climate change risks, but contributes to hone the qualitative assessment performed by ICAS analysts of key areas of firms' governance that affect its creditworthiness and on which alternative data are not available. The questions in this section investigate corporate practices in market monitoring, resource allocation for risk management, and formal control functions. In particular, we investigate the scope of governance structures and strategic planning across firms, including plans to respond to sectoral challenges and emerging risks.

Regarding *market monitoring*, 79% of 535 respondents state that they monitor trends and potential opportunities or threats in their sector of activity. Only one-third allocate specific resources to this function, with higher CQS-rated firms doing so more frequently than lower-rated ones. This practice is observed more frequently in the manufacturing sector (42%) than in the services sector (30%).

[30] Insurance coverage for asset damage caused by natural disasters was made mandatory in Italy (Law 213/2023). The Italian Budget Law for 2024 has envisaged a gradual entry into force of the obligation for Italian firms, differentiating the recipients between large, medium, small and micro enterprises (by 31 March, 1 October and 31 December 2025, respectively).

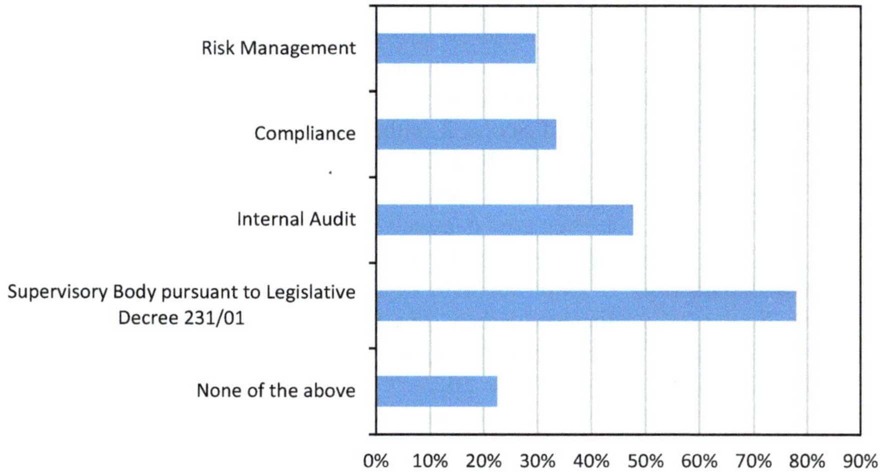

Fig. 11 Corporate control functions. *Source* ICAS Survey

For *formal control functions*, 78% of the respondents report to have a Supervisory Body under Italian Legislative Decree 231/2001. Other control functions including internal audit, compliance, and risk management, are less widespread (Fig. 11).

Regarding *social impact reporting*, 93% of firms responded, with 52% stating that they do not produce dedicated documentation, such as sustainability or social responsibility reports. Reporting is more common in sectors like utilities and construction, where 55 and 63% of firms, respectively, engage in such reporting.

6 Climate-Risk Adjusted PDs: ICAS Granular Data vs. Sectoral Approximation

To check whether firm-specific transition risk information improves the accuracy of credit risk assessment, the survey results are compared with the sectoral estimates[31] of emission data used so far in credit risk methodologies. For physical risk, the scores provided by an external provider are refined using the survey data described in previous Sections.

[31] Sectoral estimates refer to emission values and transition risk indicators derived from industry-level averages rather than firm-level data. These estimates are typically obtained by imputing energy use and emissions based on the firm's sector classification (e.g. NACE codes), employment figures, and standard energy intensities.

6.1 Transition Risk

Firstly, we perform a comparison of emission data. For each firm included in the survey, we obtain greenhouse gas emissions by aggregating data reported by firms for the Survey for Scope 1 and Scope 2 (either location-based or market-based) emissions.[32] When Scope 2 market-based data are available, we aggregate Scope 1 with Scope 2 market-based data to reflect the energy procurement choices of the firm, such as renewable energy contracts or supplier-specific emission factors. This method prioritises firm-specific information, recognising that Scope 2 market-based data offer a more accurate representation of a firm carbon footprint than Scope 2 location-based data. For firms that do not provide data on direct Scope 2 emissions, energy consumption is converted into emissions using the ISPRA emission factors (ISPRA, 2023),[33] which provide standard values for key energy sources.[34] This process ensures consistency and comparability across firms, reflecting Italy's specific energy mix and decarbonization trends as documented by ISPRA. The resulting emission dataset covers 432 firms, representing 11.5% of Italy's total emissions in 2022.

Among the 83 firms included in the survey declaring participation in the EU-ETS, 67 also reported Scope 1 emissions in the survey. For 54 of them, verified emissions from the EU-ETS registry were retrieved, showing a strong correlation (0.87) and an average standard deviation below 9%. This alignment underscores the accuracy of self-reported data and confirms the survey's potential as a validation tool for information independently collected by ICAS, despite minor discrepancies due to reference years or reporting boundaries.

The comparison over the whole set of 432 firms reveals significant discrepancies between individual and sectoral emission levels (Fig. 12). The absolute difference between emissions levels exceeds 10% in 85.4% of cases, highlighting substantial discrepancies between firm-level and sectoral estimates. A visual inspection

[32] Scope 1 emissions refer to direct greenhouse gas emissions from sources that are owned or controlled by the company, such as emissions from fuel combustion in company-operated facilities or vehicles. Scope 2 emissions are indirect emissions associated with the consumption of purchased electricity, heat, or steam, and depend on how the electricity is generated and procured. Firms provide Scope 2 data in two distinct categories: location-based and market-based, reflecting the different methodologies for accounting emissions from purchased electricity. Location-based data represent emissions calculated using the average emission intensity of the grid where the electricity is consumed, while market-based data are derived from supplier-specific emission factors or contractual instruments, such as renewable energy certificates.

[33] ISPRA (Istituto Superiore per la Protezione e la Ricerca Ambientale) is the Italian Institute for Environmental Protection and Research. It operates within the framework of the National System for Environmental Protection (SNPA) and is responsible for conducting research, providing technical-scientific support, and developing indicators and reports related to environmental protection and sustainability in Italy.

[34] For instance, emissions from natural gas are calculated using a factor of 0.001927 tCO_2e per standard cubic meter (Sm^3), while market-based electricity emissions are computed using a factor of 0.4491 tCO_2e per megawatt-hour (MWh).

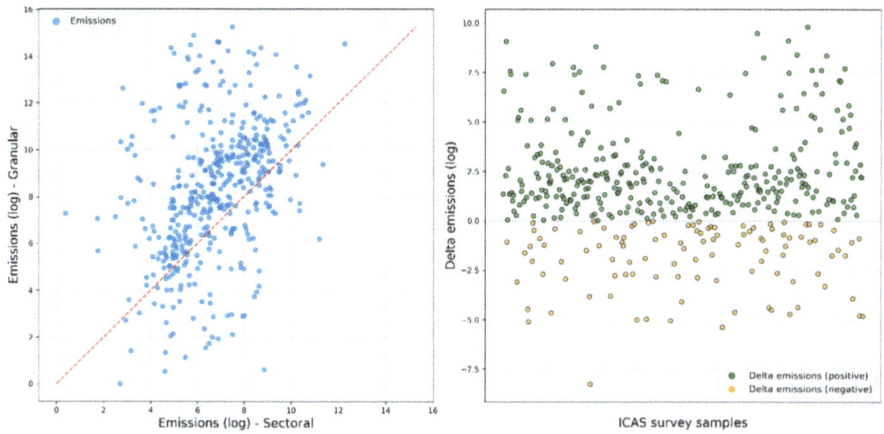

Fig. 12 Individual vs sectoral emission levels (in logarithmic scale). The left panel shows individual and sectoral emissions, while the right panel illustrates the dispersion of the difference between individual and sectoral emissions across our 432 firms. *Sources* Authors' calculations based on sectoral or individual emission data

of the scatter plot (Fig. 12) in the left panel suggests a systematic prevalence of firms whose granular emissions exceed the corresponding sectoral estimates, as evidenced by the dense concentration of points above the 45-degree line. The right panel complements this evidence by showing the distribution of the logarithmic difference between granular and sectoral emissions. The asymmetry in the distribution—particularly the predominance of green points—further confirms that firm-level data often report higher emissions than sectoral averages.

Secondly, we integrate these data into the ICAS framework to assess their impact on credit risk metrics. We incorporate individual emission data into the Bank of Italy's climate stress-testing framework, building on Bernardini et al. (2021) and Di Virgilio et al. (2024). This methodology relies on a tool that embeds the financial risk associated with climate policies into the ICAS methodology. Specifically, emission data are fed into the ICAS stress-testing framework to simulate the impact of transition risk on the PD of Italian firms. By computing energy expenditures and working out their impact over a range of financial statement items, the methodology allows for the calculation of key financial variables used as inputs to the ICAS statistical model. The mean and standard deviation of granular PDs (respectively, 0.19 and 0.65, Table 3) are higher than the equivalent figures for sectoral PDs (respectively 0.03 and 0.07),[35] as using firm-level data naturally introduces greater variability compared to assigning the same sectoral value to all firms. While this result reflects the shift from sectoral averages to firm-level

[35] Both PDs are computed at the individual firm level; the former (granular PDs) use firm-specific data collected via the ICAS survey, while the latter (sectoral PDs) are based on sectoral averages for climate change risk variables.

Table 3 Sectorial vs Individual PDs (percentage values)

Sectoral vs Individual PDs			
Method	Mean	Std. Dev	CV
Sectoral	0.03	0.07	2.36
Individual	0.19	0.65	3.35

Source Authors' PDs calculations based on sectoral or individual emission data

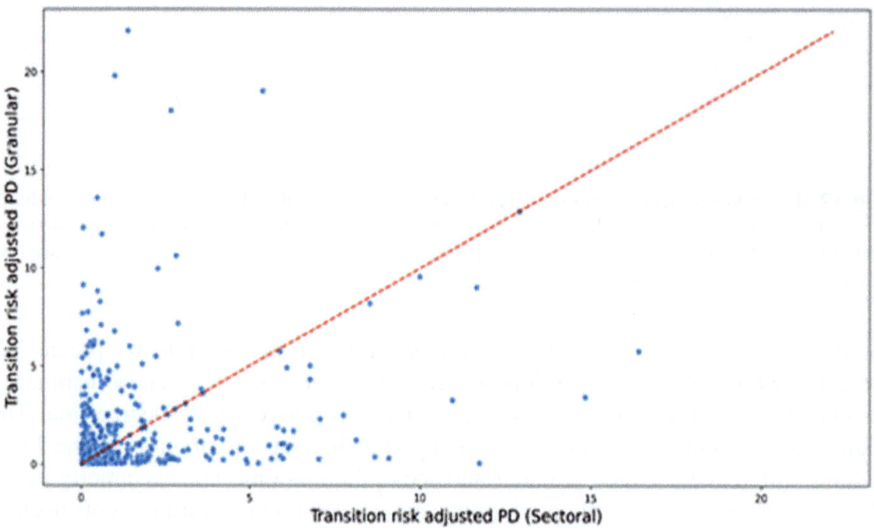

Fig. 13 Change in 1-year credit ratings (in percentage values). *Source* Authors' TR-adjusted PDs calculations based on sectoral or individual emission data

information, it is methodologically relevant: the increased dispersion and higher average PD highlight the capacity of granular data to reveal firm-specific vulnerabilities and risks that are masked when sectoral proxies are used. This finer granularity improves the ability of the ICAS framework to capture the heterogeneity of transition risks across firms, which is critical for a forward-looking credit risk assessment.

The impact of using firm-level versus sectoral data becomes even clearer when comparing the year-on-year change in transition risk-adjusted PDs derived from the two datasets (Fig. 13).[36]

The diagonal line represents perfect alignment between the two estimates, while deviations indicate firms whose 1-year PDs differ depending on whether granular or sectoral emission data are used. Out of the 172 firms for which complete Scope

[36] The individual emissions exhibit a wider dispersion and far more outliers, capturing higher variability and extreme values in the transition-risk adjusted PDs.

1 and Scope 2 data are available, 90 are assigned higher PDs and 82 lower PDs than with the use of sectoral data. The number of firms with higher and lower PDs rises to 227 and 205, respectively, when we employ the full sample of 432 firms for which individual data on either Scope 1 or Scope 2 emission data are available, through the conversion of energy consumption into emission levels.[37] These results confirm the importance of individual emission data in capturing firm-specific risks that sectoral averages fail to reflect, particularly in high-emission industries where transition risk is most pronounced.

We observe that the relationship between PD estimates based on granular and sectoral emission data ('granular PD' and 'sectoral PDs' respectively) differs notably under the stress-testing framework (Fig. 14).[38] Although the median values are comparable across the two datasets, the wider dispersion in granular PDs underscores the capacity of firm-level data to reflect a broader array of risk exposures.[39] This variability reflects the improved detection of vulnerabilities specific to individual firms, especially those in high-risk sectors.[40]

When comparing the effects of transition risk integration on ICAS ratings and CQS migrations, a higher incidence of downgrades emerges under the granular approach—25% versus 14% using sectoral data (Tables 4 and 5). This outcome reflects the circumstance that granular data, by capturing firm-level differences, allow for the identification of transition risks that are masked when using sectoral averages data. Stable ratings, referring to firms for which the stressed PD under climate risk does not result in a rating migration, remain the vast majority in both cases, accounting for 75% in granular assessments and 86% in sectoral ones.

In terms of CQS (Table 5), not surprisingly the downgrades are less frequent than those observed for rating changes, reflecting the less fine-grained nature of the CQS scale. However, individual assessments still show a higher proportion of downgrades (15%) compared to sectoral assessments (5%).

---

[37] Namely, 227 firms showed higher PD estimates based on granular emissions compared to those derived from sectoral averages, while 205 displayed lower PD values.

[38] Transition risk-adjusted PDs are computed by monetising firm-specific emissions through a carbon bill, defined as the product of excess emissions and a stressed carbon price. The resulting cost is propagated through the income statement and balance sheet via accounting rules, and the updated financials are fed into the ICAS statistical model to estimate the adjusted PD. See Cugliari et al. (2024) for methodological details.

[39] The Kolmogorov-Smirnov test yields a significant p-value (2.28×10^{-6}), confirming that PD distributions from detailed and aggregated emissions data differ. Similarly, the Mann-Whitney U test p-value (9.67×10^{-7}) supports the enhanced discriminatory power of detailed emissions data. Quartile analysis further emphasises this disparity, with PD estimates based on detailed data consistently showing higher values across all quartiles compared to those derived from aggregated data.

[40] The individual methodology's ability to detect outliers is particularly clear in the upper quartile, where the data reveal firms with significantly higher PD deltas under climate change stress scenarios. This finding helps demonstrating the asymmetric nature of climate transition risks, where a subset of firms faces disproportionately high exposure. The sectoral data, limited by their aggregate nature, fail to capture these nuances, thereby underestimating potential vulnerabilities.

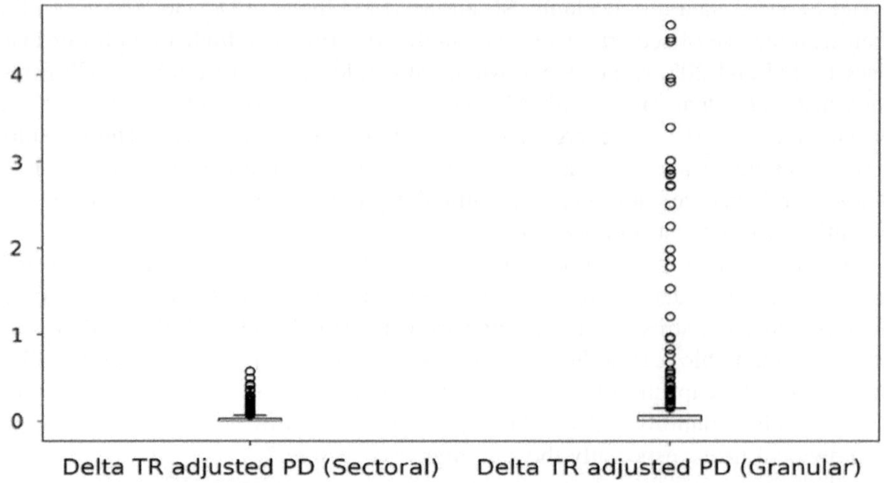

Fig. 14 Absolute difference between 1-year standard and risk-adjusted PDs (in percentage values). *Note* The left portion of the figure shows, for each firm, the absolute difference between the one-year (standard) PD and the one-year risk-adjusted PD when transition risk is proxied by sectoral averages ("Sectoral PDs"). The right portion shows the absolute difference between the one-year (standard) PD and the one-year risk-adjusted PD when transition risk is calculated through granular emissions ("Granular PDs"). *Source* Authors' TR-adjusted PDs calculations based on sectoral or individual emission data

Table 4 1-year change in credit ratings resulting from the climate stress test (percentage values)

Method	Stable	Downgrade
Sectoral	86	14
Individual	75	25

Note The stress is inherently adverse, as the extra carbon bill (either imputed or reported through the survey) resulting from the carbon tax negatively impacts financial indicators, leading to a deterioration in the PDs

Source Authors' calculations based on sectoral or individual emission data

Table 5 1-year change in CQS resulting from the climate stress test (percentage values)

Method	Stable	Downgrade
Sectoral	95	5
Individual	85	15

Source Authors' calculations based on sectoral or individual emission data

These findings confirm that, by capturing firm-specific variations and extremes in transition risk, fine-grained assessments allow for a more precise evaluation of credit risk, aligning with the goals of the Bank of Italy's forward-looking risk management framework.

Table 6 Exposure to physical risk (in unit and percentage values)

Exposure level	Baseline		Adjusted	
	Number of firms	Share	Number of firms	Share
Very high	2	0.4	1	0.2
High	14	2.7	8	1.6
Medium	63	12.3	23	4.5
Low	90	17.6	25	4.9
Negligible	342	66.9	454	88.8
Total	511	100	511	100

Source Authors' calculations based on ICAS Survey and external provider's data

6.2 Physical Risk

To evaluate the potential impact of the survey data, we adapt the ICAS methodology used to assess physical risk exposure.

This approach starts from the baseline scores provided by an external provider, which estimate individual firms' exposure to floods and landslides. These scores[41] are refined using additional information gathered from the ICAS survey. Specifically, the baseline score is adjusted upward (higher risk) when survey responses indicate that recent physical events have caused significant damage—particularly when these events have disrupted business operations in the short term. Conversely, the assessment is revised downward (lower risk) when the survey responses indicate mitigation measures, such as insurance coverage, contingency plans, or other resilience-enhancing actions. Hence, the final evaluation is an integrated view that combines the starting score with firm-reported vulnerabilities and adaptive capacity into an ICAS physical score.

This refinement is performed for the 511 firms in the survey that provide the necessary information. The results show that the incorporation of additional information generally leads to a different assessment of physical risk exposure. The resulting exposure distribution reduces the firms classified in the higher risk classes and increases those classified in the negligible class, underlying an overall shift towards lower risk classes (Table 6). This shows the value added of collecting data directly from individual firms, in order to integrate the information available to commercial providers in assessing exposure to physical risk.

[41] The external provider provides a discrete indicator of physical risk on a five-point scale (1 to 5), where higher values indicate greater exposure. The score captures the riskiness of the areas where firms' headquarters and operational units are located, based on the likelihood and impact of various natural hazard events. The assessment is derived from geo-located data on company premises, linked to census tracts, and incorporates risk from acute climate events, chronic climate phenomena, and non-climate physical hazards. The classification accounts for the type of facility exposed and sector-specific vulnerabilities. Data sources include ISPRA, Copernicus, INGV, and other public datasets.

7 Conclusions

The ICAS survey carried out by the Bank of Italy in 2024 examines the climate-related risk management practices of Italian NFCs within the context of the ICAS climate risk methodology. The survey addresses some limitations of sectoral approximations, by collecting granular data on emission strategies, risk management practices, and governance structures.

The survey identifies notable differences in climate risk management practices across sectors, geographical areas, and credit quality classes. Governance structures related to climate issues vary significantly across firms; deficiencies are more pronounced in the agriculture and services sectors, while manufacturing firms generally exhibit more structured approaches. Nearly 43% of firms have set emission reduction targets over the next five years, yet no clear correlation emerges between these commitments and firms' credit quality scores. The measurement of emissions is limited, especially for firms in sectors with medium and high emissions, and some firms quote the irrelevance of climate change risks as a reason for not monitoring greenhouse gas emissions. 58% of firms without climate insurance view climate risks as negligible; the introduction by law of insurance against damages resulting from catastrophic events should mitigate this vulnerability. Firms with higher credit standing tend to be more engaged in emission reduction. The results indicate that Italian firms have room for significant improvements in climate risk integration within their strategies, including through credible commitments to long-term mitigation goals.

The use of the survey data as inputs for the ICAS model leads to enhancements in transition and physical risk assessment. By integrating granular emission data into the ICAS methodology, the analysis reveals significant discrepancies between the PD estimates obtained with granular data and those that approximate them with sectoral data.

These enhancements allow us to fulfil the Eurosystem standards for the assessment of CCR that were introduced in 2025.

Appendix

Tables 7, 8, 9, and 10 show the composition of the ICAS sub-sample, the overall respondents' sample, the climate section respondents, and the corporate governance section respondents, respectively.

Table 7 Composition of the ICAS sub-sample (unit; percentage values)

	Number	Share
Geographical Area		
North West	843	44.1
North East	625	32.7
Center	279	14.6
South & Islands	165	8.6
Size		
Micro	0	0
Small	1	0.1
Medium	525	27.5
Large	1,386	72.5
Size		
Revenues <= € 2 m	18	0.9
€ 2 m <= Revenues < € 10 m	56	2.9
€ 10 m <= Revenues < € 30 m	346	18.1
€ 30 m <= Revenues < € 50 m	214	11.2
€ 50 m <= Revenues < € 100 m	518	27.1
€ 100 m <= Revenues < € 250 m	443	23.2
€ 250 m <= Revenues < € 1000 m	234	12.2
Revenues >= € 1000 m	83	4.3
Industry		
Manufacturing	954	49.9
Services	785	41.1
Utilities	108	5.6
Agriculture	25	1.3
Construction	34	1.8
Mining	6	0.3
Individual firm or Group		
Individual firm	1,279	66.9

(continued)

Table 7 (continued)

	Number	Share
Part of a Group	633	33.1
Participation in EU ETS		0
Participating in EU ETS	182	9.5
Not participating in EU ETS	1,730	90.5
Availability of NFD		
NFD available	65	3.4
NFD not available	1,847	96.6
Credit quality step		
CQS 1&2	153	8
CQS 3	785	41.1
CQS 4	525	27.5
CQS 5	118	6.2
CQS 6	137	7.2
CQS 7	73	3.8
CQS 8	113	5.9
CQS 9	8	0.4
Total sample	1,912	100

Table 8 Composition of the respondents' sample (unit; percentage values)

	Number	Share
Geographical Area		
North West	204	35.4
North East	192	33.3
Center	126	21.8
South & Islands	55	9.5
Size		
Micro	0	0.0
Small	1	0.2
Medium	153	26.5
Large	423	73.3
Size		0.0
Revenues <= € 2 m	4	0.7
€ 2 m <= Revenues < € 10 m	16	2.8

(continued)

Table 8 (continued)

	Number	Share
€ 10 m <= Revenues < € 30 m	104	18.0
€ 30 m <= Revenues < € 50 m	59	10.2
€ 50 m <= Revenues < € 100 m	134	23.2
€ 100 m <= Revenues < € 250 m	128	22.2
€ 250 m <= Revenues < € 1000 m	98	17.0
Revenues >= € 1000 m	34	5.9
Industry		
Manufacturing	277	48.0
Services	231	40.0
Utilities	45	7.8
Agriculture	15	2.6
Construction	8	1.4
Mining	1	0.2
Individual firm or Group		
Individual firm	356	61.7
Part of a Group	221	38.3
Participation in EU ETS		
Participating in EU ETS	87	15.1
Not participating in EU ETS	490	84.9
Availability of NFD		
NFD available	35	6.1
NFD not available	542	93.9
Credit quality step		
CQS 1&2	49	8.5
CQS 3	213	36.9
CQS 4	152	26.3
CQS 5	45	7.8
CQS 6	50	8.7
CQS 7	26	4.5
CQS 8	40	6.9
CQS 9	2	0.3
Total sample	577	100.0

Table 9 Composition of the climate section respondents' sample (unit; percentage values)

	Number	Share in the sub-sample	Share in the full sample
Geographical Area			
North West	102	32.1	17.7
North East	117	36.8	20.3
Center	68	21.4	11.8
South & Islands	31	9.7	5.4
Size			
Micro	0	0.0	0.0
Small	1	0.3	0.2
Medium	120	37.7	20.8
Large	197	61.9	34.1
Size			
Revenues <= € 2 m	4	1.3	0.7
€ 2 m <= Revenues < € 10 m	13	4.1	2.3
€ 10 m <= Revenues < € 30 m	80	25.2	13.9
€ 30 m <= Revenues < € 50 m	41	12.9	7.1
€ 50 m <= Revenues < € 100 m	72	22.6	12.5
€ 100 m <= Revenues < € 250 m	66	20.8	11.4
€ 250 m <= Revenues < € 1000 m	30	9.4	5.2
Revenues >= € 1000 m	12	3.8	2.1
Industry			
Manufacturing	181	56.9	31.4
Services	94	29.6	16.3
Utilities	31	9.7	5.4
Agriculture	9	2.8	1.6
Construction	2	0.6	0.3
Mining	1	0.3	0.2
Individual firm or Group			
Individual firm	217	68.2	37.6

(continued)

Table 9 (continued)

	Number	Share in the sub-sample	Share in the full sample
Part of a Group	101	31.8	17.5
Participation in EU ETS			0.0
Participating in EU ETS	85	26.7	14.7
Not participating in EU ETS	233	73.3	40.4
Availability of NFD			
NFD available	16	5.0	2.8
NFD not available	302	95.0	52.3
Credit quality step			
CQS 1&2	21	6.6	3.6
CQS 3	92	28.9	15.9
CQS 4	65	20.4	11.3
CQS 5	34	10.7	5.9
CQS 6	41	12.9	7.1
CQS 7	23	7.2	4.0
CQS 8	40	12.6	6.9
CQS 9	2	0.6	0.3
Total "Climate" sub-sample	318	100.0	55.1

Table 10 Composition of the corporate governance section respondents' sample (unit; percentage values)

	Number	Share in the sub-sample	Share in the full sample
Geographical Area			
North West	102	39.4	17.7
North East	75	29.0	13.0
Center	58	22.4	10.1
South & Islands	24	9.3	4.2
Size			
Micro	0	0.0	0.0
Small	0	0.0	0.0
Medium	33	12.7	5.7
Large	226	87.3	39.2
Size			
Revenues <= € 2 m		0.0	0.0
€ 2 m <= Revenues < € 10 m	3	1.2	0.5
€ 10 m <= Revenues < € 30 m	24	9.3	4.2
€ 30 m <= Revenues < € 50 m	18	6.9	3.1
€ 50 m <= Revenues < € 100 m	62	23.9	10.7
€ 100 m <= Revenues < € 250 m	62	23.9	10.7
€ 250 m <= Revenues < € 1000 m	68	26.3	11.8
Revenues >= € 1000 m	22	8.5	3.8
Industry			
Manufacturing	96	37.1	16.6
Services	137	52.9	23.7
Utilities	14	5.4	2.4
Agriculture	6	2.3	1.0
Construction	6	2.3	1.0
Mining		0.0	0.0
Individual firm or Group			
Individual firm	139	53.7	24.1

(continued)

Table 10 (continued)

	Number	Share in the sub-sample	Share in the full sample
Part of a Group	120	46.3	20.8
Participation in EU ETS		0.0	0.0
Participating in EU ETS	2	0.8	0.3
Not participating in EU ETS	257	99.2	44.5
Availability of NFD		0.0	0.0
NFD available	19	7.3	3.3
NFD not available	240	92.7	41.6
Credit quality step			
CQS 1&2	28	10.8	4.9
CQS 3	121	46.7	21.0
CQS 4	87	33.6	15.1
CQS 5	11	4.2	1.9
CQS 6	9	3.5	1.6
CQS 7	3	1.2	0.5
CQS 8		0.0	0.0
CQS 9		0.0	0.0
Total “Corporate governance” sub-sample	259	100.0	44.9

References

American Association for Public Opinion Research. (2023). *Standard definitions. Final dispositions of case codes and outcome rates for surveys* (10th edition).

Angelini, P. (2022a, ottobre 28). *Gli effetti dei cambiamenti climatici in Italia: strategie di adattamento e ruolo delle imprese assicurative.* Venezia.

Angelini, P. (2022b, November 15). *The financial risks posed by climate change: Information gaps and transition plans.* Address at Associazione nazionale per lo studio dei problemi del credito, Milan.

Angelini, P. (2023, September 26). *SMEs and the climate and environmental transition.* Speech at the Confindustria Conference Finance and ESG Disclosure, Rome.

Auria, L., Bingmer, M., Caicedo Graciano, C. M., Charavel, C., Gavilá, S., Iannamorelli, A., Levy, A., Maldonado, A., Resch, F., Rossi, A. M., & Sauer, S. (2021). *Overview of central banks' in-house credit assessment systems in the euro area* (ECB Occasional Paper Series 284).

Batteson, C., Bevan, A., Bunn, P., & Taylor, J. (2014). Quantifying catastrophic and climate-impacted hazards. *Bank of England's Quarterly Bulletin, Q2*, 219–226.

Bernardini, E., Faiella, I., Lavecchia, L., Mistretta, A., & Natoli, F. (2021). *Central banks, climate risks and sustainable finance* (Bank of Italy Occasional Paper 608).

CCRA. (2021). *The third UK Climate Change Risk Assessment Technical Report*, London.

Cugliari, M., Iannamorelli, A., Vassalli, F. (2024). *The dual face of carbon emissions: transition risk-adjusted probability of default* (Bank of Italy Markets, Infrastructures, Payment Systems Working Paper 59).

Di Virgilio, S., Faiella, I., Mistretta, A., & Narizzano, S. (2024). Assessing credit risk sensitivity to climate and energy shocks: Towards a common minimum standards in line with the ECB climate agenda. *Journal of Policy Modeling, 46*(3), 552–568.

European Central Bank. (2022). Common minimum standards for incorporating climate change risks into in-house credit assessment systems in the Eurosystem. *ECB Economic Bulletin Boxes, 6*.

Ferrando, A., Groß, J., & Rariga, J. (2023). Climate change and euro area firms' green investment and financing – results from the SAFE. *ECB Economic Bulletin Boxes, 6*.

Frigo, A., & Venturini, A. (2024). *Insurance coverage against natural risks: A preliminary analysis* (Bank of Italy Occasional Paper 830).

Gallo, R., Guazzarotti, G., Nigro, V., & Cosconati, M. (2022). *Insurance coverage against operational risks of Italian companies: Some evidence* (Bank of Italy Notes on Financial Stability and Supervision 31).

ISPRA. (2023). *Efficiency and decarbonization indicators in Italy and in the biggest European Countries.*

Kunreuther, H., Heal, G., Allen, M., Edenhofer, O., Field, C. B., & Yohe, G. (2014). Integrated risk and uncertainty assessment of climate change. In *Climate Change 2014: Impacts, Adaptation, and Vulnerability. Part A: Global and Sectoral Aspects. Contribution of Working Group II to the Fifth Assessment Report of the IPCC* (pp. 151–194). Cambridge University Press.

Lavecchia, L., Appodia, J., Cantatore, P., Cappariello, R., Di Virgilio, S., Felettigh, A., Giustini, A., Guberti, V., Liberati, D., Meucci, G., Piermattei, S., Schimperna, F., & Specchia, K. (2022). *Dati e metodi per la valutazione dei rischi climatici e ambientali in Italia* (Bank of Italy Occasional Paper 732).

MoF Platform on Sustainable Finance. (2024). *Sustainability dialogue between SMEs and banks.*

Monasterolo, I. (2020). Climate change and the financial system. *Annual Review of Resource Economics, 12*(1), 299–320.

Rising, J., Tedesco, M., Piontek, F., & Stainforth, D. A. (2022, October). The missing risks of climate change. *Nature, 610*(7933), 643–651.

The Credit Risk of Italian Firms and Collateral

Stefano Di Virgilio, Alessandra Iannamorelli, Francesco Monterisi, and Simone Narizzano

1 Introduction

Credit claims have gained prominence among the collateral asset classes used in Eurosystem refinancing operations. The assessment of firms' creditworthiness has thus become important for ensuring the smooth access to central bank refinancing, particularly during times of economic stress. In Italy, the use of ICAS assessments has facilitated banks' access to central bank liquidity, particularly during the pandemic.

This Chapter shows the evolution of credit risk for Italian firms in recent years based on the ICAS assessments, highlighting their key drivers. It also examines more generally the role of credit claims as collateral.

Italian firms' credit quality, measured by PDs, has gradually improved since 2013 (see Chap. 3). In the years 2020–2022, this improvement was mainly due to policy support measures following the pandemic, and to the subsequent economic recovery. The high cost of debt and the cyclical slowdown have resulted in a slight deterioration in PDs since 2023. Differences persist by sector, size, and region.

In the remainder of this Chapter, Sect. 2 outlines the evolution of the creditworthiness of Italian non-financial firms in terms of S-ICAS PDs; Sect. 3 describes the

S. Di Virgilio (✉) · A. Iannamorelli · F. Monterisi · S. Narizzano
Bank of Italy, Financial Risk Management Directorate, Rome, Italy
e-mail: stefano.divirgilio@bancaditalia.it

A. Iannamorelli
e-mail: alessandra.iannamorelli@bancaditalia.it

F. Monterisi
e-mail: francesco.monterisi@bancaditalia.it

S. Narizzano
e-mail: simone.narizzano@bancaditalia.it

A. Scalia (ed.), *Corporate Credit Analysis and AI*, Finance for Professionals,
https://doi.org/10.1007/978-3-032-13422-6_7

use of ICAS PDs for evaluating credit claims pledged as collateral in Eurosystem monetary policy operations; Sect. 4 concludes.

2 The Creditworthiness of Non-Financial Firms

S-ICAS PDs show a gradual improvement of the creditworthiness of Italian firms between 2013 and 2024.[1] In the aftermath of the sovereign debt crisis and up to the COVID-19 pandemic, the PDs significantly decreased in line with the economic recovery and the improvement in firms' financial structure, favoured by the accommodative monetary policy stance (Fig. 1, panel a). The sharp decline in the values corresponding to the 75th and 90th percentiles of the sample distribution indicates that the improvement has also affected weaker companies. The deterioration of credit quality following the COVID-19 outbreak prompted the worsening of the financial statement scores (Fig. 1, panel b). Such phenomenon was mitigated by the stability of the credit behaviour scores (Fig. 1, panel c), that benefited from the Government measures aimed at preserving firms' access to credit (debt moratorium and public guarantee schemes). The effects of the pandemic crisis were heterogeneous across sectors,[2] as a significant increase of the financial statement PDs was observed only near the values corresponding to the 75th and 90th percentiles of the PD distribution, while the median value remained stable (Fig. 1, panel b).

The vigorous post-pandemic economic recovery caused a decline in the PDs at the end of 2022, thanks to a significant improvement in the financial statements for 2021 and the stability of the credit behaviour component. The PDs estimated at the end of 2023 showed a slight deterioration. The mild increase in risk was entirely attributable to the changes in the macroeconomic context, considering the stability of the financial statement and of the credit behaviour components of the model. The slowdown in the domestic economic outlook, the global instability, the effects of persistent inflation, and the sharp rise in interest rates were expected to affect companies' ability to meet their debt obligations negatively. At the end of 2024, firms' creditworthiness remained stable compared to the end of 2023. According to our estimates, the default rate for Italian firms will be around 3% in 2025, driven by still high financing costs, weak economic growth and increased geopolitical risks.

The S-ICAS PDs are categorized into 18 risk classes and mapped into the credit quality steps (CQS) of the Eurosystem harmonized rating scale to compute the haircuts for the bank loans posted as collateral in monetary policy operations

[1] For a broader discussion of credit quality developments in the Italian financial and non-financial sector please refer to the Bank of Italy's Financial Stability Report. Data in this Section refer to the evaluations at the end of each year of about 370,000 firms. The most recent PDs are as of the end of 2024, based on contemporaneous NCR data and on financial statements mostly for 2023.

[2] For further details, see De Socio et al. (2020).

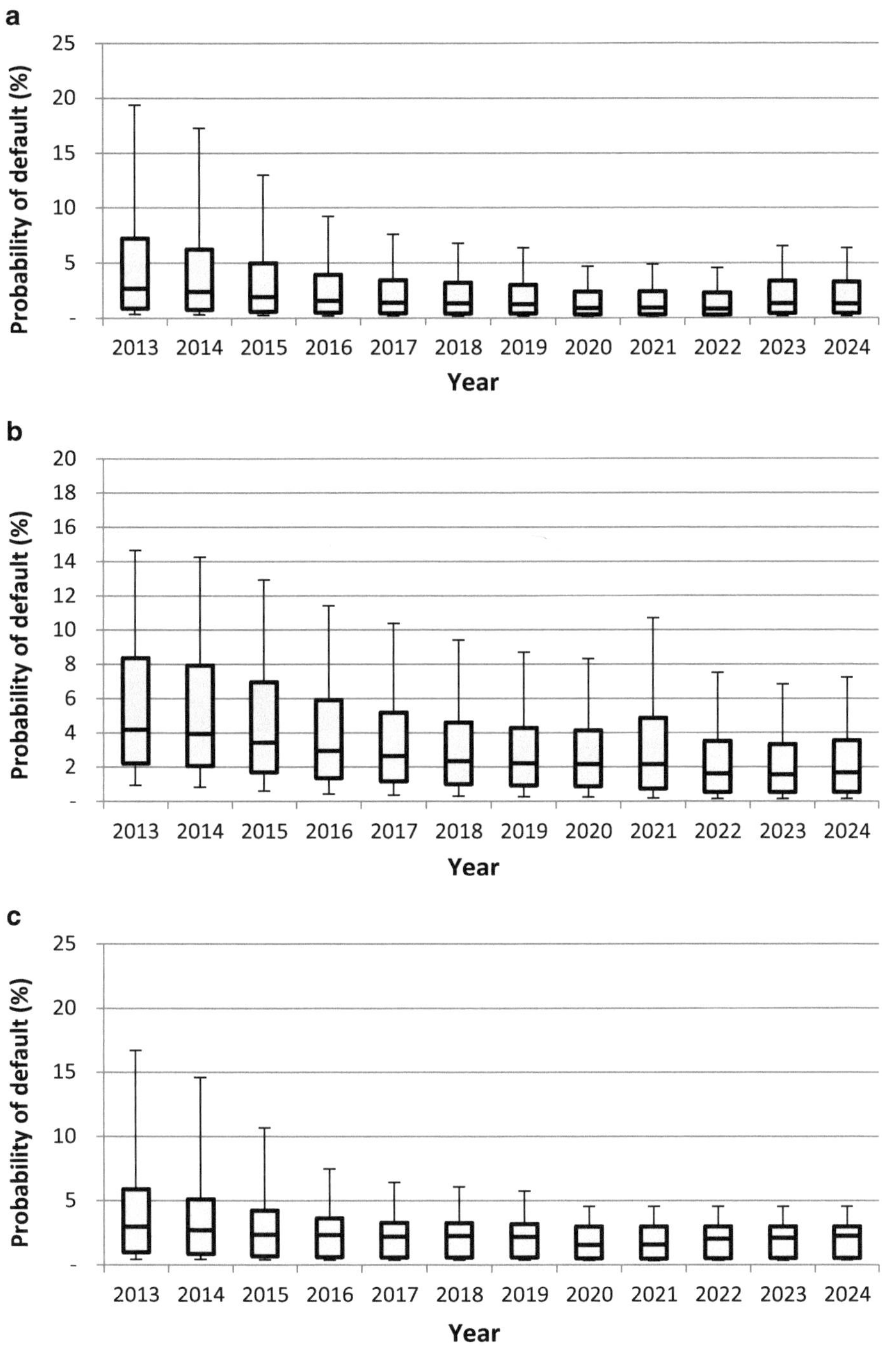

Fig. 1 Default probability (2013–2024). **a** PD distribution; **b** financial statement PD distribution; **c** Credit behaviour PD distribution. The boxplots mark the 90th, 75th, 50th, 25th and 10th percentiles of the distribution. *Source* Own calculations on Bank of Italy data

Table 1 Credit quality steps (percentage values)

Credit quality	PD min	PD max
Excellent	0	0.1
Very good	0.1	0.4
Good	0.4	1
Fair	1	1.5
Acceptable	1.5	3
Vulnerable	3	5
Very vulnerable	5	99.99
Default	100	100

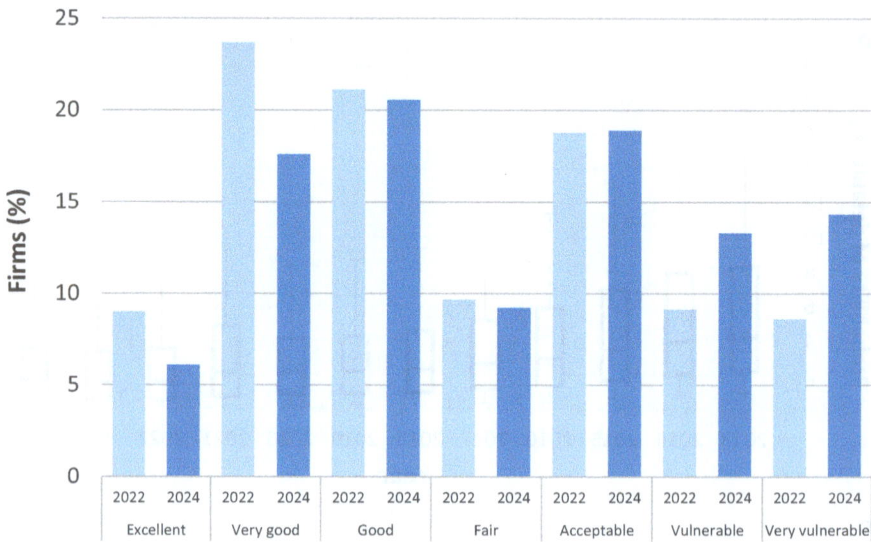

Fig. 2 Distribution of firms by credit quality step (2022–2024). *Source* Own calculations on Bank of Italy data

(see Chap. 3). Each CQS can be associated with a different degree of solvency (Table 1).

According to the statistical model, compared to 2022,[3] in 2024 Italian firms[4] have migrated towards higher risk classes (Fig. 2); however, the impact on the median statistical PD has been moderate.

[3] Considering the overall stability of the PDs between 2023 and 2024, in the rest of the Chapter, we present the evolution of PDs in the last two years.

[4] For further details, please refer to the Appendix.

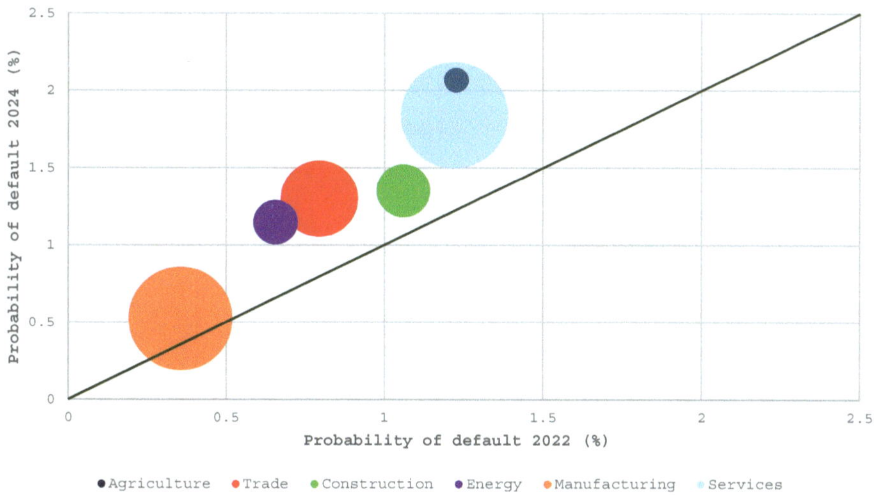

Fig. 3 Median PD by sector (2022–2024). The size of the bubble corresponds to the amount of loans to firms in each sector at the end of 2024. *Source* Own calculations on Bank of Italy data

Table 2 Capital structure by size (percentage values)

Size	Equity to total net debt
Micro	38
Small	55
Medium	70
Large	77

The manufacturing and energy sectors have proven to be the least risky over 2022–2024. In that period the statistical PDs of Italian firms rose for all sectors; the increase was more pronounced for agriculture and services[5] (Fig. 3).

Large and medium-sized firms are more creditworthy than small firms and especially micro firms. The higher riskiness of micro enterprises reflects their weaker capital structure (Table 2).

In the period 2022–2024 the PDs of micro enterprises increased more than those of the other firms (Fig. 4). The weaker financial condition of micro firms makes them more prone to the deterioration of the macroeconomic outlook.

In the period 2022–2024, firms' riskiness increased across macro-regions at a different pace. Statistical PDs in the Centre, South, and in the Islands have shown a significant deterioration; the gap with the PDs of firms in the North has widened (Fig. 5). This trend in riskiness is consistent with the different distribution of firms among macro-regions. In particular, micro firms account for about 62% of firms in the Centre, South and Islands compared to 52% in the North area. At the end of 2024 the share of firms in the vulnerable and very vulnerable classes was 31%

[5] For our purposes the services sector also includes real estate.

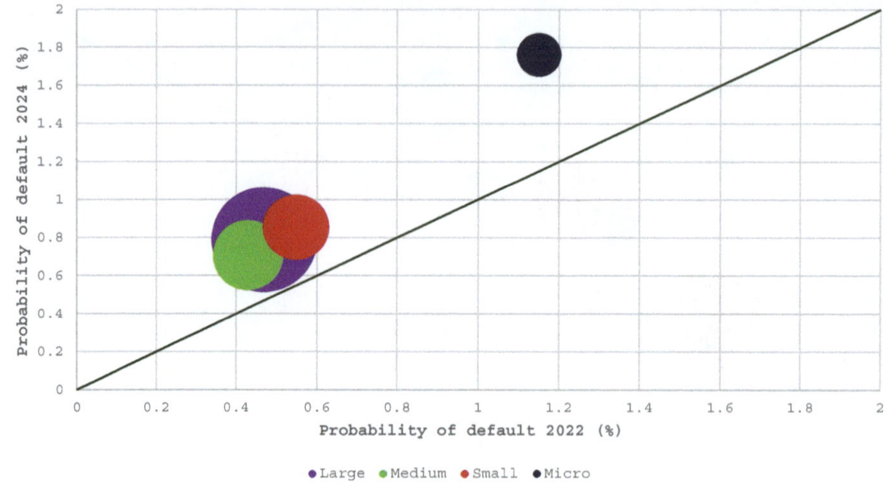

Fig. 4 Median PD by size class (2022–2024). The size of the bubble corresponds to the amount of loans to firms in each size class at the end of 2024. *Source* Own calculations on Bank of Italy data

for the Centre and South and 32% for the Islands, compared to 26% and 23%, respectively, for the North-West and North-East areas.

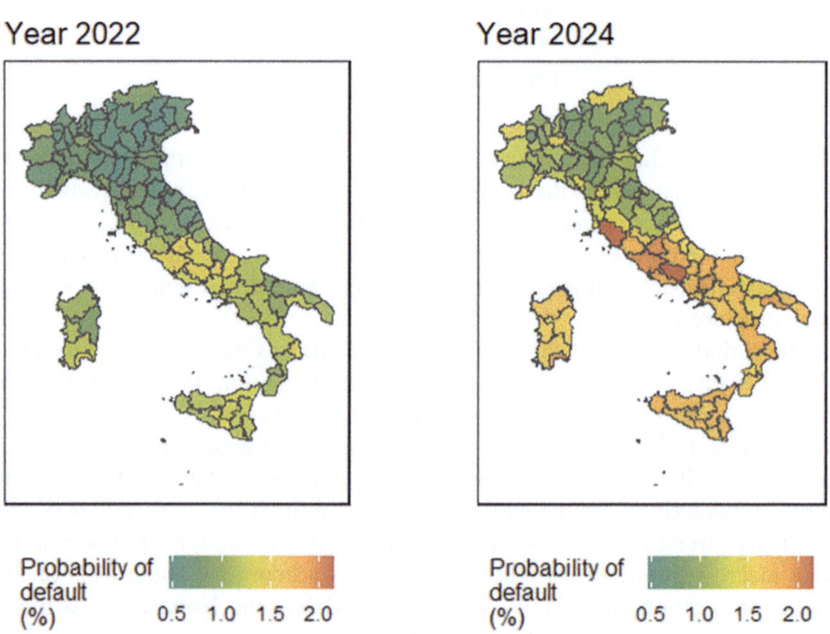

Fig. 5 Median PD by geographical areas (2022–2024). *Source* Own calculations on Bank of Italy data

3 The Evolution and the Riskiness of Bank Loans Pledged as Collateral

The Eurosystem accepts as collateral in monetary policy operations a large set of assets, including marketable debt instruments (public sector securities, corporate bonds, bank bonds, ABS) and bank loans. Bank loans are a significant component of the collateral pledged to the Eurosystem and their use—allowing banks to refinance otherwise illiquid assets—supports the provision of credit to the economy on favourable terms.[6] Starting from the second half of 2020, credit claims constitute the most important asset class as a share of the Eurosystem collateral, accounting for more than 30% of the total value of collateral pledged by euro area banks.[7]

In conducting refinancing operations, the Eurosystem is exposed to banks' default risk and to the risks associated with the collateralized assets. Collateral protects the Eurosystem in credit operations against losses that might affect its financial independence and credibility. Consequently, a robust set of rules has been defined on the financial soundness of counterparties and on the eligibility of collateral,[8,9] including the application of valuation haircuts on the assets pledged as collateral.[10] Haircuts depend on the characteristics of collateral, notably on the credit risk measured by means of the PD estimated with one of the eligible rating sources: ECAIs, IRBs, and ICASes (for more information see Chap. 3).

In the last decade, the use of ICAS by Italian monetary policy counterparties has significantly increased: the number of banks that use it for evaluating credit claims pledged as collateral was 52 at the end of 2024, with a steady growth over previous years.[11] The amount of collateral evaluated with ICAS has also

---

[6] Mésonnier et al. (2021).

[7] For more information, please refer to https://www.ecb.europa.eu/mopo/coll/charts/html/index.en.html.

[8] European Central Bank (2015).

[9] To be eligible as collateral all assets must meet certain criteria regarding the type of instrument, place of issuance, currency of denomination, country of residence of the debtor (or guarantor), and credit quality. Based on ordinary rules, bank loans must have an annual PD less than or equal to 0.40%. Besides, the collateral framework has been progressively expanded with the introduction of the Additional Credit Claims (ACC) scheme. This started in December 2011 to facilitate banks' access to monetary policy operations. Under the ACC scheme, individually pledged loans must have an annual PD less than or equal to 1.5 per cent; for loans pledged within a portfolio, an initial PD limit of 10 per cent was set; this was later removed with the subsequent measures on the collateral framework adopted in response to the pandemic. Only performing loans can be accepted as collateral.

[10] Collateral haircuts are prudential deductions applied to the value of pledged assets to calculate the net collateral value. Haircuts are intended to cover potential losses in the value of the assets in the event of counterparty default and during the time required for their sale. The haircut is proportional to the risk level of each asset, thus ensuring that the residual risk is equal for all pledged assets under the so-called risk equivalence principle.

[11] The figure considers also three counterparties that employ only pool of loans to households.

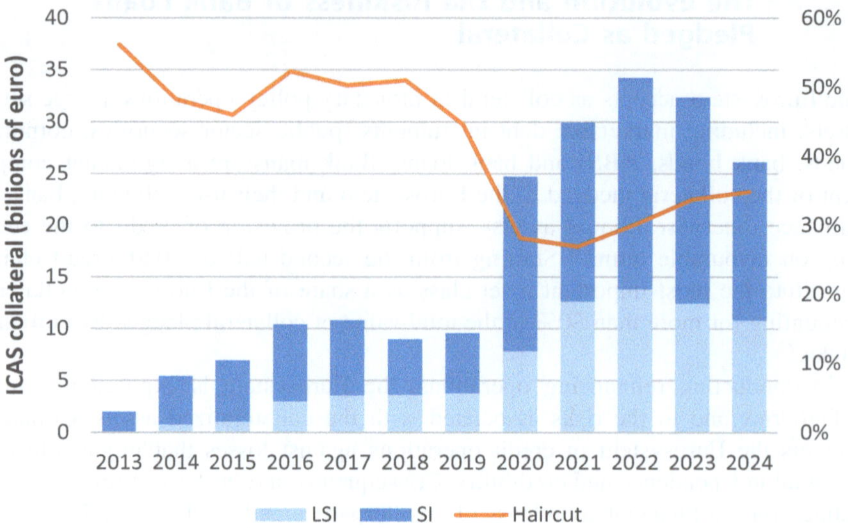

Fig. 6 Bank loans as collateral evaluated with ICAS—Distribution by bank class[13] (left hand scale) and average haircut (right hand scale). *Source* Own calculations on Bank of Italy data

significantly grown, reaching a peak at the end of 2022 (34.2 billion euros in net terms).

The sharp growth of the loans assessed with ICAS from 2019 to 2022 is related to the introduction by the Eurosystem of extraordinary measures aimed at countering the adverse effects of the pandemic crisis, by easing banks' access to central bank liquidity; in particular, in April 2020 the Eurosystem reduced the haircut applied to all eligible assets (Fig. 6).[12] In Italy the so-called Additional Credit Claims Framework was expanded to let counterparties pledge a wider range of loans as collateral in monetary policy operations. The availability of ICAS PDs for a large share of firms contributed to easing banks' access to central bank refinancing. At the end of 2024, as monetary policy normalization was underway, the amount of credit claims evaluated with ICAS decreased, to 26.1 billion euros (Fig. 6). The average haircut increased from 30% in 2022 to 35% in 2024.

ICAS evaluations are widely used by both significant banks (SIs) and less significant banks (LSIs). At the end of 2024, the net value of collateral evaluated with ICAS and provided by SIs was 15.3 billion euros (−25% compared to 2022), while LSIs used ICAS evaluations for 10.8 billion euros of loans (−22% compared to 2022; Fig. 6). The decrease of net collateral is due to the increase in the average haircut and to the decrease in the gross value of pledged loans.

[12] Valuation haircuts for marketable assets were reduced by 20 per cent (on average from 9.1 to 7.3%) and by 42 per cent for non-marketable assets (on average from 44.6 to 25.8%). For further details, see Antilici et al. (2023).

[13] Net of haircut.

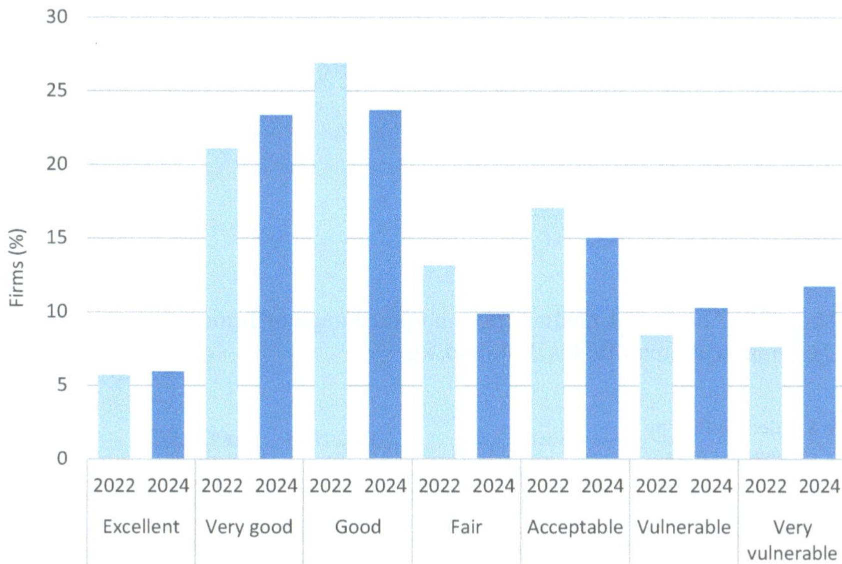

Fig. 7 Distribution of firms by credit quality step (credit claims pledged; 2022–2024). *Source* Own calculations on Bank of Italy data

In 2024 credit claims pledged as collateral showed an increase in credit risk: the weighted average PD rose from 2.39 in 2022 to 2.65%. The share of firms in the vulnerable and very vulnerable classes increased from 16% in 2022 to 22% in 2024 (Fig. 7); however, it remained lower than the corresponding share in the overall portfolio of firms evaluated by ICAS (28%; Fig. 2). The lower credit risk of the portfolio of loans pledged as collateral compared to that of the overall portfolio evaluated with ICAS is related to the risk control rules of the collateral framework that discourage the use of credit claims towards more vulnerable firms.[14]

4 Conclusion

The growing reliance on credit claims as collateral highlights their strategic role in Eurosystem monetary policy operations, as well as the importance of ICASes in assessing credit risk and facilitating access to central bank liquidity. In Italy, ICAS assessments have been instrumental in supporting banks' liquidity needs, particularly through the pandemic. Over the past decade, the credit risk profile of Italian non-financial firms has evolved considerably, shaped by macroeconomic developments and targeted policy measures. While substantial government intervention

[14] The ECB publishes on its website only the list of marketable assets, updated daily by the NCBs. The eligibility of bank loans depends on predetermined rules verified by the competent NCB.

during the COVID-19 crisis led to an improvement in firms' creditworthiness, recent economic developments have triggered a moderate rise in default probabilities, with micro enterprises and firms in southern regions exhibiting heightened vulnerability due to structural weaknesses.

Appendix

Median S-ICAS PDs

We show 2022 and 2024 median PDs and percentage of firms by sector, size class and geographical area (Tables 3, 4, and 5).

Table 3 Median PDs by sector (percentage values)

Sector	PDs 2022	PDs 2024	Firms
Agriculture	1.23	2.07	1.96
Trade	0.80	1.30	21.23
Construction	1.06	1.35	14.24
Energy	0.66	1.15	2.21
Manufacturing	0.36	0.52	21.04
Services	1.22	1.84	39.32

Table 4 Median PDs by size class (percentage values)

Size class	PDs 2022	PDs 2024	Firms
Micro	1.15	1.76	56.98
Small	0.55	0.86	32.86
Medium	0.43	0.71	8.00
Large	0.47	0.79	2.16

Table 5 Median PDs by geographical area (percentage values)

Area	PDs 2022	PDs 2024	Firms
North-West	0.73	1.12	29.48
North-East	0.60	0.91	23.12
Centre	1.03	1.54	22.40
South	1.11	1.66	17.86
Islands	1.18	1.73	7.14

References

Antilici, P., Gariano, G., Monterisi, F., Picone, A., & Russo, L. (2023). The Eurosystem collateral framework and the measures introduced in response to the pandemic emergency. In A. Scalia (Ed.), *Financial risk management and climate change risk* (pp. 55–71). Springer.

De Socio, A., Narizzano, S., Orlando, T., Parlapiano, F., Rodano, G., Sette, E., & Viggiano, G. (2020). *The Effects of the COVID-19 shock on corporates liquidity needs, balance sheets, and riskiness*. Bank of Italy, COVID-19 Notes.

European Central Bank. (2015). *The financial risk management of the Eurosystem's monetary policy operations*. European Central Bank, July

Mésonnier, J., O'Donnell, C., & Toutain, O. (2021). The interest of being eligible. *Journal of Money, Credit and Banking, 54*, 425–458.

Part III

The Models at Commercial Banks

IRB Systems

Federica Orsini and Anna Maria Rossi

1 Introduction

The Eurosystem grants credit to its counterparties for monetary policy purposes; adequate collateral is a prerequisite. Since the Eurosystem accepts a very broad variety of collateral, it has to rely on various sources of credit risk assessment: the IRB systems of the Eurosystem counterparties are one of these sources, which can be used to determine the eligibility and valuation of non-marketable assets—such as bank loans—used as collateral in monetary policy operations.

This Chapter explores the role and evolution of IRB systems within the ECAF, with a particular focus on the Italian context. The integration of IRB systems into the ECAF reflects the Eurosystem's objective of maintaining a broad and diversified collateral base while ensuring robust risk management standards. In a financial system like the euro area, where bank-based financing prevails, the inclusion of credit claims in the collateral framework has become increasingly important, especially during periods of financial stress, as demonstrated by the introduction of ACCs and the extraordinary measures adopted during the COVID-19 pandemic.

The Chapter also examines the regulatory and operational implications of using IRB systems, their interaction with other credit assessment tools (such as ICAS and external credit rating agencies), and recent regulatory developments, including the introduction of the ICAS prioritization rule in 2025. The analysis is complemented by an international comparison of how other central banks treat credit claims as

F. Orsini · A. M. Rossi (✉)
Financial Risk Management Directorate, Bank of Italy, Rome, Italy
e-mail: annamaria.rossi@bancaditalia.it

F. Orsini
e-mail: federica.orsini@bancaditalia.it

A. Scalia (ed.), *Corporate Credit Analysis and AI*, Finance for Professionals,
https://doi.org/10.1007/978-3-032-13422-6_8

collateral and by a detailed overview of the Bank of Italy's experience in managing and monitoring IRB systems.

The remainder of the Chapter is organized as follows. Section 2 outlines the main characteristics of the Eurosystem collateral framework for monetary policy implementation and discusses the importance of credit claims in this context; Sect. 3 describes the usage of IRBs for evaluating credit claims pledged as collateral in Eurosystem monetary policy operations; Sect. 4 provides a comparative overview of how different central banks assess credit claims, highlighting the unique role of IRB systems within the Eurosystem; Sect. 5 reviews the regulatory and supervisory developments affecting IRB models, from Basel II to Basel IV, and their impact on capital requirements; Sect. 6 presents the rules governing the use of IRBs within the ECAF and the experience of the Bank of Italy in implementing and monitoring these systems; finally, Sect. 7 discusses the recent introduction of the ICAS prioritization rule and its implications for the use of IRB ratings in the collateral framework of the Eurosystem.

2 The Eurosystem Collateral Framework for Monetary Policy Implementation

Collateral adequacy serves two purposes: ensuring effective risk management and supporting monetary policy implementation (Antilici et al., 2023; Bindseil et al., 2017).

On the one hand, the concept of collateral adequacy is pivotal in safeguarding the Eurosystem against potential financial losses. This protection becomes material if a counterparty defaults on its repayment obligations under the agreed terms. Ensuring that the collateral held is of sufficient quality and value is a fundamental risk management measure aimed at preserving the financial integrity of the Eurosystem balance sheet.

On the other hand, from a broader monetary policy perspective, collateral adequacy requires that there is ample collateral available. This requirement is crucial for averting scenarios in which a scarcity of eligible collateral could restrict banks' access to central bank liquidity, as such restrictions could in turn hinder the effective transmission of monetary policy to the economy. By ensuring that banks can pledge assets directly relating to their core activities as collateral, the Eurosystem mitigates the risk of impairing the flow of central bank liquidity that is essential for financial stability and economic growth.

The Eurosystem has always maintained a broad collateral framework. This includes marketable assets—which consist of debt instruments such as government bonds, bonds issued by supranational organizations, covered bonds, corporate bonds, and asset-backed securities (ABS)—as well as non-marketable assets, namely bank loans issued to businesses or individuals.

All these assets are subject to eligibility criteria, risk control measures and valuation procedures to ensure adequate risk management. Such framework is known as ECAF (see Chap. 3 for further details).

Due to the prevalence in Europe of bank-based financing over market-based financing, credit claims are the most important asset class on the balance sheet of euro-area banks.[1] Therefore, credit claims have been playing a significant role in the monetary policy collateral framework since its inception.

Notable milestones in this evolution include the establishment of the single list in 2007 which unified collateral eligibility rules, thereby creating a consistent system across the euro area.[2]

The acceptance of ACCs in 2011 marked another significant step, allowing banks to pledge loans that do not meet the standard ECAF criteria. ACCs substantially expanded the collateral pool. This turned out to be particularly important in times of financial stress, as ACCs provided banks with greater flexibility in the mobilization of assets for liquidity purposes.[3]

Another crucial evolution in this framework was the introduction of Pandemic ACCs in 2020. This was designed as a temporary measure to support banks during the unprecedented financial strains caused by the COVID-19 pandemic, further broadening the range of credit claims to be used as collateral. This was vital for maintaining liquidity in the financial system and ensuring that banks could continue to lend to the real economy during the crisis.[4]

[1] For Italian banks, loans granted to households and non-financial corporations (NFCs) account for around 33% of their assets, compared with 30% in the euro area.

[2] The Eurosystem decided to introduce the single list of collateral in 2004. It was then implemented in 2005 for marketable assets and in 2007 for credit claims (see ECB, 2005). This was a departure from the previous two-tier system in which Tier one collateral was uniformly accepted under a loss-sharing regime by all NCBs within the Eurosystem and Tier two collateral was specific to individual NCBs and operated under a no loss-sharing regime. Up to 2005–2007, the two-tier system allowed for a certain degree of flexibility but it also introduced complexity in the management of collateral across the euro area. The transition to the single list was driven by a harmonization effort. One of the main changes brought about by the single list was the expansion of eligibility to credit claims across the euro area in 2007. Previously, the acceptance of credit claims varied significantly across jurisdictions. For instance, pure bank loans were only eligible in Spain, France, Germany, and Austria; private claims were accepted in the Netherlands and mortgage-backed promissory notes in Ireland.

[3] In 2011, in the midst of the euro area sovereign debt crisis, the Governing Council decided to ease the collateral framework allowing the NCBs to accept, under a no loss-sharing scheme, the ACCs, i.e. bank loans that deviate from the standard ECAF acceptance criteria. With the ACCs, a two-tier system in the collateral framework was de facto reintroduced. Each national ACC framework required the authorization from the ECB's Governing Council, to ensure a careful control. These national frameworks are required to align with minimum common rules, preserving collateral quality and sound risk management across the euro area. This approach underscores the Eurosystem's commitment to accommodate national financial market conditions, to promote the effectiveness of the operational framework.

[4] In response to the economic crisis caused by the outbreak of the COVID-19 pandemic, the Governing Council of the ECB took extraordinary measures to support the provision of credit to households and NFCs and to stimulate the demand for goods, services, and investment. To avoid the possible collateral shortage, the Governing Council increased the risk tolerance level of the Eurosystem through a package of collateral measures along three directions: (i) easing of the risk control measures, to increase the value of collateral in a timely manner and offset potential loss of

The evolution of ACCs highlights the adaptability in the collateral framework, as the Eurosystem has sought to address emerging challenges and ensure the continuous flow of credit. These measures have enhanced the robustness and flexibility of the Eurosystem's collateral framework, making it resilient to shocks and fully equipped to support monetary policy implementation and the stability of the financial system.

2.1 Why Central Banks Accept Credit Claims

Accepting credit claims within the collateral framework of central banks facilitates credit flow to productive sectors and helps create a resilient collateral framework. This allows the system to respond effectively to market developments and episodes of stress, minimizing the need for extraordinary measures and promoting continuity.

The notion that allowing banks to refinance corporate term loans at the central bank prevents bank runs and suboptimal equilibria dates back at least to Diamond and Dybvig (1983). Such possibility has major macroeconomic benefits. By accepting credit claims as collateral, central banks act as a liquidity insurer towards commercial banks. This makes commercial banks more confident in providing longer-term loans to firms, which in turn supports aggregate investment. This channel is especially important for small banks and SMEs, which often face liquidity constraints due to limited access to capital markets and fewer funding options compared to larger institutions (Harpedanne de Belleville, 2018).

Asset liquidity, the central bank collateral framework, and regulation interact to determine the ability of the banking system to perform maturity transformation and to preserve financial stability (Bindseil, 2013). By pledging less liquid assets as collateral, banks can keep more liquid assets readily available on their balance sheet, enhancing their capacity to meet day-to-day liquidity needs—such as unexpected withdrawals or funding requirements—without disrupting operations. Furthermore, holding a larger buffer of liquid assets improves banks' resilience in times of financial distress, when the ability to convert assets into cash quickly and with minimal losses is critical for financial stability.

Central bank lending against low-quality collateral can also enhance market liquidity even when high-quality collateral is available (Choi et al., 2021). While lending against high-quality collateral may reduce central banks' credit risk, it

collateral value in a scenario of economic and financial stress (mainly via the reduction of valuation haircuts); (ii) extension of the range of eligible assets, with special reference to credit claims, to stimulate the provision of credit to the real economy (mainly through extensions of the ACC frameworks); (iii) lowering of the minimum credit quality threshold for eligible assets, to increase the resilience of the banking system to potential rating downgrades by credit rating agencies. The ACC extension involved the collateral usage, among others, of loans to SMEs or self-employed individuals that benefit from the Government guarantee schemes introduced to address the COVID-19 emergency. For a description of the collateral rules see Antilici et al. (2023).

can adversely affect market liquidity since high-quality collateral gets locked up with the central bank and no longer circulates in markets. Conversely, lending against low-quality collateral creates counterparty risk for the central bank, but it expands the available pool of outstanding collateral, improving overall market liquidity. These effects have been magnified by the introduction of supervisory liquidity requirements such as the Liquidity Coverage Ratio (LCR) and the Net Stable Funding Ratio (NSFR). These requirements raise banks' demand for high-quality liquid assets (HQLA), especially in periods of market stress, thereby intensifying the scarcity of freely circulating collateral.

Furthermore, the possibility to pledge credit claims can reduce the banks' reliance on originating asset-backed securities and covered bonds primarily for own use as collateral in central bank credit operations, preserving a level playing field for smaller banks that have limited access to the structured finance markets. These markets involve significant costs, regulatory requirements and know how in structuring complex deals. If the possibility to pledge credit claims were limited, smaller banks would face constraints in originating certain types of loans, especially mortgages and small business loans.

The March 2023 crisis involving some US regional banks provides a salient lesson on the paramount importance of reliable access to central bank financing. The crisis highlighted how the facilities available at the US Federal Reserve were lacking in certain respects and underscored the value of having a robust framework in place for the immediate liquidity provision to banks in distress. Notably, the capacity to pledge credit claims cannot be created from scratch in the midst of a crisis. It requires pre-existing operational readiness, including knowledge, tested procedures, and appropriate infrastructure, which must already be in place in normal times, both within the central bank (in terms of collateral management and credit risk assessment capability) and among commercial banks. The effectiveness of such a system depends on continuous maintenance and integration into normal times, so that it can function effectively when most needed.[5]

2.2 The Use of Collateral

Credit claims are one of the most important forms of collateral compared with other eligible assets in several euro area countries, such as France, Germany, Greece, Italy, and Cyprus. The use of credit claims as collateral in monetary policy operations plays a crucial role towards enhancing risk diversification for the Eurosystem and supporting neutrality with respect to banking business models.

In Italy, between early 2012 and February 2020, i.e. prior to the outbreak of the COVID-19 pandemic, the net value of the credit claims pledged as collateral nearly doubled, from 40 to 76 billion euros. The use of credit claims as collateral reached record volumes afterwards as a result of the introduction of the easing

[5] See Dudley (2024).

measures taken in response to the COVID-19 pandemic in 2020; it reached a peak of 170 billion euros at the end of March 2023, before decreasing to 111 billion by June 2025. As of that date, credit claims accounted for 64% of the total value of collateral pledged by Italian banks, with nearly two thirds of which of this amount mobilized under the temporary ACC framework (Figs. 1 and 2).

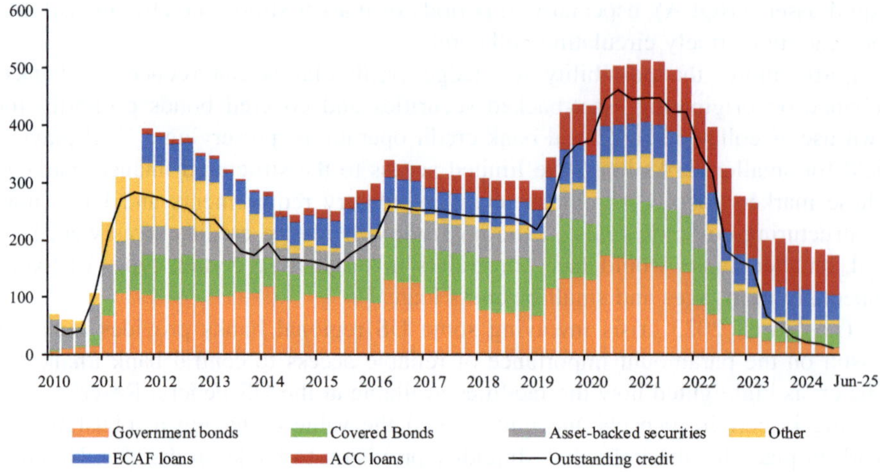

Fig. 1 Collateral pledged by Italian banks (collateral value after haircuts; EUR bln; quarterly data). *Note* "Other" includes bank bonds and securities issued by non-financial corporations and supranational organizations

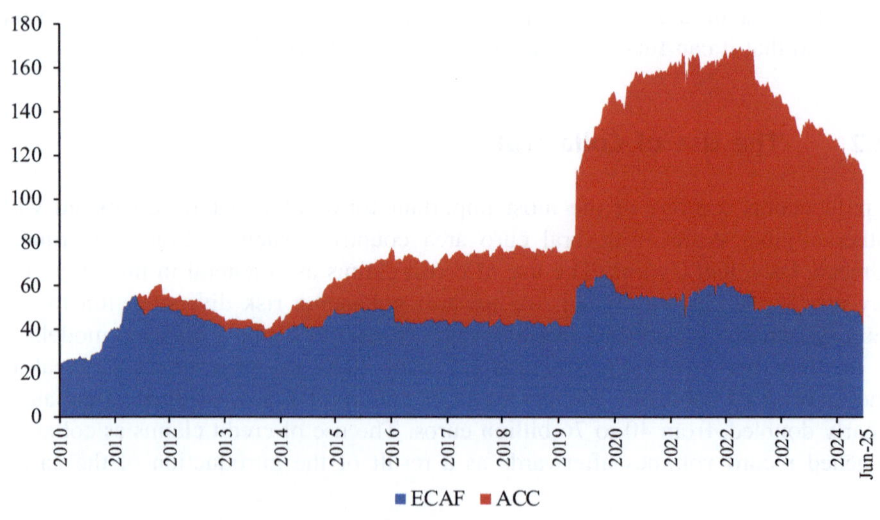

Fig. 2 Credit claims pledged by Italian banks (collateral value after haircuts; EUR bln; daily data)

3 The IRB Systems Within the ECAF

If a counterparty in liquidity-providing operations were to default, the Eurosystem would bear the credit, market and liquidity risks associated with the assets pledged by that counterparty as collateral. As a first layer of risk protection, the Eurosystem has thus defined a set of rules to ensure the financial soundness of banks that can act as counterparties in credit operations. In addition, as a second layer of protection, the Eurosystem applies risk control measures on the assets pledged as collateral.

Since the Eurosystem accepts a very broad variety of collateral, it has to rely on various sources of credit risk assessment (see Chap. 3 for further details). The IRB systems of the counterparties are one of these accepted sources in the ECAF, used by about 40 banks across the euro area.

Until recently, each counterparty was allowed to select one system from the list of available credit assessment sources as the primary source, informing the responsible NCB of the choice. The selection normally pointed to the system that best suited the counterparty's potential collateral portfolio. However, such selection mechanism has changed with the entry into force of the ICAS prioritization rule in June 2025 (see Sect. 7), which mandates the use of ICAS ratings—where available—over other sources.

With the growing importance of credit claims in the collateral pool, the reliance on credit rating agencies has declined. In Italy, IRBs are the most used rating source in both the ECAF and the ACC framework. At the end of 2024 the IRB ratings were used for the assessment of 28 billion worth of ECAF loans and 35 billion worth of ACC loans, covering 47% of the value of the credit claims pledged in monetary policy operations. ICAS ratings were also extensively used, covering almost 20% of the value of pledged loans. Ratings from ECAIs cover 15%[6] of loans (Figs. 3 and 4). IRBs are used by eight large banks, while ICAS is used by many medium and small banks.

Ratings from ECAIs and PDs from IRB systems and ICASes are mapped into the CQSs defined by the Eurosystem harmonised rating scale (see Table 1 in Chap. 3). Under the general collateral framework, all eligible assets must have a credit assessment corresponding to at least CQS3, which is equivalent to a rating not lower than BBB- or to an annual PD of the obligor/issuer less than or equal to 0.40%. Under its ACC framework, Bank of Italy accepts as collateral credit claims with higher thresholds: for individually pledged loans, it requires an annual PD of less than or equal to 1.5% (CQS 5); performing loans mobilized within portfolios of credit claims have no minimum credit quality threshold.[7]

[6] The remaining loans are mostly pools of residential mortgages, assessed via a conservative approach developed internally by Bank of Italy, and loans to Public Sector Entities (PSEs), for which specific valuation rules apply and the credit assessment is generally derived from the ECAI rating assigned to the central government of the jurisdiction in which these entities are established.

[7] On 29 November 2024 the Governing Council of the ECB approved, *inter alia*, the discontinuation of certain assets which have been eligible under the Guideline on additional temporary

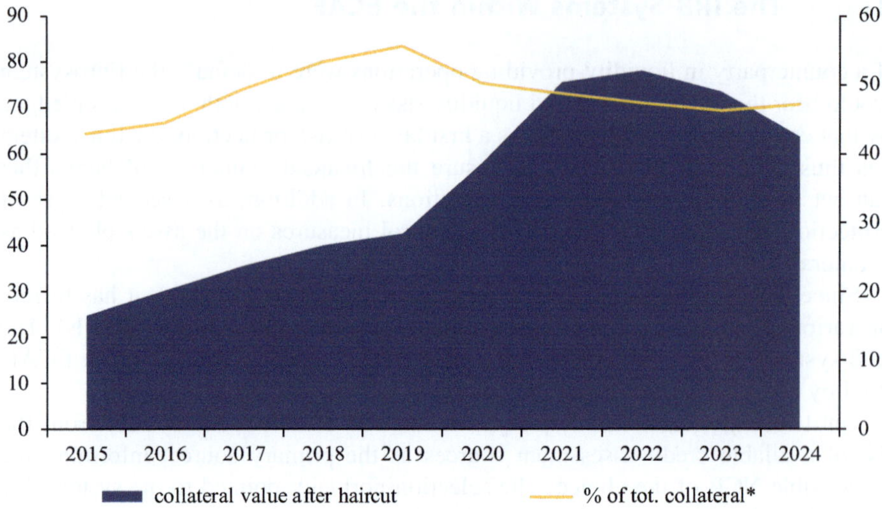

Fig. 3 The use of IRB systems for collateral assessment in Italy (EUR billions and percentage values). *Note* *Right-hand side scale

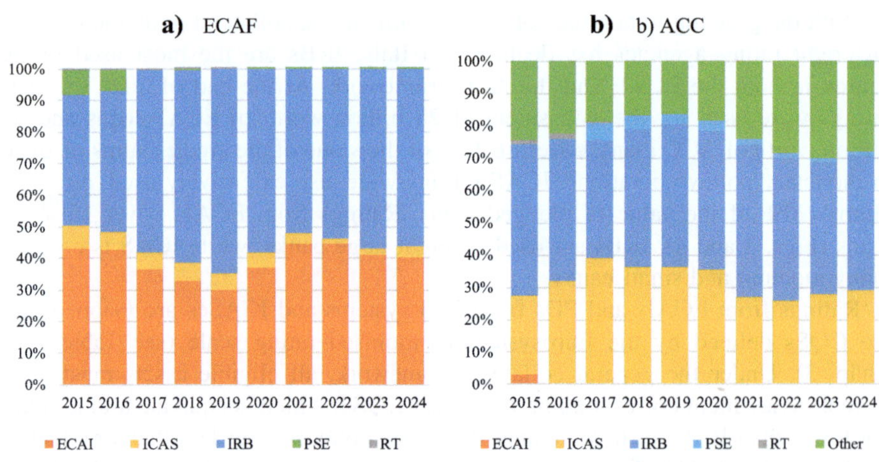

Fig. 4 Credit claims—Use of assessment systems in Italy (average percentage values). *Note* RT refers to Rating Tool, a system developed and operated by a private company for evaluating a borrower's credit risk through ratings or scores. RTs were discontinued in the ECAF in 2021. PSE refers to Public Sector Entities, for which specific rules apply and the credit assessment is generally derived from the ECAI rating assigned to the central government of the jurisdiction in which these entities are established. "Other" includes the Statistical ICAS and the conservative approaches developed internally at Bank of Italy to assess the credit quality of loan pools to non-financial corporations, mortgages, and consumer loans, along with loans backed by the state guarantee scheme

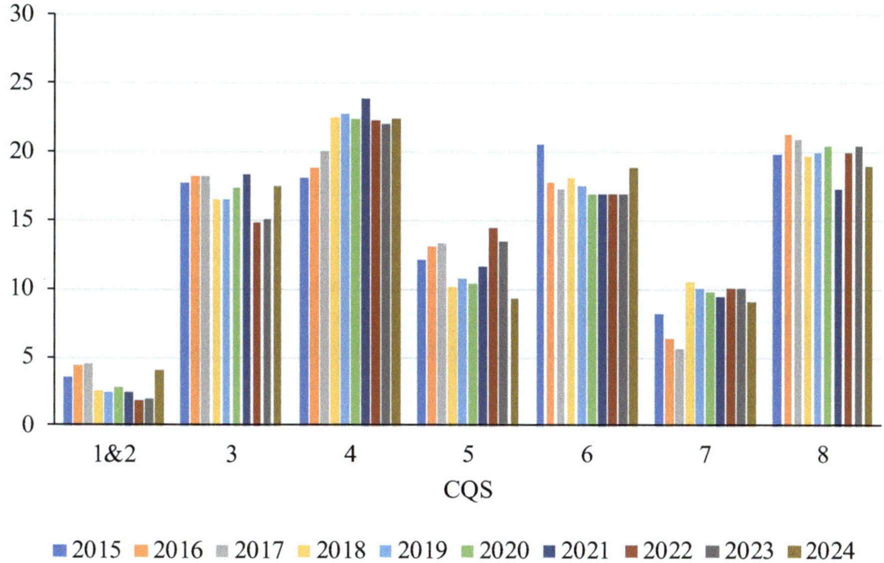

Fig. 5 CQS distribution of the companies assessed with IRBs (percentage of companies). *Note* For companies assessed by more than one IRB, the mean of the PDs has been considered

In Italy, due to the prevalence of small firms, the large majority of the companies assessed by IRBs has a PD above 0.4%, i.e. worse than the CQS3 threshold for the permanent framework. In detail, only around 20% of the companies receive a PD from IRB systems within CQS 1&2 or CQS 3. The most populated class is CQS 4 (PDs between 0.4 and 1%; Fig. 5).

Collateral Valuation

The Eurosystem trims the value of eligible assets for the calculation of the net collateral value. The valuation haircuts cover potential losses in the value of the assets in the event of the default of counterparties, over the period required to liquidate collateral in the market. Since haircuts are designed to cover credit and market risks, they are not differentiated by counterparty. Instead, the haircut level applied to each asset depends on the instrument features (such as asset type, residual maturity, and coupon type) and on its

measures relating to Eurosystem refinancing operations and eligibility of collateral (ECB/2014/31), of which individual credit claims with a credit quality below CQS 3. Such change will enter into force with the next regular update of the applicable legal framework (no earlier than the fourth quarter of 2025). In the same context, the Governing Council mandated the relevant Eurosystem committees to carry out preparatory work on the future integration of pools of non-financial corporate credit claims into the general framework.

credit quality. The haircut is independent of the maturity of the refinancing operation. Valuation haircuts are applied to the market value of marketable assets and to the nominal value of non-marketable assets.[8]

Within the ACC frameworks, credit claims can be pledged as collateral in two distinct fashions: either individually or as part of homogenous portfolios. For individually pledged loans, as in the case of marketable assets, the Eurosystem applies a haircut to each credit claim depending on its characteristics. For portfolios of ACCs, a single haircut is applied to the portfolio as a whole, taking into account the features of each credit claim as well as the risk diversification effect within the portfolio.

The Table 1 shows the current valuation haircuts for all asset types.

Table 1 Eurosystem haircut schedule

	Credit claims			
Maturity	0 ≤ PD ≤ 0.1%	0.1% < PD ≤ 0.4%	0.4% < PD ≤ 1%	1% < PD ≤ 1.5%
[0,1)	8.0%	16.0%	46.0%	54.0%
[1,3)	11.5%	25.0%	57.0%	62.0%
[3,5)	15.0%	35.0%	59.0%	64.0%
[5,7)	20.0%	42.0%	61.0%	66.0%
[7,10)	26.0%	46.0%	63.0%	68.0%
[10,15)	33.0%	48.0%	64.0%	69.0%
[15,30)	38.0%	50.0%	65.0%	70.0%
≥30	40.0%	52.0%	65.0%	70.0%

	Central Gov		Covered bonds	ABS	Corporate	
Maturity	AAA-A	BBB	AAA-A	AAA-A	AAA-A	BBB
[0,1)	0.5%	5.0%	1.0%	4.0%	1.0%	6.5%
[1,3)	1.0%	6.0%	1.5%	5.0%	2.0%	9.5%
[3,5)	1.5%	8.5%	2.5%	7.0%	3.0%	13.0%
[5,7)	2.0%	10.0%	3.5%	9.0%	4.5%	15.0%
[7,10)	3.0%	11.5%	4.5%	12.0%	6.0%	17.0%
[10,15)	4.0%	12.5%	6.5%	18.0%	7.5%	19.5%
[15,30)	5.0%	13.5%	8.0%	20.0%	9.0%	22.0%
≥30	6.0%	14.0%	10.0%	22.0%	11.0%	25.0%

[8] For example, consider an Italian government bond (with a rating of BBB+) and a credit claim, both with a residual maturity between 7 and 10 years and a nominal value of ten million euros. Assume that the price of the government bond is 101.75 and the annual PD of the loan is 0.40%. The liquidity that can be obtained with the Italian government bond amounts to 10 million *

The integration of IRB systems into the ECAF provides several benefits for the Eurosystem.

- *greater precision in credit assessment*. IRB systems rely on sophisticated models that incorporate a wide array of quantitative and qualitative information. Thanks to the ongoing relationship between banks and their clients, these models can leverage confidential borrower data. Moreover, IRB systems are subject to close supervisory oversight, which helps ensure that risk estimates are produced with a prudent degree of conservativeness.
- *facilitation of monetary policy implementation*. Especially in jurisdictions without an ICAS, the use of IRB systems for monetary policy allows banks to mobilize credit claims, thus supporting the effective transmission of monetary policy to the economy.
- *diversification of rating sources and reduced reliance on rating agencies*. IRBs are an alternative to rating agencies, at least for larger firms that have an ECAI rating, thus differentiating the rating sources available in ECAF and reducing the reliance on ECAIs, already widely used for assessing marketable assets.

However, the use of IRB systems within the ECAF also presents certain challenges for the Eurosystem:

- *reliance on external sources*. Like ECAIs, IRB systems are operated by external entities (i.e. the banks themselves), which implies limited direct control by the Eurosystem over their methodologies. Nonetheless, this limitation is largely overcome by the supervisory review and approval processes to which IRB systems are subject, thereby providing assurance regarding their soundness and consistency. For further details on the use of IRB ratings as opposed to ICAS ones in the ECAF see Calza et al. (2021) and Chap. 10.
- *complexity*. Adhering to the ECAF requirements while using complex internal models involves robust regulatory oversight and clear guidelines, together with a deep understanding of the supervisory practices. Regular validation and monitoring ensure that these models remain accurate and reliable. This entails a significant operational burden for the Eurosystem, which must allocate substantial resources to maintain the integrity and consistency of the framework.

4 An Overview on the Use of IRB Systems for Monetary Policy

Many central banks accept credit claims (such as loans to corporations, SMEs, and households) as collateral in monetary policy operations. However, eligibility criteria and valuation methods vary considerably across jurisdictions.

101.75% * (1–11.5%) = 9 million euros. In the case of the credit claim, the amount of liquidity would be: 10 million * (1–46%) = 5.4 million euros. See also Adler et al. (2023).

The assessment methods for the credit quality generally involve a combination of internal credit assessment, external credit ratings, and market-based indicators. Internal assessment relies on the central banks' own systems, which typically consider the borrower's credit profile, loan terms, and relevant factors such as the economic sector and geographic region. External credit ratings from agencies like Moody's, S&P, and Fitch are also frequently used, with rating thresholds. Additionally, market-based indicators such as the credit spread, implied default probability, or market liquidity may be considered to evaluate the quality and associated risks of each credit claim.

The Bank of England (BoE)[9] accepts a wide range of loans as collateral in its liquidity operations, which provide an effective liquidity insurance mechanism to the financial system, through the Sterling Monetary Framework (SMF).[10] Loans may be pledged individually or in portfolios and include loans to individuals on a stand-alone basis. The risk assessment is based on a combination of internal analysis and the use of credit quality criteria. There is no mention of IRBs in the public documentation on the web site of the BoE. Acceptable loans must fall into specific categories, such as commercial or residential loans, and meet manageable risk criteria. These portfolios must be well diversified and comply with some transparency requirements.

In particular, the BoE considers market information and external ratings; it also forms its own independent assessment of the risk associated with loans. Synthetic instruments or instruments with non-transparent risk characteristics are excluded. Furthermore, the BoE reserves the right to reject any collateral offered if it cannot be adequately risk assessed or managed.

The US Federal Reserve System[11] accepts a wide range of loan types as collateral. These can be used to secure discount window advances and extensions of daylight credit or master account activity, including charges associated therewith. The discount window supports banking system liquidity and stability by providing depository institutions with quick access to funding. This helps them manage liquidity risk and ensures the continued flow of credit to households and businesses.

The Fed's collateral acceptance relies on external ratings and standardized internal models. Notably, it permits the use of the banks' IRB system for assessing commercial loan portfolios. Institutions using their own IRB system must submit their internal risk rating policies to the local Reserve Bank for review. If approved,

[9] Bank of England (2025).

[10] The Bank offers three liquidity insurance facilities allowing participants to exchange a wide range of collateral, including credit claims, for very liquid assets such as central bank reserves or UK Government bonds: (i) the Indexed Long-Term Repo (ILTR), monthly operations for institutions with predictable liquidity needs; (ii) the Discount Window Facility (DWF), on-demand bilateral operations for institutions facing specific or market-wide shocks and (iii) the Contingent Term Repo Facility (CTRF), a facility activated during exceptional market stress, with terms set by the Bank according to prevailing market conditions.

[11] The Federal Reserve (2025a, 2025b).

the Reserve Bank will rely on the institution's rating system to assess the credit quality of pledged loans and establish their eligibility and collateral value.

The Bank of Japan (BoJ)[12] accepts a broad range of public and private sector credit claims as collateral in its monetary policy operations.[13] Credit claims must meet certain eligibility requirements, including quality and size thresholds. The BoJ determines collateral eligibility using its own criteria, relying more on external credit ratings and market-based data than on banks' internal assessments. While banks can provide internal information, their rating systems are not formally reviewed or approved. Creditworthiness is assessed through a combination of external agency ratings, internal evaluations, and market indicators. Legal compliance is also verified to ensure enforceability, and regular reviews keep the assessment up-to-date, especially during periods of economic instability.

The People's Bank of China (PBoC) also accepts loans as collateral in its monetary policy operations. This is primarily done through instruments like repurchase agreements and the Medium-term Lending Facility (MLF), in which commercial banks may use their loans and other assets as collateral to obtain liquidity from the central bank.

The PBoC uses loans as collateral to maintain flexibility and stability in the financial system. Only loans that meet specific quality standards, such as low default risk, are accepted. High credit ratings, either from external rating agencies or internal bank systems, are required. External ratings, favoured on account of their transparency, provide a third-party evaluation of risk, while internal ratings, often used for SMEs or specialized loans, must adhere to regulatory standards in line with Basel II or III. Internal ratings are subject to scrutiny and approval by the PBoC or other regulatory bodies to ensure that they meet certain standards of accuracy and robustness. These include adherence to strict risk management practices and oversight to avoid potential conflicts of interest. In practice, the PBoC combines external ratings with its internal assessment; for higher-risk or less transparent loans, external ratings may carry more weight and additional haircuts may be applied.

In conclusion, not all major central banks allow the use of IRB systems for the credit assessment of collateralised loans. The Eurosystem practice is part of the broader flexibility provided to banks under the collateral framework.

Most central banks rely more extensively on external credit ratings, market-based valuations, or standardized internal criteria for collateral eligibility and risk assessment. Even though some central banks may allow a certain degree of flexibility on credit claim assessment under exceptional circumstances, this typically does not extend to the use of internal risk systems such as IRBs.

---

[12] Bank of Japan (2025a, 2025b).

[13] As of 30 September 2024 the share of credit claims accepted on a stand-alone basis in total collateral stands at around 28%. See Bank of Japan (2025a, 2025b).

5 Regulation and Supervisory Issues

Prudential regulation requires banks to hold a minimum amount of regulatory capital to cover potential losses from risky assets. As the riskiness increases, the capital requirements also rise accordingly. Over the past few decades, bank regulation has sought to reinforce the link between the amount of regulatory capital of each bank and the risk level of its assets.

The Basel Accord of 1988 (Basel I) was the first major effort to establish international risk-based standards for capital regulation. Basel I required banks to maintain a minimum ratio of capital to risk-weighted assets (RWAs) of 8%. However, the approach used a basic measure of risk that did not take into account changes in risk levels within different asset types, treating all assets in each category in a similar way.

The entry into force of Basel II in 2007 marked a significant shift in the assessment of credit risk. It expanded the range of asset categories and promoted more sophisticated risk management by allowing banks to use internal models to calculate capital requirements. Specifically, Basel II introduced the Internal Ratings-Based (IRB) approaches as alternatives to the Standardised Approach (SA). While the SA applies fixed risk weights based on asset class and credit quality, the IRB framework allows banks to estimate risk parameters based on their own historical data and internal credit risk models.

Under the IRB approach, banks estimate key risk parameters such as the probability of default, the loss given default (LGD) and the exposure at default (EAD) for different categories of assets. These parameters are then used to compute the RWAs. When banks decide on the implementation of the IRB-approach, they may choose between the Foundation Internal Ratings-Based Approach (FIRBA) and the Advanced Internal Ratings-Based Approach (AIRBA). The main difference is that under FIRBA the bank only needs to establish the probability of default on its own, whereas the remaining parameters, such as EAD and LGD, rely on regulatory benchmarks. Under AIRBA all parameters must be estimated by the bank instead.

The adoption of the IRB approach had several effects on banks. Since Basel II was introduced, a growing number of banks have opted for the IRB approach, many of which have achieved substantial capital savings. However, following the financial crisis of 2007–2009, doubts were raised regarding the unwarranted variability of the output of IRB systems. Such doubts developed in parallel with the concerns of banking supervisors and external stakeholders about the complexity of IRB systems and their resulting opaqueness, which made it increasingly difficult for supervisors to assess whether risks had been estimated correctly.[14]

[14] The introduction of risk-weighted capital charges and the potential problems related to them have been discussed in several papers, e.g. Kashyap and Stein (2004), Hellwig (2010), and Behn et al. (2022). For an assessment from the regulator's perspective, see Basel Committee on Banking Supervision (1999).

After the financial crisis of 2007–2009, the reform brought about by Basel III focused on measures to increase the required amount of capital for a given size of RWAs,[15] recognizing that no model can fully account for the complexity of banking risks and that some form of model risk is unavoidable. The ensuing changes to the Basel II framework increased complexity without altering its rationale. This raised some criticism (see e.g. Haldane, 2011, 2013; Hellwig, 2010; Hoenig, 2013).

The concerns on the unwarranted variability of the IRB outcomes led to further regulatory work by the Basel Committee on Banking Supervision (BCBS) in subsequent years. In March 2016, the BCBS drafted the consultative document "Reducing variation in credit risk-weighted assets—constraints on the use of internal model approaches", which contained several proposals to reform the standardized approach and restrict the IRB approach. The final version of Basel III (commonly referred to as Basel IV), adopted at the end of 2017,[16] concluded the post-crisis review process. As concerns the IRB systems, the main innovations are as follows: i) the internal models may no longer apply to loan portfolios for which the use of statistical criteria is problematic, on account of too few observations, short time series or distributions that are hard to characterize; ii) input floors are set for the key parameters (PD, LGD, EAD); iii) an output floor is introduced, that is a limit on the capital savings that banks can attain by using internal models with respect to the requirements based on the standardized method; in practice, the final IRB RWA should be equal to at least 72.5% of the RWA obtained with the standardized approach by 2027.

In the EU the regulatory activity of the BCBS was complemented by initiatives from the European Banking Authority (EBA). One of them was the regulatory review of the IRB approach to credit risk,[17] which tried to reduce non-risk-based variability in model outcomes among banks through regulatory guidance and clarifications. The goal was to improve the comparability of risk estimates, while at the same time preserving risk sensitivity. Through its annual assessment of the consistency of internal model outcomes (the benchmarking exercises), the EBA assesses risk-weight variability for credit and market risks.

In conjunction with these regulatory initiatives, at the beginning of 2016 the ECB's direct supervision of Significant Institutions (SIs) under the Single Supervisory Mechanism (SSM), in close cooperation with the National Competent Authorities (NCAs), launched the TRIM project, a large-scale multi-year supervisory initiative with the purpose of:

[15] Common equity tier 1 (CET1) requirement of 4.5% of RWAs, capital conservation buffer, heightened capital requirements for some categories, countercyclical capital buffer, systemic buffers, etc. Basel III introduced also a leverage ratio, which should act as a protection against the failure of internal systems and therefore represents a risk insensitive backstop.

[16] See BCBS (2017).

[17] For further details see EBA (2016) and (2019).

- confirming the adequacy and appropriateness of approved Pillar I internal models used by SIs in euro-area countries, thus ensuring their compliance with regulatory requirements;
- harmonizing supervisory practices relating to internal models within the SSM.

Within the TRIM project, about 200 on-site internal model investigations (IMIs) across 65 institutions were conducted. The project was an important milestone in raising the quality standards and comparability of outcomes of internal models in use at SIs within the SSM. To ensure consistency and to support the execution of on-site IMIs, TRIM delivered the ECB guide to internal models (the 'ECB guide'), updated in February 2024,[18] which contributes to a level playing field for SIs in the area of internal models.[19] In parallel, the EBA's IRB Repair Programme—launched in 2016 and implemented through a range of regulatory products between 2017 and 2019—complemented these efforts by providing detailed regulatory guidance and harmonized expectations on the development, validation, and implementation of IRB models. By promoting convergence in both model development and supervisory assessment, the IRB Repair Programme reinforced the TRIM's objectives and contributed significantly to strengthening the overall credibility and consistency of the IRB approach across the EU.

6 ECAF Rules for IRBs and the Experience of the Bank of Italy

The Eurosystem allows the use of IRB models as an eligible source of credit quality assessment for credit claims as collateral as from 2007, following the introduction of the Single List of collateral, which sets common eligibility criteria across the Eurosystem. IRB usage increased in parallel with the importance of credit claims in the collateral framework.

About 40 banks currently use their IRB systems in ECAF. These counterparties are based in eight countries (Austria, Belgium, Germany, France, Italy, Portugal, Slovenia, Slovakia).

The IRBs in Italy were first admitted in ECAF in 2008 to expand eligible collateral. Today, almost all the Italian banks with IRBs authorized for regulatory purposes use their model also for the assessment of credit claims as collateral in monetary policy operations.

[18] ECB (2024a, February).

[19] Furthermore, internal ECB banking supervision mechanisms (e.g. several layers of managerial quality assurance, horizontal analyses and approval of supervisory decisions in batches to allow cross-comparisons) were used to ensure consistent results of TRIM on-site investigations across institutions, as well as a consistent follow-up via supervisory decisions or, where appropriate, operational acts. The TRIM project has created organisational structures and processes which ensure harmonisation by means of close cooperation among all the parties involved, gathering skilled internal model experts from across the European banking supervision.

6.1 Risk Control Framework

Acceptance Procedure

To obtain approval for an IRB system under ECAF, a counterparty must submit a request to its home NCB. The prerequisite is that the competent supervisory authority has already authorized the counterparty to use the IRB system for capital requirements. If this authorization is later withdrawn, ECAF approval is also revoked. The assessment is made by the responsible NCB.

During the acceptance period the NCB performs a due diligence on the use of the IRB system to verify the compliance with the rules set forth in the ECB's General Documentation (GD)[20] and the contractual provisions. The due diligence is based on the statistical and non-statistical information provided by the counterparties in a number of documents[21,22] devoted to:

- authorization: proof of supervisory approval to use the IRB system for capital requirements, including any conditions;
- compliance monitoring: up-to-date evaluation and required modifications by the competent authority;
- risk assessment: methodology for calculating probabilities of default and how these figures are integrated into capital requirements;
- disclosure: recent market discipline disclosures as mandated by international and EU regulations;
- regulatory contacts: identification of relevant authorities and auditors overseeing the IRB system.

[20] The General Documentation (GD) is a public document which contains the rules for monetary policy operations. The current version of it is Guideline ECB/2024/37.

[21] Art. 122 of the GD.

[22] (a) a copy of the decision by the competent authority authorizing the use of the IRB system for capital requirements, either on a consolidated or non-consolidated basis, along with any specific conditions attached to this authorization.

(b) a current assessment by the competent authority reflecting up-to-date information on all matters affecting the IRB system's use for collateral purposes, including any data relevant to the ECAF performance monitoring process.

(c) details of any modifications to the IRB system recommended or required by the competent authority, including the deadlines for implementing these changes.

(d) information on how the counterparty assigns probabilities of default to debtors, along with data on rating grades and their associated one-year probabilities of default used to determine eligible rating grades. The probability of default reported by the counterparty's IRB system should be the 'final' probability of default used for calculating own fund requirements, including any supervisory regulatory floors, add-ons, adjustments, margin of conservatism, overrides, and mapping to master scales.

(e) a copy of the latest Pillar 3 disclosures (related to market discipline) that the counterparty is required to publish regularly according to the Basel III Framework, Directive 2013/36/EU, and Regulation (EU) No 575/2013.

(f) the name and address of the competent authority and the external auditor.

An important piece of information is the data on the observed default rates by rating grade over the previous five calendar years.[23] These data must comply with the performance monitoring requirements of Article 126 of the GD (see below), as if the IRB system had been subject to these provisions during that period. Based on the track record of the counterparty's IRB default experience, the IRB rating classes or probabilities of default are mapped into the Eurosystem harmonized rating scale.[24]

The NCB informs the relevant banking supervisor of the counterparty's application to use the IRB for ECAF purposes and may ask for information and documents for the assessment and monitoring of the IRB following its acceptance in ECAF.

Due Diligence

A counterparty which has been authorized to use its IRB system for ECAF purposes is subject to reporting obligations, on an annual basis or upon request, of statistical and non-statistical information to the home NCB.[25] The counterparty must also meet any additional operational criteria specified in the contractual or regulatory arrangements set by the home NCB, including provisions related to ad hoc checks, annual audits, and timely communication of any changes regarding the eligibility of credit claims.

Performance Monitoring Exercise

The statistical information on the universe of the final debtors/obligors which are eligible for collateral purposes, the so-called static pool data, is used to perform the annual performance monitoring exercise, which involves all accepted credit assessment sources. This process ensures that the risk mapping of the Eurosystem's harmonized rating scale remains accurate and that the results from different sources are comparable.

Static pool data for credit assessment systems are reported to the respective NCB using a template that facilitates the quality checks.[26] The exercise assesses whether the estimated probability of default issued by each IRB system conforms to the required level. This involves the analysis of deviations between the estimated default probability and the realized default rate in a back-testing exercise (Coppens et al., 2007). The testing procedure is implemented via the 'traffic light approach', where a binomial distribution of independent defaults is assumed.

If the monitoring process reveals discrepancies, adjustments may be made to the mapping onto the harmonized rating scale for the individual counterparty. In this case, the Eurosystem imposes the reduction of the threshold for the acceptance of credit claims within each CQS, resulting in a reduction of the collateral value and

[23] If the IRB system was authorized during this period, the information should cover the time since the authorization was granted.

[24] ECB (2025).

[25] Art. 123 of the GD.

[26] ECB (2024b, December).

a stricter monitoring of the individual IRB system, in liaison with the Supervisory Authority. The corrective measure may be revoked once it is ascertained that the causes of the IRB's underperformance have been removed, possibly by a model change, and the performance monitoring is satisfactory.

In case of repeated failures of the performance monitoring exercise or of any violation of rules related to ECAF, the Eurosystem may suspend or remove an individual counterparty's credit assessment system from the list of accepted sources.

On-Site Visits

As part of the regular monitoring of IRB systems, the NCB conducts on-site[27] visits about the statistical data provided by counterparties to ensure that they are accurate, correct, and complete. A higher frequency for such inspections may be required if issues are detected in the performance monitoring or as a consequence of the off-site due diligence.

On-site visits are designed to thoroughly evaluate static pools and the IRB approach as a whole. The objective is to offer the NCB a clear understanding of the static pool data, as well as of the procedures for its compilation. A key procedure for these inspections is the comparison of the data submitted by the institution with the data stored in its internal database, ensuring consistency and accuracy. For data-related aspects, the counterparty must provide relevant explanations based on the key findings from the off-site due diligence, which may include performance results, inconsistencies, rating withdrawals, and analysis of rating transitions.

On the procedural side, the counterparty must describe how debtors are selected from the databases, how frequently these databases are updated and verified, and whether static pool data are cross-checked after extraction.

Additionally, on-site visits provide an opportunity to discuss non-statistical information that the counterparty must submit annually. This includes an assessment of the IRB approach by supervisors, any recommended changes to the IRB framework, and updates to the Pillar III disclosures, as required by Regulation (EU) No 575/2013 (CRR).

Since 2014 Bank of Italy has conducted 30 on-site visits, devoted to data quality, procedures, and organizational structures. The recommendations focus mainly on strengthening the safeguards to guarantee the automation of the data management process and the consistency between the information in the databases used for reporting.

[27] During the COVID-19 period the Eurosystem conducted also remote inspections.

7 The Prioritization of ICAS Ratings

In recent years, the use of IRB models for supervisory purposes has gone through an important review. A key outcome of the CRR3 is the reduction in the scope of exposures eligible for IRB models. As the European Commission aimed at increasing harmonization across the institutions and making IRB model outcomes more comparable, the IRB framework was revised to establish limits to its application.

In June 2025 the new Eurosystem collateral management system, known as ECMS, went live. In parallel, the ECB's Governing Council introduced a new rule, whereby the ICAS rating, if available for a given debtor, prevails over any alternative rating source for the same debtor. This measure is dubbed as ICAS prioritization. The existing ICAS ratings are thus used to assess the credit risk of debtors and guarantors of credit claims, determining both the eligibility of the credit claim and the applicable valuation haircuts.[28]

The prioritization concerns the full ICAS (F-ICAS) ratings, namely the ICAS evaluations enriched with the analysis carried out by financial analysts (see Chap. 5). In Italy, the prioritization applies to claims pledged both individually or in portfolios.[29,30] The IRB ratings are considered only in the absence of an available ICAS rating for the debtor and/or guarantor of a credit claim.[31]

Bank of Italy has been providing counterparties using ICAS as their primary assessment source with information that enables them to identify ex ante the debtors whose bank loans are eligible as collateral, either individually or within ACC pools. With the introduction of prioritization, this information is sent to all counterparties and enhanced with the information of the ICAS risk class (CQS) assigned to each debtor. This allows all counterparties to calculate the collateral value of loans in advance, supporting effective treasury management.

The rationale for the prioritization is to promote the internal rating capabilities of the Eurosystem and reduce the reliance on external ratings. This enhances the Eurosystem independence and improves consistency in monetary policy implementation. Encouraging the use of ICAS reinforces stability within the collateral framework. Banks without IRB models—typically smaller banks—will be on a more equal footing with banks using IRBs for the mobilisation of credit claims. In

---

[28] The ICASes of the Eurosystem operate under a set of rules established within the ECAF, aimed at ensuring both high quality standards and a consistent application across the Eurosystem. For further details see Auria et al. (2021).

[29] In November 2024 the Governing Council decided that NCBs' statistical ICASes will be accepted as an additional credit assessment source in the ECAF, subject to the development of a harmonised framework. Until then, the S-ICAS ratings will continue to be used only in the ACC framework, subject to a request by the counterparty.

[30] The prioritization applies to all claims individually pledged, both in the ordinary and the ACC framework, while each NCB with an ICAS may decide to extend such measure also to ACC portfolios. For further details on the characteristics of the Bank of Italy's ICAS see Bank of Italy (2024).

[31] For a thorough comparison of the ICAS and IRB ratings in Italy see Chap. 10.

addition, the priority rule will contribute to a consistent collateral treatment across counterparties for a given debtor or guarantor that is rated by multiple systems.

Banks that have invested heavily in developing and maintaining IRB models might in principle perceive some value loss in their efforts. However, IRB models continue to play an important role in ensuring a broad and diversified pool of collateral within the Eurosystem. These models provide credit assessment for SMEs that do not have a full ICAS rating. By covering this segment, IRB models will continue to support a wide range of eligible assets, contributing to the overall availability of collateral and the smooth implementation of monetary policy. According to the latest available data, in the Italian context, even after the introduction of ICAS prioritization IRB systems provide the credit assessment of approximately 35% of the total volume of credit claims pledged as collateral (down from 47% in 2024) and 50% of the number of debtors.

References

Adler, M., Camba-Méndez, G., Džaja, T., Manzanares, A., Metra, M., & Vocalelli, G. (2023). The valuation haircuts applied to eligible marketable assets for ECB credit operations. *ECB Occasional Paper Series, 312.*

Antilici, P., Gariano, G., Monterisi, F., Picone, A., & Russo, L. (2023). The Eurosystem collateral framework and the measures introduced in response to the pandemic emergency. In A. Scalia (Ed.), *Financial risk management and climate change risk: The experience in a central bank* (pp. 55–72). Springer.

Auria, L., Bingmer, M., Mateo, C., Graciano, C., Charavel, C., Gavilá, S., Iannamorelli, A., Levy, A., Maldonado, A., Resch, F., Rossi, A. M., & Sauer, S. (2021). Overview of central banks' in-house credit assessment systems in the euro area. *ECB Occasional Paper Series, 284.*

Bank of Italy. (2024). *The Bank of Italy's in-house credit assessment system (ICAS-BI).* https://www.bancaditalia.it/compiti/polmon-garanzie/gestione-garanzie/qualita-crediti/index.html?com.dotmarketing.htmlpage.language=1

Bank of England. (2025). *Bank of England market operations guide.* https://www.bankofengland.co.uk/markets/bank-of-england-market-operations-guide

Bank of Japan. (2025a). *Guidelines on eligible collateral.* https://www.boj.or.jp/en/mopo/measures/term_cond/yoryo18.htm

Bank of Japan. (2025b). *Collateral accepted by the Bank of Japan.* https://www.boj.or.jp/en/statistics/boj/other/col/index.htm

Basel Committee on Banking Supervision. (1988). *International convergence of capital measurement and capital standards.* Bank for International Settlements, Basel, Switzerland

Basel Committee on Banking Supervision. (1999). *Capital requirements and bank behaviour: The impact of the Basel Accord.* Bank for International Settlements, Basel, Switzerland.

Basel Committee on Banking Supervision. (2004). *Implementation of Basel II: Practical considerations.* Bank for International Settlements, Basel, Switzerland

Basel Committee on Banking Supervision. (2017). *Basel III: Finalising post-crisis reforms*. Bank for International Settlements, Basel, Switzerland. https://www.bis.org/bcbs/publ/d424.pdf

Behn, M., Haselmann, R., & Vig, V. (2022). The limits of model-based regulation. The *Journal of Finance, LXXVII*(3), 1635–1684.

Bindseil, U. (2013). Central bank collateral, asset fire sales, regulation and liquidity. *ECB Working Paper Series, 1610.*

Bindseil, U., Corsi, M., Sahel, B., & Visser, A. (2017). The Eurosystem collateral framework explained. *ECB Occasional Paper Series, 189.*

Calza, A., Hey, J., Parrini, A., & Sauer, S. (2021). Corporate loans, bank's internal risk estimates and central bank collateral: Evidence from the Euro area. *ECB Working Paper Series, 2579.*

Choi, D. B., Santos, J. A. C., & Yorulmazer, T. (2021). A theory of collateral for the lender of last resort. *Review of Finance, 2021*, 973–996.

Coppens, F., González, F., & Winkler, G. (2007) The performance of credit rating systems in the assessment of collateral used in Eurosystem monetary policy operations. *ECB Occasional Paper Series, 65.*

Diamond, D. W., & Dybvig, P. H. (1983) Bank Runs, deposit insurance, and liquidity. *Journal of Political Economy, 91*(3).

Dudley, W. C. (2024). *Bank failures and contagion lender of last resort, liquidity, and risk management* (Working Paper 329). Princeton University, Department of Economics, Center for Economic Policy Studies. https://ideas.repec.org/p/pri/cepsud/329.html

European Banking Authority. (2016, February 16). *EBA sets out roadmap for the implementation of the regulatory review of internal models.* https://www.eba.europa.eu/publications-and-media/press-releases/eba-sets-out-roadmap-implementation-regulatory-review

European Banking Authority. (2017, November). *Guidelines on PD estimation, LGD estimation and the treatment of defaulted exposures.*

European Banking Authority. (2019, July 9). *EBA publishes report on progress made on its roadmap to repair IRB models* [Press release]. https://www.eba.europa.eu/publications-and-media/press-releases/eba-publishes-report-progress-made-its-roadmap-repair-irb

European Central Bank. (2005). *Eurosystem collateral framework: Inclusion of non-marketable assets in the Single List* [Press release]. https://www.ecb.europa.eu/press/pr/date/2005/html/pr050722.en.html

European Central Bank. (2015, July). *The financial risk management of the Eurosystem's monetary policy operations.* https://www.ecb.europa.eu/pub/pdf/other/financial_risk_management_of_eurosystem_monetary_policy_operations_201507.en.pdf

European Central Bank. (2024a, February). *Guide to Internal Models.* https://www.bankingsupervision.europa.eu/ecb/pub/pdf/ssm.supervisory_guides202402_internalmodels.en.pdf

European Central Bank. (2024b, December). *Questions and answers on the compilation of the static pool for performance monitoring in the Eurosystem credit assessment framework (ECAF).* https://www.ecb.europa.eu/mopo/pdf/assets/risk/ecaf/ECAF-static-pool-questions-and-answers.pdf

European Central Bank. (2024c). Guideline (EU) 2024/3132 of the European Central Bank of 14 November 2024 repealing Guideline (EU) 2024/3130 amending Guideline (EU) 2015/510 on the implementation of the Eurosystem monetary policy framework (ECB/2024/23) and amending Guideline (EU) 2015/510 (ECB/2014/60) (ECB/2024/37), Frankfurt am Main.

European Central Bank. (2025). *Eurosystem credit assessment framework (ECAF).* https://www.ecb.europa.eu/mopo/coll/risk/ecaf/html/index.en.html

Giovannelli, F., Iannamorelli, A., Levy, A., & Orlandi, M. (2023). The Bank of Italy's in-house credit assessment system for non-financial firms. In A. Scalia (Ed.), *Financial risk management and climate change risk* (pp. 107–137). Springer.

Haldane, A. (2011). *Capital discipline, speech at the American economic association in Denver on January 9th of 2011.*

Haldane, A. (2013). *Constraining discretion on bank regulation, speech at the Federal Reserve Bank of Atlanta on April 9th of 2013.*

Harpedanne de Belleville, L. (2018). *Real effects of central bank collateral policy: Liquidity insurance at work.* Available at SSRN: https://papers.ssrn.com/sol3/papers.cfm?abstract_id=3190618

Hellwig, M. (2010). *Capital regulation after the crisis: Business as usual?.* Bonn: Max Planck Institute for Research on Collective Goods Bonn, No. 2010/31.

Hoenig, T. (2013). *Basel III capital: A well-intended illusion, speech to the international association of deposit insurers on April 9th of 2013.*

Kashyap, A. K., & Stein, C. (2004). *Cyclical implications of the Basel II capital standards.* Economic Perspectives, Federal Reserve Bank of Chicago, vol. 28(Q I), pages 18–31

The Federal Reserve. (2025a). *Collateral eligibility—Securities and loans*. https://www.frbdiscountwindow.org/pages/collateral/collateral_eligibility
The Federal Reserve. (2025b). *Pledging collateral*. https://www.frbdiscountwindow.org/Pages/Collateral/pledging_collateral

The Credit Assessment of Large Firms

Lorenzo Esposito, Marisa Franzoni, Massimo Guglielmi, Alessandra Iannamorelli, and Raffaella Sorgente

1 Introduction

As of 2026, the statistical models of ICASes (S-ICASes) are included among the ECAF sources to assess small and medium-sized enterprises (SMEs), many of which are not assessed by other sources (Duarte et al., 2025). Full ratings are required for large firms. Under this framework, the ICAS expert assessment will progressively concentrate on large firms. To support the specialization of expert assessment by firm size, we have conducted a review of methodologies used by external rating sources to assess large non-financial firms, with a view to identifying best practices and recent developments.

The review covers the credit assessment sources accepted for Eurosystem collateral purposes:

L. Esposito
Bank of Italy, Milan Branch, Milan, Italy
e-mail: lorenzo.esposito@bancaditalia.it

M. Franzoni
Bank of Italy, Bologna Branch, Bologna, Italy
e-mail: marisa.franzoni@bancaditalia.it

M. Guglielmi · A. Iannamorelli (✉)
Bank of Italy, Financial Risk Management Directorate, Rome, Italy
e-mail: alessandra.iannamorelli@bancaditalia.it

M. Guglielmi
e-mail: massimo.guglielmi@bancaditalia.it

R. Sorgente
Bank of Italy, Venice Branch, Venice, Italy
e-mail: raffaella.sorgente@bancaditalia.it

A. Scalia (ed.), *Corporate Credit Analysis and AI*, Finance for Professionals,
https://doi.org/10.1007/978-3-032-13422-6_9

- ECAIs, such as Moody's, S&P, and Fitch;
- selected ICASes with longstanding use and public documentation, including those of Banco de España, Banque de France, and Bundesbank;
- commercial banks' IRB systems;
- the two main Italian rating agencies, Cerved and CRIF.[1]

To our knowledge, this Chapter provides the first overview of rating methodologies for large firms.

We find that the rating entities rely on a wide range of financial and non-financial information. Qualitative judgement based on interviews with top management and the analysis of governance and market positioning play a key role in the evaluation of complex firms. Most systems share common features, such as the use of a sector-specific methodology (especially in industries such as real estate or energy), group-level assessment, early warning monitoring tools, and procedures for overriding the standard model output, if deemed appropriate. The analysis also shows recent methodological developments, including the integration of sustainability factors into the credit risk assessment and the use of machine learning techniques.

The remainder of the Chapter is organized as follows: Section 9.2 reviews the related literature; Section 9.3 describes the methodology of the analysis; Section 9.4 presents the results; Section 9.5 summarizes the main findings and Section 9.6 provides the conclusions.

2 Literature Review

The assessment of creditworthiness for large corporations has gained prominence in the context of market regulation, prudential supervision, and Eurosystem credit operations also due to the growing systemic importance of these firms. This is reflected in the ECAF, which has introduced expert assessment for large firms as a condition for collateral eligibility (Duarte et al., 2025). Several rating methodologies coexist in the European financial system, including those employed by ECAIs, ICASes, and IRB systems. While harmonization has progressed in terms of regulatory coordination—such as the mapping of ECAI ratings under Regulation (EC) No. 1060/2009 (European Commission, 2009), the Capital Requirements Regulation (European Parliament and Council, 2013), and common eligibility criteria for ECAF purposes (ECB, 2015)—no alignment is imposed on rating methodologies. Each source continues to operate within distinct institutional settings and objectives, combining different data sources, models, time horizons, and judgemental components.

[1] Cerved and CRIF, accepted for the assessment of Italian collateral until 2021, are also ECAIs and their ratings are issued by Cerved Rating Agency and CRIF Ratings, respectively. The latter are distinct legal entities within their respective group. Therefore, when referring to ratings, the terms "Cerved" and "CRIF" shall apply to the latter two entities.

ECAIs primarily focus on large firms that issue bonds and structured securities. ECAIs adopt globally standardized TTC rating methods to assess long-term creditworthiness (Lecomte and Torres, 2023). They are based on expert assessment and sector-specific financial analysis, enriched by interviews with senior management and the integration of macroeconomic and ESG data (Moody's Investors Service, 2024; S&P Global, 2021; Fitch, 2023). The global reach of this approach leads to highly standardized methodologies, although it might limit responsiveness to local economic conditions (Marandola, 2021).

ICASes are developed by several national central banks of the Eurosystem, that are formally recognized within the ECAF (ECB, 2015). The ICAS process starts with a statistical evaluation based on financial ratios, followed by the expert assessment, largely of qualitative nature, carried out by analysts. The analysts' effort mainly covers governance issues, market positioning, and business strategies, which are not fully reflected in quantitative models (Giovannelli et al., 2023). Although they are based on one-year default probabilities (closer to PIT rating methodology), ICAS models include forward-looking adjustments that partially align with TTC characteristics (Auria et al., 2021). ICASes assess firms of all sizes but have increasingly devoted the expert assessment to large firms in response to collateral policy changes (ECB, 2022).

IRB systems were originally developed by commercial banks under the Basel II and III frameworks to set capital requirements; as such, they are subject to supervisory validation (BCBS, 2001 and 2005, EBA, 2023b). Although general information can be found in the financial statement and the Pillar 3 documentation, public disclosure on IRB methodologies remains limited. Some studies have raised concerns about transparency and overreliance on internal benchmarks (Brunella et al., 2023). IRB systems typically rely on PIT statistical evaluation of the PD with financial ratios, sectoral indicators and, increasingly, governance factors (Ferri and Pesic, 2017; Gallo, 2021). Although formally defined as PIT under the Basel and Capital Requirements Regulation (CRR) frameworks, in practice some banks employ smoothing techniques or hybrid calibration that partially approximate the TTC approach (BCBS, 2005; EBA, 2023b). While banks apply IRB systems to a wide range of borrowers, IRB systems are often calibrated to cover the corporate loan portfolios.

Nationally-focused rating agencies, such as Cerved and CRIF in Italy, adopt proprietary methodologies based on financial statements, sector analysis, and qualitative interviews (Cerved Group, 2023; CRIF Group, 2023). They cover all firm sizes; the available documentation does not reveal whether CRAs' models differ across firm size. Their rating horizon typically ranges between one and three years. Ratings are updated more frequently in cyclical sectors such as real estate and construction. ESG issues and advanced techniques, such as machine learning and predictive modelling, are increasingly employed to improve firms' assessment.

The use of the TTC approach or the PIT approach varies across rating sources. ECAIs and IRBs generally adopt the TTC notion to assess credit risk over the economic cycle. By contrast, ICASes typically rely on the PIT notion, although expert overrides and qualitative considerations allow partial convergence with the TTC approach (Auria et al., 2021; ECB, 2022).

IRB systems may rely on the ECAI ratings as a benchmark under the so-called *shadow rating* approach, which is prominent for banks with lending portfolios concentrated on large corporations (Mediobanca, 2024). The major ECAIs are normally aligned among themselves as far as the rating of important firms is concerned (Morgan, 2002). The alignment can be more nuanced in the outlook (such as 'stable' or 'negative'), used as a signal of a possible future change in the rating (Alsakka, 2017; Livingston et al., 2020).

Several studies examine the rating methodologies. Some studies provide an overview of rating use within the Eurosystem collateral framework, focusing on regulatory practices (e.g. Lecomte and Torres, 2023). Others examine the structure and evolution of ICASes (Auria et al., 2021) or the effect of ICAS eligibility on collateral (Carpinelli et al., 2021). Other studies compare internal ratings with standardized approaches or examine how ECAI ratings are mapped and validated (Cucinelli et al., 2018; Columba et al., 2023; Gagliardone and Papadia, 2022). These studies do not address the methodological differences for large firm assessment across rating sources.

3 Review Design

To carry out the review, we analysed publications describing the criteria employed by ECAIs such as Fitch, Moody's and S&P, as well as publicly available information on the IRB systems used by commercial banks. For ICASes, we examined public documentation and information from exchanges and seminars with Banco de España, Banque de France and Bundesbank. Additionally, we conducted interviews with representatives from nearly all the rating sources, except for IRBs, to address specific issues on their methods.

We examine rating sources using homogeneous criteria as concerns the methodologies and the organization of the process. The assessment focuses on three components: the rating model architecture, the nature and sources of input data, and the process for the generation of ratings. For each system under review, we try to establish whether the approach is predominantly quantitative, qualitative, or both. In the case of statistical models, the analysis explores how the relative contribution of different categories of input data - such as balance sheet financial statements, credit register information, and alternative sources - may vary along with the firm's size, with specific attention to large corporations.

For the qualitative dimension of credit assessment, the review identifies the risk profiles considered by each rating system, as well as the criteria used to form individual assessments. In addition, we examine how each system aggregates these assessments to produce the final rating, exploring whether aggregation follows a formalized scoring algorithm, expert assessment, or both. This step helps to assess the transparency and replicability of the rating process, particularly when it involves a large degree of qualitative judgement. The analysis explores several operational features underlying the governance and reliability of rating issuance. These include the procedure for rating approval, the internal control mechanisms in place to ensure rating consistency and accuracy, and the protocols for monitoring rated entities over time. Furthermore, the review evaluates the frequency and triggers for rating updates, with the aim of understanding how timely and responsive each system is to new information or evolving risk conditions.

4 Comparison of Rating Systems

4.1 Regulatory Definitions

Each rating provider defines its methodology based on its purpose and applicable regulation. Rating purposes also influence how large companies are defined. For ECAIs, the definition of a large company is not explicit, as they mainly rate widely traded corporate bonds that are typically issued by large firms. The CRA Regulation (Regulation (EC) No 1060/2009, as amended) rules ECAIs, and ESMA supervise their methodologies. The Eurosystem recognizes their ratings for monetary policy purposes. The ESAs and EBA periodically update the mapping rules applied to the ECAI ratings (EBA 2023a). These ratings assess the issuer's ability to meet financial commitments, based on a qualitative analysis of company data.[2]

In IRB systems, corporations are classified according to the size of the respective turnover. The size thresholds for large corporations vary between banks, ranging between 150 and 500 million euros in turnover, with different approaches for consolidated groups or specific exposures. In some sectors total assets are used. The CRR regulates IRB systems, and national authorities validate them in line with Chap. 3 of the CRR and the EBA Supervisory Handbook. Art. 178 of the CRR provides the default definition for IRB systems.

ICASes currently follow the European Commission Recommendation 2003/361 to define large enterprises, i.e. those with over 250 employees and a turnover exceeding 50 million euros or total balance sheet assets exceeding 43 million euros. Under the S-ICAS framework, these systems may be authorized to operate also as statistical sources, under enhanced governance and in compliance with Eurosystem standards. With the introduction of the new S-ICAS framework, such definition will be replaced by that of Directive 2013/34/EU (the so-called Accounting Directive), as amended by Directive 2023/2775/EU. According to the new criteria, a large company fulfils at least two of the following requirements: assets above 25 million euros, turnover exceeding 50 million euros, more than 250 employees. The ECAF recognizes ICASes, which follow the default definition in Article 178 of the CRR, like IRBs.

---

[2] Rating agencies provide two rating scales for both issuers and emissions: one for the long term and one for the short term.

Cerved and CRIF operate as registered ECAIs under Regulation (EC) No 1060/2009 and are subject to the supervision of the ESMA. Regulators accept their ratings, and the EBA includes them in the credit risk mapping. For Cerved a large company is defined as a company with a turnover exceeding 150 million euros, or as a listed company with a turnover exceeding five million euros. CRIF applies different criteria by size cluster: large corporations are generally defined as firms with a turnover between 50 million euros and 200 million euros, while very large corporations exceed 200 million euros in annual revenues.

Cerved ratings evaluate the company's ability to generate cash flows for debt repayment, based on an analysis of the economic and financial situation, sector positioning and prospective sustainability. CRIF estimates the PD over a one-year horizon through its ratings. Due to their regulatory framework[3] the definition of default adopted by these agencies implies substantial convergence with the CRR definition, as operationalized for prudential purposes. Internal validation procedures apply in case of analysts' disagreement.

Despite differences in default definitions, their practical application is largely aligned across rating sources, reflecting the common objective of capturing material credit events for large corporations. The data sources, overall method and interaction with assessed entities may differ according to the institutional framework. ECAIs emphasize structured engagement and global standardization; IRBs leverage long-term bank-firm relationships; ICASes integrate statistical and expert assessment within a structured process; Cerved combines real-time monitoring with granular insight.

The methodologies of these rating sources are shaped by regulatory obligations and the need to capture the nuances of large and complex firms. While ECAIs rely largely on qualitative methods, ICASes, IRBs, and Cerved incorporate both quantitative and qualitative assessments to provide a comprehensive and adaptable evaluation of credit risk (Moody's Investors Service, 2024; Cerved Group, 2023).

4.2 ECAIs

ECAI ratings mostly focus on large firms, typically those active in international bond markets. ECAI methodologies rely on a globally standardized TTC method aimed at assessing the firm's long-term ability to meet financial obligations. The assessment is forward-looking and qualitative, integrating a wide range of data sources, including audited financial statements, sectoral benchmarks, macroeconomic indicators, and ESG information. In addition, structured interviews with senior management play a central role in evaluating qualitative factors such as corporate strategy, governance, and market positioning. For example, Moody's places particular emphasis on management quality and financial policy, which are central in the first stage of assessment. All three agencies consider ESG risks, although

[3] They are registered ECAIs under the CRA Regulation.

Table 9.1 Definitions and Regulations

Source	Definition of large firms	Definition of rating	Regulatory framework
ECAI	Implicit in mandate; only assess issuers of widely traded corporate securities, typically large firms	Forward-looking assessment of the ability to meet financial commitments	CRA Regulation (EC No 1060/2009), supervised by ESMA; included in ECAF and EBA mapping
IRB	Size thresholds vary by bank; typically, between €150 m and €500 m in turnover; in some sectors total assets are used	Quantification of credit risk for regulatory capital purposes	CRR regulation; validation by competent authorities; EBA supervisory handbook
ICAS	European Commission (2003)/361; to be replaced by thresholds in Directive 2013/34/EU and 2023/2775/EU	Probability of default over one year	ECAF; governed by Eurosystem standards; default definition from article 178 CRR
Cerved	Defined as firms with turnover > €150 m, or listed firms with turnover > €5 m	Assessment of ability to generate cash flows for debt repayment	Registered as ECAI under Regulation (EC) No 1060/2009, supervised by ESMA; included in EBA mapping.
CRIF	"Large corporations" defined as firms with turnover > €200 m	Forward-looking assessment of the ability to fulfil financial commitments	

with different intensity and methodological roles: S&P explicitly incorporates ESG factors into its credit rating criteria, while Fitch treats them as complementary elements in the overall risk analysis.

The rating process typically begins with the collection and analysis of financial and non-financial data, followed by sector-specific modelling. Sector specialization is high, with dedicated teams applying frameworks tailored to the structural and cyclical features of each industry. The output of this analysis is then integrated with input from the analysts' qualitative assessment. A rating committee discusses and validates the draft rating proposals, thus ensuring methodological consistency and independence of judgement. The rating committee acts as the final decision-making body.

ECAIs place strong emphasis on direct engagement with rated entities. Management meetings are a core component of the evaluation process, especially for first-time ratings or following material events. These meetings allow analysts to assess elements not directly observable in financial statements, such as strategic adaptability, internal control systems, and ESG positioning. This interaction does not weaken rating independence and objectivity.

Monitoring procedures are systematic and frequent. The rating is subject to ongoing surveillance and can be reassessed in case of new information or at scheduled dates. The use of watchlists and outlooks allows timely signalling of potential changes in creditworthiness. ECAIs also apply an override mechanism that is formally regulated and must be documented and explained within the internal control system.

ESG risks are increasingly integrated into ECAIs' rating system. Analysts incorporate material ESG issues into financial projections and qualitative risk assessments, in line with each rating agency's public methodology statements.

AI tools are being tested by ECAIs, although their use remains at an experimental level. They are also constrained by confidentiality requirements and regulatory considerations.

4.3 IRB Systems

Large banking groups use IRB systems to assess the creditworthiness of firms, particularly those with significant exposures. These models typically apply to medium and large firms within the banking book and are used to support internal credit decisions and capital requirement calculations. Each banking institution tailors its rating system to its own lending portfolio and risk management practices.

The methodological framework combines statistical estimation of risk parameters with qualitative assessment modules. Banks use firm-level financial data and behavioural indicators from internal datasets, often complemented by macroeconomic or sectoral variables. The resulting credit risk parameters—such as the PD—are specific to each institution and subject to supervisory review.

Credit institutions assess qualitative aspects through structured frameworks, focusing on governance, strategic outlook, and management reliability. Their weight varies across institutions and becomes more important when quantitative input is limited or volatile. Some banks segment their portfolios by industry or product type, applying different models or assessment procedures accordingly. Group-level exposures are often evaluated in a consolidated manner, especially when intra-group dependencies are material.

Interaction with firms is an integral part of the process, particularly for larger or more complex corporations. Meetings with management help validate strategic assumptions and integrate forward-looking elements into the assessment.

Override procedures allow analysts to modify the model output based on documented evidence. These interventions are subject to internal controls and regular review.

Monitoring is carried out regularly, with greater intensity for high-risk or large exposures. Dedicated teams often support portfolio surveillance and early warning activities. While the use of artificial intelligence (AI) is still limited, some banks have initiated exploratory projects in areas such as data screening and anomaly detection.

ESG factors are increasingly considered, mainly through dedicated questionnaires or desk-based analysis. Their impact on the rating remains limited, and credit institutions generally treat ESG factors as complementary to financial risk drivers.

4.4 ICASes

The ICASes of Banque de France, Deutsche Bundesbank, and Banco de España apply structured procedures to evaluatc the creditworthiness of non-financial corporations. Under the revised S-ICAS framework, the expert assessment component of these systems will progressively concentrate on large firms, due to methodological priorities and operational constraints.

The primary data source consists of financial statements, complemented by credit register information and other administrative or supervisory records when available. Depending on the institutional context, ICASes may also access tax or supervisory databases. Public sources, such as business registers, are used to complement core datasets. Banque de France and Bundesbank systematically interact with firms through interviews or structured questionnaires support the collection of forward-looking information. Banco de España does not currently conduct such interactions.

The methodological structure is modular, combining a statistical component and an expert assessment component. The statistical model estimates default probabilities using firm-level and in most cases macroeconomic variables, typically by sector and firm size. The expert module allows analysts to adjust the model output based on qualitative elements, such as sector outlook, exposure to external shocks or governance-related issues. Internal protocols define the adjustment procedures to ensure consistency and accountability. The oversight on override practices is integrated into the internal governance of the system.

The use of overrides requires appropriate documentation and internal validation. Analysts may follow scheduled cycles for reviews or be prompted by the emergence of new information.

Monitoring activities are adapted to each ICAS operational structure. Consistency checks, periodic validation, and backtesting exercises are routinely conducted to ensure the robustness of model-based and expert-based results. Rating systems are segmented by sector, size, or product type. For large firms, ICASes typically adopt dedicated statistical expert procedures and monitoring frequencies. The expert module allows analysts to consider aspects not included in the statistical models and to adjust the model output based on qualitative elements, such as sector outlook, exposure to external shocks, or governance-related issues.

ICASes currently consider ESG factors only within the expert assessment module, in line with the common minimum standards issued by the ECB. ESG information has not yet been integrated into the statistical models (Körding and Resch, 2022).

Also, the three ICASes are starting to use AI tools. Some institutions are exploring the potential use of AI in support functions such as data pre-processing or validation.

4.5 Cerved and CRIF

Cerved and CRIF provide credit ratings for a broad set of Italian firms, including SMEs and large corporations. Banks and financial institutions primarily use these assessments for commercial purposes and internal credit risk management. Users often employ them in the early stages of loan origination, portfolio segmentation, and pre-screening processes, and in some cases as auxiliary information alongside internal ratings or expert assessments.

The information base includes financial statements, official registries, payment records, and a wide range of proprietary sources. Both providers rely on statistical models that operate without direct contact with rated firms. They also offer tailored services to institutional clients, including case-by-case analytical reports or enriched datasets for specific borrower profiles.

The evaluation model combines quantitative and qualitative analysis. Quantitative analysis is based on scoring methodologies that rely on statistical models calibrated on large historical datasets. Core indicators typically include balance sheet ratios, profitability margins, liquidity metrics, and payment punctuality. They assign scores by applying thresholds to weighted composite indicators. While qualitative elements are not measured directly, external proxies approximate them such as negative events, sectoral dynamics, or payment anomalies.

Despite similarities in overall approach, Cerved and CRIF differ in various aspects, including the structure of the rating scale, the method of data updating, and the scope of sectoral granularity. For instance, Cerved incorporates data from corporate governance records and legal events. Both providers offer optional modules tailored to different sectors or enterprise types.

The standard rating output does not include override mechanisms. However, institutional clients often integrate ratings with internal evaluations or request customized solutions. For example, banks may supplement them with internal classifications for high-exposure clients or embed them into broader early warning systems.

Ratings are updated when new balance sheet or administrative data are filed. Both providers offer value-added services such as alert systems, dynamic dashboards, and benchmarking reports, supporting credit monitoring and risk portfolio management, particularly for banks with large corporate portfolios.

ESG factors are not yet included in the credit rating models. Nevertheless, both Cerved and CRIF have launched initiatives to develop ESG methodologies aligned with international standards and national guidelines, given that they are increasingly used by financial intermediaries for due diligence and sustainability reporting.

They apply machine learning and other AI technologies to optimize data classification, anomaly detection, and predictive analytics. These tools are particularly effective in supporting the pre-processing of large-scale datasets and in identifying behavioural patterns. However, they do not replace the core statistical models used for credit ratings.

5 Findings

5.1 Data Sources

Financial statements are the primary data source across all rating methodologies. All providers rely on balance sheets, income statements and cash flow statements which indicate profitability, liquidity, financial sustainability, and leverage. Financial data typically include sector-specific information. In industries such as real estate, energy, or infrastructure—where volatility and regulatory exposure are higher—ECAIs and, to a lesser extent, IRBs incorporate industry-specific performance metrics. Sectoral differentiation is also used by Cerved, CRIF, and ICASes.

Macroeconomic indicators are included to account for broader cyclical conditions. Variables such as GDP growth, inflation and interest rates are especially relevant in sectors sensitive to macroeconomic trends, such as construction and manufacturing. Macroeconomic assessment plays a bigger role in through-the-cycle models.

Non-financial data are another important input, particularly for large firms and selected sectors. Elements such as governance, ownership, competitive positioning, and business strategy are considered by all ECAIs, ICASes, and IRBs. For instance, Cerved places emphasis on management quality and strategic orientation, while IRBs incorporate governance risks in sectors where they affect credit stability.

For large firms, the weight of data drawn from credit registers tends to be lower in deciding their rating, due to their more diversified funding structure and lower reliance on short-term credit lines.

All rating sources integrate financial information with qualitative input gathered through direct interactions with firms. ECAIs routinely conduct management interviews, which are also carried out by Cerved for solicited ratings. IRBs benefit from continuous relationships with clients and may use them to gather additional insights, particularly in high-risk sectors or when covenants apply. ICASes also conduct structured interviews, although practices vary due to institutional constraints. These interactions help assess governance, market strategy and the capacity to respond to sectoral or firm-specific developments.

In addition, all models use intra-annual data (e.g., quarterly reports for large firms), corporate presentations, and updates on sectoral and firm-specific events, such as M&A transactions or business plans.

5.2 Sector Analysis

For large firms, rating providers use industry-based methodologies to reflect differences in firms' financial profile. These methods capture the heterogeneity of financial structures across sectors, including the role of fixed assets, leverage levels and regulation. These factors influence the construction and weighting of financial indicators in sectoral models.

ECAIs and some IRB systems use sector-specific models, especially when exposure to a given sector is significant. Cerved uses separate models for sectors such as utilities, construction, and real estate. Real estate and infrastructure often require tailored models, because of volatile asset values, project-based financing, and interest rate sensitivity. In ICASes, industry differentiation exists depending on internal data availability.

In addition to model segmentation, organizational structures reflect such specialization. ECAIs and Cerved assign analysts by industry to ensure that ratings are prepared and reviewed by experts. This supports consistent use of firm-level data and expert judgement. Some IRB systems follow a similar approach in the internal model validation and assignment of credit analysts.

The degree of segmentation depends on portfolio composition and operations. ECAIs serving multiple jurisdictions tend to adopt uniform sector-specific templates. Banking groups with centralized IRB systems apply industry modules across countries. For institutions with concentrated exposures in one or more sectors, sector-specific models help to improve calibration.

5.3 Group Structure and Government-Related Entities

For entities belonging to a group, rating providers assess the intensity of interlinkages between the corporation and its parent company. In some systems, when the group relationship is strong, the parent company's rating is applied to the subsidiary without a stand-alone evaluation. In intermediate cases, the group rating is used as a benchmark, and it is adjusted to reflect specific risk factors. If the link is assessed as weak, rating providers typically disregard the group rating. In all cases, they assign the subsidiary a rating that is generally not above that of the parent company.

This treatment reflects risk-sharing mechanisms and organizational efficiency. Specifically, relying on the parent's rating prevents duplicating analytical efforts when the financial and operational integration within the group is significant. Such practices are consistently observed across rating providers and are more important for subsidiaries operating as captive entities or benefiting from intra-group guarantees.

ECAIs apply a similar approach to government-related entities, whose ratings incorporate the probability of extraordinary public support in times of distress. These entities typically deliver services deemed strategic or essential and may be publicly owned or subject to close regulatory oversight. In these instances, the national sovereign rating serves either as a ceiling or is directly assigned to the corporation. ECAIs and banks employing IRB systems often use structured questionnaires to assess the strength of government links and the nature of potential support.

5.4 Override and Monitoring

In all rating systems, the analysts in charge of the expert assessment may override the model output when specific elements, not adequately captured by the standard methodology, are deemed as material. This mechanism is particularly important in assessing large firms with complex ownership, group-level guarantees, or extraordinary risk events. Overrides follow defined internal procedures and require adequate documentation. In most cases, they are submitted to a rating committee, which acts as the control body to ensure consistency and transparency.

For example, the override process is activated with mergers and acquisitions (as in the case of Banco de España's ICAS), rapid deterioration in business outlook (as in IRB systems), or major revisions of strategic plans (as in the Deutsche Bundesbank's ICAS). In IRB systems, overrides require hierarchical approval mechanisms. In ECAIs, overrides are approved by committees that typically involve multiple experts and are structured by sector or geography.

Besides the override mechanism, all systems implement ongoing surveillance procedures. These include the regular update of financial information, usually on a quarterly basis for large firms, and monitoring of qualitative signals such as changes in ownership, business plans, or market positioning. For IRB systems, surveillance is also linked to credit operations, since reviews are often triggered by new exposures or renewals.

Some rating providers—such as the Banque de France's ICAS and major ECAIs—use automated monitoring tools to identify early warning signals and changes in firm-level conditions. These tools generally complement the analysts' assessment. In the systems under review, automated and expert-based monitoring coexist, with varying degrees of integration, depending on data availability and the operational structure of the rating function.

5.5 ESG Factors

All rating sources include ESG factors in their process, although the degree and method of integration vary significantly across systems.

In general, ESG aspects are incorporated mainly through qualitative components rather than statistical models, and this applies regardless of the firm size - though larger firms may disclose more structured information.

Cerved and CRIF integrate ESG aspects via sector-specific indicators or structural questions within expert assessment modules. ECAIs follow a different practice, considering ESG information only when it is relevant to the firm's risk profile and available through public disclosures or third-party providers. Some ESG data derive from company disclosures.

ICASes adopt a more systematic approach to climate-related risks, following the introduction by the ECB of minimum standards under the ECAF (Körding and Resch, 2022). In particular, the ICASes are progressively integrating climate risk into their methodologies although the level of implementation differs across systems.

IRB systems have begun to consider ESG dimensions also in response to growing expectations from supervisory bodies such as the EBA, the ECB, and national authorities. Supervisors generally recommend gradual and proportional incorporation of ESG factors, to avoid distortions in credit supply, such as those linked to stranded assets.

5.6 AI Tools

The use of advanced data analysis and tools is expanding among credit rating systems, especially for large enterprises, because of the volume and digital nature of available information. AI and machine learning (ML) increasingly support model performance and operational efficiency, although adoption varies across providers.

ML models improve discriminatory power compared with traditional statistical techniques, particularly with limited data (Moscatelli et al., 2019). However, this data scarcity is less common for large firms, which typically provide more structured and comprehensive information. Moreover, empirical results on ML in retail credit portfolios are mixed with some studies reporting improved predictive accuracy compared with traditional models, and others highlighting limited gains or challenges related to interpretability (Bazarbash, 2019; Locatelli et al., 2022).

Cerved and CRIF are integrating AI tools mainly to support data collection, processing, and model calibration. Cerved, for example, is using big data analytics and machine learning to improve accuracy and timeliness of its credit assessment. It also employs text mining and natural language processing (NLP) techniques to extract information from large volumes of unstructured data, including online news sources.

ECAIs are experimenting with AI to a more limited extent, partly because of regulatory constraints. As regulated entities, they require prior authorization from supervisory authorities to employ ML in rating production. Furthermore, the confidential nature of some input data limits the applicability of ML tools and raises data-sharing risks. ECAIs are therefore cautious in adopting ML techniques, especially for core modelling activities.

In IRB systems, early experiences confirm the potential of ML to enhance predictive performance in specific sub-models or tasks. Nonetheless, banks must balance potential accuracy gains against explainability constraints, as ML models often operate as 'black boxes'. Limited transparency may create reputational or commercial risks in client relationships (EBA, 2023c). These concerns support the supervisory emphasis on maintaining human oversight and interpretability in credit risk models (BCBS, 2023).

Some ICASes are exploring AI applications for early warning or data quality purposes, but developments are still at an initial stage.

More broadly, AI evolution in credit risk models is influenced by the European regulatory framework. The AI Act (Regulation EU 2024/1689) introduces a risk-based approach for AI systems. Credit rating applications may fall under the 'high-risk' category, especially if they affect financial decisions or involve individuals' profiling, although the human intervention can help reduce the risk level. This classification implies stringent obligations in terms of transparency, robustness, human oversight, and data governance. Rating systems—particularly those run by public institutions—must assess their compliance accordingly, also in the light of existing General Data Protection Regulation (GDPR) provisions and EBA guidance.

6 Conclusions

The review of ECAIs, ICASes, IRB systems, and national rating agencies reveals a broad range of practices in assessing creditworthiness of large and complex firms. These differences mainly reflect the specific objectives, mandates, and regulatory constraints of each system. Still, some common features emerge across rating providers. All entities combine financial data with qualitative elements, particularly on governance and market positioning. A sector-specific analysis is often carried out, with tailored approaches for complex industries such as real estate and infrastructure. Group linkages, override mechanisms, and monitoring tools for early warning also emerge as recurrent features. Structured interviews and regular contacts with large firms are key tools for the collection of qualitative information on governance, strategic positioning, and risk outlook. Clear governance procedures support override mechanisms, allowing for the rating adjustment for firm-specific features, particularly for large, internationally active corporations. The above features represent in our view a set of best practices for the rating industry.

Although ESG integration varies across providers, it is gaining momentum in line with regulatory developments, such as the ECB common minimum standard for ICASes (Körding and Resch, 2022). AI applications are still limited, but they offer some support in data processing and anomaly detection.

Future developments could include an investigation on the regulatory impact of forthcoming EU initiatives—such as the AI Act and the ESG disclosure requirements under the Omnibus Directive package—on credit assessment systems based on expert input or hybrid methodologies. These regulatory changes will influence standards on data governance, model transparency, and oversight, especially where qualitative evaluation enters into play.

Table 9.2 Summary of the main findings

	ECAIs	IRB systems	ICASes	Cerved /CRIF
Data sources and information	Financials, sectoral data, macro, governance, interviews, infra-annual and event info	Financials, sectoral data, macro, governance, client interaction	Financials, sectoral data, macro, governance, structured interviews, climate-related data	Financials, sectoral data, governance, structured interviews (esp. Cerved), use of M&A and strategic plan info
Sector analysis	Sector models and analyst allocation by industry	Used when exposure justifies it; models and analysts may be allocated by industry	Present, depending on internal data availability and structure	Sector models (Cerved: Utilities, construction, real estate); analyst specialization by industry
Group & government	Group rating cascades to subsidiaries; sovereign ceiling applies to public sector entities	Group link assessment; government-related firms assessed with specific tools	Group logic applied, especially if guarantees/ funding are in place	Group logic applied (esp. CRIF); public support assessed and based on indirect criteria
Override and monitoring	Overrides by committees; quarterly updates; early warning tools	Overrides require approval; reviews linked to exposure changes; automated tools complement human checks	Overrides with internal procedures; monitoring via early warning tools and ECB reporting	Overrides and monitoring tools used; Cerved integrates news/ NLP for monitoring
Sustainability factors	ESG integrated case-by-case if material; sourced from disclosures or providers	ESG gradually integrated under supervisory pressure; attention to stranded assets	Coordinated implementation under ECAF; minimum standards on climate risk	ESG indicators included in sectoral models; expert assessment module considers ESG (esp. Cerved)
Use of AI tools	Limited due to regulation and explainability; experimentation ongoing	Some ML modules explored; use constrained by explainability and supervision	Exploration phase only; use for early warning or data quality under evaluation	Actively used (esp. Cerved): ML, big data analytics, NLP for text mining from unstructured sources. CRIF: Limited use due to regulation and explainability; experimentation ongoing

References

Alsakka R, ap Gwilym O, Vu H (2017) Differences of opinion in sovereign credit signals during the European crisis. Eur J Finance 23(10):859–884

Auria L, Bingmer M, Caicedo Graciano CM, Charavel C, Gavilá S, Iannamorelli A, Levy A, Maldonado A, Resch F, Rossi AM, Sauer S (2021) Overview of central banks' in-house credit assessment systems in the euro area, ECB Occasional Paper, No. 284.

Basel Committee on Banking Supervision (2001) The internal ratings-based approach. Bank for International Settlements, Basel

Basel Committee on Banking Supervision (2005) Studies on the validation of internal rating systems. Working Paper No. 14, Bank for International Settlements, Basel

Basel Committee on Banking Supervision (2023) CRE calculation of RWA for credit risk. Bank for International Settlements, Basel

Bazarbash M (2019) FinTech in financial inclusion: machine learning applications in assessing credit risk. IMF Working Papers 2019/109, International Monetary Fund, Washington

Brunella B, Marino I, Nocera G (2023) Internal ratings and bank opacity: evidence from analysts' forecasts. J Finan Intermed 56:101062

Carpinelli L, Crosignani M, Guazzarotti G (2021) Collateral eligibility and credit supply: evidence from the ECB. ECB Working Paper Series No. 2579, European Central Bank, Frankfurt

Cerved Group (2023) Cerved rating methodology. Cerved, Milan

Columba F, Orsini R, Tranquillo F (2023) Rating the raters: a central bank perspective. Markets Infrastructures Payment Syst No. 55, Bank of Italy, Rome

CRIF Group (2023) CRIF Ratings methodology. CRIF, Bologna

Cucinelli D, Di Battista ML, Marchese M, Nieri L (2018) Internal ratings vs. standardised approach: evidence from Italian banks. J Bank Regul 19(2):145–160

Duarte C, Engel J, Reichmann O, Džaja T (2025) Introducing statistical in-house credit assessment systems (S-ICASs) as an additional source of credit assessments under the general collateral framework. *ECB Economic Bulletin,* No. 3, European Central Bank, Frankfurt

European Banking Authority (2023a) Draft implementing technical standards amending implementing regulation (EU) 2016/1799 on the mapping of ECAIs' credit assessments under Article 136(1) and (3) of Regulation (EU) No. 575/2013, final report. European Banking Authority, Paris

European Banking Authority (2023b) Supervisory handbook on the validation of rating systems under the internal ratings based approach. EBA/REP/2023/29, European Banking Authority, Paris

European Banking Authority (2023c) Machine learning for IRB models. European Banking Authority, Paris

European Central Bank (2015) Guideline (EU) 2015/510 on the implementation of the Eurosystem monetary policy framework (ECB/2014/60). European Central Bank, Frankfurt

European Central Bank (2022) Overview of central banks' in-house credit assessment systems in the euro area. Occasional Paper Series No. 284, European Central Bank, Frankfurt

European Commission (2003) Commission Recommendation 2003/361/EC concerning the definition of micro, small, and medium-sized enterprises. European Commission, Brussels

European Commission (2009) Regulation (EC) No. 1060/2009 of the European Parliament and of the Council of 16 September 2009 on credit rating agencies (text with EEA relevance). European Commission, Brussels

European Parliament and Council (2013) Regulation (EU) No. 575/2013 of the European Parliament and of the Council of 26 June 2013 on prudential requirements for credit institutions and investment firms and amending Regulation (EU) No. 648/2012. Off J Eur Union L 176

Ferri G, Pesic V (2017) Bank regulatory arbitrage via risk weighted assets dispersion Journal of Financial Stability. 33:331–345

Fitch Ratings (2023) Corporate rating criteria. Fitch, London

Gagliardone L, Papadia F (2022) The credit assessment ecosystem in Europe: a comparative review. Bruegel Policy Contrib No. 16, Bruegel AISBL, Brussels
Gallo R (2021) The IRB approach and bank lending to firms. Economic Working Papers No 1347, Bank of Italy, Rome
Giovannelli F, Iannamorelli A, Levy A, Orlandi M (2023) The Bank of Italy's in-house credit assessment system for non-financial firms. In: Scalia A (ed) Financial risk management and climate change risk. The experience in a central bank. Springer, pp 107–137
Körding J, Resch F (2022) Common minimum standards for incorporating climate change risks into in-house credit assessment systems in the Eurosystem. ECB Economic Bull No. 6, European Central Bank, Frankfurt
Lecomte E, Torres C (2023) Are credit ratings procyclical? A study of French banks' capital requirements during the COVID crisis. Bull Banque de Fr 245(1). Banque de France, Paris
Livingston M, Van Ness BF, Van Ness RA (2020) Credit ratings. In: Oxford research Encyclopedia of economics and finance. Oxford University Press
Locatelli R, Pepe G, Satis F (2022) Artificial intelligence and credit risk: the use of alternative data and methods in internal credit rating. Palgrave Macmillan
Marandola G (2021) Local credit rating agencies: Is their economic role underrated? Q Rev Econ Finan 81:143–156
Mediobanca (2024) Pillar III disclosure and internal rating methodology. Relazione di trasparenza pubblica ai sensi di CRR, sezioni su PD corporate e shadow rating approach. Mediobanca, Milan
Moody's Investors Service (2024) Rating methodology for non-financial corporates. Moody's, New York
Morgan DP (2002) Rating banks: risk and uncertainty in an opaque industry. Am Econ Rev 92(4):874–888
Moscatelli M et al (2019) Corporate default forecasting with machine learning. Economic working paper no 1256, Bank of Italy, Rome
S&P Global Ratings (2021) Environmental, social, and governance principles in credit ratings. S&P, New York

IRB and ICAS: A Comparative Analysis

Francesco Columba, Federica Orsini, and Stefano Tranquillo

1 Introduction

Collateralized credit operations are a standard and widely used tool for monetary policy implementation. Central bank funding has been crucial for credit institutions' support to the real economy in the years following the financial crises and in the pandemic period, especially in the jurisdictions where the financial sector was more fragile. In 2020–2021, during the COVID-19 pandemic, the average share of Eurosystem refinancing on total Italian bank liabilities was about 12%.

In this Chapter we employ the Bank of Italy's ICAS as a benchmark to assess the ratings set by commercial banks with their IRBs and used for monetary policy purposes. We examine the distribution of ratings on bank loans pledged as collateral in monetary policy in Italy and test for risk under-reporting, found by Behn et al. (2022) and Calza et al. (2021), which might generate an unwarranted exposure for the central bank. Our goal is to detect differences, if any, in ratings between Italian IRBs and the central bank's system, and investigate their determinants.

Credit claims are an essential source of collateral for banks and the Eurosystem and the BoI employ several layers of protection against potential losses (see Chap. 8).

F. Columba (✉) · F. Orsini · S. Tranquillo
Bank of Italy, Financial Risk Management Directorate, Rome, Italy
e-mail: francesco.columba@bancaditalia.it

F. Orsini
e-mail: federica.orsini@bancaditalia.it

S. Tranquillo
e-mail: stefano.tranquillo@bancaditalia.it

A. Scalia (ed.), *Corporate Credit Analysis and AI*, Finance for Professionals,
https://doi.org/10.1007/978-3-032-13422-6_10

The accurate design of this system has ensured that the Eurosystem has never experienced losses in its credit operations so far.[1] To be accepted as collateral in Eurosystem monetary policy operations, bank loans must comply with some eligibility criteria, including a minimum credit quality threshold. The rating is a key determinant of the haircut imposed on the collateral.[2]

To shed light on the consistency of the IRB ratings for non-financial firms with those produced by the Italian central bank, while we draw inspiration from Calza et al. (2021), we use a more recent and complete dataset and we employ a richer and more robust estimation strategy. The dataset includes all domestic IRBs used for monetary policy purposes over the years 2015–2023,[3] providing a full characterization of banks' policies in this area over a full business cycle, while the ECB authors cover the 2014–2018 period. Additionally, while Calza et al. (2021) consider only credit claims pledged in the general collateral framework (known as the ECAF), we take into account also those pledged in the temporary collateral framework (ACCs).[4] Considering the whole internal rating span enables us to avoid the sample selection bias that affects the analyses based only on the ratings accepted within the general collateral perimeter (i.e. IRB's PDs below 0.4%), resulting in a potential overestimation of the average difference between IRB and ICAS ratings. Finally, as for the estimation approach, we test additional specifications to measure, if any, the degree of risk under-reporting by banks in the context of monetary policy operations.

---

[1] Few cases of counterparty default events were offset by the proceedings deriving from the posted collateral. The main case of default concerned Lehman Brothers Bankhaus AG (LBB), the German subsidiary of Lehman Brothers Holdings Inc. whose liabilities vis-à-vis the Bundesbank from monetary policy operations stood at around €8.5 billion at the time of the insolvency of the bank. The Bundesbank eventually managed to recover all the amount of LBB exposure. For further details see the press release on the Bundesbank website.

[2] A collateral valuation haircut is the deduction of a certain percentage from the valuation of an asset for the purpose of calculating the amount of liquidity that can be backed by the asset in case of counterparty default. The calibration of haircuts aims to ensure the equivalence of risk across different types of collateral assets. The loss in value of collateral that the Eurosystem expects to incur—with low probability—in an adverse scenario should be the same for the different assets and asset types. An adverse, but still reasonable scenario, is defined by the Eurosystem as the average loss occurring within the worst percentile of the loss distribution. For calibration purposes, an adverse scenario is set to correspond to the average loss in the worst one per cent of the cases, i.e. to expected shortfall at a 99%confidence level (ES[99%]). Collateral valuation haircuts are determined according to the credit risk assessment of the debtor, the residual maturity and the type of interest of the loan. An important risk component for the haircut calibration is therefore represented by default risk, which is embedded in rating assessments, even though it is not the only one. Market and liquidity risk are also other modelled sources of risk. For more detail on haircut calibration see also Chap. 8, ECB (2015) and Adler et al. (2023).

[3] The PDs reported by banks in the context of the annual ECAF exercise are those used to calculate prudential capital requirements under the European Banking Authority Common Reporting (CoRep) framework; as such, they comply both with the Capital Requirements Regulation (CRR) and any Single Supervision Mechanism bank-specific requirements.

[4] See Chap. 8 for further details.

The case of Italy is particularly fit to investigate the consistency across commercial banks and central banks' risk assessments systems, as a significant number of IRB systems are employed also for monetary policy purposes[5] and a large number of NFCs is rated by the Bank of Italy's ICAS. Banks that choose to use their IRB as a primary source in the collateral framework must use their IRB PDs for the mobilization of credit claims for all debtors rated by their IRB system.[6] The PDs are used both for the determination of the eligibility of the claim and for the calculation of the haircut.

IRBs and ICAS have different primary purposes. The primary purpose of IRBs is to compute banks' capital requirements to cover credit risk; they must be authorized by the banking supervisors. Besides, to be used for monetary policy purposes, IRBs must also be specifically authorized by the Eurosystem regulation (for further information see Chapter 8). The primary purpose of ICAS is instead to assess the credit quality of eligible loans to be used as collateral in monetary policy operations and thus to determine the corresponding valuation haircuts. For the banks that do not manage an IRB, ICASes constitute an important tool for expanding the sources of liquidity, allowing the use of bank loans as collateral.

We contribute to the literature on credit risk assessment systems by bringing new evidence, including for the post COVID-19 recovery. We study some features that to our knowledge have not been explored yet, such as the use of credit rating systems within the ACC framework, which lends itself to the analysis of loans of a lower credit quality, and of ratings produced with NCB statistical models (S-ICAS) compared with those given by IRB quantitative models (S-IRB),[7] which significantly increase the sample size and provide more robust results.[8] Overall, the evidence and the analysis of the drivers of the small differences between the credit risk assessment provided by IRBs and ICAS lead us to conclude that the evidence of an economically significant strategic management of the IRB credit systems found by Behn et al. (2022) and Calza et al. (2021) is not supported by the data for Italy.

The remainder of this Chapter is organized as follows. Section 2 discusses the literature. Section 3 describes the data and stylized facts about the two credit assessment systems. Section 4 presents the results of the performance analysis

[5] In 2023 eight out of ten Italian banks with IRB systems authorized for regulatory purposes had their IRBs approved also for monetary policy purposes. The number of Italian banks with IRB systems authorized for ECAF purposes ranges from seven in 2015 to eight in 2023, due to new authorizations and mergers. They were nine in 2020.

[6] Whenever a debtor is not covered by the IRB, the secondary source, namely the ICAS in our analysis, is used. Such selection mechanism however has changed after the inception of the ICAS prioritization rule as of June 2025 (see Chap. 8 for further details).

[7] We group the IRB models which the banks use for ECAF purposes into Statistical (S-IRB) and Full (F-IRB) ones. In the first group PDs are calculated with statistical or econometric models, while in the second PDs are calculated complementing the models with the banks' financial analysts' assessment (potentially leading to so called override). We compare F-ICAS PDs with F-IRB PDs and S-ICAS PDs with S-IRB PDs.

[8] In 2023 ICAS Full ratings were in excess of 3,000 and ICAS Statistical ratings of 330,000.

of the rating systems. Section 5 presents the results of the empirical analysis. Section 6 discusses the robustness analysis. Section 7 concludes.

2 Literature Review

With regard to the analysis of the framework of monetary operations, Calza et al. (2021) find that, based on data between 2014 and 2018 from Austria, Belgium, France, Germany, Italy, Portugal, and Slovenia, for the set of debtors whose loans are eligible as collateral, banks' ratings are on average more conservative than NCB ratings, while the opposite occurs for the subset of borrowers whose loans are pledged with the Eurosystem. Banks' ratings become less conservative as loan size and the level of central bank liquidity utilization increase.[9] These results rely mainly on observations from France, Italy, and Austria; in the authors' view, they support the hypothesis that banks strategically manage their IRBs to maximize access to central bank funding. As such, IRB leniency by banks might generate an unwarranted risk exposure for the central bank.

From the regulatory perspective, a set of studies investigate with pre-Basel II data the consistency of banks' IRBs to ascertain the role played by banks' policies within the debate on the merits of model-based capital regulation, with mixed results. Lenders may disagree on borrowers' riskiness reflecting different views on credit quality (Carey, 2002) and also because of different lending or risk management styles (Jacobson et al., 2006). Estimates of PDs can diverge significantly, but not systematically across banks.[10]

A second set of studies investigates the effect of the introduction of the model-based approach with post-Basel II data, focusing on the relation between the variability of PD estimates across IRBs and banks' characteristics. These works find that in Germany from 2008 to 2012 weakly capitalized banks may report lower PDs (Berg & Koziol, 2017) and some banks may systematically under-report risk to lower their capital requirements (Behn et al., 2022). However, there is also evidence that validated IRB models are accurate and robust, and that the introduction of the IRB approach promotes the adoption of stronger risk management practices among Western European banks[11] from 2008 to 2015 (Cucinelli et al., 2018).

[9] In contrast, the degree of capitalization of banks does not seem to have explanatory power for the difference between the ratings of the two systems for bank loans used as collateral.

[10] A feature of the Basel rules is that banks can have differences in opinions and approaches to managing and measuring credit risk, that imply different risk parameters. Persistent differences in Loss Given Default (LGD) may be attributed to banks' policies (Firestone & Rezende, 2016).

[11] From Austria, Belgium, Denmark, Finland, France, Germany, Great Britain, Ireland, Italy, Netherlands, Norway, Portugal, Spain, and Sweden.

3 The Italian Banks' IRBs and the Bank of Italy ICAS Features

General description—IRBs and ICASes are both designed to evaluate the probability of default[12] associated with credit exposures. However, they differ in their objectives, regulatory context, methodologies. In terms of objectives and regulatory context, IRBs' valuations are mainly used for the calculation of capital requirements and as important inputs in approving and pricing loans, and in managing the portfolio of a wide range of credit exposure which does not entail only the corporate ones; they are developed in line with the Basel framework. ICASes are instead specifically aimed at evaluating the creditworthiness of non-financial corporations whose credit claims are used as collateral in monetary policy operations; they are developed by central banks in line with the Eurosystem requirements.

As concerns the methodologies, both systems use statistical techniques and historical data to estimate the likelihood that a borrower will default within a specific time horizon, i.e. one year; however, the exact statistical methodology, the set of information taken into consideration and the length of the time-series used in the models may differ among the systems.[13] Another important element which may differ among IRBs and ICASes is the rating 'philosophy'. In the context of rating systems, two approaches can be adopted, one that includes cyclical effects and one that does not. The two approaches generate different rating types, commonly known as point-in-time (PIT) and through-the-cycle (TTC).[14] While often models cannot be classified as purely PIT or TTC, but are rather a hybrid combination of the two approaches, it can be said that the rating philosophy of the Bank of Italy's ICAS is point-in-time, while it is expected to be more through-the-cycle oriented for IRBs.[15]

The ICAS rating process is based on a two-stage procedure,[16] which combines a statistical model, that determines one-year default probabilities (S-ICAS PDs), and an expert assessment, that determines final PDs of the whole process, called the F-ICAS PDs.

---

[12] IRB models are also used for the estimation of other parameters apart from the PD, i.e. the LGD and the EAD.

[13] These elements may of course also differ (for the same class of debtors) from one IRB bank to another. As concerns different ICASes, while all the ICASes developed within the Eurosystem are similar in their general characteristics and comply with Eurosystem requirements, some differences can be observed, either in the sources of information or in the methodology adopted in order to calculate the ratings.

[14] PIT ratings aim at evaluating the current situation of an entity by taking into account both cyclical and permanent effects. In contrast, TTC ratings focus mainly on the permanent component of default risk and are essentially independent from cyclical changes in the entity's creditworthiness.

[15] See Paragraphs 105–106, Credit Risk Chapter of the ECB guide to internal models. Common statistical methods used by IRBs include traditional credit scoring models and machine learning algorithms. In particular, IRB models often use traditional credit scoring techniques which include discriminant analysis models and regression models (linear, logit, probit).

[16] See Chap. 3 and Giovannelli et al. (2023) for further details.

Table 1 Mapping between Eurosystem CQSs and PDs over one-year horizon

CQS	1 & 2	3	4	5	6	7	8
PD	≤0.1%	≤0.4%	≤1%	≤1.5%	≤3%	≤5%	> 5%
Employed for	ECAF; individual loans and pools of ACCs		Individual loans and pools of ACCs		Pools of ACCs		

Data—We use yearly data between 2015 and 2023 on ratings collected from ten Italian IRB systems and the Bank of Italy's ICAS during the annual Eurosystem performance monitoring exercises and on credit claims used as collateral in credit operations with BoI. In order to ensure consistency, accuracy, and comparability of the credit assessment systems used for monetary policy purposes, the Eurosystem established a framework to monitor their performance.[17] The managers of each NCB's credit assessment system are required to send to the ECB data on all firms whose bank loans are assessed to be eligible as collateral in the Eurosystem monetary policy operations. The data for ICASes and IRBs are reported to the respective NCB and include PDs assigned to debtors over a one-year horizon.[18]

Accepted credit assessment sources can use their own individual rating scales and grades. The Eurosystem maps these different grades into a harmonized rating scale to make the credit ratings comparable across systems and sources (Table 1, see also Chap. 3 for further details).

Data for ICAS and IRB systems transmitted for the annual Eurosystem monitoring exercise comprise PDs at the beginning and at the end of the year.[19] We focus on ratings assigned to NFCs that are jointly rated by the Bank of Italy's ICAS and by at least one Italian IRB system. We first consider the observations for all eligible loans from borrowers jointly rated by the ICAS and by at least one IRB system; we then construct a narrower data set focusing only on those loans actually mobilized as collateral.[20] Table 2 shows the number of firms rated by at

[17] The basic principles of the framework are included in Article 126 and Annex IX of the Guideline (EU) 2024/3132 of the European Central Bank of 14 November 2024 repealing Guideline (EU) 2024/3130 amending Guideline (EU) 2015/510 on the implementation of the Eurosystem monetary policy framework (ECB/2024/23) and amending Guideline (EU) 2015/510 (ECB/2014/60) (ECB/2024/37).

[18] See Appendix A for details on the variables employed.

[19] In our analysis we use beginning-of-year PDs. Calza et al. (2021) use end-of-year PDs, in order to benefit from greater rating variability, because beginning-of-year data are bounded by the ex-ante eligibility threshold (while end-of-year PDs may also refer to debtors that have lost eligibility throughout the year). However, in jurisdictions (like Italy) in which pools of credit claims are accepted, the credit assessment sources are requested to report debtors belonging to the full rating spectrum also at the beginning of the year; therefore, we are able to use beginning-of-year PDs without incurring in the problem of losing rating variability.

[20] In the period covered by the analysis, all the Italian banks with IRBs authorized for monetary policy purposes used the PDs calculated by their IRB systems when pledging their loans to the ECAF.

least one IRB, by ICAS and jointly by both systems, with the detail of the number of firms whose credit claims are used as collateral by Italian banks.

Stylized facts—We compare the assessments of IRBs and ICAS collected annually for the Eurosystem performance monitoring exercise.[21] F-IRB PDs have been slightly less conservative than F-ICAS ones for eligible borrowers since 2017 (Fig. 1a): the difference has been mildly larger for debtors with loans pledged as collateral. S-IRB PDs, instead, since 2016 have been overall more conservative than S-ICAS PDs (Fig. 1b), to a smaller extent for debtors with loans pledged as collateral.The differences between IRB PDs and ICAS PDs are statistically significant, according to the Student's t-test and the Wilcoxon signed-rank test, in nearly all the years and samples.

The circumstance that F-IRB PDs are only slightly less conservative than F-ICAS ones for both eligible borrowers and those with loans mobilized as collateral indicates the absence of a material underestimation of credit risk by the banks in the use of IRB to maximize the pledgeability of their loans. Moreover, the differences between the ratings of the IRBs and ICAS, which are more pronounced for the debtors with mobilized loans, may reflect the selection made by banks when assembling the collateral portfolio, contrary to the negative effect associated to the hypothesis of a strategic management of collateral. Banks may have in the first place an incentive to pledge loans with higher credit quality according to their genuine assessment to secure lower haircuts and more stable central bank liquidity.

To appreciate how a sub-sample with a higher share of debtors with lower PDs may affect the difference between IRB and ICAS PDs, we focus on the three subsamples of the general collateral framework, of the individual claims and of the pools of credit claims in the temporary collateral framework of ACCs.[22]

Within the general collateral framework sub-sample of pledged debtors (Fig. 2a) the differences between F-IRBs and F-ICAS PDs are negative, as in the full sample of pledged debtors; this is in line with the finding of Calza et al. (2021). However, when considering individual ACC claims, IRB ratings are on average less conservative than ICAS ratings only in half of the years analysed and IRB ratings are on average more conservative than ICAS ones for ACC pools. The comparison between S-IRBs and S-ICAS PDs provides a similar result, with larger differences

[21] In our analysis firms rated by more than one IRB are considered as different debtors, i.e. if a firm is rated by two different IRBs and by the ICAS it is considered twice in the sample of debtors rated in common.

[22] We proxy the three frameworks (ECAF, ACC single claims and pool of ACCs) splitting the sample into three subsamples based on IRB PD ranges; this is due to the fact that debtors can overlap between the three frameworks, especially for ACC pools, where there is not a lower PD boundary and PDs can also assume values below 1.5%. Therefore, in this paragraph when we refer to ECAF, ACC single claims and pool of ACCs we intend, respectively, credit claims with PD values: (i) up to 0.4%; (ii) from 0.4 to 1.5%; (iii) greater than 1.5%.

Table 2 Distribution of firms rated by IRBs and the Bank of Italy's ICAS

Year	No. of firms rated by at least an IRB	No. of firms rated by BoI F-ICAS	No. of firms rated by BoI S-ICAS	No. of firms rated by BoI F-ICAS and by at least 1 IRB					No. of firms rated by BoI S-ICAS Stat and by at least 1 IRB				
				Total assessed		With mobilized credit claims			Total assessed	With mobilized credit claims			
					Total	*ECAF*	*ACC single claims*	*ACC pools*		Total	*ECAF*	*ACC single claims*	*ACC pools*
2015	776,480	1,192	256,452	4,616	668	*425*	*202*	*41*	278,813	8,649	*3,988*	*2,464*	*2,197*
2016	738,471	2,057	275,096	7,935	1,658	*801*	*522*	*335*	322,472	22,486	*7,837*	*4,563*	*10,086*
2017	725,815	2,357	290,300	9,386	2,628	*1,306*	*429*	*893*	330,590	47,531	*17,842*	*4,382*	*25,307*
2018	722,134	2,374	284,526	10,463	3,376	*1,253*	*497*	*1,626*	329,697	46,709	*14,734*	*2,792*	*29,183*
2019	792,090	2,444	285,349	12,103	4,247	*1,611*	*604*	*2,032*	361,700	57,431	*16,232*	*3,400*	*37,799*
2020	803,290	2,850	268,943	14,239	4,571	*1,714*	*623*	*2,234*	353,908	54,038	*16,034*	*3,055*	*34,949*
2021	832,210	2,991	273,100	14,634	5,506	*1,655*	*717*	*3,134*	349,799	65,113	*12,278*	*4,474*	*48,361*
2022	721,533	2,925	309,889	12,849	4,400	*1,328*	*582*	*2,490*	330,549	74,248	*11,987*	*3,411*	*58,850*
2023	695,785	3,036	334,370	12,568	3,832	*1,080*	*431*	*2,321*	329,872	62,476	*9,547*	*3,087*	*49,842*
Total	6,807,808	22,226	2,578,025	98,793	30,886	*11,173*	*4,607*	*15,106*	2,987,400	438,681	*110,479*	*31,628*	*296,574*

Note Firms rated by more than one IRB are considered as different debtors, i.e. if a firm is rated by two different IRBs and by the ICAS it is considered twice in the sample of debtors rated in common (this explains why the figures in the fourth column exceed those in the second column)

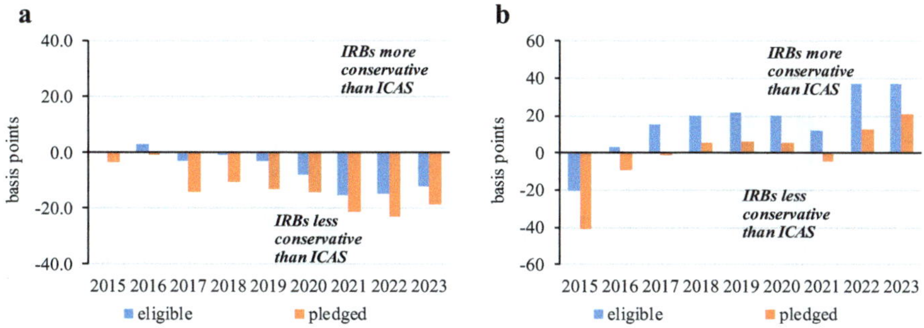

Fig. 1 IRB and ICAS assessments: eligible debtors and with pledged loans. For each debtor is reported the median difference between the IRB PD and the ICAS PD

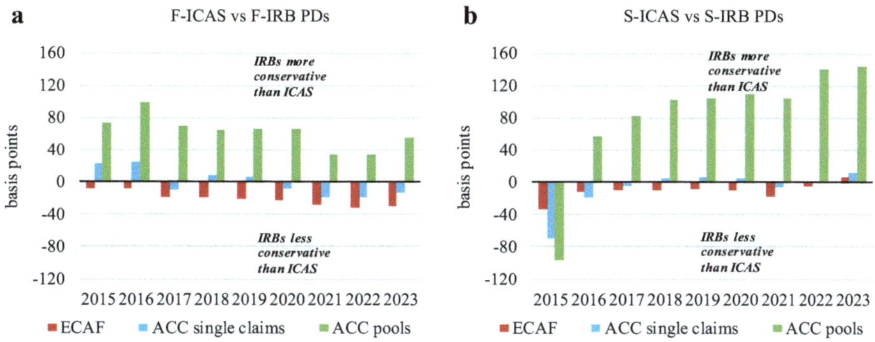

Fig. 2 IRB and ICAS assessments: debtors with pledged loans. For each debtor is reported the median difference between the IRB PD and the ICAS PD

for the ACC pools (Fig. 2b). The fact that IRB PDs are less or more conservative than ICAS PDs is mainly an effect of the considered sub-sample's selection criteria, which is based on the variable of analysis (i.e. the PD).[23]

The selection induced by the criteria of the collateral frameworks arguably leads to observed differences between the ratings of the two systems that are more pronounced in the sub-sample of pledged debtors than in the sample of eligible debtors (Fig. 3).[24] Indeed we find that the share of IRB banks' loans in CQSs 1, 2 and 3 in the sample of borrowers assessed with full ratings is 48% for pledged debtors and

[23] The PDs of borrowers whose loans are pledged by IRB banks have to be lower than 0.4%, while ICAS PDs are not upper-bounded. As for the ACC individual claims sample and the ACC pool sample, instead, a censoring of lower IRB PDs occurs, since IRB PDs cannot be lower than 0.4 and 1.5%, respectively, while ICAS PDs are not lower-bounded, contributing to the circumstance that IRBs are more conservative than ICAS in this sample.

[24] Eligible debtors are those whose loans are eligible as collateral in monetary policy operations; pledged debtors are those whose loans are pledged as collateral in such operations.

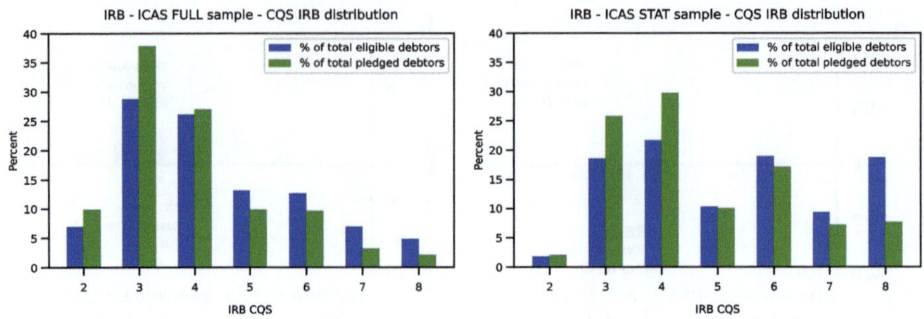

Fig. 3 IRBs CQS distribution: comparison between eligible and pledged debtors commonly rated by IRBs and ICASes

36 for eligible debtors (Fig. 3, left graph). As for the sample of borrowers assessed with statistical rating, the share of banks' loans in CQSs 1, 2 and 3 is 29% for pledged debtors and 22% for eligible debtors (Fig. 3, right graph). These figures suggest to control for IRB credit quality rating in the empirical analysis since the credit quality distribution is more skewed towards higher CQSs for pledged firms than for eligible firms.

4 The Performance of the Credit Assessment Systems

AUROC curve—One of the most widely used metric to test the performance of the credit assessment system is the AUROC curve.[25] The calculation of the area under the ROC curve is a popular way of testing the discriminatory power of the rating systems, which measures the degree with which the system is capable of assigning every entity to the correct class (in our case, the system performs a binary classification between defaulted and non-defaulted debtors). Figure 4 shows the ROC curves relative to the Italian IRB systems accepted for monetary policy purposes (considered as a whole) and to ICAS.

The AUROC is quite high for both the F-IRBs and the F-ICAS, with F-IRBs showing a steeper ROC curve (0.87 and 0.83 in Fig. 4a and b, respectively). The good results in terms of AUROC are confirmed also considering smaller samples of data for individual banks, years, and for debtors with loans pledged in monetary policy operations. Similar evidence can be detected also regarding the AUROC of S-IRBs and S-ICAS (0.87 for both systems in Fig. 4c and d). This is another element which confirms that the ability of the two credit assessment sources to properly evaluate the credit risk of the debtors they rate is satisfactory and that it does not raise concerns with respect to underestimation of credit risk.

[25] See Engelmann (2006) and Tasche (2006) for further details.

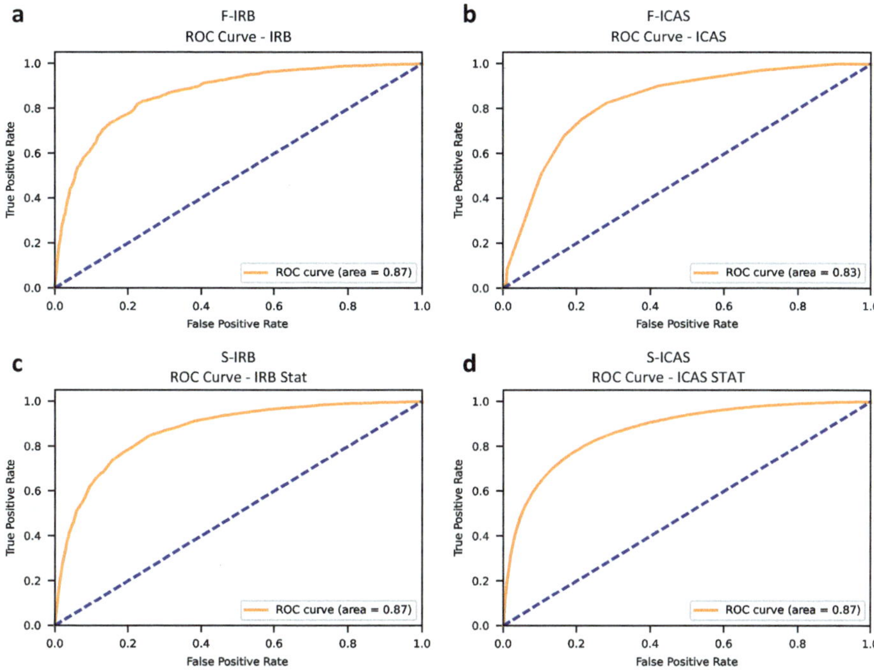

Fig. 4 ROC Curves and AUROC

Back-testing—In the previous sections we have verified that ICAS and IRB ratings are dissimilar to a certain extent, especially for pledged loans and in the more recent period. However, it is rather normal that ratings issued by two different credit assessment sources are not identical (Firestone & Rezende, 2016), as this may be due to different information sets, diverse statistical models, divergences in the expert assessment of the analysts. The true PD of a debtor is an unobservable variable; therefore, it is not possible to establish ex-ante whether a credit assessment system is correct in assigning a certain rating to a debtor, but it can be verified ex-post. From the perspective of a central bank, which receives bank loans as collateral in monetary policy operations, the satisfactory performance of the credit assessment systems evaluating these loans is of the utmost importance.

We performed a back-testing exercise[26] with the purpose to confirm that the two credit assessment systems under investigation do not underestimate the defaults in the sample of the debtors with bank loans pledged as collateral in monetary policy operations, as for the AUROC, we focus on the full rating sample in line with the goal of the Chapter. The methodology we use follows a 'traffic-light approach' (TLA) with a green zone, a yellow ('monitoring') zone and a red ('trigger') zone. These zones indicate different levels of significance of the deviations of the number

[26] The results of the tests are not reported due to confidentiality reasons.

of defaulted entities and of the corresponding default rates from the PD thresholds of the respective Eurosystem CQSs as defined in Table 1.[27]

We first calculated the back-testing on eligible debtors, as if we had a whole static pool which includes all the static pools of each IRB system. We then repeated the test only on the sub-sample of debtors in common with ICAS with loans pledged in monetary policy operations. The results indicate that, apart from some performance issues between 2015 and 2017, due to the unsatisfactory performance of some IRBs, in the last five years the F-IRB systems in aggregate showed a satisfactory performance both for the whole perimeter of eligible debtors and for the sample of debtors with pledged loans, which is the most relevant from a central bank risk management perspective.

We repeated the performance monitoring exercise for ICAS ratings on the whole sample of eligible debtors and then we focused on the sample of debtors in common with IRB banks with loans pledged as collateral; we detected some performance issues in the first years under analysis, the start-up phase of the ICAS system, which were solved from 2018 onwards.

In addition, we conducted the performance monitoring exercise also for S-IRB and S-ICAS ratings. The results for IRBs indicate that, apart from some performance issues in 2015, S-IRB systems show a good predictive capacity both on the universe of eligible debtors and on the sample of pledged debtors in common with S-ICAS. The performance is satisfactory also for S-ICAS ratings for almost the whole period; the model had some minor performance issues only in 2022,[28] then overcome with a new statistical model, developed and implemented also to address these issues, as explained in Chap. 3. In the development of the new statistical model features of traditional models (i.e. the logit regression) and machine learning components for some variables are combined, in the attempt to solve the trade-off between predictability and transparency.

In conclusion, despite some issues emerging mainly in the first years of the analysis, in the more recent period both IRBs and ICAS systems show a good performance, even when tested on bank loans pledged as collateral.

---

[27] The trigger zone indicates that the deviation is considered very significant, i.e. the probability that the credit assessment system is mis-calibrated is very high. The monitoring zone, in turn, indicates a degree of deviation that is significant, i.e. the probability that the credit assessment system is mis-calibrated is high, but not large enough for classifying this situation as a breach of good performance by the system. The green, yellow and red zones are determined on the basis of a statistical binomial test: for further insights see Coppens et al. (2007).

[28] The performance issue in 2022 was related to the micro firms class, due to the fact that a number of such firms disclosed a simplified version of the financial statements, without the breakdown required for a complete model estimation.

5 Empirical Analysis

Empirical approach—In this section we investigate the factors driving the differences between the ratings provided by banks' IRB systems and those provided by the Bank of Italy's ICASes in the collateral framework. First, we estimate the following equation in a panel setting:

$$\log\left(\frac{\mathrm{PD}_{\mathrm{IRBijt}}}{\mathrm{PD}_{\mathrm{ICASit}}}\right) = \alpha_i + \alpha_j + \beta_t \cdot D_t + \beta \cdot \mathrm{Dpledge}_{ijt} + \varepsilon_{ijt} \quad (1)$$

where i indicates the individual firm, j the bank and t the year examined, $\log\left(\frac{\mathrm{PD}_{\mathrm{IRBijt}}}{\mathrm{PD}_{\mathrm{ICASit}}}\right)$ is the log ratio between $\mathrm{PD}_{\mathrm{IRB}}$ and $\mathrm{PD}_{\mathrm{ICAS}}$, $\mathrm{Dpledge}_{ijt}$ is a dummy that is active when the loan is pledged in either of the general collateral, individual or pool temporary collateral frameworks. We include year ($\mathrm{D_t}$), firm and bank fixed effects, to control for business cycle, structural changes, businesses' and banks' unobservable characteristics, and we use the log ratio between the PDs of the IRBs and that of ICAS to address the non-linearity in the absolute differences between PDs.

As in Calza et al. (2021), we assume as a benchmark for the risk assessment of the borrower the PD assigned to the debtor by the NCB, since it has no incentive to manage strategically its rating models parameters, while commercial banks may have an incentive to optimize them to save on capital requirements (this would be the primary goal of a hypothetical strategic behaviour in the management of the internal rating systems), or to save on the collateral posted. According to this hypothesis, banks could underestimate the credit risk of the debtors whose loans are pledged to the NCB to save on the haircuts imposed on the value of the collateral in the monetary policy operation to maximize the liquidity obtained. The effect of this behaviour would materialize in a lower credit risk assessed by IRBs, with respect to ICAS, for the borrowers whose loans are pledged, while it would not alter the creditworthiness assigned by banks to the other borrowers, relative to that calculated by ICAS.

In our analysis, thanks to the richness of the data set received from the banks and used to monitor the compliance with the collateral frameworks, we can also differentiate the IRB models of banks among Statistical ones, that do not entail a credit analysts' judgement before issuance of the rating, and Full ones where analysts' judgement is layered on the outcome of the statistical model. We also have the benefit of being able to match those data with the respective ratings produced by the BoI's S-ICAS and F-ICAS. This wealth of data allows us to differentiate the models among those theoretically amenable to some strategic management of the risk assessment via the intervention of the analysts' judgement, the Full ones, and those who are not, the Statistical ones. IRB models are validated and supervised by the SSM both for supervisory purposes and for the use in the Eurosystem monetary policy purposes and their parameters are rigorously calibrated excluding the possibility that they systematically underestimate the credit risk.

Our analysis thus differs from that of Calza et al. (2021), who only consider F-ICAS models in comparison with undistinguished F- and S-IRBs[29] and interpret as strategic underestimation of the credit risk any observation of a debtor to which an IRB assigns a PD lower than the one assigned by the ICAS.

We also argue that to ascertain a hypothetical strategic behaviour of banks on the basis of the comparison between IRB and ICAS PDs for the firms whose loans are pledged (pledged firms) and for those whose loans are not (eligible firms), the effects of the criteria for acceptance of loans in the collateral frameworks on the credit quality composition of the sample of pledged loans have to be duly considered. Indeed, when we compare IRB and ICAS assessments of eligible debtors the observed borrowers are not selected and represent the universe of the debtors assessed.[30] Differently, when we consider the assessments of pledged debtors the observed sample is filtered by the selection made by the banks and, presumably, the pledged debtors are those with the best IRB rating available responding to the incentive to secure the lowest haircuts for the loans.[31]

Hence, in order to correctly measure the effect of the pledging of a loan on the difference between IRB PDs and ICAS PDs (which proxies the degree of relative conservativeness in credit risk assessment of IRB banks with respect to the NCB) the credit quality of the pledged loan has to be controlled for. In Eq. (2) we therefore control also for the credit quality of the loans, where k indicates one of the eight CQSs in which loans are classified according to the ECAF rating scale (Table 1).

$$\log\left(\frac{\mathrm{PD_{IRBijt}}}{\mathrm{PD_{ICASit}}}\right) = \alpha_i + \alpha_j + \alpha_k + \beta_t \cdot D_t + \beta \cdot \mathrm{Dpledge}_{ijt} + \varepsilon_{ijt} \tag{2}$$

We then aim to investigate what drives the differences among the IRBs and ICAS ratings for pledged debtors. In particular, we analyse the characteristics of the debtors rated by IRBs and ICAS and of the banks which rate them estimating Eq. (3) for debtors with loans pledged as collateral.

$$\begin{aligned}\log\left(\frac{\mathrm{PD_{IRBijt}}}{\mathrm{PD_{ICASit}}}\right) = {} & \alpha_i + \alpha_j + \alpha_k + \alpha_t + \alpha_i.\alpha_t + \beta_1 \cdot \mathrm{REV_{it-2}} + \beta_2 \cdot \mathrm{DEB}_{ijt} \\ & + \beta_3 \cdot \mathrm{CVAH}_{ijt} + \beta_4 \cdot \mathrm{CET1R}_{jt} + \beta_5 \cdot \mathrm{LTC}_{jt} + \varepsilon_{ijt}\end{aligned} \tag{3}$$

[29] Before the introduction of the pandemic easing measures, the Bank of Italy's ICAS was the only ICAS in the euro area to use both a Full and a Statistical stage (the latter only in the ACC framework). Therefore, in Calza et al. (2021) only F-ICAS ratings are considered. Since 2020, S-ICAS have been also used in their ACC frameworks by Oesterreichische Nationalbank, Banco de España, Banco de Portugal and Banca Slovenije.

[30] We considered all the debtors jointly assessed by at least one of the IRB systems of the banks and the ICAS system.

[31] The effects of the selection can be seen in Fig. 3, which shows that the CQS distribution is more skewed to the left in the pledged sample with respect to the distribution for all eligible borrowers.

where REV is the log of the borrower's net revenues, that proxies the size of the borrower,[32] and DEB denotes the share of the loans received by the company from bank *j*, to proxy the relationship lending intensity. CVAH is the collateral value after haircuts of the loans of the company *i* pledged by the bank *j* in monetary policy operations. CET1R is the bank Common Equity Tier 1 Ratio of bank *j*, and LTC is the loan-to-collateral ratio for bank *j*, i.e. the ratio of the central bank liquidity received in the monetary policy operation and the collateral posted by the bank.[33] We also include time, bank and firm fixed effects.

Results—The results for Eq. (1) indicate that F-IRB PDs are lower than F-ICAS PDs for the eligible debtors, as the coefficients of the time dummies are negative (Table 3),[34] also controlling for firm fixed effects, indicating that IRB models are less conservative than ICAS in credit risk assessment.[35] The (negative) difference between IRB and ICAS PDs increases when a loan is pledged, also controlling for firm fixed effects. Calza et al. (2021) find a different result for the eligible debtors, since F-IRB PDs are higher than F-ICAS ones, while their results for pledged debtors are in line with our evidence, i.e. a negative difference between F-IRBs and F-ICAS PDs; they argue that this large decrease (comparing results on eligible debtors and pledged debtors) in the difference between IRB and ICAS PDs indicates a strategic underestimation of the credit risk by commercial banks to increase the pledgeability of loans and banks' access to central bank liquidity.

The results are different for the sample of S-ratings (Table 4). The positive coefficients of the year dummies, with the exception of 2015, indicate that for eligible debtors S-IRBs are more conservative than S-ICAS, and, similarly to what observed for F-ratings, the (positive) difference decreases when considering pledged debtors.

The coefficients estimated for the dummy pledged indicate to what extent the circumstance that a debtor is pledged affects the difference between IRB PDs and ICAS PDs. The estimated effect for F-ratings is −0.40 and, controlling for bank fixed effects, it is halved, to −0.23.

The inclusion of credit quality steps in Eq. (2) yields a significant reduction by a factor of 10, to −0.027 (Table 5) for F-ratings, and from −0.18 to −0.08 for S-ratings, in both cases with an improvement in the explanatory power of the model.

This evidence further indicates that the hypothesis of Calza et al. (2021) of a sizeable strategic management behaviour of banks is not supported by the data as the coefficient of the dummy for pledged debtors significantly decreases controlling for bank fixed effects and CQS by a factor of almost 20. Indeed, the

---

[32] The variable is used with a two-year lag with reference to the PDs to conform to the data available when ratings are assigned.

[33] The rationale behind the introduction of this covariate is to test for the hypothesis that banks with a higher level of central bank liquidity utilization are more keen to strategically underestimate credit risk when pledging credit claims.

[34] The results are discussed using the same metric of Calza et al. (2021).

[35] The only exception is the 2016 coefficient for eligible loans.

Table 3 Estimation of Eq. (1)—Full ratings

Eq_1				
	(1)	(2)	(3)	(4)
Dependent Var	$\ln \frac{PD_{IRB}}{PD_{ICAS}}$	$\ln \frac{PD_{IRB}}{PD_{ICAS}}$	$\ln \frac{PD_{IRB}}{PD_{ICAS}}$	$\ln \frac{PD_{IRB}}{PD_{ICAS}}$
Year:				
2015	−0.021	0.007***		
	(0.018)	(0.021)		
2016	−0.055***	0.045***	0.068*	0.044*
	(0.015)	(0.018)	(0.021)	(0.019)
2017	−0.271***	−0.178***	−0.124***	−0.163***
	(0.014)	(0.017)	(0.021)	(0.019)
2018	−0.149***	−0.107***	−0.032***	−0.083***
	(0.012)	(0.016)	(0.022)	(0.020)
2019	−0.181***	−0.180***	−0.095***	−0.115***
	(0.011)	(0.015)	(0.021)	(0.019)
2020	−0.218***	−0.253***	−0.179***	−0.195***
	(0.010)	(0.013)	(0.021)	(0.019)
2021	−0.391***	−0.404***	−0.307***	−0.333***
	(0.010)	(0.013)	(0.021)	(0.019)
2022	−0.341***	−0.396***	−0.307***	−0.333***
	(0.010)	(0.013)	(0.021)	(0.020)
2023	−0.275***	−0.322***	−0.244***	−0.282***
	(0.010)	(0.010)	(0.021)	(0.020)
Dummy pledged			−0.396***	−0.231***
			(0.008)	(0.007)
Fixed—Effects				
Firm FE	No	Yes	Yes	Yes
Bank FE	No	No	No	Yes
Observations	90,015	89,748	89,748	89,748
R-sqr	0.05	0.34	0.36	0.45
R-sqr_adj	0.05	0.30	0.32	0.41

*** $p < .001$, ** $p < .01$, * $p < .05$

small change (i.e. −0.027) in the gap between IRB and ICAS PD associated to the pledging of a loan contrasts with the sensibly larger variation in Calza et al. (2021), who find that IRB PDs double the ICAS PDs for eligible debtors,[36] and amounts to two-thirds of ICAS PDs for pledged debtors.

[36] With positive average log-differences ranging from 0.8 to 0.95.

Table 4 Estimation of Eq. (1)—Statistical ratings

Eq_1				
	(1)	(2)	(3)	(4)
Dependent Var	$\ln \frac{PD_{IRB}}{PD_{ICAS}}$	$\ln \frac{PD_{IRB}}{PD_{ICAS}}$	$\ln \frac{PD_{IRB}}{PD_{ICAS}}$	$\ln \frac{PD_{IRB}}{PD_{ICAS}}$
Year:				
2015	−0.228***	−0.195***		
	(0.003)	(0.005)		
2016	0.051***	0.075***	0.277***	−0.213***
	(0.003)	(0.005)	(0.004)	(0.012)
2017	0.274***	0.284***	0.495***	−0.017*
	(0.003)	(0.004)	(0.004)	(0.008)
2018	0.346***	0.346***	0.556***	0.111***
	(0.003)	(0.004)	(0.004)	(0.008)
2019	0.393***	0.376***	0.587***	0.128***
	(0.003)	(0.004)	(0.004)	(0.008)
2020	0.387***	0.354***	0.567***	0.130***
	(0.003)	(0.004)	(0.004)	(0.008)
2021	0.261***	0.216***	0.433***	−0.058***
	(0.003)	(0.004)	(0.004)	(0.008)
2022	0.607***	0.541	0.761***	0.285***
	(0.004)	(0.004)	(0.005)	(0.009)
2023	0.601***	0.545***	0.766***	0.446***
	(0.004)	(0.004)	(0.005)	(0.009)
Dummy pledged			−0.149***	−0.178***
			(0.004)	(0.004)
Fixed—Effects				
Firm FE	No	Yes	Yes	Yes
Bank FE	No	No	No	Yes
Observations	1,201,177	1,141,556	1,141,556	1,141,556
R-sqr	0.09	0.54	0.54	0.55
R-sqr_adj	0.09	0.44	0.44	0.45

*** $p < .001$, ** $p < .01$, * $p < .05$

The analysis of the drivers of the difference between the assessments of IRBs and ICAS can be beneficial to the calibration of the credit risk models and it can also shed light on how the features of the rating systems interact with banks' and firms' characteristics that influence the transmission of the monetary policy.

We find that rating disagreements become less likely the larger the borrower (Tables 6 and 7), as the coefficient of REV is positive, reducing the negative gap between the IRB and the ICAS PDs: this result is in line with the fact that public

Table 5 Estimation of Eq. (2)

Eq. 2		
	FULL	STAT
	(1)	(2)
Dependent Var:	$\ln \frac{PD_{IRB}}{PD_{ICAS}}$	$\ln \frac{PD_{IRB}}{PD_{ICAS}}$
Year:		
2016	-0.029^{*}	0.241^{***}
	(0.013)	(0.003)
2017	-0.240^{***}	0.426^{***}
	(0.014)	(0.003)
2018	-0.287^{***}	0.482^{***}
	(0.015)	(0.003)
2019	-0.286^{***}	0.534^{***}
	(0.014)	(0.003)
2020	-0.353^{***}	0.537^{***}
	(0.014)	(0.003)
2021	-0.525^{***}	0.475^{***}
	(0.014)	(0.003)
2022	-0.522^{***}	0.665^{***}
	(0.014)	(0.004)
2023	-0.401^{***}	0.670^{***}
	(0.014)	(0.004)
Dummy_pledged	-0.027^{***}	-0.081^{***}
	(0.005)	(0.003)
Fixed—Effects		
Firm FE	Yes	Yes
Bank FE	Yes	Yes
CQS FE	Yes	Yes
Observations	89,748	1,141,556
R-sqr	0.72	0.70
R-sqr_adj	0.70	0.64

*** $p < .001$, ** $p < .01$, * $p < .05$

information is more easily available for larger firms, inducing a likely convergence of the ratings from different CASs, as found by Carey (2002). The results indicate also that the intensity of the lending relationship, proxied by the variable DEB, affects differently the two kinds of assessment to a very limited extent and only in the Statistical ratings sample, possibly as the use of loans as collateral is not perceived important enough to activate banks' behaviour aimed at protecting their relationships by increasing the pledgeability of the loans via a more favourable credit assessment.

Table 6 Estimates of Eq. (3) with different sets of fixed effects – Full ratings

Eq. 3				
	(1)	(2)	(3)	(4)
Dependent Var	$\ln \frac{PD_{IRB}}{PD_{ICAS}}$	$\ln \frac{PD_{IRB}}{PD_{ICAS}}$	$\ln \frac{PD_{IRB}}{PD_{ICAS}}$	$\ln \frac{PD_{IRB}}{PD_{ICAS}}$
REV	0.146^{***}	0.217^{***}		0.224^{***}
	(0.040)	(0.045)		(0.044)
DEB	0.002^{*}	0.001	0.001	0.001
	(0.001)	(0.001)	(0.001)	(0.001)
CVAH	-0.106^{***}	-0.091^{***}	-0.091^{***}	-0.101^{***}
	(0.008)	(0.008)	(0.010)	(0.008)
CET1R_Q4	0.033^{***}	0.033^{***}	0.037^{***}	0.018^{***}
	(0.001)	(0.001)	(0.002)	(0.003)
Q4_LTC	-0.009^{***}	-0.006^{***}	-0.008^{***}	0.009^{***}
	(0.001)	(0.001)	(0.001)	(0.001)
Fixed—Effects				
Firm FE	Yes	Yes	No	Yes
Year FE	No	Yes	No	Yes
FirmxYear FE	No	No	Yes	No
Bank FE	No	No	No	Yes
Observations	23,350	23,350	18,588	23,350
R-sqr	0.40	0.41	0.57	0.50
R-sqr_adj	0.31	0.31	0.33	0.42

*** $p < .001$, ** $p < .01$, * $p < .05$

We also find that more capitalized banks tend to assign more conservative ratings to their debtors, as the Common Equity Tier 1 coefficient is positive in the Full ratings sample, where assessments are constituted of the banks' analysts' judgement overlaid on the statistical models' outcome, while it is mostly not significant in the statistical ratings sample, that relies only on models' ratings. This finding suggests that, correspondingly, banks with less capital and more limited balance sheet capacity are incentivized to be less conservative in credit risk assessment to strengthen primarily their capital base, and, secondarily, their access to central bank funding, in line with Calza et al. (2021) and the literature on regulatory capital and credit risk (Behn et al., 2022; Berg & Koziol, 2017).

On the contrary, an increase in the amount of the pledged loan, proxied by the variable CVAH, increases the negative difference between the ratings of the IRBs and ICAS in the F-ratings sample, in line with the results found by Calza et al.

Table 7 Estimates of Eq. (3) with different sets of fixed effects—Statistical ratings'

Eq. 3				
	(1)	(2)	(3)	(4)
Dependent Var	$\ln \frac{PD_{IRB}}{PD_{ICAS}}$	$\ln \frac{PD_{IRB}}{PD_{ICAS}}$	$\ln \frac{PD_{IRB}}{PD_{ICAS}}$	$\ln \frac{PD_{IRB}}{PD_{ICAS}}$
REV	0.044 ***	0.056 ***		0.060 ***
	(0.010)	(0.010)		(0.010)
DEB	0.000	0.001 ***	−0.003	0.001 ***
	(0.000)	(0.000)	(0.002)	(0.000)
CVAH	−0.129 ***	−0.092 ***	−0.023	−0.082 ***
	(0.006)	(0.006)	(0.030)	(0.006)
CET1R_Q4	0.001	−0.022 ***	−0.071 ***	−0.003
	(0.001)	(0.001)	(0.004)	(0.001)
Q4_LTC	0.005 ***	−0.010 ***	−0.002	−0.006 ***
	(0.000)	(0.001)	(0.002)	(0.001)
Fixed—Effects				
Firm FE	Yes	Yes	No	Yes
Year FE	No	Yes	No	Yes
FirmxYear FE	No	No	Yes	No
Bank FE	No	No	No	Yes
Observations	93,355	93,355	2,475	93,355
R-sqr	0.71	0.72	0.72	0.73
R-sqr_adj	0.56	0.59	0.44	0.60

*** $p < .001$, ** $p < .01$, * $p < .05$

(2021).[37] This result could suggest a strategic behaviour of the banks in managing the collateral.

The effect of the loan-to-collateral ratio in the monetary policy operations in the F-ratings sample is positive, when also bank fixed effects are introduced, indicating that higher NCB liquidity utilization by banks makes the banks produce more conservative ratings.[38] This evidence contrasts with the negative effect of high liquidity utilization of banks on banks' conservativeness in the assessment of

[37] In the Statistical rating sample, the effect, statistically weaker, is of a reduction of the positive difference between IRB and ICAS ratings; we do not view this as a sign of strategic management of collateral either since banks' analysts cannot override the ratings produced by the models.

[38] The effect of higher liquidity utilization in the Statistical rating sample, statistically weaker, is of a reduction of the positive difference between IRB and ICAS ratings; we do not view this as a sign of strategic management of collateral either since banks' analysts cannot modify the ratings produced by the models. We also note that higher values of loan-to-collateral ratio do not necessarily indicate more liquidity-constrained banks, instead they can be linked to the liquidity management practices or to the specific business models of the banks under analysis.

credit risk found by Calza et al. (2021), who infer that banks interested to save on their capacity to access central bank's liquidity underestimate the credit risk of the collateral.

We then introduce among the regressors the classes of credit quality steps to control also for the effect of the criteria for acceptance of loans in the collateral framework. Such approach represents an innovation with respect to previous works, making our results not directly comparable with them. In the F-rating sample, the effect of net revenues remains positive and that of the intensity of the banking relation is not significant (Table 8). The effect of bank capital remains positive, confirming that more capitalized banks tend to assign more conservative ratings to their debtors. The effects of the collateral value after haircuts and of the LTC ratio, instead, turn out to be not significant, when all unobservable effects are accounted for, confirming the absence of a strategic behaviour of banks.[39] The results for the S-rating sample (Table 9) confirm those commented above.

Table 8 Estimates of Eq. (3) with different sets of fixed effects including CQSs—Full ratings

Eq. 3				
	(1)	(2)	(3)	(4)
Dependent Var	$\ln \frac{PD_{IRB}}{PD_{ICAS}}$	$\ln \frac{PD_{IRB}}{PD_{ICAS}}$	$\ln \frac{PD_{IRB}}{PD_{ICAS}}$	$\ln \frac{PD_{IRB}}{PD_{ICAS}}$
REV	0.423^{***}	0.583^{***}	0.000	0.565^{***}
	(0.031)	(0.035)	(0.000)	(0.035)
DEB	0.002^{**}	0.000	0.000	0.000
	(0.001)	(0.001)	(0.000)	(0.001)
CVAH	-0.027^{***}	−0.005	−0.006	−0.009
	(0.005)	(0.005)	(0.004)	(0.005)
CET1R_Q4	0.011^{***}	0.012^{***}	0.008^{***}	0.010^{***}
	(0.001)	(0.001)	(0.001)	(0.002)
Q4_LTC	-0.009^{***}	-0.005^{***}	-0.003^{***}	0.001
	(0.000)	(0.000)	(0.000)	(0.001)
Fixed—Effects				
Firm FE	Yes	Yes	No	Yes
Year FE	No	Yes	No	Yes
FirmxYear FE	No	No	Yes	No
Bank FE	No	No	No	Yes
CQS FE	Yes	Yes	Yes	Yes
Observations	23,350	23,350	18,588	23,350
R-sqr	0.73	0.74	0.94	0.74

(continued)

[39] Finally, we explore whether the disagreements could be lower if a debtor is rated by many banks (i.e. by three or more banks). The results suggest that this variable is not significant and therefore it seems not to have a role in explaining the differences among IRB and ICAS ratings.

(continued)

Eq. 3				
	(1)	(2)	(3)	(4)
R-sqr_adj	0.69	0.70	0.90	0.70

*** $p < .001$, ** $p < .01$, * $p < .05$

Table 9 Estimates of Eq. (3) with different sets of fixed effects—Statistical ratings

Eq. 3				
	(1)	(2)	(3)	(4)
Dependent Var	$\ln \frac{PD_{IRB}}{PD_{ICAS}}$	$\ln \frac{PD_{IRB}}{PD_{ICAS}}$	$\ln \frac{PD_{IRB}}{PD_{ICAS}}$	$\ln \frac{PD_{IRB}}{PD_{ICAS}}$
REV	0.139^{***}	0.133^{***}		0.133^{***}
	(0.008)	(0.008)		(0.008)
DEB	0.002^{***}	0.002^{***}	0.000	0.002^{***}
	(0.000)	(0.000)	(0.001)	(0.000)
CVAH	-0.081^{***}	-0.063^{***}	−0.017	-0.061^{***}
	(0.005)	(0.005)	(0.011)	(0.005)
CET1R_Q4	0.007^{***}	-0.006^{***}	-0.003^{*}	−0.001
	(0.001)	(0.001)	(0.002)	(0.001)
Q4_LTC	0.002^{***}	-0.006^{***}	-0.005^{***}	-0.004^{***}
	(0.000)	(0.001)	(0.001)	(0.001)
Fixed—Effects				
Firm FE	Yes	Yes	No	Yes
Year FE	No	Yes	No	Yes
FirmxYear FE	No	No	Yes	No
Bank FE	No	No	No	Yes
CQS FE	Yes	Yes	Yes	Yes
Observations	93,355	93,355	2,475	93,355
R-sqr	0.81	0.81	0.97	0.81
R-sqr_adj	0.72	0.72	0.94	0.72

*** $p < .001$, ** $p < .01$, * $p < .05$

The residual differences between IRB and ICAS PDs not explained by the abovementioned factors could be driven also by diversity across rating models along the following dimensions: (i) the rating quantification approach, i.e. the assignment of PD values to different rating classes; (ii) the set of information and statistical methodology used for the rating assignment; (iii) the length of the time-series used for PD calibration; (iv) the rating "philosophy", which is more through-the-cycle oriented for IRBs and point-in-time for ICAS, as explained in Sect. 2.

6 Robustness Analysis

In order to allay the concern on the dependence of the comparison between eligible and pledged debtors on the IRB PD distribution in the two samples we estimate Eq. (2) separately, for both F- and S-ratings, on the seven sub-samples of eligible debtors grouped by credit quality step class according to their IRB PD, which allows also for controlling more accurately for the effects of the different distribution of loans across lower and higher credit quality classes. The results confirm those found controlling directly for credit quality steps in Eq. (2).[40]

As a further robustness check, we run Eqs. (1), (2), and (3) using the absolute differences between IRB PDs and ICAS PDs as the dependent variable. The results broadly confirm the main evidence found when running the same equations with log PD ratios as the dependent variable.

Finally, we test the differences between the IRBs and ICAS in terms of ranking of borrowers' creditworthiness using proximity indicators (Appendix B). Since the relative ordering of the debtors' assessments is similar and the statistics indicate an agreement of the two kinds of systems, the evidence supports the assessment that the differences between the IRB and ICAS systems are quite low.

7 Conclusions

This Chapter aims to detect any systematic differences in the ratings issued by Italian IRB systems accepted for monetary policy purposes and by the Bank of Italy's ICAS. The data indicate that small differences exist and that IRBs tend to be less conservative than ICAS when considering the Full models, i.e. those that include the financial analysts' assessment, while the opposite occurs when considering the purely statistical models. The difference between IRB and NCB PDs mildly increases for firms with loans pledged as collateral.

We bring new evidence on credit risk assessment systems, including for the post COVID-19 recovery. We thus seek to contribute to the literature with the study of features of the internal rating models not yet explored to our knowledge, such as the pandemic related extension of the Eurosystem collateral framework, which allows the analysis of loans of lower credit quality, and ratings produced by the NCB internal models and by IRB purely quantitative models, extending the analysis to a vast number of small non-financial corporates that account for a large part of the Italian economy.

We observe that IRB and the Bank of Italy's ICAS overall show a satisfactory predictive capacity and a good discriminatory power.

We find that, for borrowers whose corporate loans are eligible as collateral, F-IRB PDs are slightly less conservative than those assigned by F-ICAS, especially

[40] We do not show the results of the regressions here for brevity.

in more recent years. We also find that the difference between F-IRB and F-ICAS PDs increases very modestly when restricting the sample to the debtors with loans mobilized as collateral and fully accounting for borrowers' creditworthiness. This evidence suggests that, when taking into account banks' common liquidity management practices in the context of the collateral framework, a strategic management of the rating of the collateral, if any, is negligible and of low economic significance. Furthermore, ratings produced by quantitative models without the judgement of analysts, S-IRBs PDs, are often more conservative than S-ICAS PDs, but to a lesser extent when considering the borrowers whose loans have been pledged.

We also characterize the factors driving the differences between the ratings issued by IRBs and ICAS. We find that the difference between PDs issued by IRBs and by ICAS decreases with the size of the borrower. We view this finding as reflecting the consideration that for larger companies and for those accessing market financing the availability of public information is larger, contributing to align the assessment of rating systems. In addition, we find that the difference between PDs is not affected by the size of the loan pledged and by the levels of central bank liquidity utilization, allowing us to conclude that IRB banks do not underestimate the PDs assigned to borrowers to mobilize strategically the largest amount of collateral. Residual differences between IRB and ICAS PDs may be ascribed also to methodological diversity across rating systems.

We also evaluate the ratings produced by the banks and ICAS as similar according to proximity measures. Overall, the evidence discussed above and the analysis of the drivers of the small differences between the credit risk assessment provided by IRBs and ICAS leads us to conclude that the hypothesis of an economically significant strategic management of the IRB credit systems is not supported by the data for Italy and that, while IRBs in some instances appear less conservative than ICAS, both IRBs and ICAS evaluate credit risk adequately, in this way contributing to minimize the risks borne by the Eurosystem and the Bank of Italy within the monetary policy collateral frameworks.

Appendix A

Dataset

Variable	Description	Unit	Source
Firm information			
ICAS PD	Probability of default (PD) over a 1-year horizon, provided by the Bank of Italy's ICAS Full or by the Bank of Italy's ICAS statistical to an individual firm	Basis points	Bank of Italy

(continued)

(continued)

Variable	Description	Unit	Source
REV	Net revenues of a firm. In the regressions, the variable is used with a two years lag with reference to the PDs to conform to the data available when ratings are assigned. The logarithmic transformation has been used	EUR million	Cerved
DEB	Share of the loans received by the firm *i* from bank *j* on its total bank loans	Percentage	Cerved
Bank information			
CET 1	Common Equity Tier 1 ratio at the end of each year	Percentage	Bank of Italy
LTC	Loan-to-Collateral ratio (ratio between the central bank credit provided by the bank and collateral mobilized by the bank) at the end of each year	Percentage	Bank of Italy
Firm-bank information			
IRB PD	PD over 1-year horizon assigned by IRB banks to firms	Basis points	Bank of Italy
CVAH	Collateral value after haircut (outstanding amount of the loan mobilized by bank *j* to a firm *i*, net of haircuts applied on the basis of the Eurosystem collateral framework rules); logarithmic transformation	EUR million	Bank of Italy

Appendix B

Proximity Statistics

The ratings of two credit assessment systems can be compared via the use of proximity measures calculated on the basis of the pairs of ratings for a sample of commonly rated entities. In order to obtain an indication of the degree of proximity between the F-IRB and F-ICAS ratings,[41] we follow Hornik et al. (2006) and use the following two measures of proximity: Association and Agreement.[42] In addition, we perform the Wilcoxon signed-rank test in order to test whether the median rating difference between the two systems is significantly different from zero. The proximity statistics are calculated on the CQSs used by the Eurosystem.

The Association indicator measures to what extent the relative pair-wise ordering produced by one credit assessment system (CAS) matches that of the other CAS. The Association indicator is also known as the Kendall Tau distance or the

[41] We do not show the results for S-IRB and S-ICAS ratings for brevity, since our main focus for these additional statistics is on the IRB judgmental systems, which proved to be less conservative than F-ICAS.

[42] Hornik et al. use a third proximity measure, i.e. the "rating bias", which measures, for every debtor rated by two credit assessment sources, the deviation between the two rating classes, subsequently scaled to the interval $[-1, +1]$. We do not present here the rating bias because this measure is very similar to the one commented in Sect. 3.

Table 10 Comparison between IRBs and ICAS Full ratings according to a set of proximity statistics

Year	Kendall-Tau (Association)		Cohen's coefficient (Agreement)		Wilcoxon test (p-values)	
	F-IRB-ICAS eligible	*F-IRB-ICAS pledged*	*F-IRB-ICAS eligible*	*F-IRB-ICAS pledged*	*F-IRB-ICAS eligible (%)*	*F-IRB-ICAS pledged (%)*
2015	0.69	0.70	0.33	0.29	0.0	0.0
2016	0.70	0.72	0.41	0.42	0.0	0.1
2017	0.71	0.71	0.48	0.45	14.8	0.0
2018	0.72	0.71	0.57	0.53	0.1	0.0
2019	0.71	0.71	0.55	0.53	12.2	0.0
2020	0.73	0.72	0.61	0.58	0.0	0.0
2021	0.72	0.71	0.57	0.52	0.0	0.0
2022	0.71	0.71	0.57	0.53	0.0	0.0
2023	0.72	0.72	0.58	0.58	0.0	0.0

Kemeny-Snell τ_x. This measure is scaled so that it can take values in the interval [0, 1], with 1 corresponding to identical orderings.

The Agreement is another measure for the proximity of two rating systems. While the Association only measures whether the rank-ordering is similar, the Agreement also depends on the rating distance between the two systems. The measure can take positive values up to 1, but is not limited by zero on the lower end. A value of 1 corresponds to a perfect agreement between the CASs, a value of 0 corresponds to the expected agreement as if the ratings were independent, and a negative value corresponds to disagreement.

Finally, as far as the Wilcoxon test is concerned, it can be used to test whether the median rating difference between the two CASs is zero.[43]

The main advantage of the Wilcoxon test is that it is non-parametric and therefore the individual distributions of both samples can be left undetermined. The test, however, requires that both samples to be tested originate from the same population, and that both systems use an ordinal scale for measurement (Table 10).

According to the Association measure, in the time span under investigation the pair-wise ordering for both CASs matches in between 65 and 73% of the cases, i.e. the internal relative ordering of the rated debtors was the same (100% is a perfect match).

The Agreement measure suggests that, at least in the more recent period, around 55% of the F-IRBs and F-ICAS provide equivalent or very close to equivalent rating assessments (a value of 100% would mean a perfect agreement) for the samples of eligible debtors. Agreement measures tend to be higher in the more

[43] The hypothesis to be tested using the Wilcoxon test is the following: $H_0 : m_A = m_B$; $H_1 : m_A \neq m_B$, where m_A and m_B are the median rating grades for CAS A and B, respectively.

recent period. Evidences are similar for the samples of pledged debtors, though on slightly lower levels, which look consistent with the results of Sect. 3.

The Wilcoxon p-values are instead very low (with a few exceptions), meaning that the null hypothesis $H_0 : m_A = m_B$ is rejected at the 5% level, and therefore that the median rating grades assigned by IRBs and ICAS do not coincide, in line with the findings of Sect. 3.

To sum up, the analysis of the proximity measures confirms that there are some differences in the way ICAS and IRBs rate debtors, as evidenced by the results of the Wilcoxon test. However, the relative ordering of the debtors' assessments is similar and the level of agreement is sufficient. A reliable benchmark to assess the level of the indicators is represented by the outcome of a cross-comparison of ICAS ratings with other credit assessment systems ECAF-accepted conducted by the ECB in the context of the works related to the prioritization of ICAS ratings. The ECB concludes, on the basis of proximity measures with levels in line with those showed above (or even lower), that the cross-comparison of ICAS ratings with IRB systems shows limited average differences overall. This evidence thus further supports the assessment that the differences between the IRB and ICAS systems are quite low.

References

Adler, M., Camba-Méndez, G., Džaja, T., Manzanares, A., Metra, M., & Vocalelli, G. (2023). *The valuation haircuts applied to eligible marketable assets for ECB credit operations* (ECB Occas Paper Ser 312).

Behn, M., Haselmann, R., & Vig, V. (2022). The limits of model-based regulation. *The Journal of Finance, LXXVII*(3), 1635–1684.

Berg, T and Koziol P (2017) An analysis of the consistency of banks' internal ratings. *Journal of Banking & Finance, 78*, 27–41.

Calza, A., Hey, J. B., Parrini, A., & Sauer, S. (2021). *Corporate loans, bank's internal risk estimates and central bank collateral: evidence from the euro area* (ECB Working Paper Ser 2579)

Carey, M. (2002). Some evidence on the consistency of banks' internal credit ratings. In M. K. Ong (Ed.), *Credit ratings: Methodologies, rationale and default risk* (pp. 449–467). Risk Books.

Coppens, F., González, F., & Winkler, G. (2007) *The performance of credit rating systems in the assessment of collateral Used in Eurosystem monetary policy operations* (ECB Occas Pap Ser 65).

Cucinelli, D, Di Battista, M. L., Marches, M., & Nieri, L. (2018). Credit risk in European banks: The bright side of the internal ratings based approach. *Journal of Banking & Finance, 93*(C), 213–229

Engelmann, B. (2006). Measures of a rating's discriminative power—Applications and limitations. In *The Basel II Risk Parameters* (pp. 263–287).

European Central Bank. (2015). The financial risk management of the Eurosystem's monetary policy operations, July.

European Central Bank. (2024). Guide to Internal Models, February.

Firestone, S., & Rezende, M. (2016). Are banks' internal risk parameters consistent? Evidence from syndicated loans. *Journal of Financial Services Research, 50*, 211–242.

Giovannelli, F., Iannamorelli, A., Levy, A., & Orlandi, M. (2023). The bank of Italy's in-house credit assessment system for non-financial firms. In A. Scalia (Ed.), *Financial risk management and climate change risk* (pp. 107–137). Springer.

Hornik, K., Jankowitsch, R., Lingo, M., Pichler, S., & Winkler, G. (2006). *Validation of credit rating systems using multi-rater information.* Available at SSRN: https://ssrn.com/abstract=871213 or https://doi.org/10.2139/ssrn.871213

Jacobson, T., Lindé, J., & Roszbach, K. (2006). Internal ratings systems, implied credit risk and the consistency of banks' risk classification policies. *Journal of Banking & Finance, 30*(7), 1899–1926.

Tasche, D (2006) Validation of internal rating systems and PD estimates. arXiv: physics/0606071.

Part IV

AI and New Risk Sources

Credit Risk Assessment with Stacked Machine Learning

Francesco Columba, Manuel Cugliari, and Stefano Di Virgilio

1 Introduction

This Chapter compares the performance of widely used machine learning (ML) methods to the performance of the S-ICAS and discusses how differences between the outcome obtained with the former and those of the S-ICAS can be treated to improve the quality of the ICAS second stage, and thus the overall assessment. We contribute to the literature in two ways. First, while earlier studies typically compare ML techniques with traditional statistical methods using a single, simplified model, we carry out this comparison with a complex model, S-ICAS, which has been employed for monetary policy purposes for over a decade, with a consistently high performance. Second, unlike previous studies in which model explainability is discussed mainly as a theoretical exercise, we propose a practical tool based on eXplainable Artificial Intelligence (XAI) methods that can be used by financial analysts in the second stage of the ICAS evaluation process.

This analysis is motivated by the significant advancements in machine learning observed in recent years—thanks to the availability of large datasets and the improvements in computational capabilities—and by the fact that ML methods, being intrinsically different from traditional statistical approaches, have the potential to provide useful results to enhance the accuracy and robustness of our

F. Columba · M. Cugliari (✉) · S. Di Virgilio
Bank of Italy, Financial Risk Management Directorate, Rome, Italy
e-mail: manuel.cugliari@bancaditalia.it

F. Columba
e-mail: francesco.columba@bancaditalia.it

S. Di Virgilio
e-mail: stefano.divirgilio@bancaditalia.it

A. Scalia (ed.), *Corporate Credit Analysis and AI*, Finance for Professionals,
https://doi.org/10.1007/978-3-032-13422-6_11

assessment of firms' creditworthiness. Classical techniques, such as logistic regression, rely on assumptions about the underlying stochastic process generating the observed data; the model's parameters are estimated from the data and subsequently used for population inference or statistical testing. In contrast, ML methods make minimal or no assumptions about the data-generating process; instead, they identify the optimal function that maps input variables into the target variable, prioritizing maximum predictive accuracy (Breiman, 2001b). These methods frequently outperform traditional statistical models (Barboza et al., 2017) as they are capable of capturing complex, non-linear and non-monotonic relationships with the dependent variable (Moscatelli et al., 2020).

One important aspect, however, is that due to the non-parametric or complex functional form, explaining ML predictions remains a challenge (Loyola-Gonzalez, 2019). As a result, their application is often restricted, particularly in regulatory environments where explainability is crucial (Cascarino et al., 2022). In contrast, most traditional statistical models—among which S-ICAS—have simpler structures and their output can be easily interpreted by financial analysts. To address this issue, a sub-field of artificial intelligence, XAI, has been developed to enhance both the explainability and the interpretability of ML models (Apley & Zhu, 2020; Ribeiro et al., 2016; Štrumbelj & Kononenko, 2014).[1] In this paper we explore whether XAI developments can be leveraged to support the analysis conducted within the ICAS framework.

In the first part of our empirical analysis, we replicate the structure of S-ICAS by training three different ML models—random forests, extreme gradient boosting, and deep learning—and assess whether these techniques can achieve significant improvements in discriminatory power compared to S-ICAS. To further enhance performance and robustness, we also develop a meta-model that, by stacking the three models, integrates their predictions. We then use XAI techniques to design an interpretation tool that identifies which factors, among those considered in the models, are more relevant in explaining the discrepancies between the PDs estimated by ML models and those produced by S-ICAS.

Our main finding is that ML models provide useful results for S-ICAS, which complement but cannot substitute it, due to their complexity, that prevents corporate credit analysis from relying only on ML to fully characterize firms' creditworthiness. This result aligns with warnings against overreliance on automated decisions when applying artificial intelligence (Narayanan & Kapoor, 2024), as human oversight remains essential (Angelini, 2025). This challenge is a source of concern also in banking regulation and supervision (European Banking Authority, 2023), which care for transparency and accountability of models. The interpretation tool, in this respect, is valuable and may streamline the analysts' work, enabling them to pay attention to the most problematic issues, specifically where

[1] A model is deemed explainable if it allows a person to understand either its internal mechanisms or the rationale behind its outputs. In the first case, the model is also called interpretable (European Banking Authority, 2020).

ML models and S-ICAS provide diverging signals (although caution is needed, since not all the cases are easily explainable). All in all, these results suggest that the use of ML models may increase the efficiency and quality of the whole ICAS process, offering insights for the calibration of its output and making it more robust, also due to the possibility of integrating additional information from unstructured databases.

The remainder of the Chapter is structured as follows. Section 2 reviews the literature related to the use of ML techniques for credit risk and of the XAI methods. Section 3 outlines the dataset and the methods employed to estimate the ML models. Section 4 presents the main results of the models. Section 5 describes the robustness checks. Section 6 introduces the tool developed to explain the differences in the PDs produced by the various models. Section 7 concludes.

2 Machine Learning for Credit Risk and XAI Methods

The literature on credit risk indicates that ML techniques frequently outperform traditional statistical models in terms of accuracy and discriminatory power (Shi et al., 2022). Several studies have compared machine learning models—especially ensemble methods, which use various learning algorithms, such as random forests and gradient boosting machines—with traditional techniques like logistic regression. These comparisons show that ML models may outperform traditional models in terms of discriminatory power and/or accuracy when predicting corporate failures and bankruptcy (Li & Wang, 2017; Moscatelli et al., 2020; Schalck & Yankol-Schalck, 2021).

Since the early 2010s, deep learning models have gained prominence in the ML literature (Alom et al., 2019; Dell, 2024), due to the increasing size of datasets and the advancements in computational power. Indeed, deep learning methods tend to outperform other ML techniques when the dataset is very large (Fig. 1).

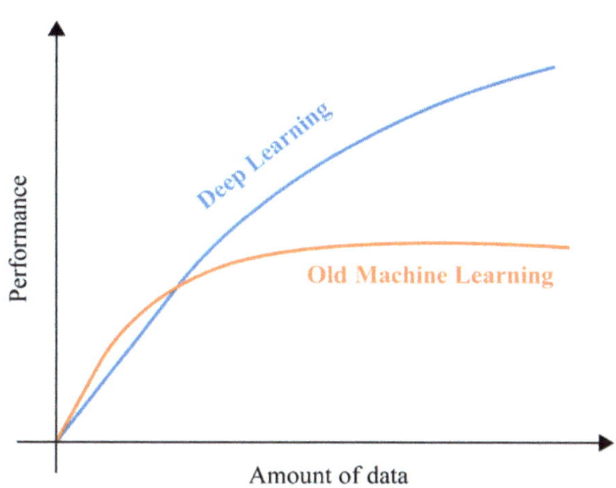

Fig. 1 Deep learning vs other ML techniques. *Source* Alom et al. (2019)

For these reasons, some authors have started to train models using also deep learning—which use artificial neural networks—to predict corporates' default and financial distress (Barboza et al., 2017; Ciampi & Gordini, 2013; Gregova et al., 2020; Petropoulos et al., 2019; Zhang et al., 2022). The performance of ML models, including deep learning, is generally superior to that of traditional models according to a number of key metrics, particularly in terms of accuracy and Area Under the Receiver Operating Characteristic (AUROC). However, when comparing deep learning to other ML techniques, the results are mixed, without a clear best performer. In the aforementioned studies, the comparison between ML and traditional statistical methods has often relied on relatively simple models constructed specifically for this purpose.

In recent years, global and local XAI techniques have also been used to improve the interpretability and the explainability of machine learning models. Global XAI methods provide insights into the model as a whole. Notable examples include the permutation variable importance method (Altmann et al., 2010; Breiman, 2001a) and accumulated local effects (ALE) plots (Apley & Zhu, 2020). The permutation variable importance method identifies the contribution of each variable to the model's discriminatory power, while ALE plots illustrate the average relationship between the independent variables and the model's predictions, making it possible to detect non-linear or non-monotonic effects.

Conversely, local XAI methods aim to explain single predictions. Examples are the 'Shapley values' (Lundberg & Lee, 2017a, 2017b; Lundberg et al., 2020; Štrumbelj & Kononenko, 2014) and 'Local interpretable model-agnostic explanations' (*LIME;* Ribeiro et al., 2016). Shapley values, derived from game theory (Shapley, 1953), are grounded in robust theoretical properties (see Sect. 6) and are used to fairly distribute the difference between a model's prediction and the average prediction among the independent variables. LIME approximates a non-linear model with a linear one, in the neighbourhood of a specific prediction. However, LIME relies on a heuristic procedure that contains different sources of uncertainty (Zhang et al., 2019).

Explaining the output of an ML model is crucial in credit risk assessment, as highlighted by Cascarino et al. (2022). Specifically, in the case of corporate default forecasting, it is essential to link a given prediction to the firm's characteristics, particularly when an automated scoring procedure directly influences the firm's ability to access credit. Furthermore, in the case of ICAS, since the output of the statistical model serves as input of the expert assessment, it is imperative to explain statistical PDs to credit analysts.

In recent years, XAI techniques have increasingly been applied to improve the explainability of ML models trained to assess companies' credit risk (Bitetto et al., 2023; Bussmann et al., 2021; Cascarino et al., 2022). In these studies, since the objective is to show how these techniques can be used to improve the models' explainability, the exercises performed by the authors are relatively simple.

Table 1 Default rates and firms

Year	Default rate (%)	Firms
2014	6.2	237,109
2015	5.3	229,134
2016	4.3	252,740
2017	3.2	260,061
2018	2.9	259,768
2019	2.7	260,985
2020	2.1	261,328
2021	1.7	246,287
2022	1.9	245,972
2023	2.0	278,186

3 Data and Methods

3.1 Dataset

The dataset extends from 2014 to 2023; financial statement and credit behaviour indicators are built using the methodology described in Chap. 3. We consider the data for 2020 and 2021 to be significantly different from the other, as these years were heavily influenced by extraordinary government measures aimed at supporting businesses during the Covid-19 pandemic.[2] These measures had an impact on the default rates recorded in those years. Consequently, the data for 2020 and 2021 are not used for training the ML models and are considered only in the robustness checks. The dataset contains about 2.5 million observations. The trend of the default rate is generally decreasing over the sample period (Table 1).

As expected, default rates are rather low, which is typical when dealing with corporate insolvencies, as default is a rare event. Consequently, the dataset is unbalanced, with far fewer companies in default compared to those not in default. In the ML literature, unbalanced datasets are often addressed through rebalancing techniques, such as undersampling (He & Garcia, 2009). Undersampling involves randomly removing observations from the majority class (in this case, companies not in default) until the dataset achieves an approximate balance. Although

[2] The Italian government implemented several economic measures to support Italian companies, following the outbreak of COVID-19 pandemic. In particular, the government introduced the possibility of benefiting from payment delays ('debt moratorium') and public guarantees for bank loans. These measures increased the amount of liquidity available to companies during the pandemic (see D.L. 'Cura Italia' and D.L. 'Sostegni').

research has shown that undersampling does not always improve the performance of ML models (Dal Pozzolo et al., 2015), we choose this technique for computational reasons.[3]

The dataset is also divided into a training set and a test set[4] for the estimation and evaluation of the models, as follows. The years 2014 and 2023, first and last year of analysis, are designated as the test set, allowing us to test the models in a year with a high default rate (2014) and in a year with a low default rate (2023). Both years are marked by challenging economic conditions[5]: during 2014, the economic cycle was still affected by the aftermath of the sovereign debt crisis, while 2023 was affected by the surge of inflation in 2021–2022 and the subsequent sharp rise in interest rates. Excluding the COVID-19 pandemic, the central years (2015–2019 and 2022) are used as the training sample. This temporal split ensures that the model is tested on an out-of-sample set from distinct economic periods.

3.2 Random Forests

Random Forests (RFs) are a combination of individual decision trees (Breiman, 2001a) which improves the overall predictive performance and robustness. RFs may handle large, high-dimensional datasets and model complex, non-linear relationships. In the context of credit risk, where the relationship between predictors and default is influenced by numerous factors, RFs mitigate overfitting by averaging multiple decision trees, thus providing more stable and accurate predictions. Additionally, RFs can be used as a feature importance ranking method, to rank the financial and behavioural indicators for credit risk, making RFs a powerful tool not only for prediction, but also for interpretation.[6]

The methodology used to estimate the RF model for predicting PDs involves several steps (see Appendix A). The pre-processing phase involves constructing

[3] Under-sampling greatly reduces the size of the dataset, speeding up the training-validation cycle of ML models.

[4] Under-sampling was only applied to the training set.

[5] See "Banca d'Italia Annual Report 2014" and "Banca d'Italia Annual Report 2023".

[6] RFs operate by constructing multiple decision trees during the training phase and then predicting the outcome by aggregating the results from all trees. In classification tasks, where the goal is to assign observations to discrete classes, the model aggregates the predictions across the trees to determine the final class. In regression tasks, where the objective is to predict a continuous value, the model combines predictions by averaging the output from all trees to generate a final, more stable prediction. Each tree is trained on a different bootstrap sample of the original data, and at each split in the tree, a random subset of features is considered for splitting. This feature generally results in better performance and reduced susceptibility to overfitting compared to individual decision trees (Louppe et al., 2013).

Table 2 Random forests hyper-parameters search space

Parameter	Type	Range
n_estimators	Integer	100 ÷ 500
min_samples_leaf	Integer	1 ÷ 1000
max_features	Categorical	[sqrt, log2, None]
bootstrap	Categorical	[True, False]
criterion	Categorical	[gini, entropy]
n_iter	Integer	200
cv	Integer	10

Note *n_estimators* is the number of trees in the forest; *min_samples_leaf*, the minimum number of samples required to be at a leaf node; *max_features*, the number of features to consider when looking for the best split; *criterion* measures the quality of a split, with 'gini' for the Gini impurity and 'entropy' for the information gain; *n_iter*, is the number of iterations for the hyper-parameter search; *cv* is the number of folds

sub-datasets by selecting variables of interest for each of the eleven financial statement models and three credit performance models.[7] Then, for each sub-model, a parameter space is defined for the hyper-parameter optimization process (Table 2).

The training dataset is then split into multiple subsets, known as folds, and cross-validation[8] is used for hyper-parameter optimization (Kohavi, 1995) to evaluate the model generalizability and mitigate overfitting. By evaluating the model performance across multiple folds, we enhance the model predictive accuracy and robustness. The cross-validation process not only assesses the model ability to generalize to unseen data, but it also plays a critical role in hyper-parameter tuning, which is critical to enhance the model performance.[9] Once the optimal hyper-parameters are identified, the final RF model is trained using the entire training dataset and subsequently evaluated on the test set to assess its performance.

[7] These eleven financial statement models reflect the structure and variables of S-ICAS, encompassing five macroeconomic sectors (industrial, trade, construction, services, and real estate) across two distinct types of financial statements (ordinary and simplified), plus an additional model for holding companies. Distinct sub-datasets are created by extracting relevant features for each sector and financial statement type. Similarly, three credit models are constructed to capture firms' credit behaviour performance.

[8] Cross-validation implies systematically training the model on a combination of the folds, while validating it on the remaining one.

[9] We employ Bayesian optimization to explore systematically the hyper-parameter space and identify the optimal combination of parameters that maximize the model's AUROC on the validation data.

3.3 Extreme Gradient Boosting

Extreme Gradient Boosting (XGB or XGBoost) is a widely recognized ML technique (Chen & Guestrin, 2016) that has been successfully applied to various predictive modelling problems, including the prediction of corporate default (Petropoulos et al., 2019; Schalck & Yankol-Schalck, 2021). XGB represents an advanced implementation of Gradient Boosting (GB), a ML technique that builds predictive models by sequentially training decision trees, where each new tree corrects the errors made by the previous ones, to optimize both computational speed and model performance. XGB aggregates the outputs of multiple weak learners, typically shallow decision trees, to form a single, more accurate predictive model. The technique incorporates advanced regularization methods to reduce overfitting and employs innovative algorithms that allow for faster training and better scalability, making it a more robust and efficient version of GB. We use XGB to predict the PD by leveraging financial and credit behavioural indicators.

The optimization process is carried out using a ten-fold cross-validation strategy for each of the sub-models to ensure robust hyper-parameter selection (Table 3). This method helps in assessing the model performance across different subsets of the data, thus providing a better generalization.

The hyper-parameters selected are those that maximize the AUROC on the validation sets. Once the optimal hyper-parameters are identified, the final XGB model is trained on the entire training set and evaluated on the test set. The model ability to rank the predicted probabilities effectively is visualized using the ROC curve,

Table 3 Extreme Gradient Boosting hyper-parameters search space

Parameter	Type	Range
n_estimators	Integer	50 ÷ 500
learning_rate	Real	0.005 ÷ 0.3
max_depth	Integer	1 ÷ 10
reg_alpha	Real	0 ÷ 500
reg_lambda	Real	0 ÷ 500
n_iter	Integer	200
cv	Integer	10

Note n_estimators is the number of trees in the forest; *learning_rate* controls the contribution of each tree to the final model, balancing model complexity and learning speed; *max_depth* determines the maximum depth of each tree and helps to control overfitting by limiting the tree's complexity; *reg_alpha* is the L1, or Lasso, regularization term on weights, which adds a penalty to the absolute values of the weights to encourage sparsity and prevents overfitting; *reg_lambda* is the L2, or Ridge, regularization term on weights, which adds a penalty to the squared values of the weights to prevent overfitting by discouraging large coefficients; *n_iter*, is the number of iterations for the hyper-parameter search; *cv* is the number of folds which represents the true positive rate against the false positive rate at various threshold settings.

An important feature of XGB is the robustness to overfitting, which is achieved through the combination of boosting and regularization techniques. In XGB, this robustness is further enhanced by the regularization parameters that add penalties for large coefficients, avoiding the risk that the model becomes overly complex and thus reducing the risk of overfitting. By controlling the size of the coefficients, regularization ensures that the model remains generalizable to new, unseen data, striking a balance between fitting the training data and maintaining predictive power on the test set.

3.4 Deep Learning

Deep learning uses artificial neural networks to perform complex computations on large amounts of data. This type of ML, which resembles the structure of the human brain, has emerged as a powerful tool in credit risk estimation. Neural networks consist of layers of interconnected nodes, or neurons, that process input data. Each neuron receives inputs, performs a computation, and passes the result to the next layer. These networks typically include an input layer, multiple hidden layers, and an output layer. In the hidden layers, neurons apply weights to the inputs and pass them through an activation function to introduce non-linearity, allowing the network to learn complex patterns. The output layer generates the final predictions. Deep learning arises when multiple hidden layers are employed within a neural network. As the number of layers increases, the network gains the ability to detect more intricate patterns and complex relationships within the data.

In classification tasks, such as credit risk assessment, neural networks categorize input data into predefined classes. The input features—such as financial ratios, payment records—are fed to the network. The network processes these features through its layers, adjusting the weights during training to minimize the error between its predictions and the actual outcomes. The final output is a probability score that indicates the likelihood of a firm defaulting. By leveraging multiple hidden layers, deep learning models can reveal hidden relationships in financial datasets, allowing for the estimation of complex, non-linear relationships (LeCun et al., 2015). This capability arises from the evolution of the weights that connect the neurons in the hidden layers. As the model is trained, these weights are adjusted through back-propagation, enabling the network to learn and model the non-linear relationships present in financial data. This approach is particularly advantageous in assessing credit risk, as it allows the model to uncover patterns that traditional linear models may overlook.

In applying deep learning to firm default prediction, the architecture of the model is crucial. The designed network consists of multiple layers, each serving a specific role in transforming the input data into a meaningful output that reflects the probability of default. The sub-models are implemented using *Keras*,[10] a high-level neural networks library that simplifies the construction and training of deep learning models. The architecture includes dense and fully connected layers with varying numbers of neurons, activation functions to introduce non-linearity, and dropout layers for regularization.

As an example, Fig. 2 illustrates the neural network architecture used to estimate the sub-model of ordinary balance sheets within the industrial macro-sector. This architecture comprises several layers (input, hidden, output), depicted at the bottom with their vector dimensions, each serving a specific function in the network overall performance. The input layer is composed of multiple nodes, each corresponding to an input variable relevant to credit analysis.[11] The network ability to generalize from the training to unseen data—i.e. data not included in the training set—is crucial for achieving reliable predictions. This capability heavily depends on configuring the hidden layers effectively, as their structure and parameters enable the network to capture underlying data patterns. This generalization allows the model to accurately assess the default risk of firms that it has not encountered during training, ensuring its robustness across scenarios. For representation purposes, the number of neurons in each hidden layer is displayed, highlighting the architecture complexity and capacity for learning intricate patterns. The final layer in the network is the output layer, which consists of a single neuron that produces the prediction of default. This output is a probability score indicating the likelihood that a firm will default based on the input variables processed through the network.

Regularization techniques are essential in neural network training to mitigate overfitting, a common issue if the model performs well on the training data, but poorly on the test data (see Appendix A). As for RFs and XGB, a thorough hyper-parameter search is conducted for this model (Table 4).

Hyper-parameter optimization through cross-validation is essential in deep learning (see Appendix A), as in all ML models. To further improve model training, *early stopping* and *reduce learning rate on plateau* techniques are used.[12] We also note that the computational demands of training multiple deep learning models necessitate the use of Graphics Processing Units (GPUs).[13]

---

[10] *Keras* is an open-source software library that provides a Python interface for artificial neural networks.

[11] See Chap. 3 for a detailed definition of the financial and credit indicators used across the various models.

[12] The first one monitors the validation loss and halts training when the loss stops to decrease, preventing overfitting. The second technique reduces the learning rate when the validation loss levels off or plateaus. This adjustment allows the model to fine-tune its weights with greater precision, adapting to smaller gradients as it approaches an optimal solution.

[13] A GPU (Graphics Processing Unit) is a specialized processor designed to accelerate the rendering of images and video, but it has become essential in deep learning due to its ability to perform parallel processing on large datasets. Unlike CPUs, which are optimized for sequential tasks, GPUs can execute thousands of operations simultaneously, making them highly efficient for training neural networks, especially when dealing with complex models and large-scale data. GPUs, such as the

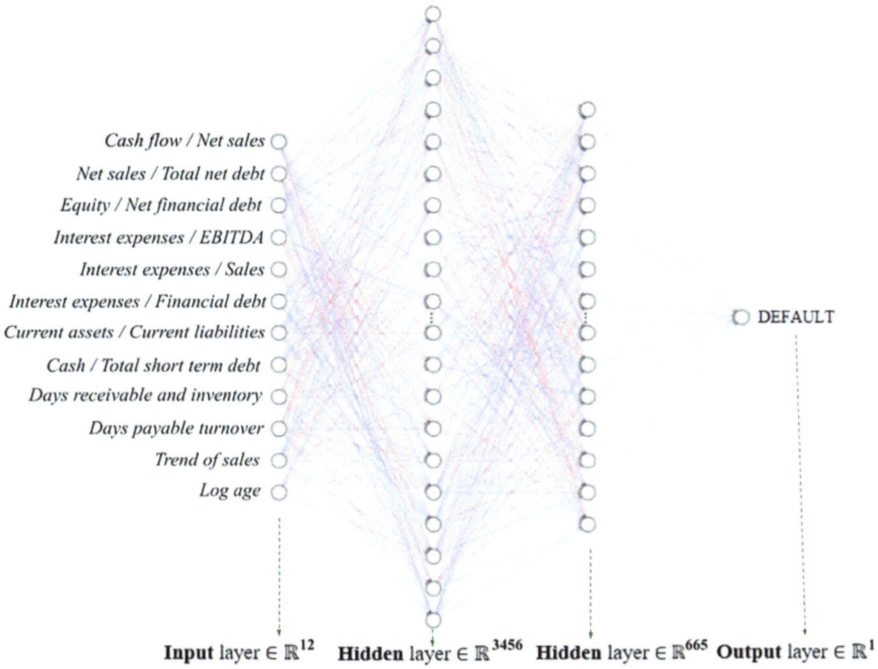

Fig. 2 Industry ordinary balance sheet neural network

Table 4 Neural network hyper-parameters search space

Parameter	Type	Range
dense_1_units	Integer	$2048 \div 6144$
dense_2_units	Integer	$2048 \div 6144$
dense_1_dropout	Real	$0.01 \div 0.99$
dense_2_dropout	Real	$0.01 \div 0.99$
learning_rate	Real	$1 \times 10^{-4} \div 5 \times 10^{-1}$
reg_strength	Real	$1 \times 10^{-6} \div 1 \times 10^{-3}$
activations	Categorical	relu, selu, elu, tanh, swish
batch_size	Integer	$32 \div 64$

Note The number of neurons in each layer is *dense_x_units*; the dropout rates are *dense_x_dropout,* for the hidden layers, the strength of regularization is *reg_strength. Batch_size* significantly affects the model performance and training stability helping to prevent overfitting, without compromising the efficiency of computation and the speed of convergence. The optimal combination of hyper-parameters is searched with Bayesian optimization, facilitated by the KerasTuner library

Finally, although the AUROC of the deep learning model on the test set may be slightly lower than traditional models like RF and XGB, its inclusion in a stacked ensemble model boosts the overall performance (see Sect. 4). The ensemble leverages the strengths of each model, resulting in better generalization, meaning that the model performs well not only on training data, but also on new, unseen data, reducing the risk of overfitting.

3.5 Stacked Model

Model stacking (Wolpert, 1992) is a powerful ensemble learning technique that combines multiple machine learning models to produce a single, more accurate predictive model. By integrating various models, stacking leverages the strengths of each model, thereby mitigating their weaknesses and enhancing the overall performance. In stacking, the base models are trained on the training data, then a meta-model is trained to make the final predictions based on the outputs of these base models.[14] This approach captures a diverse range of patterns and relationships within the data, which might be missed by a single model, thus improving generalization and robustness.

The benefits of stacking are manifold (Alexandropoulos et al., 2019; Dietterich, 2000). First, it improves predictive accuracy by incorporating the unique strengths of different models. In this study, the final model for predicting firms' defaults is derived through the stacking of RFs, XGB, and deep learning models (Fig. 3). While tree-based models, such as RFs and XGB, are best suited for structured data and the identification of non-linear relationships, deep learning models excel at capturing complex patterns and interactions within the data (Shwartz-Ziv & Armon, 2022). By combining these models, stacking ensures that the final prediction is well-rounded and robust. Second, stacking can help to reduce the risk of overfitting by allowing a meta-model to learn how to optimally combine the predictions from multiple base models. This is achieved by training the meta-model on a validation set, where it assesses the strengths and weaknesses of each base model predictions. By assigning appropriate weights to the base models according to their performance, the meta-model effectively balances their individual biases and

NVIDIA® GeForce RTX™ 4080, are designed to handle the parallel processing required for training deep learning models efficiently. The NVIDIA® GeForce RTX™ 4080 is a powerful graphics processing unit (GPU) designed for high-performance tasks like gaming, deep learning, and complex computations. Based on NVIDIA's Ampere architecture, it provides advanced features like ray tracing and AI-enhanced graphics. With its improved tensor cores and support for technologies such as DLSS (Deep Learning Super Sampling), the RTX 4080 is particularly well-suited for speeding up deep learning model training and other intensive workloads. In this project, leveraging GPU capabilities facilitated the training of sub-models across various balance sheet and credit rating models, with the entire process taking approximately 12 days.

[14] In order to train the meta-model, the output of base models is obtained through a cross-validation procedure in order to avoid overfitting (Breiman, 1996).

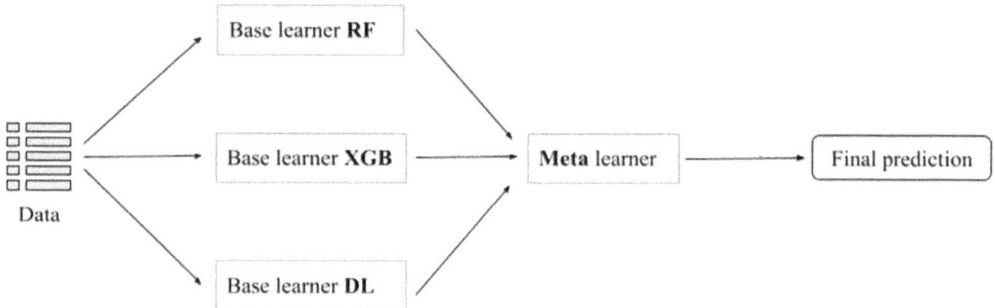

Fig. 3 ICAS stacked machine learning model for predicting firms' PDs

variances. This process results in a more generalized and robust final prediction, minimizing the overfitting risk that any single model might introduce.

The stacked model process begins with the training of the base models—RFs, XGB, and the deep learning—on the dataset. Each model generates its predictions, which serve as input features for the meta-model. The meta-model, trained with logistic regression on these predictions, is responsible for making the final decision. By learning the optimal way to combine the base model predictions, the meta-model effectively enhances the overall performance. The inclusion of deep learning in the stacking ensemble is noteworthy. While the AUROC of the deep learning model on the test set may slightly lag behind the RF and XGB models individually, its contribution to the stacked model is significant. The deep learning model unveils complex dependencies and interactions that the other models might overlook, thus enriching the feature set for the meta-model and leading to more accurate predictions.

4 Models' Results

The S-ICAS currently used by the Bank of Italy has been trained on a different dataset than the one used in this work. To properly compare the performance of the models, we decided to train not only the ML models, but also to re-train S-ICAS, using the same dataset described in Sect. 3. The performance of the models is assessed with AUROC. In the following, we report the results for each of the three main components of S-ICAS.

Table 5 AUROC for the financial component

Year	S-ICAS	Random forests	XGBoost	Deep learning	Stacked
2014	0.737	0.760	0.761	0.757	0.764
2023	0.755	0.786	0.788	0.782	0.791

4.1 Financial Component

We show the aggregated[15] AUROC of ML models and that of S-ICAS financial component (Table 5).

We first note that, in general, the models perform better in 2023. This may depend on the difference in the percentage of ordinary balance sheets available in those two years. While for 2014 the number of available ordinary balance sheets was less than half the number of simplified financial statements, for 2023 the situation was reversed. This is important because models estimated on ordinary balance sheets are superior, in terms of AUROC, to corresponding models estimated on simplified financial statements (see Appendix B). This was expected since ordinary financial statements contain more information than simplified financial statements.

In comparing the discriminatory power of the methods, we observe that the performances of RF and XGBoost are very similar, and superior to that of the S-ICAS financial component, with an approximate 2.3 to 3.3 percentage point increase in AUROC, depending on the year. Deep learning also performs better than S-ICAS, but the AUROC increments are slightly less pronounced.

To further enhance the discriminatory power, we integrate the predictions obtained from all three ML methods using the stacking method. The discriminatory power of the meta-model is slightly superior to that of RF and XGBoost (almost 0.5 percentage points), showing the potential of combining different ML approaches to achieve improved performance, and illustrating the value of ensemble and stacking techniques in ML.[16]

4.2 Credit Behaviour Component

We show the aggregated[17] AUROC of ML models and that of S-ICAS credit behaviour component (Table 6).

[15] The performance of ML models on each one of the eleven sub-component of S-ICAS financial module are reported in Appendix B.

[16] We conducted a bootstrap analysis to verify the statistical significance of these results with 95% confidence intervals for the difference between the AUROC of ML models and of S-ICAS (Appendix C, Table 12).

[17] The performance of ML models on each one of three sub-components of S-ICAS credit behaviour module are reported in Appendix B.

Table 6 AUROC for the credit behaviour component

Year	S-ICAS	Random forests	XGBoost	Deep learning	Stacked
2014	0.864	0.868	0.870	0.869	0.870
2023	0.823	0.835	0.838	0.829	0.839

Table 7 Comparison between AUROC of complete models

Year	S-ICAS	Stacked
2014	0.874	0.880
2023	0.854	0.873

First, we observe that AUROC values are far greater than the ones observed in Table 5. This was expected since the credit behaviour component is estimated using high quality NCR data, that are also available with a shorter delay than it is the case for financial statement data. Second, we note that ML models still outperform S-ICAS, but the increments in AUROC, between 0.5 and 1.5 percentage points, are less pronounced than the ones obtained for the financial component, in line with the findings of Moscatelli et al., 2020. Third, the disruptions caused by the Covid-19 pandemic blurred the information conveyed by firms' credit and financial indicators, also due to the measures which supported firms' liquidity, denting models' accuracy after the pandemic. Lastly, we observe that the model built using the stacking method has the same performance or slightly outperforms each one of the base models,[18] but the increments in AUROC are less noticeable than the ones obtained in the financial component.

4.3 Complete Model

In this Section, we present the results of the integrated models (the financial component merged with the credit behaviour component) in terms of discriminatory power. Since the best ML model is the one obtained using stacking, both for the financial and the credit behaviour component, we show the comparison between the aggregated AUROC of the meta-model and that of S-ICAS (Table 7).

As expected, the two complete models outperform both the corresponding financial and credit behaviour component in terms of AUROC. We also note that the meta-model outperforms S-ICAS in 2014 (by 0.6 percentage points), and especially in 2023 (by 1.9 percentage points). This finding likely reflects a greater robustness of the meta-model. The aftermath of the Covid pandemic, as noted in the previous sub-section, suggests that the meta-model may be more resilient to

[18] We conducted a bootstrap analysis to verify the statistical significance of these results with 95% confidence intervals for the difference between the AUROC of ML models and of S-ICAS (Appendix C, Table 13).

Table 8 Comparison between AUROC of complete models with Covid period

Year	S-ICAS	Stacked
2014	0.874	0.880
2020	0.872	0.885
2021	0.838	0.852
2023	0.854	0.873

the challenges posed to models by the decrease in the precision of credit quality information caused by the disruption to the economic activity and the associated mitigating measures.

5 Robustness

To understand if the last finding derives from the greater stability of the meta-model, we report the performance of the two models during the Covid period, 2020–2021 (Table 8).

The performance gap (in terms of AUROC) between the meta-model and S-ICAS widens over the years: in 2014, the difference is 0.6 percentage points; in 2020, at the onset of the Covid crisis, the gap increases to 1.3 percentage points; and in 2021, it reaches 1.4 percentage points. Moreover, in 2023, in the aftermath of the pandemic, even if there are still effects of the Covid-19 crisis on the variables used by the models,[19] the performance of both models improves. However, the difference between the two AUROC grows further, and it is equal to 1.9 percentage points.[20]

Thus, we conclude that: (i) the meta-model is less affected by the disruptions that occurred in 2020 and 2021 than S-ICAS; (ii) the meta-model performance appears to have recovered, after the pandemic, more than S-ICAS. We believe that the greater robustness of the meta-model depends on: (i) the ability of ML models to capture non-linear and non-monotonic effects, as noted in Moscatelli et al., 2020; (ii) the use of stacking, which improves robustness as it aggregates different base models.

[19] To predict 2023 PDs, 2021 financial statements data are used.

[20] We conducted a bootstrap analysis to verify the statistical significance of these results with 95% confidence intervals for the difference between the AUROC of the stacked model and of S-ICAS (Appendix C, Table 14).

6 Forecast Explanations

The default probabilities generated by ML models can significantly differ from those produced by S-ICAS. For instance, Fig. 4 shows the normalized histogram of the statistical distribution of the difference between the PDs produced by the meta-model and by S-ICAS for 2023.

These differences can be substantial, given that the average default probabilities produced by both models are around 1.5 percentage points. As shown in the previous Sections, the meta-model consistently outperforms and is more robust than S-ICAS. Consequently, if the probability of default produced by the meta-model significantly differs from that generated by S-ICAS for the same firm, it could indicate that S-ICAS faces a challenge in the assessment of the riskiness of the company. This discrepancy could serve as the basis for an alert system that flags such cases to the financial analysts in charge of the expert assessment stage. However, without any hints on the main reasons behind the difference between the two PDs, the utility of the tool would be limited. Hence, we are interested in a methodology capable of offering insight into the contribution of each input variable to the difference between the two PDs. Such information would allow financial analysts to concentrate on the most problematic areas, to understand if S-ICAS PD has indeed appropriately captured the company's credit risk. It is possible to associate

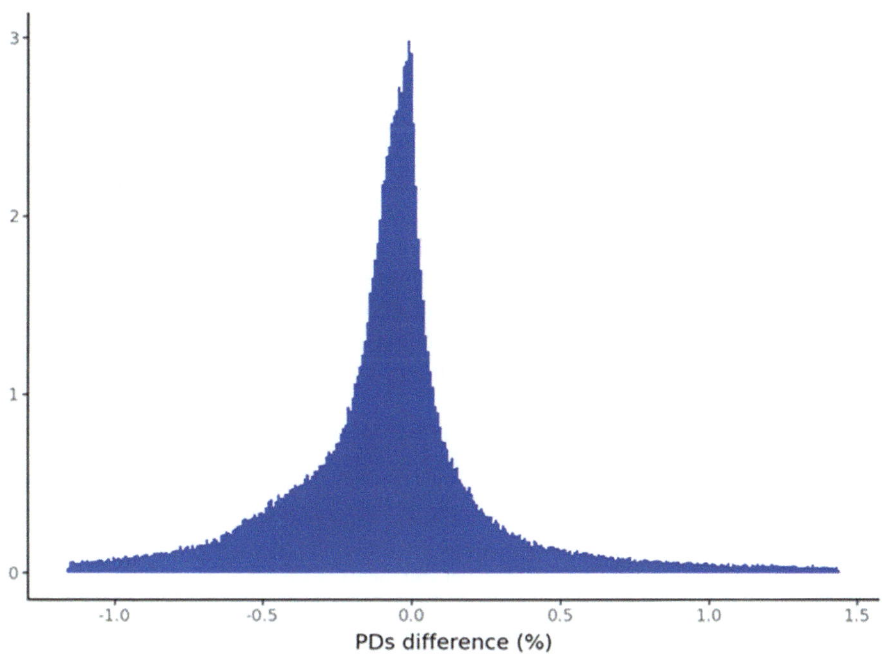

Fig. 4 Statistical distribution of the difference between meta-model and S-ICAS PDs

each variable with its contribution to the prediction of any model using a specific XAI technique, the Shapley values, as discussed below.

6.1 Shapley Values

Shapley values, originating from game theory (Shapley, 1953), provide a method to fairly distribute the total expected payout in a cooperative game among its participants, ensuring that certain desirable properties are satisfied (see Appendix D).[21] In recent years, this technique has been applied to machine learning (Štrumbelj & Kononenko, 2014).

The application is straightforward; let's assume we have a model that maps variables $\boldsymbol{x} = (x_1, x_2, \ldots, x_K) \in \mathbb{R}^K$ to a prediction $f(\boldsymbol{x}) \in \mathbb{R}$. To determine the contribution of each variable to a specific prediction $f(\boldsymbol{x}^*)$ we can find its Shapley values ϕ_k (for $k = 1, 2, \ldots K$), where: (i) the values of the model's variables $\boldsymbol{x}^*$ take on the role of players; (ii) the value of the prediction $f(\boldsymbol{x}^*)$ takes on the role of the total expected payout; (iii) the average prediction $E\left[f(x)\right]$ takes on the role of the fixed payout of the game. In this case, the sum of all Shapley values is equal to the difference between $f(\boldsymbol{x}^*)$ and $E\left[f(x)\right]$.[22] Formally:

$$\sum_{k=1}^{K} \phi_k = f(\boldsymbol{x}^*) - E\left[f(x)\right]. \tag{1}$$

In order to calculate Shapley values, it is necessary to know (or to approximate) the joint distributions of the K variables $\boldsymbol{x}$.. Besides, due to the computational burden of the exact Shapley value calculation, several approximation algorithms have been developed, such as the 'Shapley sampling value' (Štrumbelj & Kononenko, 2014)[23] and the 'Kernel SHAP' (Lundberg & Lee, 2017a, 2017b). While the latter is more computationally efficient, both methods assume that the variables are independent (see Appendix D). This type of approximation is not accurate in many cases, such as in S-ICAS, where there is a non-negligible correlation among variables. To address this problem, Aas et al. (2021) develop some approximation algorithms that compute more accurate Shapley values, taking into consideration the variables' correlation. In this work, we use their methods to compute the Shapley values.[24]

---

[21] In this context, a player's Shapley value corresponds to the payout he deserves, i.e. it quantifies the player's contribution to the team's win. Moreover, the sum of all the Shapley values is equal to the difference between the total expected payout and the fixed payout of the game (if the latter is different from 0).

[22] If we do not know the value of any variable, the best possible prediction is the expected value of the model output.

[23] This method has been applied for explaining ML predictions in Cascarino et al. (2022).

[24] The algorithms developed in Aas et al. (2021) are available in an R package, *shapr*, and in a Python package, *shaprpy*, which is a wrapper of the R package.

6.2 Shapley Values for ICAS Expert Assessment

We build an application to obtain, for a given firm, the Shapley values related to the difference between the PD forecast with the meta-model and the one produced with S-ICAS. This application is built to explain the difference in the financial PDs or the difference in the credit behaviour PDs, since financial analysts look at the two components separately during their analysis.

It is possible to show (see Appendix D) that, by calculating the Shapley values related to the difference in the predictions between the two models, for a specific observation $\boldsymbol{x}^*$ we approximately get:

$$\sum_{k=1}^{K} \phi_k \approx f_m(\boldsymbol{x}^*) - f_s(\boldsymbol{x}^*), \tag{2}$$

where ϕ_k, for $k = 1, 2, \dots K$, are the Shapley values, $f_m(\boldsymbol{x}^*)$ is the PD produced by the meta-model and $f_s(\boldsymbol{x}^*)$ is the one produced by S-ICAS.[25] This approximation holds for the most problematic cases, the ones where the two PDs are very different from each other. For example, it holds when the two PDs belong to two not adjacent Credit Quality Steps (CQSs).[26] In those cases, the sum of Shapley values is approximately equal to the difference between the two PDs.

Next we present an example from this tool.[27] Consider an industrial firm where the S-ICAS financial component predicts a default probability of 0.51%, while the meta-model predicts a PD of 1.57%. The meta-model deems the firm as much riskier. The Shapley values explaining the difference between the two PDs provide insights into the variables which mostly influence the higher risk signalled by the meta-model (Fig. 5).

In this example, the variables '*interest expenses divided by EBITDA*', '*days payables turnover*'[28] and '*cash flow divided by net sales*' have the largest Shapley value. Consequently, these indicators are the ones that contribute more to the positive difference in PDs.[29]

[25] The expected value in Eq. (1) has vanished. Since each S-ICAS sub-model uses specific indicators, Eq. (2) needs to be applied separately for each sub-model.

[26] The CQSs are the core of the Eurosystem's harmonized rating scale. For further details, see European Central Bank (2015) and Chap. 3.

[27] We present a second example in Appendix E.

[28] The average number of days it takes a company to pay back its accounts payable.

[29] To better understand this point, we consulted a financial analyst to assess the firm's financial condition. The analyst, paying attention to the three variables reported above, said that the firm had low margins and a good part of the company liquidity was absorbed by suppliers. This analysis reveals that the company has limited available liquidity and a low capacity for cash generation, which could become problematic, especially during periods of financial distress. For these reasons, a PD of 0.51% seems to be too low when compared to the true riskiness of the firm, while a PD of 1.57% is more appropriate. There are also variables with a negative Shapley value. These variables contribute negatively to the difference between the two PDs, i.e. they indicate that, for the meta-model, there are some aspects of the firm's financial situation that S-ICAS has judged

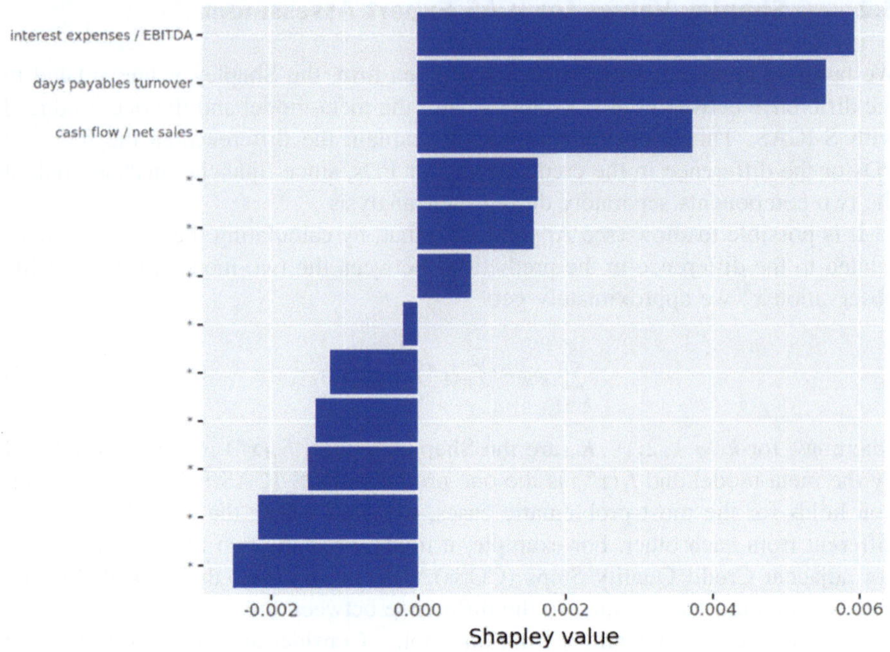

Fig. 5 Shapley values for the industrial company

In the example we show how Shapley values can clarify aspects that may have represented a challenge for S-ICAS. We believe that the issue often lies in the presence of interaction effects among variables. In fact, S-ICAS is a multivariate logistic model that is additive in its nature. In some cases, a combination of some variables could have a strong positive or negative effect on a firm's conditions, and this effect might not be reflected accurately in S-ICAS PD. While it is true that Shapley values are not always straightforward to interpret,[30] in cases where there is a dominance of highly positive (or negative) Shapley values, this tool may be an effective support for ICAS financial analysts.

7 Conclusions

In this Chapter we use three machine-learning models—random forests, extreme gradient boosting and deep learning, as well as a meta-model that integrates predictions from the three models, to replicate the Bank of Italy's ICAS statistical

too negatively. However, in this case these variables have a small weight, so they provide a small contribution.

[30] It is possible to have at the same time both high positive and negative Shapley values. These situations can be hard to interpret.

model, which is estimated with logistic regressions. The dataset includes financial and credit behaviour variables for hundreds of thousands of Italian non-financial companies, from 2014 to 2023.

Within the financial component of S-ICAS, we observe that RF and XGBoost yield an improvement of the discriminatory power, as measured by the AUROC, of 2.3 to 3.3 percentage points over logistic regressions, while deep learning yields slightly less pronounced increments. ML models provide an increase in discriminatory power, though smaller, also in the credit behaviour component (between 0.5 and 1.5 percentage points). We also find that the meta-model that integrates the predictions from the three ML models outperforms the individual models. When looking at the complete model, the meta-model consistently outperforms the discriminatory power of S-ICAS by 0.6 to 1.9 percentage points depending on the year. Furthermore, the meta-model performance is less affected by the disruptions that occurred in 2020 and 2021 and shows a stronger performance recovery than S-ICAS in the post-pandemic period.

Meta-model PDs could be used by financial analysts in the expert assessment stage to improve ICAS ratings, by focusing on aspects where ML models and S-ICAS provide different signals. To make this information explainable, we build a tool that provides financial analysts with the contribution of each variable of the model to the PD difference, using Shapley values. This tool can highlight aspects that may have not been fully grasped by S-ICAS, enabling analysts to focus on the most problematic areas of the analysis. Nevertheless, caution is needed, since the interpretation of Shapley values may be challenging, especially when both highly positive and highly negative values are present. These conditions also show that the credit assessment process cannot rely only on ML models, reflecting also regulatory concerns, due to their complexity which makes them difficult to be interpreted and understood by all the relevant stakeholders. Overall, our results indicate that ML models have the potential to enhance both the efficiency and quality of the ICAS process, refining and reinforcing it through a comprehensive and effective analysis of firm-related information.

Appendix A

Methods

Cross-Validation and Optimization

As for cross-validation, in stratified K-fold cross-validation, the data is divided into K folds, ensuring a proportional representation of each class in every fold. The model is iteratively trained on K-1 folds and validated on the remaining fold, with this process repeated K times so that each fold is used as a validation set exactly once. This approach provides a comprehensive evaluation of the model performance across different data splits, reducing the variance associated with a single train-test split. We set the number of folds to 10, as specified by the *cv* parameter, ensuring a thorough and reliable evaluation.

Cross-validation is used to maximize the validation AUROC, guiding the search process toward configurations that enhance the model ability to discriminate between default and non-default cases. The search inside the hyper-parameter space is conducted using Bayesian optimization, which is a probabilistic, model-based approach that constructs a surrogate model to approximate the objective function. It uses this surrogate to select the most promising hyper-parameters to evaluate, balancing exploration and exploitation. This method is particularly effective for complex search spaces, as it converges to optimal solutions more efficiently than grid or random search methods.[31]

In the context of hyper-parameter optimization, there are several specialized software libraries designed to efficiently search for the best combination of parameters. Among these, *scikit-optimize* stands out as a particularly effective tool. This library provides advanced algorithms for Bayesian optimization. The decision to use scikit-optimize is based on its flexibility in handling various types of hyper-parameters (including both continuous and categorical variables). Compared to other libraries, *scikit-optimize* offers a balance between ease of use and powerful optimization techniques, making it one of the best choices for hyper-parameter tuning in machine learning models.

Regularization and Training in Deep Learning

Regularization in deep learning involves adding penalties to the loss function for larger weights, preventing the model from becoming overly complex and overfitting the training data. By discouraging the network from assigning excessive importance to any single feature, regularization ensures that the model generalizes better to new, unseen data, ultimately leading to more robust predictions. Dropout, a different form of regularization, operates by randomly deactivating a fraction of neurons during each training iteration. This operation avoids that the network becomes too dependent on any single neuron or small group of neurons, which might otherwise capture patterns specific only to the training data. As a result, the network is forced to distribute the learning process across multiple neurons, leading to the development of a more robust and diverse feature representation.

Stochastic Gradient Descent (SGD) is a fundamental optimization method employed in training deep learning, especially in the backpropagation process. In the context of backpropagation, SGD iteratively adjusts the model weights by computing the gradient of the loss function with respect to each weight. Instead of calculating the gradient over the entire dataset, SGD uses a randomly selected subset of the data (a mini-batch) to update the weights, making the process faster and more scalable for large datasets. This iterative adjustment helps the model minimize the loss function and gradually converge toward the optimal set of weights, improving accuracy. For all the sub-models estimated, the optimizer chosen is

[31] For a survey on optimization algorithms see, for example, Yu and Zhu (2020).

Table 9 AUROC for the financial component - ordinary financial statement

Sector	S-ICAS	Random forests	XGBoost	Deep learning
Industry	0.832	0.854	0.852	0.849
Trade	0.781	0.809	0.806	0.804
Construction	0.783	0.807	0.812	0.803
Services	0.782	0.801	0.801	0.796
Real estate	0.820	0.837	0.830	0.834

Table 10 AUROC for the financial component—simplified financial statement

Sector	S-ICAS	Random forests	XGBoost	Deep learning
Industry	0.774	0.789	0.795	0.792
Trade	0.738	0.771	0.770	0.769
Construction	0.713	0.739	0.741	0.738
Services	0.741	0.759	0.761	0.757
Real estate	0.759	0.774	0.776	0.774
Holding	0.750	0.773	0.785	0.757

Adam,[32] renowned for its adaptive learning rate capabilities, which combines the benefits of two other extensions of stochastic gradient descent, namely *AdaGrad*[33] and *RMSProp*.[34] The loss function selected is the *binary cross entropy*, which is well-suited for binary classification tasks as it measures the performance of the model by comparing the predicted probabilities to the actual binary labels, thereby guiding the model to improve its predictions through gradient descent.

Appendix B

S-ICAS and ML Sub-Models Performance

In Tables 9 and 10 we report the discriminatory power, calculated in terms of AUROC on the entire test set, of S-ICAS and ML models, for each financial sub-component.

[32] *Adam* is an adaptive optimizer widely used in deep learning, known for efficiently handling sparse gradients and noisy data. It adjusts the learning rate dynamically for each parameter during training, which helps to improve convergence and model performance in a variety of tasks.
[33] *AdaGrad* (Adaptive Gradient Algorithm) is an optimization method that adapts the learning rate for each parameter, improving convergence on sparse data.
[34] *RMSProp* (Root Mean Square Propagation) is an optimization algorithm that adjusts the learning rate for each parameter based on the moving average of recent gradient magnitudes.

Table 11 AUROC for the credit behaviour component

Size	S-ICAS	Random forests	XGBoost	Deep learning
Micro	0.856	0.862	0.864	0.861
Small	0.884	0.891	0.892	0.888
Medium-large	0.871	0.873	0.873	0.871

In Table 11 we report the discriminatory power, calculated on the entire test set, of S-ICAS and ML models, for each credit behaviour sub-component.

Appendix C

AUROC Confidence Intervals

The superior discriminatory power of ML models showed in Sects. 4 and 5 is statistically significant. Using bootstrap, we construct 95% confidence intervals for the difference in the AUROC of ML models and the AUROC of S-ICAS. As we can see from Tables 12, 13, and 14, the lower limit of all the confidence intervals is always greater than zero.

Table 12 95% confidence intervals for AUROC difference—ML vs S-ICAS financial component

Year	Random forests	XGBoost	Deep learning	Stacked
2014	(0.020, 0.025)	(0.022, 0.027)	(0.018, 0.022)	(0.025, 0.029)
2023	(0.027, 0.035)	(0.030, 0.038)	(0.023, 0.031)	(0.033, 0.040)

Table 13 95% confidence intervals for AUROC difference—ML vs S-ICAS credit component

Year	Random forests	XGBoost	Deep learning	Stacked
2014	(0.002, 0.004)	(0.004, 0.006)	(0.004, 0.005)	(0.005, 0.007)
2023	(0.010, 0.015)	(0.013, 0.018)	(0.005, 0.008)	(0.014, 0.018)

Table 14 95% confidence intervals for AUROC difference—ML vs S-ICAS complete models

Year	Stacked
2014	(0.005, 0.007)
2020	(0.012, 0.015)
2021	(0.011, 0.015)
2023	(0.017, 0.021)

Appendix D

Mathematical Theory Behind Shapley Values

In a cooperative game with K players the goal is to maximise a payout v, with the function $v : S \rightarrow v(S)$ associating each subset $S \subseteq M = \{1, 2, \ldots, K\}$ of players with the expected payout they can win together. Shapley values distribute the total expected payout $v(M)$ among the K players, ensuring that some desirable properties are met.

For a player k, with $k = 1, 2, \ldots K$, the payout portion (his contribution to the team's win) is called Shapley value, denoted as ϕ_k. These values uniquely satisfy the following desirable properties (Shapley, 1953):

(1) (*Additivity*) The total payout is distributed additively among players:

$$\sum_{k=0}^{K} \phi_k = v(M), \tag{3}$$

where ϕ_0, if it differs from 0, represents a fixed payout not dependent on the players' contributions.

(2) If two players i, j contribute equally to the payout regardless of the other players participating, i.e.:

$$v(S \cup \{i\}) = v(S \cup \{j\}), \tag{4}$$

for every $S \subseteq M \backslash \{i, j\}$, then their Shapley values ϕ_i and ϕ_j are equal.

(3) If a player's inclusion does not increase the expected payout for any group, i.e.:

$$v(S \cup \{i\}) = v(S), \tag{5}$$

for every $S \subseteq M \backslash \{i\}$, then its Shapley values ϕ_i is equal a 0.

(4) (*Linearity*) For two games with payout functions v and w, a player's Shapley value for the combined game equals the sum of his Shapley values for each game:

$$\phi_k(v + w) = \phi_k(v) + \phi_k(w), \tag{6}$$

for each $k = 1, 2, \ldots, K$. Additionally, for any real constant α: $\phi_k(\alpha v) = \alpha\phi_k(v)$.

Now, let's assume that we have a model that maps variables $\boldsymbol{x} = (x_1, x_2, \ldots, x_K) \in \mathbb{R}^K$ to a prediction $f(\boldsymbol{x}) \in \mathbb{R}$. If we want to explain a specific prediction $f(\boldsymbol{x}^*)$ we can find its Shapley values, where:

(1) The values of the K variables $\boldsymbol{x}^* = \left(x_1^*, x_2^*, \ldots, x_K^*\right)$ take on the role of players.

(2) The prediction $f(\boldsymbol{x}^*)$ takes on the role of the payout $v(M)$ and the expected value of the prediction of the model $E[f(\boldsymbol{x})]$ represents the fixed payout that does not depend on the contribution of the variables/players (ϕ_0). The property of additivity (Equation A.1) can then be rewritten:

$$\sum_{k=1}^{K} \phi_k = f(\boldsymbol{x}^*) - E[f(\boldsymbol{x})]. \tag{7}$$

To compute Shapley values, the reward function $v : S \rightarrow v(S)$ must be known for every subset S of the model's variables. Consistently with the definition provided earlier, the reward function for each subset S can be defined (Štrumbelj & Kononenko, 2014) as the expected value of the model's prediction knowing only the values of the variables $\boldsymbol{x}^*$ present in S (denoted as $\boldsymbol{x}_S^*$):

$$v(S) = E[f(\boldsymbol{x})|\boldsymbol{x}_S = \boldsymbol{x}_S^*]. \tag{8}$$

In other words, $v(S)$ represents the contribution that the knowledge of the value of the variables in S gives to the prediction.

Therefore, in order to calculate Shapley values, it is necessary to know (or to approximate) the joint distributions of the variables $\boldsymbol{x}$. Besides, due to the computational burden of the exact Shapley value calculation, several approximation algorithms have been developed. The algorithms that are most used in the literature have been defined in Štrumbelj and Kononenko (2014) and in Lundberg and Lee (2017b). However, those methods assume that the variables are independent, i.e. the conditional distribution of each subset of variables $\overline{S} = M \backslash S$ does not depend on the variables in S:

$$p(\boldsymbol{x}_{\overline{S}}|\boldsymbol{x}_S = \boldsymbol{x}_S^*) = p(\boldsymbol{x}_{\overline{S}}). \tag{9}$$

Instead, algorithms developed more recently in Aas et al. (2021) approximate $p(\boldsymbol{x}_{\overline{S}}|\boldsymbol{x}_S = \boldsymbol{x}_S^*)$ without using the independence assumption.

When applying Shapley values to the difference in the predictions between two models, using the additivity property (Eqs. A.1 and A.5), for a specific observation $\boldsymbol{x}^*$ we get:

$$\sum_{k=1}^{K} \phi_k = f_m(\boldsymbol{x}^*) - f_s(\boldsymbol{x}^*) - (E[f_m(\boldsymbol{x})] - E[f_s(\boldsymbol{x})]), \tag{10}$$

where $f_m(\boldsymbol{x}^*)$ is the PD produced by the first model and $f_s(\boldsymbol{x}^*)$ is the PD produced by the second model.

The two expected values in Eq. (A.8), $E[f_m(\boldsymbol{x})]$ and $E[f_s(\boldsymbol{x})]$, can both be approximated with the average prediction of the corresponding model on the training set. If the two models had been trained on the same dataset, this difference is generally small but in some cases it can be not negligible. However, if we concentrate on explaining the most problematic cases, where the PDs produced by the two models are very different from each other, we can simplify Eq. (A.8) and write:

$$\sum_{k=1}^{K} \phi_k \approx f_m(\boldsymbol{x}^*) - f_s(\boldsymbol{x}^*), \tag{11}$$

since in those cases $f_m(\boldsymbol{x}^*) - f_s(\boldsymbol{x}^*) \gg E[f_m(\boldsymbol{x})] - E[f_s(\boldsymbol{x})]$. This means that the sum of Shapley values is approximately equal to the difference between the two PDs.

Appendix E

Example on the Explainability of the Credit Behaviour Component

We consider a medium-large firm where S-ICAS credit behaviour component predicts a default probability of 0.99%, while the meta-model predicts a credit behaviour PD of 2.42%. The meta-model judges the company much riskier. Below we plot the Shapley values relative to the difference of the two PDs (Fig. 6).

As we can see, the variable "*number of months with overdraft on current account revolving credit lines*"[35] has by far the greatest Shapley value and contributes the most to the difference in PDs. The financial analyst, examining the company's situation, observed that not only the number of months with overdraft is high, but the company has also a discrete amount of "*unpaid amount on account receivables credit lines compared to net sales*" and of the variable "*drawn divided by granted on short term credit lines*" (in the last six months). According to the analyst's opinion, the combination of these aspects is enough to raise suspicions on the credit soundness of the company and on the value of S-ICAS PD, which has a very low value.

[35] The value is calculated looking at the past six months.

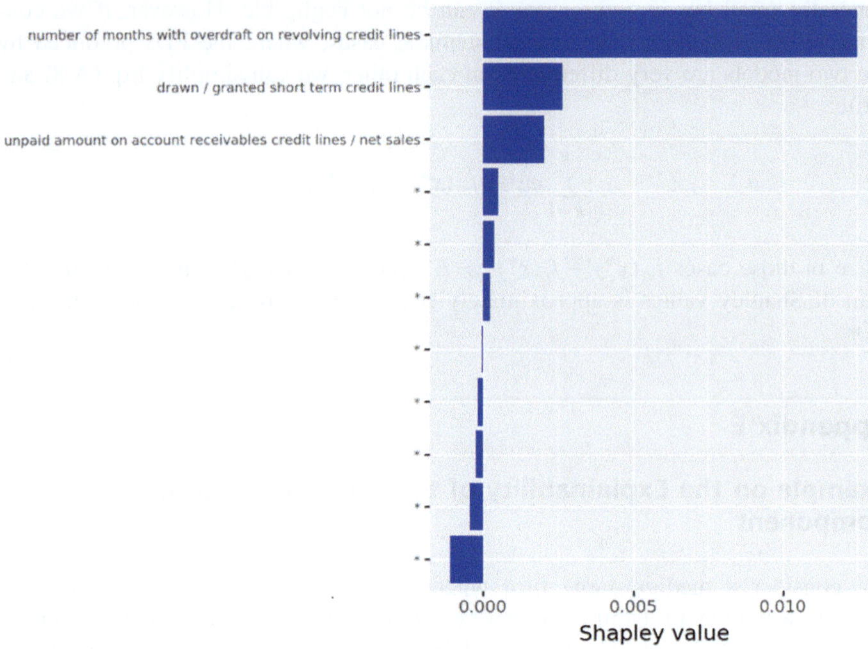

Fig. 6 Shapley values for the medium-large company[36]

References

Aas, K., Jullum, M., & Løland, A. (2021). Explaining individual predictions when features are dependent: More accurate approximations to Shapley values. *Artificial Intelligence, 298*, Article 103502.

Alexandropoulos, S.-A.N., Aridas, C. K., Kotsiantis, S. B., & Vrahatis, M. N. (2019). Stacking strong ensembles of classifiers. *Artificial Intelligence applications and innovations* (pp. 545–556). Springer.

Alom, M. Z., Taha, T. M., Yakopcic, C., Westberg, S., Sidike, P., Nasrin, M. S., & Asari, V. K. (2019). A state-of-the-art survey on deep learning theory and architectures. *Electronics, 8*(3), 292.

Altmann, A., Toloşi, L., Sander, O., & Lengauer, T. (2010). Permutation importance: A corrected feature importance measure. *Bioinformatics, 26*(10), 1340–1347.

Angelini, P. (2025). Data Science in Central Banking. *Remarks at the 4th workshop on "Data science in Central Banking"*, Banca d'Italia, 20 February 2025.

Apley, D. W., & Zhu, J. (2020). Visualizing the effects of predictor variables in black box supervised learning models. *Journal of the Royal Statistical Society Series B, Statistical Methodology, 82*(4), 1059–1086.

Barboza, F., Kimura, H., & Altman, E. (2017). Machine learning models and bankruptcy prediction. *Expert Systems with Applications, 83*, 405–417.

[36] For simplicity, only variables with the greatest Shapley values are reported.

Bitetto, A., Cerchiello, P., Filomeni, S., Tanda, A., & Tarantino, B. (2023). Machine learning and credit risk: Empirical evidence from small-and mid-sized businesses. *Socio-Economic Planning Sciences, 90*, Article 101746.

Breiman, L. (1996). Stacked regressions. *Machine Learning, 24*, 49–64.

Breiman, L. (2001a). Random forests. *Machine Learning, 45*, 5–32.

Breiman, L. (2001b). Statistical modeling: The two cultures (with comments and a rejoinder by the author). *Statistical Science, 16*(3), 199–231.

Bussmann, N., Giudici, P., Marinelli, D., & Papenbrock, J. (2021). Explainable machine learning in credit risk management. *Computational Economics, 57*(1), 203–216.

Cascarino, G., Moscatelli, M., & Parlapiano, F. (2022). Explainable artificial intelligence: interpreting default forecasting models based on machine learning. *Bank of Italy Occas Pap* 674.

Chen, T., & Guestrin, C. (2016). Xgboost: A scalable tree boosting system. In *Proceedings of the 22nd ACM SIGKDD International Conference on Knowledge Discovery and Data Mining* (pp. 785–794).

Ciampi, F., & Gordini, N. (2013). Small enterprise default prediction modeling through artificial neural networks: An empirical analysis of italian small enterprises. *Journal of Small Business Management, 51*(1), 23–45.

Dal Pozzolo, A., Caelen, O., & Bontempi, G. (2015). When is undersampling effective in unbalanced classification tasks? In *ECML PKDD 2015*, Porto, September 7–11, 2015 (pp. 200–215). Springer.

Dell, M. (2024). Deep learning for economists. *NBER Work Pap* 32768

Dietterich, T. G. (2000). Ensemble methods in machine learning. In *Multiple classifier systems* (pp. 1–15). Springer.

European Banking Authority. (2020). *EBA report on big data and advanced analytics.*

European Banking Authority. (2023). *Machine learning for IRB models. Follow-up Report from the Consultation on the Discussion Paper on Machine Learning for IRB Models.*

European Central Bank. (2015). *The financial risk management of the Eurosystem's monetary policy operations*, July.

Gregova, E., Valaskova, K., Adamko, P., Tumpach, M., & Jaros, J. (2020). Predicting financial distress of Slovak enterprises: Comparison of selected traditional and learning algorithms methods. *Sustainability, 12*(10), 3954.

He, H., & Garcia, E. A. (2009). Learning from imbalanced data. *IEEE Transactions on Knowledge and Data Engineering, 21*(9), 1263–1284.

Kohavi, R. (1995). A study of cross-validation and bootstrap for accuracy estimation and model selection. In *Proc 14th Int Joint Conf Artif Intell (IJCAI'95)* (pp. 1137–1143).

LeCun, Y., Bengio, Y., & Hinton, G. (2015). Deep learning. *Nature, 521*(7553), 436–444.

Li, Y., & Wang, Y. (2017). Machine learning methods of bankruptcy prediction using accounting ratios. *Open Journal of Business Management, 6*(1), 1–20.

Louppe, G., Wehenkel, L., Sutera, A., & Geurts, P. (2013). Understanding variable importances in forests of randomized trees. *Advances in Neural Information Processing Systems, 26*, 431–439.

Loyola-Gonzalez, O. (2019). Black-box vs. white-box: Understanding their advantages and weaknesses from a practical point of view. *IEEE Access, 7*, 154096–154113.

Lundberg, S. M., Erion, G., Chen, H., DeGrave, A., Prutkin, J. M., Nair, B., & Lee, S. I. (2020). From local explanations to global understanding with explainable AI for trees. *Nature Machine Intelligence, 2*(1), 56–67.

Lundberg, S. M., & Lee, S. I. (2017a). *Consistent feature attribution for tree ensembles.* arXiv: 1706.06060

Lundberg, S. M., & Lee, S. I. (2017b). A unified approach to interpreting model predictions. *Advances in Neural Information Processing Systems, 30*, 4765–4774.

Moscatelli, M., Parlapiano, F., Narizzano, S., & Viggiano, G. (2020). Corporate default forecasting with machine learning. *Expert Systems with Applications, 161*, Article 113567.

Narayanan, A., & Kapoor, S. (2024). *AI snake oil: What artificial intelligence can do, what it can't, and how to tell the difference.* Princeton University Press.

Petropoulos, A., Siakoulis, V., Stavroulakis, E., & Klamargias, A. (2019). A robust machine learning approach for credit risk analysis of large loan level datasets using deep learning and extreme gradient boosting. *IFC Bulletins Chapters, 49.*

Ribeiro, M. T., Singh, S., & Guestrin, C. (2016). "Why should I trust you?" Explaining the predictions of any classifier. In *Proc 22nd ACM SIGKDD Int Conf Knowl Discov Data Min* (pp. 1135–1144).

Schalck, C., & Yankol-Schalck, M. (2021). Predicting French SME failures: New evidence from machine learning techniques. *Applied Economics, 53*(51), 5948–5963.

Shapley, L. (1953). A value for n-person games. In H. Kuhn & A. Tucker (Eds.), *Contributions to the Theory of Games II* (pp. 307–317). Princeton University Press.

Shi, S., Tse, R., Luo, W., D'Addona, S., & Pau, G. (2022). Machine learning-driven credit risk: A systemic review. *Neural Computing and Applications, 34*(17), 14327–14339.

Shwartz-Ziv, R., & Armon, A. (2022). Tabular data: Deep learning is not all you need. *Information Fusion, 81*, 84–92.

Štrumbelj, E., & Kononenko, I. (2014). Explaining prediction models and individual predictions with feature contributions. *Knowledge and Information Systems, 41*, 647–665.

Wolpert, D. H. (1992). Stacked generalization. *Neural Networks, 5*(2), 241–259.

Yu, T., & Zhu, H. (2020). *Hyper-parameter optimization: A review of algorithms and applications.* arXiv:2003.05689

Zhang, Y., Song, K., Sun, Y., Tan, S., & Udell, M. (2019). *Why should you trust my explanation? Understanding uncertainty in LIME explanations.* arXiv:1904.12991

Zhang, W., Yan, S., Li, J., Tian, X., & Yoshida, T. (2022). Credit risk prediction of SMEs in supply chain finance by fusing demographic and behavioral data. *Transportation Research Part E: Logistics and Transportation Review, 158*, Article 102611.

Physical-Risk Adjusted Credit Analysis

Manuel Cugliari, Simone Narizzano, and Federica Vassalli

1 Introduction

Climate change is reshaping the natural environment and catalysing more frequent and intense natural disasters. These events have significant economic and business consequences, that may affect firms' soundness.Natural hazards can result in the destruction of tangible assets and prolonged operational disruption, potentially leading to insolvency (Monnin, 2018). However, assessing physical risks remains challenging, as the most severe events, such as floods and landslides, are typically localised. At the same time, precise data on the geographic distribution of firms' assets are often unavailable.

In Italy, the increasing frequency and severity of floods and landslides (collectively referred to as hydrogeological events, or HG) cause considerable damage and pose significant threats to the population (Guzzetti & Reichenbach, 1994; Guzzetti & Tonelli, 2004; Gatto, et al., 2023). The Italian Agency for Environmental Protection and Research (ISPRA) annual report reveals that 7,423 Italian municipalities (93.9%) are at risk of landslides, floods, or coastal erosion. Industries and services located in high and very high landslide hazard areas are over 84,000, with 220,000 employees exposed to risk. Additionally, in a medium-risk flood scenario, over 640,000 employees (13.4% of the total) are exposed to flooding risk. Flooding is particularly notable for its economic devastation

M. Cugliari · S. Narizzano · F. Vassalli (✉)
Bank of Italy, Financial Risk Management Directorate, Rome, Italy
e-mail: federica.vassalli@bancaditalia.it

M. Cugliari
e-mail: manuel.cugliari@bancaditalia.it

S. Narizzano
e-mail: simone.narizzano@bancaditalia.it

A. Scalia (ed.), *Corporate Credit Analysis and AI*, Finance for Professionals,
https://doi.org/10.1007/978-3-032-13422-6_12

(Barredo, 2009; Bower et al., 2010; Lugeri et al., 2010; Barredo et al., 2012) and it is Europe's most significant natural risk (Arrighi et al., 2018). In Europe, the expected annual loss by 2100 due to flood amounts to €44 billion, which could be substantially reduced by detention areas (Dottori et al., 2023). Notably, insurance coverage for asset damage caused by natural disasters, including HG risks, has recently been made mandatory in Italy (Law 213/2023), though its implementation is still pending.

The growing regulatory attention and the rising frequency of extreme events have heightened firms' awareness of climate-related risk. In 2014, only 7% of Italian firms considered nature and climate risk as highly relevant (Salvati et al., 2014), whereas by 2022 this proportion had increased to 73% (Gallo et al., 2022). Also, non-financial firms affected by HG events are 7.3% more likely to exit the market than unaffected firms. Indeed, physical risk can negatively impact cash flows through several channels, such as production disruption, due to direct damages, work absenteeism or supply chain interruptions, lower sales (e.g. demand shock in the affected area) and increase in capital costs for restoring damaged assets (Monnin, 2018). These firms also experience an average decline by 4.9% in revenue and 2.3% in employees (Clò et al., 2024).

Thus, it is crucial to understand the extent to which Italian firms are exposed to HG risk and how this impacts their creditworthiness and the possible side effects, such as limited access to credit and reduction in collateral value that underpin credit (Monnin, 2018). Between 2012 and 2016, 5.3% of firms in Italy experienced losses or incurred expenses to restore their businesses following floods or landslides, subsequently facing difficulty in the access to credit (Faiella & Natoli, 2018). Furthermore, loans are often collateralized, and there is a significant overlap between the location of debtor companies and the real estate collateral offered as a guarantee. Therefore, loan exposure is highly correlated with collateral exposure, potentially increasing the PD and the LGD if climate risk materializes (Meucci & Rinaldi, 2022).

Hence, integrating climate related factors into credit risk assessment is a topical issue for credit risk management, both at the corporate level (Brogi et al., 2022) and within central banking institutions (Angelini, 2022). However, several complexities arise in this context (Redondo & Aracil, 2024): (i) data gaps: usually, only the firm's headquarters is known, with insufficient information on the location of other facilities, such as production plants; (ii) natural hazard maps are often not accurate; (iii) when reliable hazard maps are available, the empirical evidence on the impact of natural hazards on businesses is insufficient, hindering the estimates of potential damages.

In this Chapter, we evaluate the effect of physical HG risk on the one-year default probability of a large sample of Italian non-financial firms, trying to overcome the above-mentioned data issues. First, we derive the exact geographic location of each firm's primary and local units using data from the Italian Business Registry (Infocamere). Second, we assign specific flood and landslide exposure levels to each firm matching geographic local unit location with the 'ISPRA mosaic risk maps' (Loberto & Spuri, 2023). In doing so, we define three discrete risk indicators: one for flood, one for landslides and one for the overall HG risk for each firm, accounting, alternatively, for all local units and for the headquarters only.

We find that roughly 38% of Italian non-financial firms are exposed to HG events, particularly floods. Accounting for local units is important: when considering the headquarters location only, the risk estimation is misrepresented for almost 10% of firms, and 23% if we exclude firms with only one local unit that coincides with the headquarters.

HG risk is especially concentrated in certain regions. Firms in Emilia-Romagna and Tuscany regions are significantly exposed to HG risks in absolute numbers regarding local units and employees. In Emilia-Romagna, almost 55% of local units and 60% of employees are exposed to flood risk. Liguria and Calabria have the highest share of local units exposed to the most severe risk category (7.7%). For landslide risk, Tuscany, Lombardy, and Campania have the highest absolute numbers of exposed employees, whereas Aosta Valley has the most significant relative share, with nearly 40% of employees exposed to landslide risk.

As a third and final step, to assess the effect of natural hazards on firms' creditworthiness, we compute a risk-adjusted financial statement by quantifying the expected damage based on property type (e.g. warehouse, shed, store, etc.) weighted by the risk level. To translate the risk-adjusted financial statement into a one-year PD, we rely on the S-ICAS (see Chap. 3). Given that S-ICAS rates Italian non-financial firms, whose credit claims serves as collateral, the impact of physical risk on firms' credit profile has implications for collateral availability.

Our estimates indicate that 38% of firms experience a mild deterioration in PDs. However, the overall impact—in terms of CQS scale (see Ch. 3)—is limited, as only 0.43% of firms transitions to a worse rating class.[1] Exposure to HG risk appears positively correlated with firm size, as larger firms exhibit higher average PD changes; this result may be explained by the fact that large firms have more branches and this is consistent with the findings of Loberto and Russo (2024a). The most affected sectors are "Agriculture", "Transportation and Storage" and "Accommodation and Food Services". On average, firms in Liguria show the worst deterioration of PD, followed by Aosta Valley and Calabria.

Insurance coverage stands out as a key risk mitigation factor. An analysis based on data from a survey carried out by the Bank of Italy in 2024[2] indicates that, for a subsample of firms, insurance against natural hazard can reduce the average PD deterioration by nearly 50%. This finding is particularly noteworthy given that banks usually do not differentiate between firms insured or uninsured (Gallo et al., 2024). Also, insurance against climate risk contributes to financial stability (De Polis, 2025).

---

[1] Each CQS corresponds to a broad range of PD values; therefore, minor PD increases may not result in a change of CQS. For further details, see Table 13.

[2] See Chap. 6.

Despite the high concentration of HG risks in certain regions, and the fact that firms most exposed to HG risks exhibit a notable increase in average PD, our findings indicate that the impact on firms' creditworthiness is, on average, not economically significant and may be meaningfully reduced with insurance coverage. The average effect on collateral is also negligible and at this stage it does not pose a significant constraint on the refinancing capacity of Italian banks.

Our analysis relies on ISPRA hazard maps, whose probabilities are derived from historical observations until 2021. However, climate change is driving a substantial increase in the frequency of extreme natural events globally (World Meteorological Organization, 2025), with particularly pronounced effects observed in Italy. In 2023 floods and river overflows increased by 170% with respect to 2022, landslides triggered by heavy rainfall by 64%, and flooding events by 12.4% (Legambiente, 2024). Therefore, our results should be interpreted as reflecting an average[3] historical scenario, while recognizing that, in the absence of targeted policy interventions, the frequency and severity of extreme events are expected to rise further (Emambakhsh et al., 2023). When we increase the frequency of HG events using the upper bound available, PD increases double or even triple compared to the baseline with an average PD increase of 32 bp for firms in the highest risk category.

The remainder of this Chapter is organised as follows: Sect. 2 provides an overview of the state of the art in the assessment of HG risk; Sect. 3 describes the data sources; Sect. 4 explains the methodology and Sect. 5 presents the results. Section 6 provides an analysis about the potential effect on collateral pledged for monetary policy operations and Sect. 7 concludes.

2 Modelling Hydrogeological Risk

2.1 Flood

Assessing exposure to natural disasters involves matching flood risk (hazard) data with the share of firms in floodplain areas within each municipality (exposure). Hazard data are typically sourced from the ISPRA mosaic hydrogeological map, providing risk indicators for floods and landslides at the municipal level. For exposure, ISTAT provides the concentration of buildings by municipality. Vulnerability is crucial in assessing the annual potential loss, especially when considering mitigation policies (e.g., insurance or preventive interventions like drainage areas) and flood depth.[4] A study analyses Dutch banks' exposure to flooding risk, considering mitigation policies and water depth (Caloia & Jansen, 2021). The author uses private and commercial real estate data, including property quality, the number of

[3] Average scenario refers to the return period. Return period is an average time statistically measured on extended historic data between floods or landslide to occur.

[4] Flood depth refers to the vertical distance between the ground level and the surface of the floodwater during a flood event.

floors, and flood depth associated with return periods. Risk mitigation measures, such as insurance covering recovery costs, are also considered.

In Italy, such detailed analysis presents significant challenges, particularly with respect to the availability and accuracy of flood depth data. While the ISPRA hazard maps are the official national reference, they do not provide flood depth information. Alternatively, flood depth maps published by the Joint Research Center (JRC) of the European Commission are available, but they lack the precision required for firm-level analysis (Loberto & Spuri, 2023). A key difference between the two sources lies in the way spatial information is represented. JRC maps are based on raster data, grids of cells where each cell represents a given value. The spatial resolution and accuracy of raster data depend on the size of these grid cells; larger cells lead to less precise boundary definitions. Conversely, ISPRA maps rely on vector data, where features are defined by coordinates in several geometric elements, offering greater accuracy in mapping boundaries and locations. Notably, the JRC itself acknowledges that their maps cannot be considered official flood hazard maps.

Several efforts have been made to estimate flood depth and associated damage. A basic approach involves constructing an index based on historical flood raster data as a proxy for flood depth (Dottori et al., 2018). This index also accounts for flood risk mitigation measures, such as flood management strategies and building elevation. Although useful for assessing exposure in complex scenarios, this methodology remains indicative and untested. JRC has also published a mainstream study estimating the so-called Flood Damage Function (Huizinga et al., 2017). This study derives a damage function for each country with available historical data, quantifying the relationship between hydraulic parameters and asset-specific damage in real terms. However, the economic estimation of direct damages remains subject to significant uncertainty, driven by simplifying assumptions and data constraints. In countries without established damage models, transferring damage functions from other regions is necessary, but this can lead to large discrepancies, as such functions often vary substantially. These uncertainties in quantitative damage modelling strongly affect the reliability of detailed economic assessments (Scorzini & Leopardi 2017). Moreover, model validation is essential when extending hydrogeological risk models to other countries (Molinari et al., 2019). Replicability is only feasible when geomorphological characteristics and precipitation patterns are comparable; otherwise, damages are likely to be underestimated or overestimated (Molinari et al., 2020).

In this context, the River Po District implements a model for hydrogeological risk assessment (MOVIDA, 2021) explicitly trained on Italian data to meet the requirements of the Flood Directive. MOVIDA assesses risk for the populations, economic activities, infrastructure, plants, and cultural heritage by considering hazards, exposure, vulnerability, flood depth, damage functions by building type, and recovery costs.

2.2 Landslides

Assessing landslide vulnerability is complex and should consider multiple dimensions, including physical and socioeconomic factors. The physical vulnerability of buildings and infrastructure depends on the intensity of the landslide event and the resistance level of the exposed elements. Studies on landslide risk assessment primarily focus on technical aspects (see UNISDR, 2009; Arrogante-Funes et al., 2021; Roccati et al., 2021; and Novellino et al., 2024 among others). Due to the geological and morphological characteristics of the Italian territory, which is 77% mountainous-hilly, landslides are ubiquitous. Thus, comprehensive inventory projects are essential for landslide risk assessment. The Inventory of Landslide Phenomena in Italy (IFFI Project), carried out by ISPRA and the Regions and Autonomous Provinces, classifies landslides that have occurred nationwide using standardized and shared methods (APAT, 2007). The IFFI Inventory is Italy's most comprehensive and detailed landslide database (Trigila et al., 2010), though it presents some limitations stemming from the heterogeneity of regional sources, subjectivity in mapping procedures, and lack of temporal and typological consistency (Loche et al., 2022).[5] Despite the availability of alternative sources (e.g., IRPI-CNR inventories or local studies), both the scientific community and public authorities consistently rely on ISPRA maps. These maps are the official tool adopted at both national and European levels for hydrogeological risk reporting and management (EU Floods Directive 2007/60/EC), as they ensure methodological harmonization, regional comparability, and institutional legitimacy, while still reflecting the inherent limitations of the underlying models and inventories.

Landslide hazard reflects the probability of a potentially destructive phenomenon of a certain intensity occurring in a given period and area (Varnes, 1984). The primary challenge in landslide hazard analysis is obtaining information on landslide activation dates, which then enables the study of recurrence times. Susceptibility or spatial hazard analysis is typically conducted to identify areas with the highest likelihood of landslide occurrence (Trigila et al., 2013). Unlike flood risk assessment, which often relies on quantitative approaches, landslide risk assessment primarily follows a qualitative methodology. This approach integrates the probability of occurrence with the associated risk level and event magnitude (Iadanza et al., 2021).

[5] These differences generate significant spatial biases: in some areas (e.g., Sicily and Calabria), landslide hazard is systematically underestimated, while in other regions such as Piedmont or Lombardy, data coverage is more complete. Moreover, the preferential nature of surveys (e.g., along infrastructure or in areas of particular interest) and the uneven use of detection techniques further reduce the reliability of the data at the national scale. Indeed, ISPRA is committed to continuously updating its mosaic.

3 Data

We rely on three data sources: (i) ISPRA georeferenced maps to identify floodable areas and areas exposed to landslide, (ii) the Infocamere database with information about the location of primary and secondary units, (iii) S-ICAS firms' financial variables.

3.1 Hazard—ISPRA

Given the complex nature of the Italian terrain, with 42% hilly, 35% mountainous, and only 23% flat,[6] detailed local investigations have led to the zonation of landslide and flood hazards. This work was initially formalised through the 'Piani di Assetto Idrogeologico' (PAI),[7] which later evolved into 'Piani di Gestione Rischio Alluvioni' (PGRA).[8] Each of the seven Italian District Basin Authorities (ABD) manages and updates its own PGRA every six years. The current PGRA, covering the period 2021–2027, defines flood scenarios and provides guidance for the design of defensive structures and mitigation strategies. ISPRA periodically updates the hydrogeological hazard maps collecting detailed data about floods and landslides from the ABDs.

Based on the ISPRA maps, a recent study offers a new methodology for assessing flood risk in Italy for residential property (Loberto & Spuri, 2023). Flood risk is assessed through a two-step process: (i) identification of potentially floodable areas based on past events and a forward-looking evaluation, partly accounting for climate change effects; (ii) attribution of a risk level to each area. The risk level differs for flood and land. Flood risk levels convey information about flood return times, while landslide risk levels also provide information about the magnitude of the phenomenon (see Table 1).

Unlike the flood hazard mosaic, where an area may be subject to flooding under one or more of three different probability scenarios, the landslide hazard mosaic assigns each portion of the territory to a single hazard class. Therefore, the total area of landslide hazard zones in Italy is equal to the sum of the areas of the four hazard classes.

It is important to notice that ISPRA mosaic risk maps are subject to the typical uncertainties of hydrogeological modelling, such as parameter selection, boundary conditions, calibration, and conceptual structure. However, ISPRA mosaic is embedded within the regulatory framework of the EU Floods Directive (2007/60/EC) and serves as the official tool for hydraulic risk management and assessment

---

[6] Data available at https://www.istat.it/it/archivio/137001.

[7] Legislative decree 23 February 2010, no. 49. Transposition of the Floods Directive 2007/60/EC Concerning Flood Risks Assessment and Management.

[8] 2019. ProteggItalia. National Plan for Landslide and Flood Risk Mitigation, Restoration and Protection of the Environment. For a detailed evolution of policies, see Vitale and Meijerink (2023).

Table 1 ISPRA risk category for flood and landslide[9]

Flood	Landslide
HPH—High Probability Hazard (flood return time between 20 and 50 years)	P4—high (1–30 years) and medium (30–100 years) frequency, high damage magnitude
MPH—Medium Probability Hazard (flood return time between 100 and 200 years)	P3—high (1–30 years) and medium (30–100 years) frequency, medium damage magnitude OR low frequency (100–300 years), high damage magnitude
LPH—Low Probability Hazard (flood return time longer than 200 years)	P2—high (1–30 years) frequency, low damage magnitude OR low frequency (100–300 years), medium damage magnitude
	P1—medium (30–100 years) and low (100–300 years) frequency, medium and low damage magnitude

at both national and European levels. When ISPRA collects data from the various ADB, it applies harmonization and quality control procedures to ensure consistency and compliance with EU guidelines, and the European Commission itself validates the data. While the maps do not report confidence intervals or uncertainty zones, they are expected to reflect the highest possible level of reliability. Technical literature also highlights that uncertainty is particularly associated with flood depth and flow velocity; variables not yet considered in this work.

3.2 Exposure—Infocamere and Cebi/Cerved

When assessing HG risk, it is essential to account for exposure, namely the value of activities susceptible to such events. To this end, we use data from Infocamere to determine the location of primary and local units for each firm assessed by the S-ICAS model (Sect. 3.2). Infocamere provides information on the establishment, modification, and cessation of all enterprises, regardless of their legal form or economic sector of activity, with headquarters or local units (e.g., offices, plants, warehouses) within the national territory, as well as other entities mandated by law. Hence, we retrieve detailed information on company headquarters (*Sede Legale*) and local units (*Unità Locali*) across Italy, including their functional type. Given that Infocamere classifies local units into over 100 types, we consolidate these into four primary categories based on their roles in the production cycle: warehouses

[9] ISPRA's hazard classifications are based on the most recent PGRA, covering the period 2021–2027. Although the PGRA adopts a forward-looking framework, the definition of return periods is still grounded in historical observations. As a result, these return periods may underestimate the true frequency of such events, particularly in light of the recent surge in extreme weather occurrences. Between 2022 and 2023 alone, floods and river overflows increased by 170%, landslides by 64%, and flooding events by 12.4% (Legambiente, 2024).

Table 2 Distribution of industrial building by category and NACE sector[10] (percentage values)

Sector	Office	Plant	Shop	Warehouse	Other	Total
Agriculture	0.1	1.3	0.1	0.2	0	1.8
Mining	0	0.1	0	0.1	0	0.3
Manufacturing	1.9	13.6	1.5	2.2	0.1	19.4
Electricity	0.4	1	0.1	0	0	1.5
Waste management	0.3	0.7	0.1	0.2	0	1.3
Construction	1.6	0.3	0.5	8.5	0.1	11
Trade	2	0.7	9.2	14.1	0.3	26.3
Hosting services	2.8	0.2	0.3	3.3	0.1	6.8
Transporting	0.3	0.1	7	0.2	0.2	7.8
ICT	2.8	0	0.2	0.1	0	3.1
Real Estate	0.3	0	0	0	0.1	0.4
Professional services	0.6	0.1	6.1	0.1	0	6.8
Administrative services	4.3	0.1	0.2	0.1	0.1	4.9
Education	2.7	0.1	0.5	0.3	0	3.7
Health services	0.5	0.1	0.1	0	0.4	1
Entertainment	0.8	0.1	2	0	0	3.1
Other services	0.1	0	1.1	0	0	1.3
Total	21.9	18.6	28.9	29.5	1.6	100

(supply and storage), plants (production), shops (sales), and offices (administrative functions). Warehouses and Shops have the highest shares (around 29% in both cases) of the industrial building distribution, followed by Offices (Table 2). The overall distribution aligns with the core activities and patterns of the NACE sectors. Trade accounts for 26.28% of the total buildings, followed by Manufacturing (19.44%) and Construction (10.97%). Additionally, Trade holds the largest shares of shops (9.17%) and warehouses (14.07%), whereas Manufacturing features the highest proportion of plants (13.60%), reflecting the primary business activities of these sectors.

To evaluate the significance of each local unit, we follow a hierarchical approach that prioritizes employment information while ensuring that all premises are considered in the assessment of exposure. We use employee distribution data at the municipal level for each firm. In cases where a single building exists within a municipality, we get the exact number of employees for each location. For municipalities with multiple buildings, we assume a uniform distribution: the proportion

[10] See Appendix A for full NACE Rev. 2 sector definitions. From now on, we refer to NACE sector with letters.

of employees relative to the total number of buildings in the municipality determines the relative importance of each unit.[11] The employment information is then complemented with an alternative allocation based on the number of premises. By construction, this step assigns a residual weight also to premises without employees, which would otherwise be disregarded in the assessment of risk exposure. The final distribution combines the two dimensions, with a higher weight given to employment (75%) and a smaller but non-negligible weight to premises (25%).

Our dataset includes 745,370 local units, corresponding to 366,799 active firms as of December 31, 2023, employing a total of 7.2 million workers. We integrate Infocamere data with firms' financial statement data for 2022, sourced from the *Sistema Informativo Economico-Finanziario* (SIEF) of the Bank of Italy. SIEF incorporates data from Cebi (*Centrale dei Bilanci*) and Cerved databases. While the Cebi database primarily covers medium and large Italian firms and a limited number of small firms, Cerved provides a broader scope, encompassing nearly all small and micro limited-liability firms (Giovannelli et al., 2020).

The average number of employees varies significantly across NACE sectors (Table 3—Panel A). The mean number of employees by firm is 26, with peaks in Hosting services at 60, and Administrative services at 67. However, the median number of employees is much lower at 6, reflecting the dominance of micro firms, which constitute 67% of the sample. Firms have, on average, two buildings, while the median remains one, again influenced by micro-firm prevalence. The average asset value is €8 million while revenues average €7 million. For both total assets and revenues, Electricity records the highest average, respectively at €41 million and €53 million.

When analysing firm characteristics by size,[12] the averages become closer to the median values (Table 3—Panel B). Micro firms on average have 5 employees, small firms 18, medium firms 69, and large firms 565, although the latter exhibit significant variability, with a standard deviation approximately equal to 6,000. Large firms average 14 local units, compared to just one for micro firms. The average asset value ranges from €228 million for large firms to €1 million for micro firms. Average revenues vary similarly, from €1 million for micro firms to much higher values for larger firms. The final dataset is obtained by merging the firm information in the S-ICAS database with information about the geographic location of primary and local units, the number of employees for each firm's unit, and the risk level based on ISPRA maps.

[11] This is the best proxy available to provide a municipal-level approximation of the number of employees, and it has also been used in other studies (Trigila et al., 2021; Meucci & Rinaldi, 2022; Loberto & Spuri, 2023; Loberto & Russo, 2024a).

[12] According to the European Commission definition (Recommendation 2003/361/EC).

Table 3 Summary statistics

	Firms (#)	Employees (#)			Business units (#)			Assets (€ mln)			Revenues (€ mln)		
	366,799	Mean	SD	Median	Mean	SD	Median	Mean	SD	Median	Mean	SD	Median
Panel A: Nace sector													
Agriculture	7,241	15	47	6	2	1	1	5,101	18,817	1,439	2,879	20,916	453
Mining	827	12	17	8	2	2	2	7,176	18,924	2,787	3,656	12,665	1,472
Manufacturing	76,103	29	175	11	2	3	1	10,229	102,909	1,945	10,120	115,132	1,923
Electricity	3,881	34	434	4	3	12	2	40,603	712,313	2,044	52,687	1,115,254	308
Waste management	3,351	45	184	12	3	6	2	14,331	75,573	2,605	9,493	28,916	2,592
Construction	52,606	12	37	6	1	1	1	3,725	26,434	1,146	2,667	11,532	983
Trade	78,859	16	147	5	2	9	1	5,168	87,474	1,073	8,901	168,486	1,385
Hosting services	16,322	60	3,426	9	3	103	1	14,097	915,618	1,056	6,394	87,619	1,289
Transporting	27,349	17	101	7	2	5	1	2,573	15,376	500	1,316	7,956	497
ICT	11,453	26	157	6	2	3	1	8,882	212,225	690	4,281	58,295	528
Real Estate	40,137	11	92	1	1	1	1	4,738	22,326	1,316	502	2,660	142
Professional services	16,685	15	105	4	2	4	1	2,655	16,073	655	2,242	17,437	520
Administrative services	11,815	67	791	7	2	6	1	4,754	71,232	675	4,294	41,024	685
Education	2,132	15	34	6	2	3	1	1,447	4,689	466	1,167	3,881	419
Health services	9,080	47	181	9	3	5	1	3,734	19,787	701	3,066	14,076	759

(continued)

Table 3 (continued)

	Firms (#)	Employees (#)			Business units (#)			Assets (€ mln)			Revenues (€ mln)		
	366,799	Mean	SD	Median	Mean	SD	Median	Mean	SD	Median	Mean	SD	Median
Entertainment	5,158	15	83	3	2	2	1	2,808	24,525	505	1,681	13,117	351
Other services	3,800	14	52	5	2	2	1	1,432	5,111	370	1,104	2,887	385
Panel B: Firm size													
Large	5,191	569	6,323	217	15	187	4	226,635	1,833,720	73,887	219,727	1,222,443	78,007
Medium	27,677	70	119	53	3	5	2	19,513	26,824	14,852	18,306	17,440	14,294
Small	117,283	18	34	13	2	2	1	4,044	6,514	2,917	3,492	3,702	2,612
Micro	216,638	5	19	4	1	1	1	874	2,225	559	646	727	450

4 Methodology

4.1 Geo-Referencing Local Units

A prerequisite for quantifying physical risk is the geographical location of the firm's primary and secondary local units. This process, known as geocoding, entails converting textual addresses into latitude and longitude coordinates. To ensure accurate geolocation of local units, a geocoding server is essential, as it facilitates the reliable mapping of entities to their physical locations. Given the critical nature of this task, we opted for the ESRI—a worldwide leader in Geographic Information Systems (GIS)[13]—paid APIs,[14] which stand out for their exceptional accuracy and reliability in geospatial data processing.

Geocoding in the ESRI system consists in a multi-step process that converts addresses into geographic coordinates with high accuracy. First, addresses are cleaned and standardized to ensure consistency in formatting—this means fixing abbreviations, punctuation, and other inconsistencies. Then, each part of the address (like street name, house number, and postal code) is checked against official reference data. Once the address is properly formatted, we send it to the ESRI API, which generates possible location matches and ranks them based on similarity. Each match receives a confidence score, and only those above 90% are automatically accepted. If an address does not meet this threshold, it is flagged for manual review. To further improve accuracy, we compare ESRI's results with other geocoding services like Nominatim[15] (OpenStreetMap) and Google Maps.[16] This helps validate the 90% confidence threshold and ensures the best balance between accuracy and reliability.[17]

Using data from Infocamere, we identify 366,799 primary offices and 378,571 local units for the firms evaluated by the S-ICAS model as of December 31, 2023.

[13] GIS refers to a technological framework designed for collecting, managing, analysing, and visualizing geospatial data, enabling the exploration of spatial patterns, relationships, and trends across various disciplines, including urban planning, environmental science, and risk assessment.

[14] API (Application Programming Interface) is a structured set of protocols, routines, and tools that enables different software systems or components to communicate and exchange data, often facilitating the integration of third-party functionalities into applications. The ESRI paid APIs integrate customizable advanced algorithms for address parsing, candidate location identification (both in rural and urban areas), and scoring mechanisms that ensure robust geocoding results.

[15] Nominatim is a geocoding tool provided by OpenStreetMap that transforms textual addresses into geographic coordinates and vice versa, utilizing open-source geospatial data curated and maintained by a global community.

[16] Google Maps is a comprehensive geospatial platform developed by Google, offering services such as geocoding, mapping, and navigation through APIs, supported by an extensive and regularly updated global dataset.

[17] For further details about the geocoding algorithm see Appendix C.

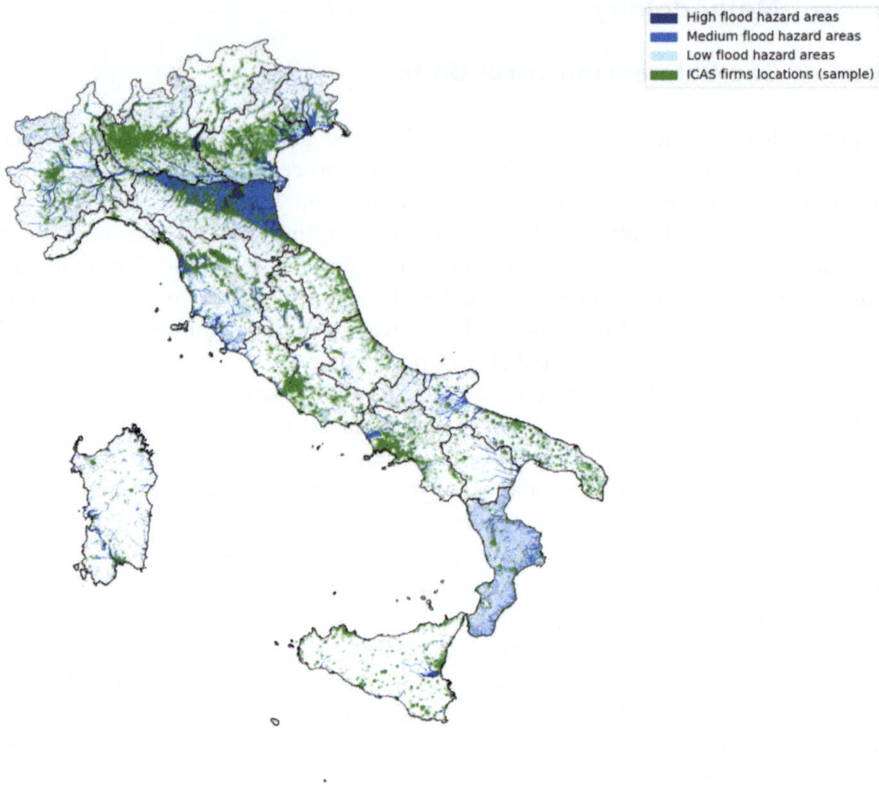

Fig. 1 ISPRA mosaic risk maps for flood and a sample of about 60.000 S-ICAS firms' distribution (green dots). See Fig. 11 in Appendix C for Italy's political map at regional level

We validate the locations on a sample basis through web access to Telemaco[18] and verification of business registry records. We also exclude foreign local units. In total, there are 745,370 positions to be geocoded. This comprehensive dataset forms the foundation for our geocoding analysis, ensuring that all relevant local units are accurately accounted for in the subsequent risk assessment.

The resulting dataset enriches the geocoded data with risk attributes for both flood and landslide hazards. Each local unit is assigned a risk level, and for those falling within multiple hazard zones, attributes for each distinct risk are stored. The outcome provides a granular risk profile that captures the multi-dimensional nature of hydrogeological threats (Fig. 1).

[18] Telemaco is the online access method to the Italian Business Registry databases and it allows the consultation of ordinary and historical business records, company financial statements, and documents of all enterprises, providing the primary legal, economic, and administrative information.

To validate the integration, we manually cross-check a subset of local unit coordinates against the ISPRA hazard maps using an external GIS tool (Loberto & Russo, 2024b). The results show the spatial alignment between the mapped local units and the ISPRA-defined flood and landslide hazard zones (Figs. 1, 2). The left panel highlights flood risk zones, with darker shades indicating higher risk levels, while the right panel shows landslide risks using a gradient of red to represent severity. The green dots marking local unit locations show their spatial correspondence with the hazard zones.

This enriched geospatial dataset forms the backbone for subsequent risk analysis, enabling the calculation of firm-level risk indicators that aggregate hazard exposure across all local units. These indicators are weighted by the operational importance of each unit, providing a comprehensive measure of hydrogeological exposure for integration into financial and credit risk models.

As described in Sect. 2, each risk category for flood and landslide is associated with a range of return time. In order to compute risk-adjusted financial statements,

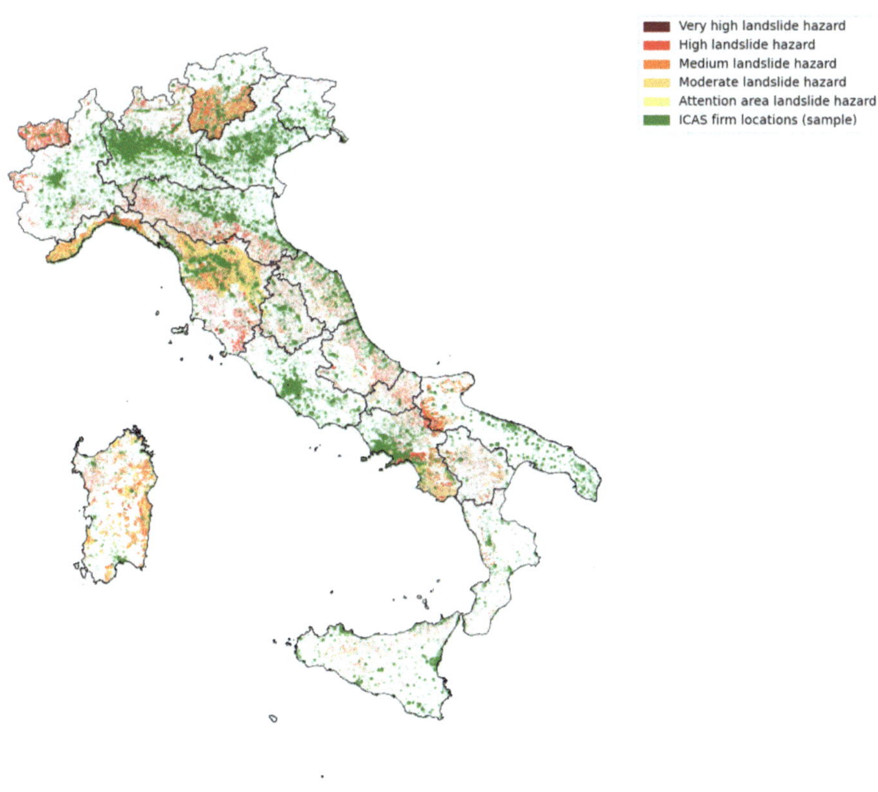

Fig. 2 ISPRA mosaic risk maps for landslide and a sample of about 60.000 of S-ICAS firms' distribution (green dots). See Fig. 11 Appendix C for Italy political map at regional level

Table 4 Annualised probability of occurrence of the HG events

Flood	Landslide
HPH: T = [20; 50] → $\overline{T}$ = 35 → p = 0.028	**P4**: T = [1; 30] → $\overline{T}$ = 15 → p = 0.067
MPH: T = [100; 200] → $\overline{T}$ = 150 – p = 0.007	**P3**: T = [30; 100] → $\overline{T}$ = 65 → p = 0.015
LPH: T > 200 → $\overline{T}$ = 200 → p = 0.005	**P2**: T = [100; 300] → $\overline{T}$ = 200 → p = 0.005
	P1: T > 300 → $\overline{T}$ = 300 → p = 0.003

Note The table reports for flood and landslides the risk category, the range of return time, the average time and the average annualised probability of occurrence. For the lowest risk category, we have adopted a prudential approach by applying the highest available frequency (own calculation on ISPRA data)

we need to convert the return period into the annual probability of occurrence of the HG event.

To do so, we rely on the hydraulic engineering formula in Eq. (1). Given that T is the average return time, the annualised probability of occurrence is:

$$p = 1 - \left(1 - \frac{1}{T}\right)^{N} \quad \text{with } N = 1 \tag{1}$$

In our case, we set $N = 1$ since we are interested in the probability of the event occurring within the current year. However, when the event is associated with a time interval $[T_1, T_2]$, selecting a single representative value requires a methodologically sound approximation. In this paper, we choose to use the probability corresponding to the average return period, calculated as the arithmetic mean of the two return periods defining the interval (Table 4).[19] Studies in the field of extreme value processes, such as Raschke (2021), show that the mean of two return periods can be used to derive a so-called *combined return period*, defined as $T_c = \frac{T_1+T_2}{2}$, whose exceedance frequency is therefore $1/T_C$.

As pointed out in Sect. 2, the Infocamere database also provides detailed information about the type of industrial building. We provide the distribution of local units by risk category for flood and landslide (Table 5). For both flood and landslide, most of the industrial buildings are in a non-risk area (69.7% and 92.4% respectively). Nevertheless, 6% and almost 12% of local units are exposed, respectively, to the highest and medium flood risk categories (Table 5—Panel A).

As a final step, we include information from the Infocamere database about the number of employees for each firm at municipal level. By matching these data with the locations, we can determine the number of employees for each local unit at municipal level. If the location is not available or cannot be matched, we assume a uniform distribution of the firm's total number of employees across its local units. This step is crucial for assigning the relative importance of each local unit to the overall firm operations.

[19] The assumptions regarding return time are critical for the estimation of the expected losses due to HG risks. See Appendix D for alternative hazard probability calculations.

Table 5 Distribution of industrial building by risk category (percentage values)

ISPRA risk category	Office	Plant	Shop	Warehouse	Other	Total
Panel A: Flood						
0	15.7	12.6	20	20.4	1	69.7
LPH	2.7	2.4	3.8	3.6	0.2	12.7
MPH	2.4	2.4	3.2	3.5	0.2	11.6
HPH	1.2	1.1	1.9	1.8	0.1	6
Panel B: Landslide						
0	20.5	17	26.5	27.1	1.4	92.4
P1	0.7	0.6	1	1	0.1	3.3
P2	0.6	0.5	0.8	0.8	0.1	2.8
P3	0.2	0.2	0.3	0.3	0	1
P4	0.1	0.1	0.2	0.2	0	0.6

4.2 Risk-Adjusted Firms' Financial Statement

Drawing from probability theory, we consider two states of the world: (i) the HG event occurs this year with probability *p*, and (ii) the HG event does not occur this year, with probability *1-p*. Based on this framework, we can estimate the financial impact of HG events by assessing potential production disruptions on the income statement and evaluating expected asset losses on the balance sheet.[20] A production halt directly affects the revenue stream, which in turn influences other key financial variables such as costs, value added, EBITDA, EBIT, and net income. To quantify this impact, we follow a two-stage approach.

First, we determine the contribution of each local unit to total revenues, starting from local unit relative importance (see Sect. 3.2). In this step, we assign greater weight to local units that play a critical role in production and sales activities, such as warehouses, plants, and retail stores. The weighting procedure involves two steps: (i) the weights of the critical assets are rescaled to sum to 100%; (ii) the final weight is computed as a convex combination of the rescaled weights (75%) and the original employee-based weights (25%), thereby preserving a residual contribution from non-critical local units.[21] This procedure ensures that the revenues expected loss estimation appropriately reflects the operational relevance of each local unit.

Second, we assume that production or revenue generation at the affected site ceases for a duration that varies based on the level of flood or landslide risk. Specifically, operations are disrupted for 6, 4, and 2 months depending on the flood

[20] Financial statement data refer to 2022.

[21] For example, consider a firm owning three premises: a retail store (40%), a production facility (30%), and an office (30%). The store and facility are identified as critical. Their rescaled weights become approximately 57.14% and 42.86%, respectively. The final weights are then calculated as follows: store 52.86%, facility 39.64%, office 7.5%.

risk category, and for 8, 6, and 4 months in the case of landslides, as reflected in Eq. (1). This structured approach enables a systematic assessment of the financial consequences of extreme events on firms. Then the expected loss of revenues for firms i is:

$$ELrevenues_i = revenues_i \sum_k \left[exposure_{i,k} \times \sum_j \left(hazard_{k,j} \times distruption_{k,j} \right) \right] \tag{2}$$

where $revenues_i$ is the total revenues for firm i, $exposure_{i,k}$ is the relative importance of site k for firm i, $hazard_{k,j}$ is the probability of occurrence of the j-th HG event (flood or landslide) in site k and $disruption_{k,j}$ is the number of months in a year (in percentage) in which the production is disrupted in site k for the occurrence of the j-th HG event. Then, the HG risk-adjusted value of revenues for firm i is defined as follows:

$$Revenues_i^{HG} = Revenues_i^{2022} - ELrevenues_i^{2022} \tag{3}$$

where $Revenues_i^{2022}$. are the revenues of firm i realized in fiscal year 2022. From a different point of view, going back to probability theory, the HG risk-adjusted revenues could be computed as the sum of the variable in the two states of the world for each local unit k (the j-th HG event happens with probability $hazard_{k,j}$ and the j-th HG event does not occur with probability $1\text{-}hazard_{k,j}$):

$$\begin{aligned} Revenues_i^{HG} &= revenues_i^{2022} \left\{ \sum_k \left[\left(exposure_{i,k} \times \sum_j \left(1 - hazard_{k,j} \right) \right] \right. \right. \\ &\left. + \sum_k \left[exposure_{i,k} \times \sum_j \left(hazard_{k,j} \times \left(1 - distruption_{k,j} \right) \right) \right] \right\} \end{aligned} \tag{4}$$

Additionally, a production disruption reduces costs. We assume that the reduction of revenues is transmitted to variable and labour costs using elasticities estimates at NACE sector level (see Appendix B for further details on elasticity estimation). A percentage reduction g_R in revenues corresponds to a percentage change in variable costs $g_{VC,R} = \eta_{VC} g_R$ and a percentage change in labour costs $g_{LC,R} = \eta_{LC} g_R$, where η_{VC} and η_{LC} are the elasticity of variable costs to revenues and the elasticity of labour cost to revenues, respectively (De Socio et al., 2020). Therefore, we reduce variable and labour costs accordingly. For the remaining variables in the income statement, we adopt the simplifying assumption of zero elasticity of interest expenditures to revenues. Fixed costs, such as amortization and depreciation, are assumed to remain stable.

We augment impairment losses, reflecting the expected loss in assets due to HG risk. We evaluate the expected losses due to an HG event on the balance sheet asset side and adjust the liabilities side accordingly. An HG event can directly affect Property, Plant, and Equipment (PPE) and Warehouse Inventories (WI). To compute the expected loss for PPE, we consider the annualised probability of the HG event associated with the specific local unit (hazard). The contribution to the total value of this balance sheet item is computed as the relative share of employees for the local unit times the total value of PPE (exposure). For WI, we follow the same approach used for revenues and overweight the relative importance of warehouses that are obviously more suited for the storage of raw materials and inventories.

To determine the expected loss, we assume that the assets lose 60% of their value in case of a flood event (Huizinga et al., 2017; Loberto & Spuri, 2023).[22] For landslides, given that a magnitude class is associated with each risk category, we apply different assumptions about the asset damage according to different risk areas. Thus, P4 is associated with a loss of 80% of the asset value, P3 of 60%, P2 of 40% and P1 of 20% (vulnerability).

Hence, the expected loss on the *l-th* asset (PPE or WI), given the contribution of site *k* for firm *i* in case of flood, landslide or both is given by:

$$\mathrm{EL}asset_{i,l} = \sum\nolimits_{k} [exposure_{i,k} \times asset_l \times \sum\nolimits_{j} (vulnerability_{k,j} \times hazard_{k,j})] \quad (5)$$

Hence, from the expected loss, we derive the new value of asset *l* for firm *i*:

$$IV_{i,l}^{HG} = IV_{i,l}^{2022} - \mathrm{EL}asset_{i,l} \quad (6)$$

where $IV_{i,l}^{HG}$ is the *l-th* item new value that accounts for HG risk, $IV_{i,l}^{2022}$ is the *l-th* asset value recorded in the 2022 balance sheet. The total amount of the expected losses for all the assets of the firm is equal to the impairment losses considered in the risk-adjusted income statement. Finally, to calculate net income, we apply a tax rate of 28% to pre-tax income, corresponding to the median effective tax rate and aligning with the IRES and IRAP tax rates (De Socio et al., 2020).

After the calculation of the HG risk-adjusted income statement, it is possible to re-compute all the balance sheet variables. For the accounting principle, we get the firm's equity at the end of the year by adding the net profits or losses for the year to the equity recorded at the end of the previous year. Similarly, we also consider a potential reduction in liquidity due to the HG expected losses. If the resulting expected liquidity shortfall cannot be fully offset by the beginning-of-period liquidity, the residual liquidity requirement is assumed to be met through an increase in short-term financial debt.[23]

In conclusion, based on the revenues and cost changes and the estimation of the reduced values of balance sheet assets, we compute the HG risk-adjusted income statement and the HG risk-adjusted balance sheet (Tables 6, 7 respectively). A '+' ('−') indicates an increment (reduction) in the HG risk-adjusted value compared to the original financial statement. Variables with '=' are assumed to remain stable.

[22] See Appendix D for simulations with other values, such as 30% and 90%.

[23] We assume a maximum reduction of liquidity equal to 90% of the initial value. This hypothesis derives from the fact that firm prefer, whenever possible, to keep a minimum amount of liquidity for operating needs (De Socio et al., 2020).

Table 6 Transmission of the HG risk on Income Statement

Income statement (Reclassified)	Effect
+ Net revenues	$-\Delta$Rev
– Variable costs	$-\Delta_{\%}$ Rev $\times \eta_{VC}$
Gross Profit	–
– Labour costs	$-\Delta_{\%}$ Rev $\times \eta_{LC}$
EBITDA	–
– Depreciation and Amortisation	=
EBIT	–
+ Financial income	=
– Interest expenses	=
– Impairment losses	$-\sum \text{ELasset}_i$
EBT	–
– Tax expenses	ΔEBT $\times$ (1-t)
Net Income (Loss)	–

Note Reclassified Income Statement. Items on the LHS column, effects on the items on the RHS column. $-\Delta$ is a pure variation, $-\Delta\%$ is a percentage variation, EL is the expected loss. (1) From Eqs. (2) and (3), we get that $\Delta \text{Rev} = \text{Revenues}^{2022} - \text{Revenues}^{HG}$; (2) Percentage change in variable costs depending on the percentage reduction in revenues and on the elasticity of variable costs to revenues; (3) Percentage change in labour costs depending on the percentage reduction in revenues and on the elasticity of labour costs to revenues; (4) total amount of the expected losses for all the assets of the firm (from Eq. (4)); (5) Tax saving due to the decrease of pre-tax income (EBT)

The results of the financial statement HG risk-adjusted recalculation under the assumption of two states of the world, are then plugged into the S-ICAS model to determine the HG risk-adjusted PDs of Italian non-financial firms.

5 Results

5.1 Discrete Indicators

To evaluate the risk exposure of Italian non-financial firms, we develop three discrete indicators, each ranging from 0 (no risk) to 3 (highest risk). These indicators assess exposure to flood, landslide, and aggregate HG risks. Using risk categories assigned to individual sites by ISPRA, we calculate a firm-level indicator based on the sum of the weighted exposure of each local unit to the corresponding risks. We subsequently reclassify these scores into discrete values between 0 (no risk) and 3 (highest risk). We adopt a conservative approach for the aggregate HG risk indicator, taking the highest risk value (flood or landslide).

Table 7 Transmission of the HG risk on Balance Sheet

Balance sheet (assets)	Effect
Fixed assets	–
Property, plant and equipment	$-\sum ELPPE_i$
Current assets	–
Cash and equivalents	–
Inventories	$-\sum ELWI_i$
Total assets	–
Balance sheet (Liabilities and equity)	**Effect**
...	
±Net income (loss)	– ΔNet Income
Equity	–
...	
Long-term debt	=
...	
Short-term debt	+
Short-term financial debt	+
Total liabilities and equity	–

Note Balance sheet—Asset side and Liabilities side. Items on the LHS column, effects on the items on the RHS column. (1) Sum of the expected loss on local units classified as PPE computed as in Eq. (4); (2) Sum of the expected loss on WI computed as in Eq. (4); (3) Change in Net Income resulting from the changes in Income Statement

Most firms are in areas with no significant HG risk (Table 8—Panel A). Flood risk is more widespread than landslide risk, particularly at lower severity levels. Approximately 33% of Italian non-financial firms are exposed to flood risk, while 8% are vulnerable to landslides. These Fig. 12 are broadly in line with the latest ISPRA report (Trigila et al., 2021), which estimates that around 40% of local units face flood risk, and 6% are at risk of landslides. Overall, based on the aggregate HG risk indicator, approximately 38% of Italian non-financial firms are exposed to some level of HG risk, compared to 34% of firms when considering the headquarters only (Table 8—Panel b). These findings highlight the importance for risk assessment of locating local units beyond the headquarters in risk assessment. Ignoring branches, as has been common in previous studies (e.g., Fatica et al., 2024; Clò et al., 2024), can alter the risk exposure estimation. Our analysis shows that focusing solely on headquarters locations has some limitations. Specifically, when exposure is measured at the headquarters level, risk could be overestimated or underestimated depending on the headquarters location compared to other local units. In our sample, discrepancy in risk classification occurs for almost 9% of the

Table 8 Physical risk indicators

Risk indicator	Flood (% firms)	Landslide (% firms)	HG (% firms)
Panel A: All local units			
0	66.7	91.8	62.1
Low	15.5	4.3	16.8
Medium	12.7	2.7	14.9
High	5.1	1.2	6.2
Panel B: Headquarters only			
0	70.6	92.8	66.3
Low	12.3	3.2	13.3
Medium	11.4	2.7	13.5
High	5.6	1.4	6.8

Note Indicators based on own calculations accounting for all local units (Panel A) and for headquarters only (Panel B). The first column refers to flood risk, the second one to landslide risk and the third one to HG risk

firm.[24] However, this percentage rise to 23% if we exclude firms with only one local unit that coincides with the headquarters.[25]

Emilia-Romagna and Tuscany are the most affected regions by flood risk, both in the absolute number of local units and in their share within the region (Fig. 3). In Emilia-Romagna, almost 55% of local units are in risky areas; the percentage is similar for Tuscany (54%); however, in most cases this concerns the least severe risk category. Liguria and Aosta Valley also exhibit a remarkable exposure, with nearly 35% and 32% of local units in risky areas. Liguria and Calabria have the highest share of local units exposed to the most severe risk category (7.7%).

The picture slightly changes when landslide risk is considered (Fig. 4). Tuscany, Campania, and Liguria are the most affected regions in absolute terms. In Tuscany, nearly 7,000 local units are in areas categorized at low or medium risk levels (approximately 13% of the total). Campania has nearly 4,000 units in the low risk level. About 17% of branches in Liguria are exposed to the lowest risk category, while 6% face medium risk. Aosta Valley exhibits the highest overall share of local units exposed to risk (32%) and the highest proportion of premises in the most severe risk category (3.3%).

The exposure of employees broadly mirrors the distribution of local units (Fig. 5). Emilia-Romagna, Tuscany, Veneto, and Lombardy are the most affected regions in terms of absolute number of employees. In Emilia-Romagna, 466,260 employees are exposed to flood risk, Tuscany accounts for three quarters as many exposed employees as Emilia-Romagna, and Veneto for a half. In percentage

[24] Risk estimates based only on headquarters lead to underestimation of HG risk for 6% of firms and overestimation of risk for 3% of firms.

[25] Almost 60% of firms in our sample are micro firms that usually have just one local unit.

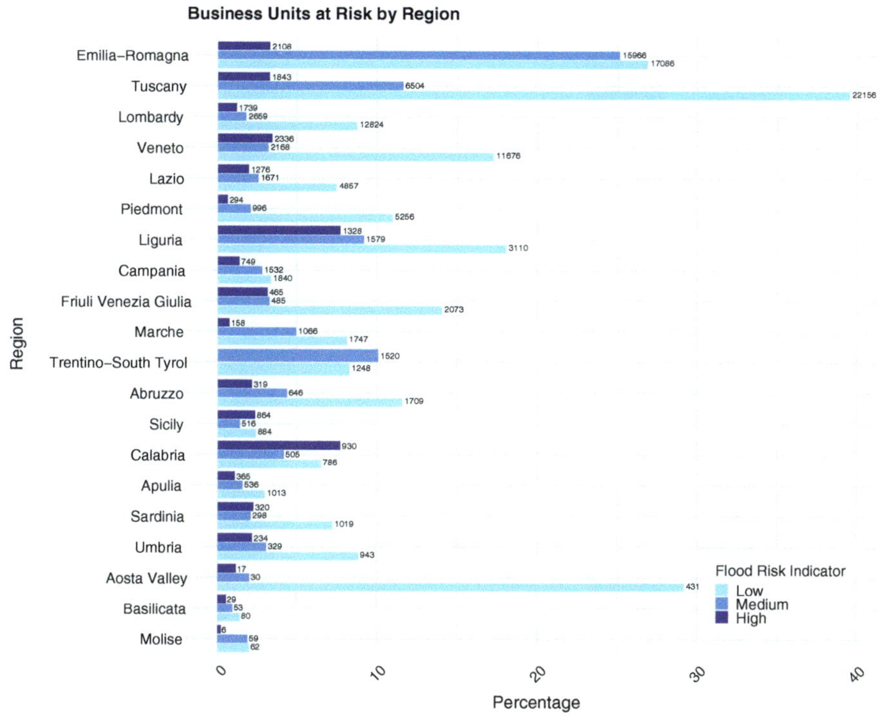

Fig. 3 Share and number of local units exposed to flood risk by region. Absolute numbers are shown near the bars, while shares are along the horizontal axis

terms, Emilia Romagna and Tuscany have the highest share of exposed employees (roughly 65%). Liguria and Calabria have the highest relative exposure (almost 10%) in the most severe category.

For landslide risk, Tuscany, Campania, and Lombardy have the highest absolute numbers of exposed employees (Fig. 6). Aosta Valley has the most significant relative share, with nearly 40% of employees exposed to landslide risk, followed by Liguria (30%). Basilicata has the highest share of employees in the most severe risk area (8.4%).

5.2 Physical-Risk Adjusted PD

We now assess the impact of HG risk on firms' creditworthiness using he S-ICAS model, focusing on the financial consequences of expected losses due to floods and landslides. The analysis quantifies physical risk by computing the expected loss associated with these hazards and evaluating their effect on firms' financial health. Our approach allows us to derive risk-adjusted financial statements, incorporating

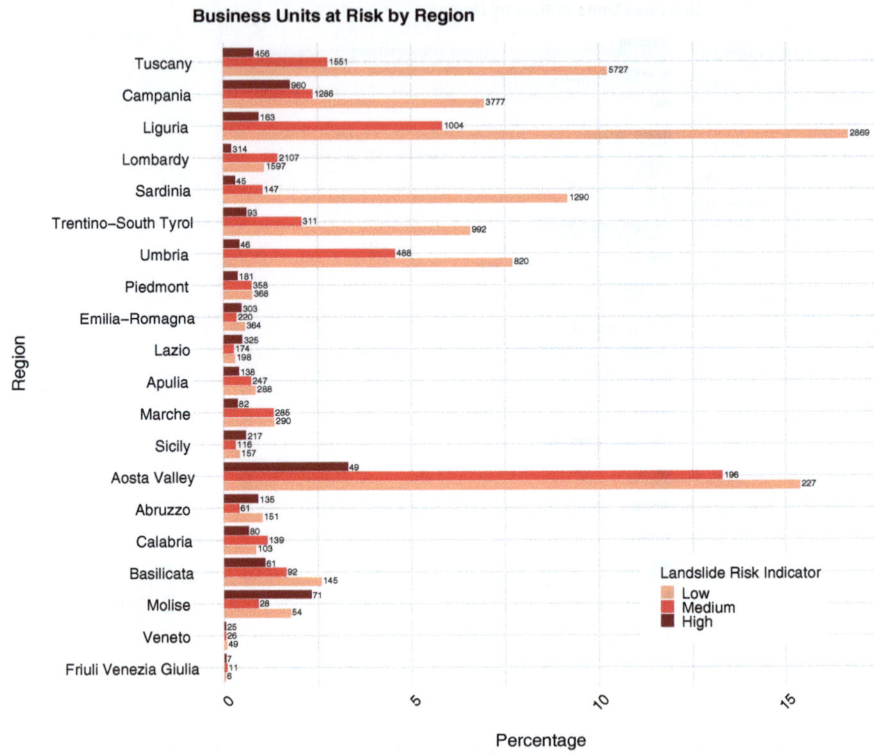

Fig. 4 Share and number of local units exposed to flood risk by region. Absolute numbers are shown near the bars, while shares are along the horizontal axis

the impact of HG risk into both income statement and balance sheet figures (see Sect. 4.2).

A key finding is that when accounting for all local units instead of the headquarters only, the total expected revenue loss due to HG risk amounts to €3.5 billion, of which €3 billion stems from flood risk and €0.5 billion from landslide risk. In contrast, considering the headquarters only, the estimated total revenue expected loss is nearly €3 billion. This adjustment translates into an average HG risk-adjusted revenue loss of -0.2% per firm, compared to -0.1% when focusing solely on headquarters (Eq. 1). On the asset side, the most significant loss occurs in PPEs, with an expected value reduction of €1.37 billion, of which €1.20 billion is due to floods. Similarly, WIs register an expected loss of nearly €0.65 billion. On average, PPEs and WIs experience value reductions of -0.2%, respectively. These results underscore the material financial impact of HG risk.

With S-ICAS, we convert the risk-adjusted financial statements into physical-risk adjusted PDs. Hence, we examine the breakdown of PD changes of firms overall and across HG risk indicator (Table 9), NACE sectors (Table 10), size (Table 11) and region (Table 12) analysing 'Changed Firms' or 'Unchanged

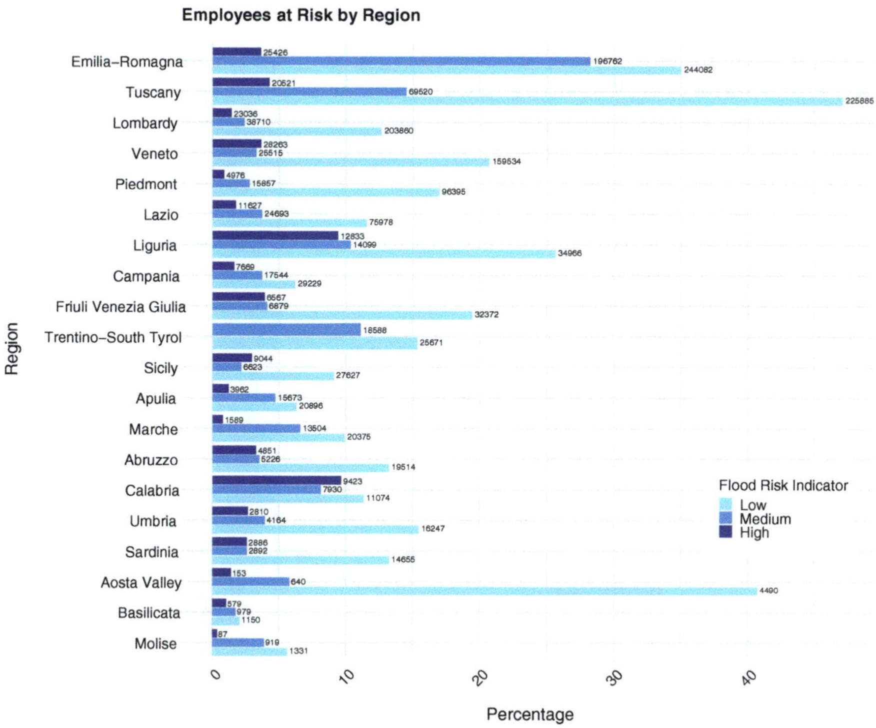

Fig. 5 Share and number of employees exposed to flood risk by region. Absolute numbers are shown near the bars, while shares are along the horizontal axis

Firms', along with their respective percentage shares and average PD increments in basis point (bp).

We find that approximately 38% of firms experience an increase in their PD, with an average PD deterioration of 1 bp (Table 9—Panel A). This relatively modest PD increase is primarily driven by the high concentration of firms in risk category 0, which remains unaffected by any PD changes (Table 9—Panel B). However, the extent of the average PD deterioration intensifies as firms are exposed to higher risk level in the baseline scenario. In the highest risk category, the average PD increase reaches 9 bp, significantly exceeding the overall average PD changes and those observed across NACE sectors (Table 10) and firm size categories (Table 11). However, if high-impact HG events become more frequent, PD deterioration would intensify, particularly for firms located in the most exposed areas. When we calculate the probability of HG events using the average of the interval bounds and the upper bound (see Table 24), the PD increases double or even triple compared to the baseline with an average PD increase of 32 bp for firms in the highest risk category (Table 9—Panel B). This shows that, if the frequency and severity of extreme events continue to rise as expected (Emambakhsh et al., 2023), the economic impact could be substantial. In 2025, a year characterised by

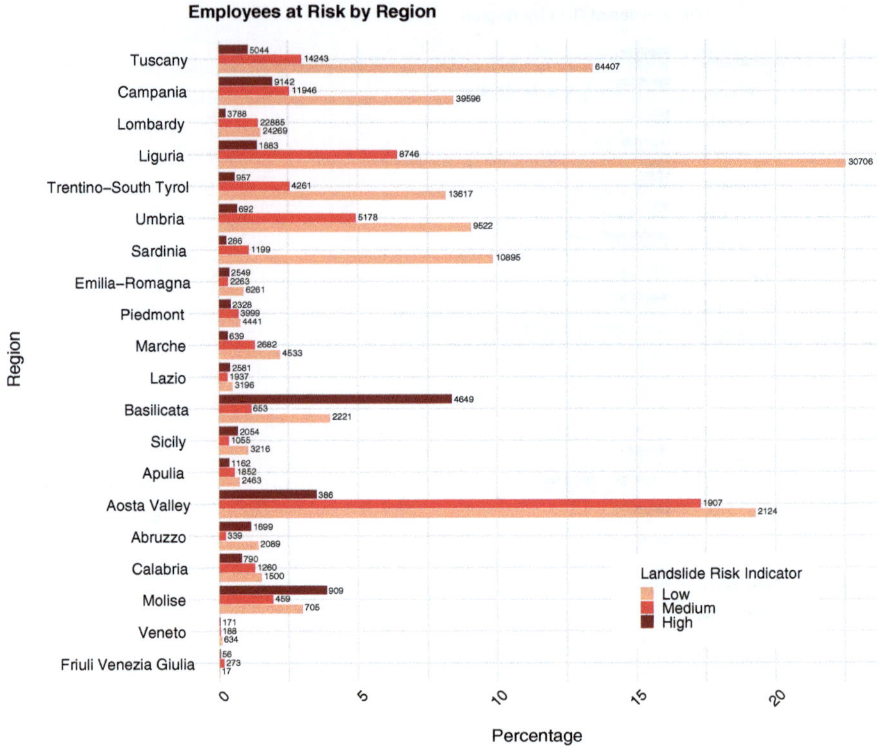

Fig. 6 Share and number of employees exposed to landslides risk by region. Absolute numbers are shown near the bars, while shares are along the horizontal axis

Table 9 one-year change in probability of default by HG risk indicator

	Firms (#)	Firms (%)	Average PD increments (bp)			
			Baseline	Lower bound	Average	Upper bound
Panel A: Firms						
Total	366,799		1.0	0.6	1.7	2.8
Panel B: HG risk indicator—Max level						
0	227,591	62.1	0.0	0.0	0.0	0.0
Low	61,520	16.8	0.9	0.7	1.0	1.4
Medium	54,864	14.9	1.8	1.1	2.5	3.8
High	22,824	6.2	9.1	4.4	18.9	32.0

Table 10 One-year change in PD by NACE sector

Sector	Migrated (# of firms)	Migrated (% total)	Migrated (% sector)	Stable (# firms)	Stable (% total)	Stable (% sector)	Average PD increment (bp)
Agriculture	2,724	0.7	37.6	4,517	1.2	62.4	1.9
Mining	342	0.1	41.4	485	0.1	58.6	1
Manufacturing	29,539	8.1	38.8	46,564	12.7	61.2	1
Electricity	1,542	0.4	39.7	2,339	0.6	60.3	0.7
Waste management	1,253	0.3	37.4	2,098	0.6	62.6	0.6
Construction	18,012	4.9	34.2	34,594	9.4	65.8	1.3
Trade	31,342	8.5	39.7	47,517	13	60.3	0.9
Hosting services	6,614	1.8	40.5	9,708	2.6	59.5	1.9
Transporting	11,188	3.1	40.9	16,161	4.4	59.1	1.3
ICT	4,400	1.2	38.4	7,053	1.9	61.6	0.8
Real Estate	14,390	3.9	35.9	25,747	7	64.1	0.6
Professional services	6,195	1.7	37.1	10,490	2.9	62.9	0.7
Administrative services	4,601	1.3	38.9	7,214	2	61.1	1.2
Education	853	0.2	40	1,279	0.3	60	1
Health services	3,248	0.9	35.8	5,832	1.6	64.2	1.1
Entertainment	2,116	0.6	41	3,042	0.8	59	0.8
Other services	1,482	0.4	39	2,318	0.6	61	1.1

Note Variations with respect to all firms and within the sector

Table 11 One-year change in probability of default by size

Size	Migrated (# of firms)	Migrated (% total)	Migrated (% size)	Stable (# firms)	Stable (% total)	Stable (% size)	Average PD increment (bp)
Large	3,083	0.8	59.4	2,108	0.6	40.6	1.9
Medium	12,684	3.5	45.8	14,993	4.1	54.2	1.2
Small	46,104	12.6	39.3	71,179	19.4	60.7	1.1
Micro	77,970	21.3	36	138,668	37.8	64	0.9

Table 12 One-year change in probability of default by region

Region	Migrated (# of firms)	Migrated (% total)	Migrated (% region)	Stable (# firms)	Stable (% total)	Stable (% region)	Average PD increment (bp)
Abruzzo	2,724	0.7	35.4	4,964	1.4	64.6	1.4
Aosta Valley	532	0.2	74.9	178	0.1	25.1	2.1
Apulia	2,492	0.7	14.4	14,790	4	85.6	0.5
Basilicata	522	0.1	19.7	2,123	0.6	80.3	0.8
Calabria	2,282	0.6	35.4	4,171	1.1	64.6	2.2
Campania	8,966	2.4	31.3	19,675	5.4	68.7	1.4
Emilia Romagna	26,286	7.2	78.4	7,253	2	21.6	1.6
Friuli Venezia Giulia	2,702	0.7	39.1	4,206	1.2	60.9	0.7
Lazio	8,742	2.4	23.6	28,316	7.7	76.4	1.3
Liguria	5,822	1.6	82.8	1,212	0.3	17.2	3.3
Lombardy	18,053	4.9	23.1	60,003	16.4	76.9	0.4
Marche	3,220	0.9	28.3	8,154	2.2	71.7	0.5
Molise	322	0.1	22	1,143	0.3	78	1.5
Piedmont	6,491	1.8	29.6	15,478	4.2	70.5	0.5
Sardinia	2,663	0.7	43.6	3,442	0.9	56.4	1.2
Sicily	2,720	0.7	14.1	16,556	4.5	85.9	1
Tuscany	25,827	7	89.5	3,032	0.8	10.5	1.8
Trentino-South Tyrol	3,042	0.8	37.5	5,061	1.4	62.5	0.5
Umbria	2,255	0.6	39.7	3,431	0.9	60.3	0.8
Veneto	13,374	3.7	37.9	21,918	6	62.1	0.8

extreme climate events, the estimated total losses from floods in Italian regions are around 4.6€ billion, expected to rise to 14.2€ billion in 2029. This is equivalent to 0.23% of national GVA in 2025 and 0.72% in 2029 (Usman et al., 2025).

Trade, and Manufacturing sectors dominate in terms of PD changes (8.5% and 8.1%, respectively). Specifically, these sectors exhibit the highest absolute numbers of firms experiencing PD changes (31,342 and 29,539 firms, respectively).

Looking at the shares of firms changed against firms unchanged within each sector, Mining and Hosting services show a notable proportion of firms experiencing changes within the sector (41.4% and 40.9%, respectively). These Fig. 102s are above the overall average increase of 38.6%, indicating that these sectors are particularly sensitive to risk-related adjustments. Conversely, Construction, and Health services display the highest proportion of firms remaining unchanged. The highest average PD increments are observed in Agriculture and Transportation

(1.9 bp), followed by Hosting services (1.3 bp). Whereas Real Estate and Waste management exhibit lower average PD variations (0.6 bp). Sectors Trade and Manufacturing stand out for having a higher proportion of firms with PD changes and relatively higher average PD variations.

Figure 7 illustrates the range (black whiskers) and the average PD increase (orange dot) in bp for firms, categorized by their respective NACE sectors. This shows the heterogeneous distribution of PD increments, revealing that some sectors are significantly more exposed to physical risk than others. Among the sectors, Agriculture emerges as the most vulnerable, exhibiting both the highest average PD increase and the largest peak increment, reaching approximately 13 bp. This is followed by Transportation, with a peak of nearly 11 bp, and Construction, where the PD increase reaches 9 bp.

As to firm size (Table 11), micro firms exhibit the highest change in absolute terms, however large firms vary the most in PD changes within their size category, with 59.4% of firms affected and 40.6% remaining unchanged. Micro firms have the lowest proportion of PD changes (36.0%) within their size class, indicating greater stability. Similarly, small firms exhibit a slightly higher rate of PD changes (39.3%) than micro firms. Medium firms fall between these extremes, with 45.8% of firms experiencing changes. Besides, large firms display the highest average PD variation (1.9 basis point), followed by medium (1.2 basis point), lastly small and

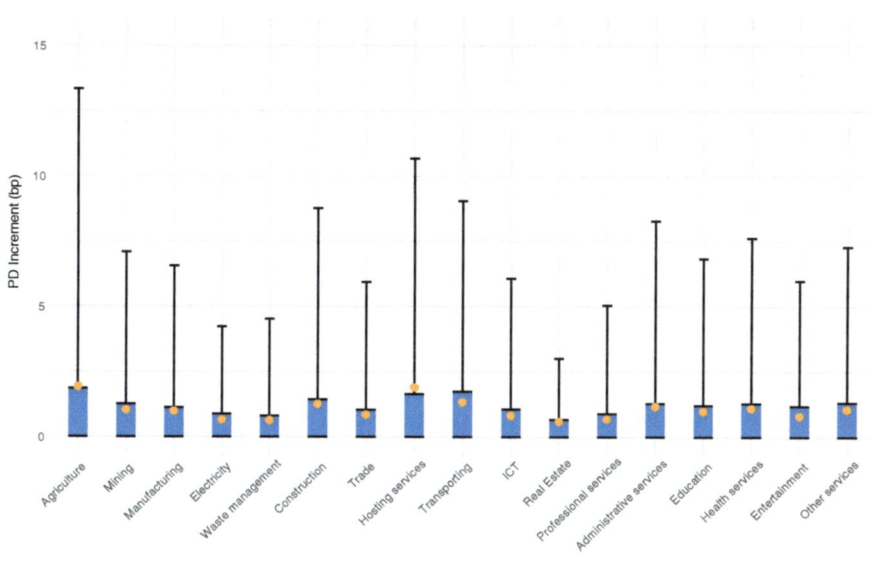

Fig. 7 One-year probability of default sensitivity to physical risk by NACE sector. The box plots illustrate PD increments in bp across different NACE sectors. The black whiskers represent the variation range, covering the 50th to the 97.5th percentile, while the box spans from the 50th to the 90th percentile. This design provides a more accurate representation of PD increments, given that the median value is 0, effectively capturing the upper tail of the distribution

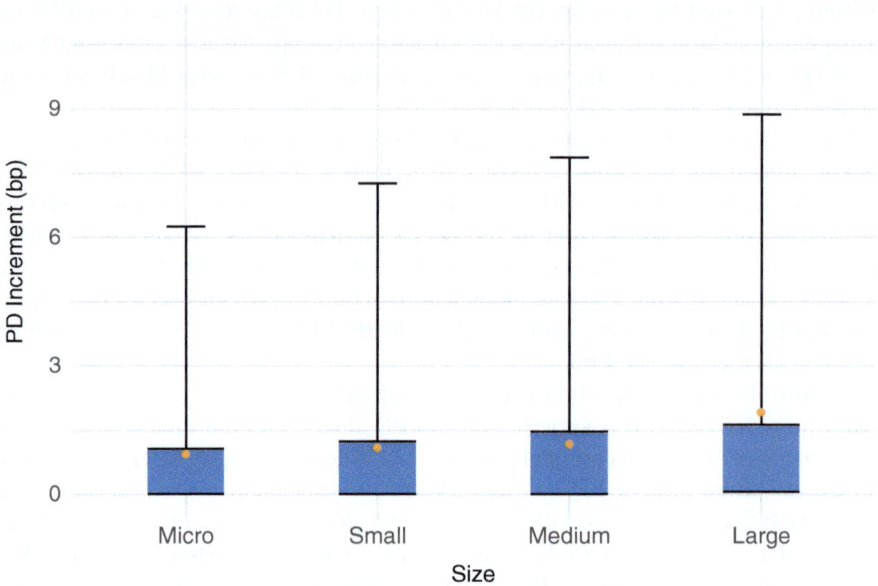

Fig. 8 One-year probability of default sensitivity to physical risk by firm size. The box plots illustrate PD increments in bp across different NACE sectors. The black whiskers represent the variation range, covering the 50th to the 97.5th percentile, while the box spans from the 50th to the 90th percentile. This design provides a more accurate representation of PD increments, given that the median value is 0, effectively capturing the upper tail of the distribution

micro firms (1.1 basis point and 0.9 basis point, respectively). Figure 8 provides graphical insights into the distribution of PD increments and average PD changes by firm size. A visual inspection reveals a linear relationship between firm size and PD increments, suggesting that larger firms experience greater PD deterioration. This trend seems attributable to the fact that large firms with many branches are more likely to be exposed to HG risk (as in Loberto & Russo, 2024a).

Finally, the results at regional level[26] show that Emilia Romagna, Tuscany and Lombardy are the regions with the highest share of firms with PD changes, consistently with exposure at local units and employees level: Emilia Romagna has 7.2% of firms with a PD deterioration, followed by Tuscany (7.1%) and Lombardy (4.9). In relative terms, for four regions in the Centre-North of Italy the percentage of firms experiencing PD changes is above 70%. Conversely, two regions in the South exhibit the lowest percentage of firms changed (14%). In terms of average PD increments, Liguria is the most exposed region with a PD increase of 3.2 bp, followed by Aosta Valley and Calabria with average PD increments above 2 bp. Figure 9 provides graphical details about the distribution of PD increments and

[26] We refer to the headquarter location for summarising the results.

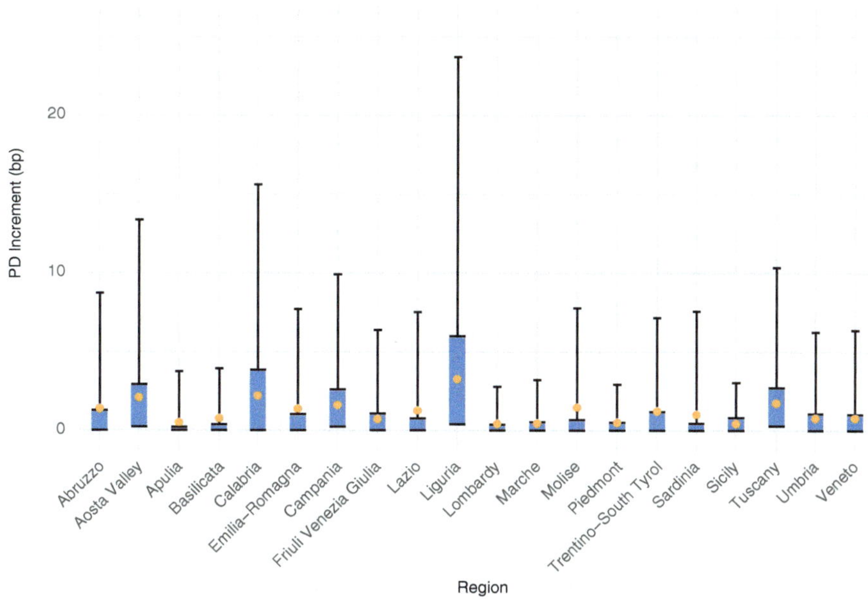

Fig. 9 One-year probability of default sensitivity to physical risk by region. The box plots illustrate PD increments in bp across different NACE sectors. The black whiskers represent the variation range, covering the 50th to the 97.5th percentile, while the box spans from the 50th to the 90th percentile. This design provides a more accurate representation of PD increments, given that the median value is 0, effectively capturing the upper tail of the distribution

the average increases by region, highlighting that Liguria, Calabria and Aosta Valley also experience the highest PD increment peaks, reaching 24, 16 and 13 bp, respectively. These findings underscore the regional disparities and vulnerability of firms operating in these areas.

The results of our analysis reveal a significant heterogeneity across sectors in terms of PD changes. Sectors with a larger number of firms tend to have a balanced distribution between firms with and without PD changes, while some smaller sectors exhibit a higher relative proportion of firms experiencing a change. Besides, the analysis reveals a clear relationship between firm size and risk. Larger firms face higher risk, as shown by the greater proportion of PD changes within their size category and higher average PD increment. This finding is consistent with the fact that large firms operate with several branches. The regional analysis discloses significant disparities in PD changes and stability. Tuscany, Emilia-Romagna, Liguria and Aosta Valley exhibit the largest proportion of firms experiencing PD changes (as expected from the exposure analysis in Sect. 5.1), whereas Liguria, Aosta Valley and Calabria exhibit the highest increase in the average PD.

Finally, to verify the robustness of our results, we repeat the analysis using a different geo-locating server (see Appendix D for the results) and test the correlation between the difference in physical risk adjusted PDs and baseline PDs and the

HG risk discrete indicator. The Spearman correlation test shows 89% correlation, which is statistically significant at the 1% level. This is consistent with ex-ante expectations: a higher risk level corresponds to higher PD deterioration.

6 Further Results

6.1 The Impact on Collateral in Monetary Policy Operations

The Bank of Italy's ICAS model plays an important role in evaluating collateral used in monetary policy operations. Several banks rely on ICAS to assess the quality of the collateral they pledge when accessing Eurosystem refinancing operations. In these operations, the Eurosystem accepts both marketable assets and credit claims. These claims typically arise from loans granted by banks to the public sector, corporates, and small- and medium-sized enterprises. Physical risk could impair the banks' ability to pledge collateral, potentially reducing their refinancing capacity and affecting liquidity management.

To gauge the impact of changes of firms' creditworthiness on collateral value we analyse shifts within the harmonised rating scale of the ECAF: the CQS. Under this framework,[27] one-year PD ranges define the CQS classes, from the safest (CQS 1 and 2) to the riskiest (CQS 8. See Table 1 in Chap. 3). In the ordinary ECAF framework, only assets rated at least in CQS 3 are eligible as collateral. By contrast, in the ACCs, individual loans up to CQS 5 are eligible, while pools of credits can include loans up to CQS 8.[28] Based on the CQS rating, the Eurosystem applies a haircut to the collateral value; a bank's borrowing capacity is determined by the net collateral value after this reduction. As of December 2023, BI-ICAS had evaluated almost 27% of the credit claims pledged by Italian banks as collateral in monetary policy operations (both individual loans and pools), whit an outstanding amount equal to €29 billion.[29]

An examination of transition dynamics across risk classes shows that the safest CQS classes are largely stable (Table 13). CQS1and2, the most stable classes, experience a minor outflow of 101 firms (−0.5%), while CQS3 loses 177 firms (−0.3%). All firms that shift away from CQS 3 are no more eligible as collateral for monetary policy operations in the ordinary ECAF framework. Middle classes

[27] Article 82 of Guideline ECB/2014/30.

[28] ACCs are a temporarily extension of the types of assets eligible as collateral to ensure that banks have full access to central bank liquidity, even in adverse economic condition. ACCs are credit claims that do not fulfil all the eligibility criteria applicable under the general collateral framework, as lowering credit quality. Italian ACCs is regulated by "Condizioni generali relative alle garanzie 2024.1".

[29] Given the prioritization of ICAS rating, we expect this percentage to increase (Columba et al., 2024).

Table 13 One-year change in Eurosystem credit risk quality

CQS	Migrated (#)	Migrated (%)	Stable (#)	Stable (%)	Delta (#)	Delta (%)	Average PD increment (bp)
CQS1and2	19,208	5.2	19,107	5.2	−101	−0.5	0
CQS3	63,172	17.2	62,997	17.2	−175	−0.3	0.1
CQS4	72,701	19.8	72,708	19.8	7	0	0.3
CQS5	32,612	8.9	32,551	8.9	−61	−0.2	0.6
CQS6	64,981	17.7	64,947	17.7	−34	−0.1	0.9
CQS7	48,633	13.3	48,761	13.3	128	0.3	1.3
CQS8	65,241	17.8	65,477	17.9	236	0.4	3.2

Table 14 Overall migration in one-year default probability and in credit quality class

Variation	Migrated (#)	Migrated (%)	Stable (#)	Stable (%)	Average PD increment (bp)
PD	139,841	38.1	226,958	61.9	1.02
CQS	1,571	0.4	365,228	99.6	1.02

(CQS 4–CQS6) shifts are negligible, indicating strong stability within this segment. CQS7 and CQS8 experience small increases, gaining 128 firms (+0.3%) and 236 firms (+0.4%), respectively. These results suggest that, in percentage terms, the deteriorations in PD are more numerous in the lower quality classes.

Overall, the magnitude of these shifts is minimal. Although physical risks lead to a deterioration in PD for about 38% of cases, the direct impact on credit quality is limited, with only 0.4% of firms experiencing a downgrade in their CQS rating (Table 14). The stability in the middle and high-quality classes, alongside the modest increase in the riskiest classes, produces a marginal deterioration in the value of collateral of 0.4% (individual loans and pools). Thus, the overall effect on collateral value is economically insignificant.

6.2 Does Insurance Matter?

Many studies in this field do not consider the role of insurance against natural hazards and mitigation policies due to data limitations. In Italy, insurance against natural hazards will become mandatory for all firms across all sectors (except agriculture) seeking access to public restoration funds in case of disasters (DL 202/2024).

The new law requires that insurance policies cover at least 85% of damages to plants, buildings, and land, with insurance companies mandated to immediately pay out at least 30% of the insured amount upon damage assessment (Law 213/2023).

According to the INVIND survey,[30] 68% of Italian firms currently hold insurance against natural hazards. Among those without coverage, the primary obstacle is the high cost of insurance premiums (Gallo et al., 2022). Despite this relatively high reported coverage rate, European data present a stark contrast, indicating that only 5% of potential losses incurred by Italian firms are actually insured (European Environment Agency, 2023). This discrepancy suggests that while firms may hold some level of coverage, this is generally insufficient to offset the financial risks associated with extreme events.

The Bank of Italy carried out a survey in 2024, designed for ICAS purposes (see Chap. 6). This initiative aimed at the collection of granular data on firms' greenhouse gas emissions, energy consumption, financial exposure to climate-related events, and insurance coverage, providing insights into their vulnerability and risk mitigation strategies. This allows us to extend our analysis by examining the mitigation effects of insurance coverage for firms that responded to the survey.[31]

Since insurance premiums are recorded under "Service Costs" in the 2023 income statement, no additional expense is considered. This is important, as purely quantitative credit scoring models do not account for insurance coverage. Moreover, the insurance premium is typically treated as an operational cost, and the insurance financial benefits are only recognised in the financial statement when a covered adverse event occurs. As a result, a firm that insures against HG risks may be assessed with a higher PD than an otherwise identical firm (i.e. one with the same financial statement) that chooses not to insure. Our methodology, which incorporates a HG risk-adjusted financial statement, accounts for the potential financial benefit of insurance against HG risks.

Regarding insurance coverage for potential damages, we make the following assumptions based on the upcoming regulation (Law 213/2023):

- Reduced Business Disruption: As insurers must immediately reimburse 30% of damages, we assume business disruption time is halved following a HG event (see Sect. 4.2).
- Asset Value Adjustment: Since insurance covers at least 85% of damages to plants, buildings, and land, we reduce the PPE's value by 15% only in case of an HG event. This adjustment does not apply to WI.

Our findings indicate that insurance coverage significantly reduces the PD increase following HG events—by nearly half, regardless of NACE sector, region, or HG intensity indicator (Fig. 10). This result is noteworthy, as banks currently do not differentiate between firms with or without insurance coverage (Gallo et al., 2024).

[30] The survey conducted by the Bank of Italy annually collects information on investments, revenue, employment, and other economic variables of Italian industrial and service enterprises with at least 20 employees.

[31] This extension applies to 228 firms only. While not fully representative of the S-ICAS sample, it serves as a valuable starting point for assessing the potential impact of insurance coverage.

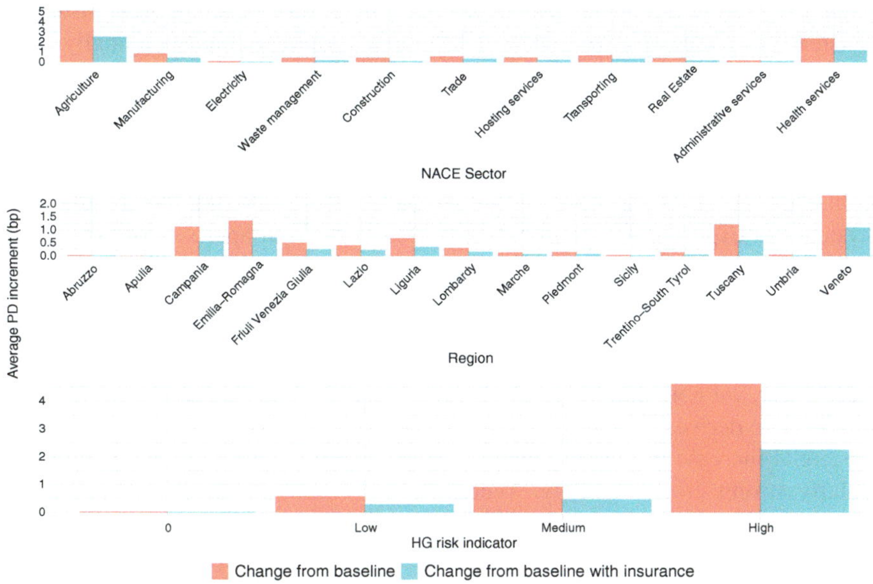

Fig. 10 Average PD increase with and without insurance coverage

7 Conclusion

This Chapter advances the assessment of credit risk for non-financial firms by integrating climate change-related physical risks into firms' PD estimation. We focus on HG risk (flood and landslide), which is particularly relevant in Italy due to its distinctive geographical characteristics. Our methodology leverages ISPRA's mosaic risk map, which provides granular flood and landslide data, to estimate physical risks at the local unit level. To evaluate the impact of physical risk on firms' creditworthiness, we examine how damages and business disruptions caused by HG events affect firms' financial statements. Our methodology addresses a critical gap in previous studies by incorporating the full geographic exposure of firms' operations.

Our findings show that nearly 38% of Italian firms are exposed to HG risks when accounting for all local unit. In most cases, floods and landslides have limited effect on the one-year PD with an average PD deterioration of about 1 bp and a small number of rating migrations. Nevertheless, firms located in high-risk areas, classified in the worst category of our risk indicator, may face significant financial losses, with an average PD deterioration of 9 bp, far beyond the overall average. The impact on collateral value is economically negligible: the deterioration in the value of collateral is of 0.37% (both individual loans and pools).

Insurance coverage emerges as a key risk mitigation factor. Our results indicate that, for a subsample of firms, insurance against natural hazard can reduce the average PD deterioration by nearly 50%. This finding is particularly noteworthy given available evidence that banks usually do not differentiate between firms insured or uninsured. A widespread presence of insurance coverage could potentially lower borrowing costs, making bank loans more affordable for insured firms, in addition to contributing to the stability of the financial system.

Our methodology, based on expected loss estimation, differs from traditional stress testing and scenario-based approaches, which often rely on assumptions about extreme events that have yet to materialize. By combining the granularity of physical risk exposure with a probabilistic framework, our approach offers a robust and flexible model that can be integrated into credit risk assessment frameworks, including ICAS and IRB systems. Such integration can improve PD forecasting accuracy, helping all type of lenders to better manage risks associated with HG events.

However, we note that our analysis relies on ISPRA hazard maps, whose probabilities are derived from historical observations. Climate change is driving a substantial increase in the frequency of extreme natural events globally, with particularly strong effects in Italy. Therefore, our results should be interpreted as reflecting an average historical scenario. In the absence of targeted policy interventions, the frequency and severity of extreme events are expected to rise further, triggering larger economic impacts for firms located in highly exposed areas. If we consider the current worst scenario, the PD deterioration is more than three times larger than in the baseline scenario, with an average PD increase of 32 bp for firms in the highest risk category.

Moreover, ISPRA mosaic risk maps are subject to the uncertainties of hydrogeological modelling, yet ISPRA mosaic is embedded within the regulatory framework[32] and serves as the official tool for hydraulic risk management and assessment at national and European levels. We acknowledge these limitations to enhance transparency and lay the groundwork for future research, such as incorporating flood depth data and industrial building characteristics to enhance vulnerability assessment. Together with a broader dataset on firms' insurance coverage, this would lead to more accurate expected loss estimation.

Appendix A

NACE Sector Classification

See Table 15.

[32] EU Floods Directive (2007/60/EC).

Table 15 List of NACE sectors, letter and activities denomination

Letter	Short Name	Long Name
A	Agriculture	Agriculture, forestry and fishing
B	Mining	Mining and quarrying
C	Manufacturing	Manufacturing
D	Electricity	Electricity, gas, steam and air conditioning supply
E	Waste management	Water supply; sewerage; waste management and remediation activities
F	Construction	Construction
G	Trade	Wholesale and retail trade
H	Transporting	Transporting and storage
I	Hosting services	Accommodation and food service activities
J	ICT	Information and communication
K	Financial Services	Financial and insurance activities
L	Real Estate	Real estate activities
M	Professional services	Professional, scientific and technical activities
N	Administrative services	Administrative and support service activities
P	Education	Education
Q	Health services	Human health and social work activities
R	Entertainment	Arts, entertainment and recreation
S	Other services	Other services activities

Appendix B

Elasticity of Costs to Revenues

We estimate variable costs and personnel costs elasticity at NACE sector level. For each sector s, we use financial statement data for limited firms from 2010 to 2018 to estimate $\eta_{j,s}$ with $j = VC, LC$ using the following equation (De Socio et al., 2020):

$$\log y_{i,t} = \eta_{j,s} \log r_{i,t} + \gamma X_{i,t-1} + \theta_t + \xi_i + \varepsilon_{i,t} \tag{7}$$

where s is the i-th firm's sector, $r_{i,t}$ is the i-th firm's revenues, $X_{i,t-1}$ is a vector of control variables including total assets and net income, θ_t and ξ_i are time and firm fixed effect. We exclude from the sample firms whose total assets and total revenues are less than 500.000 euros. Table 16 reports the estimated elasticities.

Table 16 Estimated elasticity for NACE sector

NACE	Variable cost	Personnel cost
Agriculture	0.64	0.23
Mining	0.75	0.3
Manufacturing	0.78	0.25
Electricity	0.87	0.12
Waste management	0.77	0.27
Construction	0.68	0.21
Trade	0.92	0.1
Hosting services	0.68	0.25
Transporting	0.7	0.26
ICT	0.63	0.24
Financial services	0.72	0.21
Real estate	0.62	0.22
Professional services	0.71	0.21
Administrative services	0.64	0.2
Education	0.66	0.22
Health services	0.71	0.19
Entertainment	0.55	0.33
Other services	0.71	0.19
Agriculture	0.62	0.28

Note Own estimates based on Cerved data. Some companies that have a special format for financial statements ("real estate companies") are excluded

Appendix C

Geocoding Algorithm

The ESRI geocoding system involves a multi-layered process designed to maximize accuracy. Initially, addresses are parsed and standardized according to regional norms, ensuring consistency in format. This involves resolving inconsistencies in address notation, such as abbreviations, punctuation, and formatting conventions, to align with the input requirements of the ESRI API. Address components, such as street names, house numbers, postal codes, and administrative divisions, are segmented and validated against reference datasets. The pre-processing step is crucial for improving the likelihood of obtaining accurate matches from the geocoding service.

Each pre-processed address is then sent to the ESRI API, which generates a list of potential candidate locations. The API evaluates these candidates based on their similarity to the input address and assigns a confidence score to each match. The algorithm selects the candidate location with the highest score, provided it meets or exceeds a confidence threshold of 90%. Addresses failing to meet this threshold are flagged for manual review to ensure that no critical data are omitted. To further enhance precision, we implement a validation mechanism where a subset of geocoded addresses is cross-referenced with manually verified locations and output from alternative providers. Specifically, we analyse a subset of enterprises using results from Nominatim (OpenStreetMap) and Google Maps, comparing their geocoding accuracy with that of the ESRI system. This analysis informs the empirical justification for the 90% threshold, demonstrating its efficacy in balancing precision and recall while minimizing false positives.

The algorithm developed for this process incorporates additional safeguards to ensure robustness. It supports batch processing, allowing multiple addresses to be geocoded simultaneously, and employs parallelization techniques to optimize computational efficiency. The standardized output format provided by the ESRI API ensures consistent representation of address components, facilitating seamless integration with other datasets, such as the ISPRA mosaic risk maps. These standardized data form the basis for mapping firms' local units to their respective hydrogeological risk zones, enhancing the accuracy of physical risk-adjusted PD models.

The decision to set a 90% confidence threshold is informed by an extensive analysis of geocoding results across different providers. By comparing the accuracy of ESRI's results with those from Nominatim and Google Maps on a representative subset of firms, we find that matches below the 90% threshold often lead to incorrect or imprecise geolocations. Conversely, matches meeting or exceeding this threshold consistently align with ground-truth data. This empirical validation underscores the reliability of the ESRI system when operate within these parameters.

The geocoded data serves as a foundation for mapping firms' local units to their respective hydrogeological risk zones, as defined by the ISPRA mosaic risk maps. By ensuring high-precision geocoding, we mitigate the risk of misclassification, thereby enhancing the accuracy of our physical risk-adjusted PD models. Furthermore, the standardized geocoded data facilitates seamless integration with other geospatial datasets, enabling a comprehensive analysis of risk exposure at both the firm and regional levels.

Building on the geocoded data, the integration process with the ISPRA hydrogeological risk maps establishes a robust link between each local unit and its corresponding hazard zones. The procedure begins by aligning the datasets through the standardization of coordinate reference systems to ensure spatial compatibility. The ISPRA maps, detailed as shapefiles, provide polygons that categorize flood and landslide risks based on factors such as probability and intensity.

A spatial join operation matches the geocoded local unit coordinates to these hazard zones, appending specific risk attributes to each unit. For locations positioned near the boundaries of risk polygons, buffering techniques refine the spatial assignment, ensuring accurate alignment. This process is critical for mitigating errors that may arise from overlapping or closely adjacent zones.

Fig. 11 Italy political map

Appendix D

Robustness Checks—OpenStreetMap Geolocalisation

We repeat our analysis with OpenStreetMap/Nominatim geolocalisation as consistency check (Tables 17, 18, 19, 20, 21, 22, 23, Figs. 12, 13).

Table 17 Distribution of industrial building per risk category. Percentage values

ISPRA risk category	Office	Plant	Shop	Warehouse	Other	Total
Panel A: Flood						
0	16.42	13.29	20.67	21.33	1.05	72.76
LPH	2.46	2.03	3.38	3.14	0.18	11.19
MPH	2.12	2.05	2.88	3.05	0.21	10.32
HPH	1.2	0.99	1.81	1.63	0.12	5.74
Panel B: Landslide						
0	20.61	16.86	26.39	26.92	1.36	92.15
P1	0.63	0.51	0.93	0.83	0.09	2.99
P2	0.51	0.48	0.77	0.69	0.05	2.51
P3	0.28	0.32	0.41	0.44	0.03	1.49
P4	0.16	0.18	0.23	0.26	0.02	0.86

Table 18 Discrete risk indicators. Percentage values

Risk Indicator	Flood (% firms)	Landslide (% firms)	HG (% firms)
Panel A: All local units			
0	70.05	91.59	64.64
Low	14.12	3.92	15.57
Medium	11.07	2.5	13.11
High	4.76	1.99	6.68
Panel B: Headquarters only			
0	73.85	92.69	68.98
Low	10.73	2.79	11.79
Medium	10.09	2.35	11.88
High	5.33	2.17	7.35

Robustness Checks—Alternative Hazard Probability

We calculate all PDs, disaggregated by risk indicator, NACE sector, firm size, and region, using hazard probabilities associated with upper and lower bounds of the time range for each risk category and derived as the average between the upper and lower probabilities (Table 24).

Our results show that the average increase in PD exceeds 0.7 basis points in the average scenario and is nearly three times higher in the upper-bound scenario. The most significant variations occur in the highest HG risk category, as well as in sectors and regions that were already among the most exposed in the baseline scenario (Table 25). Hence, the assumptions regarding return time are the most

Table 19 One-year change in probability of default for NACE sectors with respect to all firms and within the sector

Sector	Migrated (# of firms)	Migrated (% total)	Migrated (% sector)	Stable (# firms)	Stable (% total)	Stable (% sector)	Average PD increment (bp)
Agriculture	2,573	0.7	35.54	4,667	1.27	64.46	1.99
Mining	302	0.08	36.52	525	0.14	63.48	0.91
Manufacturing	27,787	7.57	36.47	48,402	13.18	63.53	1.05
Electricity	1,475	0.4	38.03	2,404	0.65	61.97	0.93
Waste management	1,171	0.32	34.92	2,182	0.59	65.08	0.66
Construction	16,808	4.58	31.94	35,821	9.76	68.06	1.4
Trade	29,329	7.99	37.13	49,655	13.52	62.87	0.82
Hosting services	6,162	1.68	37.72	10,173	2.77	62.28	1.55
Transporting	10,581	2.88	38.64	16,801	4.58	61.36	1.31
ICT	4,134	1.13	36	7,350	2	64	0.81
Real Estate	13,643	3.72	33.99	26,500	7.22	66.01	0.59
Professional services	5,874	1.6	35.17	10,830	2.95	64.83	0.68
Administrative services	4,340	1.18	36.69	7,489	2.04	63.31	1.17
Education	799	0.22	37.44	1,335	0.36	62.56	0.9
Health services	3,139	0.85	34.55	5,946	1.62	65.45	1.15
Entertainment	1,976	0.54	38.26	3,188	0.87	61.74	0.87
Other services	1,417	0.39	37.18	2,394	0.65	62.82	1.11

Table 20 One-year change in probability of default for all firms and within size

Size	Migrated (# of firms)	Migrated (% total)	Migrated (% size)	Stable (# firms)	Stable (% total)	Stable (% size)	Average PD increment (bp)
Large	2,999	0.82	57.65	2,203	0.6	42.35	2.03
Medium	12,106	3.3	43.68	15,609	4.25	56.32	1.16
Small	43,538	11.86	37.1	73,823	20.11	62.9	1.12
Micro	72,867	19.85	33.6	144,015	39.22	66.4	0.94

Table 21 One-year change in probability of default for all firms and within region

Region	Migrated (# of firms)	Migrated (% total)	Migrated (% region)	Stable (# firms)	Stable (% total)	Stable (% region)	Average PD increment (bp)
Abruzzo	2,907	0.79	37.84	4,775	1.3	62.16	1.67
Apulia	2887	0.79	15.31	15,971	4.35	84.69	0.48
Basilicata	834	0.23	31.54	1,810	0.49	68.46	1.06
Calabria	1859	0.51	28.81	4,593	1.25	71.19	1.49
Campania	5,213	1.42	36.58	9,039	2.46	63.42	2
Emilia Romagna	24,932	6.79	74.41	8,576	2.34	25.59	1.64
Friuli Venezia Giulia	2,445	0.67	39.23	3,788	1.03	60.77	0.94
Lazio	7,054	1.92	19.04	29,994	8.17	80.96	1.02
Liguria	5,361	1.46	76.27	1,668	0.45	23.73	2.92
Lombardy	16,720	4.55	21.42	61,340	16.71	78.58	0.54
Marche	3,129	0.85	27.51	8,244	2.25	72.49	0.47
Molise	258	0.07	17.61	1,207	0.33	82.39	0.49
Piedmont	5788	1.58	26.35	16,181	4.41	73.65	0.49
Sardinia	2,446	0.67	35.06	4,531	1.23	64.94	1.07
Sicily	2,529	0.69	13.12	16,746	4.56	86.88	1.1
Tuscany	25,126	6.84	87.18	3,696	1.01	12.82	1.88
Trentino-South Tyrol	2,933	0.8	36.15	5,180	1.41	63.85	0.51
Umbria	1,806	0.49	31.8	3,874	1.06	68.2	0.62
Aosta Valley	483	0.13	68.41	223	0.06	31.59	4.99
Veneto	13,330	3.63	37.68	22,051	6.01	62.32	0.91

Table 22 One-year change in ICAS and Eurosystem credit risk quality

CQS	Migrated (#)	Migrated (%)	Stable (#)	Stable (%)	Delta (#)	Delta (%)
CQS1and2	19,220	5.23	19,118	5.21	−102	−0.53
CQS3	63,214	17.22	63,031	17.17	−183	−0.29
CQS4	72,744	19.81	72,711	19.8	−33	−0.05
CQS5	32,635	8.89	32,620	8.88	−15	−0.05
CQS6	65,042	17.71	65,008	17.71	−34	−0.05
CQS7	48,700	13.26	48,813	13.29	113	0.23
CQS8	65,617	17.87	65,871	17.94	254	0.39

Table 23 One-year change in ICAS PD

	Migrated (#)	Migratede (%)	Stable (#)	Stable (%)
PD	131,510	35.82	235,662	64.18

impactful. However, the baseline assumption—averaging the return time and converting it into a probability of occurrence—is the mainstream method for obtaining a combined return period (Raschke, 2021).

Robustness Checks—Alternative Flood Vulnerability Measure

To further corroborate our findings, we extend our analysis by considering two alternative measures of flood vulnerability. Specifically, we examine two scenarios: (i) a mild scenario, in which PPE and WI lose 30% of their value; (ii) an extreme scenario, in which PPE and WI lose up to 90% of their value. No significant differences arise with respect to the baseline, hence, assumptions about vulnerability are not crucial (Table 26).

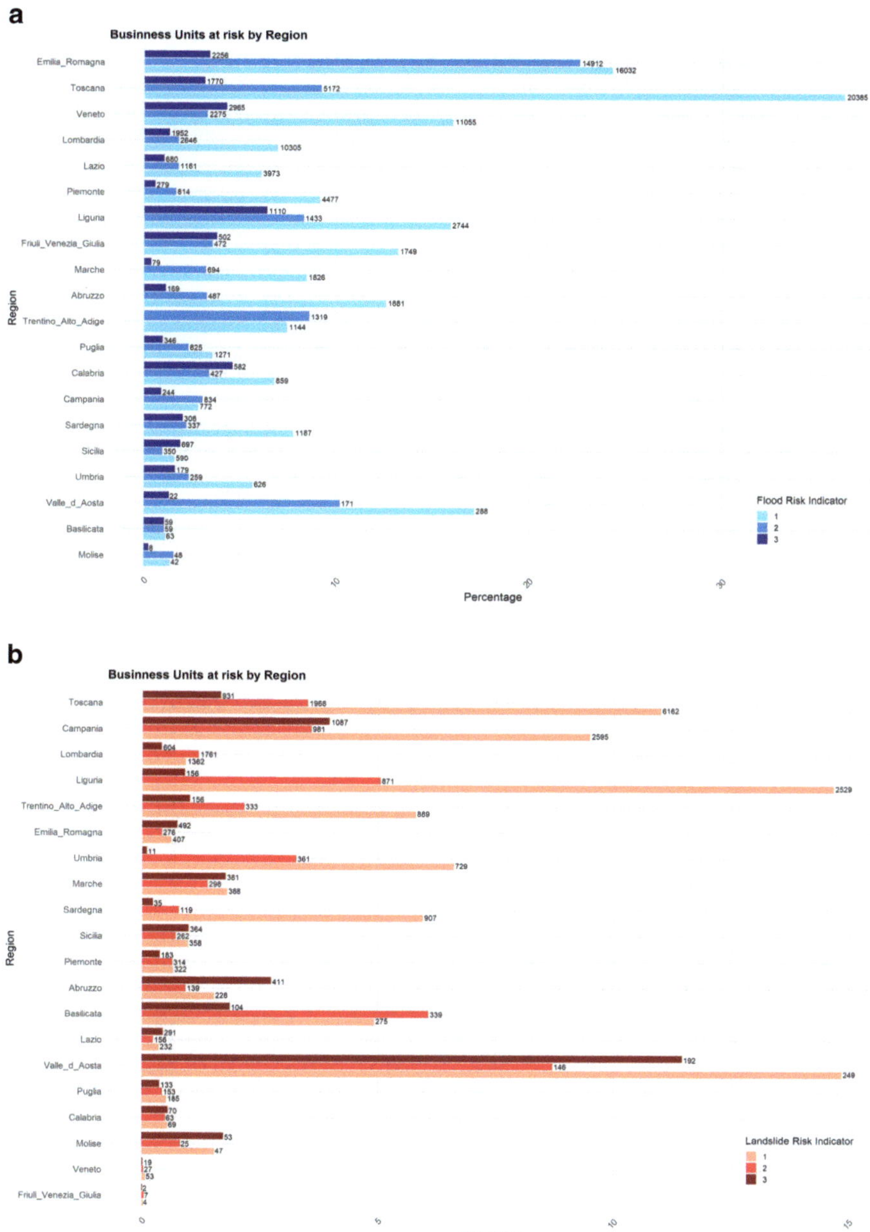

Fig. 12 Share and number of exposed local units by region. **a** Flood hazard; **b** Landslide hazard. Absolute numbers are shown near the bars, while shares are along the horizontal axis. Source: Nominatim/OpenStreetMap geolocalisation server

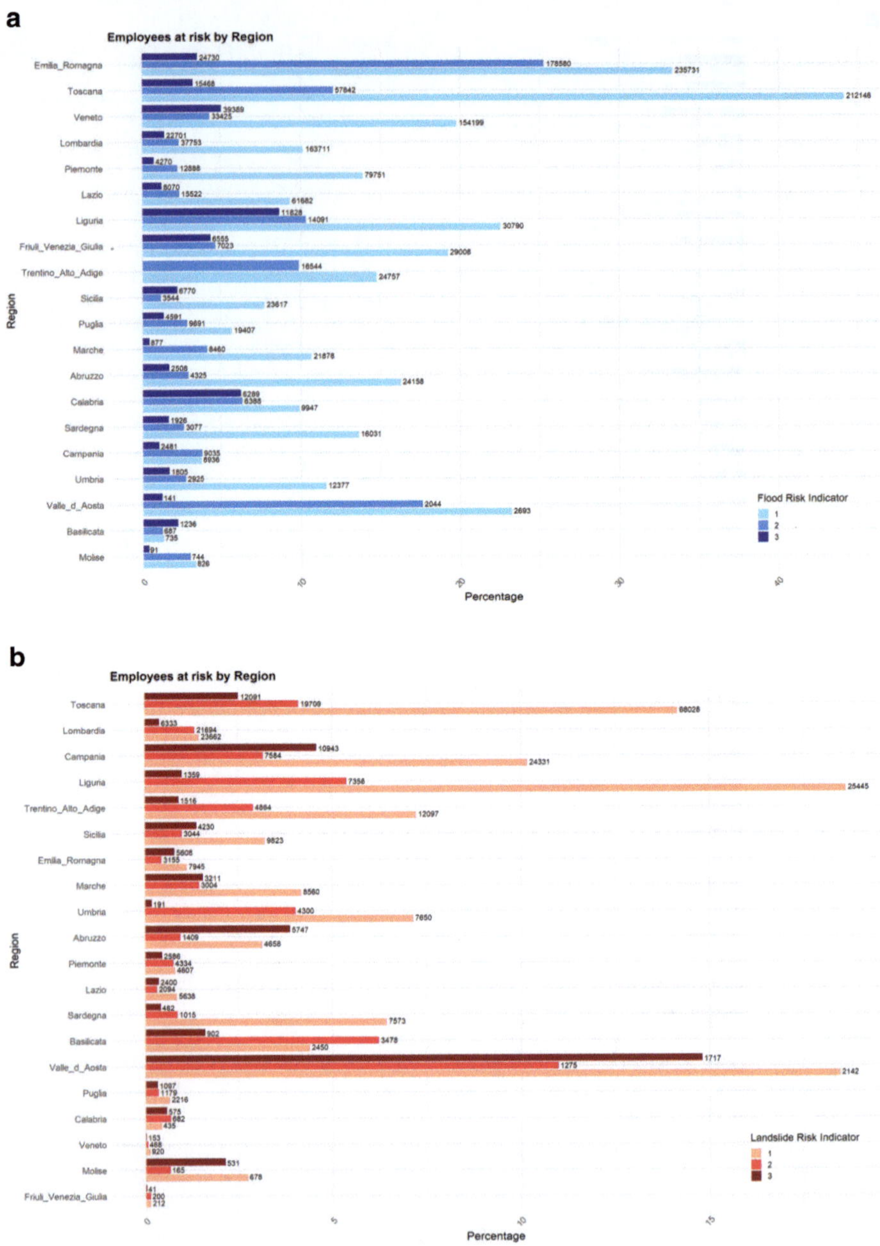

Fig. 13 Share and number of exposed employees by region. **a** Flood hazard; **b** Landslide hazard. Absolute numbers are shown near the bars, while shares are along the horizontal axis. Source: Nominatim/OpenStreetMap geolocalisation server

Table 24 Annualised probability of occurrence of the extreme HG events. Alternative hazard probability

Flood	Landslide
HPH: T = [20; 50] $\rightarrow p_u = 0.02; p_l = 0.05 \rightarrow \overline{p} = 0.035$	**P4**: T = [1; 30] $\rightarrow p_u = 0.033; p_l = 1 \rightarrow \overline{p} = 0.517$
MPH: T = [100; 200] $\rightarrow$ $p_u = 0.005; p_l = 0.01 \rightarrow \overline{p} = 0.0075$	**P3**: T = [30; 100] $\rightarrow p_u = 0.01; p_l = 0.033 \rightarrow \overline{p} = 0.0217$
LPH: T > 200 $\rightarrow p_u = 0.002; p_l = 0.002 \rightarrow \overline{p} = 0.002$	**P2**: T = [100; 300] $\rightarrow p_u = 0.003; p_l = 0.01 \rightarrow \overline{p} = 0.0067$
	P1: T > 300 $\rightarrow \overline{p} = 0.0033$

Table 25 One-year change in ICAS PD for different hazard probability

	Average PD increments (bp)			
	Baseline	Lower Bound	Average	Upper Bound
Panel A: Firms				
Total	1.0	0.6	1.7	2.8
Panel B: HG risk indicator				
0	0.0	0.0	0.0	0.1
Low	0.9	0.7	1.0	1.4
Medium	1.8	1.1	2.5	3.8
High	9.1	4.4	18.9	32.0
Panel C: NACE Sector				
Agriculture	1.9	1.2	5.2	8.7
Mining	1.0	0.6	3.7	6.9
Manufacturing	1.0	0.6	1.8	2.8
Electricity	0.7	0.3	1.4	2.8
Waste management	0.6	0.3	1.6	2.6
Construction	1.3	0.7	2.5	3.7
Trade	0.9	0.4	1.3	2.3
Hosting services	1.9	1.1	3.2	4.8
Transporting	1.3	0.7	2.3	4.0
ICT	0.8	0.4	0.9	1.4
Real Estate	0.6	0.4	0.8	1.3
Professional services	0.7	0.4	0.8	1.2
Administrative services	1.2	0.6	1.6	2.5
Education	1.0	0.7	1.2	1.8
Health services	1.1	0.6	1.7	2.6

(continued)

Table 25 (continued)

	Average PD increments (bp)			
	Baseline	Lower Bound	Average	Upper Bound
Entertainment	0.8	0.5	1.6	2.4
Other services	1.1	0.7	1.6	2.5
Panel D: Size				
Large	1.9	1.4	2.3	3.4
Medium	1.2	0.6	1.9	3.1
Small	1.1	0.6	1.9	3.0
Micro	0.9	0.5	1.7	2.7
Panel E: Region				
Abruzzo	1.4	0.7	4.0	6.8
Aosta Valley	2.1	1.1	6.5	11.1
Apulia	0.5	0.2	1.3	2.3
Basilicata	0.8	0.4	1.8	3.0
Calabria	2.2	1.0	3.5	6.0
Campania	1.4	0.6	4.2	7.5
Emilia Romagna	1.6	1.1	2.1	3.1
Friuli Venezia Giulia	0.7	0.4	0.6	0.9
Lazio	1.3	0.6	2.1	3.6
Liguria	3.3	1.7	3.2	4.4
Lombardy	0.4	0.2	0.6	0.9
Marche	0.5	0.3	0.6	0.8
Molise	1.5	0.7	5.6	9.2
Piedmont	0.5	0.3	1.2	2.1
Sardinia	1.2	0.7	1.7	2.3
Sicily	1.0	0.4	1.9	3.2
Tuscany	1.8	0.2	0.4	0.6
Trentino-South Tyrol	0.5	1.3	2.6	3.9
Umbria	0.8	0.5	0.9	1.3
Veneto	0.8	0.5	0.8	1.2

Table 26 One-year change in ICAS PD for different vulnerability level

	Average PD increments (bp)		
	Baseline	Mild	Extreme
Panel A: Firms			
Total	1.0	1.0	1.0
Panel B: HG risk indicator			
0	0.0	0.0	0.0
Low	0.9	0.9	1.0
Medium	1.8	1.8	1.9
High	9.1	8.9	9.3
Panel C: NACE Sector			
Agriculture	1.9	1.9	2.0
Mining	1.0	1.0	1.1
Manufacturing	1.0	1.0	1.0
Electricity	0.7	0.6	0.7
Waste management	0.6	0.6	0.6
Construction	1.3	1.2	1.3
Trade	0.9	0.8	0.9
Hosting services	1.9	1.9	1.9
Transporting	1.3	1.3	1.4
ICT	0.8	0.8	0.8
Real Estate	0.6	0.5	0.6
Professional services	0.7	0.7	0.7
Administrative services	1.2	1.2	1.2
Education	1.0	1.0	1.0
Health services	1.1	1.1	1.1
Entertainment	0.8	0.8	0.8
Other services	1.1	1.1	1.1
Panel D: Size			
Large	1.9	1.6	2.2
Medium	1.2	1.2	1.2
Small	1.1	1.1	1.1
Micro	0.9	0.9	1.0
Panel E: Region			
Abruzzo	1.4	1.4	1.4
Aosta Valley	2.1	2.1	2.2
Apulia	0.5	0.5	0.5
Basilicata	0.8	0.8	0.8
Calabria	2.2	2.2	2.3
Campania	1.4	1.4	1.4
Emilia Romagna	1.6	1.6	1.7

(continued)

Table 26 (continued)

	Average PD increments (bp)		
	Baseline	Mild	Extreme
Friuli Venezia Giulia	0.7	0.7	0.8
Lazio	1.3	1.2	1.3
Liguria	3.3	3.2	3.3
Lombardy	0.4	0.4	0.4
Marche	0.5	0.4	0.5
Molise	1.5	1.5	1.5
Piedmont	0.5	0.5	0.5
Sardinia	1.2	1.2	1.3
Sicily	1.0	1.0	1.1
Tuscany	1.8	0.4	0.5
Trentino-South Tyrol	0.5	1.7	1.8
Umbria	0.8	0.8	0.8
Veneto	0.8	0.8	0.8

References

Angelini, P. (2022). *I rischi finanziari posti dai cambiamenti climatici: carenze informative e piani di transizione.* Associazione nazionale per lo studio dei problemi del credito.

APAT (2007). Trigila, A. (ed.). Rapporto sulle frane in Italia – Il Progetto IFFI: Metodologia, risultati e rapporti regionali. Rapporti 78/2007

Arrighi, C., Rossi, L., Traforini, E., Rudari, R., Ferraris, L., Brugioni, M., Franceschini, S., & Castelli, F. (2018). Quantification of flood risk mitigation benefits: A building-scale damage assessment through the RASOR platform. *Journal of Environmental Management, 207*, 92–104.

Arrogante-, P., Bruzón, A., Arrogante-Funes, F., Ramos-Bernal, R., & Vázquez-Jiménez, R. (2021). Integration of vulnerability and hazard factors for landslide risk assessment. *International Journal of Environmental Research and Public Health, 18*(22), 11987.

Barredo, J. (2009). Normalised flood losses in Europe: 1970–2006. *Natural Hazards and Earth Systems Sciences, 9*(1), 97–104.

Barredo, J. I., Sauri, D., & Llasat, C. (2012). Assessing trends in insured losses from floods in Spain 1971–2008. *Natural Hazards and Earth Systems Sciences, 12*(5), 1723–1729.

Bower, L., Bubeck, P., & Aerts, J. (2010). Changes in future flood risk due to climate and development in a Dutch polder area. *Global Environ Change, 20*(3), 463–471.

Brogi, M., Lagasio, V., & Porretta, P. (2022). Be good to be wise: Environmental, social, and governance awareness as a potential credit risk mitigation factor. *Journal of International Financial Management and Accounting, 33*(3), 1–26.

Caloia, F., & Jansen, D. J. (2021) Flood risk and financial stability: Evidence from a stress test for the Netherlands. *De Nederlandsche Bank Work Pap 730.*

Clò, S., David, F., & Segoni, S. (2024). The impact of hydrogeological events on firms: Evidence from Italy. *Journal of Environmental Economics and Management, 124*, 102942.

Columba, F., Orsini, F., & Tranquillo, S. (2024). Rating the raters: A central bank perspective. *Bank of Italy Markets, Infrastructures, Payment Systems Working Paper 55.*

De Polis, S. (2025). *L'assicurazione obbligatoria delle imprese per i danni catastrofali.* Sapienza Università di Roma.

De Socio, A., Narizzano, S., Orlando, T., Parlapiano, F., Rodano, G., Sette, E., & Viggiano, G. (2020). Gli effetti della pandemia sul fabbisogno di liquidità, sul bilancio e sulla rischiosità delle imprese. *Note Covid-19, Bank of Italy.*

Distretto del Fiume Po. (2021). *Relazione metodologica: MOdello per la Valutazione Integrata del Danno Alluvionale (MOVIDA).* Autorità di Bacino Distrettuale del Fiume Po.

Dottori, F., Martina, M., & Figueiredo, R. (2018). A methodology for flood susceptibility and vulnerability analysis in complex flood scenarios. *Journal of Flood Risk Management, 11*, S632–S645.

Dottori, F., Mentaschi, L., Bianchi, A., Alfieri, L., & Feyen, L. (2023). Cost-effective adaptation strategies to rising river flood risk in Europe. *Nature Climate Change, 13*(2), 196–202.

Emambakhsh, T., Fuchs, M., Kordel, S., Kouratzoglou, C., Lelli, C., Pizzighello, R., & Spaggiari, M. (2023). The road to Paris: Stress testing the transition towards a net-zero economy. *ECB Occas Pap 328.*

European Environment Agency. (2023). *Economic losses from weather- and climate-related extremes in Europe.*

Faiella, I., & Natoli, F. (2018). Natural catastrophes and bank lending: The case of flood risk in Italy. *Bank Ital Occas Pap 457.*

Fatica, S., Katay, G., & Rancan, M. (2024). *Floods and firms: Vulnerabilities and resilience to natural disasters in Europe.* SSRN.

Gallo, R., Guazzarotti, G., & Nigro, V. (2024). Rischi operativi delle imprese e coperture assicurative—evidenze dall'indagine RBLS presso le banche. *Note Stabil Finanza Vigilanza, 37*, 1–9.

Gallo, R., Guazzarotti, G., Nigro, V., & Cosconati, M. (2022). Le coperture assicurative contro i rischi operativi delle imprese italiane. *Note Stabil Finanza Vigilanza, 31*, 1–15.

Gatto, A., Clò, S., Martellozzo, F., & Segoni, S. (2023). Tracking a decade of hydrogeological emergencies in Italian municipalities. *Data, 8*(10), 151.

Giovannelli, F., Iannamorelli, A., Levy, A., Orlandi, M. (2020). The in-house credit assessment system of Bank of Italy. *Quest Econ Finanza 586.*

Guzzetti, F., & Reichenbach, P. (1994). Towards a definition of topographic divisions for Italy. *Geomorphology, 11*(1), 57–74.

Guzzetti, F., & Tonelli, G. (2004). Information system on hydrological and geomorphological catastrophes in Italy (SICI). *Geo-Databases Nat Hazards Risk Assess, 4*(2), 213–232.

Huizinga, J., De Moel, H., & Szewczyk, W. (2017). *Global flood depth-damage functions: Methodology and the database with guidelines.* Joint Research Centre.

Iadanza, C., Trigila, A., Starace, P., Dragoni, A., Biondo, T., & Roccisano, M. (2021). IdroGEO: A collaborative web mapping application for landslides and floods in Italy. *ISPRS International Journal of Geo-Information, 10*(2), 89.

International Institute for Sustainable Development. (2009). UNISDR says landslide impacts can be reduced. SDG Knowledge Hub, 12 August. https://sdg.iisd.org/news/unisdr-says-landslide-impacts-can-be-reduced/

Legambiente. (2024). Città Clima: Bilancio finale 2024. https://www.legambiente.it/wp-content/uploads/2025/06/Citta-Clima-Bilancio-finale-2024.pdf

Loberto, M., & Russo, R. (2024a). The exposure of Italian manufacturing firms to hydrogeological risk. *Questioni di Economia e Finanza* 1–50.

Loberto, M., & Russo, R. (2024b). Climate risks and firms: a new methodology for assessing physical risks. *mimeo.*

Loberto, M., & Spuri, M. (2023). L'impatto del rischio di alluvione sulla ricchezza immobiliare in Italia. *Bank Ital Occas Pap 768.*

Loche, M., Alvioli, M., Marchesini, I., Bakka, H., & Lombardo, L. (2022). Landslide susceptibility maps of Italy: Lesson learnt from dealing with multiple landslide types and the uneven spatial distribution of the national inventory. *Earth-Science Review, 232*, Article 104125.

Lugeri, N., Kundzewicz, Z., Genovese, E., & Hochrainer-Stigler, S. (2010). River flood risk and adaptation in Europe. *Mitigation and Adaptation Strategies for Global Change, 15*, 621–639.

Meucci, G., & Rinaldi, F. (2022). Bank exposure to climate-related physical risk in Italy: An assessment using AnaCredit data. *Bank Ital Occas Pap 706*.

Molinari, D., De Bruijn, K., Castillo-Rodríguez, J., Aronica, G., & Bouwer, L. (2019). Validation of flood risk models. *International Journal of Disaster Risk Reduction, 33*, 441–448.

Molinari, D., Scorzini, A., Arrighi, C., Carisi, F., Castelli, F., Domeneghetti, A., & Ballio, F. (2020). Are flood damage models converging to reality? *Natural Hazards and Earth Systems Sciences, 20*(11), 2997–3017.

Monnin, P. (2018). Integrating climate risks into credit risk assessment. *Council on Economic Policies, Discussion Note, 4*(2018), 1–24.

Novellino, A., Pennington, C., Leeming, K., Taylor, S., Alvarez, I., McAllister, E., Arnhardt, C., Winson, A. (2024). Mapping landslides from space: A review. *Landslides*, 1–12.

Raschke, M. (2021). About the return period of a catastrophe. *Natural Hazards and Earth Systems Sciences, 2021*, 1–18.

Redondo, H., & Aracil, E. (2024). Climate-related credit risk: Rethinking the credit risk framework. *Global Policy, 15*, 21–33.

Roccati, A., Paliaga, G., Luino, F., Faccini, F., & Turconi, L. (2021). GIS-based landslide susceptibility mapping. *Land, 10*(2), 162.

Salvati, P., Bianchi, C., Fiorucci, F., Giostrella, P., Marchesini, I., & Guzzetti, F. (2014). Perception of flood and landslide risk in Italy. *Natural Hazards and Earth Systems Sciences, 14*(9), 2589–2603.

Scorzini, A., & Leopardi, M. (2017). River basin planning: From qualitative to quantitative flood risk assessment. *Natural Hazards, 88*, 71–93.

Trigila, A., Frattini, P., Casagli, N., Catani, F., Crosta, G., Esposito, C., Iadanza, C., Lagomarsino, D., Scarscia, G., Segoni, S., Spizzichino, D., Tofani, V., & Lari, S. (2013). Landslide susceptibility mapping at national scale: The Italian case. *Landslide Science and Practice, 1*, 287–295.

Trigila, A., Iadanza, C., Lastoria, B., Bussettini, M., & Barbano, A. (2021). *Dissesto idrogeologico in Italia: pericolosità e indicatori di rischi*. ISPRA.

Trigila, A., Iadanza, C., & Spizzichino, D. (2010). Quality assessment of the Italian Landslide Inventory using GIS. *Landslides, 7*, 455–470.

Usman, S., Parker, M., & Vallat, M. (2025) *Dry-roasted NUTS: early estimates of the regional impact of 2025 extreme weather* (September 14, 2025). Available at SSRN.

Varnes, D. (1984). *Landslide hazard zonation: A review of principles and practice*.

Vitale, C., & Meijerink, S. (2023). Flood risk policies in Italy: A longitudinal institutional analysis. *International Journal of Water Resources Development, 39*(2), 211–235.

World Meteorological Organization. (2025). State of the global climate. *WMO, 1368*, 1–42.

Transition-Risk Adjusted Credit Analysis

Manuel Cugliari, Alessandra Iannamorelli, and Federica Vassalli

1 Introduction

Embedding climate-related transition risk[1] into the ICAS credit risk assessment framework is a key element of the ECB strategic plan to integrate CCR into its regulatory frameworks (European Central Bank, 2021).[2] Besides, central banks must address CCR to safeguard their balance sheets from related financial risks (Boneva et al., 2021). Detailed data are essential to evaluate firm-specific risks in the context of climate change (Financial Stability Board, 2021). However, the scarcity of granular firm-level data on climate exposures poses some challenges for the assessment of CCR.

To address this issue for the purpose of transition risk assessment, we set out to employ a granular dataset on verified emissions from the European Union Emissions Trading System (EU-ETS) and estimate the effect of carbon-price related transition risk on the one-year PD of Italian non-financial firms. Our methodology unfolds in three steps.

[1] In the broader context of climate change risk, transition risk refers to investment losses from economic activities affected by climate policies.

[2] See also Chaps. 5 and 6.

M. Cugliari · A. Iannamorelli (✉) · F. Vassalli
Bank of Italy, Financial Risk Management Directorate, Rome, Italy
e-mail: alessandra.iannamorelli@bancaditalia.it

M. Cugliari
e-mail: manuel.cugliari@bancaditalia.it

F. Vassalli
e-mail: federica.vassalli@bancaditalia.it

A. Scalia (ed.), *Corporate Credit Analysis and AI*, Finance for Professionals,
https://doi.org/10.1007/978-3-032-13422-6_13

First, we design a bottom-up approach to calculate direct emissions precisely (Scope 1), using verified emissions data from the EU-ETS—the largest carbon market in the world for trading emission allowances, covering around 40% of the EU greenhouse gas (GHG) emissions (DG Clima, 2023). EU-ETS data provide direct insights into individual firm emissions and production-related carbon costs. Our method differs from the standard top-down approaches, that rely on sectoral averages and proxies such as employee counts (Faiella et al., 2022). It also differs from bottom-up methods based on estimated or self-reported data under the Non-Financial Reporting Directive (NFRD), which may suffer from quality issues (Grundmann et al., 2023).

Second, we generate multiple carbon price scenarios using stochastic simulations of EU-ETS futures, which are highly liquid and sensitive to current and expected climate policies (Dhamija et al., 2017; Kanzig, 2023). Departing from Grundmann et al. (2023), we apply the conditional Value at Risk (CVaR) to select a risk-tailored extreme scenario, capturing the average of the worst 5% of simulated price outcomes (Ordonez, 2022).

Third, we conduct a scenario analysis to estimate transition risk-adjusted PDs via the S-ICAS model on a baseline and an extreme carbon price scenario (see Chap. 3). This analysis covers both listed and unlisted firms, incorporating carbon cost projections into firm financial statements. Unlike traditional stress tests that focus solely on downside risks, our framework also accounts for potential upside: firms emitting below their allocated quota can sell surplus allowances, generating additional revenue. This dual perspective reflects the firms' capacity to mitigate emissions and generate financial opportunities from proactive climate strategies.

Our main finding is that the PDs derived from EU-ETS-based scenarios exhibit greater sensitivity to transition risk than those based on the Network for Greening the Financial System (NGFS) scenarios.[3] This allows for a more realistic assessment of rating migrations, capturing both downgrades and upgrades.

The remainder of this Chapter is organized as follows: Sect. 2 reviews the relevant literature; Sect. 3 describes the emission data collection and compares our bottom-up approach with a standard top-down methods; Sect. 4 and 5 present, respectively, the empirical methodology and the results. Section 6 performs a robustness exercise, while Sect. 7 concludes.

[3] The NGFS is a group of central banks and regulatory authorities established in 2017 after the Paris Agreement to enhance international cooperation to reach the target of keeping the maximum temperature rise below 2 °C with respect to the pre-industrial levels. The NGFS Climate Scenarios explore the impacts of climate change and climate policy to provide a common reference framework. The Orderly and Disorderly scenarios explore a transition consistent with limiting global warming to below 2 °C. The Hothouse world scenario leads to severe physical risks.

2 Literature Review

2.1 The EU-ETS Market

Market-based environmental policy tools are classified into quantity-based mechanisms like 'cap and trade' and price mechanisms, like carbon taxes (Stavins, 2003). The EU-ETS belongs to the 'cap and trade' class, implying that a maximum limit for GHG emissions produced by participating firms' installations is set at the European Economic Area level. Participating firms can buy or sell quotas as needed. One European Emission Allowance (EUA) equals 1 ton of CO_2 (or an equivalent amount of another GHG). Every year, participating firms must return allowances for each ton of CO_2 equivalent ($tCO_2eq.$) emitted. A limited number of emission quotas is assigned free of charge to selected firms based on harmonised rules. Firms not provided with free allowances, or exceeding their free allocations, must buy allowances either at auctions or from firms having them in excess. Non-compliance leads to sanctions.

In contrast with a carbon tax system, where the price is fixed per 'unit of pollution' while the quantity is free to vary, in a carbon market like EU-ETS, the total quantity of emissions is fixed, and the price can change based on the demand for certificates. Therefore, the price of the certificates can be high during an economic expansion and low during a recession (Taschini, 2023). The EU-ETS market flexibility compared to price-based mechanisms lies in the quota allocation, in the trading systems, and in the predetermined quota reduction, helping firms in planning and selecting cost-effective energy compositions and long-term investments to reduce emissions (Bustamante & Zucchi, 2022).[4] Within the European Union legislation, Italy adopted the EU-ETS as the main measures for the reduction of greenhouse gas emissions. Thus, Italian firms belonging to the sectors with the greatest impact on climate change are expected to manage their emissions through EU-ETS.

The EU-ETS supply cap was set to decrease at a predetermined rate in each of the four phases of the system (Phase I-IV).[5] However, other factors affect the supply side, including the opportunity to save or borrow certificates over time, as well as a plan for global integration. On the other side, demand for certificates mainly arises from three categories of entities: energy producer firms, energy consumer

[4] In low-emission years, member states can save unused allowances for subsequent years and in high-emission years borrow a limited amount of emissions from subsequent years (European Commission, 2023).

[5] The first two phases (Phase I and II, 2005–2012) involved national emission limits (National Allocation Plans - NAPs) with free allocations for most polluting sectors. Phase III (2013–2020) transitioned to a single emission limit at the European level, with free allocations based on a sectoral benchmark. Phase IV (2021–2030) introduced a decreasing European emission limit recalibrated against the benchmark, aiming at a 62 per cent reduction in GHG emissions by 2030 compared to 2005.

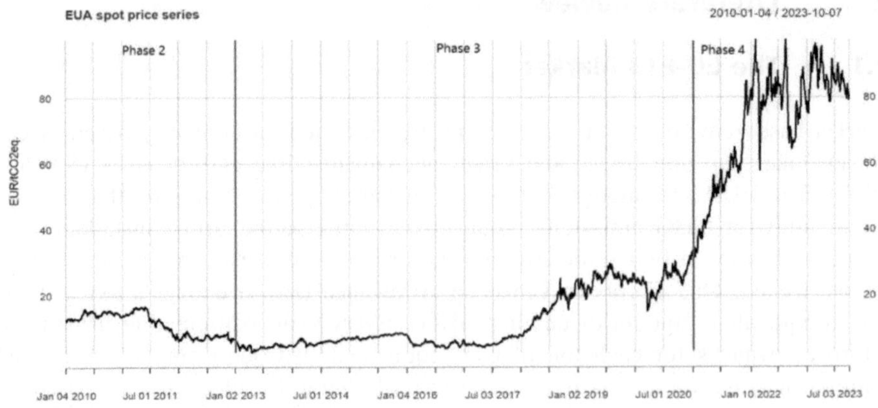

Fig. 1 EU Carbon Price measured by the spot price of EUA contracts traded on the EEX market. *Source* Own calculation from Bloomberg

firms (i.e. those belonging to other industrial sectors), and financial firms or investment funds. Demand-side price drivers include borrowing, auctioning (Chevallier, 2012) and energy prices (Krokida et al., 2020 and Gargallo et al., 2021), the transition from fossil fuels to renewable sources, as well as extreme weather conditions (Alberola et al., 2008; Christianen et al., 2005; Mansanet-Bataller et al., 2007).

For these reasons, the EU-ETS market price dynamics have been heterogeneous across phases (see Fig. 1). The initial decentralised emission limitation system led to an aggregated CO_2 volume limit higher than the actual emissions, reducing prices. In Phase III, the introduction of stringent limits and an auction system was expected to lead to an increase in prices of allowances. However, the sovereign debt crises had a significant impact on overall productive activities, leading to a decrease in economic output and, consequently, in carbon prices. The low surplus in emissions and low carbon prices discourage green technology investment, thus hindering the goal of a 'cap-and-trade' system in mitigating and contrasting climate change. In 2019, the European Commission established the Market Stability Reserve (MSR)[6] to address the surplus of allowances. MSR purpose is to improve the system resilience to major shocks by adjusting the supply of allowances to be auctioned. In March 2023, the MSR was extended until 2030 to protect the EU from CO_2 price drops due to external shocks like COVID-19. Several studies recognise that environmental policy announcements affected price formation during Phases I and II of the EU-ETS market (Fan et al., 2017; Guo et al., 2018; Yu et al., 2022). In Phase IV, stricter CO_2 and trade limits helped further increase prices, especially with the adoption of more restrictive measures by the European Commission in July 2021 (European Commission, 2021).

[6] EU Commission Climate Action: https://climate.ec.europa.eu/eu-action/eu-emissions-trading-system-eu-ets/market-stability-reserve_it#market-stability-reserve.

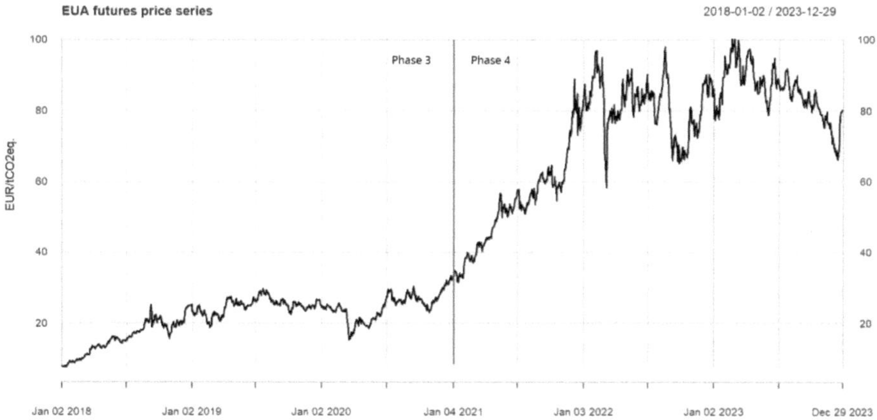

Fig. 2 EU Carbon Price measured by the price of EUA futures contracts traded on the EEX market. *Source* Own calculation from Bloomberg

EUA certificates are traded on both spot markets, such as the Blue Next in Paris, the European Energy Exchange (EEX) in Leipzig or the Nord Pool in Oslo, and futures markets, such as the EEX and the ICE in London, with the latter markets being particularly liquid (Rittler, 2012 and Stefan & Wellenreuther, 2020). The liquidity feature of futures EUA markets, has led the literature to model price volatility using GARCH (Engle, 2002). Through VaR analysis, milestone works by Benz and Truck (2008) and Taschini and Paolella (2008) demonstrate the predictive capabilities of simple GARCH models with an asymmetric component. Further studies show the asymmetric behaviour of EU-ETS spot and derivative market (Arouri et al., 2012; Brauneis, 2016; Byun, 2013; Daskalakis, 2009; Dutta, 2018). Following such initial studies, the analysis focused on observing EUA futures returns to identify the typical motivations for choosing the GARCH model, such as non-constant volatility, volatility clustering and leverage effects (Wang & Ghysels, 2015; Zivot, 2009) (Fig. 2).

2.2 Climate-Related Credit Risk

The participation in the EU-ETS, which may affect the firms' profit and loss account, has been studied for listed firms during Phase I to III. Typically, this research focuses on the 'carbon premium' and involves classifying firm portfolios as 'dirty' or 'clean' based on the number of free carbon allowances received by the firm. Namely, 'dirty' portfolios are related to a significant number of free certificates,[7] and vice versa for 'clean' ones. Due to environmental policy uncertainty,

[7] Recall that during Phase I and II the most polluting sectors received the highest number of free certificates.

in the initial EU-ETS phases, 'dirty' portfolios yielded higher returns than 'clean' ones, confirming the existence of a carbon premium (Oestreich & Tsiakas, 2015 and Wen et al., 2020). However, in Phase III, policies became more explicit, and the carbon premium proved to be directly linked to the difference between verified emissions and free-allocated allowances. With rising certificate costs, firms with emissions exceeding free quotas experienced a drop in stock prices, while firms with excess free quotas experienced an increase in stock prices (Bolton et al., 2023). In other words, investors tend to demand a premium to be compensated for CO_2 emission risk exposure (Bolton & Kacperczyk, 2021).

Besides, the research has increasingly focused on the integration of transition risk into credit risk assessment, with more attention paid to transition risk over physical risk due to the unpredictability of extreme natural events (Bernardini et al., 2021). After initial studies on transition risk transmission to the financial system (Faiella & Malvolti, 2020 and Monasterolo, 2020), the analysis has evolved towards Credit Default Swap (CDS) spreads. Namely, firms are classified into 'green' or 'brown' portfolios based on their emissions (Scope 1 and 2),[8] as estimated in quantile distributions. By calculating the difference between the median CDS premium of green and brown firms, a transition risk exposure factor (Carbon Risk—CR) is obtained. Several studies have found a positive correlation between transition risk and the term structure of CDS, suggesting a significant long-term impact of transition risk on credit risk (see Blasberg et al., 2021; Zhang & Zhao, 2022; Zhang et al., 2023 among others). Currently, the prevalent approach for long-term integration of transition risk into credit risk assessment relies on NGFS-based scenario analysis (NGFS, 2021). NGFS scenarios combine long-term transition policy paths with short-term macroeconomic projections, factoring in recent energy prices and consumption data. Banks and supervision authorities use stress test exercises to assess the impact of the green transition on non-financial firms' and households' creditworthiness, incorporating energy dynamics and sectoral interactions. Scenario analyses usually employ Integrated Assessment Models (IAMs) for both stress test development (Emambakhsh et al., 2023; European Central Bank, 2022) and general transition risk-adjusted credit risk assessments (Battiston et al., 2023; Billio & Giacomelli, 2023). Ordonez (2022) employs stochastic simulations to create multiple scenarios, projecting macroeconomic indicators and firm asset values in log returns. This risk-metric analysis performs tail risk assessments, including Value-at-Risk (VaR) and Expected Shortfall (ES), to analyse the impact of low-probability, high-impact events on portfolios.

Other authors apply carbon tax shocks to energy prices consistent with NGFS scenarios. For instance, Faiella et al., (2022) assess the effects of different carbon taxes on the credit quality of Italian firms considering energy demand elasticity to price. The analysis employs a top-down approach for deducing energy demand

[8] The Task Force on Climate-Related Financial Disclosure (TCFD) defined a harmonised set of rules to classify emissions (*Greenhouse Gas Protocol*) in three categories: Scope 1, 2 and 3. Scope 1 includes direct emissions related to the production, and Scope 2 covers indirect emissions, such as those related to acquired energy. Scope 3 emissions are all those related to the supply chain.

and emissions, proportionally allocating sectoral emissions to firms based on Eurostat data and employee numbers. Aiello and Angelico (2023) implement a similar methodology to evaluate the vulnerability of Italian banks to transition risk. This risk originates from the exposure of borrower firms to the transition risk factors. The authors' microsimulation model detects sector-specific impacts, correlating firm financial vulnerability with carbon taxation. The most considerable impact is on agriculture and services due to their less elastic energy demand. Di Virgilio et al., (2024) further develop this approach, using sectoral attribution to estimate emissions for the Bank of Italy's ICAS sample firms. The NGFS scenarios projections on firms' balance sheets showed different effects on production costs, liquidity, income statements, and balance sheets, varying impacts across sectors. Such a top-down approach, while useful, has inherent limitations in precisely estimating individual emission levels and PDs. In response to the ECB recommendations, some central banks are investigating the use of EU-ETS market data for the assessment of firm-specific emissions. Such choice addresses the inaccuracies of the top-down approach by enabling precise calculation of emission levels and costs without relying on a generic carbon tax assumption. Grundmann et al., (2023) describe the Bundesbank's bottom-up method as applied to EU-ETS data to integrate climate risk into the German ICAS. Despite the fact that a modest share of firms evaluated by the German ICAS participate to the EU-ETS, their contribution to the total volume of firm emissions in Germany is significant. The proposed method considers two scenarios: one related to the current average EUA price and an extreme scenario aligned with the NGFS *Below 2 °C* scenario. The extra cost of emission certificates is calculated as the difference between the average past price for EUA certificates and the price for the following year, multiplied by the number of needed EUA certificates beyond free allocation. The extra cost is passed through both the income statement and the balance sheet to recalculate PDs. The results show little change in corporate riskiness under the current scenario, but a significant increase in the number of firms that may suffer a one or two-level rating downgrade in the extreme scenario.[9]

Against this background, our analysis makes a contribution by offering a more accurate perspective on credit rating changes in response to climate-related financial data. The existing literature mainly focuses on listed firms and computes a risk premium - the 'carbon premium' - linked to their emissions (Blasberg et al., 2021 among others). Our methodology instead applies to both listed and unlisted firms, since the transition risk impact on PDs is derived from the balance sheet stress rather than from the market risk premium. Last, we align transition risk-adjusted PDs to the typical one-year horizon of credit risk, facilitating regular updates of credit ratings.

[9] Regarding the rating scale, we refer to the ICAS risk classes.

3 Data

This Chapter relies on three data sources: *(i)* EU-ETS firm-level data,[10] *(ii)* prices and volumes for spot and futures allowances sourced from Bloomberg, and *(iii)* detailed information on firms' financial variables, obtained from the ICAS database (see Chap. 3).

3.1 EU-ETS Data

According to the EU-ETS rules, every year, each registered entity has to submit to the climate-competent national authority a quantity of emission certificates at least equivalent to its verified emissions for the previous year. The National Registry of Emissions and Removals (RNER) collects the submitted certificates. The RNER, established under the European Commission Decision No. 389/2013/EU, is the authorities' monitoring instrument for all activities linked to emission allowances, including their initial allocation to firms and subsequent transactions up to cancellation. For Italy, the national authority is the Institute for Environmental Protection and Research (ISPRA). As RNER's managing bodies, national authorities like ISPRA ensure data transparency, security, and integrity. This role encompasses validating CO_2 emissions produced by Italian corporations and supervising their compliance with European and domestic regulations.

As an open system, the EU-ETS allows regulated and unregulated members, including firms and individuals, to transact emission permits. An essential system component is the electronic registry, the European Union Transaction Log (EUTL), which facilitates and records the transfer of all participant certificates. As a central element of the EU ETS' settlement infrastructure, the EUTL involves several stakeholders, from corporate entities and their intermediaries to regulatory bodies and market operators, each with a dedicated account. Figure 3 describes the structure of the EUTL registry.

In the EU-ETS framework, installations represent the regulated entities. The responsibility for submitting emission certificates and the associated recording are managed at the installation level. Certificate transfers, or transactions, are conducted at the account level, with each installation linked to an 'Operator Holding Account' (OHA) managed by its operator. Regulatory authorities operate through 'Administrative Accounts' (AA) for allocating and receiving permits. Non-regulated participants, like intermediaries, use 'Person Holding Accounts' (PHA). The EUTL records each account's primary contact and tracks transactions between holders, allocating firms and regulatory authorities into the registry through their respective account holders to facilitate inter-system connections. From the EUTL records, we collected data on free allocated quotas and traded quotas at the firm

[10] EU-ETS data include verified emissions levels, firm compliance levels, and allocation of free allowances.

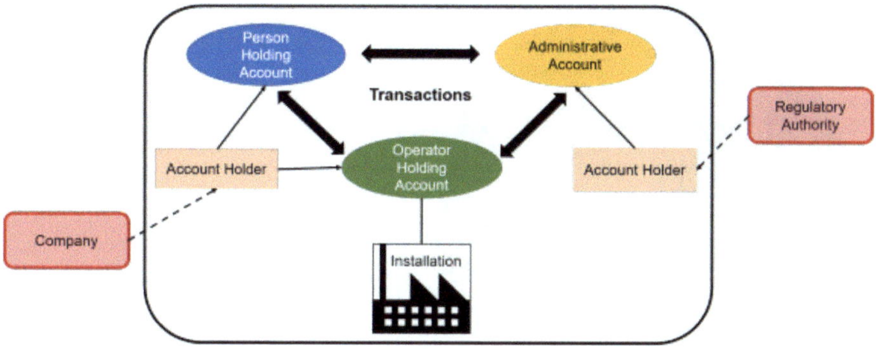

Fig. 3 Entities operating within the EU-ETS system. *Source* Letout, 2022

Table 1 Contribution to national emissions in 2022 by Italian EU-ETS firms and ICAS firms (Source: ISPRA, EUTL and ICAS dataset)

Emissions	tCO_2eq	per cent	N of firms	per cent
National emissions (ISPRA)	369,000,000	/	1,021,618	/
EU- ETS emissions	138,272,559	37	1,200	0.12
ICAS emissions	103,738,358	28	542	0.05

level. Since each EUA quota represents 1 tCO_2eq, we can calculate the total emissions for each firm (Table 1). In 2022, 37% of Italy's national emissions were traded as EUA quotas in the EU-ETS markets. A group of 542 ICAS firms (roughly 0.05% of Italian non-financial firms), for which we have mapped transactions in EUA certificates, accounted for 75% of the EU-ETS traded emissions, representing 28% of Italy's total GHG emissions (Fig. 4).

3.2 Market Data

The second pillar of the data for this study relates to the dynamics of EUA certificate trading, focusing on price trends and volume metrics as recorded in the EEX. From 2018 to 2023, we derive a time series of both spot and futures prices of EUA certificates from Bloomberg.

3.3 Firms' Financial Data

The ICAS database is the third data source. We obtain the final dataset by merging the firm information in the ICAS database with emission and transaction information included in the EU-ETS.

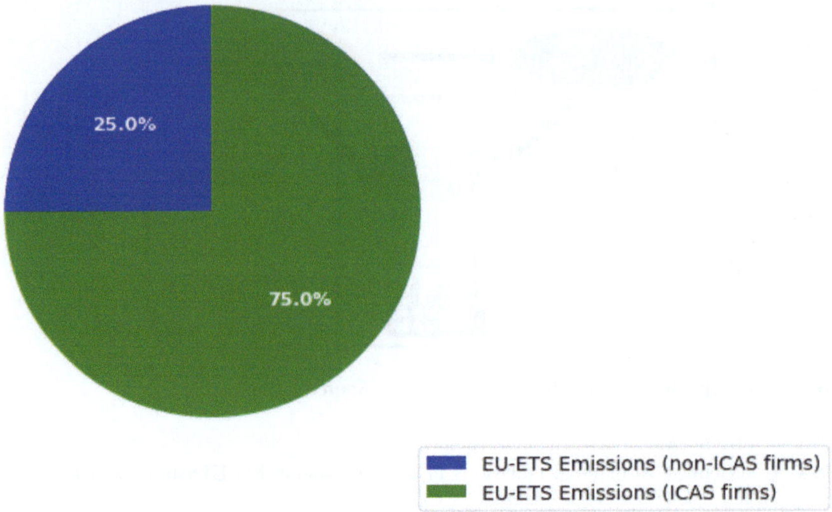

Fig. 4 Contribution of S-ICAS firms' emissions to the total Italian EU-ETS emissions. *Source* own calculation on EUTL and ICAS dataset

The above-described information is publicly accessible. However, to merge the EU-ETS database with ICAS for our study, structured relationships are needed. The merge is costly since no database that hierarchically represents the relationships among EU-ETS entities is available. Starting from the publicly available data from the European Commission, Abbrell (2022) develops a relational database for European installations, integrating various components of the EUTL registry to analyse firms' compliance with EU-ETS requirements and market behaviours. Letout (2022) further expands this work by linking the EU-ETS account holders to the Bureau van Dijk database,[11] achieving extensive coverage and high accuracy in identifying firms. Using the described methods, we create a new dataset by merging EUTL data with the ICAS database, effectively combining the two sources. The fundamental element for implementing the merging process, which enables the association of installations with the ICAS sample firms, is the information on Italian plants, available within a non-public database managed by ISPRA.[12] Using a specialised algorithm combining different matching techniques (see Appendix A), we reconstruct emissions data for 572 listed companies in the ICAS sample.

[11] Bureau van Dijk is a Moody's Analytics Company that aggregates personal and financial information, ratings, shareholders, shareholdings and MandA on companies, banks and insurance companies from all over the world.

[12] Within its mandate to ensure monetary and financial stability, the Bank of Italy can access information on installation-level commitment with the EU-ETS requirements, like annual reports produced by the firm's installation managers and assessments of plant energy consumption.

From now on, we will refer to these entities as the ICAS sample. Table 1 and Fig. 3 report the coverage of the ICAS sample for the year 2022.

3.4 Bottom-Up vs Top-Down Approach

To measure the gain in accuracy obtained by using a bottom-up approach rather than a top-down approach, we compare verified firm-reported emissions in the EUTL registry from the previous year with sector-attributed emissions for the ICAS sample.[13] The traditional method of estimating emissions by matching sector-based Physical Energy Flow Account (PEFA)[14] data with data on firms' employee numbers provides a broad sectoral emission perspective, but lacks in precision at the firm level. With its detailed records of traded certificate volumes, the EU-ETS market provides a more accurate representation of each firm's emissions and a clearer understanding of emission costs. The comparison, focusing on ICAS-registered companies in the EU-ETS, highlights the need to refine and broaden the traditional approach, proposing an alternative way to compute corporate emissions.

By comparing EUTL granular data for firms assessed by ICAS with the corresponding sectoral estimation of Scope 1 CO_2 emissions (tCO_2eq), we find that sectoral attribution underestimates emissions, as most data points lie above the 45° line (Fig. 5). The average difference between the emissions reported by EU-ETS firms and sectoral imputation-based emissions is 246,000 tCO_2eq. The positive correlation of 0.51 indicates a significant monotonic relationship between sectoral and EU-ETS datasets. This suggests that, despite biases in magnitude, sectoral emissions estimates tend to follow the same general trend as EU-ETS-reported emissions. The discrepancy can be partly explained by the scope of the EU-ETS, which focuses on certified emissions from carbon-intensive activities, such as electricity and heat generation, energy-intensive industries, aviation, and maritime transport. Only high emitters participate in the EU-ETS, leaving smaller emitters out of its coverage. By contrast, sectoral imputation, relies on average estimates calibrated according to individual firm number of employees, which do not capture the variability in emissions among firms of the same size. The reliance on average values limits accuracy of sectoral attribution, especially for extreme emitters (Unnewehr et al., 2022).

[13] To carry out the comparison the following data sources have been used: *i)* Eurostat for sectoral consumption and employees; *ii)* National Social Security Institute (INPS) for the number of company employees.

[14] PEFA, available in Eurostat, is an accounting statistical system that measures and quantifies energy flow within an economy – including its production, transformation, and consumption. This system provides crucial data for environmental and economic analyses, offering insights into energy utilisation and its impacts on various sectors.

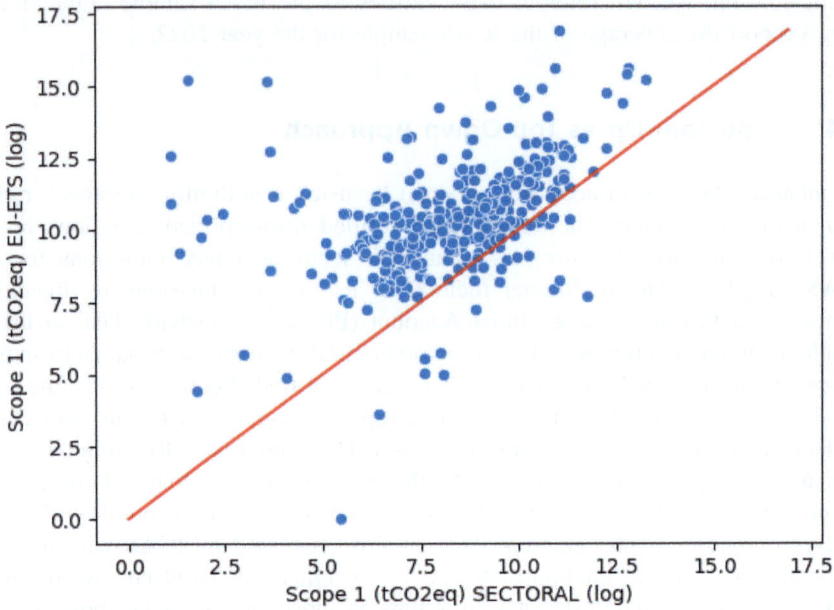

Fig. 5 EU-ETS verified firms' emissions versus sectoral imputation-based emissions. *Source* Own calculation on EUTL and Eurostat Scope 1 emissions

4 Empirical Methodology

4.1 A Model for EU-ETS Price Dynamic

We treat CO_2 emissions as a production input to estimate the additional costs implied by firm excess emissions based on the certificate prices. We focus on the futures market for EU-ETS allowances due to its liquidity and informative content (Stefan & Wellenreuther, 2020), in particular about future price expectations (Gorenflo, 2013). In Sect. 2, we conduct an in-depth analysis of the primary factors influencing the prices within the EU-ETS. We examine the period from 2018 to 2023, which covers the transition from Phase III to Phase IV. During these phases, the European Commission clearly defined the policy measures, minimising the likelihood of unexpected shifts in climate policy as the system's structure is predetermined and known to all stakeholders. We develop alternative price scenarios, which can be regularly updated, by modelling the volatility of futures prices and using stochastic simulations. This approach enables us to account for periods of high or low prices, which may arise from speculative bubbles, energy shocks, or policy-related shocks.

The *first estimation step* involves modelling price volatility of futures contracts on EUA certificate. To this aim, we use GARCH models for estimating the variance of EUA futures certificate returns.[15]

We perform some data analysis (Zivot, 2009 and Wang & Ghysels, 2015), to show that the above features of financial returns also hold true for futures contracts on EUA certificates, thus enabling the choice of GARCH to model their volatility. Among GARCH models, we opt for an asymmetric parametric model in the form of GJR-GARCH (*p, K q*) (Glosten, 1993), allowing for a leverage effect. The leverage effect implies that negative returns have a greater influence on future volatility than do positive returns. In fact, we observe that there is a negative correlation between volatility and past returns. Further details on model selection are provided in Appendix B. The general GARCH specification is the following:

$$r_t = \mu_t + \varepsilon_t \tag{1}$$

$$\mu_t = E(r_t|F_{t-1}) \tag{2}$$

$$\sigma_t^2 = Var(r_t|F_{t-1}) \tag{3}$$

where r_t is the daily return, μ_t is the expected value of returns, ε_t is a generic shock to the conditional volatility σ_t^2 at time t, F_{t-1} is the information set at time $t-1$. In the GJR-GARCH, σ_t^2 evolves according to the following equation:

$$\sigma_t^2 = \omega + \sum_{i=1}^{p} \alpha_i \varepsilon_{t-i}^2 + \sum_{k=1}^{K} \gamma_k I_{t-k} \varepsilon_{t-k}^2 + \sum_{j=1}^{q} \beta \sigma_{t-i}^2 \tag{4}$$

$$I_{t-i} = \begin{cases} 0 if r_{t-i} \geq \mu \\ 1 if r_{t-i} < \mu \end{cases} \tag{5}$$

where $\omega > 0, \alpha_i \geq 0, \beta_j \geq 0$ are bounded parameters representing a sufficient condition to ensure a positive variance. The shock ε_t can be written as $\varepsilon_t = \sigma_t z_t$, with z_t quantile from the Normal distribution. The indicator function in Eq. 5 is typical of GJR-GARCH specification. It assigns a coefficient γ_i to below-average returns to account for the leverage effect. Parameters p and q are the lags for the shocks and for the autoregressive conditional volatility, respectively; K is the number of asymmetric parameters. Using the Bayesian optimization procedure (Naik et al., 2020), the model is set with $p = 2, q = 2, K = 1$. This setup allows modelling conditional volatility for $T + h$ periods ahead through Monte-Carlo simulations of the ε_{t-i}^2 shock. In our case h amounts at 252 days, equivalent

[15] Log return are commonly defined as: $r_t = \log(P_t) - \log(P_{t-1})$, where r_t is the daily return of EUA certificates, obtained as log difference of closing prices of adjacent days (P_t and P_{t-1}). We model via GARCH the variance σ^2 of EUA certificate futures returns, linked to EUA certificate futures price volatility through the standard relationship: $\sigma^2 = Var(r_t)$.

to one year. Using standard tests, such as the Unconditional Coverage test (UC, Kupiec, 1995), the Conditional Coverage test (CC, Christoffersen, 1998), and the Dynamic Quantile test, we validate the VaR of GJR-GARCH model for variance (see Appendix B for further details). To construct the scenarios, we use the average variance for the baseline scenario and extract an extreme scenario by considering tail variances (Ordonez, 2022). By exploiting the volatility and the relation $r_t = \mu_t + \sigma_t z_t$, we get one-year ahead trajectories for EUA futures certificate price. Note that scenarios are not price forecasts, but descriptions of market trajectories.

The *second estimation step* consists in estimating the extra production cost that firms must bear for GHG emissions. Building upon Grundmann et al. (2023), we get the extra cost as follows:

$$EC_{i,t} = ExtraEUA_{i,t} \times \left(\hat{P}_{EU-ETS,t+1} - P_{EU-ETS,t}\right) \tag{6}$$

where $ExtraEUA_{i,t}$ represents the EUA certificates exceeding the free allocated quotas for firm i traded in the current year, $\hat{P}_{EU-ETS,t+1}$ is the simulated unit price 12 month ahead estimated via the GJR-GARCH, while $P_{EU-ETS,t}$ is the volume weighted average certificate price over the last 12 months.[16] The additional cost of EU-ETS quotas can be positive or negative. Firms exceeding their free allocated certificate limits face a deficit and must buy certificates. Conversely, firms with emissions below their allocation have a surplus and can sell their excess quotas. Transition plans may improve carbon efficiency, supporting the surplus channel. However, since transition plans are typically designed for long-term implementation, their impact on the one-year timeframe of our analysis may be less significant compared to that of short-term certificate management policies. Considering the extra cost, which adjusts the current year's cost against the previous one, the approach effectively accounts for the impacts of high or low-price phases, including when depending on bubbles, energy, and policy shocks.

Grundmann et al. (2023) explore both a current and a stressed scenario. In the current scenario, the price is set at the average EUA price in 2022, while in the extreme scenario, a price consistent with the NGFS' orderly transition' scenario is assumed. They compute the additional costs based on these prices and stress the balance sheet accordingly.

In this study, we employ stochastic simulations to generate alternative price scenarios. The baseline scenario builds upon the average certificate price projected over a year through 10,000 GJR-GARCH model runs via Monte Carlo simulations. Based on such simulated price trajectories, the extreme scenario is defined by the CVaR approach, focusing on the average of the worst 5% outcomes in the extra cost distribution. In doing so, we also align the transition risk estimation horizon with standard practices in credit risk assessment.

[16] For each firm i, $ExtraEUA_{i,t}$ is calculated as the difference between EUA certificates exceeding the free allocated. See Sect. 3.1 on how we get free allocated and traded quotas at firm level.

This method is sensitive to price fluctuations allowing for frequent updates of PD estimates. Also, it incorporates the market risk faced by firms in the EU-ETS market.

4.2 The Transmission of Transition Costs Through Firm Balance Sheet

We focus on the S-ICAS to stress-test financial statements with additional costs related to EUA certificates. We rely on the reclassified financial statement indicators to examine how deficit or surplus scenarios in emission quotas affect the PD estimations. This assessment is reflected in the latest firm balance sheet (2022).

In the first scenario (firms in deficit), based on the accounting principles defined by the Organismo Italiano di Contabilità (OIC),[17] we assume that the firm adds the extra cost to the income statement following the need to buy extra quotas[18] to align ex post emissions with the allowed ones (' $+ C_{add}$' in Table 2). The corresponding balance sheet item is cash outflow. Suppose cash and equivalents are not large enough to cover the cash outflow. In that case, we assume that the firm negotiates a new short-term debt, which implies an increase in interest expenses (' $+ C_{int}$').[19] The higher costs reduce operating margins and net income, negatively affecting equity. The deterioration of the balance sheet is partially offset by a reduction in taxation ('- E_{tax}')[20] resulting from a lower taxable income. Overall, the net effect on the financial component of the PD estimation is negative (see Tables 2 and 3).[21]

In the second scenario (firm in surplus), we assume that the firm sells the extra quotas, generating a non-operating revenue (' $+ R_{add}$') with the subsequent

[17] OIC is an accounting Italian institution that consistently sets and updates national accounting principles with international standards.

[18] For the analysis, we do not consider the balance sheet effects of a hypothetical scenario where firms with surplus EUA certificates store them for future use. While this behaviour is typical in normal operations, we assume that a company would prefer to sell immediately these certificates for short-term liquidity in case of financial distress. Aligning with national accounting principles, a 'storage' scenario would not affect excess free certificates. However, for a surplus of previously purchased certificates, there would be a reduction in previously recorded costs, offset by a deferred income entry, maintaining cash flow effects and limiting PD variation.

[19] The cost of new debt is assumed equal to the estimated debt cost for the current year (Return on Debt 'ROD').

[20] The reduction in taxation is obtained as $E_{tax} = (C_{add} + C_{int}) \times t$, where t is the tax rate equal to 27.9%.

[21] The firm financial statements analysis also considers the 'net liability approach'. This approach involves recording free quotas as intangible assets at nominal (zero) value. Purchased quotas are recorded as fixed assets with an indefinite useful life and are not subject to depreciation. However, they are recognised in the income statement in the relevant period under miscellaneous operating expenses. Given the analysis assumptions, the methodology described and the one used can be considered equivalent.

Table 2 Transmission of extra-costs of emissions on Income Statement (firms in deficit)

Income Statement (Reclassified)	Effect
+ Net sales	
+ Other revenues	
- Cost of goods sold	
Gross Profit	
- Operating expenses	$+ C_{add}$
EBITDA	
- Amortisation and Depreciation	
EBIT	
± Net financial income	
- Interest expenses	$+ C_{int}$
EBT	
- Tax expenses	$- E_{tax}$
Net Income (Loss)	-

Table 3 Transmission of extra-costs of emissions on Balance Sheet (firms in deficit)

Balance Sheet (Assets)	Effect
Fixed Assets	
…	
Current Assets	
Cash and cash equivalents	$- C_{add} - C_{int} + E_{tax}$
…	
Total Assets	–
Balance Sheet (Liabilities and Equity)	**Effect**
…	
± Net Income (Loss)	$- C_{add} — C_{int} + E_{tax}$
Equity	
…	
Long-Term Debt	
…	
Short-Term Debt	
Short-term financial debt	$+ C_{add} + C_{int} — E_{tax}$ (if cash is not enough)
Total Liabilities and Equity	–

increase in cash and equivalents. Selling quotas implies an improvement in the financial component of the PD estimation. The new revenue positively contributes to cash, margins and operating results, thus reducing leverage. In this case, we consider the fiscal effect consisting of higher taxation (‘ + E_{tax}’), due to higher income (see Tables 4 and 5).

Table 4 Transmission of extra-costs of emissions on Income Statement (firms in surplus)

Income Statement (Reclassified)	Effect
+ Net sales	
+ Other revenues	+ R_{add}
- Cost of goods sold	
Gross profit	
- Operating expenses	
EBITDA	
- Amortisation and Depreciation	
EBIT	
±Net financial income	
- Interest expenses	
EBT	
- Tax expenses	+ E_{tax}
Net Income (Loss)	+

Table 5 Transmission of extra-costs of emissions on Balance Sheet (firms in surplus)

Balance Sheet (Assets)	Effect
Fixed Assets	
…	
Current Assets	
Cash and cash equivalents	+ R_{add} - E_{tax}
…	
Total Assets	+
Balance Sheet (Liabilities and Equity)	**Effect**
…	
±Net Income (Loss)	+ R_{add} - E_{tax}
Equity	
…	
Long-Term Debt	
…	
Short-Term Debt	
Short-term financial debt	
Total Liabilities and Equity	+

5 Results

5.1 Transition Risk for Italian Firms

In the baseline scenario (cyan points), the probabilities are close to the 45° line, indicating a slight variation of transition risk-adjusted PDs from standard estimates (Fig. 6). In contrast, the extreme scenario (scattered red points) shows more significant PD variability than the baseline scenario. Points above the 45° line represent firms with worsened PDs due to increased certificate prices and extra costs. Points below the line represent companies with improved PDs due to reduced emissions compared to their free certificate allocation, leading to extra revenues. The baseline scenario analysis found no significant PD changes, indicating that firms capable of absorbing carbon costs continue to do so. Only the abrupt shifts in carbon pricing affect firm creditworthiness, leading to notable changes in their PD levels.

The CVaR-based extreme scenario is more cautious, preserving the credit rating for only 83% of firms, as opposed to 90% in the baseline scenario. Notably, the extreme scenario leads to more downgrades (about 14% of firms) and more upgrades in credit ratings compared to the baseline (3% versus 1%. Table 6). Migration dynamics provide supporting evidence for the sensitivity and effectiveness of the EU-ETS-based methodology. It demonstrates that transition risk affects firms through price shifts that have not yet been absorbed, both positively and negatively.

Moreover, we show that the baseline scenario has a tighter cluster of PD variations around zero. In contrast, the extreme scenario exhibits a more dispersed PD distribution, reflecting a wider range of variations in the PDs (Fig. 7).

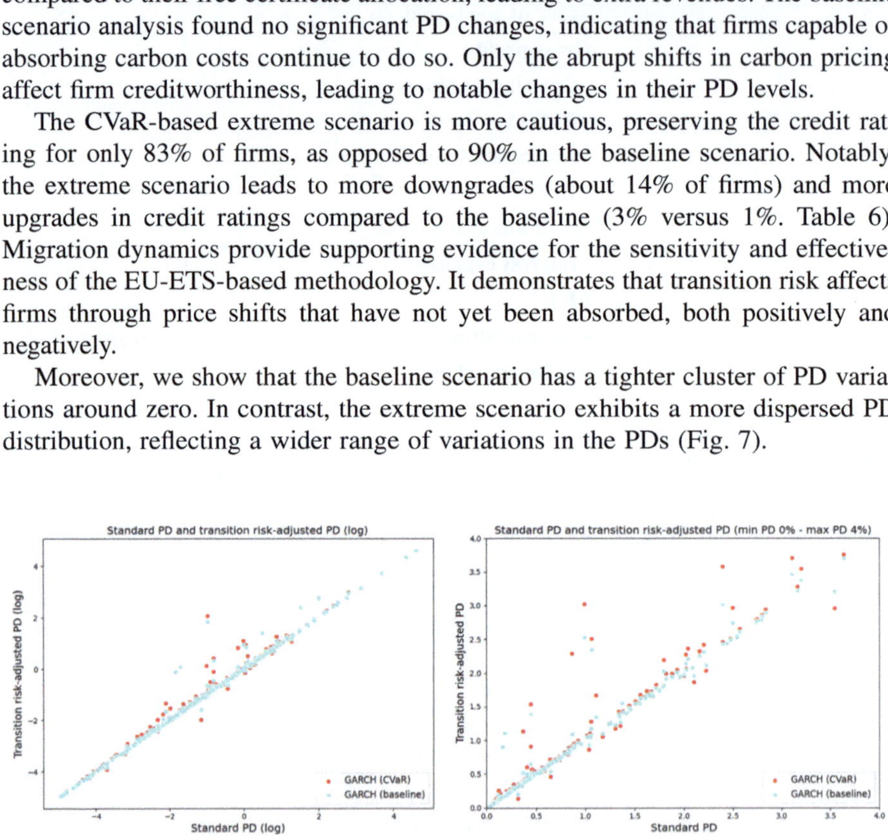

Fig. 6 Transition risk-adjusted PDs obtained in the two scenarios (y-axis) against the standard ICAS PDs (x-axis). **a** Baseline scenario and CVaR scenario, data for the entire sample (logarithmic scale); **b** Baseline scenario and CVaR scenario, PD at a maximum value of 4% (percentage values). Cyan points represent the baseline scenario PDs, and red points represent the CVaR scenario PDs

Table 6 One-year change in credit ratings for GJR-GARCH baseline and CVaR (ICAS rating scale; percentage values)

Method	Stable	Upgrade	Downgrade
GJR-GARCH (base)	90	1	9
GJR-GARCH (CVaR)	83	3	14

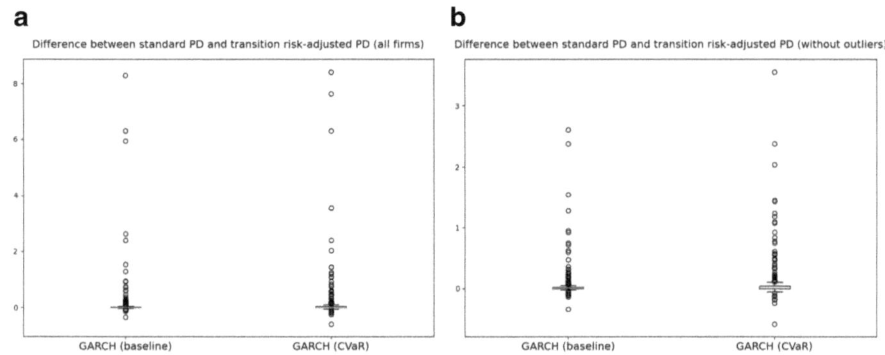

Fig. 7 One-year probability of default variation under the baseline scenario and the extreme scenario. **a** Box-whisker plots illustrating the difference between transition risk-adjusted and standard PDs for both the extreme and the baseline scenarios; **b** Box-whisker plots illustrating the difference between transition risk-adjusted and standard PDs without outliers. The Y-axis displays the absolute difference between standard PDs and transition risk-adjusted PDs in percentage values

5.2 EU-ETS vs NGFS-Based Scenario Analysis

The one-year horizon of our proposed methodology contrasts with the common practice of relying on long-term (8/10 years) NGFS scenarios (Emambakhsh et al., 2023). Through ICAS, we compare the sensitivity of firm PDs to the transition risk assessed via EU-ETS data against the transition risk assessed via NGFS scenarios. To perform the comparison, first we shorten the NGFS scenarios to a one-year timeframe by front-loading the price impact on the first year, and then we associate to each NGFS scenario three possible carbon taxes: *Below 2 °C*—40€/tCO_2eq., *Net Zero 2050*—90€/tCO_2eq and *Delayed Transition*—140€/tCO_2eq (Di Virgilio et al., 2024). The comparison resulted in differing responses of firm PDs to transition risk quantified by carbon market data or by a fixed carbon tax. The baseline EU-ETS scenario (cyan points) exhibits more variability than the adverse NGFS scenario (blue points), with a broader dispersion around the line (Fig. 8). The PDs for the average NGFS scenario (green points) and the adverse NGFS scenario (blue points) align more closely with the 45° line, indicating small deviations from standard PD estimates. The extreme EU-ETS scenario (red points) shows more significant variability, with data points widely scattered above and below the 45° line, suggesting significant fluctuations in transition risk-adjusted PDs.

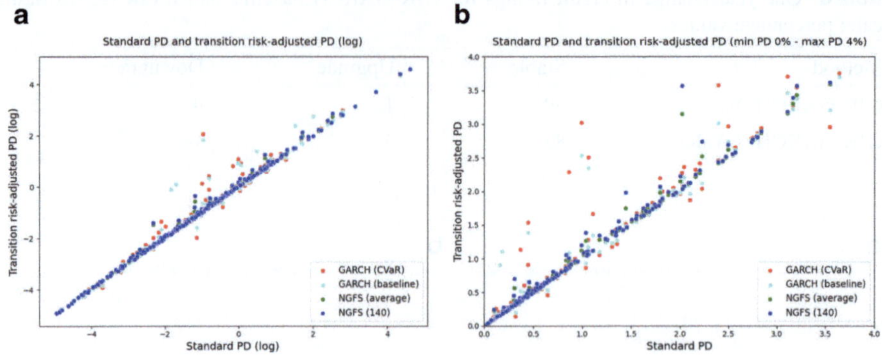

Fig. 8 **a** One-year probability of default under the baseline ETS scenario, extreme CVaR ETS scenario, average NGFS scenario, and adverse NGFS scenario (logarithmic scale); **b** One-year probability of default under the baseline ETS scenario, extreme CVaR ETS scenario, average NGFS scenario, and adverse NGFS scenario, PD at a maximum value of 4% (percentage values)

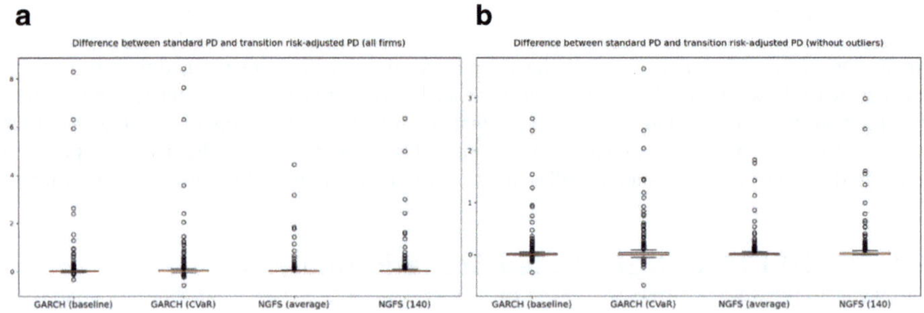

Fig. 9 One-year probability of default variation under alternative scenarios. **a** Box-whisker plots illustrating the differences across baseline, CVaR, NGFS (average), NGFS worst PDs scenarios; **b** Box-whisker plots illustrating the differences across baseline, CVaR, NGFS (average), NGFS worst PDs scenarios without outliers. The Y-axis displays the absolute difference between standard PDs and transition risk-adjusted PDs in percentage values.

The new methodology, both in baseline and CVaR scenarios, shows a more responsive approach in adjusting risk classes, especially in terms of improvements (Table 7), compared to the carbon tax and sectoral data emission estimation approach (see Sect. 3.2). The NGFS scenarios, despite their varying carbon tax values, tend to keep around 90% of firms in the same risk class, indicating a lower sensitivity to transition risk. The underestimation of emissions in sectoral approaches and the lack of a mechanism to reward environmentally responsible firms, like selling quotas in the EU-ETS market, lead to lower sensitivity. Additionally, NGFS scenarios focus only on policy-driven decarbonisation targets, based on pre-defined assumptions on their implementation. In contrast, the EU-ETS-based approach incorporates market dynamics, to which participating firms are inherently

Table 7 Migration of 1-year credit rating classes generated by the alternative methodologies (per cent)

Method	Stable	Upgrade	Downgrade
GJR-GARCH (CVaR)	83	3	14
GJR-GARCH (base)	90	1	9
Below 2 °C (40 €/tCO_2)	94	0	6
Net Zero 2050 (90 €/tCO_2)	91	0	9
Delayed Transition (140 €/tCO_2)	88	0	12
Average of NGFS scenarios	91	0	9

exposed beyond the effects of transition policies, including both general speculative movements and those specific to the EU-ETS. When carbon prices rise, firms selling certificates in the EU-ETS market gain additional revenue, enhancing their creditworthiness. In the baseline scenario, 1% of firms benefit from trading EUA certificates, while 3% improve their rating class in an extreme scenario. In addition, in the extreme EU-ETS scenario, when firms incur additional costs, we observe 14% of firms being downgraded. This contrasts with a 12% downgrade under the extreme NGFS scenario (Delayed Transition).

Finally, we rank the alternative methodologies based on the average difference in transition risk-adjusted PDs compared to the standard PD (Table 8). The methodology proposed in this research is more responsive to transition risk estimated through carbon price shocks, as indicated by the higher sensitivity and lower concentration of the EU-ETS-based approach than the NGFS ones. The Gini Index and the CV scores under the stochastic method reflect less concentration due to specific rather than sectoral data.

Despite the broader variability observed in the outcomes, the central tendencies, such as the mean adjusted PDs, remain broadly aligned with those derived from NGFS scenarios. This similarity in magnitude reflects a convergence of transition risk impacts at an aggregate level. However, the added granularity of our model provides insights into firm-level risks and their dispersion across sectors, capturing heterogeneity in transition risk profiles that sectoral averages may overlook.

Table 8 Descriptive statistics about variations 1-year probability of default across alternative methodologies (percentage values)

Method	Mean	Std. Dev	CV	Gini Index
GJR-GARCH (CVaR)	0.06	0.22	3.65	10
Delayed Transition (140 €/tCO_2)	0.05	0.13	2.75	78
GJR-GARCH (base)	0.04	0.15	4.21	11
Net Zero 2050 (90 €/tCO_2)	0.03	0.08	2.7	78
Average of NGFS scenarios	0.03	0.08	2.68	78
Below 2 °C (40 €/tCO_2)	0.01	0.04	2.67	77

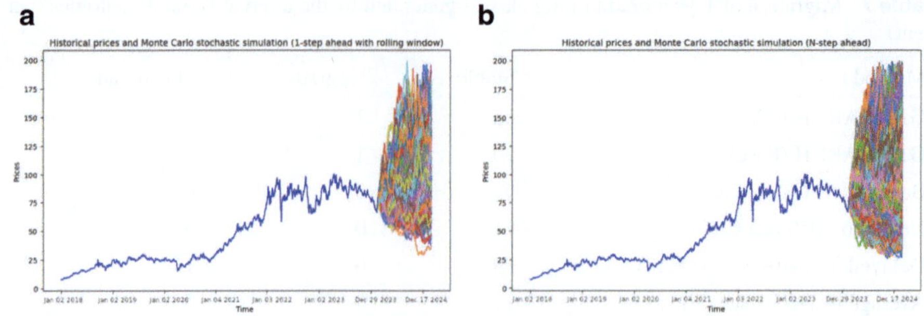

Fig. 10 EU-ETS price and the 10.000 estimated trajectories one year ahead **a** Comparison of price simulated trajectories with 1-step ahead rolling window; **b** Comparison of price simulated trajectories with N-step ahead

While NGFS scenarios utilise sectoral averages that compress the tails of the distribution, smoothing extreme variations, our approach captures real-world market fluctuations, including firm-specific emissions data. This results in a broader range of predicted PDs and a higher sensitivity to transition risks (Fig. 10).

To further investigate the two methodologies based on EU-ETS allowances price evolutions and NGFS scenarios, we compare the relevant PD distributions. The comparison involves all the firms in the ICAS sample participating in the previously analysed EU-ETS scheme and a subset excluding firms with more free certificates than emissions (Table 9). The Kolmogorov-Smirnov and Mann-Whitney U tests confirms different distributions for the two samples. The Spearman correlation coefficient (0.67) indicates some agreement in stress intensity between methodologies, decreasing to 0.41 when including firms with lowered default probabilities.

Table 9 Tests on statistical distribution on 1-year probability of default under alternative methodologies

Method	Kolmorogov-Smirnov (p-value)	Mann-Whitney U (p-value)	Spearman (%)
GJR-GARCH CVaR vs Average NGFS scenario (only firms experiencing costs)	0	0	43
GJR-GARCH CVaR vs Average NGFS scenario (including virtuous firms)	0	0	69

Table 10 Comparison in migration of credit rating classes (per cent)

Method	Stable	Upgrade	Downgrade
N-steps ahead			
GJR-GARCH (CVaR)	90	1	9
GJR-GARCH (base)	83	3	14
Rolling window			
GJR-GARCH (CVaR)	91	1	8
GJR-GARCH (base)	86	1	13

6 Consistency Check

Our findings are robust and not dependent on the estimated conditional volatility of EUA futures prices. In the literature, asymmetric GARCH models, particularly the GJR-GARCH model, are preferred for modelling the volatility of EUA allowances during Phases III and IV. Our stochastic simulation method uses a Monte Carlo n-step ahead simulation for the error term, producing multiple return trajectories based on one-year average volatility. Using a 252-day rolling window, we forecast 1-step ahead volatility, leading to 10,000 one-year return paths and corresponding price trajectories. These trajectories remain within a consistent range (Fig. 10).

There is no significant variation in credit rating migration resulting from the two techniques to project trajectories, affirming the robustness and reliability of our results (Table 10).

7 Conclusion

This Chapter integrates transition risk into the estimation of firms' credit risk assessment by estimating transition risk-adjusted PDs. Our methodology employs EU-ETS market data, including prices and transaction details, to estimate transition risks accurately.

Our findings show that EU-ETS market data enable a more accurate and responsive transition risk assessment compared to top-down sectoral emissions estimations and NGFS scenario-based methods. By capturing both cost increases and potential revenue gains from emissions trading, our approach reflects the full spectrum of transition impacts. Environmentally responsible firms, which emit less than their allocated quotas, can benefit financially by selling surplus allowances—leading to potential rating improvement. Conversely, firms with high emissions face increased costs and potential downgrade.

The dual impact has important implications. For the banking sector, changes in PDs affect the valuation of collateral eligible for monetary policy operations, affecting risk management and asset pricing. For firms, higher emissions may translate into tighter borrowing conditions, reinforcing the financial incentives for decarbonization (Altavilla et al., 2023).

Future research could consider transition plans as a risk mitigation tool,[22] and explore scenarios where environmentally virtuous firms save excess allowances for future use, while non-virtuous firms pass additional costs onto consumers, with the overall impact depending on the price elasticity of their products.

Appendix A

EU-ETS Transactions Functioning

We show in a diagram the interconnectedness within the primary structures of the EUTL database (Fig. 11). On the right side, every installation relates to multiple records in the compliance and surrender sectors. For each installation under the EU-ETS, the compliance dimension focuses on distributing and submitting permits alongside annually confirmed emissions. When it comes to surrendering, each installation corresponds to a specific entry in the surrender log, which is distinguished by the type and provenance of the surrendered item. At any given moment, a single operator's holding account is uniquely connected to an Installation. However, this representation of an Installation by an OHA can shift over periods.

Consequently, an installation may have connections to numerous OHAs. Post the 2012–13 overhaul of the EUTL, most installations are linked to a past operator's holding account (type 120–0) and a current one (type 100–7), leading to at least two linked accounts for most. Every account is directly associated with a solitary account holder, who may have links to multiple accounts. This connection helps in identifying accounts that are collectively owned. For instance, a prominent electricity firm operating several power stations would register multiple OHAs, one for each facility, often under a single account holder. Such a firm could also be linked to a PHA managing its trade through a centralised account. EUETS.INFO facilitates the exploration of these patterns by enabling searches of accounts via account holders and identifying related accounts based on the same holders.

Transactions are defined by two accounts, identified as the donor and recipient of allowances. Each account partakes in numerous transactions, serving in both capacities. OHAs annually engage in at least two transactions, acquiring allowances to match their verified emissions. To comply with EU-ETS regulations, OHAs must then surrender these units, thus participating in a transaction as a donor. The algorithm developed for establishing connections initially uses

[22] A climate transition plan is a detailed action plan that outlines how a firm will modify its business model to achieve net zero carbon emissions by 2050. Transition plans are essential for showing stakeholders that the firm is committed to reducing emissions and ensuring the business remains profitable in a net-zero carbon economy. Thus, we consider incorporating the transition plans' impact on carbon emissions into the calculation of the difference between produced emissions and allocated quotas, which should be annually reduced by the fixed established percentage (see Sect. 2).

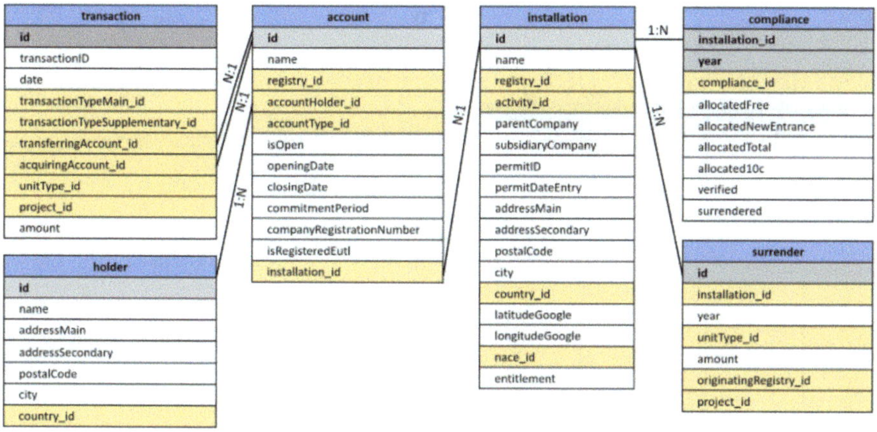

Fig. 11 EUTL database relational model (Abbrell, 2022)

Table 11 ICAS enterprises within EU-ETS grouped by correspondence criteria

ICAS firms within EU-ETS	572
Legal entity identifier	342
Tax code	61
Fuzzy logic	169

the Legal Entity Identifier (LEI) or tax code as identifiers for the firms. In its final stage, the algorithm employs approximate matching techniques (fuzzy logic) between the demographic data of OHAs and specific details of ICAS firms (standardised name, postal code, and geolocation information). This algorithm generates a likelihood score between the EUTL and ICAS entries. This score allows the ranking of the combinations of data acquired: valid matches realise when the score for each of the three identifying details of the company exceeds a certain threshold. The number of ICAS enterprises included within the EU-ETS is 572, distinguishing them based on the various matching techniques (Table 11).

Appendix B

GARCH Stylised Facts

The features of EUA certificate futures returns are analysed through the examination of 'stylized facts' (Zivot, 2009 and Wang & Ghysels, 2015). The analysis, covering data from 2018 to 2023, reveals characteristics like non-constant volatility (conditional heteroscedasticity) and, less prominently, volatility clustering. This phenomenon is more apparent in the squared returns series. The autocorrelation function (ACF) chart indicates no autocorrelation, consistent with the series'

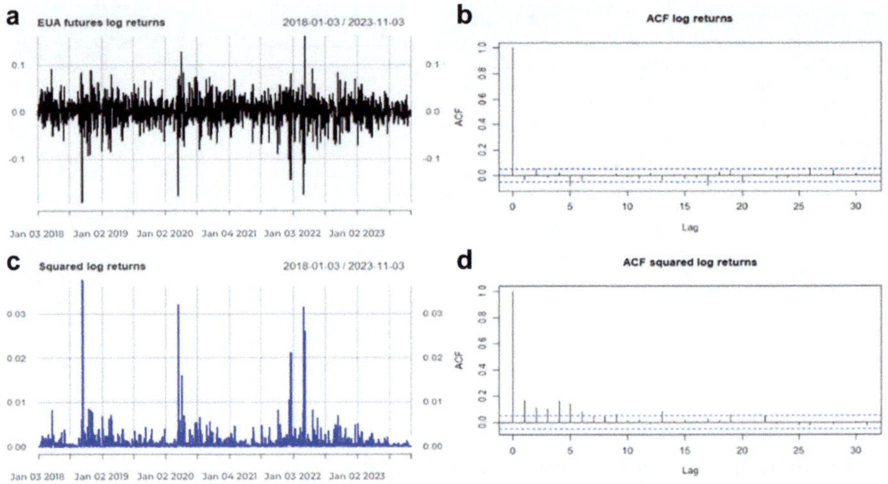

Fig. 12 **a** Time series of log returns; **b** ACF for log returns; **c** squared log returns; **d** ACF for squared log returns

nature, but shows correlation in squared returns. These findings suggest modelling the variance (second moment) of the futures price distribution rather than the series trend (see Fig. 12).

To analyse the distribution of EU-ETS returns, we use the Quantile-Quantile (QQ) plot and the estimation of data density compared to a normal distribution. Both panels reveal deviations from the normal in the tails (Fig. 13). Specifically, the data distribution shows heavy tails (kurtosis = 7.89) and a leftward skew (skewness index = −0.6).

The graphical inspection of the correlation between volatility and past returns, and the scatter plot between the two, reveals a negative correlation (Fig. 14). This finding confirms the presence of a significant leverage effect, although it's less pronounced in the second analysis.

Our next step involves testing various GARCH specifications to identify the most suitable model for capturing the volatility of EUA certificates. We start with the simplest specification and progress to the more complex GARCH-MIDAS, which incorporates the monthly price of crude oil as a lower frequency variable. Initially, we assess model performance using the Akaike Information Criterion (AIC), as shown in Table 12, selecting the model with the lowest AIC value. Subsequently, we conduct a back-test analysis on VaR at 5% confidence (Taschini & Paolella, 2008). This process involves comparing expected versus actual VaR violations (as shown in the AE column of Table 12) and testing the statistical properties of the VaR. We utilise several tests for this purpose: the Unconditional Coverage test (UC, Kupiec, 1995), the Conditional Coverage test (CC, Christoffersen, 1998), and the Dynamic Quantile test (DQ, Engle & Manganelli, 2004). These tests evaluate whether the rate of VaR violations aligns with expectations

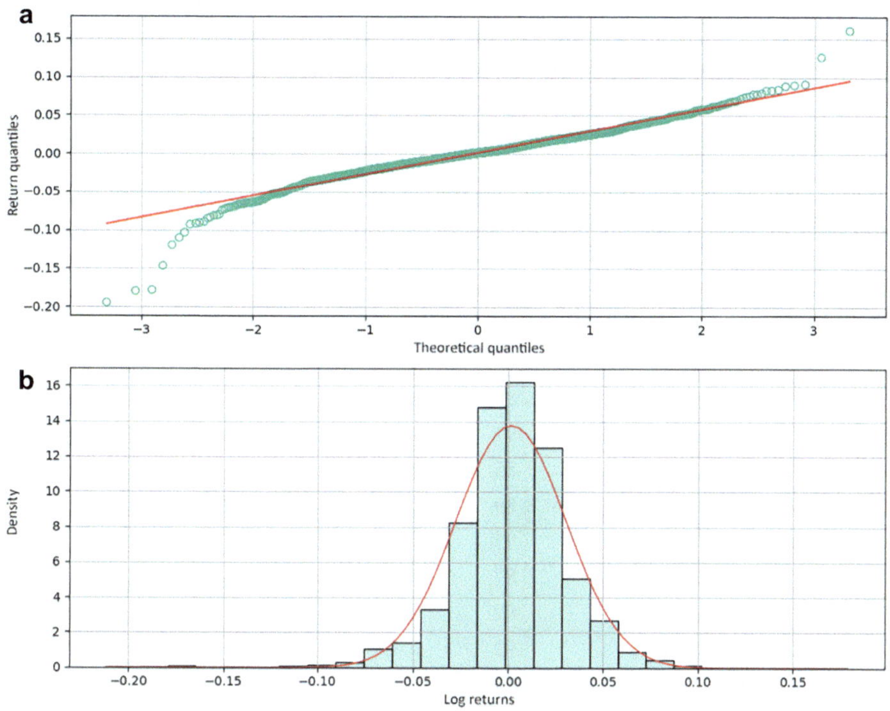

Fig. 13 **a** QQ plot; **b** returns distribution

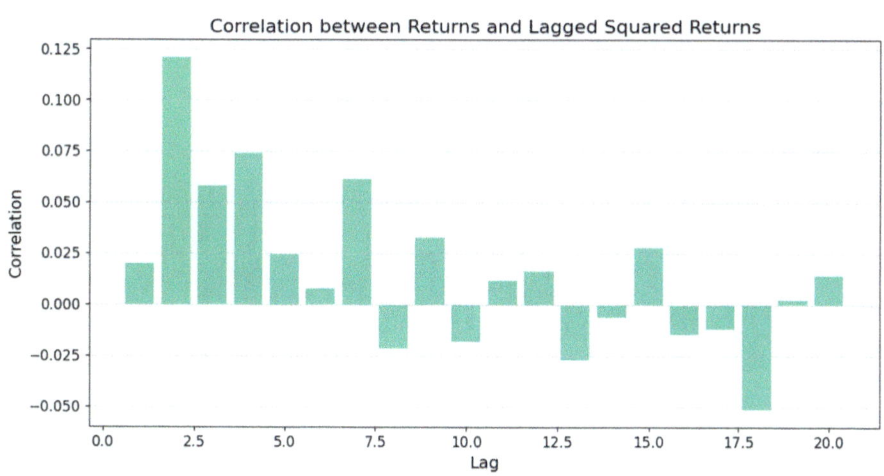

Fig. 14 Correlation between returns and volatility up to 20 lags

and whether these violations are independently distributed over time. The DQ test, which also assesses the independence of VaR violations and the accuracy of violation counts (similar to the CC test), is more powerful (Berkowitz et al., 2011). Based on the results in Table 12, we choose the GJR-GARCH(2,1,2) model, with optimal parameters determined through Bayesian optimization (Naik et al., 2020). Figure 15 illustrates the 5% VaR estimation against EUA returns, demonstrating the model's ability to closely mirroring the series. For the sake of exposition, we report in Fig. 16 all the estimated models.

Table 12 Statistical properties of GARCH models

	AIC (test score)	AE (%)	UC (p-value)	CC (p-value)	DQ (p-value)
GARCH-N	−4.37	85	0.19	0.41	0.7
GARCH-t	−4.42	91	0.41	0.56	0.2
GARCH skew-t	−4.42	85	0.19	0.37	0.1
EGARCH-N	−4.37	89	0.34	0.64	0.7
EGARCH-t	−4.42	95	0.64	0.84	0.2
GJR-N	−4.37	87	0.23	0.48	0.6
GJR-t	−4.41	92	0.48	0.59	0.2
GJR-t 22	−4.41	92	0.48	0.77	0.5
GARCH-MIDAS	−6.56	89	0.34	0.64	0.4
GARCH-MIDAS-t	−8.33	92	0.48	0.77	0.3
DAGM	−6.56	89	0.34	0.64	1.6
DAGM-t	−8.32	92	0.47	0.77	0.3

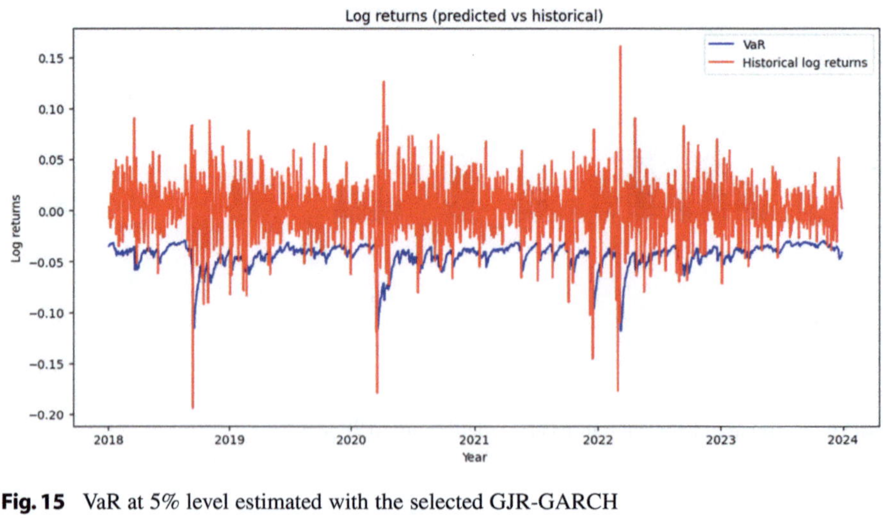

Fig. 15 VaR at 5% level estimated with the selected GJR-GARCH

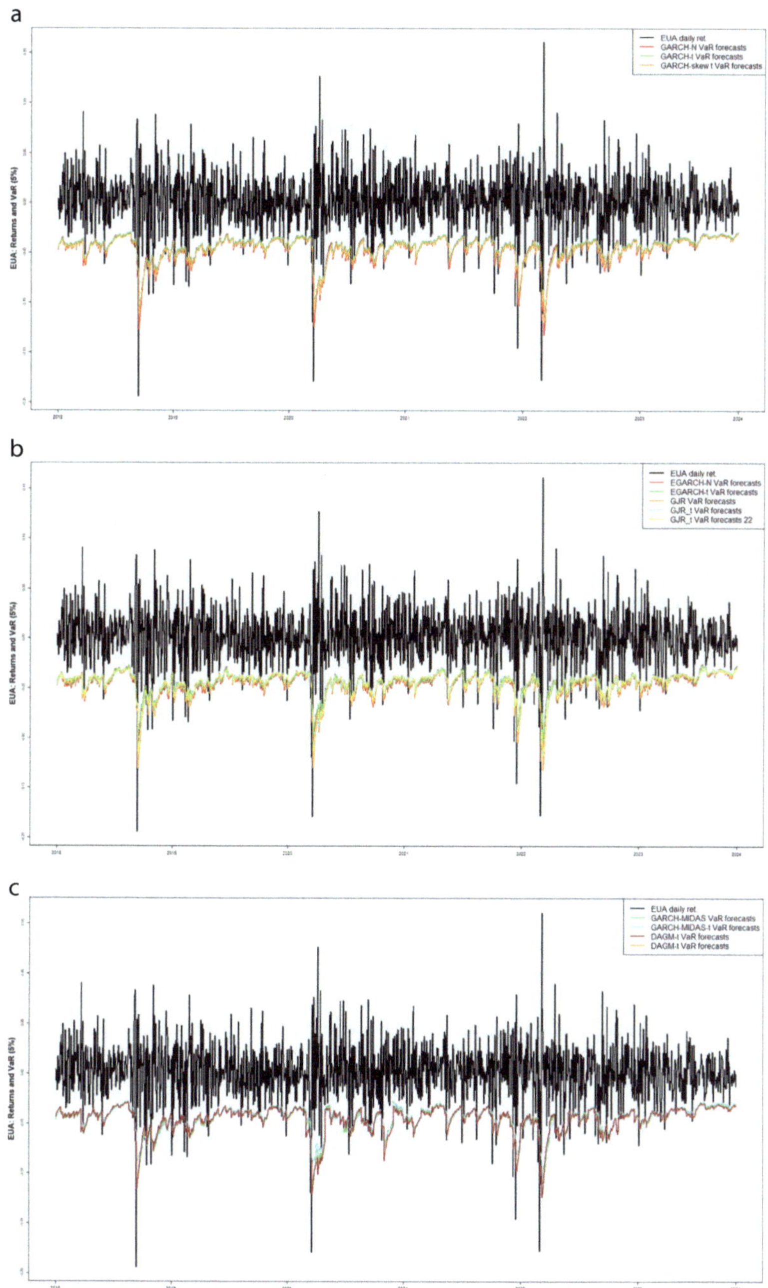

Fig. 16 Estimated VaR. **a** Simple model; **b** Advanced model; **c** MIDAS model

References

Abbrell, J. (2022) EU ETS info. Retrieved from April 24, 2024, from https://www.euets.info/
Aiello, A., & Angelico, C. (2023). Climate change and credit risk: The effect of carbon taxes on Italian banks' business loan default rates. *Journal of Policy Modelling, 45*(1), 187–201.
Alberola, E., Chevallier, J., & Cheze, B. (2008). The EU emissions trading scheme: The effects of industrial. *The International Economy, 116*, 93–125.
Altavilla, C., Bouchina, M., Pagano, M., Polo, A. (2023). Climate risk, bank lending, and monetary policy. Centre for studies in economics and finance 687.
Arouri, M., Jawadi, F., & Khuong, D. (2012). Nonlinearities in carbon spot-futures price relationships during Phase II of the EU ETS. *Economic Modelling, 29*(3), 884–892.
Battiston, S., Mandel, A., Monasterolo, I., Roncoroni, A. (2023). Climate credit risk and corporate valuation. Retrieved from April 24, 2024, from https://ssrn.com/abstract=4124002
Benz, E., & Truck, S. (2008). Modeling the price dynamics of CO_2 emission allowances. *Energy Econ, 31*(1), 4–15.
Berkowitz, J., Christoffersen, P., & Pelletier, D. (2011). Evaluating value-at-risk models with desk-level data. *Management Science, 57*(12), 2213–2227.
Bernardini, E., Faiella, I., Lavecchia, L., Mistretta, A., & Natoli, F. (2021). Central banks, climate risks, and sustainable finance. Quest Econ Finanza 608.
Billio, M., Giacomelli, A. (2023). ESG-adjusted credit rating: The indirect approach. Accessed 24 Apr 2024.
Blasberg, A., Kiesel, R., & Taschini, L. (2021). Climate default swap: Disentangling the exposure to transition risk through CDS. Accessed 24 Apr 2024.
Bolton, P., & Kacperczyk, M. (2021). Do investors care about carbon risk? *Journal of Financial Economics, 142*(2), 517–549.
Bolton, P., Lam, A., Muuls, M. (2023). Do carbon prices affect stock prices? Accessed 24 Apr 2024.
Boneva, L., Ferrucci, G., & Mongelli, F. P. (2021). To be or not to be "green": How can monetary policy react to climate change? *ECB Occas Pap Ser, 285*, 1–40.
Brauneis, A. Z. (2016). Modeling carbon spot and futures price returns with GARCH and Markov switching GARCH models. *Central European Journal of Operations Research, 24*, 149–176.
Bustamante, M. C., & Zucchi, F. (2022). *Dynamic carbon emission management* (ECB Work Pap 2885).
Byun, S. J. (2013). Forecasting carbon futures volatility using GARCH models with energy volatilities. *Energy Econ, 40*, 207–221.
Carbone, S., Giuzio, M., Kapadia, S., Kramer, J., Nyholm, K., & Vozian, K. (2021). The low-carbon transition, climate commitments, and firm credit risk. *ECB Work Pap, 2631*, 1–70.
Chevallier, J. (2012). *Econometric analysis of carbon markets*. Springer.
Christianen, A., Arvanitakis, A., Tangen, K., & Hasselknippe, H. (2005). Price determinants in the EU emissions trading scheme. *Clim Policy, 1*(5), 15–30.
Christoffersen, P. (1998). Evaluation of interval forecasts. *International Economic Review, 18*(2), 111–128.
Daskalakis, G. D. (2009). Modeling CO_2 emission allowance prices and derivatives: Evidence from the European trading scheme. *Journal of Banking & Finance, 33*(7), 1230–1241.
DG Clima. (2023). Participation in the EU ETS markets. Europe Economics.
Dhamija, A., Surendra, S., & Jain, P. (2017). Forecasting volatility of carbon under EU ETS: A multi-phase study. *Environmental Economics and Policy Studies, 19*, 299–335.
Di Virgilio, S., Faiella, I., Mistretta, A., & Narizzano, S. (2024). Assessing credit risk sensitivity to climate and energy shocks. Towards a common minimum standards in line with the ECB climate agenda. *Journal of Policy Modeling, 46*(3), 552–568.
Dutta, A. (2018). Modeling and forecasting the volatility of carbon emission market: The role of outliers, time-varying jumps, and oil price risk. *Journal of Cleaner Production, 172*, 2773–2781.

Emambakhsh, T., Fuchs, M., Kordel, S., Kouratzoglou, C., Lelli, C., Pizzighello, R., & Spaggiari, M. (2023). *The road to Paris: Stress testing the transition towards a net-zero economy* (ECB Occas Pap 328).
Engle, R. (2002). New frontiers for ARCH models. *J Appl Econom, 17*(5), 425–446.
Engle, R., & Manganelli, S. (2004). CAViaR: Conditional autoregressive value at risk by regression quantiles. *J Bus Econ Stat, 22*(4), 367–381.
European Central Bank. (2021). ECB presents action plan to include climate change considerations in its monetary policy strategy. Retrieved from April 24, 2024, from https://www.ecb.europa.eu/press/pr/date/2021/html/ecb.pr210708_1~f104919225.en.html
European Central Bank (2022) ECB takes further steps to incorporate climate change into its monetary policy operations. Retrieved from April 24, 2024, from https://www.ecb.europa.eu/press/pr/date/2022/html/ecb.pr220704~4f48a72462.en.html
European Commission. (2021). Fit for 55: Delivering the EU's 2030 climate target on the way to. Retrieved from April 24, 2024, from https://eur-lex.europa.eu/legal-content/EN/TXT/?uri=CELEX:52021DC0550
European Commission. (2023). Our ambition for 2030. Retrieved from April 24, 2024, from https://climate.ec.europa.eu/eu-action/eu-emissions-trading-system-eu-ets/our-ambition-2030_en?prefLang=it
Faiella, I., & Malvolti, D. (2020). The climate risk for finance in Italy. Quest Econ Finanza 545.
Faiella, I., Mistretta, A., & Lavecchia, L. (2022). A climate stress test on the financial vulnerability of Italian households and firms. *Journal of Policy Modelling, 44*(2), 396–417.
Fan, Y., Jia, J. J., Wang, X., & Xu, J. H. (2017). What policy adjustments in the EU ETS truly affected the carbon prices? *Energy Policy, 103*, 145–164.
Financial Stability Board. (2021). The availability of data with which to monitor and assess climate-related risks to financial stability.
Gargallo, P., Lample, L., Miguel, J., & Salvad, M. (2021). Co-movements between EU ETS and the energy markets: A VAR-DCC-GARCH approach. *Mathematics, 9*(15), 1787.
Glosten, L. R. (1993). On the relation between the expected value and the volatility of the nominal excess return on stocks. *J Finance, 48*(5), 1779–1801.
Gorenflo, M. (2013). Futures price dynamics of CO_2 emission allowances. *Empirical Economics, 45*, 1025–1047.
Grundmann, J., Silberbach, A., & Auria, L. (2023). *Including carbon taxation risk in Deutsche Bundesbank's in-house credit assessment system (ICAS): An empirical analysis* (Deutsche Bundesbank Tech Pap).
Guo, J., Su, B., Yang, G., Feng, L., Liu, Y., & Gu, F. (2018). How do verified emissions announcements affect the comoves between trading behaviors and carbon prices? *Evidence from EU ETS. Sustainability, 10*(9), 3255.
Kanzig, D. (2023). *The unequal economic consequences of carbon pricing* (NBER Work Pap Ser: 1–44).
Krokida, S.-I., Lambertides, N., Savva, C., & Tsouknidis, D. (2020). The effects of oil price shocks on the prices of EU emission trading system and European stock returns. *Eur J Finance, 26*(1), 1–13.
Kupiec, P. H. (1995). Techniques for verifying the accuracy of risk measurement models. *The Journal of Derivatives, 95*(24).
Letout, S. (2022). Corporate micro-data in the EU Emission Trading System (EU ETS). Publ Off Eur Union.
Mansanet-Bataller, M., Pardo, A., & Valor, E. (2007). CO_2 prices, energy, and weather. *Energy, 28*(3–5), 73–93.
Monasterolo, I. (2020). Climate change and the financial system. *Annual Review of Resource Economics, 12*, 299–320.
Naik, N., Mohan, B. R., & Jha, R. A. (2020). GARCH-model identification based on performance of information criteria. *Procedia Computer Science, 171*, 1935–1942.
NGFS. (2021). NGFS: Climate scenarios for central banks and supervisors.

Oestreich, A., & Tsiakas, I. (2015). Carbon emissions and stock returns: Evidence from the EU emissions trading scheme. *Journal of Banking & Finance, 58*, 294–308.
Ordonez, G. (2022). Moody's integrated risk analysis. Moody's Analytics.
Rittler, D. (2012). Price discovery and volatility spillovers in the European Union emissions trading scheme: A high-frequency analysis. *Journal of Banking & Finance, 36*(3), 774–785.
Stavins, R. N. (2003). Experience with market-based environmental policy instruments. *Handbook of environmental economics* (Vol. 1, pp. 355–435). Elsevier.
Stefan, M., & Wellenreuther, C. (2020). London vs. Leipzig: Price discovery of carbon futures during Phase III of the ETS. *Economics Letters, 188*, 108990.
Taschini, L. (2023). Carbon pricing and carbon markets. LSE Executive Education.
Taschini, L., & Paolella, M. S. (2008). An econometric analysis of emission allowance prices. *Journal of Banking & Finance, 32*(10), 2022–2032.
Unnewehr, J. F., Weidlich, A., Gfüllner, L., & Schäfer, M. (2022). Open-data based carbon emission intensity signals for electricity generation in European countries—Top-down vs. bottom-up approach. *Cleaner Energy Systems, 3*, 100018.
Wang, F., & Ghysels, E. (2015). Econometric analysis of volatility component models. *Economet Theory, 31*(2), 362–393.
Wen, F., Wu, N., & Gong, X. (2020). China's carbon emissions trading and stock returns. *Energy Economics, 86*, 104678.
Yu, H., Wang, H., & Liang, Z. L. (2022). Carbon market volatility analysis based on structural breaks: Evidence from EU-ETS and China. *Exp Sci, 10*, Article 973855.
Zhang, Y., Liu, Y., & Wang, H. (2023). How credit default swap market measures carbon risk. *Environmental Science and Pollution Research, 30*(34), 82696–82716.
Zhang, Z., & Zhao, R. (2022). Carbon emission and credit default swaps. *Finance Res Lett, 50*, Article 103286.
Zivot, E. (2009). Practical issues in the analysis of univariate GARCH models. *Handbook of financial time series* (pp. 101–136). Springer.

S and G Pillars in Credit Analysis with AI

Manuel Cugliari, Stefano Di Virgilio, Enrico Foscolo, and Alessandra Iannamorelli

1 Introduction

In recent years, the assessment of corporate default risk has evolved beyond traditional approaches relying on financial indicators. The integration of broader ESG considerations is increasingly important to develop a comprehensive framework for risk assessment. The PD estimation for small and medium-sized enterprises benefits from the integration of S and G indicators, such as board gender composition, managers' age, management experience, employee tenure, and firing and hiring ratios. Similarly, sound governance practices, such as an independent board and audit function, effective control systems, and transparent communication, can contribute to corporate success, mitigate fraud and conflicts of interest, and improve the firm's creditworthiness (Moody's Ratings, 2025; S&P Global, 2021). The extant literature on social issues mostly examines gender diversity and financial literacy (e.g., Ballacci et al., 2021; Belás et al., 2018).

This Chapter investigates whether the social and governance pillars may improve the accuracy of corporate default prediction for Italian non-financial firms, as assessed within the Bank of Italy's S-ICAS.

M. Cugliari · S. Di Virgilio · E. Foscolo (✉) · A. Iannamorelli
Bank of Italy, Financial Risk Management Directorate, Rome, Italy
e-mail: enrico.foscolo@bancaditalia.it

M. Cugliari
e-mail: manuel.cugliari@bancaditalia.it

S. Di Virgilio
e-mail: stefano.divirgilio@bancaditalia.it

A. Iannamorelli
e-mail: alessandra.iannamorelli@bancaditalia.it

A. Scalia (ed.), *Corporate Credit Analysis and AI*, Finance for Professionals,
https://doi.org/10.1007/978-3-032-13422-6_14

While the literature mainly deals with bankruptcy (Altman, 1968; Altman et al., 1977; Barboza et al., 2017; Ciampi, 2015; Ciampi & Gordini, 2013; Cultrera, 2020; García & Herrero, 2021; Norden & Weber, 2010; Paraschiv et al., 2024; Tian et al., 2015), the default definition that matters for ICAS relies on Article 178 of Regulation (EU) No 575/2013 (see Chap. 3). For this reason, the default status is generally reversible, unlike bankruptcy. We investigate the role of explanatory variables such as ownership structure, external audit firm appointments, board stability and independence, board experience and effectiveness, wages, and employee turnover. We thus adopt a similar approach as the Omega score developed by Altman et al., (2023). While the governance pillar is usually employed by credit analysts in the expert assessment of ICAS, which involves a qualitative judgment based on various information sources, to our knowledge this study provides the first attempt to include a wide range of S and G indicators within statistical credit assessment in the Eurosystem framework. The sample size, including hundreds of thousands of non-financial firms, provides robustness to the analysis.

We leverage traditional and novel data to construct the S and G indicators. Our sources include the Italian National Social Insurance Agency (INPS) and a proprietary knowledge graph dataset termed KG19, developed by the Bank of Italy and based on information from the Italian Business Register. The INPS dataset contains detailed information on Italian firms and employees. It allows the extrapolation of social indicators, such as workforce characteristics and employment patterns, that can affect corporate performance. The KG19 dataset enables automated reasoning and probabilistic analysis to obtain governance indicators (Bellomarini et al., 2019).

In line with the S-ICAS framework, we first group firms by size and perform feature selection for the S and G indicators, combining visual inspection and variable importance ranking with univariate logistic regressions and random forests. We thus construct a list of statistically significant indicators according to firm size (from now on, the watchlist; see, e.g., James et al., 2023). In particular, random forests help to identify non-monotonic and possibly non-linear effects and reduce the number of variables in each watchlist. Afterwards, we assess company default risk with two independent scores, one based on the social watchlist (the S score) and the other on the governance watchlist (the G score), both obtained with multivariate logistic regressions.

Our findings support the conclusions of Altman et al. (2023). Social indicators, such as *layoff*, *turnover rate*, and *average wage* enhance the discriminatory and predictive power in assessing default risk. Employment stability and workforce engagement are correlated with financial health. A higher layoff rate is associated with a higher PD, suggesting that workforce volatility may signal financial or operational challenges (Mawdsley & Somaya, 2016). Conversely, firms with relatively high *average wage* exhibit a lower PD than the rest of the industry. These findings support the view that investment in human capital is important for long-term financial sustainability (Houston et al., 2024).

Governance factors impact the S-ICAS PD differently based on firm size. For instance, *board age diversity* emerges as a statistically significant predictor for all classes, while *board size* does so for micro and small firms only. Overall, this seems consistent with the notion that board composition matters for corporate stability (Altman et al., 2023; Aulia & Wijaya, 2020).

In the final step of the analysis, the S and G scores are integrated into the baseline S-ICAS, which relies on financial and credit behaviour scores. Rather than revising the whole framework of S-ICAS, our contribution builds upon its existing structure. We investigate whether the inclusion of social and governance variables—derived from the INPS and KG19 datasets—can enhance the baseline model's predictive and discriminatory power. This approach allows us to assess the incremental value of the S and G dimensions without altering the econometric design of S-ICAS.

We do not seek to establish causality between social and governance variables and the firm's default status; we simply investigate the predictive power of the new set of variables for the default one year ahead. We find that the augmented S-ICAS—with the inclusion of the S and G scores—improves the discriminatory power of the baseline model, as measured by the out-of-sample AUROC. Specifically, the AUROC increase ranges between 0.5 and 0.9 percentage points for micro and small firms. While such an increase may seem relatively modest in absolute terms, it should be assessed considering the high baseline AUROC, which lies between 84 and 90%. For medium-sized firms, we observe similar results, with increments between 0.6 and 0.8 percentage points; in this case the governance score is not statistically significant. For large firms, the governance score and the AUROC increment are not significant. Overall, the augmented S-ICAS shows higher predictive power than the baseline model or, in other words, the augmented model leads to more precise PD estimates and rating classes than the baseline.

The modest statistical significance of the governance score in predicting default of larger firms is not necessarily at odds with the existing literature on the importance of fair governance practices for corporate health. Integrating governance variables with credit behaviour and/or financial ratios usually improves default predictions (Altman et al., 2023; Aulia & Wijaya, 2020). We divide firms into four different size classes and conduct a separate analysis for each class. For large firms the relatively low number of companies and the low occurrence of defaults—driven by very adverse circumstances—are a technical challenge for the statistical model. In summary, while the governance dimension is statistically significant only for micro and small firms, social issues emerge as important default predictors in all groups, making them strong candidates for integration into S-ICAS.

The remainder of the Chapter is organised as follows. Section 2 presents the literature review. Section 3 describes the data sources and presents the selection process of the S and G indicators. Section 4 presents the results of the social and governance logistic regression outcomes and the integration of the S and G scores into S-ICAS. Section 5 concludes.

2 Literature Review

Several studies show the important role of governance structure, ownership dynamics, and succession planning in influencing firm performance and mitigating credit risk. Robust governance mechanisms reduce default risk (Altman et al., 2023; Aulia & Wijaya, 2020) and improve financial outcomes (Baltrunaite et al., 2019, 2024). Altman et al. (2023) and Aulia and Wijaya (2020) examine default risk using traditional default risk measures[1] along with standard E, S and G indicators. The authors point out that introducing governance can improve the accuracy of default predictions. Tufford et al. (2024) show that U.S. companies which displayed governance leadership, according to the MSCI governance pillar score, have consistently outperformed governance laggards between 2015 and 2023, with an excess annualised return of 2.7%. On a global scale, country effects largely impact performance: good governance is generally associated with higher profitability, lower volatility, and lower earnings variability in developed markets, but it tends to be less significant in emerging markets.

The impact of social factors, including gender diversity, on credit risk management is also clearly established. Altman et al. (2023) show how S (in addition to G) indicators can improve the estimation of PD of small and medium companies. The performance of a firm led by a female CEO increases with the share of female workers, suggesting that female leadership positively influences wages and firm productivity (Flabbi et al., 2019). This evidence is consistent with the over-performance of companies with the highest scores on the social pillar of the MSCI ESG Ratings compared with their lowest-scoring peers across North America, Asia, Pacific, and Europe when adjusted for size and sector (Houston et al., 2024). Specifically, companies with superior human capital, product liability, and stakeholder opposition outperform those with the lowest scores. Among these three key social themes, human capital is the most universally significant factor for companies, underlining the important role of employee contribution in driving corporate success.

To summarise, the literature shows the significant role of governance and social factors in corporate performance. Integrating these factors into risk models might improve a company's risk evaluation.

3 Data

To investigate the improvement of the predictive and discriminatory power of the statistical model due to the inclusion of S and G variables, we construct a dataset that uses the following two sources in addition to the ICAS information:

[1] Such as Altman's Z-score and a PD from RMI-NUS. The studies examine the euro area and Indonesia, respectively.

Table 1 Firms and default rate by year

Year	Number of firms	Default rate (per cent)
2014	237,108	6.24
2015	229,132	5.35
2016	252,739	4.28
2017	260,056	3.20
2018	259,765	2.93
2019	260,983	2.66
2020	261,324	2.08
2021	246,283	1.69
2022	245,969	1.86
2023	278,179	2.04

- *INPS dataset*: INPS runs the Italian public retirement system. All employed and most self-employed workers are enrolled with INPS. It maintains an extensive dataset containing comprehensive information on Italian employees and firms;
- *Infocamere Knowledge Graph dataset*: the Bank of Italy's KG19 is a knowledge graph designed to structure detailed information from the Italian Business Register.

The following sections describe the ICAS company sample and the content of the INPS and Infocamere Knowledge Graph datasets, focusing on the selection process of social and governance indicators.

3.1 ICAS Firms

The ICAS dataset covers the years from 2014 to 2023, providing a longitudinal view of corporate financial health and credit performance. The number of firms and the default rate for each year are reported (Table 1).

The annual default rate in the sample exhibits a general downward trend over the period, reflecting improving creditworthiness within the Italian non-financial corporate sector. The sharp decline in the default rate during 2020 and 2021 was largely driven by the extraordinary policy measures implemented by the Italian government in response to the COVID-19 pandemic.[2] These measures—including a debt moratorium, exemptions from default reporting, and the provision of state-backed loans—resulted in a substantial liquidity support, which temporarily stabilised the firms' financial conditions. The increase in defaults observed in 2022 and 2023 partly reflects a rebound following the expiry of the support measures. Considering the distortions introduced by the pandemic-related interventions, the data for 2020 and 2021 have been excluded from the analysis.

[2] See legislative decrees 'Cura Italia' and 'Sostegni'.

Table 2 Firms and default rate by size

Size	Number of firms	Default rate (per cent)
Micro	1,535,493	3.64
Small	900,961	3.33
Medium	228,163	2.98
Large	51,754	2.23

Table 3 Social Key Issue Hierarchy

Pillar	Key Issues	Involved Indicators	Type
Social	Age	Employees' age entropy	Continuous
	Occupation	Hire rate	Continuous
		Employees' turnover rate	Continuous
		Layoff rate	Continuous
		Fixed-term contract rate	Continuous
	Sex	Female employment rate (compared to the industry)	Categorical
	Wage	Average wage (compared to the industry)	Categorical

Micro firms represent the largest class in the sample when classified by size, reflecting their widespread presence in the Italian productive system. The default rate is inversely related to firm size: larger companies may benefit from greater financial resilience, diversified revenue streams, and enhanced access to credit (Table 2).

3.2 Social Indicators

The INPS dataset contains information on Italian employees and firms. Each year, INPS provides the Bank of Italy with a dataset comprising aggregate data on all Italian firms with at least one statement of social security contributions for the year. The dataset includes wage, occupation, and age categories for each firm. Based on this source, we identify seven social company-level indicators (Table 3). A description of each indicator is available in Appendix A. By construction, all the indicators have a strong link with employment.

Some of these indicators are part of the GRI Standards[3] (e.g., hire and turnover rate), while others measure employee well-being and help to reveal the firm non-financial performance (Siegerink et al., 2022).

[3] The Global Reporting Initiative (GRI) Standards help organizations to be more transparent on how their actions affect sustainable development. The Standards cover relevant themes across the economic, environmental and social dimensions.

Table 4 Firms in INPS dataset and default rate by year

Year	Number of firms	Default rate (per cent)
2017	204,589	3.07
2018	206,852	2.88
2019	208,137	2.66
2020	209,258	2.07
2021	201,425	1.69
2022	197,979	1.84
2023	227,572	2.04

Note For each year *t* under analysis, INPS data refer to year *t*-2

The INPS dataset distribution of defaulted companies over time mirrors the one shown in Table 1, since the majority of ICAS companies have at least one statement of social security contributions (Table 4).

For the reasons explained in Sect. 3.1, we exclude the period 2020–2021 from our analysis.[4] We begin our exploratory analysis with a visual inspection, plotting each social variable's default rate by decile (or value, depending on the type of the variable).

In the case of micro firms, when examining the *hire rate*, *employees' turnover rate*, *layoff rate* and *fixed-term contract rate*, we observe a flat pattern for the lower deciles (Fig. 1).[5] Except for this evidence, the social indicators generally correlate monotonously with the ICAS default rate. There is also a clear association between *average wage* and default, with lower default rates associated with higher wages (compared to the industry). In contrast, *employees' age entropy* and *female employment rate* (compared to the industry) do not show a clear relationship with default.

The patterns for small firms are similar to those for micro firms (Fig. 2). However, for small firms, there are spikes in default rates in the first deciles of *fixed-term contract rate, hire rate, employees' turnover rate.*

The plots for medium- and large-sized companies exhibit broadly U-shaped relationships for *fixed-term contract rate, hire rate,* and *employees' turnover rate* (Fig. 3). The spikes observed in Fig. 2 are even more evident in this case. The non-monotonic effects are present in the first deciles, where the underlying variables are equal to zero. Therefore, these effects could be captured by introducing binary variables.

To rank the social indicators, we estimate univariate logistic regressions where default is the dependent variable; then, we compute the AUROC for each variable

[4] The resulting dataset is then subjected to the pre-processing procedure, as follows: exclusion of firms with missing data (< 1 per cent); handling of borderline cases (e.g., division by zero); winsorisation of continuous variables at the 95th percentile.

[5] The flat trends result from zero-valued variables for many firms. For instance, *layoff rate* is zero for over 80% of firms.

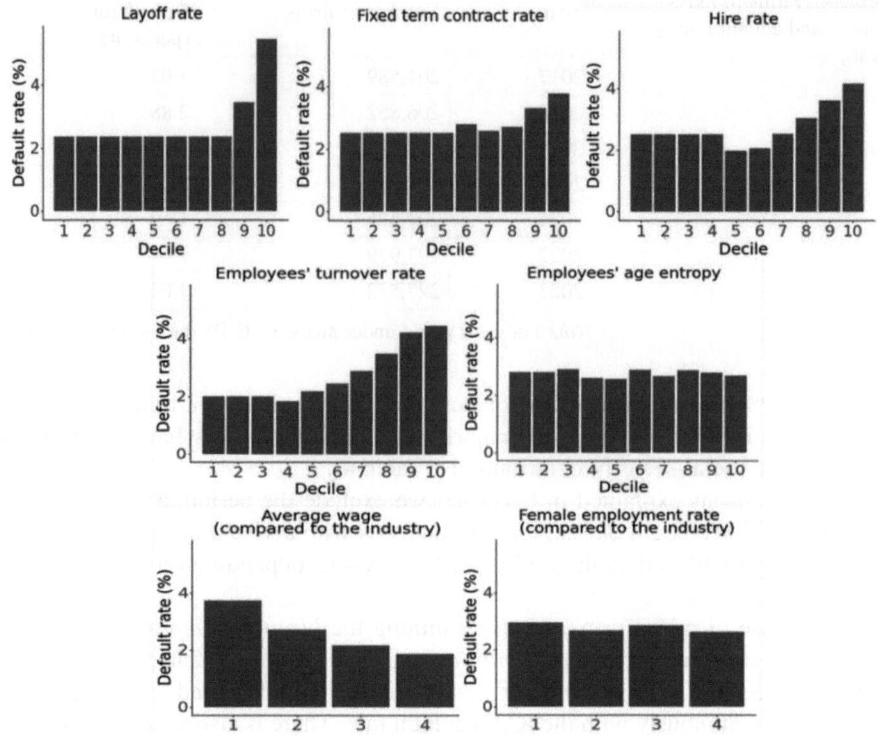

Fig. 1 Micro firms' default rate by social indicator (*Source* Own calculations on INPS and ICAS data). *Average wage (compared to industry)* and *female employment rate* plots have only four bars since these variables are categorical and take four different values (from 1 to 4); see Appendix A

based on regression outcomes. The evidence is similar across the three groups of firms: *layoff rate*, *hire rate*, *employees' turnover rate*, and *average wage* exhibit good discriminatory power (with average AUROC greater than 55%), while the remaining variables show worse performance.[6]

Since the standard logistic regression assumes a linear relationship between the predictors and the log-odds of the outcome, which implies a monotonic effect of each predictor on the probability of the default, we investigate the strength of possible non-linear relationships by running random forest models using all the seven indicators as independent variables (Figs. 4, 5, and 6).[7] At this step, assuming a multivariate (nonparametric) approach with the random forest is useful

[6] Detailed tables for the univariate AUROC values of each social indicator are available upon request.

[7] Nonmonotonic or highly non-linear effects require variable transformations within the logistic framework. To estimate the random forest models, a hyperparameter search has been conducted (see Appendix B).

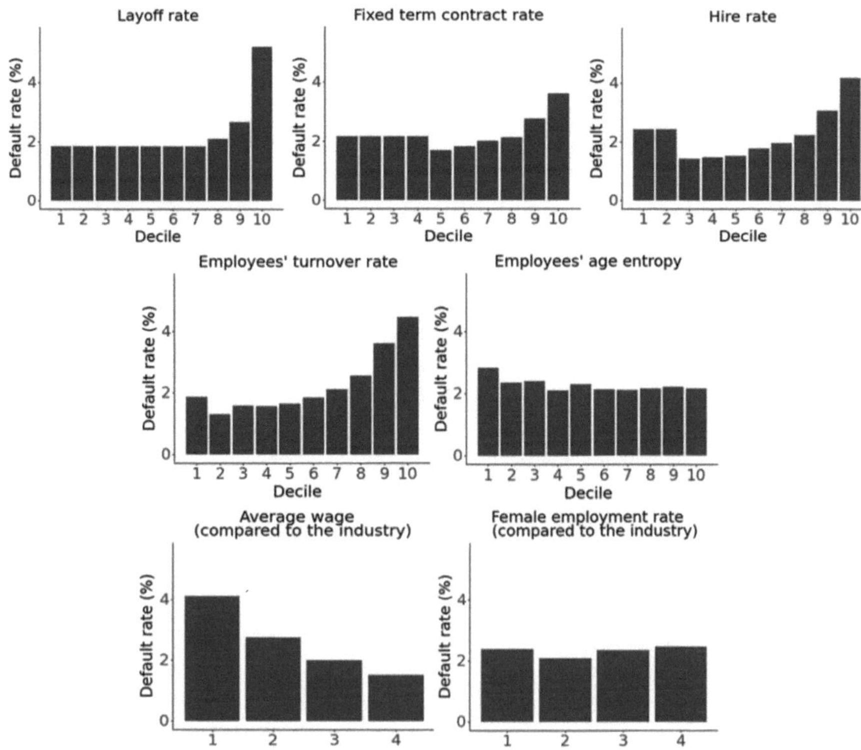

Fig. 2 Small firms' default rate by social indicator (*Source* Own calculations on INPS and ICAS data). *Female employment rate* and *average wage (compared to industry)* plots have only four bars since these variables are categorical and take four different values (from 1 to 4); see Appendix A

not only for inspecting complex interactions, but also for identifying potential overlaps or redundancies among the indicators before the new risk dimension is tested for the inclusion into the baseline S-ICAS.

Random forest feature rankings mostly confirm the visual inspection and the univariate logistic regression outcomes. The variables *layoff rate*, *hire rate*, *employees' turnover rate*, and *average wage* are in the highest positions of the rankings, while *female employment rate* stands at the lowest position. Based on this evidence, the graphical inspection, and the regression outcome, we exclude *female employment rate* from further analyses. Besides, the variable *fixed-term contract rate* is deemed less important than *employees' age entropy*. It could depend on the presence of weak non-linear effects or interactions for *employees' age entropy*, not captured by univariate logistic regressions, and the loss of significance of *fixed-term contract rate* due to the presence of the other variables. Since: i) we are interested in estimating a logistic regression model in line with the structure of S-ICAS; ii) there are no strong indications of non-linear effects that could hinder the estimation phase; iii) from visual inspection a clearer relation between default

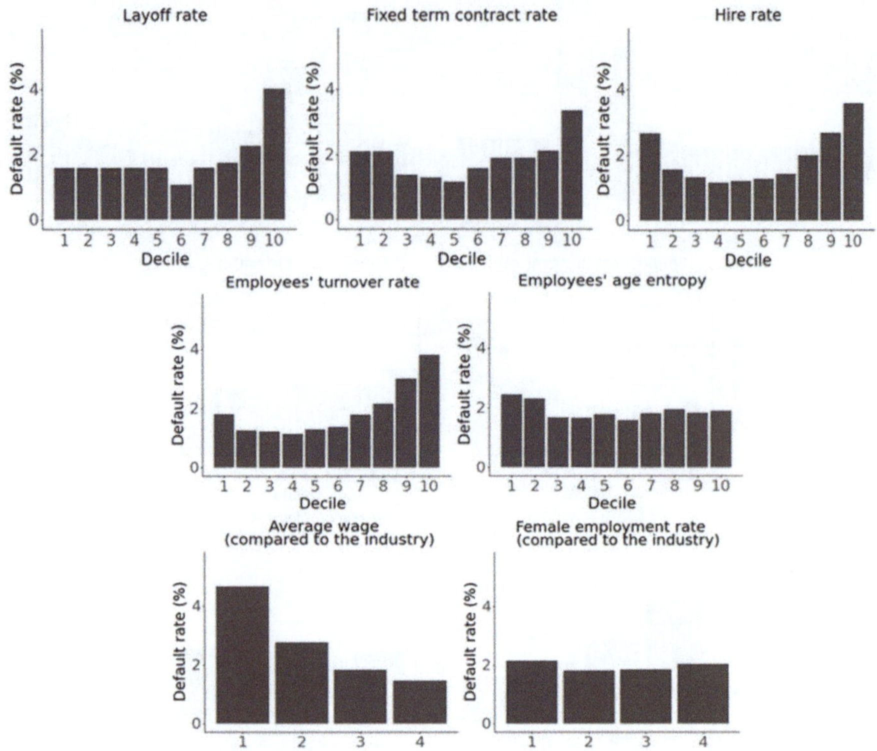

Fig. 3 Medium and large firms' default rate by social indicator (*Source* Own calculations on INPS and ICAS data). *Female employment rate* and *average wage (compared to industry)* plots have only four bars since these variables are categorical and take four different values (from 1 to 4); see Appendix A

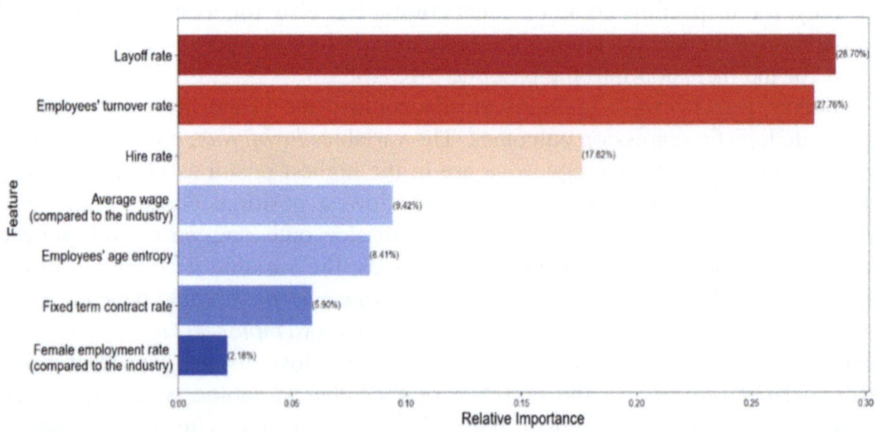

Fig. 4 Random forest feature importance for social indicators—Micro firms (*Source* Own calculations on INPS and ICAS data)

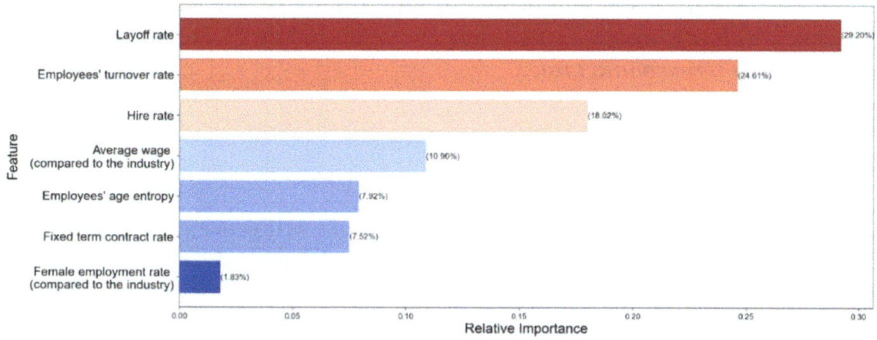

Fig. 5 Random forest feature importance for social indicators—Small firms (*Source* Own calculations on INPS and ICAS data)

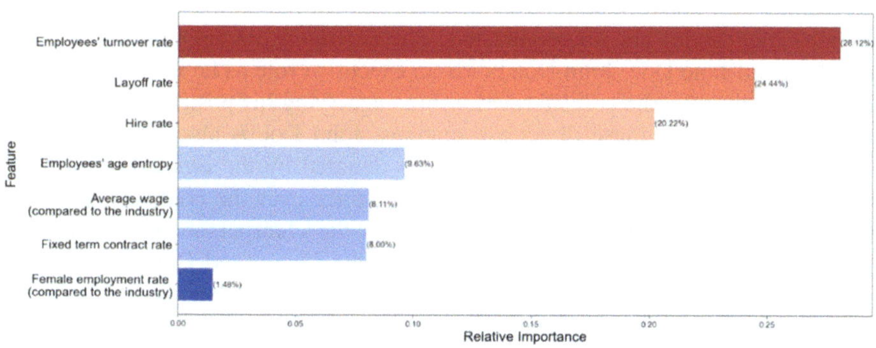

Fig. 6 Random forest feature importance for social indicators—Medium and large firms (*Source* Own calculations on INPS and ICAS data)

rate and *fixed-term contract rate* appears, we exclude *employees' age entropy* from further investigations.

Finally, we perform an empirical correlation analysis for each size class based on the Spearman rank correlation coefficient among the remaining five indicators.[8] The two variables that show a higher correlation are *hire rate* and *employees' turnover rate*. Since the correlation between these variables is approximately 0.9 and the latter shows a better association with the default rate (Figs. 1, 2, and 3), we exclude *hire rate* from the social watchlist.[9]

[8] Spearman's rank correlation is a nonparametric measure of the strength and direction of association between two ranked variables. Unlike Pearson's correlation, which assumes linearity, Spearman's method ranks the data and measures monotonic relationships, making it robust to outliers and non-linear associations.

[9] Detailed data on the correlation analysis are available upon request.

We thus identify a single watchlist of four key social variables for all groups of firms: *layoff rate*, *average wage* (relative to the industry), *employees' turnover rate*, and *fixed-term contract rate*.

3.3 Governance Indicators

Knowledge graphs (KGs) are key tools of artificial intelligence (AI), especially in the deductive AI field. Unlike inductive AI, which primarily relies on machine learning and statistical models to uncover patterns in large datasets, deductive AI uses logical reasoning over structured data to generate new knowledge. A knowledge graph consists of entities representing core elements—individuals, organisations, or abstract concepts—and relationships that capture the inner connections. Figure 7 illustrates an example of knowledge graph where the relationships between John Doe, Jane Doe, and several corporations are reported. It is represented as a network structure where entities (firm—orange nodes—and individuals—blue node) are interconnected. The *is_sibling_of* relationship connects John Doe and Jane Doe. John Doe holds an executive role as he is linked to Alpha Corporation through the *ceo_of* relationship, signifying his position as chief executive officer. Beyond these direct associations, John Doe is also identified as the ultimate controller of Alpha Corporation, as denoted by the *ultimate_controller_of* relationship, indicating his overarching influence over the company. Jane Doe is also involved in corporate structures. She is the chairperson of Gamma Corporation. Moreover, she holds shares in both Beta Group and Delta Corporation. Finally, Jane Doe is a board member of Delta Corporation, as shown by the *board_member_of* relationship. By encoding temporal and hierarchical attributes, the graph facilitates advanced queries and analyses, offering a dynamic view of cross-linking governance features and how ownership concentration and role dispersion impact governance trends and corporate stability.

KG19, developed by the Bank of Italy (Bellomarini et al., 2019), represents an enterprise implementation of knowledge graph. KG19 extracts detailed information from the Italian Business Register and enables us to identify 47 quantitative governance indicators for each firm from 2012 to 2022 (Table 5).[10]

Henceforth, we examine the relationship between each indicator and corporate default. As discussed in Sect. 3.1, data from 2020 to 2021 have been removed from the analysis.[11] Given the large set of governance indicators, only graphs related to the indicators showing the clearest association with the default rate are reported.

Micro- and small-sized companies show similar patterns (inverse relation) for *internal–external ratio* and *shareholders with at least 5% ownership* (Figs. 8 and 9). In the case of micro firms, the same picture seems valid for *board size* and *board age diversity*—an index of diversity in the age distribution of board members.

[10] The Cypher query language within KG19 enhances its analytical capabilities.

[11] The resulting dataset was subjected to the pre-processing schema described in note 4, Sect. 3.2.

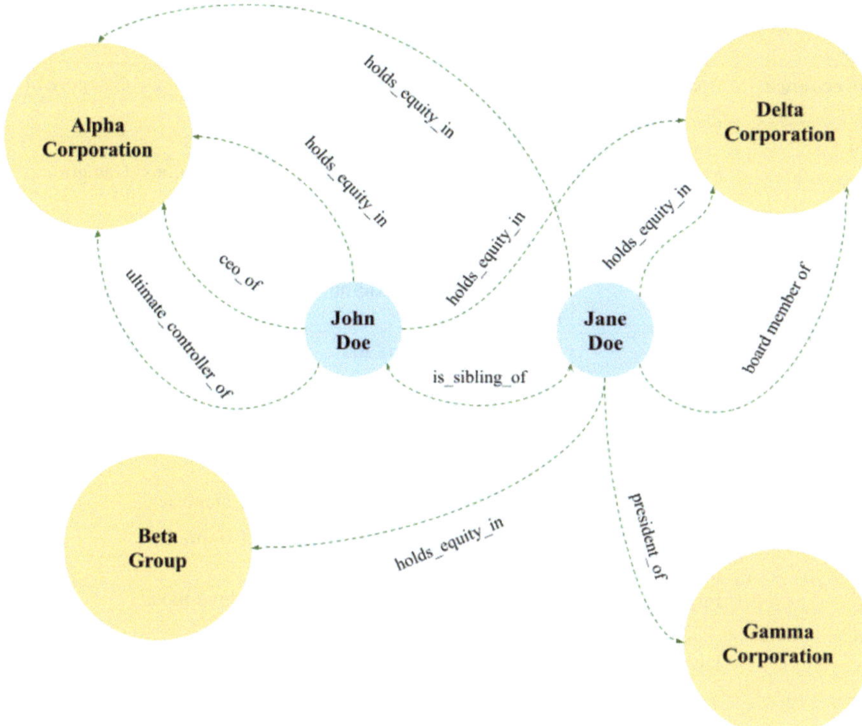

Fig. 7 Example of a knowledge graph

Herfindahl–Hirschman index and *board ownership concentration* show a U-shaped pattern for both groups of firms.

For medium- and large-sized companies, we observe an increase in default rate in the highest deciles of *average board age* (Fig. 10). The *board size* and *board age diversity* patterns illustrate an inverse relationship with default rate, like what has been detected for micro firms. Finally, *board stability* exhibits a distinct pattern where firms with less stable boards (lower deciles) show significantly higher default rates than those with more stable governance structures.

To rank the indicators, we first estimate univariate logistic regressions and compute the AUROC for each variable, as in Sect. 3.2.[12] Then, to account for the possible non-linear and non-monotonic relationships, we replicate the random forest feature importance selection analysis.

Board size and *board age diversity* are confirmed at the top two places in the list of the three best predictors for all groups of firms. *Internal–external ratio* shows a high discriminatory ability for micro and small firms, reaching an average

[12] Detailed figures for the univariate AUROC values of each governance variable are available upon request.

Table 5 Governance Key Issue Hierarchy

Pillar	Key Issues	Groups of indicators	Type
Governance	Board	Size, age, stability, instability, gender, location, ownership, diversity	Continuous/ Categorical
	Management	Size, age, stability, instability, gender, location, experience, family relations	Continuous/ Categorical
	Ownership	Concentration, major owner, diversity, change, external influence, depth	Continuous/ Categorical
	Gender	Gender ratio (board and management)	Continuous
	Audit	Audit size, percentage, firm presence, stability, concentration	Continuous/ Categorical
	Turnover	CEO turnover	Categorical
	Stability	Stability of board, management, audit	Continuous
	Instability	Instability of board, management, audit	Continuous
	Diversity	Age, gender, location (board and management)	Categorical

Note Appendix A provides a description of each indicator

AUROC equal to 55. For medium and large firms, *audit size* provides valuable insights (average AUROC equal to 60).

The results of the random forest feature importance selection are presented in Figs. 11, 12, and 13 for micro, small, and medium and large enterprises, respectively.

Since we handle a large set of indicators, we filter the watchlists initially obtained from univariate logistic regressions with the random forest features ranking. To do so, we apply a cumulative variable importance threshold of 90%: only the most influential variables that reach a relative importance of at least 90% of the total are retained for further analysis.[13] Since the governance score will be obtained through a logistic regression, to handle the variables with the most

[13] The existing literature supports the rationale behind choosing a 90 per cent threshold. For example, Guyon and Elisseeff (2003) argue that feature selection methods should balance the trade-off between model complexity and performance by focusing on the most informative variables, often captured within the top 80 per cent-90 per cent of cumulative importance in ensemble methods like random forests. Similarly, in their review of feature selection techniques, Bolón-Canedo et al. (2015) show that selecting variables based on cumulative feature importance can improve the model's interpretability without sacrificing predictive accuracy.

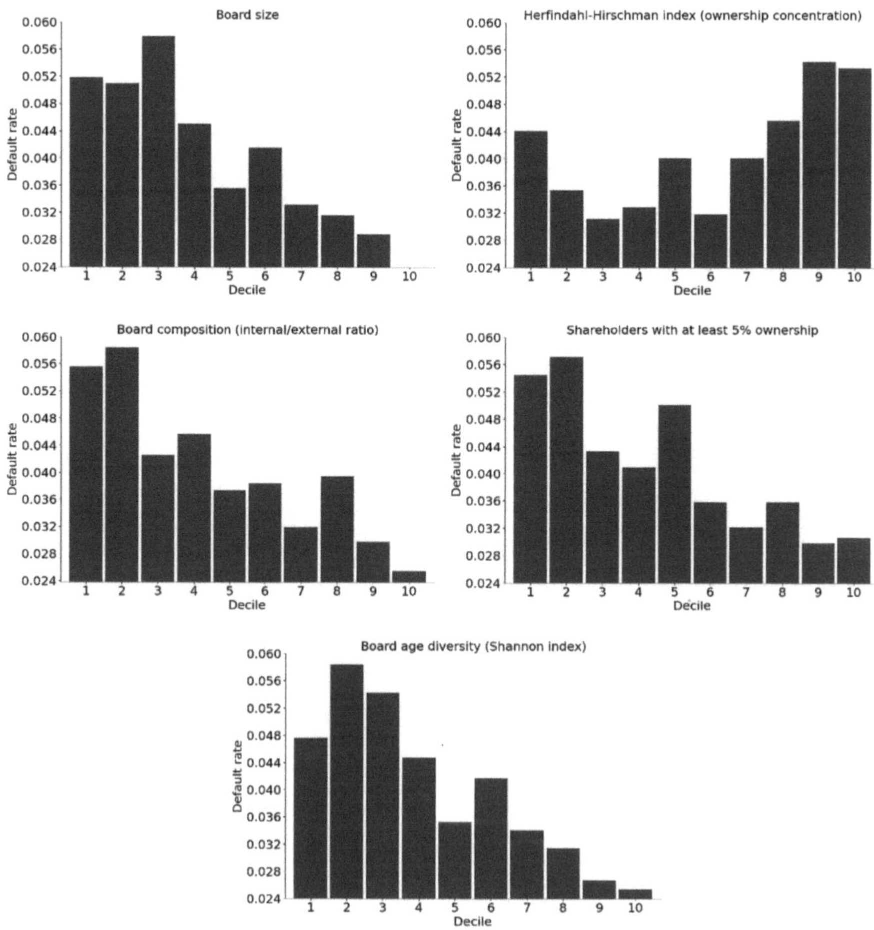

Fig. 8 Micro firms' default rate and governance indicators (*Source* Own calculations on KG19 and ICAS data)

prominent non-monotonic relation with the default rate,[14] we apply a discretisation process using decision trees.[15] This method transforms each non-monotonic variable into a new monotonic variable by assigning a rank based on the predicted default probabilities derived from a decision tree.[16]

[14] As emerged from visual inspection.

[15] Due to the limited number of nonmonotonic relations detected with the social indicators, we restrict the use of the discretisation process to the governance indicators.

[16] Specifically, a decision tree classifier is trained using the training dataset for each variable, where the default status serves as target variable. The tree's predicted PDs are then used to rank the data, ensuring a monotonic relationship with the default rate.

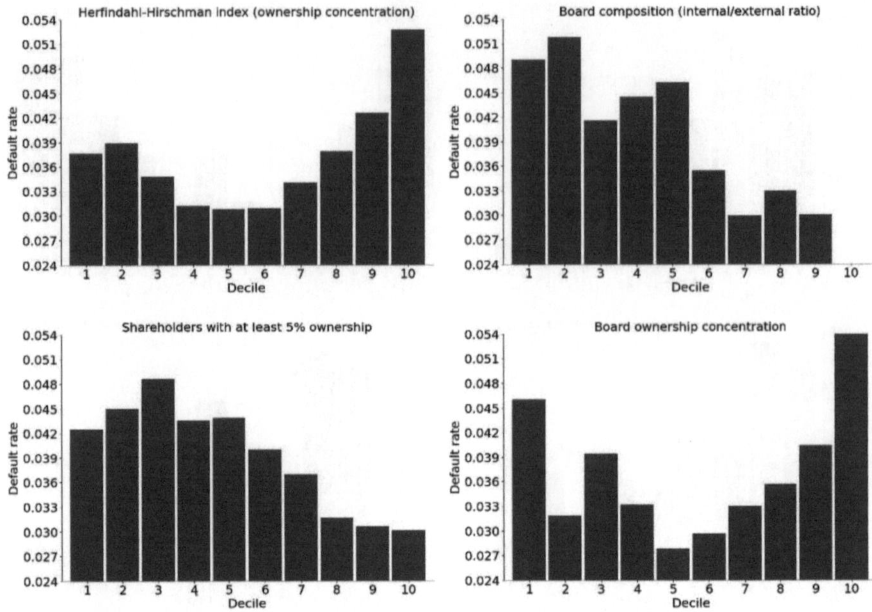

Fig. 9 Small firms' default rate and governance indicators (*Source* Own calculations on KG19 and ICAS data)

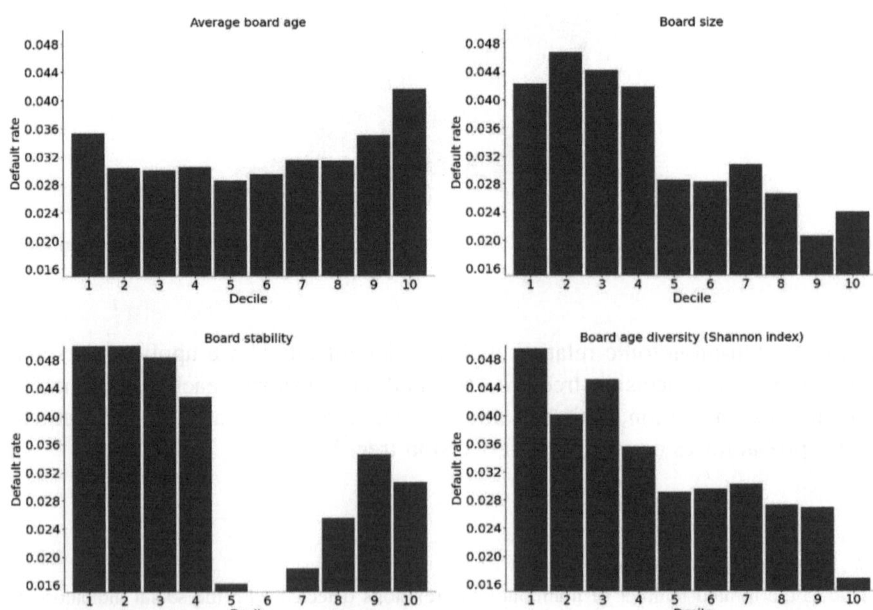

Fig. 10 Medium and large firms' default rate and governance indicators (*Source* Own calculations on KG19 and ICAS data)

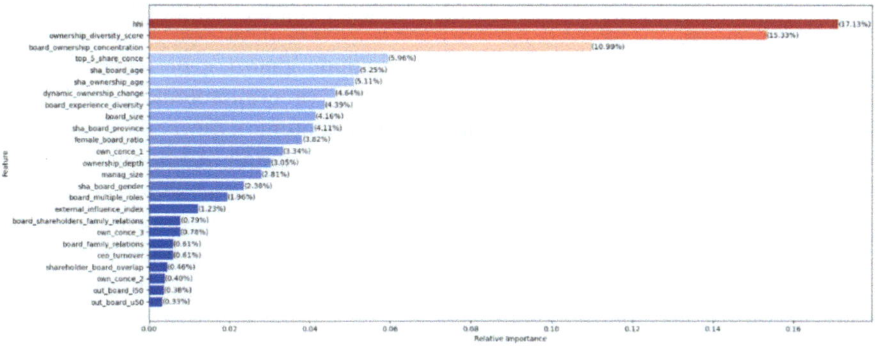

Fig. 11 Random forest feature importance for governance indicators—Micro firms (*Source* Own calculations on KG19 data)

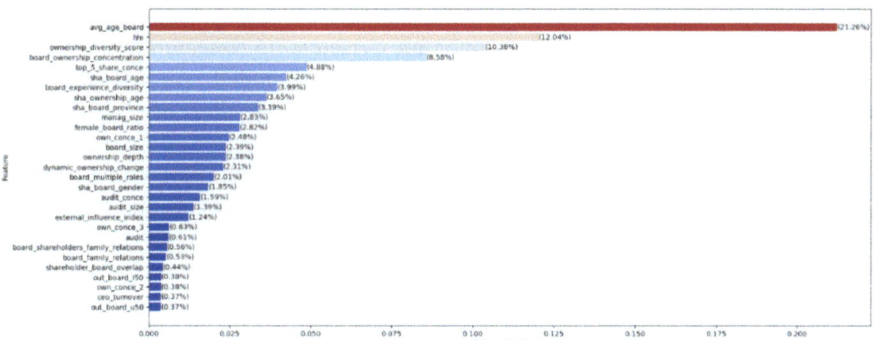

Fig. 12 Random forest feature importance for governance indicators—Small firms (*Source* Own calculations on KG19 data)

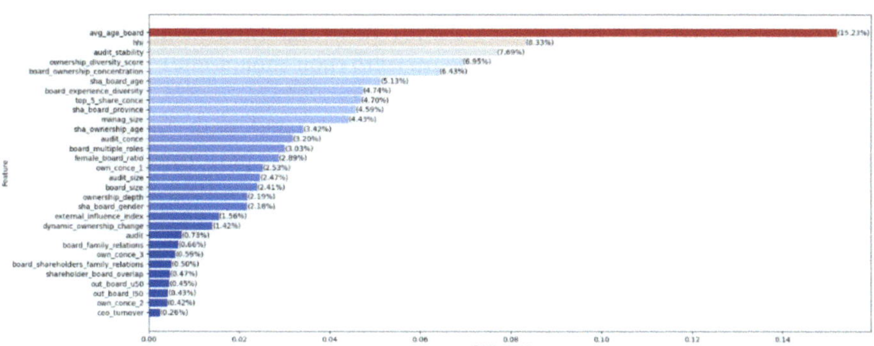

Fig. 13 Random forest feature importance for governance indicators—Medium and large firms (*Source* Own calculations on KG19 and ICAS data)

We finally provide distinct watchlists for micro, small, and medium and large firms.

The key variables for the micro firms include *board experience diversity* (non-monotonic) *board ownership concentration* (non-monotonic), *board size* (monotonic), *Herfindahl–Hirschman index* (non-monotonic), *ownership concentration 1* (non-monotonic), and *board age diversity* (monotonic). Additionally, factors such as, *Shannon board province* (non-monotonic), and *ownership age diversity* (non-monotonic) have been included. Other variables such as *ownership diversity score* (non-monotonic), *shareholders with at least 5% ownership* (non-monotonic), *dynamic ownership change* (non-monotonic), *female board ratio* (non-monotonic), and *ownership depth* (non-monotonic) are also part of the selected features for this firm size category. We thus exclude *internal–external ratio* from the final list due to the poor performance in the multivariate setting.

In the case of small firms, the watchlist includes variables such as *average age board* (non-monotonic), *board experience diversity* (monotonic), *board multiple roles* (non-monotonic), and *board size* (monotonic). Governance aspects such as *Herfindahl–Hirschman index* (non-monotonic), *ownership concentration 1* (monotonic), and *ownership depth* (monotonic) are also included. Additional factors are *ownership diversity score* (non-monotonic), *board age diversity* (monotonic), *Shannon board province* (monotonic), *ownership age diversity* (monotonic), *top 5 share concentration* (non-monotonic), *management size* (non-monotonic), *female board ratio* (non-monotonic), and *dynamic ownership change* (non-monotonic). As before, we exclude *internal–external ratio* from the final list.

For medium- and large-sized firms, the watchlist includes *average age board* (non-monotonic), *board experience diversity* (monotonic), *board multiple roles* (non-monotonic), *board ownership concentration* (non-monotonic), and *board size* (monotonic). *Herfindahl–Hirschman index* (non-monotonic), *board age diversity* (monotonic), and *Shannon board province* (monotonic) are also considered. Audit stability, audit concentration, and audit size are included too (all non-monotonic cases). Furthermore, *ownership diversity score* (non-monotonic), *top 5 share concentration* (non-monotonic), *management size* (non-monotonic), *ownership age diversity* (monotonic), *female board ratio* (non-monotonic), and *ownership concentration 1* (monotonic) are added to the list.

Since governance indicators are typically associated with financial performance outcomes, a multicollinearity analysis is finally performed between the watchlists and indicators from the financial statements involved in the baseline S-ICAS. We use Spearman's rank correlation and the Maximal Information Coefficient (MIC).[17] However, correlation analysis does not suggest the presence of multicollinearity and, consequently, any exclusion.

[17] The Maximal Information Coefficient (MIC), part of the Maximal Information-based Nonparametric Exploration (MINE) family of statistics, identifies complex relationships between variables. MIC is particularly effective in detecting linear and non-linear associations, providing a measure of association that remains high across a range of functional relationships.

4 The Inclusion of S and G in S-ICAS

Based on the previous section's exploratory analysis, we provide separate PD estimates that capture social and governance factors. Second, we map the governance and social PDs into scores (via the logit function) and merge them with the integration module of S-ICAS, resulting in an augmented statistical model with a broader set of risk dimensions. In the augmented version, the S-ICAS PD results from the combination of four components: the financial statement score, the credit behaviour score, the social score, and the governance score. In the final step, we perform a comparative analysis of the performance of the augmented PDs and baseline PDs based on the AUROC and binomial tests.

To properly handle the separate estimation of the governance and social PDs, we employ a stepwise backward regression approach to estimate logistic regression models for each firm size class with the smallest set of indicators. Stepwise backward regression starts with the watchlists outlined in Sects. 3.2 and 3.3.[18] This approach allows for the identification of the most important variables, while reducing overfitting.

4.1 The Social PD

For small firms, we observe a monotonic relationship between default rate and both *employees' turnover rate* and *fixed-term contract rate*, except in the first deciles, where these variables are equal to zero (Fig. 2). To adequately capture these features, we introduce dummy variables for both predictors, with values set to one where the corresponding indicator is zero. However, since the correlation between *fixed-term contract rate* and its dummy is below −0.7 and the spike in the first deciles is not too high, we exclude it from model estimation. Similarly, for medium and large firms, we consider dummy variables for *employees' turnover rate*, *fixed-term contract rate*, and *layoff rate*. However, we exclude the dummies related to *fixed-term contract rate* and *layoff rate* from the estimation due to the very high correlation with their corresponding indicators.

For robustness, we employ an expanding window approach. Starting from 2017 and extending to 2022,[19] the logistic regression is iteratively trained using data from 2017 up to year t and subsequently tested on data from year $t + 1$. For

[18] Although stepwise backward regression can technically be applied to all variables, in the present Chapter it is restricted to those showing a more promising (and possibly monotonic) relationship with the default rate, as discussed in the exploratory analysis.

[19] As mentioned in Sect. 3.1, we exclude data for 2020 and 2021. The sample evidence starts in 2017 (Table 14.4).

Table 6 Regression results by firm size—Social

a) Micro firms			
	coef	***std err***	***P*** > |z|
Const	−3.50	0.03	0.00
layoff rate	2.04	0.07	0.00
employees' turnover rate	0.13	0.01	0.00
average wage (compared to industry)	−0.13	0.01	0.00
b) Small firms			
	coef	***std err***	***P*** > |z|
const	−3.44	0.04	0.00
layoff rate	3.09	0.12	0.00
employees' turnover rate	0.14	0.01	0.00
average wage (compared to industry)	−0.19	0.01	0.00
dummy employees' turnover rate	0.12	0.04	0.00
c) Medium and Large firms			
	coef	***std err***	***P*** > |z|
const	−3.38	0.10	0.00
layoff rate	3.51	0.28	0.00
fixed term contract rate	1.09	0.24	0.00
average wage (compared to the industry)	−0.23	0.03	0.00
dummy employees' turnover rate	0.43	0.10	0.00

the sake of simplicity, regression results are reported for the largest window only (Table 6).[20]

Across all firm size categories, a higher *layoff rate* is significantly associated with an increase of the PD. The interpretation deserves some caution. Rather than implying a causal relationship between layoffs and financial distress, the evidence may suggest that firms experiencing difficulties tend to reduce their workforce. A similar rationale applies to *average wage*. Firms that offer wages below the industry benchmark exhibit a higher likelihood of default. This evidence may reflect weaker underlying financial health rather than a direct causal effect of wage policy on creditworthiness.[21] The *employees' turnover rate* may also reflect some organisational instability associated with financial distress. Collectively, these variables may act as early warning indicators of deteriorating conditions. Overall, we also note that the estimated coefficients for key variables like *layoff rate, employees'*

[20] For clarity, estimated coefficients, standard errors, and p-values in tables with values reported as 0.00 do not indicate zero values. Instead, they represent values less than the assumed reporting threshold of 0.01.

[21] Further investigation employing methods such as difference-in-differences or lagged variable models would allow a test of reverse causality in these relationships.

Table 7 Social PD—Out-of-sample AUROC (percentage values)

Out-of-sample year	Micro	Small	Medium-Large
2022	62	65	63
2023	63	65	63

turnover rate, and *average wage* (*compared to the industry*) tend to increase in magnitude as firm size increases.

Finally, the social PD's out-of-sample performance in AUROC is moderate, with AUROC values ranging from 62 to 65%, suggesting better performance in the case of small firms (Table 7).

4.2 The Governance PD

We replicate the expanding window strategy for model testing described in Sect. 4.1. Starting in 2012 and progressing through 2022, the logistic regression is successively trained on data from 2012 to year t and evaluated on data from year $t + 1$. As in Sect. 4.1, regression results are reported for the largest window for the sake of simplicity (Table 8).[22]

Despite differences across firm sizes, some patterns stand out. Firstly, *board size* shows a negative coefficient across micro and small firms, indicating that larger boards are generally associated with reduced default risk. Secondly, *board age diversity* exhibits a negative coefficient for all size classes. In contrast, *average age board* does not confirm its predictive role as suggested by the exploratory analysis.

The governance PD's out-of-sample performance in terms of AUROC is relatively modest, with AUROC values between 58 and 65% (Table 9). These results indicate a level of discriminatory power in line with or slightly smaller than the 'S' outcome. Compared with the 'S', we observe better results for medium and large companies in 2023.

4.3 The Augmented S-ICAS PD

Sections 4.1 and 4.2 introduce the estimated governance and social PDs separately. Each of the two PDs provides some discriminatory power. To disentangle the contribution of the two new dimensions, we introduce the social and governance scores—obtained via the logit function—into the baseline S-ICAS. Specifically, we perform logistic regressions using financial, credit behaviour, social, and

[22] In Sect. 3.1, we exclude data related to 2020 and 2021.

Table 8 Regression results by firm size—Governance.

a) Micro firms			
	coef	*std err*	*P* > |z|
const	−2.88	0.01	0.00
dynamic_ownership_change	0.25	0.03	0.00
hhi	0.13	0.01	0.00
board_size	−0.21	0.01	0.00
sha_board_age	−0.23	0.02	0.00
b) Small firms			
	coef	*std err*	*P* > |z|
const	−3.02	0.04	0.00
board_size	−0.15	0.01	0.00
sha_ownership_age	−0.12	0.01	0.00
board_experience_diversity	−0.15	0.02	0.00
sha_board_age	−0.26	0.02	0.00
Hhi	0.07	0.02	0.00
avg_age_board	2.96E-03	6.07E-04	0.00
c) Medium and Large firms			
	coef	*std err*	*P* > |z|
const	−2.81	0.10	0.00
ownership_diversity_score	0.03	0.03	0.01
sha_board_age	−0.30	0.02	0.00
Hhi	1.44E-03	3.70E-04	0.00
avg_age_board	2.63E-03	7.94E-04	0.00

Table 9 Governance PD—Out-of-sample AUROC (percentage values)

Out-of-sample year	Micro	Small	Medium-Large
2022	61	64	58
2023	61	65	65

governance scores as predictors of default by firm size.[23] Each regression is estimated using a backward elimination procedure. We employ the expanding window approach already adopted in Sects. 4.1 and 4.2, except for large firms for which we adopt a single window.[24] Due to the limited evidence affecting the social indicators, 2017 is the first year in the estimation process. Unlike regressions estimated

[23] We normalise the four scores to compare regression coefficients and assess the strength of each score in determining the final PD.

[24] The dataset's total number of large companies' defaults is extremely low (below 150), which prevents the adoption of the expanding window approach.

Table 10 Logistic regression results for Micro firms—integration module

	coef	*std err*	*P* > |z|
const	−4.56	0.02	0.00
financial score	0.62	0.01	0.00
credit score	1.09	0.01	0.00
social score	0.20	0.01	0.00
governance score	0.23	0.01	0.00

Table 11 Comparison of the integrated PD AUROC—Micro firms (percentage values)

Out-of-sample year	Model with Governance and Social scores	Model without Governance and Social scores
2022	84.3	83.6
2023	84.9	84.1

in Sects. 4.1 and 4.2, where medium and large firms were grouped, large firms are separately processed in the integration step, as in S-ICAS.[25]

Micro Firms

For micro firms, both the social and governance scores are significant in each estimation window (Table 10 reports the largest window-based results).

The credit behaviour score has the highest coefficient, reflecting the critical role of creditworthiness for these firms, for which access to financing is often limited, and default risk is tightly linked to external credit relationships. The financial score is also important. Although the social and governance scores play a secondary role, our results support the notion that poor governance practices and weak social performance are correlated with credit risk.

Next, we compare the AUROC of the augmented S-ICAS with the baseline model obtained by integrating only the financial and credit behaviour scores (Table 11).[26]

The model with the social and governance score has a larger AUROC. The increments in AUROC are statistically significant[27] and range between 0.7 and 0.8 percentage points.

[25] The integration module of the standard S-ICAS has a separate model for medium and large firms, respectively.

[26] We estimate the baseline model on the same dataset as the one employed to estimate the governance and social scores.

[27] The bootstrap confidence intervals of the AUROC increments are available upon request.

Table 12 Logistic regression results for Small firms—integration module

	coef	*std err*	*P* > |z|
Const	−4.92	0.02	0.00
financial score	0.73	0.02	0.00
credit score	1.07	0.01	0.00
social score	0.21	0.01	0.00
governance score	0.23	0.02	0.00

Table 13 Comparison of the integrated PD AUROC—Small firms (percentage values)

Out-of-sample year	Model with Governance and Social scores	Model without Governance and Social scores
2022	86.9	86.4
2023	87.4	86.5

Small Firms

Our results are similar to those for micro firms. The social and governance scores are significant in each estimation window (Table 12 reports the results for the largest window).

The larger coefficient for the financial score indicates that financial health becomes more important as firms grow. As with micro firms, the credit score remains critical, though it is slightly less important, possibly reflecting improved access to credit for small firms. The social and governance scores maintain their limited but significant effect.

Next, we compare the out-of-sample AUROC of the augmented S-ICAS with the baseline model (Table 13).

The model estimated with the social and governance score has a larger AUROC. The increments are all statistically significant and range between 0.5 and 0.9 percentage points.

Medium Firms

The social score is statistically significant for medium-sized firms in all estimation windows. Instead, the governance score is significant only in the last two windows. For this reason, we exclude the governance score from the augmented S-ICAS (Table 14 reports the results for the largest window).

Table 14 Logistic regression results for Medium firms—integration module

	Coef	*std err*	*P* > |z|
const	−4.95	0.06	0.00
financial score	0.90	0.06	0.00
credit score	0.87	0.03	0.00
social score	0.18	0.03	0.00

Table 15 Comparison of the integrated PD AUROC—Medium firms (percentage values)

Out-of-sample year	Model with Social score	Model without Social score
2022	85.2	84.6
2023	88.3	87.5

Table 16 Logistic regression results for Large firms—integration module

	coef	***std err***	***P > |z|***
const	−5.25	0.16	0.00
financial score	1.09	0.14	0.00
credit score	0.90	0.08	0.00
social score	0.18	0.07	0.01

The financial score has the highest influence among the three scores, reflecting medium-sized firms' growing operational complexity and reliance on sound financial management to preserve financial stability. The credit behaviour score is still significant, though slightly less influential than the financial score. The effect of social factors further diminishes in medium-sized firms, suggesting that such firms can offset deficiencies in social issues with stronger financial and operational capabilities.

Next, we compare the out-of-sample AUROC of the augmented S-ICAS with the baseline model (Table 15).

The model that includes the social score has a larger AUROC. The increments are statistically significant and range between 0.6 and 0.8 percentage points.

Large Firms

Owing to the few occurrences of default for large firms, we estimate the model only once using the largest available window, from 2017 to 2022.

The financial score bears the largest contribution to default risk assessment, reflecting the critical importance of financial stability and operational performance in large organisations (Table 16). While still significant, the impact of the credit behaviour score is lower than that of the financial score, as already observed for medium firms. The social score has a limited impact on default risk, possibly due to the ability of large firms to mitigate social inefficiencies through their financial structure. Finally, governance does not significantly influence default risk, likely due to the maturity and robustness of governance systems in large organisations.

The model estimated using the social score has a larger AUROC than the baseline model, with an increment of 0.4 percentage points (Table 17).

Predictive Power

The augmented S-ICAS exhibits greater discriminatory power than the baseline model. Discriminatory power refers to a model's ability to rank firms from the riskiest to the safest. Predictive capacity (or calibration) measures the ability to assign the correct PD to a group of homogeneous borrowers.

Table 17 Comparison of the integrated PD AUROC—Large firms (percentage values)

Out-of-sample year	Model with Social score	Model without Social score
2023	90.8	90.4

Table 18 Comparison of predictive power (percentage values)

Rating class	2022		2023	
	Baseline model	**Augmented model**	**Baseline model**	**Augmented model**
CQS 1&2	0.04	0.04	0.10	0.07
CQS 3	0.17(*)	0.19	0.22	0.23
CQS 4	0.82(**)	0.74	0.76(**)	0.69
CQS 5	1.38	1.21	1.48(**)	1.36
CQS 6	2.20	2.31	2.46(**)	2.42(**)
CQS 7	4.50(**)	4.28(**)	5.25(**)	4.98(**)

To evaluate the predictive power of the augmented S-ICAS, we employ a procedure commonly used in the Eurosystem (see Chap. 3).[28] From best to worst, we categorise companies into rating classes identified by their CQS. Next, we conduct a two-tailed binomial test within each rating class to establish whether the observed default rate aligns with the out-of-sample insolvency probability. The null hypothesis is that the number of defaults within each rating class is in line with the expected one, given by the number of companies in the rating class multiplied by the average PD.[29] The results are reported (Table 18). Each cell shows the observed default rate for the corresponding rating class. Asterisks highlight anomalies: a single asterisk indicates that the model is overly conservative (overestimating risk), while two asterisks signal insufficient caution (underestimating risk). Cells without asterisks represent successful tests. Overall, the augmented S-ICAS model delivers higher precision than the baseline, improving predictive performance, particularly in the lowest risk classes, where firms exhibit minimal credit risk.

[28] The binomial test used by the Eurosystem to evaluate ICASes' predictive power is slightly different from the one adopted in this work. It is a one-tailed binomial test in which the null hypothesis is that the number of actual defaults within each rating class is smaller than the number of expected defaults. In this work, we test a stronger hypothesis using a two-tailed binomial test: the actual defaults within each rating class are consistent with the expected number. According to the Eurosystem monitoring framework, the analysis is carried out on firms irrespective of their size.

[29] The test is passed if the p-value is greater than 0.05.

5 Conclusions

This Chapter contributes to the empirical literature on credit risk assessment by estimating the effect of social and governance factors on the probability of default within the framework of S-ICAS in use at the Bank of Italy. We adopt its existing structure as a benchmark to evaluate whether the integration of social and governance indicators can improve performance. This approach allows us to pin down the marginal contribution of these additional dimensions. We employ random forest feature importance ranking to assess the significance of the variables across firm size, providing a hierarchy of S and G factors correlated with default. In addition, decision tree discretisation for non-monotonic variables enables us to capture complex relationships that may not fit the standard logistic model.

Our goal is not to establish causal relationships between social and governance indicators and corporate default. In line with the ICAS objectives, we assess the incremental contribution of these variables to the model's performance. Our results show that the augmented model improves the discriminatory power over the baseline statistical model. Besides, the augmented S-ICAS shows better predictive power than the baseline model, especially in the initial risk classes, populated by low credit risk companies.

The overall contribution of the S and G variables seems moderate. For medium and large firms, the governance variables do not provide a significant improvement, and the social indicators offer marginal gains.

G indicators for large firms will continue to be considered in the second building block of ICAS, namely the expert assessment performed by credit analysts. This involves the analysis of qualitative information on the transparency of governing bodies, the reputational standing of top managers, and the existence of legal disputes; these elements, obtained from various sources, are difficult to embed in the statistical model.

The integration of the S and G indicators into the statistical framework is a subject for further investigation. This will involve a careful estimation and validation of the added value of these indicators, with a possible distinction according to the firms' business sector.

Appendix A

Feature Description

We briefly describe each social variable in Table 3 (Sect. 3.2):

- *Average wage (compared to the industry)*: defined as the position of the yearly average wage of the firm in the corresponding sectoral distribution (NACE 2 digits) of the same year. It is equal to 1 if the average wage is less than the first quartile of the distribution; it is equal to 2 if the average wage is between the first and the second quartile; it is equal to three if the average wage is between the second and the third quartile; it is equal to four in the remaining case;

- *Female employment rate (compared to the industry)*: defined as the position of a firm's yearly female employment rate in the same year's corresponding sectoral distribution (NACE 2 digits). The indicator is equal to 1 if the female employee's rate is less than the first quartile of the distribution; it is equal to 2 if the female employees' rate is between the first and the second quartile; it is equal to three if the female employees' rate is between the second and the third quartile; it is equal to four in the remaining case;
- *Fixed-term contract rate*: defined as the number of employees with a fixed-term contract in a certain year divided by the mean number of employees in the same year;
- *Employees' age entropy*: INPS data contain, for each firm and year under analysis, the information on the number of employees in three different age groups: between 15 and 34 years old, between 35 and 54 years old, and older than 55 years old. This indicator is simply the entropy of the distribution of the number of employees in these three age groups;
- *Employees' turnover rate*: defined as the sum of the number of hires and terminations in a certain year, divided by the average number of employees in the same year;
- *Hire rate*: defined as the number of hires in a certain year divided by the mean number of employees in the same year;
- *Layoff rate*: defined as the number of dismissals in a certain year divided by the number of employees with a permanent contract in the same year.

We briefly describe each governance variable in Table 5 (Sect. 3.3).

- *Audit* (stored variable name: 'audit'): percentage of audits in the company;
- *Audit concentration* (stored variable name: 'audit_conce'): ratio of the number of audit members to the number of board members;
- *Audit firm* (stored variable name: 'audit_firm'): the presence of an audit firm in the company;
- *Audit instability* (stored variable name: 'audit_instability'): index of audit instability calculated annually for each company. Formula: c = (number of entries+number of exits) / audit members. Annual formula: inst_year_k = sum from 0 to k of (c_k) / k;
- *Audit size* (stored variable name: 'audit_size'): number of audit members in the company;
- *Audit stability* (stored variable name: 'audit_stability'): audit stability (analogous to board_stability);
- *Average age delta* (stored variable name: 'avg_age_delta'): average age difference between the board and the management;
- *Average age management* (stored variable name: 'avg_age_manag'): average management age;

- *Average board age* (stored variable name: 'avg_age_board'): average age of the board;
- *Board age diversity* (stored variable name: 'sha_board_age'): Shannon index for age on the board;
- *Board diversity* (stored variable name: 'board_diversity'): measures the diversity of the board in terms of its members;
- *Board experience diversity* (stored variable name: 'board_experience_diversity'): measures the diversity of the board in terms of past experience;
- *Board family relations* (stored variable name: 'board_family_relations'): family relationships within the board;
- *Board instability* (stored variable name: 'board_instability'): index of board instability calculated annually for each company. Formula: c = (number of entries+number of exits) / board members. Annual formula: inst_year_k = sum from 0 to k of (c_k) / k;
- *Board management family relations* (stored variable name: 'board_manag_family_relations'): family relationships between the board and management;
- *Board multiple roles* (stored variable name: 'board_multiple_roles'): proportion of board members with multiple roles;
- *Board ownership concentration* (stored variable name: 'board_ownership_concentration'): ownership concentration among board members. Measured as the sum of ownership shares held by board members divided by the number of board members holding shares;
- *Board size* (stored variable name: 'board_size'): size of the company's board;
- *Board stability* (stored variable name: 'board_stability'): board stability (consecutive years of an unchanged board). If there is a change, the indicator is reset to zero. It is not collinear with the analogous instability monitoring;
- *Ceo turnover* (stored variable name: 'ceo_turnover'): 1 if there has been a change in CEO in the last two years;
- *Dynamic ownership change* (stored variable name: 'dynamic_ownership_change'): ownership change based on the annual variation of shares;
- *External Influence Index* (stored variable name: 'external_influence_index'): ratio of board members without shareholding to those with shareholding. Measures ownership influence on company management;
- *Female board ratio* (stored variable name: 'female_board_ratio'): percentage of women on the board;
- *Female management ratio* (stored variable name: 'female_manag_ratio'): percentage of women in management;
- *Herfindahl–Hirschman index* (stored variable name: 'hhi'): a low value indicates concentration among few entities;
- *Internal–external ratio* (stored variable name: 'internal_external_ratio'): the ratio between board and ownership. The ratio of internal board members (those who hold shares) to external board members (those who do not hold shares);
- *Management board experience ratio* (stored variable name: 'management_board_experience_ratio'): ratio of management members with board experience;

- *Management instability* (stored variable name: 'management_instability'): index of management instability calculated annually for each company. Formula: c = (number of entries+number of exits) / management members. Annual formula: inst_year_k = sum from 0 to k of (c_k) / k;
- *Management size* (stored variable name: 'manag_size'): size of the company's management;
- *Management stability* (stored variable name: 'management_stability'): management stability (analogous to board_stability);
- *Out board lower 50%* (stored variable name: 'out_board_l50'): 1 if the sum of shares of board members is between 0 and 50% (exclusive), 0 otherwise;
- *Out board upper 50%* (stored variable name: 'out_board_u50'): 1 if the sum of shares of board members is between 50% and 100%, 0 otherwise;
- *Ownership age diversity* (stored variable name: 'sha_ownership_age'): Shannon index for age of the owners;
- *Ownership concentration 1* (stored variable name: 'own_conce_1'): number of owners with at least 5% of shares;
- *Ownership concentration 2* (stored variable name: 'own_conce_2'): 1 if at least one owner holds more than 20% of shares;
- *Ownership concentration 3* (stored variable name: 'own_conce_3'): 1 if at least one owner holds more than 50% of shares;
- *Ownership depth* (stored variable name: 'ownership_depth'): measures the depth of company ownership quantified by the number of distinct levels of shareholder percentages. Higher values indicate greater diversification;
- *Ownership diversity score* (stored variable name: 'ownership_diversity_score'): ownership diversity score. Combines the number of unique shareholders with the distribution of their shares;
- *Shannon board gender* (stored variable name: 'sha_board_gender'): Shannon index for gender on the board;
- *Shannon board province* (stored variable name: 'sha_board_province'): Shannon index for geographic location on the board;
- *Shannon management age* (stored variable name: 'sha_management_age'): Shannon index for age in management;
- *Shannon management gender* (stored variable name: 'sha_management_gender'): Shannon index for gender in management;
- *Shannon management province* (stored variable name: 'sha_management_province'): Shannon index for geographic location in management;
- *Shareholder board overlap* (stored variable name: 'shareholder_board_overlap'): overlap between shareholders and board members, indicating 1 if at least one board member is also a shareholder;
- *Shareholders with at least 5% ownership* (stored variable name: 'top_5_share_conce'): ownership concentration among the top 5 shareholders.

Appendix B

Random Forest and Hyperparameter Optimisation

Random forests are an ensemble learning method widely used in classification tasks due to their robustness and ability to handle large datasets with complex interactions. By aggregating multiple decision trees, each trained on a different subset of the data, random forests reduce overfitting and improve predictive accuracy. Each tree in the forest is trained independently, and the final output is determined through a majority voting system, making the model less sensitive to noise and individual tree errors. The model's performance, however, relies on carefully tuned hyperparameters, which control issues such as the structure of each tree, the depth of exploration, and the breadth of features under consideration.

Hyperparameter optimisation is important in random forests to achieve optimal performance, as it directly influences the model's classification ability. This process involves systematically searching the hyperparameter space to find combinations that effectively maximise the model's ability to differentiate between classes. Through techniques like grid search and random search, hyperparameters can be fine-tuned to yield an optimal configuration for the classification task.

The hyperparameters have been tuned to optimise model performance based on their impact on the overall classification task (Table 19). Specifically, the *n_estimators* represents the forest's number of trees, with values between 100 and 500. The *min_samples_leaf* parameter controls the minimum number of samples required at a leaf node, ranging from 1 to 1000. *Max_features* stands for the number of features to consider when looking for the best split, where we have tested options like 'sqrt', 'log2', and 'None' (considering all features). *Bootstrap* represents the categorical parameter that controls whether bootstrap samples are used when building trees, evaluated as both True (enabling) and False (disabling). *Criterion* refers to the function used to measure the quality of a split, with both the Gini impurity and entropy explored. The *n_iter* refers to the number of iterations performed during the random search process, set at 50 iterations. *CV* is the number of cross-validation folds (set at 5) to evaluate the model's performance. Lastly, *scoring* indicates the evaluation metric used—in this case, the AUROC—which measures the classifier's ability to distinguish between classes.

Table 19 Random Forest sub-models hyperparameters search space

Parameter	Type	Range
n_estimators	Integer	100 ÷ 500
min_samples_leaf	Integer	1 ÷ 1000
max_features	Categorical	[sqrt, log2, None]
bootstrap	Categorical	[True, False]
criterion	Categorical	[gini, entropy]
n_iter	Integer	50
cv	Integer	5
scoring	Categorical	AUROC

References

Altman, E. I. (1968). Financial ratios, discriminant analysis and the prediction of corporate bankruptcy. *The Journal of Finance, 23*(4), 589–609.

Altman, E. I., Haldeman, R. G., & Narayanan, P. (1977). ZETA^{TM} analysis A new model to identify bankruptcy risk of corporations. *J Bank Financ, 1*(1), 29–54.

Altman, E. I., Balzano, M., Giannozzi, A., & Srhoj, S. (2023). Revisiting SME default predictors: The omega score. *Journal of Small Business Management, 61*(6), 2383–2417.

Aulia, A. S., & Wijaya, C. (2020). The effect of corporate governance quality on default risk of companies listed in Indonesia stock exchange (IDX) period 2013–2017. *Am Int J Bus Manage, 3*(5), 36–44.

Ballacci, F., Baltrunaite, A., Ciavarella, A., Cucinotta, F., Benedetto, M. D., Stefano, G. D., Fabrizio, R., Sgroi, A., Signoretti, R., & Torchella, V. (2021). La partecipazione femminile negli organi di amministrazione e controllo delle società italiane. Rapporto dell'osservatorio inter istituzionale sulla partecipazione femminile negli organi di amministrazione e controllo delle società italiane, Banca d'Italia, Dipartimento delle Pari Opportunità, Consob

Baltrunaite, A., Brodi, E., & Mocetti, S. (2019). *Assetti proprietari e di governance delle imprese italiane: nuove evidenze e effetti sulla performance delle imprese* (Bank of Italy, Occas Pap 514.

Baltrunaite, A., Formai, S., Linarello, A., & Mocetti, S. (2024). Ownership, governance, management and firm performance: Evidence from Italian firms. *Ital Econ J, 10*(3), 993–1027.

Barboza, F., Kimura, H., & Altman, E. (2017). Machine learning models and bankruptcy prediction. *Expert Systems with Applications, 83*, 405–417.

Belás, J., Smrcka, L., Gavurova, B., & Dvorsky, J. (2018). The impact of social and economic factors in the credit risk management of SME. *Technol Econ Dev Eco, 24*(3), 1215–1230.

Bellomarini, L., Fakhoury, D., Gottlob, G., & Sallinger, E. (2019). Knowledge graphs and enterprise AI: The promise of an enabling technology. In 2019 IEEE 35th International Conference on Data Engineering (ICDE).

Bolón-Canedo, V., Sánchez-Maroño, N., & Alonso-Betanzos, A. (2015). Recent advances and emerging challenges of feature selection in the context of big data. *Knowledge-Based Systems, 86*, 33–45.

Ciampi, F., & Gordini, N. (2013). Small enterprise default prediction modeling through artificial neural networks: An empirical analysis of Italian small enterprises. *Journal of Small Business Management, 51*(1), 23–45.

Ciampi, F. (2015). Corporate governance characteristics and default prediction modeling for small enterprises. An empirical analysis of Italian firms. *Journal of Business Research, 68*(5), 1012–1025.

Cultrera, L. (2020). Evaluation of bankruptcy prevention tools: Evidences from COSME programme. *Economic Bulletin, 40*(2), 978–988.

Flabbi, L., Macis, M., Moro, A., & Schivardi, F. (2019). Do female executives make a difference? The impact of female leadership on gender gaps and firm performance. *The Economic Journal, 129*(622), 2390–2423.

García, C. J., & Herrero, B. (2021). Female directors, capital structure, and financial distress. *Journal of Business Research, 136*, 592–601.

Guyon, I., & Elisseeff, A. (2003). An introduction to variable and feature selection. *Journal of Machine Learning Research, 3*(Mar), 1157–1182.

Houston, L., Shah, D., & Wang, X. (2024). Social risks and opportunities for corporates: Long-Term performance in global equity markets. *MSCI Research.* https://www.msci.com/www/blog-posts/social-risks-and-opportunities/04829288964?utm_source=pardot&utm_medium=email&utm_campaign=2024_MSCI+Weekly_08-08

James, G., Witten, D., Hastie, T., Tibshirani, R., & Taylor, J. (2023). *An introduction to statistical learning: With applications in Python.* Springer Nature.

Mawdsley, J. K., & Somaya, D. (2016). Employee mobility and organizational outcomes: An integrative conceptual framework and research agenda. *J Manage, 42*(1), 85–113.

Moody's Ratings. (2025). General principles for assessing environmental, social and governance risks. *Cross-Sector Rating Methodology.*

Norden, L., & Weber, M. (2010). Credit line usage, checking account activity, and default risk of bank borrowers. *The Review of Financial Studies, 23*(10), 3665–3699.

Paraschiv, F., Schmid, M., & Wahlstrøm, R. R. (2024). Bankruptcy prediction of privately held SMEs using feature selection methods. https://doi.org/10.2139/ssrn.3911490

Siegerink, V., Shinwell, M., & Žarnic, Ž. (2022). *Measuring the non-financial performance of firms through the lens of the OECD well-being framework: A common measurement framework for "Scope 1" Social performance* (OECD Papers on Well-being and Inequalities, No. 3, OECD Publishing, Paris). https://doi.org/10.1787/28850c7f-en

S&P Global. (2021). The evolution of ESG factors in credit risk assessment: Corporate governance. https://www.spglobal.com/market-intelligence/en/news-insights/research/the-evolution-of-esg-factors-in-credit-risk-assessment-corporate-governance

Tian, S., Yu, Y., & Guo, H. (2015). Variable selection and corporate bankruptcy forecasts. *J Bank Financ, 52*, 89–100.

Tufford, H., Wang, X., & Shah, D. (2024). Corporate governance: Market matters. *MSCI Research.* https://www.msci.com/www/blog-posts/corporate-governance-market/04784692180?utm_source=pardot&utm_medium=email&utm_campaign=2024_MSCI+Weekly_07-18

Sentiment Analysis with AI

Manuel Cugliari and Giulio Gariano

1 Introduction

As discussed in the previous Chapters, ICAS consists of two components: a statistical rating model and an expert judgment process carried out by financial analysts. The expert judgment on each firm involves several data types, including qualitative information that is available online, such as press news, interviews, reviews, and corporate websites. However, a structured analysis of qualitative information is currently not available.

Natural language processing (NLP) techniques have greatly expanded the possibilities for integrating unstructured textual data into a quantitative framework. For instance, Lu et al. (2016) show that sentiment scores derived from financial news significantly enhance the predictive accuracy of CDS spreads, showing the value of qualitative data in complementing traditional financial indicators. More recently, large language models (LLMs) have emerged as powerful tools, offering unprecedented capabilities in processing and interpreting complex linguistic data. These tools are useful to discern nuanced sentiment within financial narratives (Zhang & Zhao, 2024).

We leverage state-of-the-art LLMs, including Bidirectional Encoder Representations from Transformers (BERT), Large Language Model Meta AI 3 (LLaMA 3), Microsoft's Phi 3 and Google's Gemma 2 to extract sentiment indicators

M. Cugliari · G. Gariano (✉)
Bank of Italy, Financial Risk Management Directorate, Rome, Italy
e-mail: giulio.gariano@bancaditalia.it

M. Cugliari
e-mail: manuel.cugliari@bancaditalia.it

A. Scalia (ed.), *Corporate Credit Analysis and AI*, Finance for Professionals,
https://doi.org/10.1007/978-3-032-13422-6_15

from a dataset of company-related news sourced from the Dow Jones Factiva database. These models bridge the gap between qualitative and quantitative analyses, enabling a comprehensive evaluation of corporate creditworthiness.

While advanced predictive models based on large language models (LLMs) offer great potential, one concern is the risk of manipulation if the qualitative data sources they rely on become widely known. In theory, this could lead to attempts to distort the information environment to influence the model's outputs. However, in the specific context of our study, this risk is minimal. This is due to the nature of the data sources, the statistical aggregation method we use, the capabilities of the NLP models involved, and the institutional framework of the rating system.[1]

By applying compression techniques that reduce the computational load of these models, while preserving their performance to a considerable extent, this study achieves a balance between analytical precision and computational efficiency, while also ensuring compliance with the Bank of Italy's operational and confidentiality standards. Our findings reveal that sentiment indicators derived from LLMs enhance the discriminatory power of ICAS and establish a robust framework for incorporating unstructured data into predictive models.

The remainder of this Chapter is organized as follows: Sect. 2 reviews the relevant literature, tracing the evolution of textual analysis in credit risk assessment. Sections 3 through 5 describe the data, the LLMs and the methodology. Section 6 presents the results. Section 7 concludes with insights into the implications of our findings and suggestions for future research.

2 Literature Review

Traditional credit risk models are based on quantitative indicators derived from company balance sheets and market data (Altman, 1983). These indicators can be easily included in multivariate regressions or, more recently, in machine learning models (Altman et al., 2017; Ciampi & Gordini, 2013). In contrast, a wide range of qualitative information contained in notes and comments on company financial statements, in company press releases and in news articles is not exploited by the above models.

Recent literature shows that the use of textual information can increase the accuracy of credit risk models. Lu et al. (2016) construct a sentiment score based on quarterly reports of US companies with quoted CDS as well as related press

[1] Several factors help reduce this risk in our case. First, the news sources used are reputable national outlets with strong editorial and fact-checking standards. Second, sentiment analysis is based on a large and time-distributed set of articles, which helps dilute the impact of any outliers. Third, modern NLP models can detect and downweight texts that are potentially biased or of low quality. Moreover, the ICAS ratings produced by the Bank of Italy are not publicly available, which limits the incentive for targeted manipulation. Finally, in the context of Italian SMEs, economic motivations for such manipulation are weak, due to the low share of listed companies and the importance of direct, long-term business relationships.

reports and show that this score improves the forecast of CDS spreads. Similarly, Cathcart et al. (2020) show that a news sentiment score obtained via the Thomson Reuters News Analytics service is a significant variable in forecasting sovereign CDS spreads.

The use of alternative textual bases such as social networks and search engines is the object of a rich literature. González-Fernández and González-Velasco (2020) use the Google Trends service to build a sentiment index for bank credit risk, in alternative to classic CDS-based indices. Lau et al. (2018) extract an 'emotion indicator' from Twitter messages that can complement the usual financial indicators to forecast company ratings. Bozzon et al. (2020) extract information from the Facebook pages of Dutch SMEs to build indicators that complement financial data in a credit risk model.

Gariano and Viggiano (2022) show that credit sentiment indicators derived from press news and tweets using a dictionary approach improve the discriminating power of the ICAS model.

The incorporation of financial news as a source of unstructured data has been shown to enhance the performance of credit risk models. Tran-The (2020) shows that incorporating news sentiment into predictive models significantly improves the ability to forecast credit downgrades, achieving significant gains along several accuracy metrics. Similarly, Lei et al. (2024) propose a framework combining linguistic features from financial news with quantitative indicators, which outperforms traditional models in predicting credit risk. These findings show the growing importance of textual data, particularly press news, in complementing conventional financial indicators.

In parallel, the application of NLP techniques has emerged as a pivotal advancement in harnessing unstructured textual data for credit risk assessment. Lis et al. (2023) employ NLP-based clustering methods to validate credit risk models, demonstrating their efficacy in uncovering latent patterns and addressing structural inconsistencies. These techniques have proven to be more effective than traditional approaches, especially in processing large-scale textual datasets. Dolphin et al. (2024) further show the potential of augmented NLP methods in extracting structured insights from financial news, offering innovative ways to build sentiment indicators that enrich the analytical framework of credit risk models.

More recently, LLMs have shown a better performance than classical NLP techniques in analysing textual data for credit risk applications. Sanz-Guerrero and Arroyo (2024) employ BERT to extract sentiment indicators from loan descriptions on peer-to-peer lending platforms, demonstrating superior predictive power compared to traditional NLP models. Mo et al. (2024) fine-tune the Gemma 2-7B model for analysing financial headlines, achieving significant improvements in accuracy over existing NLP-based classifiers. These advancements underline the ability of LLMs to capture complex linguistic nuances, providing deeper insights into financial narratives and enhancing the predictive capabilities of credit risk models.

Table 1 Companies dataset (2016–2020)

Number of companies	6,006
Number of companies defaulting at least once in sample	500
Number of records	351,755
Number of records of defaulting companies	5,490

3 Data

We employ three data sources: ICAS, InfoCamere, and Factiva. ICAS provides credit risk quantitative indicators and default information on a monthly basis for a sample of Italian companies. InfoCamere offers detailed company registry information. Factiva supplies news, articles and data from journalistic sources, news agencies and business publications on a daily basis.

To enable a comparison with previous work (Gariano & Viggiano, 2022), the analysis spans the same five-year period, from January 2016 to December 2020.

3.1 ICAS

The sample companies are those that receive a comprehensive ICAS rating in the survey period: about 6,000 companies, of which 500 became insolvent, according to the ICAS definition, at least once in the sample period (Table 1).[2] The one-year average default rate in the sample is around 1.6 percent (roughly 100 companies defaulting each year).

Taking into account the monthly frequency of ICAS data (each company is considered for the 60 months in the sample period[3]), the number of records is above 350,000.

The dataset includes, for each company and reference date: (i) the S-ICAS score and (ii) the default 'flag' of the company. The former is a monotone function of the probability of default, while the latter is a binary variable indicating whether the company defaults within the subsequent 12 months (1 for default, 0 otherwise).

The dataset predominantly features medium and large companies, which represent 80 percent of the sample. About 75 percent of these firms are located in Northern Italy, in line with the geographic concentration of economic activity within the region (Table 2).

[2] Unlike bankruptcy, insolvency is a reversible event.

[3] Some company are considered for less than 60 months, for example if they were rated only after January 2016 or if they defaulted before December 2020.

Table 2 Company distribution by size and geographical area (percentage values)

	North-West	North-East	Centre	South	Total
Micro	3	2	1	1	7
Small	6	4	2	1	13
Medium	19	16	7	5	48
Large	13	11	5	3	32
Total	41	34	15	10	

Table 3 Managers dataset

Number of managers	66,415
Minimum number of managers by company	1
Maximum number of managers by company	62
Average number of managers by company	11

3.2 InfoCamere

Infocamere offers detailed company registry information, including the list of managers of the companies in our sample. The names of the managers are important since some of them might be involved in legal proceedings cited in news articles. As shown in Gariano and Viggiano (2022), news articles on legal proceedings are among the most relevant news for credit analysis.

On average, approximately 11 managers by company are identified in the sample period, for a total of approximately 66,000 managers (Table 3).

3.3 Factiva

The Factiva database contains approximately 800,000 press articles per year, obtained from over 60 news sources. This dataset is extracted from the Dow Jones Factiva service, applying a preliminary filter to include only articles related to economics and finance, thereby making its size manageable for our purposes (for a similar approach, see Aprigliano et al., 2021).

Each article provides access to the title, summary, main text, date, and source, along with some metadata designed to facilitate analysis, including a list of companies mentioned in the article.

To ensure that the analysis considers only relevant articles, some exclusions are applied, such as: (i) articles containing an extensive number of numerical values, and (ii) articles referencing a large number of companies. Such filters are implemented to exclude generic articles, such as those summarizing daily stock market closures, which are frequent in the database but not informative for the purposes of this Chapter.

Table 4 Factiva dataset

Year	Number of articles	Number of articles on sample companies	Number of company-date pairs
2016	590,117	23,134	3,587
2017	612,303	31,011	4,777
2018	659,798	43,981	5,994
2019	1,138,076	56,796	6,510
2020	1,255,528	56,513	5,961
Total	4,255,822	211,435	26,829

Following this initial screening, all articles mentioning one of the companies in our sample are identified. As in Gariano and Viggiano (2022), this identification relies on metadata analysis when available. Where metadata are not provided, a raw search of the company name or company managers within the text is conducted.

Table 4 provides a breakdown for each year of the total number of articles available, the number of articles mentioning at least one company in our dataset, and the number of distinct company-date pairs. While the total number of articles exceeds 4 million, only 211,435 of them (about 5 percent) explicitly mention at least one company from our sample. Since companies, when mentioned, typically appear in multiple articles within the same month—on average, eight articles per month—the number of distinct company-month pairs is even lower (26,829). This measure is particularly important, as the default flag is defined on a monthly basis, meaning that all articles referencing the same company within the same month must be aggregated. Overall, we find news for 2,772 companies, out of 6,006 companies in our dataset.

Before processing the articles from the Factiva database with LLM for inference, a comprehensive pre-processing pipeline is implemented to ensure data quality and consistency. Using the SpaCy[4] library, several steps are undertaken to clean and structure the text. Special characters, extraneous whitespace, and HTML tags are removed to eliminate noise that could affect model performance. URLs and embedded hyperlinks are stripped, while redundant or irrelevant metadata commonly found in Factiva articles, such as publication dates and author credits, are filtered out. Furthermore, text encoding inconsistencies are resolved to standardize the input format.

This preparation ensures that the text fed into the LLM is optimized for accurate sentiment analysis, to extract meaningful insights from company-related news.

[4] SpaCy is an advanced open-source library for NLP in Python, designed for efficient and scalable text processing. It provides a wide range of features, including tokenization, named entity recognition, part-of-speech tagging, dependency parsing, and text vectorization, making it a versatile tool for linguistic analysis and pre-processing tasks.

4 Large Language Models

LLMs are a cornerstone in the evolution of NLP and artificial intelligence. Their inception dates to the emergence of pre-trained transformer-based architectures,[5] most notably BERT, introduced by Devlin et al. in 2019. BERT pioneered the use of bidirectional context during training, marking a paradigm shift in text representation and understanding. Since then, the field has witnessed the rapid proliferation of more advanced and larger models, including LLaMA 3, Phi 3, and Gemma 2, each making advancements to the state of the art. These innovations testify the relentless drive towards models capable of capturing increasingly complex linguistic structures, enabling them to understand and generate text with human-like proficiency.

The transformative capabilities of LLMs lie in their ability to leverage vast training datasets. By ingesting trillions of tokens from diverse sources, they develop a sophisticated understanding of syntax, semantics, and pragmatics. This pre-training phase equips LLMs with the ability to generalize across domains, making them adaptable to a wide range of downstream tasks. One area where LLMs have demonstrated exceptional utility is sentiment analysis. Financial news, in particular, present a unique challenge due to the specialized language, the nuanced sentiment conveyed, and the significant implications for decision-making. LLMs not only extract sentiment with remarkable precision, but also integrate these insights into predictive models for credit risk assessment, enhancing the discriminatory power of traditional metrics (Chen et al., 2023; Zhang & Zhao, 2024).

Sentiment analysis in finance requires a granular approach. The language employed in financial news is replete with subtleties and implicit cues that traditional models often fail to capture. LLMs excel by leveraging their contextual awareness, trained on extensive *corpora* that include financial texts. This contextual depth allows them to discern the latent sentiment embedded in narratives.

The architecture of an LLM is governed by several settings that define its functionality and adaptability. Context length is a pivotal factor, determining the volume of preceding text the model can consider when generating responses. A longer context window enables the model to maintain coherence over extended narratives. This is particularly valuable in financial discourse where connections between events and implications often span multiple sentences or paragraphs. Tokenization is another foundational aspect, converting text into discrete units, or

---

[5] Transformer-based architectures are a class of neural networks introduced by Vaswani et al. (2017) that rely on self-attention mechanisms to process and generate sequences of data. They have become the foundation for modern natural language processing models due to their ability to capture contextual relationships between words in a sequence efficiently, regardless of distance, making them highly effective for tasks such as machine translation, text summarization, and sentiment analysis.

tokens,[6] that the model processes. This step ensures that the model can handle complex linguistic constructs while maintaining computational efficiency. Temperature, that controls the randomness of output generation, allows fine-tuning of the model responses. Adjusting the temperature can yield output that range from deterministic to creative, a flexibility that is especially useful in exploratory sentiment analysis.

LLMs are computationally demanding. Their inference requires substantial processing power, posing challenges for real-time applications or deployments in resource-constrained environments. The sheer number of parameters in these models, often running into billions, necessitates high memory bandwidth and parallel processing capabilities. A pragmatic solution to this requirement is quantization, a compression technique that maps high precision parameters to lower precision ones, reducing the computational load while preserving the model performance to a considerable extent. This Chapter employs quantization techniques to enable the deployment of advanced models like Gemma 2 and Phi 3 within operational constraints, achieving a balance between accuracy and efficiency. The evolution of LLMs is intrinsically tied to advancements in hardware and software. The advent of graphics processing units (GPUs)[7] and tensor processing units (TPUs)[8] has been instrumental in scaling these models, enabling training and inference at an unprecedented scale. Concurrently, software frameworks like PyTorch[9] and TensorFlow[10] have streamlined model development, fostering innovation and accessibility.

One notable challenge in deploying LLMs for non-English contexts lies in their training data composition. Most LLMs are predominantly trained on English-language *corpora*, leading to potential biases and limitations when applied to other languages. We address this gap by employing multilingual models which offer robust support for Italian language alongside other languages, ensuring relevance and accuracy in the analysis of Italian company-related news.

We leverage four state-of-the-art LLMs: BERT, LLaMA 3, Phi 3, and Gemma 2. These models are selected for their advanced capabilities, robust architecture, and proven performance in sentiment analysis. Their training on extensive and

[6] In NLP, a token is a discrete unit of text, such as a word, sub word, or character, that serves as the fundamental element for analysis and processing in language models. Tokenization is the process of splitting text into these units to enable computational manipulation and interpretation.

[7] Graphics Processing Units (GPUs) are specialized hardware initially designed for rendering graphics but now widely adopted in parallel computing tasks, including training and inference of deep learning models due to their ability to handle large-scale matrix operations efficiently.

[8] Tensor Processing Units (TPUs) are application-specific integrated circuits (ASICs) developed by Google, designed to accelerate machine learning workloads, particularly for tensor-based operations in neural networks, offering both efficiency and scalability for large models.

[9] PyTorch is an open-source machine learning framework developed by Facebook's AI Research lab. It provides flexibility for building and training deep learning models, offering dynamic computation graphs and strong support for research and production environments.

[10] TensorFlow is an open-source machine learning framework developed by Google Brain. It is widely used for developing, training, and deploying machine learning models, offering tools for scalable computation on a range of platforms from mobile devices to high-performance clusters.

diverse datasets ensures adaptability to the intricacies of financial language, while their tuning for the Italian context addresses the linguistic challenges inherent in this domain. By combining these models, this Chapter harnesses their collective strengths.

To ensure data confidentiality and compliance with the Bank of Italy's operational standards, all computations involving the LLMs are conducted locally. This approach mitigates the risk of sensitive information being transmitted to external servers, thereby complying with stringent data protection protocols. Inference for the LLMs is conducted with LM Studio[11] 0.3.5, a robust platform for deploying LLMs in localized environments. The inference process complies with OpenAI standards,[12] ensuring consistency and precision in the model's output.

The computational experiments involving all LLMs employed in this Chapter are conducted on an NVIDIA® GeForce RTX™ 4080,[13] a high-performance graphics processing unit (GPU) with advanced computational capabilities.

The following sub-sections provide essential information on the four LLMs used in the Chapter.

4.1 BERT

BERT is a major milestone in the development of natural language processing and large language models. Introduced by Devlin et al. in 2019 as part of Google's research efforts, BERT changed the way text is represented by applying a bidirectional training method, which allows the model to learn context from both earlier and later words in a sentence. This advancement overcomes the limits of traditional unidirectional models and enables a better understanding of linguistic structure, idioms, and contextual meaning.

The main idea behind BERT is based on its two training tasks: masked language modelling (MLM) and next sentence prediction (NSP). In MLM, some words in a sentence are masked, and the model learns to predict them from surrounding

[11] LM Studio is an open-source platform designed for deploying and interacting with localized LLMs. It provides a user-friendly interface and robust backend capabilities for running models on constrained hardware, supporting advanced configurations such as quantization and parameter optimization. LM Studio facilitates efficient inference while maintaining data privacy by ensuring all computations occur locally, eliminating the need for cloud-based processing.

[12] OpenAI standards refer to a set of best practices and protocols for implementing LLMs, ensuring consistency, reliability, and reproducibility in their output. These standards encompass guidelines for model configuration, including temperature settings, token limits, and inference batch sizes, enabling developers to achieve optimal performance tailored to specific tasks.

[13] The NVIDIA GeForce RTX 4080 is a high-performance GPU designed for demanding computational tasks, including machine learning and deep learning applications. Equipped with 16GB of GDDR6X memory and advanced tensor cores, it delivers exceptional performance in handling complex models and large datasets. The RTX 4080 supports efficient parallel processing and is optimized for AI frameworks, making it a suitable choice for tasks such as LLM inference and training.

context, improving its knowledge of grammar and meaning. NSP helps the model understand if two sentences are connected, reinforcing its ability to model relationships in text. Combined with the attention mechanisms of the transformer, these tasks help BERT capture detailed connections between words and phrases.

Several studies highlight BERT's strong performance in extracting sentiment from a variety of textual sources, including financial news and social media. For instance, Chen et al. (2023) show that BERT-based models are effective in identifying subtle sentiment changes in financial texts, helping to anticipate market movements. Likewise, Yang and Yu (2020) show that it can detect fine sentiment shifts, which is especially important in credit risk analysis where small changes in tone may carry significant meaning.

In this Chapter, a multilingual version of BERT, fine-tuned for sentiment analysis, is employed. This model, available through the Hugging Face[14] platform, supports six languages: English, Dutch, German, French, Spanish, and Italian. Its adaptability ensures the seamless integration of non-English textual data, a crucial feature given the multilingual nature of financial reporting and news coverage.

4.2 LLaMA 3

LLaMA 3 is the latest advancement in Meta's series of LLMs, designed to deliver state-of-the-art performance while maintaining computational efficiency. As shown by Touvron et al. (2024), LLaMA 3 introduces architectural innovations that optimize the balance between model size and usability, addressing the increasing demand for powerful yet accessible LLMs. It is designed with a decoder-only architecture,[15] that simplifies the inference process by generating output conditioned solely on the input sequence, reducing the computational overhead that is typically associated with bidirectional architectures.

The 8-billion parameter[16] variant of LLaMA 3 employed in this Chapter is a multilingual fine-tuned version of the model, as outlined in Devine (2024).

[14] Hugging Face is an open-source platform and library for natural language processing, offering pre-trained language models, tools, and datasets. It facilitates the development, fine-tuning, and deployment of LLMs for a wide range of applications, enabling researchers and practitioners to leverage state-of-the-art NLP technologies efficiently.

[15] Decoder-only architecture refers to a transformer design where only the decoder component is used, generating output conditioned on the input sequence. Unlike the encoder-decoder architecture, which processes input through an encoder before the decoder generates the output, decoder-only models are streamlined for tasks like text generation, reducing computational overhead while maintaining contextual understanding.

[16] In LLMs, parameters are the learned weights that define how the model processes and generates text. These values are adjusted during training to optimise the model's predictions, enabling it to capture linguistic nuances and complex patterns. The number of parameters directly influences the model's capacity to handle intricate tasks; larger models with billions of parameters generally show greater precision and versatility. However, this also increases computational requirements for

This specific configuration offers a balanced solution, combining computational feasibility with the advanced capabilities required for sophisticated text analysis.

To adapt LLaMA 3 for local deployment, a quantized version with 4-bit precision is employed, significantly reducing its computational demands. This precision enables the model to perform inference efficiently without compromising on accuracy. The model configuration (see Appendix A) is carefully calibrated to optimize its output for the specific use case. The temperature is set at 0.30, prioritizing deterministic responses while allowing some flexibility in text generation.

4.3 Phi 3

Phi 3 is a key innovation within Microsoft's Phi family of models, that makes a significant leap in balancing computational efficiency with linguistic precision (Abdin et al., 2024). Phi 3 offers multiple configurations ('variants') tailored to various computational and analytical needs, ranging from smaller models optimized for efficiency to larger models designed for high precision. The medium variant, featuring 14 billion parameters, strikes a balance between these extremes, providing advanced capabilities for resource-constrained environments.

The architecture of Phi 3 is rooted in a decoder-only structure, optimized for generating coherent and contextually accurate text output. Unlike bidirectional models, the decoder-only approach prioritizes streamlined processing, focusing on efficient generation without compromising on contextual understanding. The open design of Phi 3 emphasizes its versatility, offering pre-trained and instruction-tuned variants to suit a wide range of applications.

The Phi 3 model employed here features an 8-bit quantization setup, a strategic choice to minimize computational overhead. Specific settings (see Appendix A) are optimally configured to enhance the model performance for our objectives. The temperature is set at 0.20, ensuring deterministic and precise output with minimal randomness.

4.4 Gemma 2

The last of the four LLMs is developed by Google. This family of lightweight, state-of-the-art LLMs stems from the same research and technology behind the Gemini models,[17] though tailored for broader accessibility. As a text-to-text, decoder-only LLM, Gemma 2 is specifically designed to excel in diverse tasks

training and inference. The 8-billion parameter variant of LLaMA 3 is a carefully balanced configuration, offering significant analytical power while maintaining efficiency, making it suitable for applications that demand both accuracy and resource-conscious deployment.

[17] Gemini is Google's advanced generative AI systems designed for a wide range of applications, including conversational AI, content creation and complex reasoning.

such as question answering, summarization, and logical reasoning. Its design prioritizes versatility and scalability, allowing for the deployment on limited-resource environments. This approach fosters innovation while ensuring broader access to cutting-edge AI technologies (Riviere et al., 2024).

The Gemma 2 model used in this Chapter, with 27 billion parameters, strikes a balance between scale and practicality, offering high performance without the computational overhead of larger models. Its open-source nature enhances its adaptability, providing both pre-trained and instruction-tuned variants to suit a variety of use cases. To optimize the local deployment of Gemma 2, a quantized version with 4-bit precision is employed. Key configurations are fine-tuned to optimize performance for this study (see Appendix A). The temperature is set at 0.25, minimizing randomness in the model responses and prioritizing determinism.

5 Methodology

This Section describes how we construct credit sentiment indicators derived from articles with the LLMs described in Sects. 4.1–4.4: BERT, LLaMa, Phi, and Gemma.[18]

We ask LLMs to classify each article as: 'very good', 'good', 'neutral', 'bad' or 'very bad'.

When the length of the article exceeds the LLM's maximum length (see Appendix A), the text is divided into shorter segments to ensure compatibility with the model input constraints. Each segment is processed independently by the LLM, generating separate sentiment predictions. To obtain a final sentiment prediction for the entire *corpus*, an ensemble[19] method is employed, aggregating the predictions from all segments. This approach allows the model to handle extensive textual data while maintaining the integrity of the analysis.

While the output of LLaMa, Phi and Gemma is the actual classification, the output of BERT is a vector of five probabilities: the probability that the article is 'very good', the probability that it is 'good', etc. In Fig. 1[20] we present a comparative example illustrating the sentiment classification outcomes generated by the

[18] For brevity, the specific versions of the LLMs are omitted in the text from this point onward. However, all references to these models pertain exclusively to the configurations described in Sects. 4.2–4.4.

[19] Ensemble refers to a technique in machine learning where multiple models or predictions are combined to improve overall accuracy and robustness. In the context of sentiment analysis with LLMs, ensemble methods aggregate predictions from text segments, ensuring that the final output reflects the broader context while minimizing biases or inconsistencies from individual predictions. This approach is widely used to enhance performance in complex tasks. We assign greater weight to segments classified with negative sentiment, as adverse signals in financial news are often more informative for credit risk assessment. This weighting approach ensures that potential distress signals receive appropriate emphasis in the final sentiment indicator.

[20] The original prompt submitted to the LLMs is in Italian. It has been translated into English to ensure linguistic uniformity throughout the text.

LLMs. Gemma and LLaMA classify the example article as 'bad', while Phi categorizes it as 'very bad', showing a slight divergence in sentiment interpretation, possibly due to variations in their fine-tuning strategies or training *corpora*. BERT, unlike the other models, provides probabilistic output for each sentiment category. In this instance, the highest probability, 85%, is assigned to 'very bad', showing a strong agreement with Phi while also offering a more nuanced breakdown of sentiment probabilities across all categories.

For convenience, we treat the output of LLaMa, Phi, and Gemma as a vector of five binary variables, one for each state, all equal to zero except one. Therefore, for each article, we have 20 variables: 5 probabilities from BERT, 5 binary variables from LLaMA, 5 binary variables from Phi, 5 binary variables from Gemma. In the following, we refer to these variables as $X^{i,j,a}$, where $i \in$ {bert, llama, phi, gemma}, $j \in$ {very bad, bad, neutral, good, very good} and a indexes the article.

Before moving on, we need to address the potential issue of hallucination. Hallucination occurs when an LLM generates output that appears plausible but is factually incorrect or inconsistent with the input data (Huang et al., 2023). In the context of sentiment analysis for credit risk assessment, this issue could compromise the reliability of the predictions, particularly when dealing with unstructured

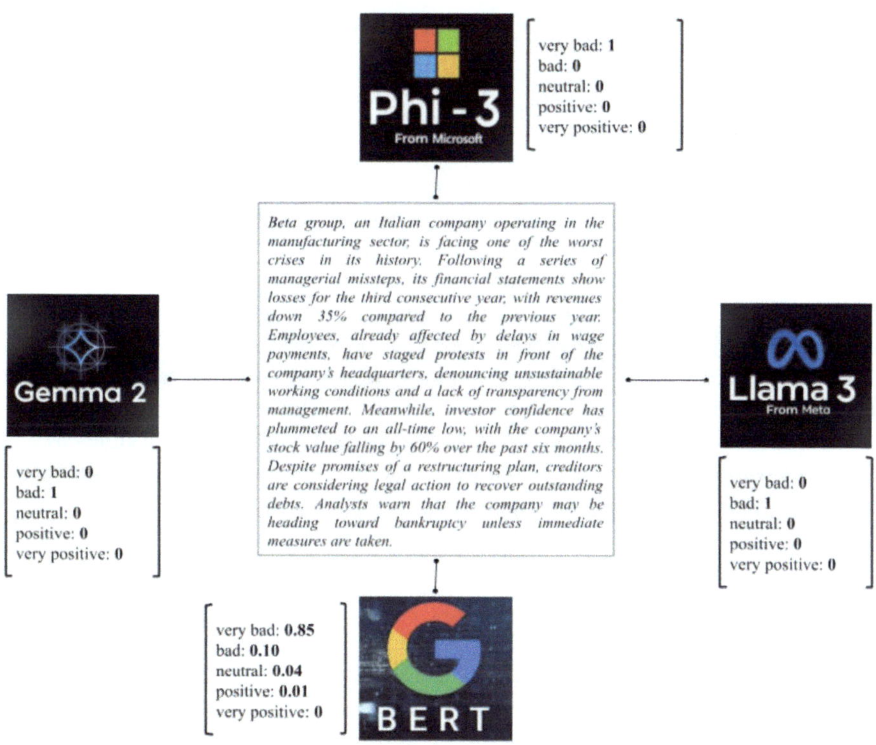

Fig. 1 Illustration of sentiment classification outcomes produced by LLMs

textual data. To mitigate this concern, a robustness check is implemented by comparing sentiment predictions derived from two levels of textual representation: the full text (*corpus*) of articles and their corresponding snippets (the concise summaries) provided by the Dow Jones Factiva database. This approach allows for an assessment of consistency in sentiment classification across different textual granularities, thereby reducing the risk of spurious output. The results of this analysis are presented in Appendix B.

In the next step, we aggregate the information from different articles. Since the default flag is defined on a monthly basis, we need to aggregate all articles mentioning the same company in the same month. Additionally, one could assume that older articles (e.g., those of the previous month, or those of two months before, etc.) are predictive of the default as well. In line with Gariano and Viggiano (2022), we aggregate the articles of the last six months. This means that each article is used for six consecutive months to predict the defaults of the company. The length of the time window (six months) is chosen taking into account the discriminatory power of the resulting model.

The aggregation is based on the average and maximum functions. More specifically, for each model i, for each state j, for each company c, and for each month m we compute:

$$A^{i,j,c,m} = \text{Average}\left(X^{i,j,a}\right)$$

$$M^{i,j,c,m} = \text{Max}\left(X^{i,j,a}\right)$$

where the average and maximum functions are computed on the articles of the last six months (from month m until month m-5, included) mentioning company c.

The purpose of the 'average' variables is to capture the average sentiment of the available articles, while the purpose of the 'maximum' variables is to detect the presence of extreme articles, which might otherwise get diluted among several neutral articles.

For Gemma, LLaMA and Phi, the interpretation of these variables is straightforward: the variables $A^{i,j,c,m}$ show the fraction of articles mentioning company c in the last six months that model i classifies in state j, while the variables $M^{i,j,c,m}$ are binary variables which are equal to 1 only if in the last six months there is at least one article (mentioning company c) classified by model i in state j.

For BERT, whose output is a set of probabilities, the interpretation is less straightforward[21]: the variables $A^{\mathrm{bert},j,c,m}$ are the average probabilities that the articles mentioning company c in the last six months are of type j, while the variables $M^{\mathrm{bert},j,c,m}$ are the maximum probabilities that the articles mentioning company c in the last six months are of type j.

Other aggregation approaches are also considered, such the use of the mode[22] or the conversion of the categorical variable into a scalar.[23] These alternatives have been discarded due to their lower discriminatory power compared to the proposed approach.

6 Results

In Sect. 6.1–6.4 we analyse the models on a standalone basis, while in Sect. 6.5 we analyse the models jointly. We consider discriminatory power since predictive power, the other important feature of a credit assessment system, is not significantly affected by LLMs.[24]

We find that, when considered individually, the BERT model does not add information to the S-ICAS, while the other three models (marginally) do. However, the best model, capable of materially improving the ICAS, is the LLMs ensemble obtained by combining all the LLMs together.

The dataset used for the estimation consists of 60,571 records, of which 967 are defaults. These records are a relatively small fraction (about 17%) of all records in the original ICAS dataset (which are 351.755, see Table 1). This is mainly due to two reasons:

[21] Alternatively, we could have converted the five probabilities of BERT into a single categorical variable looking at the highest probability (e.g., 'very bad' in the example of Fig. 1). This approach, however, would be recommended only if BERT tends to assign high probability to one state and negligible probabilities to the other four (like in the example of Fig. 1). Unfortunately, this is not the case: in the large majority of cases BERT tends to produce similar probabilities for different states: the highest probability of the five is lower than 30% for more than half of the sample, and it is lower than 50% for 95% of the sample.

[22] Under this alternative approach, for each company and for each month, we take the classification ('very bad', 'bad', etc..) that appears more often. For BERT, we take the classification with the highest aggregate probability.

[23] Under this alternative approach, for each article, the classification is converted into a scalar (eg. 'very bad' $= 2$, 'bad' $= 1$, 'good' $= -1$, 'very good' $= -2$, or other values). For BERT, the scalar is obtained as weighted average. Subsequently, the average/maximum functions are computed on these scalars.

[24] Broadly speaking, discriminatory power is the ability of a system to sort the companies by riskiness, while predictive power is the ability of a system to assign probabilities of default aligned with the observed default rates. The former is generally measured by the area under the ROC curve (AUROC), while the latter is usually verified with binomial tests.

- 54% of companies are never mentioned in the news articles available in the database;
- the remaining 46% of companies are mentioned, but not for all dates in our sample (on average, taking into account the six months' window of the articles, each company is mentioned in 22 out of 60 months).

Since sometimes the LLM fails to classify an article, the dataset shrinks a little further in the next Sections, depending on the model used.

In the following Sections we use a stepwise regression to select the significant variables (we only keep variables with a p-value $< 5\%$). Furthermore, variables with the wrong sign[25] are removed from the estimation as well.

We use pre-trained versions of LLMs, without a fine-tuning on our default data. Therefore, our dataset can be considered completely out-of-sample.

6.1 BERT

In this Section we show the results for the BERT model described in Sect. 4.1.

We consider the two following logistic models:

$$g(P[\text{def}_c = 1]) = \alpha_0 + \sum_j \left(\beta_j \cdot A^{\text{bert},j,c} + \gamma_j \cdot M^{\text{bert},j,c}\right) \tag{1}$$

$$g(P[\text{def}_c = 1]) = \alpha_0 + \alpha_1 \cdot S_c + \sum_j \left(\beta_j \cdot A^{\text{bert},j,c} + \gamma_j \cdot M^{\text{bert},j,c}\right) \tag{2}$$

where c is the company, def is the default binary variable (equal to 1 if and only if an ICAS default has occurred), $g(\pi) = log(\pi/(1-\pi))$ is the logistic function, S is the S-ICAS score, $A^{\text{bert},j,c}$ and $M^{\text{bert},j,c}$ are the two credit sentiment indicators described in Sect. 5, with $j \in$ {very bad, bad, neutral, good, very good}.

The first model uses the credit sentiment indicators to predict the defaults, while the second model uses both the S-ICAS and the credit sentiment indicators. The purpose of the first model is to test whether the credit sentiment indicators built with BERT have good predictive power, while the purpose of the second model is to test whether the credit sentiment indicators, in addition to having good predictive power, are also able to add discriminatory power to the S-ICAS.

BERT fails to classify 14% of the articles. As a result, the dataset used for the regressions shrinks by 3 percent to 58,953 records,[26] of which 962 are defaults.

[25] Sign must be positive for $j \in$ {very bad, bad} and negative for $j \in$ {good, very good}. Any sign for $j =$ neutral is considered acceptable.

[26] An article in six months is enough to keep a record, therefore a 14% reduction in the number of articles results in a much lower (3%) reduction in the number of records.

Table 5 BERT models

	def	
	(1) (News)	(2) (News + ICAS)
α_0	−4.0805*** (0.1391)	1.1653*** (0.1805)
α_1		1.2145*** (0.0279)
β_{bad}	3.4645*** (0.4098)	2.2640*** (0.4466)
β_{neutral}	−3.6995*** (0.7017)	−4.6090*** (0.7597)
AUROC	0.580	0.864

Note * p-value < 0.01; ** p-value < 0.001; *** p-value < 0.0001

Table 5 summarizes the results, reporting estimates, standard errors and p-values for the selected variables and the area under the ROC curve (AUROC).[27]

The first model shows weak performance, with an AUROC of only 58%. An analysis of the variables confirms this outcome. Maximum variables ($M^{\text{bert,j,c}}$) are not selected. Average variables ($A^{\text{bert,j,c}}$) are selected only for 'bad' and 'neutral' articles. The fact that we have a 'bad' variable without a 'very bad' variable is suspicious (in principle, 'very bad' articles should be more informative in predicting default than simply 'bad' articles). The fact that we have a 'neutral' variable with negative sign (it reduces the probability of default) without 'good' and 'very good' variables is suspicious as well (in principle, 'good' and 'very good' articles should be more informative in predicting non-default than simply 'neutral' articles).

The second model considers the BERT variables in addition to the S-ICAS. The selected variables are the same of the previous model: only the average variables for 'bad' and 'neutral' articles add information to the S-ICAS: the overall AUROC increases by 0.2% (from 86.2 to 86.4%) with respect to the S-ICAS alone.

6.2 LLaMA

In this Section we show the results of the LLaMA model described in Sect. 4.2. We consider the same logistic models of previous Section, except that LLaMA variables are used instead of BERT ones:

$$g(P[\text{def}_c = 1]) = \alpha_0 + \sum_j \left(\beta_j \cdot A^{\text{llama},j,c} + \gamma_j \cdot M^{\text{llama},j,c}\right) \tag{3}$$

[27] For further information on the AUROC see Chap. 3. Credit scoring models based on financial statement data typically reach AUROC values around 0.7; the ICAS statistical model, using both financial statement and Credit Register data, reaches a value around 0.86.

Table 6 LLaMA models

	def	
	(3) (News)	(4) (News + ICAS)
α_0	−3.8643*** (0.0749)	0.6683*** (0.1063)
α_1		1.2129*** (0.0280)
β_{neutral}	−0.3024 (0.1310)	
$\beta_{\text{very good}}$	−0.8601*** (0.1172)	−0.5150*** (0.1215)
$\gamma_{\text{very bad}}$	0.3267*** (0.0704)	0.3736*** (0.0733)
γ_{good}	−0.2593*** (0.0665)	
AUROC	0.604	0.868

Note: * p-value < 0.01; ** p-value < 0.001; *** p-value < 0.0001

$$g(P[\text{def}_c = 1]) = \alpha_0 + \alpha_1 \cdot S_c + \sum_j \left(\beta_j \cdot A^{\text{llama},j,c} + \gamma_j \cdot M^{\text{llama},j,c}\right) \quad (4)$$

LLaMA fails to classify 17% of the articles. As a result, the dataset used for the regressions shrinks by 4% to 58,166 records (a few hundred records less than the BERT one), of which 944 are defaults.

Table 6 summarizes the results, reporting estimates, standard errors and p-values for the selected variables and the AUROC.

Four variables are selected for the first model: one for the ‘very good’ articles, one for the ‘good’ articles, one for the ‘neutral’ articles and one for the ‘very bad’ articles. The variable for the ‘neutral’ articles has negative sign (it reduces the probability of default), and—unlike the previous BERT models—its presence is justified by the fact that ‘good’ and ‘very good’ articles are also considered. The fact that the coefficient of the ‘very good’ articles is bigger (in absolute value) than that of the ‘neutral’ articles is expected as well (in principle, ‘very good’ articles should be more informative in predicting non-default than ‘neutral’ articles). The AUROC is 60.4%, better than BERT but still not high.

When considering LLaMA variables together with the S-ICAS, only two variables remain: one for the ‘very good’ articles and one for the ‘very bad’. The less extreme articles (‘neutral’, ‘good’) add no information to the S-ICAS. The

Table 7 Phi models

	def	
	(5) (News)	(6) (News + ICAS)
α_0	−4.4334*** (0.0569)	0.4031** (0.1085)
α_1		1.2058*** (0.0280)
$\beta_{\text{very bad}}$	0.6200*** (0.1501)	0.4665* (0.1641)
β_{bad}	0.4798** (0.1343)	
$\beta_{\text{very good}}$	−1.0706*** (0.2753)	−0.8660** (0.2712)
γ_{bad}	0.4082*** (0.0971)	0.5565*** (0.0723)
AUROC	0.616	0.868

Note * p-value < 0.01; ** p-value < 0.001; *** p-value < 0.0001

AUROC increases by 0.4% (from 86.4 to 86.8%[28]) with respect to the S-ICAS alone.

6.3 Phi

In this Section we show the results of the Phi model described in Sect. 4.3. We consider the same logistic models of previous Sections, except that Phi variables are used here:

$$g(P[\text{def}_c = 1]) = \alpha_0 + \sum_j \left(\beta_j \cdot A^{\text{phi},j,c} + \gamma_j \cdot M^{\text{phi},j,c}\right) \tag{5}$$

$$g(P[\text{def}_c = 1]) = \alpha_0 + \alpha_1 \cdot S_c + \sum_j \left(\beta_j \cdot A^{\text{phi},j,c} + \gamma_j \cdot M^{\text{phi},j,c}\right) \tag{6}$$

As LLaMA, Phi fails to classify 17% of the articles. As a result, the dataset used for the regressions shrinks by 4% to 58,096 records, of which 941 are defaults.

Table 7 summarizes the results, reporting estimates, standard errors and p-values for the selected variables and the AUROC.

[28] The AUROC of the S-ICAS was 86.2% in previous Section and 86.4% in this one. This difference is due to the fact that the datasets slightly differ in the two Sections (the latter is a little bit smaller than the former).

Four variables are selected for the first model: one for the 'very good' articles, one for the 'very bad' articles, two for the 'bad' articles. The fact that the coefficient of the 'very bad' articles is bigger (in absolute value) than that of the 'bad' articles is as expected. The AUROC is 61.6%, marginally better than LLaMA.

When considering Phi variables together with the S-ICAS, three variables remain: one for the 'very good' articles, one for the 'very bad' articles and one for the 'bad' articles. The AUROC increases by 0.4% (from 86.4 to 86.8%) with respect to the S-ICAS.

6.4 Gemma

For Gemma (see Sect. 4.4) we consider the same logistic models of the previous Sections, except that Gemma variables are used here:

$$g(P[\mathrm{def}_c = 1]) = \alpha_0 + \sum\nolimits_j \left(\beta_j \cdot A^{\mathrm{gemma},j,c} + \gamma_j \cdot M^{\mathrm{gemma},j,c}\right) \quad (7)$$

$$g(P[\mathrm{def}_c = 1]) = \alpha_0 + \alpha_1 \cdot S_c + \sum\nolimits_j \left(\beta_j \cdot A^{\mathrm{gemma},j,c} + \gamma_j \cdot M^{\mathrm{gemma},j,c}\right) \quad (8)$$

Gemma fails to classify 19% of the articles. As a result, the dataset used for the regressions shrinks by 5% to 57,622 records (a few hundred records less than LLaMA and Phi), of which 922 are defaults.

Table 8 summarizes the results, reporting estimates, standard errors, and *p*-values for the selected variables and the AUROC.

Table 8 Gemma models

	def	
	(7) (News)	(8) (News + ICAS)
α_0	−3.9169*** (0.0596)	0.6043*** (0.1020)
α_1		1.2081*** (0.0282)
β_{good}	−0.3663*** (0.0922)	
$\beta_{\mathrm{very\ good}}$	−3.0401*** (0.3727)	−2.2111*** (0.3736)
$\gamma_{\mathrm{very\ bad}}$		0.2013* (0.0800)
γ_{bad}	0.2750*** (0.0722)	0.3191*** (0.0793)
AUROC	0.613	0.871

Note * p-value < 0.01; ** p-value < 0.001; *** p-value < 0.0001

Three variables are selected for the first model: one for the 'very good' articles, one for the 'good' articles and one for the 'bad' articles. The fact that the coefficient of the 'very good' articles is bigger (in absolute value) than that of the 'good' articles is as expected. The fact that we have a 'bad' variable without a 'very bad' variable is suspicious (in principle, 'very bad' articles should be more informative in predicting default than simply 'bad' articles). The AUROC is 61.3%, slightly lower than Phi's.

When considering Gemma variables together with the S-ICAS, three variables are selected: one for the 'very good' articles, one for the 'bad' articles and one for the 'very bad' articles. The AUROC increases by 0.5% (from 86.6 to 87.1%[29]) with respect to the S-ICAS.

6.5 LLMs Ensemble

In this Section we use all LLMs described in Sect. 4.

We consider the following logistic models:

$$g(P[\mathrm{def}_c = 1]) = \alpha_0 + \sum_{i,j} \left(\beta_{i,j} \cdot A^{i,j,c} + \gamma_{i,j} \cdot M^{i,j,c} \right) \tag{9}$$

$$g(P[\mathrm{def}_c = 1]) = \alpha_0 + \alpha_1 \cdot S_c + \sum_{i,j} \left(\beta_{i,j} \cdot A^{i,j,c} + \gamma_{i,j} \cdot M^{i,j,c} \right) \tag{10}$$

Table 9 summarizes the results, reporting estimates, standard errors, and *p*-values for the selected variables and the AUROC.

Six variables are selected for the first model: two for the 'very good' articles, two for the 'neutral' articles, one for the 'bad' articles and one for the 'very bad' articles. Based on their significance, we have one BERT variable, three Phi variables and two Gemma variables. We note that no LLaMA variables are selected, while one BERT variable is, despite the fact that LLaMA is stronger in terms of discriminatory power than BERT on a standalone basis. This means that, when combining all LLMs together, BERT still has something to say (i.e., it is less correlated to the other models), while LLaMA seems to be redundant. The AUROC is 65.1%, a fairly decent value, and better than those of the previous Sections.

When considering all variables together with the S-ICAS, six variables are selected again, mostly those of the previous model, except that a 'neutral' variable from the Gemma model is replaced by a 'neutral' variable from the Phi model. Overall, we have four Phi variables out of six. The AUROC increases by 0.9% (from 86.2 to 87.1%) with respect to the S-ICAS.

[29] The AUROC of the S-ICAS was 86.2% in Section 6.1, 86.4% in Sections 6.2 and 6.3 and 86.6% in this Section. These differences are due to the fact that the datasets slightly differ in the four Sections.

Table 9 LLMs ensemble

	def	
	(9) (News)	(10) (News + ICAS)
α_0	−3.6050*** (0.1028)	1.2718*** (0.1511)
α_1		1.1940*** (0.0279)
$\gamma_{\text{bert,neutral}}$	−3.4365*** (0.4475)	−3.8454*** (0.5267)
$\beta_{\text{phi,very good}}$	−0.5778 (0.2578)	−0.5168 (0.2611)
$\gamma_{\text{phi,very bad}}$	0.3282*** (0.0790)	0.3232*** (0.0851)
$\gamma_{\text{phi,bad}}$	0.6938*** (0.0722)	0.5939*** (0.0769)
$\gamma_{\text{phi,neutral}}$		0.1934 (0.0865)
$\beta_{\text{gemma,neutral}}$	0.2336* (0.0929)	
$\beta_{\text{gemma,very good}}$	−2.5259*** (0.3737)	−1.9767*** (0.3622)
AUROC	0.651	0.871

Note * p-value < 0.01; ** p-value < 0.001; *** p-value < 0.0001

Each model analysed in previous Sections demonstrates unique strengths in extracting and interpreting sentiment, but their combined use yields the most robust results, reflecting the synergetic potential of the LLM approach.

We recall that our LLMs are not trained on default data. This means that, for example, LLMs may classify as 'bad' or 'very bad' some articles whose content is overall negative, but without relevance to the possible default of the company. Despite this limitation, LLMs are able to increase the AUROC of the ICAS by almost one percentage point, as shown in this Section. We expect that LLMs trained on ICAS default data can perform even better; this is left for future research.

7 Conclusions

This Chapter shows the ability of large language models (LLMs) to enhance the accuracy of credit risk assessment systems through the integration of sentiment indicators derived from company-related news. By systematically processing vast amounts of unstructured textual data, the models employed are able to capture nuanced sentiment cues that traditional methods often overlook. The integration of these indicators into the ICAS framework complements quantitative metrics and addresses the complexities inherent in qualitative assessments.

The results indicate that LLM-driven sentiment analysis improves the discriminatory power of the S-ICAS, by one percentage point in terms of area under the ROC curve. This result is significant, considering that improvements in AUROC become more and more difficult as the starting level increases, and that the current model, with an AUROC of around 85 percent, is already above the levels generally reported in the literature or by other credit assessment systems.

The application of quantized versions ensures computational efficiency while maintaining high levels of accuracy, complying with operational constraints and data protection standards. Each model shows individual strengths in extracting and interpreting sentiment. Their combined use yields the most significant results, reflecting the synergetic potential of this approach.

Future developments could involve the integration of even larger LLMs and the application of fine-tuning techniques, such as training on default data. Further developments could also involve sectorial analysis, rather than company-based analysis. In particular, the extraction of information on economic sectors from the news could overcome the main limitation of the current approach, namely the fact that we did not find articles for a large share of companies.

More generally, as technology advances, the role of LLMs in credit risk assessment is likely to become even more transformative, paving the way for finer and innovative financial decision-making.

Appendix A

LLMs Prompt and Model Settings

In this Appendix, we describe the model settings employed for the large language models (LLMs) used in this study: LLaMA 3, Phi 3, and Gemma 2. These configurations are carefully selected and fine-tuned to balance computational efficiency and predictive accuracy, ensuring reliable sentiment analysis. Among the key elements, the temperature controls the randomness of the model output, with lower values such as 0.2 producing more deterministic predictions suitable for this context (see Table 10).

Table 10 Impact of temperature on LLMs output for sentiment analysis

Temperature	LLaMA 3	Phi 3	Gemma 2
0.2	'negativo'	'molto negativo'	'negativo'
0.8	The company's outlook seems decidedly negative given its ongoing crisis	The financial situation indicates significant distress and a negative outlook	Conditions suggest the company is experiencing severe financial challenges

To ensure consistent and reliable sentiment analysis, the prompt construction is carefully standardized across all LLMs. It is explicitly designed to instruct the models to perform a sentiment classification task, minimizing ambiguity and encouraging deterministic output. The instruction requires the model to classify the sentiment of a given text into one of five categories: 'molto negativo', 'negativo', 'neutrale', 'positivo', or 'molto positivo'. An example of the prompt is as follows:

You are a sentiment analysis model in the financial domain. Analyze the following TEXT and respond with one of the following categories: 'very negative', 'negative', 'neutral', 'positive', or 'very positive'. If possible, reply with the category only

TEXT: *Beta group, an Italian company operating in the manufacturing sector, is facing one of the worst crises in its history. Following a series of managerial missteps, its financial statements show losses for the third consecutive year, with revenues down 35% compared to the previous year. Employees, already affected by delays in wage payments, have staged protests in front of the company's headquarters, denouncing unsustainable working conditions and a lack of transparency from management. Meanwhile, investor confidence has plummeted to an all-time low, with the company's stock value falling by 60% over the past six months. Despite promises of a restructuring plan, creditors are considering legal action to recover outstanding debts. Analysts warn that the company may be heading toward bankruptcy unless immediate measures are taken*

The carefully structured nature of this prompt ensures that the models deliver concise and relevant output, in line with the objective of sentiment classification. The temperature plays a crucial role in regulating the randomness and variability of the output generated by LLMs. When the temperature is set at a low value (e.g., 0.2), the models prioritize the most likely and deterministic response and gives a direct sentiment classification. Conversely, higher temperature values (e.g., 0.8 or 1.0) introduce variability in token sampling, often leading to longer output or less constrained responses.

Table 10 illustrates simulated output from the three models when tasked with analysing the example text at different temperature settings:

This example shows how the temperature setting influences the models' response, with lower values ensuring concise and reliable sentiment labels, and higher values allowing for more descriptive output. For the purposes of this Chapter, a low temperature was adopted to prioritize deterministic and consistent predictions, in line with the requirement for precise sentiment analysis in credit risk assessment.

The maximum number of tokens defines the length of the output, tailored to capture sentiment concisely while accommodating the necessary details. The batch size for prediction, which determines the number of input samples processed simultaneously during a single inference pass, is uniformly set at 1024 across all models. This choice strikes a balance between computational efficiency and throughput, allowing multiple inputs to be processed in parallel. A minimum token limit of 5 was specified to ensure the brevity of output, while a maximum token threshold of 2048 allows the models to handle complex textual input. The top-p value, used for nucleus sampling, determines the diversity of the output by

Table 11 LLMs settings

	LLaMA 3	Phi 3	Gemma 2
Temperature	0.30	0.20	0.25
Max tokens	14	7	7
Predicted batch size	1024	1024	1024
N minimal tokens	5	5	5
N maximal tokens	2048	2048	2048
Top-p	0.80	0.85	0.90
Presence penalty	0	0	0
Frequency penalty	0	0	0
Stop	None	None	None
Logit bias	0	0	0
N	1	1	1
Best of	1	1	1

considering the cumulative probability of top token options. Both the presence penalty and frequency penalty were set at 0.0 to avoid penalizing token repetition excessively, ensuring the generation of coherent and contextually relevant text. Additional elements, such as the stopping criteria, are kept at their default values to maintain neutrality and to comply with the OpenAI standard for configuring large language models.

The optimal configurations for LLaMA, Phi, and Gemma are determined through an iterative process of experimentation and fine-tuning. Starting from default settings, adjustments are made based on the models' performance on a validation subset of the dataset. Temperature, maximum token limit, and batch size were systematically optimized to balance computational efficiency, inference speed, and the accuracy of sentiment predictions. This approach ensures that each model's configuration is in line with the objectives of this Chapter and the characteristics of the input data. Table 11 shows the results.

Appendix B

Chi-Squared Test for Sentiment Consistency

A challenge for LLMs is hallucination, where output appears plausible but is factually incorrect or inconsistent with the input data. In credit risk analysis, this can undermine the reliability of sentiment indicators extracted from textual data. To address this issue, we compare the sentiment predictions generated from two representations of the articles: the full text (*corpus*) and the corresponding snippets (concise summaries) provided by the Dow Jones Factiva database. This comparison ensures consistency in sentiment classification across different text granularities.

Table 12 Chi-squared test results for LLaMA sentiment distribution

	Chi-squared statistic	*p*-value
Very bad	1.87e-01	0.510
Bad	1.65e-01	0.883
Neutral	6.21e-01	0.445
Positive	3.58e-01	0.478
Very positive	1.63e-01	0.863

The Chi-squared test used for this analysis is particularly suitable for comparing distributions of discrete variables, such as the sentiment levels considered in this study: very bad, bad, neutral, good, and very good. A *p*-value greater than 0.05 indicates no statistically significant difference between the two distributions, thereby supporting the consistency of predictions.

Table 12 presents the results for LLaMA. The Chi-squared statistics and corresponding *p*-values for all sentiment categories confirm that there are no statistically significant differences between the predictions based on the *corpus* and snippet analyses.

The results for Phi are shown in Table 13. Across all sentiment categories, the *p*-values are well above 0.05, indicating high consistency in predictions between the full texts and snippets.

For Gemma, as shown in Table 14, the *p*-values across all sentiment levels also exceeded the 0.05 threshold, further confirming that there are no statistically significant differences between the sentiment distributions of the *corpus* and snippets.

The results of the Chi-squared tests show that the sentiment predictions generated by the three LLMs—LLaMA, Phi, and Gemma—remain consistent across full

Table 13 Chi-squared test results for Phi sentiment distribution

	Chi-squared statistic	*p*-value
Very bad	3.86e-01	0.290
Bad	9.63e-01	0.626
Neutral	2.73e-01	0.188
Positive	6.67e-01	0.104
Very positive	1.05e-01	0.478

Table 14 Chi-squared test results for Gemma sentiment distribution

	Chi-squared statistic	*p*-value
Very bad	2.33e-01	0.788
Bad	1.99e-01	0.795
Neutral	3.58e-01	0.202
Positive	3.35e-01	0.292
Very positive	1.00e-01	0.936

texts and snippets. This analysis suggests that the output of the models is robust and reliable, validating their suitability for large-scale sentiment analysis tasks.

References

Abdin, M., et al. (2024). *Phi-3 technical report: A highly capable language model locally on your phone.* arXiv preprint arXiv:2404.14219

Altman, E. I. (1983). *Corporate financial distress: A complete guide to predicting, avoiding, and dealing with bankruptcy.* Wiley Interscience, John Wiley and Sons.

Altman, E. I., Barboza, F., & Kimura, H. (2017). Machine learning models and bankruptcy prediction. *Expert Systems with Applications, 83*, 405–417.

Aprigliano, V., Emiliozzi, S., Guaitoli, G., Luciani, A., Marcucci, J., & Monteforte, L. (2021) The power of text-based indicators in forecasting the Italian economic activity. *Bank of Italy Work Paper, 1321*

Auria, L., Bingmer, M., Mateo, C., Graciano, C., Charavel, C., Gavilá, S., Iannamorelli, A., Levy, A., Maldonado, A., Resch, F., Rossi, A. M., & Sauer, S. (2021). Overview of central banks' in-house credit assessment systems in the euro area. *ECB Occasional Paper Series, 284*

Bozzon, A., Putra, S. G. P., Joshi, B., & Redi, J. (2020). A credit scoring model for SMEs based on social media data. *International conference on web engineering* (pp. 113–129). Springer.

Cathcart, L., Gotthelf, N. M., Uhl, M., & Shi, Y. (2020). News sentiment and sovereign credit risk. *European Financial Management, 26*(2), 261–287.

Chen, Y., Liu, Z., & Wang, H. (2023). Financial sentiment analysis using BERT-based models. *The Journal of Finance and Data Science, 5*(2), 45–58.

Ciampi, F., & Gordini, N. (2013). Small enterprise default prediction modeling through artificial neural networks: An empirical analysis of Italian small enterprises. *Journal of Small Business Management, 51*(1), 23–45.

Devlin, J., Chang, M. W., Lee, K., & Toutanova, K. (2019). BERT: Pre-training of deep bidirectional transformers for language understanding. *Proceedings of NAACL-HLT, 1*, 4171–4186.

Devine, P. (2024). *Tagengo: A multilingual chat dataset.* arXiv preprint arXiv:2405.12612

Dolphin, R., et al. (2024). *Extracting structured insights from financial news: An augmented LLM driven approach.* arXiv preprint arXiv:2407.15788

Gariano, G., & Viggiano, G. (2022). *Press news and social media in credit risk assessment: The experience of Bank of Italy's in-house credit assessment system.* Markets, Infrastructures, Payment Systems Series.

Giovannelli, F., Iannamorelli, A., Levy, A., & Orlandi, M. (2023). The Bank of Italy's in-house credit assessment system for non-financial firms. In A. Scalia (Ed.), *Financial risk management and climate change risk* (pp. 107–137). Springer.

González-Fernández, M., & González-Velasco, C. (2020). An alternative approach to predicting bank credit risk in Europe with Google data. *Finance Research Letters, 35*, Article 101281.

Huang, L., et al. (2023). *A survey on hallucination in large language models: Principles, taxonomy, challenges, and open questions.* arXiv preprint arXiv:2311.05232

Lau, R. Y., Li, C., Yuan, H., & Wong, M. C. (2018). Mining emotions of the public from social media for enhancing corporate credit rating. In *IEEE international conference on e-business engineering (ICEBE)* (pp. 25–30).

Lei, Y., et al. (2024). FinLangNet: A novel deep learning framework for credit risk prediction using linguistic analogy in financial data. *Journal of Computational Finance, 18*(3), 123–140.

Lis, S., et al. (2023). Analyzing credit risk model problems through NLP-based clustering and machine learning: Insights from validation reports. *Proceedings of an International Conference on Financial Engineering and Risk Management*, 112–120

Lu, H. M., Hung, M. W., & Tsai, F. T. (2016). The impact of news articles and corporate disclosure on credit risk valuation. *Journal of Banking & Finance, 68*, 100–116.

Mo, K., et al. (2024). *Fine-tuning Gemma 2–7B for enhanced sentiment analysis of financial news headlines*. arXiv preprint arXiv:2406.13626

Riviere, M., et al. (2024). *Gemma 2: Improving open language models at a practical size*. arXiv preprint arXiv:2408.00118

Sanz-Guerrero, M., & Arroyo, J. (2024). *Credit risk meets large language models: Building a risk indicator from loan descriptions in P2P lending*. arXiv preprint arXiv:2401.16458

Touvron, H., et al. (2024). *LLaMA 3: Open and efficient foundation language models*. arXiv preprint arXiv:2405.00360

Tran-The, T. (2020). *Modeling institutional credit risk with financial news*. arXiv preprint arXiv: 2004.08204

Vaswani, A., et al. (2017). *Attention is all you need*. arXiv preprint arXiv:1706.03762

Yang, X., & Yu, H. (2020). BERT-based sentiment analysis for financial news. *Procedia Computer Science, 174*, 122–127.

Zhang, L., & Zhao, X. (2024). Leveraging LLaMA 3 for sentiment analysis in financial news. *International Journal of Computational Finance, 12*(1), 78–92.

The Cyber Risk of Non-Financial Firms

Francesco Columba, Manuel Cugliari, Marco Orlandi, and Federica Vassalli

1 Introduction

The increasing digitalization of business operations and the growing interconnectivity of corporate internal processes and systems, favoured by rapid technological innovation and accelerated by the COVID-19 pandemic, have amplified the exposure of firms to cyber risks (Jamilov et al., 2023).[1] Globally, reported attacks to firms have almost doubled since 2020 (International Monetary Fund, 2024); the average number of incidents per month reached 295 in 2024, up from 156 in 2020, and the risk of extreme losses has increased.

This global trend is mirrored in Italy; between 2020 and 2024, the number of cyberattacks targeting non-financial firms grew by 39% (CLUSIT, 2025). Ninety percent of Italian firms acknowledge the risk of a cyberattack. Despite high awareness, mitigation efforts remain limited: many firms, especially smaller enterprises, lack dedicated cybersecurity functions and internal capabilities to effectively manage cyber risk (Bencivelli & Mongardini, 2024).

[1] We consider cyber risk as 'any risk emerging from intentional attacks on information and communication technology systems that compromises the confidentiality, availability or the integrity of data or services' (Giudici & Raffinetti, 2021).

F. Columba · M. Cugliari · M. Orlandi (✉) · F. Vassalli
Bank of Italy, Financial Risk Management Directorate, Rome, Italy
e-mail: m.orlandi@bancaditalia.it

F. Columba
e-mail: francesco.columba@bancaditalia.it

M. Cugliari
e-mail: manuel.cugliari@bancaditalia.it

F. Vassalli
e-mail: federica.vassalli@bancaditalia.it

A. Scalia (ed.), *Corporate Credit Analysis and AI*, Finance for Professionals,
https://doi.org/10.1007/978-3-032-13422-6_16

Financial firms are highly exposed to cyber risk, representing one fifth of the total attacks in the last two decades, and they are closely monitored due to their importance for macro-financial stability (Adelmann et al., 2020; Kotidis & Schreft, 2022). Indeed, also non-financial firms face a broad spectrum of cyber threats, spanning from data breaches and intellectual property theft to supply chain vulnerabilities and human vulnerability.[2] Hackers may target non-financial firms to steal sensitive business information, trade secrets, and proprietary research, leading to financial and competitive disadvantages (Anderson, 2021; Mavani et al., 2024; Mitnick at al., 2019). Non-financial firms depend on extensive networks of suppliers, making them vulnerable to cyberattacks targeting third-party vendors and service providers (Benaroch & Chernobai, 2017; Crosignani et al., 2023; Trautman et al., 2024).

Cyber incidents can have material consequences for credit risk. They can disrupt operations, impair cash flows, and trigger reputational or legal costs (Amir et al., 2018; Harrel, 2019; Kamiya et al., 2021; Lawrence et al., 2018; Mikhed & Vogan, 2018; Rosati et al., 2019), often resulting in significant losses. These effects can increase the cost of credit and capital of firms, as lenders and investors demand compensation for heightened default risk (Agarwal et al., 2024; Huang & Wang, 2021; Sheman, 2022).

Conceptually, the vulnerability of a firm to cyber risk is the likelihood of suffering a cyberattack and the potential severity of its consequences (Ordoñez and Caro Rincón, 2023). Mapping this vulnerability into financial risk indicators can help to estimate the potential impairments to the firm's financial and economic performance.[3] These impairments, such as increased costs, lost revenues, or reputational damage, can adversely affect profitability indicators and, ultimately, deteriorate the firm's creditworthiness.

This Chapter is the first study, to our knowledge, to develop a comprehensive measure of the vulnerability to cyber risk of Italian firms, while the estimation of the impact of cyber risk on firms' creditworthiness will be pursued in future work. In this work, first, we develop a new taxonomy for the assessment of cyber risk exposure, tailored to the Italian case. The taxonomy is based on approximately 300 semantically disjoint concepts and covers six areas: (i) regulatory provisions, which reflect a firm's compliance with EU regulatory frameworks (e.g. Network and Information System Directive—NIS2 Directive, and the General Data Protection Regulation—GDPR); (ii) certifications, including international

[2] Human vulnerability to cyberattacks refers to the susceptibility of individuals to actions or behaviours that can be exploited by malicious actors to gain unauthorized access to systems, data, or networks. This form of vulnerability arises not from technical flaws in software or hardware, but from human factors such as errors, lack of awareness, poor security practices, or psychological manipulation.

[3] The average loss due to malicious attacks can be estimated by stochastic simulation techniques (Giudici & Raffinetti, 2021; Mukhopadhyay et al., 2019).

standards like ISO-27001[4]; (iii) technological defences (e.g. firewalls, endpoint detection, and backup systems); (iv) processes for managing cyber risk; (v) reported cyberattacks; (vi) affiliation to international organisations that set cyber security standards. The information on cyber risk is extracted from financial statement disclosures, web scraping of corporate cybersecurity communications, and newspaper articles reporting cyber incidents. Mapping word-term patterns within the taxonomy enhances the understanding of the cyber risk disclosure aspects that firms prioritize, and it enables a structured extraction of cyber related information.

Second, building on existing methodologies (Florackis et al., 2024; Masoud & Al-Utaibi, 2022), we apply large language models (LLM) and machine learning techniques to the database obtained with the application of the taxonomy to assess: (i) firm-reported cyber risk signals and defensive actions, categorized through a supervised learning algorithm trained on the new cyber risk taxonomy; (ii) cyber incidents and mitigation measures. The classification of unstructured textual content informs the scoring of the firm-level cyber risk indicator that increases with an increase in cyber vulnerability.

Third, we use this indicator to assess the distribution of cyber risk vulnerability across firms, providing new evidence on the exposure for a large sample of Italian non-financial, and mostly non-listed, firms to cyber risk.[5]

We find that firms assessed by S-ICAS have experienced a steady increase in both the frequency and diversity of cyberattacks since 2019.[6] The number of recorded incidents in our sample increases sharply from 14 in 2019 to 232 in 2023, reflecting a marked acceleration in the frequency of cyber events. The most frequently targeted sectors include Manufacturing, Professional, Scientific and Technical Services, Wholesale and Retail, and Vehicle Repair. Each sector faces distinct cyber threats based on its operational models, digital exposure and the type of data it manages. Data breaches are the most widespread type of attack across all sectors, while ransomware is prominent in manufacturing, professional services, and retail industries. Phishing is common in transport, manufacturing, and IT sectors, whereas malware frequently targets professional services, manufacturing, and retail. The frequency and extent of these threats confirms the need for a systematic monitoring and robust assessment of firms' cyber risk.

We also find that since 2020 the value of the cyber risk index remains high, in line with the observed increase in the frequency and heterogeneity of cyberattacks, suggesting a structural weakness in firms' cybersecurity profile. Moreover,

[4] The International Standard Organisation (ISO) defines the requirements for product quality, service performance, management systems, and processes across various sectors, including Technology, Manufacturing, Environment, Occupational health and safety, Medicine, Compliance, and Food safety, among others, each identified by a sequence of numbers.

[5] The literature on cyber risk deals mainly with the effect on listed firms, proposing a methodology for assessing the effect on firm's creditworthiness (Ordoñez & Caro Rincón, 2023) or on stock returns (Grodon et al., 2011; Uddin et al., 2020; Rosati et al., 2019; Masoud & Al-Utaibi, 2022; Huang & Murthy, 2024; Florackis et al., 2024) or on public institutions (Curti et al., 2024).

[6] For the full set of types of cyberattack, see Appendix A—Table 11.

for firms that have experienced a cyber incident, we observe a marked increase in the cyber risk index, that is coherent with a heightened exposure and underlying weakness. Finally, we document that, in the aftermath of a cyberattack, firms are more likely to disclose cyber risk-related information in their financial statements, as in previous studies (Masoud & Al-Utaibi, 2022; Bryson et al., 2023; Wang et al., 2013).

By assessing the exposure to cyber risk, we believe that our contribution to the literature on the financial implications of cyber risk is twofold: First, our approach enables the systematic and replicable transformation of unstructured information into numerical data suitable for business risk analysis, leveraging AI techniques. Second, our taxonomy addresses dimensions of cyber risk that have so far not been considered within a unified methodological framework, particularly for the Italian firms.

Existing contributions in the literature, to our knowledge, either do not employ a taxonomy or rely on more limited taxonomies that are not tailored to the Italian case. Florackis et al. (2024) perform a similar textual analysis of disclosures on cyber risk included in annual filings submitted by publicly listed U.S. companies to the Securities and Exchange Commission, but they do not develop a taxonomy of the underlying risk components. As for the existing cyber risk taxonomies reviewed by Rabitti et al. (2024), two main limitations emerge: (i) the taxonomies deal with individual aspects of cyber risk, such as attack types or potential operational damages, without offering an integrated framework; and (ii) they are developed in English and are therefore not directly applicable to the textual analysis of Italian-language sources, such as financial reports or press coverage of cyber incidents.

The vulnerability index, which does not rely only on firms' self-reporting of cyber incidents, provides a foundation for the future integration of cyber risk into the PD estimation within the Bank of Italy's ICAS for non-financial firms. In operational terms, the cyber risk index will be mapped into a firm-specific probability of experiencing a cyberattack (Ordonez & Caro Rincon, 2023; Mukhopadhyay et al., 2019). Conditional on this probability, the associated expected loss will be estimated using Monte Carlo simulations from a Gamma distribution (Giudici & Raffinetti, 2021; Mukhopadhyay et al., 2019). This loss will then be embedded within the firm's financial statements to simulate the adverse effects of a cyber incident. By applying the S-ICAS to the stressed financial statement, we will be able to derive a cyber risk–adjusted PD,[7] which captures the incremental vulnerability associated with cyber threats. This adjusted PD will serve as an additional input in expert assessment, covering an emerging risk profile.

The remainder of this Chapter is organized as follows: Sect. 2 describes the methodology and data sources used for constructing the cyber risk indicator; Sect. 3 presents the empirical findings; and Sect. 4 concludes.

[7] For further details on how to stress S-ICAS firms financial statement refer to Di Virgilio et al. (2024).

2 Cyber Risk Exposure

2.1 Taxonomy

A taxonomy is necessary for measuring cyber risk, since the data on its components are often unstructured (Curti et al., 2019). We develop a taxonomy to support the extraction and the semantic analysis of cybersecurity-related content, ensuring the standardization of concepts. The taxonomy, tailored to the Italian case, is narrowly defined, unlike the more widespread taxonomies,[8] which are coarse (Rabitti, *op.cit.*) or limited only on technical defense measures (Cremer et al., 2022; Pool and Venter, 2022). We combine insights from previous studies applied to US firms (Curti et al., 2019) with the analysis of the financial statement of Italian non-financial firms. This approach allows the taxonomy to incorporate recognised cyber risk notions and terms that emerge from firms' business operations. The taxonomy comprises nearly 300 distinct items, each corresponding to a specific term relevant to cyber risk, and it is organized into six main categories.

The first category, regulations and standards (henceforth *Regulations*), encompasses regulatory frameworks, standards, and legislative instruments that define firms' cybersecurity obligations and best practices. Compliance with these frameworks mitigate exposure to cyber threats and signals robust risk management to investors, counterparties, and supervisory authorities. Relevant frameworks are the GDPR,[9] the NIS2[10] and the ISO 27001 standard.[11]

The second category, professional certifications (henceforth *Certifications*), covers certifications that validate technical and managerial expertise in cybersecurity. These certifications demonstrate a firm ability to manage cyber risks effectively, ensuring the presence of qualified personnel. Two certifications stand out for their importance and widespread adoption: MITRE ATT&CK Defender™ (MAD)

---

[8] The taxonomies commonly employed have been proposed by Cebula and Young (2010), Rea Guamàn et al. (2018), Zadeh et al. (2023); recently updates have been proposed by Malvasi et al., 2024; Rabitti *op. cit.*.

[9] The GDPR (Regulation EU 2016/679), entered into force in May 2018, establishes stringent data protection requirements and imposes heavy penalties for non-compliance, making it central to cybersecurity governance for firms processing personal data. The update to GDPR 2 is still under discussion.

[10] The NIS2 Directive (Directive (EU) 2022/2555) updates and extends the scope of the initial NIS framework (Directive (EU) 2016/1148), enhancing duties for risk management, incident reporting and supply chain security across a wider set of sectors, with particular emphasis on essential and important entities.

[11] ISO 27001 is a globally recognised standard for information security management systems (ISMS). A list of the regulations and standards included in the taxonomy, along with their detailed descriptions, is in Appendix A, where similar information is provided for all other categories.

and the Global Information Assurance Certification (GIAC) Security Operations Certified (GSOC).[12]

The third category, technologies and systems (henceforth *Technologies*), covers technological solutions, platforms, and security mechanisms that firms implement to safeguard their infrastructure, data, and digital operations. The technological layer constitutes the operational foundation of firms' cyber defences, making the identification and the evaluation of this layer essential in a comprehensive risk assessment. Vulnerability assessment, data loss prevention (DLP), and penetration testing play a critical role in strengthening firms' cybersecurity posture. Vulnerability assessment involves the systematic identification, classification, and prioritisation of security weaknesses in IT systems, applications, and networks. DLP solutions aim at preventing the unauthorised access, transfer, or exfiltration of sensitive data, enforcing policies to protect information across endpoints, networks, and cloud environments. Penetration testing simulates cyberattacks to identify exploitable vulnerabilities before they can be leveraged by adversaries, enabling firms to enhance their resilience. These technologies are particularly important for firms handling critical or regulated data, mitigating the risks associated with accidental or malicious data leaks.

The fourth category, processes and management strategies (henceforth *Processes*), includes organisational and procedural cybersecurity measures. It encompasses governance structures, security policies, and risk management frameworks that dictate how firms address cybersecurity threats. Within this category, three processes warrant particular attention: IT risk governance, threat intelligence, and incident response plan. IT risk governance ensures that cybersecurity risks are effectively identified, assessed, and managed, integrating security measures into corporate governance. Threat intelligence involves gathering and analysing cyber threat data to anticipate attacks and strengthen defences. The incident response plan establishes structured protocols for handling security breaches, minimizing disruptions, and ensuring rapid recovery.

The fifth category, cyberattacks (henceforth *Attacks*), classifies cyber threats targeting firms' digital infrastructure and assets, providing a framework for assessing exposure to malicious activities. Among the most prominent threats are ransomware, phishing, malware, and Denial of Service (DoS) attacks. Ransomware encrypts data and demands payment, often disrupting operations and causing financial losses. Phishing uses social engineering to deceive individuals into providing sensitive information or enabling cyber intrusions. Malware encompasses various malicious software types (trojans, worms, spyware) designed to infiltrate systems and steal or manipulate data. A DoS attack overloads systems with excessive traffic, disrupting operations and access to critical services. This classification

[12] MITRE ATT&CK Defender trains cybersecurity professionals on the ATT&CK framework, a widely adopted model for analysing adversarial tactics and techniques. GSOC is designed for professionals working in security operations centres. It covers key areas such as threat monitoring, log analysis, incident handling, and digital forensics, ensuring that practitioners have the necessary skills to detect, respond to, and mitigate security incidents effectively.

provides a structured approach to assessing an organization's exposure to hostile actions.

The sixth category, national and international organisations (henceforth *Organisations*), includes the membership of regulatory bodies and global institutions that establish cybersecurity standards, promote best practices, and facilitate international cooperation. Notable entities include the European Organisation for Security (EOS) and the European Union Agency for Cybersecurity (ENISA). EOS encourages collaboration between industry, research institutions, and policymakers to enhance Europe's cybersecurity resilience, while ENISA provides operational support, policy guidance, and cybersecurity certification while fostering cooperation between national and EU cybersecurity authorities.

These six categories provide exhaustive and mutually exclusive criteria to capture the vulnerability to cyber risks. For each item in the taxonomy, at least ten terminological variants have been identified and mapped, enhancing the robustness of the subsequent semantic similarity analysis, as shown in Appendix A.

2.2 Dataset

The construction of a synthetic index measuring firms' vulnerability to cyber risk relies on the integration of multiple unstructured data sources, each contributing with a distinct perspective to the definition of a firm cyber posture. The analytical framework that underpins the construction of the cyber risk index draws on three primary sources.

The first source consists of data gathered through the systematic analysis of specialized web platforms and portals dedicated to cybersecurity. This source includes sites that monitor cyberattacks and data breaches, providing a stream of information on incidents affecting Italian firms.

The second source is the Factiva database, which aggregates articles from national and international newspapers, business journals and trade publications. This source broadens the spectrum of cyber incidents captured with the first one, including those reported outside sector-specific channels.

The third source consists of the financial statements of the firms in the sample. These documents, supplied by Cerved[13] in PDF format, are a critical input for the profiling of firms with respect to all six categories defined by the taxonomy. Financial statements, through both narrative and quantitative disclosures, provide information relevant not only with respect to cyberattacks, but also to the adoption of regulations, certifications, technologies, processes, and affiliations with organisations. The cross-referencing of information extracted from financial statements

[13] Cerved is a leading provider of business information and credit risk assessment services in Italy. It offers extensive data on corporate financial statements, creditworthiness, and sectoral insights, supporting risk evaluation and decision-making processes.

Table 1 Data sources (2019–2024)

Balance sheets (Cerved)	24.544[14]
Press news (Factiva)	7 mln
Relevant web sources	10

with those derived from web platforms and press news enables a comprehensive assessment of firms' cyber posture, incorporating evidence of both preventive measures and suffered incidents.

The analysis covers data collected between 2019 and 2024. The resulting dataset ensures granularity in capturing firms' vulnerability and responses to cyber risk (Table 1).

Given the unstructured and heterogeneous nature of financial statements, we implement a targeted selection strategy to identify the sections most likely to contain references to cyber risk. The analysis examines specific areas within the annual reports: the explanatory notes, management commentaries, audit reports, and sections addressing investments, intangible assets, provisions, financial income and expenses, and related party transactions. This approach increases the likelihood of capturing informative content, ensuring that the extracted information reflects firms' actual practices, disclosures, and experiences related to cybersecurity.

2.3 Integrated AI Architecture

The extraction of relevant information from unstructured data sources requires the systematic application of AI techniques. This requirement stems from the features of the data, which are presented in natural language across diverse formats and sources. The architectures[15] have significantly improved the capacity to analyse unstructured textual data, as rule-based or deterministic approaches would fail to capture the implicit relationships and the nuances of the language. These advancements have enabled models to move beyond keyword matching and surface-level text analysis,[16] allowing for the contextual interpretation of entire documents, thereby enhancing the accuracy and completeness of the extraction.

The goal of this Chapter is to develop a firm-level cyber risk vulnerability index. This index integrates two components: (i) a measure of a firm cyber risk defensive readiness, captured through alignment with the cyber risk taxonomy categories *Technology* and *Processes* outlined in Sect. 2.1. Defensive readiness

[14] The number of balance sheets reflects the product between the roughly 4,000 firms assessed annually with S-ICAS and ICAS expert assessment and the number of observation years.

[15] Transformers are a class of neural network architectures based on attention mechanisms, widely used in natural language processing tasks for their ability to model complex dependencies in sequential data without relying on recurrence. A widespread transformer is BERT (Devlin et al., 2019).

[16] These are approaches that rely primarily on keyword matching or simple pattern recognition without understanding context or semantic relationships.

involves technological processes, that is operational aspects of cybersecurity, such as the implementation of firewalls, intrusion detection systems, or data backup protocols; (ii) a measure of the cyber risk management practices, including references to regulatory compliance, cybersecurity certifications, governance structures and past cyber incidents. Cyber risk management practices are captured through alignment with the cyber risk taxonomy categories *Regulation*, *Certifications*, *Attacks*, and *Organisations*.

To construct the index, we design a modular AI-based architecture that processes and integrates data from the three sources described in Sect. 2.2. Each one is handled through a processing pipeline, which is subsequently merged into a unified framework (Fig. 1). The pipelines are distinguished by colour: purple for financial statement data, orange for web-based sources, and green for press news. Each pipeline has one or more analytical modules (represented as rectangular boxes), some of which are common across data streams. The colour scheme reflects the specialized analytical workflows tailored to each source and shows the convergence points where the outputs are integrated to compute the final cyber risk index.

The modules in common to all data sources are:

- **Data curation layer**: this first step consists in a set of modules that perform the initial harmonisation and cleansing of the raw input data, transforming them into a format suitable for natural language processing (NLP) techniques (yellow boxes). All texts, regardless of the source, are subjected to a uniform pre-processing set of modules that applies standard cleaning procedures to remove extraneous characters, harmonise encoding inconsistencies, and normalise structural anomalies. Following this initial processing, the entire corpus is segmented into individual sentences, that are filtered to retain only those in Italian or English. This step excludes irrelevant content and ensures linguistic consistency for each analytical pipeline;
- **Prompting**: prompting refers to the practice of formulating input instructions that guide LLM in generating task-specific responses (green box). Clear and structured prompts allow the model to extract relevant textual evidence, apply consistent criteria, and avoid speculative reasoning and feed the subsequent module[17];
- **LLM**: through targeted prompting, the LLM determines whether there is compliance of content with certification, regulation, affiliation with a relevant organisation, or cyber incident (pink orange box)[18];
- **Score system:** the financial statement pipeline delivers two outputs for taxonomy alignment: one for the firm defensive readiness, capturing the level of technological and procedural defensive measures, and one for the firm cyber

[17] Further details on prompts design and model configuration are provided in Appendix B.

[18] This module leverages on Microsoft Phi-4 (Abdin et al., 2024), a 14-billion parameter LLM, to extract pertinent information. Further details on the configuration of the model are provided in Appendix B, ensuring reproducibility of the analysis.

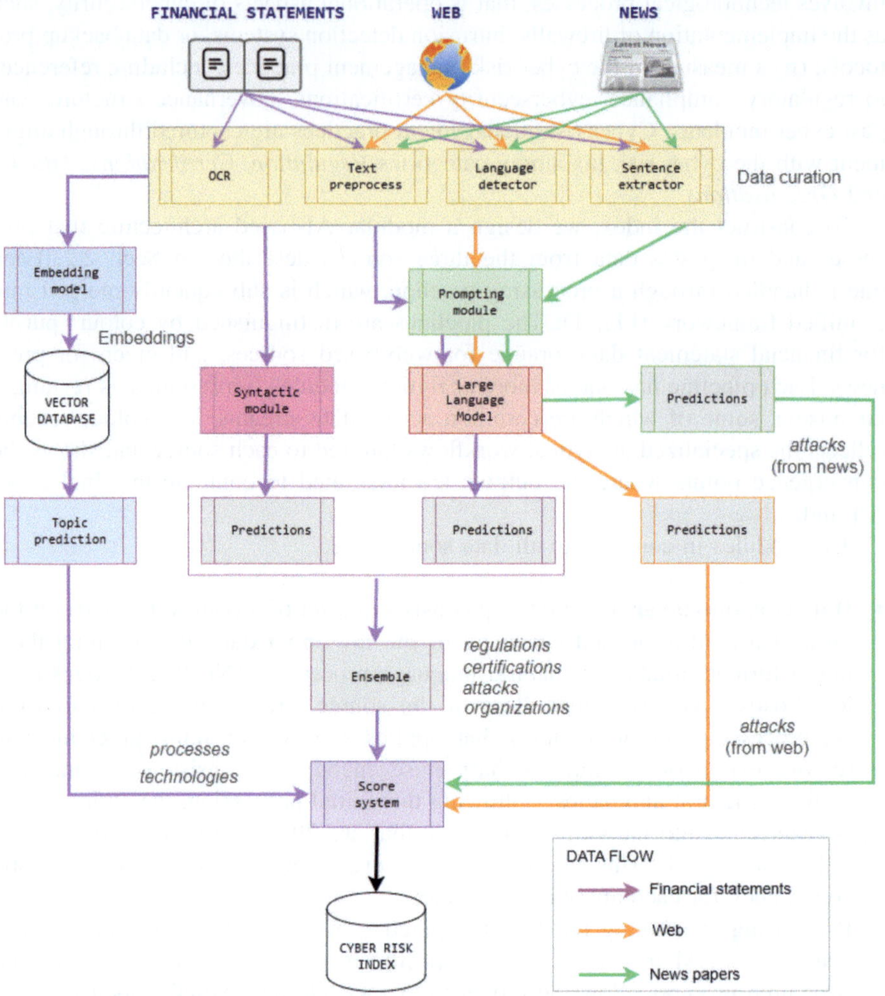

Fig. 1 AI architecture. Optical Character Recognition (OCR) refers to the process of converting different types of documents, such as scanned paper documents, PDFs, or images captured by a digital camera, into editable and searchable text

risk management practises, capturing the extent of compliance with regulations and cybersecurity standards, affiliation to international organisations and reported cyber incident. Factiva and web pipelines result in two distinct exposure grades based on reported incidents. The outputs of each pipeline are combined to get the final score (purple box). A full description of the scoring system is provided in Sect. 2.4.

Next, we describe the three pipelines, where each pipeline performs source-specific pre-processing, transformation, and analysis, ensuring that the heterogeneity of the input data is appropriately addressed.[19]

Financial statement. The financial statement pipeline measures the firm alignment with the taxonomy, providing two sub-scores, for the firm defensive readiness and for the cyber risk management practises, respectively.

This pipeline employs two complementary approaches. The first approach involves technological processes, such as the implementation of firewalls, intrusion detection systems, or data backup protocols. These elements are typically described through a detailed technical language, which requires deeper inspection than high-level topic classification. In doing so, we rely on embedding-based[20] similarity analysis to capture matches between firm disclosures and predefined taxonomic elements in the *Technologies* and *Processes* categories. This part of the pipeline assesses the firm defensive readiness, as it captures the presence of the technical measures designed to prevent cyber threats.

The second approach applies to cyber risk management practices, including references to regulatory compliance, cybersecurity certifications and affiliations with international organisation, and past cyber incidents. These topics, included in the other taxonomy categories (*Regulation*, *Certifications*, *Attacks,* and *Organisations*), are typically expressed in more formalized, declarative language (e.g., compliance statements or references to standards), making them well-suited for semantic classification and inference via LLM. This part of the pipeline assesses the cyber risk management practices, since the lack of alignment with regulatory frameworks or the reporting of past cyber incidents signals potential weakness in managing cyber risk.

For the defensive readiness sub-score, following the data curation layer, we transform the sentences extracted from financial statements into embeddings using a model provided by Hugging Face, that we fine-tune for the Italian language.[21] To assess cybersecurity-related disclosure, we compare these embeddings with the predefined taxonomy topics from the *Technologies* and *Processes* categories,[22] which are also converted into embeddings. This enables a direct, semantically consistent comparison, performed through similarity analysis. For each topic, the highest similarity score among all sentences serves as an indicator for that topic coverage within the financial statement. This structured approach measures the extent to which the financial statement aligns with the cybersecurity taxonomy.

[19] For technical details refer to Appendix B.

[20] Embeddings represent each sentence as a high-dimensional vector, encoding semantic information rather than surface-level lexical features.

[21] Hugging Face is a leading open-source platform providing pre-trained machine learning models and libraries for natural language processing, computer vision, and other AI tasks. Through its Model Hub, Hugging Face facilitates the distribution, fine-tuning, and deployment of transformer-based architectures, including the SentenceTransformer models used in this work.

[22] See Sect. 2.1 and Appendix A.

The similarity outcome contributes to the taxonomy vulnerability defensive readiness, which reflects the firm's engagement with cybersecurity-related technologies and process.

For the cyber risk management practices sub-score, we include the components from the *Regulation*, *Certifications*, *Attacks* and *Organisations* categories of the taxonomy to assess firm compliance with regulations, possession of professional certifications, affiliations with national or international organisations and reporting of cyber incidents. These elements are assessed through an ensemble module (grey box) that combines the syntactic module (deep pink box) with the LLM module (pink orange box). The syntactic module analyses the grammatical structure of sentences differentiating between general mentions of the sector of the firm and firm-specific statements. It identifies key relationships (such as subject-verb-object) to extract explicit claims about regulatory compliance, certification possession, organisational affiliation and cyber incident. This structured approach helps minimise false positives that could be associated with the description of a general content. The semantic module and the subsequent LLM prediction module (the two grey boxes in the purple bordered rectangle) result in a probability estimate of the likelihood that a firm meets specific criteria, such as regulatory compliance, certifications, affiliation, or it has suffered a cyberattack. The ensemble module combines these probabilities through a weighted aggregation process that assigns different reliability weights based on the type of information extracted to obtain the cyber risk management practices sub-score.

The taxonomy defensive readiness and cyber risk management practices sub-scores from the financial statement pipeline serve as inputs for calculating the firm's cyber risk index.

Factiva. The Factiva pipeline processes large-scale extractions of Italian press articles to identify cyber risk-related content, complementing the financial statement analysis (green flow). Following the data curation layer, articles mentioning cyber risk are segmented and filtered to retain only those mentioning cyberattacks, based on the *Attacks* taxonomy category.

Once relevant articles are identified, the pipeline employs the prompting module (green box) to instruct the LLM module such that it determines whether the article describes a cyberattack and, if so, to extract the name of the affected company. This LLM-based entity extraction improves accuracy over traditional methods, for example by addressing inconsistencies in company name variations. The LLM subsequent prediction module results in a probability estimate of the likelihood that a firm has suffered a cyberattack.

The sub-score resulting from the Factiva pipeline is another input of the scoring module that calculates the cyber risk index.[23]

[23] If a cyberattack is reported in both Factiva news and the company's balance sheet, it is counted only once to prevent double counting, ensuring an accurate representation of the firm's cyber risk exposure.

Web. The web pipeline is used for the inclusion of web-based sources, and it follows a systematic approach that leverages open-source intelligence (OSINT)[24] to monitor cyber incidents affecting firms. Dedicated websites that track ransomware campaigns, data breaches, and cybersecurity advisories provide a stream of unstructured text, collected through automated scraping techniques. This process ensures comprehensive coverage of publicly disclosed attacks, complementing press news and financial statement analysis. Extracted texts undergo the data curation layer, as in the previous two pipelines.

As in the Factiva pipeline, once the filtering phase is completed, the pipeline employs the prompting module (green box) to instruct the LLM module such that it checks for a given text describing a cyberattack. Also, when applicable, the LLM detects the involved firm, by resolving inconsistencies in naming conventions and recognising company references across different formats. The structured information is then cross-checked against firm registries to ensure consistency, mitigating the risk of erroneous matches. Even in this pipeline the LLM subsequent prediction module results in a probability estimate of the likelihood that a firm has suffered a cyberattack.

The sub-score from the web pipeline is the last input of the scoring module that yields the cyber risk index.[25]

Overall design. We design the AI Architecture with modular flexibility, allowing each component to be independently updated as new advancements in LLMs and NLP techniques become available. Additionally, the underlying taxonomy that supports the risk assessment is built to evolve over time. It allows for the expansion of existing categories and the incorporation of new ones in response to emerging cyber threats and changes in regulatory frameworks. This adaptability ensures that the system remains aligned with the changes of cyber risk and of the regulatory environment, preserving the accuracy of the vulnerability assessment.

2.4 Scoring System

The objective of the proposed methodology is the development of an indicator measuring firms' cyber risk. The indicator leverages the comprehensive set of information extracted through the AI-driven techniques built upon the taxonomy. The taxonomy organises the firm cyber risk profile into six key dimensions, each contributing to the final score through a hierarchical weighting scheme. The

[24] OSINT refers to Open-Source Intelligence, a methodology for collecting and analysing publicly available information from various online sources, including news websites, specialized cybersecurity platforms, social media, and government reports. In the context of cyber risk assessment, OSINT enables the systematic retrieval of data on cyber incidents, regulatory developments, and threat actor activities, supporting the identification of firms affected by cyberattacks.

[25] If a cyberattack is reported in both Factiva news and the company's balance sheet, it is counted only once to prevent double counting, ensuring an accurate representation of the firm's cyber risk exposure.

hierarchical structure allows for appropriate differentiation; for example, general references to cybersecurity processes weigh less than confirmed occurrences of severe cyber incidents.

For topics extracted via semantic similarity within the *Technologies* and *Processes* categories, we assign a sub-score computed as the product between the value associated with the topic—ranging between 1 and 3—and the semantic similarity—ranging between 0 and 1.[26] The contribution of *Regulations, Certifications, Organizations,* and *Attacks* is captured through sub-scores derived from the predictions provided by the LLM. For these four categories we assign a negative value for the topic—ranging between -15 and -8—when a firm discloses a cyberattack, while we attribute positive values—ranging between 1 and 9—for confirmed compliance with regulatory frameworks, possession of cybersecurity certifications, or affiliation with international or national cybersecurity organizations.[27] Unlike the first two categories assessed using semantic similarity, these dimensions do not incorporate similarity values. Instead, they rely on direct binary classifications produced by the LLM, which returns definitive responses concerning the firm's actual possession of a certification, the factual occurrence of a cyberattack, or its formal affiliation with a cybersecurity organisation. This approach reflects the nature of these categories, where the presence or absence of a specific attribute carries distinct meaning and does not require the graded interpretation enabled by semantic similarity. Thus, the final scoring model captures the balance between direct cyber threats and proactive risk mitigation efforts, assigning higher values to firms that exhibit greater vulnerability and lower levels of activities of cyber defence. A firm experiencing multiple attacks over time accumulates negative contributions in the *Attacks* category, as each confirmed incident is recorded individually. This mechanism ensures that repeated attacks to the same firm are reflected in the score as a signal of heightened vulnerability and insufficient mitigation capacity.

As the indicator does not rely on a predefined range, its minimum and maximum values are endogenously determined by the distribution of scores across the

---

[26] This approach ensures that only those topics demonstrating a high degree of alignment with the predefined cybersecurity taxonomy contribute materially to the final score. In this context, similarity is computed using cosine similarity, a measure of the angular distance between two vectors in a high-dimensional space. It estimates how closely the embedding of a sentence aligns with that of a reference topic, independently of their magnitude. The similarity ranges between 0, indicating orthogonality or absence of semantic overlap, and 1, indicating complete alignment in direction and thus maximum semantic correspondence.

[27] The scoring ranges adopted for the six categories of the taxonomy have been calibrated on the basis of their relative contribution to the firm's cybersecurity posture, as emerged from the empirical calibration phase. In this phase, particular attention was paid to preserving a consistent relationship between positive and negative signals within each dimension. The values range from 1 to 6 for regulatory compliance, from 1 to 9 for professional certifications, and from 1 to 3 for technological and procedural topics extracted via semantic similarity. For cyberattacks, scores range between -15 and -8, depending on the severity and specificity of the incident. Lastly, membership in national or international organisations is assigned a positive score between 2 and 4, reflecting their relative reputational and informational value.

sample. Accordingly, a higher score reflects a higher level of cyber risk exposure, signalling weaker alignment with established cybersecurity practices and greater susceptibility to hostile events (see Sect. 3.2 for details on the distribution). This logic is formally expressed as:

$$S_t = \sum\nolimits_{i \in \{Processes, Technologies\}} \sum\nolimits_j P_{ijt}.\sigma_{ijt} + \sum\nolimits_{k \in \{Regulations, Certitifications, Organizations, Attacks\}} \sum\nolimits_j P_{kjt}.1_{\{\mathrm{LLM_{kjt}=True}\}} \quad (1)$$

where S_t denotes the synthetic score at time t, P_{ijt} represents the value of topic j within category i at time t, and σ_{ijt} is the cosine similarity associated with that topic. For the categories *Regulations*, *Certifications*, *Organizations*, and *Attacks*, the identity function activates P_{ijt} only if the LLM prediction returns a positive outcome. To illustrate this mechanism, Appendix E presents a case study for a firm of the Professional Services sector, describing how the cyber risk index evolves in the aftermath of a documented cyber incident.

3 Results

The analysis of cyberattacks affecting firms evaluated under the ICAS framework (Sect. 3.1), together with the examination of the cyber risk index (Sect. 3.2) offers a detailed perspective on the threats that the Italian non-financial firms face. On average, every four days one of the almost 4,000 firms in our sample experiences a cyberattack. The cyber risk index exhibits a significant decline following an attack, reflecting a deterioration in firms' cyber resilience (Sect. 3.2). Furthermore, cybersecurity disclosure in financial statement increases over time (Sect. 3.3) and in the aftermath of a cyber incident (Sect. 3.4), underscoring the adjustments firms make in risk communication and management practices in response to the attacks (Masoud & Al-Utaibi, 2022).

3.1 Awareness of Firms

By combining structured information extracted from financial statements with information gathered from external sources, we identify and classify approximately affecting Italian firms over the period 2019–2024 The number of recorded incidents increases sharply from 14 in 2019 to 232 in 2023, reflecting a marked acceleration in the frequency of cyber events (Table 2).[28] In 2023, the firms in the

[28] As indicated in Table 2, data for 2024 were still incomplete when we carried out the analysis. The overall dataset includes approximately 700 distinct incidents over the 2019–2024 period.

Table 2 Cyberattacks per year

Year	Attacks
2019	14
2020	64
2021	118
2022	143
2023	232
2024	124*

Note *Preliminary financial statements will become available gradually during 2025

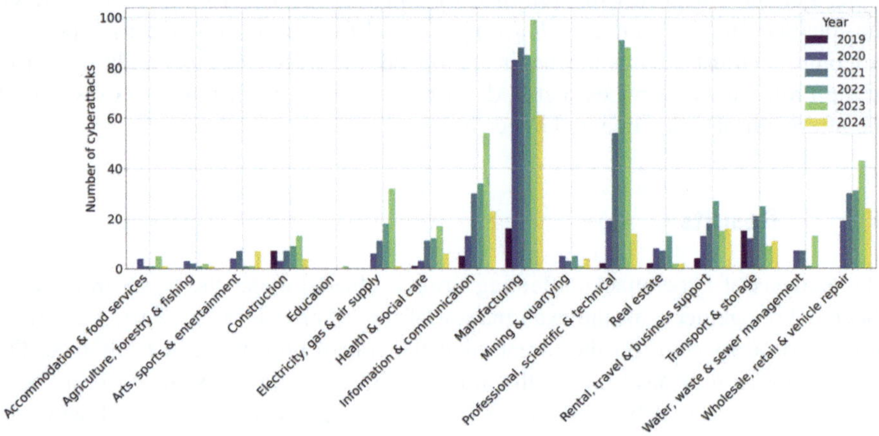

Fig. 2 Cyberattacks across sectors

sample experienced, on average, one cyberattack approximately every two days, underscoring the growing frequency of such incidents.[29]

The distribution of cyberattacks shows substantial heterogeneity in exposure across sectors (Fig. 2).

Manufacturing is the most affected sector, with 416 documented incidents. This pattern reflects the increased digitalisation and interconnection of industrial systems associated with Industry 4.0,[30] which expands the surface of operational technology environments exposed to attacks. This sector also exhibits the strongest growth in cyberattacks (Table 3), with a sharp increase between 2019 and 2020,

[29] This represents a marked acceleration compared to the average over the entire 2019–2024 period, during which one cyberattack was recorded every four days.

[30] Industry 4.0 refers to the ongoing transformation of industrial production through the integration of digital technologies, such as cyber-physical systems, the Internet of Things (IoT), and advanced data analytics, which enable increased automation, interconnectivity and real-time monitoring across manufacturing processes.

followed by a more stable trend. By contrast, in other sectors the growth appears more gradual or concentrated in recent years, suggesting sector-specific patterns in the diffusion of cyber threats. Cyberattacks also grow strongly in the Professional, Scientific and Technical sector consistently with the sector's exposure to risks associated with intellectual property and specialised business services. The pronounced increase in cyberattacks in the Wholesale, Retail and Vehicle Repair sector reflects the vulnerabilities linked to customer data management, extensive supplier networks and reliance on digital payment systems. These findings align with recent evidence provided in national threat intelligence reports (CLUSIT, 2021, 2022, 2023, 2024).

Overall, the cyberattacks across sectors grew in both frequency and intensity with digitalisation acting as a key driver of exposure (Buck et al., 2023). The evidence confirms that cyber risk has evolved into a systemic concern, transcending sectoral boundaries and becoming a core element in firms' risk profiles. Moreover, the distribution of attack types across sectors illustrates how different industries are exposed to specific cyber threats shaped by their operational structure, digital dependencies, and the nature of their data assets (Fig. 3).

Ransomware emerges as the most common threat, and it is more severe in Manufacturing, Professional, Scientific and Technical, and Wholesale, Retail and

Table 3 Growth in cyberattacks (2019–2024, percentage values)

Sector	CAGR*
Accommodation and food services	71
Agriculture, forestry and fishing	–
Arts, sports and entertainment	–
Construction	77
Education	–
Electricity, gas and air supply	44
Financial and insurance	–
Health and social care	68
Information and communication	71
Manufacturing	108
Mining and quarrying	−20
Other services	–
Professional, scientific and technical	105
Real estate	18
Rental, travel and business support	68
Transport and storage	56
Water, waste and sewer management	6
Wholesale, retail and vehicle repair	81

Note *Compound annual growth rate

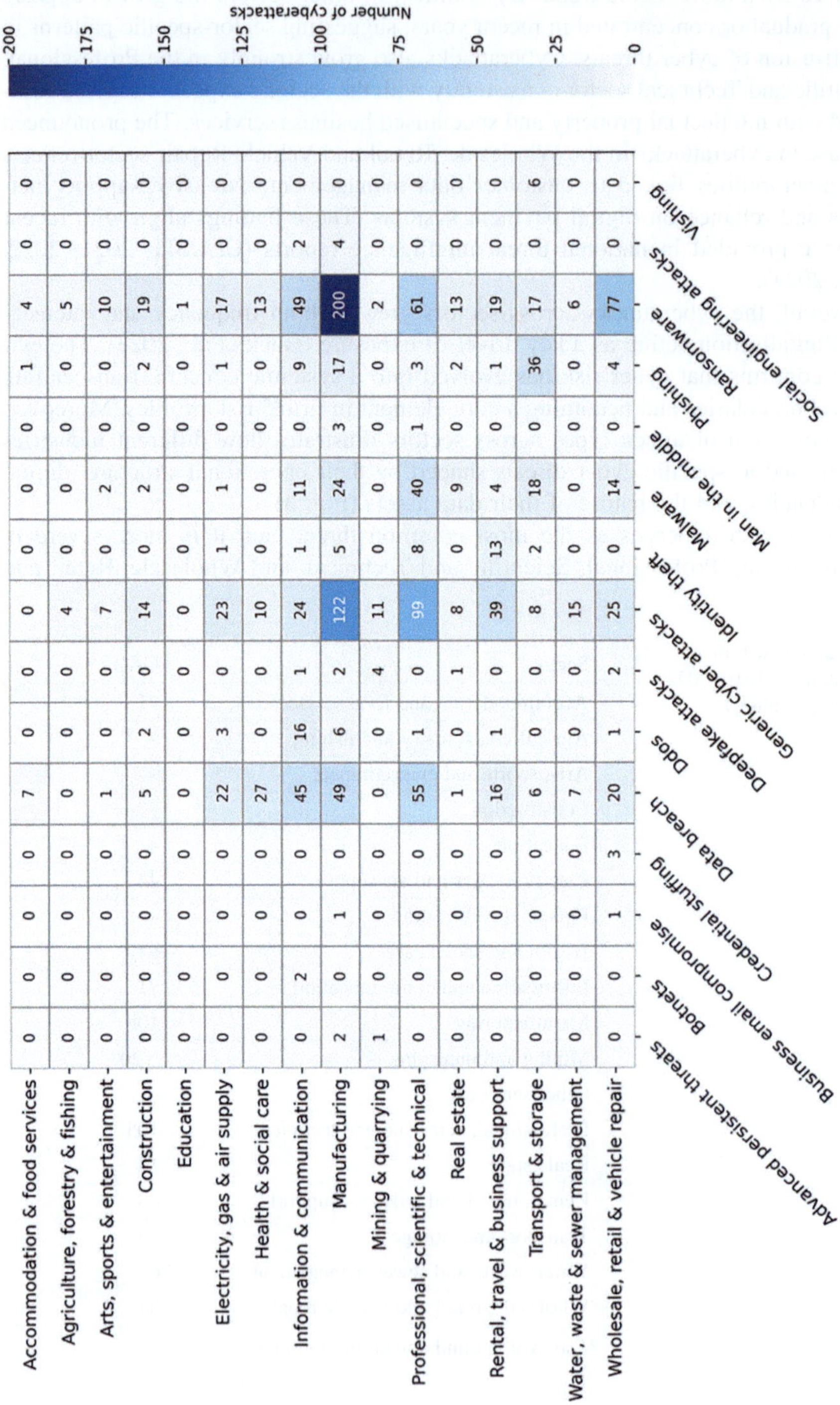

Fig. 3 Cyberattack types by sector

Vehicle repair, where operational disruptions can be swiftly leveraged by attackers for financial gain (CLUSIT, 2024).

Data breaches represent another major typology of attack, indicating attackers' interest in acquiring data for purposes that typically involve financial exploitation, industrial espionage and collection of strategic information on firms' operations, technologies or supply chains. Phishing is prominent in Transport and Storage, Manufacturing, and Information and Communication, pointing to the effectiveness of social engineering techniques in sectors where operational processes depend heavily on human interaction with digital. Malware is detected in Professional, Scientific and Technical Services, Manufacturing, and Wholesale, Retail and Vehicle Repair, underlining its role in breaching systems and spreading within networks. These findings are in line with the 2024 Report on the State of the Cybersecurity in the Union (ENISA, 2024), which identifies these domains among those most frequently targeted by this specific type of cyberattack.

A few advanced persistent threats (APTs) have been reported in Manufacturing and Mining and Quarrying, suggesting that firms in these sectors attract the attention of highly sophisticated entities capable of conducting prolonged, targeted campaigns of threats. Finally, a substantial share of incidents is also classified as generic attacks, reflecting cases in which the information sources analysed did not provide sufficient detail to identify the specific typology of the cyberattack.

3.2 Cyber Risk Index

The methodology outlined in Sect. 2.4 results in the development of a composite cyber risk index for the firms considered in the analysis, scaled between 0 and 100 following the normalization. Firms with scores near zero exhibit low cyber risk exposure, while those with values approaching 100 demonstrate a high vulnerability.

This analysis covers the period from 2020 to 2023. We excluded 2024 due to the incomplete availability of financial statements for that year at the time of the study. We also excluded 2019, since the limited occurrence of cyber incidents in 2019 and the scarcity of relevant information on firms' financial statements for that year could introduce statistical distortions into the temporal comparison, undermining its interpretative consistency. The persistently high values of the cyber risk index since 2020 indicate a structural weakness in firms' cybersecurity posture (Table 4). The average score remains nearly unchanged over the four-year period, slightly declining, from 83 in 2020 to 82 in 2023. This apparent stability, at a high level of risk, might stem from opposing forces: on one side, the increasing intensity and sophistication of cyber threats; on the other, the gradual reinforcement of corporate mitigation strategies, which require time to become effective (ENISA, 2024).

The growth in the standard deviation of the index suggests increasing heterogeneity across firms, which may reflect differences both in exposure to cyber threats and in the capacity to adopt mitigation strategies, such as risk management

Table 4 Cyber risk index[31]

Year	$\bar{x}$	σ	Min	Q_1	$\tilde{x}$	Q_3	Max
2020	83.2	6.9	0.8	83.1	85.3	86.4	96.2
2021	82.9	7.4	3.8	82.8	85.3	86.4	99.0
2022	82.1	8.4	8.5	82.0	85.1	86.2	99.4
2023	82.0	8.4	7.9	81.8	85.1	86.1	97.9

[31] Note: $\bar{x}$ denotes the arithmetic mean; σ is the standard deviation; min and max indicate the minimum and maximum values; Q_1, $\tilde{x}$, and Q_3 represent the first quartile, median, and third quartile, respectively.

practices, technological investments, or governance integration. Additional distributional indicators confirm the persistence of widespread exposure. The median value remains stable around 85, and the first and third quartiles shift only slightly, indicating that the overall structure of the distribution is largely unchanged. The interquartile range remains narrow, pointing to a persistent concentration of firms in the upper segment of the risk scale. At the extremes, the minimum score increases from below one to eight, while the maximum remains close to 100 across all years. These figures suggest that while a marginal share of firms may have improved their posture, significant disparities in cybersecurity readiness appear to persist.

The distribution of the cyber risk index over the period 2020–2023 indicates a concentration of firms at the higher end of the risk scale (Fig. 4). Most observations fall between 80 and 90, suggesting that a large share of firms remains highly vulnerable to cyber threats. Although the median exceeds 85 throughout the period, the distribution shows signs of slight flattening and widening, particularly in the lower tail, which suggests a growing heterogeneity in cyber risk exposure.

This pattern could reflect structural challenges that firms may face in achieving and maintaining cyber resilience. Despite growing regulatory requirements and the broader adoptions of certifications and defensive technologies, a notable portion of the Italian non-financial firms appears to remain highly exposed. While some firms may be strengthening their cybersecurity posture, others may still lack the capabilities or incentives to mitigate their vulnerability. Consequently, the aggregate risk profile seems to show limited signs of improvement over time. These

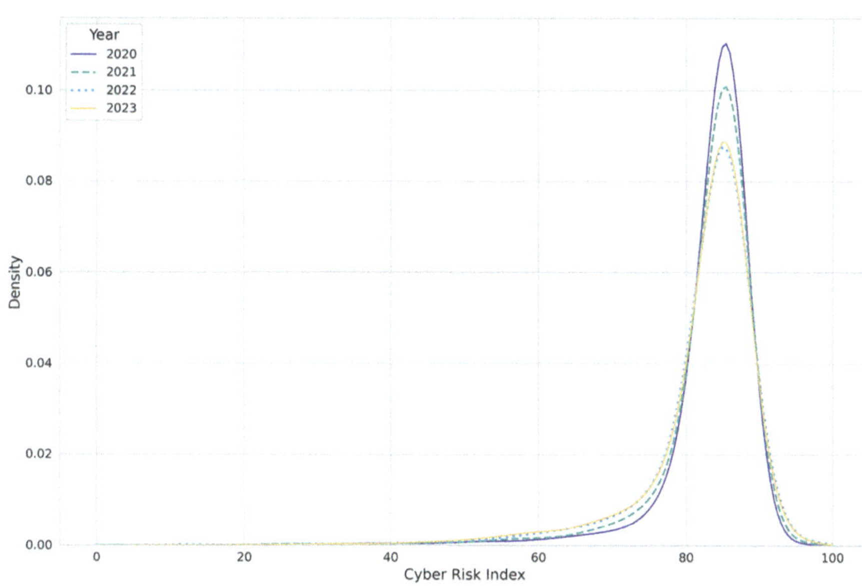

Fig. 4 Cyber risk index distribution

findings may point to the need for targeted policy actions and a more effective allocation of resources to support firms persistently lagging in preparedness, as their vulnerability could represent fault lines in the cyber resilience framework.

3.3 Semantic Space Dynamics

The classification of semantic topics performed by the AI models yields structured insights within the categories *Technologies* and *Processes*, capturing the growing attention toward cybersecurity risk in the financial statements of ICAS firms. The analysis of the 2020–2023 period displays a notable expansion in both the breadth and depth of topic coverage within financial statements. In this context, breadth refers to the number of distinct topics addressed, while depth captures the semantic intensity and recurrence of each topic. These dimensions are visually represented in the *Processes* category radar plot (Fig. 5): the radial extent across topics indicates breadth, whereas the surface area enclosed by each yearly trace reflects the depth of disclosure. Within this category, there is emphasis on the governance of IT risk, indicating the firms' efforts to manage cyber threats.

The prominence of threat intelligence, that is the systematic collection and analysis of information about cyber threats, further reflects the shift towards a proactive security posture, with firms increasingly investing in anticipatory measures to detect and mitigate risks. Additionally, the importance of data privacy

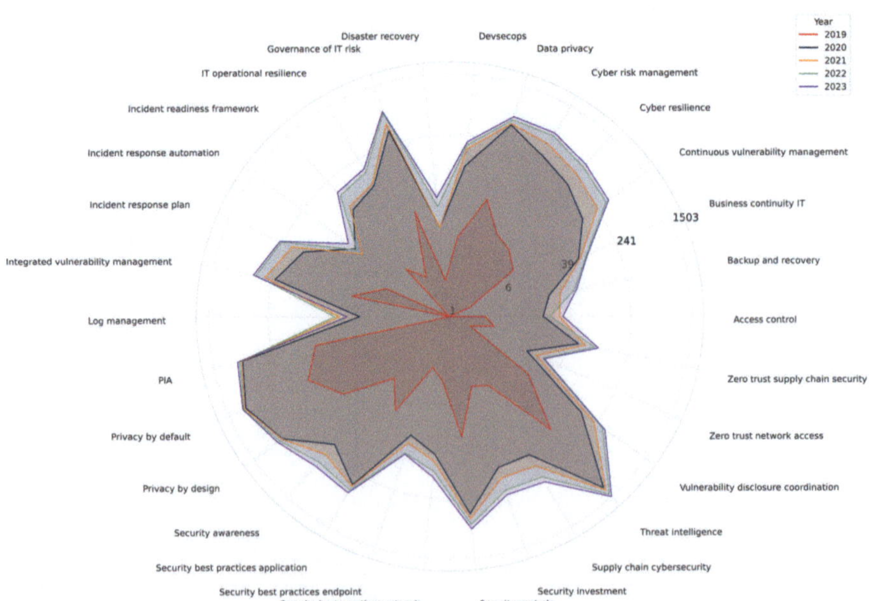

Fig. 5 Semantic coverage in processes

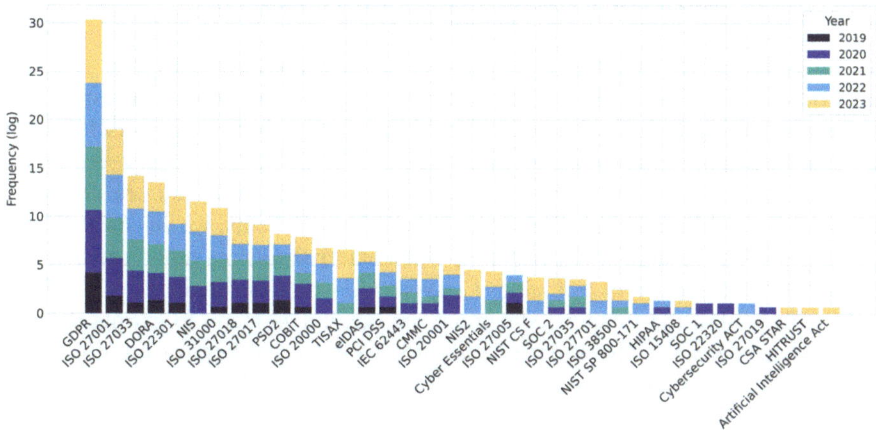

Fig. 6 Regulation and standards across firms[32]

topics indicates the growing importance of regulatory compliance, particularly in response to GDPR obligations, and signals the integration of data protection principles into the broader corporate risk management framework. This trend mirrors external regulatory and societal pressures that are encouraging firms to move beyond reactive measures and adopt more systematic and embedded cybersecurity strategies.

Overall, the presence and diversification of these topics within financial statements indicate that companies are progressively institutionalising cybersecurity governance, transitioning from ad hoc responses to comprehensive and anticipatory risk management practices. Moreover, the granularity and consistency of semantic extraction confirm the capability of structured information retrieval to track the evolution of corporate cybersecurity maturity and sophistication. A parallel trend is observed within the *Technologies* category, as shown in Appendix C.

The trends in *Regulations* further reinforce this trajectory, with financial statement disclosures indicating a steady increase in compliance with international standards (Fig. 6).

The dominance of GDPR and ISO 27001 within *Regulations* reflects the pervasive impact of privacy and information security requirements on corporate governance. These frameworks have become key reference points for firms aiming to strengthen their resilience and meet regulatory obligations. The trends of categories *Certifications* and *Organizations* are reported in Appendix C.

[32] For a detailed definition of regulations and standards, as well as professional certifications, see the taxonomy outlined in Appendix A.

3.4 Pre and Post Cyberattack: What Happens?

The analysis further investigates the causal relationship between cyber incidents and firms' cybersecurity posture by assessing whether an attack corresponds to measurable changes in both the predicted level of cybersecurity disclosure in financial statements and the cyber risk index.

By integrating data from external sources, including web sources and press releases, with information extracted from financial statements, we can establish the timing of each cyberattack. For instance, when external sources report the incident, the date of occurrence is available. Conversely, when the incident is disclosed exclusively within the financial statement, no attempt is made to extract the date of occurrence; instead, the event is attributed to the fiscal year of the document. This approach enables the construction of a timeline, facilitating the comparison between the content of the financial statements preceding the attack and those corresponding to the subsequent reporting period.

Financial statement disclosure We test whether firms identified as victims of cyberattacks exhibit a significant improvement in cybersecurity disclosure within their financial statements following the incident. We try to assess whether the experience of a cyberattack prompts firms to enhance the transparency and depth of their reporting on cybersecurity practices, governance measures, and risk mitigation efforts. To measure the extent to which the volume and diversity of cybersecurity-related content increases following a cyberattack, we perform a statistical test. It assesses whether, after a cyberattack, there is an increase in the volume of cybersecurity-related content disclosed (total number of identified elements) and its diversity (number of distinct taxonomy concepts), as captured through topic-based analysis and large language model classifications. Positive classifications by the LLM correspond either to explicit references to compliance with recognised standards within regulations or to the documented possession of certifications. The results of the statistical tests indicate a significant and systematic increase in both the total and distinct cybersecurity-related content disclosed after the attack. The Mann–Whitney U test confirms the robustness of this result, showing that firms, once affected by a cyber-incident, tend to enrich the content of their financial statements with a broader set of cybersecurity-related elements (Table 5).

We extend the same statistical tests to the individual categories of the taxonomy to assess whether the observed increase in cybersecurity-related content is uniformly distributed or concentrated in specific areas (Table 6).

We find that the occurrence of a cyberattack is associated with an increase in the number of references within *Regulations*, *Certifications*, *Technologies*, *Processes*,

Table 5 Statistical tests on the increase in cybersecurity content after a cyberattack

Taxonomy	Measure	Mann–Whitney U (p value)
Topic + LLM	Total	2.30E−11
Topic + LLM	Distinct	2.10E−10

Table 6 Statistical tests on the increase in cybersecurity content after a cyberattack (by taxonomy category)

Taxonomy	Measure	Mann–Whitney U (p value)
Regulations (LLM)	Total	1.55E−08
Regulations (LLM)	Distinct	4.40E−05
Certifications (LLM)	Total	1.51E−04
Certifications (LLM)	Distinct	1.15E−04
Technologies (topic)	Total	6.12E−12
Technologies (topic)	Distinct	2.04E−11
Processes (topic)	Total	3.06E−11
Processes (topic)	Distinct	4.37E−10
Attacks (LLM)	Total	2.63E−15
Attacks (LLM)	Distinct	8.39E−15
Organizations (LLM)	Total	1.59E−01
Organizations (LLM)	Distinct	1.76E−01

and *Attacks* categories. This pattern suggests that firms respond to incidents not only by strengthening their technological and procedural defences, but also by formalising their compliance with recognised standards and acquiring certifications that demonstrate the adoption of enhanced security practices.

The increase in references to cyberattacks within financial statements confirms that firms disclose past incidents, either with risk disclosure sections or under corporate governance and risk management framework. Conversely, no increase emerges with respect to *affiliations* category. This indicates that, although firms demonstrate growing awareness of cybersecurity risks, they do not systematically strengthen or emphasize their institutional ties with external organizations active in the field. This outcome may reflect the discretionary nature of such affiliations, which are not uniformly perceived as critical to risk mitigation strategies and are often underreported or omitted from formal financial disclosures.

Cyber risk index We compare the cyber risk index in the year of the attack—when the incident has occurred but is not yet documented in the firm's financial statement—with the index in the following year, when the related information is expected to appear in the financial statements. This approach ensures that the temporal window of observation of the cyber risk aligns with that of the credit risk in ICAS, which is set at twelve months.

The cyber risk index exhibits a systematic increase after an attack with a 99% confidence level.[33] The observed increase in the cyber risk index following a cyberattack reflects how such event is captured and weighted within the scoring

[33] We perform the Mann–Whitney U statistical test (p value 3.09E−08). The test remains reliable when the normality assumption for the underlying distribution does not hold, as in the case of the cyber risk index.

model. Specifically, the disclosure of a cyber incident in the financial statement triggers a direct penalty in the *Attacks* category, which contributes negatively to the overall index. This effect is both immediate and substantial, given that an actual incident is treated as a concrete signal of heightened vulnerability.

As discussed earlier, statistical tests on the post-attack financial statements reveal a significant increase in the volume and diversity of cybersecurity-related disclosures, indicating that many firms increase their attention to cybersecurity following an incident. However, at the aggregate level, the additional cybersecurity-related content detected—such as references to technologies, processes, or compliance—does not offset the negative contribution associated with the attack itself.[34] As a result, the index tends to rise, reflecting the predominance of the signals of exposure relative to the mitigating elements identified in the same reporting window. This mechanism is illustrated in Appendix E through a case study in which the index increases following a cyberattack, despite the continued presence of relevant cybersecurity practices. The example shows how the post-incident penalty is only partially offset by the defensive actions implemented after the attack, and that observable improvements in cyber resilience tend to emerge gradually over a longer time horizon.

4 Conclusions

This Chapter builds a cyber risk index for Italian non-financial firms based on advanced AI analysis of unstructured data, such as financial statements, corporate cybersecurity communications, and news. By defining a taxonomy of cyber risk areas and constructing a scoring system, we obtain a firm-level indicator that captures cyber risk vulnerability, based on incident reporting in financial statements and news, technical defensive measures, compliance with regulatory and industry standards, and affiliation with international organisations. This Chapter thus addresses dimensions of cyber risk that have so far not been considered within a unified methodological framework, particularly for Italian firms. Existing contributions in the literature either do not employ a taxonomy or they rely on limited ones that are not suited for the Italian case.

We document a sharp increase in the incidence of cyberattacks on non-financial firms since 2019. The Manufacturing sector exhibits the most pronounced acceleration, with a marked rise in cyberattack frequency between 2019 and 2020,

[34] The taxonomy includes five categories that contribute positively to the score when evidence of a cybersecurity related activity is detected: *Technologies, Processes, Regulations, Certifications, and Organizations*. These categories reflect the presence of mitigating elements such as security systems, risk governance practices, compliance with regulatory frameworks, and professional preparedness. Conversely, only one category—*Attacks*—introduces a direct negative contribution to the index, associated with the confirmed disclosure of a cyber incident. The net variation in the index thus depends on whether the positive signals outweigh the penalisation introduced by the attack.

followed by a more stable trajectory in subsequent years. Sectors such as Professional, Scientific and Technical Services and Wholesale, Retail Trade, and Motor Vehicle Repair display a gradual increase or a concentration of attacks in more recent years. These patterns point to sector-specific dynamics in the evolution and diffusion of cyber threats.

The cyber risk index significantly increases following a cyberattack, reflecting the immediate recognition of the incident as a signal of heightened vulnerability, that outweighs the mitigating effects of any defensive actions implemented in the aftermath of the attack. We observe, though, an increase in the volume and detail of cybersecurity-related disclosures in the aftermath of an attack, suggesting that firms tend to enhance transparency and reporting on defensive measures once a breach has occurred.

The frequency of the incidents and the potential losses reveal the need for a systematic monitoring of firms' vulnerabilities to integrate cyber risk into credit evaluations. Indeed, cyber incidents can have material consequences for credit risk, as they may disrupt operations, impair cash flows, and trigger reputational or legal costs, often resulting in significant financial losses. The proposed vulnerability indicator may be employed to assess the impact of cyber risk on the PD estimates within the ICAS framework. Therefore, future developments will include the integration of the cyber risk index and a cyber risk–adjusted PD into the set of early warning indicators monitored by analysts as part of the expert assessment module of ICAS.

Appendix A

Taxonomy

Tables 7, 8, 9, 10, 11, 12 provide a comprehensive representation of the taxonomy developed for the classification and analysis of cyber risk across six distinct categories. Each category encompasses a set of items, reflecting the semantic space relevant to firms' cyber exposure and preparedness. The taxonomy has been constructed through a process combining the outcome of a review of the literature and of the pertinent regulatory frameworks with an analysis of corporate financial statements, examining disclosures related to cyber risk management, technology investments, regulatory compliance, and reported incidents.

This iterative approach has ensured the alignment between the conceptual structure of the taxonomy and the expressions commonly found in firms' financial disclosures, particularly those referring to cybersecurity certifications, compliance with regulations, and incident reporting. Each item within the tables is accompanied by a brief description. The appendix thus serves as a reference point, offering a transparent view of the classification logic underpinning the topic detection and similarity assessment methodologies applied in the study.

Table 7 Regulation and standards

Item	Description	Significance
Artificial Intelligence Act	EU regulation ensuring the safe and transparent use of artificial intelligence technologies	Important
BSI IT Grundschutz	German framework for IT security providing comprehensive guidelines for risk management and protection	Peripheral
CCRP	Certified Cyber Resilience Professional certification specialized in organisational cyber resilience	Important
CMMC	Cybersecurity Maturity Model Certification framework for assessing cybersecurity practices	Important
COBIT	Control Objectives for Information and Related Technologies framework for IT governance and management	Important
CSA CCM	Cloud Security Alliance Cloud Controls Matrix, a framework for cloud security controls	Important
CSA STAR	Cloud Security Alliance Security, Trust and Assurance Registry certification for cloud service providers	Peripheral
Cyber essentials	UK certification scheme defining basic cybersecurity controls for organisations	Peripheral
Cybersecurity Act	EU regulation enhancing cybersecurity across the Digital Single Market through certification schemes	Important
DORA	Digital Operational Resilience Act, ensuring the financial sector's ICT risk management and operational resilience	Core
Cyber Hygiene	Italian regulation introducing mandatory cyber hygiene measures for critical infrastructure operators	Important
EU Cyber Resilience Act	EU regulation ensuring the cybersecurity of digital products and connected devices	Core
FISMA	Federal Information Security Management Act defining US federal information security standards	Important
GDPR	General Data Protection Regulation, setting requirements for personal data protection across the EU	Core
HIPAA	Health Insurance Portability and Accountability Act, regulating health data privacy and security in the US	Important
HITRUST	Common Security Framework providing a certifiable security framework for healthcare and other industries	Important
IEC 62443	International standard for cybersecurity of industrial automation and control systems	Core
ISO 20000	International standard for IT service management systems	Peripheral
ISO 22237	Standard defining requirements for data centres' design and operation	Important
ISO 22301	Standard for business continuity management systems	Core
ISO 22320	Standard for emergency management and incident response	Important

(continued)

Table 7 (continued)

Item	Description	Significance
ISO 27001	Widely adopted standard for information security management systems	Core
ISO 27002	Code of practice for information security controls	Important
ISO 27005	Standard providing guidelines for information security risk management	Important
ISO 27017	Guidelines for information security controls specifically for cloud services	Important
ISO 27018	Code of practice for protecting personal data in the cloud	Core
ISO 27019	Guidelines for information security management in the energy sector	Core
ISO 27035	Standard for information security incident management	Important
ISO 27701	Standard for privacy information management systems	Core
ISO 29100	Privacy framework providing guidelines for information privacy	Important
ISO 31000	International standard for risk management principles and guidelines	Peripheral
ISO 27003	Guidance on the implementation of information security management systems	Important
ISO 27004	Guidance on monitoring, measurement, analysis and evaluation of ISMS	Important
ISO 27033	Guidance on network security	Important
ISO 27034	Guidelines for application security	Important
ISO 27036	Guidance for security of supplier relationships	Peripheral
ISO 27037	Guidelines for digital evidence collection	Important
ISO 27038	Guidelines for digital redaction and anonymization	Important
ISO 27039	Guidelines for intrusion detection and prevention systems	Core
ISO 27040	Guidance for storage security	Important
ISO 27050	Guidelines for electronic discovery processes	Peripheral
ISO 15408	Common Criteria standard for IT security evaluation	Important
ISO 21878	Guidelines for crisis management	Important

(continued)

Table 7 (continued)

Item	Description	Significance
ISO 38500	Guidance for IT governance	Peripheral
ISO 42001	AI management system standard for ensuring trustworthy AI	Core
ISO 24762	Guidance for disaster recovery services	Important
NERC CIP	Standards for securing bulk electric systems in North America	Core
NIS	EU Network and Information Systems Directive setting cybersecurity requirements for critical operators	Core
NIS2	Revised NIS Directive expanding the scope and obligations for cybersecurity across the EU	Core
NIST CS F	NIST Cybersecurity Framework providing voluntary guidelines for managing cyber risks	Core
NIST SP 800-30	NIST guide for conducting risk assessments	Core
NIST SP 800-37	NIST Risk Management Framework for system lifecycle security	Core
NIST SP 800-53	Security and privacy controls for US federal information systems	Core
NIST SP 800-171	Guidelines for protecting controlled unclassified information in non-federal systems	Core
PCI DSS	Payment Card Industry Data Security Standard for protecting payment card data	Core
PSD2	Revised EU Payment Services Directive enhancing payment security and consumer rights	Important
SOC 1	Audit standard addressing financial reporting controls	Important
SOC 2	Audit standard addressing information security controls	Core
SWIFT CSP	SWIFT Customer Security Programme ensuring secure financial messaging	Important
TISAX	Certification scheme for information security in the automotive industry	Important
eIDAS	EU regulation on electronic identification and trust services	Peripheral

Table 8 Professional certifications

Item	Description	Significance
CISSP	Certified Information Systems Security Professional, globally recognised certification validating comprehensive cybersecurity expertise across multiple domains	Core
CISM	Certified Information Security Manager, certification concerned with information risk management, governance, and oversight of enterprise-wide security programs	Core
CEH	Certified Ethical Hacker, validating hands-on ethical hacking and penetration testing skills, preparing professionals to identify and mitigate vulnerabilities	Important
CISA	Certified Information Systems Auditor, addressing competencies in auditing, controlling, and assuring information systems, centered on covering governance and compliance	Core
OSCP	Offensive Security Certified Professional, renowned technical certification requiring hands-on demonstration of advanced penetration testing techniques	Core
GIAC GSEC	GIAC Security Essentials Certification, validating practical skills in identifying and preventing common cybersecurity threats	Important
CCSP	Certified Cloud Security Professional, addressing security architecture, governance, and risk management in cloud environments	Core
CRISC	Certified in Risk and Information Systems Control, aimed at identifying and managing IT and enterprise risk with an emphasis on control frameworks	Important
CIPP	Certified Information Privacy Professional, covering global privacy laws, regulatory frameworks, and organisational data protection strategies	Important
GIAC GPEN	GIAC Penetration Tester Certification, validating advanced penetration testing techniques for identifying and exploiting vulnerabilities	Core
GIAC GCIH	GIAC Certified Incident Handler, covering processes and methodologies for managing and responding to security incidents	Core
CDPSE	Certified Data Privacy Solutions Engineer, focusing on integrating privacy into technology platforms and systems by design	Important

(continued)

Table 8 (continued)

Item	Description	Significance
CCISO	Certified Chief Information Security Officer, designed for executive-level professionals overseeing information security strategies and governance	Core
ISO 27001 Lead Auditor	Certification for professionals conducting audits of information security management systems based on the ISO 27001 standard	Core
CHFI	Computer Hacking Forensic Investigator, addressing digital forensics techniques to investigate and analyse cyber incidents	Important
ECIH	EC-Council Certified Incident Handler, dealing with structured incident response processes and containment strategies	Important
CASP+	CompTIA Advanced Security Practitioner, validating advanced technical skills required for enterprise-level cybersecurity roles	Important
CIPT	Certified Information Privacy Technologist, aimed at embedding privacy into IT infrastructure, applications, and business processes	Peripheral
CGEIT	Certified in the Governance of Enterprise IT, assessing knowledge of IT governance frameworks and strategic alignment with business goals	Peripheral
GSLC	GIAC Security Leadership Certification, with an emphasis on security program management, governance, and risk oversight at the organisational level	Peripheral
CSSA	Certified SCADA Security Architect, validating knowledge of securing industrial control systems and SCADA environments	Core
CICP	Certified Industrial Cybersecurity Professional, addressing specific cybersecurity challenges for operational technology and industrial networks	Important
IoT SFC	IoT Security Foundation Certified, focusing on identifying and mitigating security risks in Internet of Things ecosystems	Important
ICS SCADA Security	Certifications dedicated to securing industrial control systems, addressing threats to critical infrastructure	Important

(continued)

Table 8 (continued)

Item	Description	Significance
HCS	Healthcare Cybersecurity Specialist, designed for professionals managing cybersecurity in healthcare environments	Important
CCRM	Certified Cybersecurity Risk Manager, addressing proactive identification, analysis, and mitigation of cybersecurity risks at the enterprise level	Important
CQSP	Certified Quantum Security Practitioner, addressing cybersecurity risks associated with quantum computing and post-quantum cryptography	Important
ACSP	Advanced Cloud Security Professional, validating skills in securing complex multi-cloud environments and distributed cloud infrastructure	Important
CRRE	Certified Ransomware Recovery Expert, addressing recovery strategies, backup management, and incident response for ransomware attacks	Important
CAIDS	Certified AI Defence Specialist, designed for professionals addressing cybersecurity risks posed by artificial intelligence systems	Important
GIAC GRID	GIAC Response and Industrial Defence, oriented towards incident response and threat management for industrial control environments	Core
IEC 62443 Expert	Certification validating expertise in applying IEC 62443 standards for industrial automation and control system security	Core
DPO	Data Protection Officer Certification, addressing the regulatory role and responsibilities of the DPO under GDPR and other privacy laws	Important
CCSK	Certificate of Cloud Security Knowledge, providing a foundational understanding of cloud security principles and best practices	Important
GCSA	GIAC Cloud Security Automation, targeted at automating security operations in cloud environments to enhance agility and responsiveness	Important
PCIP	PCI Professional, validating expertise in implementing and maintaining compliance with Payment Card Industry Data Security Standards	Important

(continued)

Table 8 (continued)

Item	Description	Significance
MAD	MITRE ATT&CK Defender, focusing on threat hunting, detection, and adversary emulation using the MITRE ATT&CK framework	Important
CAMS	Certified AI and Machine Learning Security Expert, addressing security implications and risk management for AI and machine learning systems	Core

Table 9 Technologies and systems

Item	Description	Significance
AI driven threat detection	AI-powered platforms capable of continuously analysing vast data streams to identify emerging cyber threats through advanced pattern recognition	Important
AI incident response	Automated incident response systems leveraging artificial intelligence to accelerate the detection, analysis, and containment of security incidents	Core
AI powered phishing protection	Advanced phishing protection solutions using AI to analyse email content, detect malicious intent, and block phishing attempts in real time	Important
Antivirus	Software designed to monitor, detect, and remove known malware threats across endpoints and servers, providing a foundational layer of defence	Peripheral
Behavioral analytics	Technology applying machine learning to baseline user behaviour and detect deviations indicative of insider threats or account compromises	Peripheral
Blockchain security	Security techniques applying blockchain's decentralised architecture to ensure data integrity, transaction transparency, and resistance to tampering	Peripheral
Cloud security	Comprehensive set of policies, controls, and technologies designed to protect data, applications, and infrastructure in cloud environments	Important
Cyber threat intelligence	Structured process of gathering, analysing, and interpreting threat data from diverse sources to proactively anticipate and mitigate cyberattacks	Important
DPI	Deep Packet Inspection technologies capable of analysing network traffic at a granular level to detect malicious activity within legitimate communications	Important
Data loss prevention	Technologies that monitor, detect, and prevent the unauthorised movement or disclosure of sensitive data both inside and outside the organisation	Peripheral
Deepfake detection AI	AI-powered solutions designed to detect synthetic media generated by deep learning techniques, often used in disinformation campaigns or fraud	Peripheral

(continued)

Table 9 (continued)

Item	Description	Significance
Digital forensics technology	Specialized tools for preserving, analysing, and reconstructing digital evidence following security incidents or breaches	Important
Email security	Solutions providing protection against phishing, spoofing, and malware delivered through email channels, including advanced filtering and encryption	Peripheral
Encryption	Techniques and protocols ensuring data confidentiality and integrity through encoding, both at rest and in transit, using cryptographic algorithms	Core
Endpoint security	Comprehensive security measures applied at endpoint devices to protect against malware, unauthorised access, and exploitation	Important
Firewall	Network security system designed to monitor, filter, and control incoming and outgoing network traffic based on predetermined security rules	Peripheral
ITDR	Identity Threat Detection and Response platforms that monitor identity-based attacks and anomalous behaviours to detect and block account compromises	Important
Identity and access management	Integrated systems for managing user identities and access rights, ensuring that only authorised individuals access specific resources	Core
Industrial control system security	Specialized security measures protecting industrial control systems and operational technology environments from cyber threats	Core
Intrusion Detection System	Network or host-based systems that monitor and detect signs of unauthorised or malicious activity within IT environments	Important
Intrusion prevention System	Advanced systems combining detection capabilities with automatic threat blocking to prevent identified attacks from succeeding	Important
Multi factor authentication	Authentication approach requiring users to provide multiple credentials (e.g., password and token) to verify their identity	Core

(continued)

Table 9 (continued)

Item	Description	Significance
Network security	Comprehensive framework of technologies and policies safeguarding the organisation's network infrastructure against internal and external threats	Important
SOC	Modern Security Operations Centre equipped with automation, threat intelligence, and machine learning to enhance detection and response	Core
OT Security	Security controls and technologies protecting operational technology systems used in industrial environments, distinct from traditional IT security	Core
Patch management	Systematic process of distributing and applying software updates to close security vulnerabilities and improve system resilience	Peripheral
Penetration testing	Authorised simulated attacks conducted to evaluate the security of systems and identify vulnerabilities before they are exploited	Important
Quantum cryptography	Emerging cryptographic methods using quantum mechanics to secure data transmission and protect against computational attacks	Core
Quantum resistant encryption	Cryptographic algorithms designed to resist future decryption capabilities of quantum computers, ensuring long-term data security	Core
SASE	Secure Access Service Edge framework combining network security and wide-area networking capabilities into a unified cloud-delivered service	Peripheral
SCADA security	Specialized cybersecurity measures tailored to protect Supervisory Control and Data Acquisition systems used in industrial automation	Core
SIEM	Security Information and Event Management platforms aggregating logs and event data to provide centralised visibility and threat detection	Core
Smart mobility security	Security solutions designed to protect connected and autonomous vehicles, intelligent transport systems, and supporting infrastructure	Peripheral
Threat detection and response	Comprehensive capabilities for identifying, analysing, and mitigating cyber threats across multiple layers of IT infrastructure	Important

(continued)

Table 9 (continued)

Item	Description	Significance
Threat deception	Deception technologies deploying fake assets and traps to lure attackers, detect their presence, and gather intelligence on attack techniques	Peripheral
Threat hunting	Proactive search activities performed by security analysts to identify undetected threats lurking within the organisation's systems	Important
Virtual patching	Temporary security controls applied at network or application layers to block exploitation of vulnerabilities before patches are applied	Important
Vulnerability assessment	Systematic process of scanning and analysing IT assets to identify security weaknesses, rank their severity, and recommend remediation	Peripheral
Web application firewall	Security solution monitoring and filtering HTTP traffic to and from web applications, protecting against web-based attacks	Important
XDR	Extended Detection and Response platform integrating multiple security products to provide holistic detection and response across environments	Core
Zero trust	Security model assuming no implicit trust, requiring continuous verification of users, devices, and systems attempting to access resources	Core

Table 10 Processes and management strategies

Item	Description	Significance
Access control	Processes ensuring only authorised individuals can access systems and data based on clearly defined permissions	Important
Backup and recovery	Structured processes ensuring regular data backups and the ability to restore operations after a cyberattack	Important
Business continuity IT	Plans and processes ensuring critical IT services remain operational during and after disruptive cyber events	Important
Continuous vulnerability management	Ongoing identification, assessment, and remediation of vulnerabilities across systems and applications	Important
Cyber resilience	Holistic strategies ensuring organisations can anticipate, withstand, and recover from cyberattacks with minimal disruption	Core
Cyber risk management	Formalised processes for identifying, assessing, mitigating, and monitoring cyber risks within the organisation	Important
Data privacy	Policies and processes ensuring personal and sensitive data are collected, processed, and stored in compliance with regulations	Core
DevSecOps	Integration of security practices into the entire software development lifecycle, ensuring security is considered from design to deployment	Important
Disaster recovery	Technical and procedural strategies ensuring rapid restoration of IT systems after a major cyber incident or disaster	Peripheral
Governance of IT risk	Framework for defining, overseeing, and continuously improving how IT and cyber risks are managed across the organisation	Important
Incident readiness framework	Comprehensive set of policies, tools, and processes ensuring the organisation is prepared to handle cyber incidents	Important
Incident response automation	Automation of incident response workflows to accelerate containment, investigation, and recovery processes	Important

(continued)

Table 10 (continued)

Item	Description	Significance
Incident response plan	Documented process outlining the steps, roles, and tools needed to effectively respond to cybersecurity incidents	Core
Integrated vulnerability management	Consolidated approach combining asset discovery, vulnerability scanning, risk prioritisation, and remediation tracking	Important
Log management	Centralised collection, storage, and analysis of security logs to support monitoring, investigation, and compliance	Peripheral
PIA	Privacy Impact Assessments evaluating the potential privacy risks of new projects, processes, or systems	Peripheral
Privacy by default	Design principle ensuring data protection measures are applied automatically without requiring user action	Peripheral
Privacy by design	Embedding privacy considerations into systems and processes from the earliest stages of development	Peripheral
Operational IT resilience	Processes ensuring IT systems can maintain essential functions under adverse cyber conditions	Peripheral
Security awareness	Ongoing education and training programs aimed at enhancing employees' understanding of cyber risks and best practices	Peripheral
Security best practices application	Adoption of proven security methodologies across software development and system operations	Peripheral
Security best practices endpoint	Implementation of recommended security configurations and practices for endpoint devices	Peripheral
Security best practices network	Enforcement of security policies and controls to protect network infrastructure and data flows	Peripheral
Security controls	Collection of administrative, technical, and physical safeguards to protect organisational assets	Peripheral
Security investment	Structured processes for budgeting and prioritising cybersecurity investments aligned with risk exposure	Important
Supply chain cybersecurity	Processes ensuring third-party vendors and service providers comply with cybersecurity standards	Important
Threat intelligence	Structured process for gathering and analysing information about current and emerging cyber threats	Important

(continued)

Table 10 (continued)

Item	Description	Significance
Vulnerability disclosure coordination	Processes enabling external researchers to responsibly report discovered vulnerabilities	Important
Zero trust network access	Access model requiring continuous verification of user identity, device posture, and application context	Core
Zero trust supply chain security	Extension of zero trust principles to ensure the integrity of supply chain partners and service providers	Core

Table 11 Types of cyberattacks

Item	Description	Significance
Advanced Persistent Threat	Long-term, covert cyber operations conducted by well-resourced adversaries, often state-sponsored, aiming to infiltrate networks and maintain persistent access for intelligence gathering or sabotage	Core
AI disinformation campaigns	Coordinated efforts using AI-generated content to spread false information, influence public opinion, or destabilise organisations or governments	Important
AI manipulation attacks	Exploiting vulnerabilities in AI algorithms to manipulate outputs, bypass security controls, or influence automated decision-making processes	Important
AI powered cyberattacks	Cyberattacks enhanced by artificial intelligence, using machine learning to automate target selection, craft personalised phishing messages, or evade detection systems	Core
BLE spoofing	Exploiting weaknesses in Bluetooth Low Energy protocols to impersonate devices, intercept data, or manipulate device behaviour	Peripheral
Blockchain exploits	Exploiting vulnerabilities in blockchain protocols, smart contracts, or consensus mechanisms to manipulate transactions or steal assets	Peripheral
Bluetooth attacks	Exploiting vulnerabilities in Bluetooth protocols to intercept communications, inject malicious commands, or gain unauthorised access to devices	Peripheral
Botnets	Networks of compromised devices remotely controlled by attackers to conduct large-scale malicious operations such as spam distribution, credential attacks, or DDoS campaigns	Important
Business email compromise	A targeted cyberattack where attackers gain access to or impersonate corporate email accounts to deceive employees into transferring funds or disclosing sensitive data	Core
Cloud API exploitation	Attacks targeting insecure or exposed cloud service APIs to gain unauthorised access to data, manipulate services, or disrupt operations	Important
Cloud misconfiguration exploits	Attacks exploiting security misconfigurations in cloud platforms, such as overly permissive access settings, unencrypted data storage, or exposed administrative consoles	Important

(continued)

Table 11 (continued)

Item	Description	Significance
Container escape attacks	Techniques that allow attackers to break out of isolated container environments, gaining access to host systems or neighbouring containers	Important
Credential stuffing	An automated attack where credentials leaked from prior data breaches are systematically tested across multiple websites and services to gain unauthorised access to user accounts	Important
Critical infrastructure attacks	Coordinated cyberattacks targeting infrastructure essential for public services, economic stability, or national security, including energy, transport, and healthcare systems	Core
Critical infrastructure sabotage	Deliberate cyber or physical actions designed to disrupt, damage, or destroy critical infrastructure essential to public services or national security	Core
Cross site scripting	A web application vulnerability where attackers inject malicious scripts into otherwise trusted websites, which are then executed by users' browsers to steal cookies, credentials, or perform unauthorised actions	Important
Cryptographic backdoor attacks	Introducing hidden vulnerabilities into cryptographic algorithms or systems, enabling secret access or weakening encryption strength	Core
Data breach	Incidents where sensitive, protected, or confidential data is accessed, disclosed, or stolen by unauthorised individuals, often resulting in severe reputational and regulatory consequences	Core
Data poisoning	A technique used to corrupt machine learning models by injecting manipulated data into training datasets, degrading model performance and reliability	Core
DDoS	A coordinated attack in which a network or service is overwhelmed with a flood of traffic from multiple sources, making it inaccessible to legitimate users, often used to extort victims or mask further cyber intrusions	Core
Deepfake social engineering	Using AI-generated deepfake content, such as fake videos or voice recordings, to impersonate trusted individuals and manipulate targets	Important
DNS spoofing	A manipulation technique that corrupts DNS responses, redirecting users to malicious websites impersonating legitimate ones, enabling credential theft or malware delivery	Important

(continued)

Table 11 (continued)

Item	Description	Significance
Drive-by downloads	A method of delivering malware where users' devices are infected simply by visiting compromised websites, without any need for user interaction, exploiting browser or plugin vulnerabilities	Important
Exploit kits	Pre-packaged collections of exploits that automate the process of compromising vulnerable systems, often delivered via malicious websites or advertisements	Important
Fileless attacks	A stealthy attack technique where malicious code is executed directly in memory without leaving traditional file traces, making detection and forensic investigation more difficult	Important
Firmware attacks	Cyberattacks that target the low-level software controlling hardware components, often providing attackers with persistent and difficult-to-detect access to compromised systems	Core
Formjacking	A technique where attackers inject malicious code into online forms, enabling them to intercept and steal data entered by users, such as payment details	Peripheral
Hardware hacking	Physical tampering or manipulation of hardware devices to alter functionality, extract sensitive data, or insert malicious components during the manufacturing or operational phases	Core
Insider threats	Cybersecurity risks posed by employees, contractors, or trusted insiders who misuse their authorised access to harm the organisation, either intentionally or negligently	Peripheral
IoT attacks	Cyberattacks targeting Internet of Things devices, which often have weak security, to gain access to networks or use the devices in botnets and other coordinated attacks	Important
Juice jacking	A physical attack where compromised public charging stations are used to inject malware into connected devices or steal data during charging	Peripheral
Keyloggers	Malicious programs that secretly record all keystrokes made on an infected device, capturing sensitive information such as passwords, payment card data, and personal messages	Important
Live streaming abuse	The misuse of live streaming platforms to broadcast illegal content, coordinate attacks, or manipulate public opinion in real time	Important
MaaS	Malware-as-a-Service offerings in underground markets, allowing unskilled actors to rent ready-made malware tools and infrastructure	Core

(continued)

Table 11 (continued)

Item	Description	Significance
Malvertising	The delivery of malware through malicious online advertisements, often placed on legitimate websites to increase reach and credibility	Important
Malware	A broad category of malicious software, including viruses, worms, trojans, and spyware, designed to infiltrate, damage, or disrupt systems, steal sensitive data, or gain unauthorised access to networks	Important
Mobile attacks	Cyberattacks targeting mobile devices through malicious apps, unpatched vulnerabilities, or phishing, aiming to steal data, intercept communications, or take control of devices	Peripheral
OT malware	Malware specifically designed to compromise operational technology systems, which control industrial processes, often targeting critical infrastructure such as power grids or manufacturing plants	Core
Password spraying	A type of brute-force attack that tries a small set of commonly used passwords across a large number of accounts to evade account lockout mechanisms	Core
Phishing	A deceptive attack technique aiming to trick users into revealing sensitive information by impersonating legitimate entities through emails, websites, or messages	Important
QR code phishing	Embedding malicious URLs in QR codes, tricking users into scanning them to visit compromised websites or download malware	Peripheral
Ransomware	A type of malicious software that encrypts files, systems, or entire networks, demanding a ransom payment in exchange for a decryption key, often severely disrupting business operations and leading to significant financial and reputational damage	Core
Rogue certificates	The use of fraudulent or compromised digital certificates to impersonate trusted entities, enabling man-in-the-middle attacks and data interception	Peripheral
Scada attacks	Targeted cyberattacks against Supervisory Control and Data Acquisition systems, which control critical infrastructure processes, with the aim of causing operational disruption or sabotage	Core
Serverless attacks	Targeting vulnerabilities in serverless computing architectures, where functions run in ephemeral containers managed by cloud providers	Core

(continued)

Table 11 (continued)

Item	Description	Significance
Session hijacking	An attack technique where an attacker intercepts and takes control of an active user session, gaining unauthorised access to systems without needing credentials	Important
Shadow it exploitation	Cyberattacks exploiting unauthorised or unmanaged IT assets within an organisation, which typically lack proper security controls or monitoring	Core
Side-channel attacks on IoT	Attacks that extract sensitive information from IoT devices by analysing indirect signals, such as power consumption or electromagnetic emissions	Important
Sim swapping	A technique where attackers fraudulently transfer a victim's phone number to their own SIM card to intercept SMS messages and bypass two-factor authentication	Peripheral
Social engineering attacks	Tactics that manipulate individuals into divulging confidential information or performing actions that compromise security, often by exploiting human trust, curiosity, or fear	Peripheral
SQL injection	An attack technique that exploits vulnerabilities in web applications by injecting malicious SQL code into database queries, enabling attackers to access, modify, or delete sensitive data	Core
Synthetic identity fraud	A fraud technique where real and fabricated data are combined to create fake identities used to open accounts or obtain credit, making detection complex	Peripheral
Vishing	A form of social engineering conducted via voice calls, where attackers impersonate legitimate entities to extract sensitive information or convince victims to perform harmful actions	Important
Voice cloning fraud	Using AI-based voice synthesis to impersonate trusted individuals in phone calls, facilitating fraud or impersonation scams	Peripheral

Table 12 National and international organizations

Item	Description	Significance
ENISA	The European Union Agency for Cybersecurity, providing expertise and support to EU institutions and member states in strengthening cybersecurity policies, capabilities, and operational cooperation	Core
CERT-Italia	Italy's national Computer Emergency Response Team, coordinating cyber incident responses and promoting proactive security measures across critical infrastructures and public administrations	Core
ECSO	European Cyber Security Organisation, fostering collaboration between industry, research, and governments to advance European cybersecurity innovation and resilience	Core
FIRST	Forum of Incident Response and Security Teams, a global network enabling collaboration and knowledge exchange among security teams to improve global incident response capabilities	Peripheral
NATO CCDCOE	The NATO Cooperative Cyber Defence Centre of Excellence, conducting research, training, and exercises to enhance NATO and allied nations' cyber defence capabilities	Core
Global Cyber Alliance	An international organisation aimed at unifying communities to eliminate systemic cyber risks through concrete solutions and global cooperation	Peripheral
CLUSIT	The Italian Association for Information Security, promoting awareness, training, and research on cybersecurity issues within Italy's public and private sectors	Important
OASIS	A global non-profit standards organisation developing open standards for cybersecurity, including frameworks for information sharing and structured threat intelligence formats	Important
ITU-T	International Telecommunication Union Standardization Sector, responsible for developing global technical standards, including guidelines for cybersecurity and network resilience	Important
ISO	International Organization for Standardization, publishing widely adopted standards for cybersecurity, including ISO 27001 and related frameworks	Peripheral
NIST	National Institute of Standards and Technology, providing globally influential guidelines such as the NIST Cybersecurity Framework and standards for risk management	Peripheral
ISACA	Global professional association offering certifications, training, and research in IT governance, cybersecurity, risk management, and audit	Important

(continued)

Table 12 (continued)

Item	Description	Significance
ISF	Information Security Forum, an independent global organisation delivering research and practical tools to help organisations manage cybersecurity risks effectively	Peripheral
CSA	Cloud Security Alliance, developing best practices and frameworks to secure cloud environments, ensuring compliance and resilience in cloud service adoption	Important
OWASP	Open Worldwide Application Security Project, offering freely available tools, standards, and methodologies to enhance application security globally	Core
MITRE	A non-profit organisation maintaining the ATT&CK framework, providing a globally recognised knowledge base for understanding adversary tactics, techniques, and procedures	Core
SANS	Leading cybersecurity training and certification organisation, offering expert-developed courses and maintaining open research initiatives like the Internet Storm Center	Peripheral
CIF	Cyber Intelligence Forum, a collaborative platform for governments, industry, and academia to share intelligence and coordinate responses to global cyber threats	Important
Cyber Peace Institute	An independent non-profit advocating for human rights and responsible behaviour in cyberspace, protecting vulnerable communities from cyber threats	Peripheral
GFCE	Global Forum on Cyber Expertise, an international platform promoting capacity building and global cooperation to strengthen cybersecurity capabilities in developing regions	Core
Europol EC3	European Cybercrime Centre at Europol, supporting member states in combating cybercrime through operational coordination, intelligence sharing, and forensic expertise	Core
Interpol Cybercrime Directorate	Interpol's specialized cybercrime unit facilitating global cooperation between law enforcement agencies to investigate and prevent cybercrime	Core
G7 Cyber Expert Group	A working group bringing together cybersecurity experts from G7 nations to align policies, improve financial sector resilience, and coordinate international responses to cyber threats	Core

Appendix B

AI Models Deep Dive

In what follows we describe the data flow within the AI architecture. Figure 1 in the main text provides a schematic overview of the system's modular architecture, where data from each source undergoes a dedicated processing pipeline before being consolidated into the integrated analytical framework. Each module, defined by a box, performs source-specific pre-processing, transformation, and analysis steps, ensuring that the heterogeneity of the input data is appropriately addressed. The visual representation assigns distinct colours to the three primary flows, distinguishing the financial statement data flow in violet, the web data flow in orange, and the press news flow in green. This colour scheme reflects the tailored analytical processes applied to each source type and shows the points of convergence where outputs from the three streams are combined for the calculation of the cyber risk index.

The data curation layer performs the initial harmonisation and cleansing of the raw input data, transforming it into a format suitable for natural language processing techniques. PDF financial statements are processed to extract machine-readable text, with optical character recognition[35] applied to any sections presented as embedded images. Once extracted, the text, regardless of the source, is subjected to a uniform pre-processing pipeline that applies standard cleaning procedures to remove inessential characters, harmonise encoding inconsistencies, and normalise structural anomalies. Following this initial processing, the entire corpus is segmented into individual sentences using SpaCy,[36] providing the analytical granularity required for downstream processing. A subsequent filtering step performed using langdetect[37] by Meta, ensures that only sentences in Italian or English are retained, thereby excluding irrelevant content and ensuring linguistic consistency across the analytical pipeline.

The analysis of financial statements, which follows the violet flow depicted in Fig. 1, proceeds with the transformation of extracted sentences into embeddings[38]

---

[35] In this context, we apply OCR to extract textual content from image-based sections within corporate financial statements to ensure comprehensive coverage of all available information.

[36] SpaCy is an advanced open-source library for NLP in Python, designed for efficient and scalable text processing. It provides a wide range of features, including tokenization, named entity recognition, part-of-speech tagging, dependency parsing, and text vectorization, making it a versatile tool for linguistic analysis and pre-processing tasks.

[37] langdetect, developed by Meta, is a lightweight and language-agnostic library for automatic language identification. It assigns a probabilistic score to each supported language, allowing the selection of text segments written in the target languages (Italian and English) to ensure analytical consistency across all processed content.

[38] The embeddings used in this research are generated using *paraphrase-multilingual-mpnet-base-v2* through Sentence Transformers. This model has been selected among the available open source embedding models for its superior balance between semantic precision, multilingual coverage,

using an Italian fine-tuned model provided through Hugging Face.[39] Embeddings represent each sentence as a high-dimensional vector, encoding semantic information rather than surface-level lexical features. This representation enables the comparison of sentences based on meaning, facilitating the identification of semantically similar content even in the absence of shared terminology. The adoption of embeddings represents a shift away from earlier topic modelling techniques, such as Latent Dirichlet Allocation,[40] which gained prominence in the early 2000s and relied on statistical co-occurrence patterns. These techniques often struggled to capture thematic coherence within sparsely populated or highly technical texts.

The sentence embeddings generated through this process are stored within a vector store, a specialized data structure optimised for the efficient retrieval and comparison of high-dimensional vectors. Unlike traditional keyword-based retrieval systems, vector stores enable the identification of relevant content through semantic similarity,[41] providing a more effective mechanism for topic identification and thematic mapping. The vector store adopted in this architecture is FAISS,[42] developed by Meta, selected for its scalability and its performance in approximate nearest neighbour search across large corpora. In parallel with the processing of financial statements, the predefined taxonomy topics belonging to the technologies and processes categories, as shown in Appendix A, are also transformed into embeddings, and inserted into the same FAISS instance. This allows for direct comparison between the embedded content of the financial statements and the embedded representations of the taxonomy topics, ensuring that the comparison is performed in a consistent semantic space.

---

and computational efficiency, making it particularly suitable for the analysis of heterogeneous corporate disclosures.

[39] Hugging Face is a leading open-source platform providing pre-trained machine learning models and libraries for natural language processing, computer vision, and other AI tasks. Through its Model Hub, Hugging Face facilitates the distribution, fine-tuning, and deployment of transformer-based architectures, including the SentenceTransformer models used in this research.

[40] Latent Dirichlet Allocation (LDA) is a probabilistic generative model used to discover the underlying thematic structure of a text corpus. Each document is represented as a distribution over topics, and each topic is characterised by a distribution over words. While originally introduced in the early 2000s for topic modelling in unstructured text corpora, LDA tends to struggle when applied to technical documents with sparse thematic content or where topics evolve across highly specialized terminology, limiting its effectiveness in contexts requiring fine-grained semantic analysis.

[41] Semantic similarity refers to the capacity of sentence embeddings to capture meaning beyond exact word matching. This allows semantically related expressions to be considered close in the vector space, even if they do not share lexical components. A well-known example illustrates this property through vector arithmetic: subtracting the embedding of 'man' from 'king' and adding that of 'woman' yields a vector that is geometrically close to the embedding of 'queen'. This demonstrates how embeddings encode analogical and contextual relationships between terms, enabling more nuanced and meaningful retrieval of information.

[42] FAISS (Facebook AI Similarity Search) is an open-source library developed by Meta for efficient similarity search and clustering of dense vectors. It is designed to handle high-dimensional vector spaces, enabling fast approximate nearest neighbour search, even on large-scale datasets, making it particularly suitable for the semantic retrieval tasks described in this research.

The semantic coverage of each topic within the financial statement is measured through similarity calculations performed between each topic embedding and all sentence embeddings extracted from the document. For each topic, the highest similarity score observed across all sentences serves as the coverage indicator for that topic. This process provides a measurement of the degree to which the financial statement covers the semantic space defined by the cybersecurity taxonomy. These similarity values determine the contribution of the first component of Eq. (1) in Sect. 2.4, which reflects the firm's engagement with technologies and processes relevant to cybersecurity.

Additional components are added to capture the firm's conformity to regulations, possession of professional certifications, exposure to cyberattacks, and affiliations with national or international organisations. These elements are assessed through an ensemble framework comprising two distinct analytical flows. The first flow performs syntactic parsing on candidate sentences identified within the financial statements. This parsing process conducted using Stanford CoreNLP,[43] decomposes the grammatical structure of each sentence, identifying subject-verb-object relationships and other syntactic dependencies. This structural analysis supports the extraction of explicit claims relating to regulatory compliance, certification possession, organisational affiliation, and the disclosure of cyber incidents. By anchoring the analysis in a syntactic structure, this approach reduces the risk of extracting false positives from general descriptive content and enhances the reliability of the extracted information.

The second flow leverages the predictive capabilities of LLM. A LLM is a deep learning architecture trained on extensive excerpts of text to capture complex linguistic patterns, contextual relationships, and domain-specific nuances. These models have recently attracted attention due to their ability to process unstructured textual data across application domains, including finance, healthcare, legal analysis, and related fields. The ability of these models to understand context and linguistic subtleties has enabled them to perform effectively in natural language processing, computer vision, and related fields. In the context of natural language processing, LLMs have delivered substantial improvements across tasks including text generation, summarisation, and domain-specific information extraction, providing a significant enhancement over traditional rule-based and statistical approaches.

The LLM deployed in this architecture is Microsoft Phi-4 (Abdin et al., 2024), a 14-billion parameter model selected for its balance between computational efficiency and reasoning capabilities. Phi-4 has demonstrated effectiveness in handling domain-specific inference tasks, especially in contexts requiring the evaluation of long-form financial and regulatory texts. Interaction with the model

[43] Stanford CoreNLP is a natural language processing suite developed by the Stanford NLP Group, offering a comprehensive set of tools for syntactic and semantic analysis. Its syntactic parser, used in this research, provides a deep grammatical analysis of each sentence, identifying the hierarchical relationships between words to support structured information extraction.

is mediated through a dedicated prompting[44] module, which constructs targeted queries designed to extract specific information from the financial statement. These prompts direct the LLM to assess whether a given sentence or paragraph supports the firm's possession of a specific certification, adherence to a particular regulation, affiliation with a relevant organisation, or experience of a defined cyberattack. Special attention is given to distinguish between generic mentions and firm-specific declarations, ensuring that the analysis reflects actual disclosures rather than general references to industry practices. Further details on the construction of these prompts are provided in Appendix C, while Appendix D documents the specific configuration parameters used to ensure reproducibility of the LLM outputs.

The outputs generated by the syntactic parser and the LLM are combined through a weighted aggregation process that assigns different reliability weights to each component, depending on the type of information being extracted. The calibration of these weights was carried out through a manual refinement procedure, which led to the assignment of a weight of 0.2 to the syntactic parser and 0.8 to the LLM, reflecting the latter's higher reliability in capturing semantic nuances within unstructured disclosures. These combined probability estimates measure the likelihood that the firm possesses each assessed attribute, whether related to regulations, certifications, organisations, or cyberattacks. These probabilities, together with the topic coverage scores derived from the embedding-based analysis, are the final inputs into the overall scoring framework that calculates the firm's cyber risk index. This ensemble approach, combining evidence derived from both syntactic parsing and advanced language model inference, ensures that the final probability estimates are both linguistically grounded and contextually validated, providing a balanced assessment of the firm's declared and inferred cybersecurity attributes.

The Factiva pipeline processes large-scale extractions of Italian press articles to identify cybersecurity-related content. The initial step involves bulk retrieval of news articles from the provider's database, ensuring broad coverage of publicly reported cybersecurity incidents. Once extracted, all texts undergo the data curation phase, which standardises the content for subsequent processing. This phase includes text cleaning, removal of non-informative elements, and structural normalisation, aligning the textual data with the analytical framework applied to other sources.

Following curation, the articles are segmented into individual sentences, providing the necessary granularity for downstream analysis. SpaCy is employed to identify sentences containing references to cybersecurity topics as defined in the taxonomy. This step filters out irrelevant content, concentrating only on news that includes mentions of cyberattacks, regulatory frameworks, technologies, organisational affiliations, or other cybersecurity-related aspects. The identification of taxonomy-relevant sentences ensures that only meaningful content advances to the

[44] Prompt engineering is the practice of designing and optimising input queries provided to a Large Language Model to elicit accurate and contextually appropriate responses. Effective prompt design is particularly critical when using LLMs for domain-specific tasks, ensuring that the model interprets the input correctly and produces outputs aligned with the analytical objectives.

next processing stage, where advanced natural language processing techniques are applied.

Once relevant articles are identified, the pipeline leverages Microsoft Phi-4 to extract and structure key information. The system generates two dedicated prompts to interact with the LLM. The first prompt evaluates whether the article describes a cyberattack. If the model detects a reference to an attack, a second prompt is issued to extract the name of the affected company. This structured query-response interaction enables precise extraction of affected entities without relying on conventional string-matching techniques, which are often susceptible to errors arising from variations in company names.

The use of an LLM for entity extraction addresses a fundamental challenge in processing financial and corporate texts. Traditional methods, such as regular expressions or dictionary-based matching, often struggle with inconsistencies in how company names are reported. Variations in legal suffixes, abbreviations, and the inclusion of subsidiary or holding structures complicate rule-based approaches, leading to misclassification or incomplete extraction. By leveraging the contextual understanding of the LLM, the system can accurately isolate the firm's name, reducing noise and improving the precision of entity recognition. This approach enhances the reliability of cybersecurity incident attribution, ensuring that reported attacks are correctly linked to the affected firms.

The extracted information is integrated into the overall cyber risk scoring framework. If an attack is identified through press sources, it is incorporated into the firm's risk profile. However, mechanisms are in place to prevent double counting when the same incident is also disclosed in the financial statements. If a cyberattack is reported in both Factiva news and the company's balance sheet, it is counted only once in the final computation. This ensures that the firm's exposure to cyber threats is accurately reflected without inflating the risk score.

Appendix C

Technologies, Certifications, and Organizations

The analysis of cybersecurity-related topics illustrates a progressive enlargement over time of their semantic coverage within corporate reporting, reflecting evolving awareness and adoption of protective technologies among ICAS firms (Fig. 7). The semantic footprint across topics expanded o, revealing a process through which cybersecurity themes progressively permeate the discussion within corporates. Notable is the emphasis placed on AI-driven technologies such as threat detection and phishing protection, underscoring a deliberate move towards automated security solutions capable of pre-emptive threat management. Concurrently, the increase of data loss prevention points to heightened concern among firms regarding data protection and privacy, likely driven by regulatory developments and the practical challenges associated with the management of sensitive information.

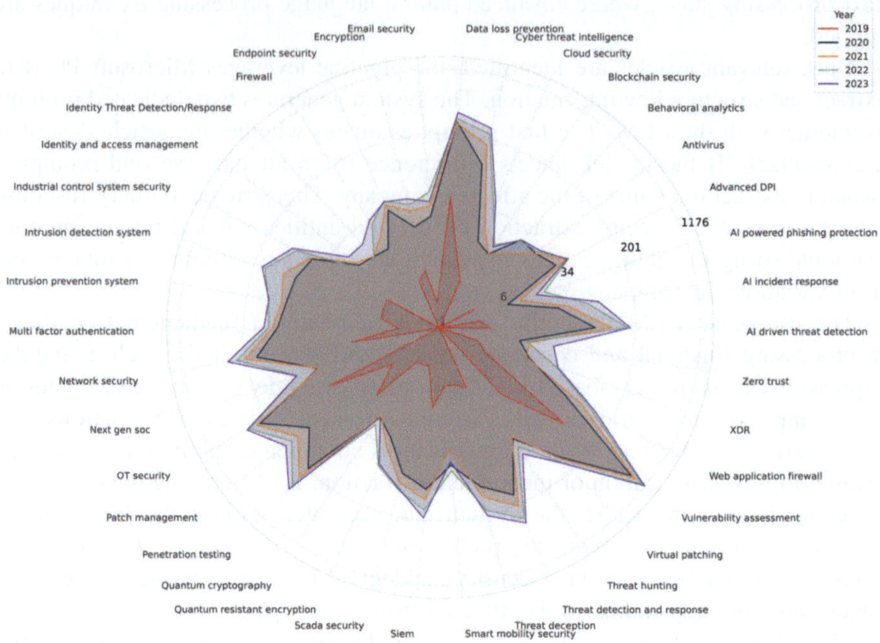

Fig. 7 Expansion of semantic coverage in the technologies

The expansion observed in cloud security and behavioural analytics reflects an industry-wide shift towards cloud computing and the necessity for sophisticated monitoring of user behaviours within digital environments. Such trends indicate that companies recognize the vulnerabilities of digital infrastructures, thereby integrating advanced protective technologies into their operational practices. Traditional cybersecurity approaches, including multi-factor authentication, firewall deployments, and intrusion detection systems, are widespread, revealing a balanced adoption strategy that combines established security practices with emerging technological solutions. This balance reflects the pragmatism of firms in managing cyber risks through comprehensive and layered defences.

Moreover, the progressive widening of the semantic area occupied by cybersecurity topics shows an increased sophistication and diversification in firms' security priorities. The semantic expansion implies a progressively deeper integration of cybersecurity within firms' strategic and operational considerations. The importance of specific advanced topics, particularly zero trust architecture and cloud security, further reflects an adjustment to evolving digital business models and the security implications associated with greater reliance on distributed computing infrastructures.

Collectively, these trends portray a maturation trajectory within the cybersecurity posture of the sample firms, shaped by both external compliance drivers and internal strategic recognition of cyber risks as key elements of business continuity and resilience. Such developments underline the broader organisational shift towards structured cybersecurity governance.

In *certifications*, the presence of the MAD program stands out, signalling the growing adoption of structured methodologies for cyber threat detection and response (Fig. 8). The increasing formalization of security practices, as reflected in both regulatory adherence and professional certification trends, suggests that cybersecurity considerations are progressively embedded into corporate risk management frameworks, extending beyond compliance-driven initiatives, to become components of strategic resilience planning.

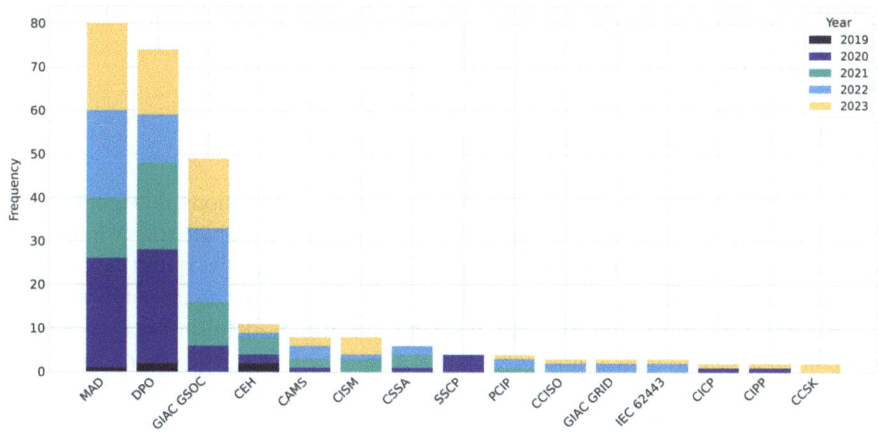

Fig. 8 Professional certifications among firms (percentage values)

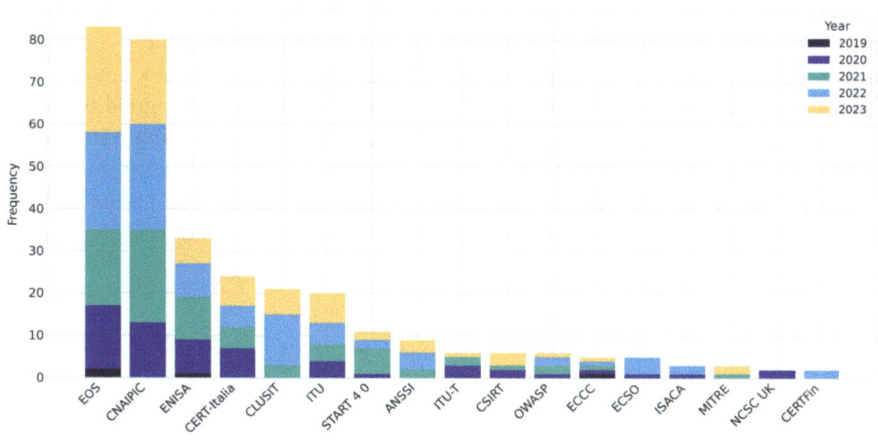

Fig. 9 Firm memberships and affiliations

The *organizations* category follows a comparable pattern, with firms demonstrating an increasing tendency to establish connections with national and international cybersecurity organisations (Fig. 9). This trend shows the role of affiliations as mechanisms for knowledge sharing, industry coordination, and incident response. Of particular importance is the growing engagement with the EOS, suggesting that firms are actively participating in cooperative security initiatives at the European level. Similarly, interactions[45] with CNAIPIC[46] point to a structured approach to incident reporting, likely linked to the formal communication of data breaches and ransomware attacks. These affiliations provide further evidence of firms' improvement of cybersecurity posture, reflecting not only compliance-driven duties, but also a broader integration of external support networks into their security strategies.

Appendix D

LLM Prompting and Parameters

Prompting refers to the practice of formulating input instructions that guide LLM in generating task-specific responses. Prompting plays a crucial role when interacting with large language models, as it directly influences the quality, precision, and importance of the generated output. Effective prompting is essential not only for reducing ambiguity, but also for ensuring that the model consistently adheres to the intended analytical framework. In the context of risk assessment and, more specifically, cyber risk evaluation, clear and structured prompts allow the model to identify and interpret the most relevant textual evidence, apply consistent criteria, and avoid speculative reasoning. Well-designed prompts are particularly important when models are deployed in operational settings, where the output must align with pre-defined classification schemes, analytical standards, and regulatory requirements.

In this work, the Phi-4 model is used to assess whether specific cyberattacks have affected firms by evaluating textual excerpts from corporate documents. The prompt adopted for this purpose, reported in Fig. 10, has been designed to ensure that the model provides binary, standardised responses, thus enabling its seamless integration into the broader risk assessment framework. This configuration reflects a balance between flexibility—necessary for interpreting diverse textual formulations—and the need for binary, standardised output required for quantitative

[45] A detailed description of the LLM prompt used for extracting membership status or related activities between firms and organizations is provided in Appendix D.

[46] CNAIPIC (Centro Nazionale Anticrimine Informatico per la Protezione delle Infrastrutture Critiche) is the Italian law enforcement unit dedicated to investigating and preventing cyber threats targeting critical infrastructure. Operating under the Polizia di Stato, it collaborates with national and international entities to counter cybercrime, safeguard strategic sectors, and enhance cybersecurity resilience.

"""You are a model specialised in detecting the presence of cyberattacks.

🔍 Analyse the following TEXT and determine whether the {attack} has been suffered.

Respond **exclusively** with one of the following categories:

- "attack suffered" (if the text indicates that the {**attack**} occurred successfully).
- "attack not suffered" (if there is no evidence of a successful {**attack**}).

📌 **Evaluation criteria:**

- "attack suffered": if the text clearly states that the {**attack**} had a negative impact on the company, such as a breach, operational disruption, data theft, or system compromise.
- "attack not suffered": if the text contains no evidence of the {**attack**}, or refers only to preventive measures, unsuccessful attack attempts, or hypothetical scenarios without confirmed harm.

⚠ **Do not add explanations, reasoning, or any other words. Respond only with one of the two options.**"""

Fig. 10 Prompt for the detection and classification of cyberattack

modelling of cyber risk exposure. This approach also supports the development of historical cyber risk profiles for individual firms, which are crucial for the estimation of their exposure and vulnerability within the proposed cyber risk index.

Figures 11 and 12 present, respectively, the prompt used to assess the possession or adoption of corporate certifications and the prompt designed to evaluate a firm's affiliation with specific organisations. Both prompts, similarly to the one adopted for cyberattacks, are structured to enforce a standardized response format, ensuring that the model provides consistent outputs across different entities and documents.

LLMs are differentiated by their parameter sets, which are instrumental in determining their accuracy and performance. The number of parameters within an LLM influences its ability to generalize across diverse linguistic constructs, improving its capacity to interpret and generate coherent and contextually appropriate text. These parameters govern the complexity of the model's decision boundaries, affecting not only predictive accuracy, but also response variability.

The configuration of an LLM is shaped by a series of hyperparameters that regulate its generative behaviour, which are explicitly declared to ensure transparency and facilitate the reproducibility of results (Table 13). Among these, *temperature* is particularly influential as it modulates the degree of randomness in the model's output. Temperature may vary between 0 and 1. A lower temperature value encourages more deterministic responses by reducing the probability distribution's entropy, leading to more predictable and consistent text generation. Conversely, higher temperature values introduce greater variability, fostering diversity in responses at the expense of coherence. This mechanism is critical in balancing creativity and precision, especially in applications where the trade-off between innovation and reliability must be managed carefully.

"""You are a model specialised in analysing the presence of corporate certifications.

Analyse the following TEXT and determine whether the company possesses or adopts the **{certification}** standard.

Respond **exclusively** with one of the following categories:

- "certification held" (if the text clearly indicates that the company has obtained the **{certification}**).
- "compliant with the standard" (if the text indicates that the company follows the guidelines of the **{certification}** standard, but does not specify whether it has obtained the certification).
- "certification not held" (if there is no evidence in the text confirming either the certification or the adoption of the standard).

Evaluation criteria:

- "certification held": applies if the text explicitly states that the company has obtained the **{certification}** or is officially certified.
- "compliant with the standard": applies if the text suggests that the company follows the guidelines or requirements of the **{certification}** standard, without indicating a formal certification.
- "certification not held": applies if the text does not mention the certification or if it is unclear whether the company follows the standard.

Do not add explanations, reasoning, or any other text. Respond with one of the three options only."""

Fig. 11 Prompt to assess the possession or adoption of corporate certifications

The *maximum tokens* parameter imposes a ceiling on the length of generated text, increasing computational efficiency while constraining verbosity. The *predicted batch size* determines the number of sequences processed simultaneously, optimising memory allocation and processing speed. *Top-p sampling* introduces an additional constraint by limiting token selection to a subset whose cumulative probability reaches a predefined threshold, refining response coherence while preserving contextual diversity.

Presence penalty and *frequency penalty* function as regulatory mechanisms to mitigate repetition, respectively discouraging the reintroduction of tokens based on their previous presence in the sequence and their frequency of occurrence. The *stop* parameter specifies termination conditions for text generation, preventing output continuation beyond a designated endpoint. *Logit bias* allows targeted adjustments to token probabilities, influencing token selection during inference. The *N* and *best-of* parameters define the number of response variations considered, affecting the selection of the optimal outcome from multiple token generations.

"""You are a model specialised in analysing a company's affiliation with an organisation.

🔍 Analyse the following TEXT and determine the level of the company's affiliation with **{organization}**.

📌 **Evaluation criteria:**

- **"affiliated"**: the TEXT **explicitly** states that the company is a member, partner, certified, accredited, or officially registered with **{organization}**.
- **"organisation-related"**: the TEXT suggests an indirect relationship, such as participation in initiatives, collaborations, or references to joint activities with **{organization}**, without clearly indicating formal affiliation.
- **"not affiliated"**: the TEXT **does not clearly mention** any affiliation with **{organization}**, or uses ambiguous wording that could refer to something else.

⚠ **If the term "{organization}" appears in isolation, without clear context of affiliation, classify the company as "not affiliated".**
⚠ **If the text contains only the acronym "{organization}" without a clear reference to the organisation, classify the company as "not affiliated".**

Respond **exclusively** with one of the following categories:

- "affiliated"
- "organisation-related"
- "not affiliated"

⚠ **Do not add explanations, reasoning or any other text. Respond with one of the three options only."""**

Fig. 12 Prompt to assess the affiliation of firms with specific organisations

Table 13 Phi-4 parameters

Temperature	0.25
Maximum tokens	20
Predicted batch size	1024
Top-p sampling	0.85
Presence penalty	0
Frequency penalty	0
Stop	None
Logit bias	0
N	1
Best of	1

Appendix E

A Case Study

This case study examines a large Italian firm operating in the management consultancy segment of the Professional, Scientific and Technical services sector, which suffered a cyberattack in 2022. We assess the impact of this event on the firm's cyber risk index by comparing its cybersecurity disclosures across two consecutive financial statements and evaluating the resulting variation in the associated risk level.

In 2022, prior to the incident, the firm's financial reporting presents a robust cybersecurity posture. The disclosure encompasses a broad range of technological solutions, including penetration testing, Security Information and Event Management (SIEM) platforms, intrusion detection and prevention systems, behavioural analytics, quantum-resistant encryption, AI-driven threat detection, and others, totalling approximately 54 points in the *Technologies* category. The *Processes* domain reveals a similarly structured approach, with the presence of cyber risk management, data privacy, threat intelligence, security awareness, integrated vulnerability management, and other procedural safeguards, adding up to 42 points. Furthermore, the firm demonstrates compliance with key international regulatory frameworks, including ISO 31000, GDPR, CMMC, and Cyber Essentials, yielding 14 points under *Regulations*. No professional certifications are mentioned, and no cyberattack is reported, resulting in no deductions from the *Attacks* category.

The cumulative score for 2022 is therefore given by:

$$S_{2022} = S_{Technologies} + S_{Processes} + S_{Regulations} = 54 + 42 + 14 = 110$$

Once normalised to a 1–100 scale and inverted to reflect the risk interpretation of the index—where higher values indicate greater vulnerability—the cyber risk index scores 46.9. In the following year, the same firm reports the occurrence of a cyberattack, which introduces a penalizing factor in the *Attacks* category. The confirmed data breach leads to a deduction of -15 points, in accordance with the scoring architecture. While several cybersecurity elements remain present across *Technologies* and *Processes*—including SIEM, penetration testing, cyber risk management, data privacy, and threat intelligence—the overall structure of the firm's cyber posture does not exhibit significant reinforcement in the aftermath of the incident. Consequently, the penalty induced by the attack is not fully counterbalanced by additional mitigating components.

The cumulative score for 2023, excluding insurance and certifications, is:

$$S_{2023} = S_{Technologies} + S_{Processes} + S_{Regulations} - S_{Attacks} = 41 + 47 + 14 - 15 = 87$$

Applying the same transformation the cyber risk index scores 55.7. The increase from 46.9 to 55.7 in the risk index reflects a clear shift in the firm's cybersecurity condition following the attack. The deduction associated with the incident is the primary driver of this variation. The framework detects the presence of critical exposure events and integrates their impact into a comprehensive risk measure. This case illustrates the ability of the cyber risk index to capture latent vulnerability that is not necessarily neutralised by partial continuity in governance practices or previously implemented controls. It also highlights the structural persistence of exposure in the period immediately following an attack, offering valuable insight into the variations of risk observable through financial reporting.

References

Abdin, M., Aneja, J., Behl, H, Bubeck, S., Eldan, R., Gunasekar, S., & Zhang, Y. (2024). *Phi-4 technical report*. Microsoft Research.

Adelmann, F., Elliot, J., Ergen, I., Gaidosch, T., Jenkinson, N., Khiaonarong, T., & Wilson, C. (2020). Cyber risk and financial stability: It's a small world after all. *Staff Disc Note, 007*, 1–32.

Agarwal, N., Agarwal, S., & Chatterjee, C. (2024). Data breach notification laws and the cost of private debt. *The British Accounting Review*, 101518.

Amir, E., Levi, S., & Livne, T. (2018). Do firms underreport information on cyber-attacks? Evidence from capital markets. *Review of Accounting Studies, 23*, 1177–1206.

Anderson, R. (2021). *Security engineering: A guide to building dependable distributed systems* (p. 1232). Wiley.

Benaroch, M., & Chernobai, A. (2017). Operational IT failures, IT value-destruction, and board-level IT governance changes. *MIS Quarterly, 41*(3), 69.

Bencivelli, L., & Mongardini, M. (2024). La sicurezza cibernetica delle imprese italiane: percezione dei rischi e pratiche di mitigazione. *Questioni di Economia e Finanza* 1–23.

Bryson, A., Curti, F., Gerlach, J., & Stacey, S. (2023). *Improving data for managing cyber risk*. SSRN.

Buck, C., Clarke, J., Oliveira, R. T., Desouza, K. C., & Maroufkhani, P. (2023). Digital transformation in asset-intensive organisations: The light and the dark side. *Journal of Innovation & Knowledge, 8*(2), 100335.

Cebula, J. J., & Young, L. R. (2010). A taxonomy of operational cyber security risk. *Software Engineering Institute.*

CLUSIT. (2021). Rapporto 2021 sulla sicurezza ICT in Italia.

CLUSIT. (2022). Rapporto 2022 sulla sicurezza ICT in Italia.

CLUSIT. (2023). Rapporto 2023 sulla sicurezza ICT in Italia.

CLUSIT. (2024). Rapporto 2024 sulla sicurezza ICT in Italia.

CLUSIT. (2025). Rapporto Clusit 2025.

Cremer, F., Sheehan, B., Fortmann, M., Kia, A., Mullins, M., Murphy, F., & Materne, S. (2022). Cyber risk and cybersecurity: A systematic review of data availability. *The Geneva Papers on Risk and Insurance, 47*, 698–736.

Crosignani, M., Macchiavelli, M., & Silva, A. F. (2023). Pirates without borders: The propagation of cyberattacks through firms' supply chains. *Journal of Financial Economics, 147*(2), 432–448.

Curti, F., Gerlach, J., Kazinnik, S., Lee, M., & Mihov, A. (2019). Cyber risk definition and classification for financial risk management. *Fed Reserve Bank Richmond White Pap.*

Curti, F., Ivanov, I., Macchiavelli, M., & Zimmermann, T. (2024). *City hall has been hacked! The financial costs of lax cybersecurity*. SSRN:56.

Devlin, J., Chang, M. W., Lee, K., & Toutanova, K. (2019). BERT: Pre-training of deep bidirectional transformers for language understanding. In *Proc 2019 Conf NAACL* (pp. 4171–4186).

Di Virgilio, S., Faiella, I., Mistretta, A., & Narizzano, S. (2024). Assessing credit risk sensitivity to climate and energy shocks. *Journal of Policy Modelling, 46*(3), 552–568.

ENISA. (2024). *Report on the state of the cybersecurity in the Union.*

Florackis, C., Louca, C., & Micaely, R. (2024). Cybersecurity risk. *The Review of Financial Studies, 36*, 351–407.

Giudici, P., & Raffinetti, E. (2021). Cyber risk ordering with rank-based statistical models. *Advances in Statistical Analysis, 105*(3), 469–484.

Grodon, L., Loeb, M., & Zhou, L. (2011). The impact of information security breaches: Has there been a downward shift in costs? *Journal of Computer Security, 19*(1), 33–56.

Harrel, E. (2019). *Victims of identity theft, 2016*. Bur Justice Stat.

Huang, H. H., & Wang, C. (2021). Do banks price firms' data breaches? *The Accounting Review, 96*(3), 261–286.

Huang, J., & Murthy, U. (2024). The impact of cybersecurity risk management strategy disclosure on investors' judgments and decisions. *International Journal of Accounting Information Systems, 54*, 1000696.

International Monetary Fund. (2024). *Cyber risk: A growing concern for macrofinancial stability.* Glob Financ Stab Rep, (pp. 1–26).

Jamilov, R., Rey, H., & Tahoun, A. (2023). *The anatomy of cyber risk*. Inst New Econ Think Work Pap Ser 206.

Kamiya, S., Kim, J. K., Kim, J., Milidonis, A., & Stulz, R. M. (2021). Risk management, firm reputation, and the impact of successful cyberattacks on target firms. *Journal of Financial Economics, 139*(3), 719–749.

Kotidis, A., & Schreft, S. (2022). Cyberattacks and financial stability: Evidence from a natural experiment. *Finance and Economics Discussion Series*, 1–55.

Lawrence, A., Minutti-Meza, M., & Vyas, D. (2018). Is operational control risk informative of financial reporting deficiencies? *Auditing: Journal of Practice & Theory, 37*(1), 139–165.

Malvasi, M., Peters, G., & Truck, S. (2024). *Cyber risk taxonomies: Statistical analysis of cybersecurity risk classifications*. SSRN.

Masoud, N., & Al-Utaibi, G. (2022). The determinants of cybersecurity risk disclosure in firms' financial reporting: Empirical evidence. *Research in Economics, 76*, 131–140.

Mavani, C., Hirenkumar, A., Ripalkumar, P., & Goswami, A. (2024). The role of cybersecurity in protecting intellectual property. *International Journal on Recent and Innovation Trends in Computing and Communication, 12*(2), 1–10.

Mikhed, V., & Vogan, M. (2018). How data breaches affect consumer credit. *Journal of Banking & Finance, 88*, 192–207.

Mitnick, K., Simon, W. L., & Wozniak, S. (2019). *The art of deception: Controlling the human element of security* (p. 368). Wiley.

Mukhopadhyay, A., Chatterjee, S., Bagchi, K., Kirs, P., & Shukla, G. (2019). Cyber risk assessment and mitigation (CRAM) framework using logit and probit models for cyber insurance. *Information Systems Frontiers, 21*(5), 997–1018.

Ordonez, G., Caro Rincon, A. (2023). *The impact of cybersecurity management practices on the likelihood of cyber events*. Moody's Analytics Whitepaper (pp. 1–21).

Pool, J. H., & Venter, H. (2022). A harmonized information security taxonomy for cyber physical systems. *Applied Science, 12*(16), 8080.

Rabitti, G., Chokami, A., Coyle, P., & Cohen, R. (2024). A taxonomy of cyber risk taxonomies. *Risk Analysis, 45*(2), 376–386.

Rea Guamàn, A. M., San Feliu, T., Calvo-Manzano Villalón, J. A., & Sánchez García, I. (2018). Systematic review: Cybersecurity risk taxonomy. *Trends and Application in Software Engineering: CIMPS, 6*, 137–146.

Rosati, P., Deeney, P., Cummins, M., van der Werff, L., & Lynn, T. (2019). Social media and stock price reaction to data breach announcements. *Research in International Business and Finance, 47*, 458–469.

Sheman, A. (2022). *Cybersecurity risk and the cost of debt*. SSRN:58.

Trautman, L., Shackelford, S., Elzweig, B., & Ormerod, P. (2024). Understanding cyber risk: Unpacking and responding to cyber threats. *University of Miami Law Review, 78*(3), 1–78.

Uddin, H., Ali, H., & Kabir Hassan, M. (2020). Cybersecurity hazards and financial system vulnerability: A synthesis of literature. *Risk Management, 22*(4), 239–309.

Wang, T., Ulmer, J., & Kannan, K. (2013). The textual contents of media reports of information security breaches and profitable short-term investment opportunities. *Journal of Organizational Computing and Electronic Commerce, 23*(3), 200–223.

Zadeh, A., Lavine, B., Zolbanin, H., & Hopkins, D. (2023). A cybersecurity risk quantification and classification framework. *Decision Analytics Journal, 9*, 100328.

MIX
Papier aus verantwortungsvollen Quellen
Paper from responsible sources
FSC® C105338

If you have any concerns about our products,
you can contact us on
ProductSafety@springernature.com

In case Publisher is established outside the EU,
the EU authorized representative is:
Springer Nature Customer Service Center GmbH
Europaplatz 3, 69115 Heidelberg, Germany

Printed by Libri Plureos GmbH
in Hamburg, Germany